# STEPHEN CRANE

*BY R. W. STALLMAN*

THE HOUSES THAT JAMES BUILT

THE CRITIC'S NOTEBOOK (Ed.)

STEPHEN CRANE: AN OMNIBUS (Ed.)

THE ART OF JOSEPH CONRAD: A CRITICAL SYMPOSIUM (Ed.)

STEPHEN CRANE: SULLIVAN COUNTY TALES AND
SKETCHES (Ed.)

STEPHEN CRANE: LETTERS (Ed. with Lillian Gilkes)

THE WAR DISPATCHES OF STEPHEN CRANE (Ed. with E. R.
Hagemann)

THE NEW YORK CITY SKETCHES OF STEPHEN CRANE (Ed.
with E. R. Hagemann)

STEPHEN CRANE: A BIBLIOGRAPHY *In preparation*

11/6/81

# STEPHEN CRANE

## A BIOGRAPHY

BY

R. W. STALLMAN

*Robert ovster* 1911—

GEORGE BRAZILLER

NEW YORK

*For Virginia*

# ✑ *Preface*

"BIOGRAPHY is a deadly job and not for a million dollars would I tackle it again," Thomas Beer wrote a friend shortly after the publication of his *Stephen Crane* in 1923. "As this communication can be of no further value to you," he added, "pray destroy it."

Beer had spent "the leisure part of three years in shearing away improbable facts from the narrative," and his publisher had engaged a detective agency to help him in his research. The biography, he said, was "the demolition of a romantic myth."

But while erroneous reports and rumors of certain scandals involving his subject were properly discredited, Beer also deliberately suppressed the romantic love story of Stephen Crane and Cora Taylor, hostess of a Jacksonville night club called the Hotel de Dream, so as not to offend the Crane family. In October, 1922, he wrote Edmund Crane (who had died in September) that if his brother Stephen had never been formally married, he (Beer) could "evade the matter very easily" because "I am anxious to avoid offending your wishes. Tell me exactly what you know, or rather exactly what you want known."

In early 1923, before his book was in galleys, he wrote Edmund's daughter, Edith, that the legends about her uncle "are all nonsense. The net result of his supposedly scandalous career comes down to the facts that he lent an actress [Amy Leslie] some money and married a woman who was supposed to have a 'past'—whatever that means. As I can find out nothing about Mrs. Crane's past or present I have reduced her to a minimum."

In "a last desperate hunting" for facts Beer sailed for England and interviewed Edward Garnett and Joseph Conrad, but he did not use any information they gave him about Cora except a single descriptive item: she was a "fair, affable woman" older than Stephen. He also reduced Amy Leslie to a minimum in the appendix to the biography, and did not mention two other romances of considerable importance in Crane's life—with Nellie Crouse and Mrs. Lily Brandon Munroe—probably because their correspondence was unknown to him. Nevertheless, he concluded that

Crane had been "a thoroughly romantic lover who had not made exactions in love and probably knew precious little about women." This simplification would seem to be somewhat inadequate for a man who lived for a time in a rooming house of street-walkers and who, while in Jamaica, went to bed with a native woman—to change his luck, as he said.

"Without doubt I shall be accused of 'whitewashing' Crane," says Beer disarmingly. He admits that he removed from Crane's letters "some hasty estimates of living people in England and America," again so as not to offend them. But he not only tampered with the letters; he also, apparently, destroyed all the Crane letters quoted in his book, since not a single one of them has ever reached the manuscript market in over forty years.

On the basis of the evidence, I reluctantly came to this conclusion and tested it before the Bibliographical Society of America in an address at the Pierpont Morgan Library in January 1963. To date my inference has not been disproved.

In the early 1900's, Willis Clarke had collected copies of letters for a life of Stephen Crane he intended to write but abandoned; "he was so baffled by conflicting statements," Beer says, "that he dropped the work." (Beer also reports that Henry McBride spent ten years planning a study of Crane and ended "by deciding there was no such animal, although I knew him for eleven years." However, McBride denied having ever intended to write such a study.)

Willis Clarke turned over to Beer the letters he had collected, along with a shorthand report of his interview with Crane at Brede Place. Clarke was also "the donor of letters from Mrs. Bolton Chafee, Julian Ralph, Robert Barr, Acton Davies and Henry Davies Hume, and of a passage in the diary of the late Charles Gary Griswold," says Beer in the appendix of his book. None of this material, nor copies of any of the letters he published in his *American Mercury* article for March, 1934—"Mrs. Stephen Crane"— remains in the Beer papers which Miss Alice Beer kindly let me examine a decade ago.*

In short, Beer's biography remains our sole source for the letters he quoted, with their doctored dates and scrambled texts. "This book is probably filled with errors," he confessed. Not only this book. In *Vanity Fair* (1922), Beer has Crane dying in his thirtieth year. He died at the age of twenty-eight.

Berryman's short biography added new insights and some new material. He rightly complained of Beer's incompleteness, his "grand inaccuracy, expurgation, and distortion." But Berryman's own book is faulted for the same reasons. For instance, he states that Crane was buried in Elizabeth,

---

* Four letters from the Beer papers were published in *Stephen Crane: Letters*, edited by R.W. Stallman and Lillian Gilkes (1960).

New Jersey. With seeming accuracy, he claims that the body "was dropped into the fifth position front," in the Crane plot in Evergreen Cemetery in Elizabeth. But the fact is that Crane was not buried in the family plot but in Hillside, which has never been a part of Elizabeth. Again, the hamlet of Hartwood, so important to our knowledge of Crane's youth, as Berryman describes it would seem to be purely his own invention.

Since 1950 no one has challenged Berryman's notion that Crane, in his *Press* account of the *Commodore* disaster, falsified the number of men in the dinghy; there were five men, he conjectures, and not four as Crane reported. But this ignores, for one thing, the telltale log of the Revenue Cutter *Boutwell,* which lists twenty-seven passengers aboard the steamer *Commodore,* so that there could have been only four men in the dinghy, exactly as Crane said.

The curious reader of Crane's life, Berryman remarks in his Preface to the 1962 edition of his biography, "is still stuck with either my picture or Thomas Beer's." But as Berryman himself is stuck with Beer's dominating thesis of fear, there isn't much difference between the two pictures.

"Let it be stated that the mistress of this boy's mind was fear. His search in aesthetic was governed by terror as that of tamer men is governed by the desire of women." So says Beer, although in fact we know of very few occasions where Crane was terrified, and always in those moments of fear he proved to be the grittiest person on the scene. To mention the earliest instance: When Stephen was not yet five years old he almost drowned in the Raritan River. The water's depth gradually increased, "came up to his chin, then to his mouth, and then to his eyes, but he kept steadily on, and I plucked him out, gasping but unscared, just as his yellow hair was going under. We boys were naturally delighted with his grit," his brother Edmund remembered.*

In "The Color of this Soul," one of the essays appended to his life of Crane, Berryman summarizes his Freudian thesis that Crane's "general war upon Authority" was "rooted rather in jealousy and hatred of the father" and that as a child he wished to "rescue" his mother and save her for himself. This sensational news is contradicted by the known evidence, which Berryman manipulated to fit his psychoanalytical theory.

Not the slighest evidence exists for the notion of hatred of the father, a kindly man without guile whom the son revered and who died when Stephen was eight years old. Busy with Methodist journalism, his parents let Stephen's sister Agnes run the household and attend to the boy. His mother was a good if domineering woman with whom, said Stephen, "you could argue just as well with a wave."

As Berryman himself admits in his 1951 Preface, "psychological inquiry

---

* In Thomas L. Raymond's *Stephen Crane,* a short biographical essay appearing in the same year as Beer's biography (1923).

is certainly not literary criticism." In his 1962 Preface he adds: "The most serious omission is an absence of consecutive detailed investigation of the major works."

In fairness to Beer and Berryman, it should be mentioned here that a number of vital documents were not available to them when they wrote their books. Not known to Berryman, for instance, were the manuscripts of *The Red Badge of Courage,* of a dozen poems and three dozen sketches; also a considerable number of New York City sketches and war dispatches, a hundred Crane letters, fifty Cora letters and two hundred letters about Crane (collected in *Stephen Crane: Letters*); and finally much secondary material that has come to light since 1950. The important Cora Crane papers, which had then disappeared, Berryman knew about but could not draw upon. He was not permitted to quote from the Nellie Crouse letters or the manuscript of C.K. Linson's *My Stephen Crane,* not published until 1958, although Mr. Linson aided him with "the damnable early chronology." Since the early 1950's a whole library has been written about Crane (more than 600 articles).

*Stephen Crane: Letters* (1960) settled old controversies by providing new materials, filled innnumerable gaps in the Crane chronology, corrected dates and facts previously misrepresented, "and what is most important, sharpened the focus on the real Crane," to quote the New York *Times.* These letters, as James Stronks wrote in *College English* (October 1960), "make it possible for Beer's undocumented, unobjective portrait and Berryman's derivative, thesis-ridden Freudian one to be superseded by a definitive critical biography."

Grants in aid for research, from the University of Connecticut Research Foundation, provided me the expert assistance of my former graduate students Miss Kelly Flynn, Paul Gabriner and Thomas Jones. For criticism of various chapters prior to my recasting them, I am also indebted to the graduate students in my English seminar (Spring, 1967)—Ashton Crosby, Brock Haussmen, Allen Hirsch, Thomas Jones and William Scruggs. I am grateful to Mrs. Ruth Farber, a former editor at the New York University Press, whose appraisal of my first draft bolstered my then sagging prospects of ever completing the work, and to my wife for having typed the manuscript and especially for having read and corrected it.

I wish to thank Professor George Rumney of the University of Connecticut, an oceanographer intimately acquainted with the Florida coastal waters; he rendered me invaluable aid in deciphering the mysteries of wind velocities and sea conditions at Daytona Beach for January 1–4, 1897, and interpreting the logs of the *Boutwell* and the *Newark,* during the *Commodore* disaster. For new material on that important event I am indebted to my friend Odell Hathaway, recently deceased, whose father was with Crane at Claverack College.

My acknowledgments include grateful thanks to Miss Roberta Smith, Reference Librarian at the University of Connecticut Library, and Mr. Harold Merklen, Research Librarian of the New York Public Library, for their constant aid of my Crane research during the past seventeen years. To Andrew K. Peters, Librarian at St. Lawrence University, I am indebted for a new Crane letter (dated March 24, 1896). For aid on the genealogy of the Crane family I wish to thank David C. Munn, Reference Librarian of the State of New Jersey Library at Trenton. My thanks to librarians at Harvard, Yale, and other libraries have already been recorded in my previous Crane volumes, but here I wish to thank James B. Rhoads of the National Archives and Records Service in Washington, D.C.; Miss Jane F. Smith, Acting Chief of the Office of Civil Archives; Mrs. Ann Bowden of the University of Texas Humanities Research Center; and Charles F. Cummings, Senior Librarian at the Public Library of Newark, New Jersey.

My thanks, also, to the Reverend Eric Kullberg of the Drew Methodist Church in Port Jervis for records on the Reverend Jonathan Townley Crane; Richard N. Wright, President of the Onondaga Historical Association at Syracuse, for his writing me about the City of Syracuse in the 1890's; Professor Jack W. Higgins of the University of Arizona for his aid in identifying Crane's journey on the Southern Pacific Railway in 1895; Elbert Hubbard II of East Aurora, New York, for new Crane–Hubbard information and documents (now in the Barrett Crane Collection); Mrs. W. S. Woytinsky for translating from the Russian certain books sent me by my friend Olga Vasilievskaya of Moscow, U.S.S.R.; Federal Judge E. J. Dimock for his gift of an undated press clipping in his family papers entitled "The Last of the Mohicans," which I traced to the New York *Tribune* for 1892 and thereby discovered five more new Sullivan County sketches—also for Mr. Dimock's unpublished address to the Minisink Valley Historical Society, "Stephen Crane and the Minisink Valley" (in Syracuse University Library); Mrs. Andrew E. Durham of Milford, Pike County, Pennsylvania, for a photograph of Crane's Twin Lakes camp.

I also wish to thank Miss Lillian Gilkes, whose *Cora Crane* (1960) has been an indispensable guide even where I differ from her findings. Our correspondence going back to 1955 becomes now a very useful reminder of certain problems in the Crane and Cora chronology of events and also of my debt to Miss Gilkes for much detective work and scholarship. I find now that *The War Dispatches of Stephen Crane* (1964) failed to make acknowledgment to Professor Margaret Schlauch for obtaining in London my photocopy set of the *Westminister Gazette's* series of Crane's

"With Greek and Turk." I am grateful to B. J. R. Stolper, who generously sent me years ago the set of Ernest McCready letters used in the present book largely for the first time (some of them were first quoted in *Stephen Crane: Letters,* 1960.); to Nicolas A. Pease for letters to R. W. S. (1962) pertaining to the Cranes at Ravensbrook; to Louis Zara, author of *The Dark Rider: A Novel Based on the Life of Stephen Crane* (1961), for a list of correction notes pertaining to *Stephen Crane: Letters* and for random data on Crane's brothers; to Joseph Katz, editor of *Stephen Crane Newsletter,* for providing me a copy of a new Crane letter (July 16, 1896); to Professor William Gibson of New York University for sharing his discovery of an addition to the Crane canon: "A Birthday Word from Novelist Stephen Crane" (New York *Journal*: November 8, 1896); to Professor James Stronks for constant kindnesses; to Professor Scott Osborn for the gift copy of his unpublished doctoral dissertation, *Richard Harding Davis* (University of Kentucky, 1953).

I am much indebted also to the following sources: Mr. Charles Feinberg of Detroit for providing me Crane letters, and Mr. Clifton Waller Barrett for his constant aid and solicitude. To the Barrett Crane Collection at the University of Virginia I am indebted for new Crane letters, additional to *Stephen Crane: Letters* (1960). For some new Crane letters appearing in Anita Leslie's *Mr. Frewen of England* (1966), I thank Miss Leslie for permission to quote; also Alfred A. Knopf for permission to quote from *Letters of Wallace Stevens* (1966) the New York *Tribune*'s story on Crane's funeral (1900), written by Wallace Stevens, then a reporter for that paper.

Finally, I wish to thank Edwin Seaver, editor-in-chief at George Braziller, Inc., for his unstinting efforts in my behalf in final preparation of the manuscript for publication.

R. W. S.

Storrs, Conn.
October 28, 1967

# Contents

# ⊑ List of Illustrations

*STEPHEN CRANE*

# I

## ⊂⊃ Origins and Beginnings

PARISHIONERS of the Central Methodist Church in Newark, New Jersey, were all agog that Mrs. Crane, the wife of the Reverend Jonathan Townley Crane, should be having still another baby. Mrs. Crane was in her forty-fifth year, and she had lost her four previous offspring, each dying within one year of birth.[1]

That Wednesday morning—November 1, 1871—Dr. Crane jotted down in his journal: "This morning at 5:30 our fourteenth child was born. We call him Stephen, the name of the ancestor of the Elizabethan Cranes, who was one of the company of 'Associates' who settled at E. town in 1665; also of S. Crane of Revolutionary times, who was prominent in patriotic labor and counsel for 15 years."

The same day he wrote a letter which he was too busy to mail until the next day, when he changed its date to November 2 because "I was interrupted yesterday and did not send this to the Post Office." (What interrupted him was not the arrival of Stephen but the tumble Master Edmund—age thirteen—had taken down the steep steps of the parsonage.) "Mrs. Crane sends her regards. The new baby is a boy and we have named him Stephen for his ancestor who signed the Declaration."

The Crane family was quite ancient and honorable, but Dr. Crane was mistaken in his belief that the baby's namesake—Stephen Crane, President of the Colonial Assemblies—had signed the Declaration of Independence. When the troubles with England began, New Jersey sent him to the Continental Congress in Philadelphia, but after serving there until about a week before the Declaration was signed he was obliged to return home and serve as speaker in the colony's assembly because the Tories were making too much trouble in New Jersey. He died in his old homestead while the British troops were marching past Elizabethtown en route to their defeat at Trenton.

H. G. Wells and other English friends of Stephen Crane in his maturity considered him "a New Englander of Puritan lineage, but his ancestors were founded "deep in Jersey soil (since the birth of Newark)," he told an inquirer, "and I am about as much of a Jerseyman as you can find." Montclair, New Jersey, had been called Cranetown when Jasper and Azariah Crane founded it.

His Revolutionary War ancestor—the Stephen Crane who was President of the Colonial Assemblies—was the grandson of the original Stephen Crane who had come to the new world from England or Wales as early as 1665.[2] The patriot Stephen had the family coat of arms painted on the flaps of his saddle bag. His eldest son, William, was Colonel of the Sixth Regiment in the New Jersey Infantry and had attained the rank of Major-General in the regular army at his death (from an old wound received in the expedition to Quebec). William's brother became the ranking Commodore in the Navy at the time when the title of Admiral was unknown here. Another son served in the Essex Militia, and his youngest (to quote another Stephen Crane) was captured by some Hessians, "and upon his refusing to tell the road by which they intended to surprise a certain American outpost, they beat him with their muskets and then having stabbed him with their bayonets, they left him dead in the road. In those old times the family did its duty." Some members of the family suffered in the British prison-ships in the harbor of New York City, according to Stephen's niece Edith (his brother Edmund's daughter). She remembered her uncle Stephen, in a tirade against the English when he lived at Edmund's house in Hartwood, saying: "Our family has little cause to love the gentle Britisher." During the American Revolutionary War against the British "the Cranes were pretty hot people," he wrote in one of his letters.

If he took pride in his military ancestors, he was less pleased to be named after the Biblical martyr. Once when asked if Stephen Crane was a *nom de guerre* he replied, "It is my own name. In childhood I was bitterly ashamed of it and now [1896], when I sometimes see it in print, it strikes me as being the homeliest name in created things." However, in the same year that he scoffed at his name he scribbled it over and over again while keeping score for a poker game: "Stephen Crane, Chauncey Depew, Stephen Crane."

Although in his *Black Riders* poems he repudiated the damnatory Methodism of his mother's family, he was proud of both branches of his family tree, which produced as many clergymen as soldiers. As his friend, Clarence Loomis Peaslee, remarked in 1896, illuminating at one stroke the whole wellspring of Crane's life: "It is an interesting study in heredity to note the influence of these two professions in Mr. Crane's literary work, the one furnishing the basis of style, the other of incident."[3]

The Methodist parsonage where Stephen was born was a small three-storied, red-brick house of high ceilings with scrollwork, located on the then fashionable Mulberry Place. Facing it was the house of a rich and powerful gentleman who owned most of Newark, a city which Jasper Crane and others had founded in 1666.[4] On that prim street, where every family knew every neighbor, was the house of Bishop Darlington, while further down was the yellow clapboard house of the county sheriff. Neighbors spoke of the Cranes as people they wouldn't mention "as much as two or three times" because they saw so little of them. They said Mrs. Crane was a fine woman, but that "she spent so much time doing good work outside her home that her children and the house were not as well looked after as they should have been."

As his parents had no time to expend in nurturing their unexpected seedling, they delegated parental authority to Agnes, who was fifteen years older than Stephen—that "adorable baby." His sisters, said a friend of the Crane circle, were "nice pretty young ladies," but in fact Agnes Elizabeth was not pretty. Very plain in appearance, she kept a diary in which she wrote: "I am my mother's ugly duckling." Agnes kept the household going while the Reverend and his wife managed the cause of Christ and Methodism.

The Reverend Dr. Crane was a most successful preacher; but it was said of this genial, dignified and compassionate man that "in his home life he perhaps shone the brightest." He noted in his journal for the spring of 1873: "Little Stephen has a bad cold this week." Thomas Beer in his *Stephen Crane* (1923) says that Dr. Crane halted a sermon in the Central Methodist Church with the blunt statement that Stephen was ill and needed him, but we should not infer from this that he was then pastor of the Newark church. Although he had been the pastor there in 1862–64, in the years of Stephen's earliest childhood he had no official connection with any particular church and only occasionally preached at the Central Methodist; he was busy with Methodist journalism and with his job as Presiding Elder of sixteen Methodist churches in the Newark district (1869–73). As no baptismal records in the Central Methodist Church mention Stephen Crane, it seems likely that he was baptized at home—in the parsonage at No. 14 Mulberry Place.

During his childhood he was afflicted with constant colds, and he dried his nose on a great silk handkerchief of red. Blue and red remained his favorite colors. He once followed the red skirt of a young lady visiting the family and, unnoticed, walked out the front door and down the steep steps to the corner of Mulberry Place. With the lady in red was a young man whom we shall encounter in after years as the Editor of the *Century Magazine,* Richard Watson Gilder. Stephen told his fraternity brother Frank W. Noxon that Goethe's analysis of "the effect which the several colors have upon the human mind" had made a profound impression on him and that he had utilized this idea "to produce his effects."

When he was three or four years old he was held on the back of a white horse and told by his mother not to be afraid, but he remembered that white horse as a savage beast. Mrs. Crane, influential in Methodist church affairs as speaker and as journalist, took him along the shore to a new

Methodist settlement at Ocean Grove, and the little boy thought he saw black riders on black horses riding out of the surf, and then he dreamed of these sea-riders and woke up again and again in the night screaming. It was this haunting image that years later inspired the title poem for *The Black Riders:*

> *Black riders came from the sea.*
> *There was clang and clang of spear and shield,*
> *And clash and clash of hoof and heel,*
> *Wild shouts and the wave of hair*
> *In the rush upon the wind:*
> *Thus the ride of Sin.*

The poem expresses the fear of retribution which had been instilled in the boy by the emotional frenzy of revival Methodism preached by his parents and his clerical forebears.

"Upon my mother's side," Crane remarked, "everybody as soon as he could walk became a Methodist clergyman—of the ambling-nag, saddle-bag, exhorting kind." His mother's uncle was Bishop Jesse T. Peck, from whom Stephen inherited—in 1881 when he was ten years old—a copy of his *What Must I Do to be Saved?* (1858), a hortatory tract "redolent with the fumes of sulphur and brimstone." Against the inhumanity of that creed (" 'the wrath of God abideth on you,' condemned already, already lost!"), Stephen was to write many of his *Black Riders* poems, a dozen of them on the kinship of fallen sinners.

> *I stood upon a high place,*
> *And saw, below, many devils*
> *Running, leaping,*
> *And carousing in sin.*
> *One looked up, grinning,*
> *And said, "Comrade! Brother!"*

Stephen's mother, Mary Helen Peck, daughter of the Reverend George Peck of Wilkes-Barre, Pennsylvania, married the Reverend Jonathan Townley Crane on January 8, 1848. That same year he published an *Essay on Dancing*—he was against it. Born on January 19, 1819 at Connecticut Farms (now a part of Union, near Elizabeth, New Jersey), he worked in a Newark trunk factory to earn money to enter the College of New Jersey (Princeton University).[5] When he was eighteen, at New Providence he was converted from the Presbyterian faith because he could not subscribe to the theory of infant damnation. In *Holiness the Birthright of All God's Children* (1874) he rejected the doctrine of sin remaining in the regenerate and insisted that regeneration induces the holy quality, attainment of which needs no "second distinct work." He expounded the gospel which Wesley had preached in England a century earlier: "He who is born of God doth not commit sin." Having forsaken Calvinistic determinism, he accepted the Arminian position that salvation may be attained through faith—he that believeth is saved. However, "He that believeth not is condemned"; his condition is "one of inexpressible evil. He is guilty, condemned, corrupt, helpless, the wrath of God resting on him, and hell waiting his coming, with its eternal darkness and despair." Youngster Stephen heard much about the fiery pit and a wrathful Jehovah not only from his father, but also from his mother whom he described as a single-minded woman who "lived in and for religion."

Dr. Crane impressed his contemporaries as "an unusually noble mind straitened by dogma and a narrow education." Gentlemanly in controversy and charitable in judgments, he recorded that at a ministerial meeting, "We did not so much argue as simply state our positions, with all good humor. I confess that I was surprised to find the most repulsive features of old style Calvinism advanced with scarce an apology for their deformities." His religion was less narrow than that of Bishop Jesse Truesdell Peck whose doctrine embraced natural depravity: "A mass of loathesome corruption alone can show how vile is the depravity of man." Bishop Peck, pastor of the Methodist Church in Syracuse in the year of Stephen's birth, was one of the founders of Syracuse University, and no doubt through his prestige and that of his window in 1891 Stephen obtained admission there. One of his brothers was George Peck, D. D., an eloquent Methodist minister and at one time editor of the *Christian Advocate,* to which Jonathan Townley was a frequent contributor.

About theologians with single-track minds Stephen Crane later wrote: "I didn't know clever people had mental tracks. I thought it was a privilege of the theologians." Stephen, whose ruling passion was curiosity, detested dogmas and fixed moral principles because he distrusted anything disengaged from life's realities. He spent his life exploring these realities, and thus contradicted the solipsism of his father whose logical mind was so disconnected from the world that he could only suspect its viciousness. He nowhere denied that man was a fallen sinner, but as an artist he preferred to identify with fallen humanity. His writings are haunted by his religious background. "He disbelieved it and hated it, but he could not free himself from it," said Amy Lowell. "Crane's soul was heaped with bitterness and this bitterness he flung back at the theory of life which had betrayed him."[6]

The Reverend Dr. Crane excused Noah's lapse from temperance: "The Scriptures tell us that Noah planted a vineyard and on one occasion drank of the wine until he was drunken. Very possibly the process of fermentation had not before been noticed, the results were not known, and the consequences were wholly unexpected." In *Popular Amusements* (1869) he advocated abstinence from reading novels and biographies, excepting those about good men and women, because the habit of novel-reading "creates an overgrowth of the passions . . . a morbid love of excitement somewhat akin to the imperious thirst of the inebriate." Stephen appraised his father as "a great, fine, simple mind," and he admired him for this because he himself was anything but a simple mind. Innocent and unworldly, Dr. Crane had yet much practical common sense. Although his *Arts of Intoxication,* an 1870 tract against tobacco, opium and alcohol, had sold four thousand copies and had been praised by the Sons of Temperance, he had some misgivings about the Christian Temperance Union League when four ladies from Ohio came to consult with his wife in 1873. "Mrs. Crane is much impressed by this project. I do not think it exactly practical." Mrs. Crane, nevertheless, joined the New Jersey Women's Christian Temperance Union and became its eloquent spokeswoman for the rest of her life.

Stephen's father and mother endured a hectic life in the service of the church; they were always on the move with their large family—"such an oyster-like family," Agnes called it. From Newark they moved in 1874 to Bloomington on the Raritan, across from Bound Brook, and then on to Paterson, New Jersey, where Dr. Crane was pastor of the Cross-Street Church from 1876 to 1878. "He worked himself to death, my people thought," said Stephen in after years. His job as presiding elder of the Methodist Conference exhausted him. By October 1876 he had visited six hundred parishioners since taking over the Methodist Church in Paterson, and illness and fatigue resulted from his strenuous devotion to his congregation there. "Much encouragement in my work," he noted on February 3 (1877). "Still, thus far, no wave of power has come sweeping all before it, as we sometimes see. Perhaps it will, if we hold on our way, doing our duty."

Unknown to his mother, four year old Stephen paddled naked in the Raritan and almost drowned. Once during a sermon Dr. Crane was interrupted by the child's wails; he had dropped his monstrous red handkerchief in the aisle. On another occasion Dr. Crane shook out a folded handkerchief in the face of his congregation only to find to his horror that it was a baby's undershirt. One Sunday morning two of his children—one of them quite likely Stephen—came down the aisle of the church and waved a rat trap at him crying: "Here it is, Father. You said to bring it to you as soon as we found it." Father's dignity was rather compromised, but he had a great sense of humor and was so much noted for it that a movement was once made to publish a collection of his witticisms. He was fond of boys and said that they "should be handled with great kindness and care as they have often notions about justice in conduct far beyond their years." Himself the youngest of six children, he felt particular sympathy for his own youngest offspring.

The boy inherited his father's idealism, forbearance and pride, and his incorrigible independence and will power; the itinerant father produced an itinerant and restless son always seeking impossible horizons. Dr. Crane, said the *Christian Advocate* in its 1874 review of *Holiness the Birthright of*

*All God's Children,* "explores for himself with careful, cautious, wise navigation the great, the illimitable oceans of truth." Stephen was to explore it too, but his navigation was never careful and cautious; often it was imprudent.

The Methodist Church in Paterson had difficulty in paying Dr. Crane his annual salary of $1800, and though "a determination was expressed to make up $200" to add to the $1600 paid him, he noted in March 1878 that his brethren "talked despondingly and seemed to take it for granted that they can not give me what they know I need." He obtained appointment as pastor of the Drew Methodist Church in the more attractive country town of Port Jervis in the New York hills (near the junction of New Jersey and Pennsylvania). He was not quite sixty. Mrs. Crane came to like the sanctity of provincial Port Jervis; and her husband remarked: "I am much more concerned that we should live truthfully and kindly here than that we should be busy in condemning the luxuries and sins of New York."

Stephen was nearly seven now, but he had not yet been to school. A delicate child, he had been nursed by his sister Agnes during the previous year, and perhaps the question of his health was one of the reasons for the family's settling in Port Jervis with its mountain air in nearby Hartwood. It was Agnes who saw after Stephen's education in his early years. She combed his long curls, which were not shorn until he was eight, and taught him whatever he learned about nature lore, science and literature. She said she wanted to be a "Christian lady" first of all and then to write. Very proud of her brother's first writings, she remained his closest companion until her death when she was only twenty-eight.

Actually Stephen did not begin his regular schoolboy routine until his eighth birthday. He had no difficulty in getting through two grades in six weeks. That "sounds like the lie of a fond mother at a teaparty," he recalled, "but I do remember that I got ahead very fast and that father was pleased with me. He used to take me driving with him to little places near Port Jervis where he was going to preach or bury somebody. Once we got mixed up in an Irish funeral near a place named Slate Hill. Everybody was drunk and father was scandalized. . . . He was so simple and good that I often think he didn't know much of anything about humanity. Will, one of my brothers, gave me a toy gun and I tried to shoot a cow with it[7] over at Middletown [near Port Jervis] when father was preaching there and that upset him wonderfully. He liked all kinds of animals and never drove a horse faster than two yards an hour even if some Christian was dying elsewhere." Stephen, too, liked all kinds of animals, especially dogs and horses. "I think that if he had not been a writer he would have been a mounted policeman! He would almost rather ride a horse than play ball," said his friend C. K. Linson. Stephen (as his sister-in-law Mrs. George Crane remembered him) "was a lovable boy, full of life and animal spirits. He possessed manly characteristics, which he displayed when scarcely more than a child."[8]

Fierce winds from the North froze up everything in February, 1880, but on the 8th Dr. Crane preached on "a Christian indeed" and again that evening against the Christian Liberals "he preached so long that we omitted the Prayer meeting." Then he went to Newark with his daughter Agnes to find employment for a lad named Sam Weller—a strict Methodist had discharged Sam from his shop for having denied Hell. On returning to Port Jervis, he caught a cold, but he nevertheless preached that Sunday. He died the next day—Monday, February 16, 1880—after one hour of sickness from "paralysis of the heart."[9]

In the parlor of the parsonage Stephen polished the coffin's silver-handles while in the kitchen some country women sang hymns. "We tell kids that heaven is just across the gaping grave and all that bosh and then we scare them to glue with flowers and white sheets and hymns," he declared twenty years later. "We ought to be crucified for it! I have forgotten nothing about this, not a damned iota, not a shred."

After his father's death in February 1880, his mother moved the family from the Methodist parsonage in Port Jervis to a boarding-house in Roseville outside Newark. But when Stephen developed scarlet fever she brought him back to the healthier climate of Port Jervis, where he had previously recovered from severe colds in the nearby forested hills of Hartwood. From Newark's Roseville the family moved in 1883 to a small house in Asbury Park on the New Jersey coast. That summer Stephen (now eleven) exhumed from the ocean sands a little chap whom he pretended a burial squad had buried on the "battlefield." The "corpse," with an imaginary canteen full of whiskey on him, was the nephew of Miss Olive Brett, and when she discovered poor Johnny buried in the sands she "rescued" him and spanked youngster Crane. (Or perhaps she only tried to, for it is difficult to spank an eleven-year-old boy.) Miss Brett had let Stephen look through the flat tomes of her Harper's illustrated *History of the Rebellion* and other worthwhile books—like the Reverend James Dixon's tour of America. She had also tried to read Dickens' *A Christmas Carol* to him but he fell asleep. Some twelve years later, when Stephen was doing research for his Civil War novel, Miss Brett—by then Mrs. Armstrong—was to lend him Century's *Battles and Leaders,* which her father assured him was accurate.

At eight, when his brother Edmund had given him a quarter for the barber to shear off his long curls (much to his mother's distress), Stephen became interested in a child character named Little Goldie Brighteyes, "and I wrote a story then which I called after this fascinating person." It was around this time that his mother made him a pair of mittens of brightest red to match his red-topped boots. When he was about ten, Agnes gave him *Sir Wilfred's Seven Flights,* the adventures of a rake who always ends in some frustrating predicament (as does Crane's rakish hero in *The O'Ruddy*). He also had "a bully time" playing games patterned on *The Terror of the Sagebrush* and on *Black Dick of the Pony Express.* It was from these various incidents that he later fashioned two of his Whilomville stories.

Stephen loved to play at soldiers, and partly because of his fondness for everything military his mother was induced to send him to the military school at Claverack in his seventeenth year. Long after his happy years at Claverack, Stephen wrote his brother William not to give away the two swords he had worn with his uniform.

Meanwhile he attended school at Asbury Park, where his oldest sister, Mary Helen Hamilton, was an art instructor, and his brother Jonathan Townley of the Newark *Advertiser* operated a summer news-reporting agency for the New York *Tribune.* Brother Wilbur Fiske, a medical student, spent summer vacations gathering shore news for Townley, and so did their mother. Ambitious and educated, although not college bred,[10] "Mother wrote articles for Methodist papers and reported for the *Tribune* and the [Philadelphia] *Press,*" Stephen later recalled. Every August she went to Ocean Grove, adjacent to Asbury Park on the New Jersey coast, "and reported proceedings at the Methodist holy show there." After Dr. Crane died, "We had very little money"; nevertheless, Mrs. Crane managed to put three of her sons into college, thanks to some stock in coal mines she had inherited.

Asbury Park was advertised as a seaside resort free from sin. When a certain girl became pregnant, Mrs. Crane took care of the unwedded mother. "My brothers tell me that she got herself into trouble, before I was old enough to follow proceedings, by taking care of a girl who had an accidental baby. Inopportune babies are not part of Methodist ritual but mother was always more of a Christian than a Methodist and she kept this girl at our house in Asbury until she found a home elsewhere. Mother's friends were mostly women and they had the famous feminine aversion to that kind of baby. It is funny that women's interest in babies trickles clean off the mat if they have never met papa socially." Stephen concluded that his mother—"a very religious woman"—was not as narrow as most of her friends or her Peck family.

In May 1884 Agnes Elizabeth died, and perhaps to mitigate Stephen's grief over the death of his dearest friend and teacher he was given a retired trick circus-pony to ride—a gift from Townley. He rode the pony "Pudgy" from Asbury Park south as far as the Shark River, and then back again to the Asbury beach to show off to the other children by plunging into the ocean while clinging to the pony's bare back. Four years later he took the pony Pudgy with him to the Claverack military school.

During the summers at Asbury Park he achieved some small measure of fame as a member of the uniformed Asbury Park baseball team, although he was one of the youngest and lightest members of that youngster ballclub. When he was fifteen he wrote his friend Wallis McHarg that he was going to be a professional ballplayer. "But ma says it's not a serious occupation and Will says I have to go to college first." McHarg replied from Chicago that they both ought to go to college first—unless they enlisted in the army. Stephen boasted that no one could pitch a baseball that he could not catch barehanded; he disdained to wear a glove.

Just to prove that he was also a writer he interrupted his ballgames long enough to write an essay for a twenty-five cent prize. Even at that early age he could coin words to suit his meaning. "A boy of fourteen who can use *irascible, pyrotechnic, impartial,* and *memorial* correctly in an impromptu essay written between two hot games of baseball is not as other American boys of fourteen. He had a passion for outlandish words and even invented one, a verb, *higgle.*" (To higgle is to behave in the manner of a schoolteacher.) He was brilliant and his mother was delighted at his brilliance in his studies other than algebra. His prodigious predilection for words no doubt began when as a child he made symbols on a piece of paper in imitation of brother Townley's handwriting and asked: "Ma, how do you spell O?" At fourteen he wrote a tale about an old farmer who on visiting the big town almost brought out the fire engine by pulling on a bell-handle which he didn't recognize as one, and that incident comprises "Uncle Jake and the Bell-Handle"—Crane's earliest known manuscript.

In the summer of 1884 Stephen saved Wallis McHarg from the surf at Asbury Park and then threatened the older boy that he would punch him in the jaw if McHarg squealed that they had been swimming on a Sunday. This same summer he was riding his pony Pudgy on the beach when he saw a white girl stabbed by her Negro lover. At home he said nothing about it, although he was sweating with fright. Seven years later he had another terrifying experience when an angry Port Jervis mob lynched a Negro named Robert Lewis on a high tree in front of the Baptist Church. The white man who claimed to have captured him told the mob that the Negro had confessed that he had assaulted a white girl, Lena McMahon. The mob exploded. Someone threw a thick rope around the Negro, and then he was pulled by waiting hands up the hill, past the park, past two churches. Women threw garbage at him as he stumbled by, and men flicked him with their riding-whips. The Negro writhed and twisted as he was dragged along East Main Street, his clothing was torn from him down to the waist, and then the thick rope was moved from his waist to his neck and thrown over the sturdy branch of a tree on the corner of Ferguson Avenue. Stephen and his brother William, then thirty-eight, tried in vain to pull the rope down but were pushed aside. In the depraved mob were young ruffians, many of them thieves and loafers, and many of them drunk. Crashes of thunder lit the sky "as if God was trying to say something" that

Thursday afternoon of June 2, 1892. "Depravity not Justice," declared the New York *Tribune,* in an article no doubt written by Jonathan Townley Crane.[11]

In the summer of 1888, when he was "about sixteen," Stephen began to write for the New York *Tribune* in articles unsigned and submitted by Townley at his Asbury Park agency, "doing correspondence from Asbury Park and other places." Townley paid out of his own pocket for what Stephen wrote up, or for the shore data his kid brother collected. Some of these early articles were written by Townley, some by Mrs. Crane, with portions contributed by Stephen.

Mrs. Crane, who was sorely pressed by duties—lecturing for the Women's Christian Temperance Union and writing for Methodist papers such as *The Heathen Woman's Friend*—turned to Stephen to gather data for her *Tribune* articles. Pale-faced and hungry-looking, always seeming more fragile than he was, he covered miles of hot sandy roads on a bicycle to collect the names of hotel guests arriving for Ocean Grove's Methodist assemblies. At fashionable Asbury Park there were sailing parties and clambakes to report, and at the nearby resort of Avon-by-the-Sea he gathered news about the Chautauqua Seaside Assembly's program for summer education.

Ocean Grove offered religion, Asbury Park entertainment, and Avon-by-the-Sea culture. The only Ocean Grove amusements were donkey and soap-bubble parties. However, the New York *Tribune,* in an article probably written by secret agent Stephen, hinted that "the seductive game of poker is played here nightly in two of the hotels in rooms which are securely bolted and locked before the game opens." Who but brother Townley was playing poker behind those locked doors? Ocean Grove, advertised as "The Summer Mecca of American Methodists," prohibited not only poker-playing and liquor and tobacco, but Sunday newspapers and novels as well. Also prohibited was the shocking new bathing suit for women, as noted in the *Tribune* ("Gay Bathing Suit and Novel Both Must Go),[12] and dancing too. But daring young Methodists could sneak off across Wesley Lake (named after the English founder of the Methodist faith) to dance in the gayer hotels of Asbury Park, where they could sin also by reading Sunday newspapers, drinking liquor and smoking tobacco.

Ocean Grove with its "Methodist Holy side show," as Crane called it, commemorated the centenary of the 1788 massacre of men, women, and children tomahawked by the Indians in the fort at Wyoming, Pennsylvania, by erecting a mock-stockade on the beach between Ocean Grove and Asbury Park. A hundred summer residents dressed themselves as warlike redskins, while others enacted the role of the doomed settlers. The horde of yelling "savages" in war-paint and feathers stormed it amid the shrieks of the "butchered victims." Stephen undoubtedly had read about these doomed settlers in Pennsylvania's Wyoming Valley, and their struggle against the Indians and the Tories, in the history book entitled *Wyoming* (1858), by George Peck (father of his mother). George Peck had married the daughter of Mary Myers Bennett; the author of *Wyoming* was thus related to the Bennett who figures in Stephen Crane's " 'Ol' Bennet' and the Indians," for which Wyoming tale Crane lifted passages right out of his grandpa's book. Brother Wilbur owned a copy of *Wyoming* and brought it with him on his visit to Stephen in England in 1899. He must also have taken it back home with him; it is not listed in Crane's "List of Books at Brede Place."

On the exhibition grounds outside the palisade hawkers sold various kinds of gewgaws, balloons, stick-candy, and even beer. Stephen and his friend George Wheeler got there by horse-car from Asbury Park, each with twenty-five cents to spend. The boys were separated from their mothers all afternoon, Mrs. Crane going to Ocean Grove in Mrs. Wheeler's family buggy. Outside the entrance gate of the palisade sat a huge Pennsylvania Dutchman with an upturned box supporting beer mugs in a row and a sign: "Beer 10 cents." Brash Stephen placed a dime on the box and demanded: "Gimme one." He said it with such an air of purpose that young George Wheeler's blood chilled. "I can still see the man's rotund face as he bent down over his keg and surveyed Stevie's diminutive figure," wrote Wheeler later. "'Hey?' he said. 'I said gimme a beer,' said Stevie. The man's fingers had closed on the eloquent coin. 'You gimme a beer or gimme back my dime,' said Stevie in a shrill falsetto. The man held a mug with a dab of foam in it toward him, but Stevie regarded it with fine scorn. 'That ain't half full!' he said indignantly. 'You fill it up.' The tap was turned then and Stevie drank slowly, while I watched in stupefaction. We walked through the gate. 'How does it taste?' I asked. 'Tain't any better'n ale,' he said. 'I been saving that dime for it all afternoon.' I was still in a daze when we came to the streetcar. Beer! Right in the crowd, too . . . 'Stevie,' I whispered as the driver whipped up the horses and the bells clanged, 'how'd you dast do it?' 'Pshaw,' said Stevie. 'Beer ain't nothing at all.' Then he added, defensively but emphatically, 'How was I going to know what it tasted like less'n I tasted it? How you going to know about things at all less'n you *do* 'em?' "[13]

On another occasion Mrs. Crane and Mrs. Wheeler, both leading members of the Women's Christian Temperance Union, went by train to Atlantic City to hear the celebrated Frances E. Willard speak. Very pale and graceful in her gestures, in gray with a white scarf falling down to her waist, Miss Willard looked like a nun. Her purity of mind and appearance impressed the ladies. She had proclaimed a decade ago that it was an unchristian thing for a boy to appear naked, or undressed outside his home. After the lecture Stevie and George Wheeler rode home to Asbury Park in the smoker of the day coach. (While their mothers were listening to Mrs. Willard's temperance lecture, they had secretly been watching a gloveless prize fight in a barn.) For boys to smoke was in those days to dare it, to challenge manhood. Between covert glances backward to the car where his mother was sitting, Stevie puffed at his Sweet Caporal cigarette, and persuaded George to try one.

As a center for religious and mental culture Ocean Grove took first rank, wrote Mrs. Crane in one of her unsigned *Tribune* reports, entitled "The Rise of Ocean Grove" (other of her reports bore such titles as "Temperance Women at the Seaside" and "Interested in Bible Lessons"). At Ocean Grove "the soul hungry for intellectual pabulum can feast to its fulness"; even the black man was here the white man's brother. But Stephen, even though he attended the Sunday School Assembly and was exposed to such Biblical lore as the eight important mountains discussed in Bible geography lessons, took a more cynical view than his idealistic mother. In after years he recalled in "The Monster" the social ostracism of a Port Jervis Negro who horrified the townfolk by his ugly disfigured face.

Mrs. Crane declared that she planned her campaigns against intemperance just as an army general would marshal his forces before battle. In her crusade against the vices of her sinful times she was trying, she said, to "catch Time by the fetlock." Stephen, who loved his mother but could not help teasing her now and then, told her she might get her head kicked off if she were not more careful to distinguish between fetlock and forelock.

His brother William would try to argue with their mother on religious subjects but he always gave up. It wasn't that their mother "was bitter or mean but it hurt her that any of us should be slipping from Grace and giving up eternal damnation or salvation or those things," Stephen recalled. "She was always sailing off when she felt well enough to some big prayer meeting or experience meeting and she spoke very well. Her voice was something like Ellen Terry's but deeper. She spoke as slowly as a big clock ticks and her effects were impromptu. . . . It is in me to think that she did good work for the public schools. One of my sisters [Agnes] was a teacher, and mother tried for years to get women placed on the school boards and to see that whiskey was not sold to boys under age." When the sale of alcohol to New Jersey school children had become a scandal, she proposed to stop it, and her work on this project brought her some recognition by women of various religious sects. They admired her dignity as a speaker on the platform.[14]

Mrs. Crane remarked to some women friends: "Stevie is like the wind in Scripture. He bloweth where he listeth." "I used to like church and prayer meetings when I was a kid," Crane said, "but that cooled off and when I was thirteen or about that, my brother Will told me not to believe in Hell after my uncle had been boring me about the lake of fire and the rest of the sideshows. . . . Once when I was fourteen an organ grinder on the beach at Asbury gave me a nice long drink out of a nice red bottle for picking up his hat for him. I felt ecstatic walking home and then I was an Emperor and some Rajahs and Baron de Blowitz[15] all at the same time. I had been sulky all morning and Mother was tickled to death. And, mind you, all because this nefarious Florentine gave me a red drink out of a bottle. I have frequently wondered how much mothers ever know about their sons, after all. She would not have found it much of a joke."

In one of Crane's Cuban War tales a father says to his son: "I guess you are no damned good." Stephen's father would never have said that, but his son felt about himself that way. He felt himself unworthy of his father because he fell short of his father's moral principles and his nobility of spiritual outlook.

"Yeh must allus remember yer father," says Henry Fleming's mother in *The Red Badge of Courage*. "Remember he never drank a drop of licker in his life, and seldom swore a cross oath."

Revolt against the fathers is the common lot of sons, but in Stephen Crane's life it is exemplified more clearly than in any other American writer. He came to revel in all the vices his father preached against. At a very early age he began smoking incessantly, drinking beer, and swearing —"Hully Gee" and "Ho Hell" were his favorite poolroom cuss-words while at Claverack military school. One of his early sketches, "The Camel," depicts a convocation of Methodist ministers surprised by a drunken camel smiling at them "with an expression of foolish good nature," whereupon the astonished clergymen take flight by climbing up into trees. It was "the first time I had seen a clergyman climbing a tree." They had assembled in the prohibitionist State of Maine, and the camel had crossed the border carrying the illegal cargo of a dozen bottles of scotch. This cynical camel is, as it were, Stephen Crane who likewise crossed into forbidden territories and transgressed the frontiers not only of alcohol, tobacco and swearing, but also of pool and poker playing, baseball and dancing, and other out-of-bounds and unholy regions such as the theatre and the house of prostitution.

The Reverend Dr. Crane, father of fourteen children, declared in his *Arts of Intoxication* that total abstinence is the guiding rule for the proper conduct of life, and he properly abstained from everything—from everything but sex; he doesn't mention sex in his *Popular Amusements* (1869). He prophesied that baseball was in decline because so many vices cluster around the ballground that "everyone connected with it seems to be regarded with a degree of suspicion." As for dancing, "the dancing-master is the devil's drill-sergeant, just as the theatre is the devil's church."

In his satirical sketch "Dan Emmonds" Stephen converts the Reverend Dr. Crane into a saloon keeper, as it were. Unable to support his son, the Irish saloon keeper sends Dan to sea. The ship is about to sail for Australia when his father discovers and removes from his baggage some cases of liquor which the youth had sequestered from the saloon. "But in truth my father never extremely admired me, for some reason or another. 'You should have been the son of a big brewer, Dan,' he often said to me."

Dan Emmonds asks the ship's captain, when the ship runs into a storm while approaching Australia, not to let the ship founder until he has first of all drunk a bottle of rum. Shipwrecked, he reaches an island and addresses some cannibals on matters of religion so as to assure them that he is not a religious bigot. He avows his willingness "to worship anything from fire and the sun to a large stone kitten if it will be a comfort to the people of the country." He tells the cannibals: "May the light of the sun illumine the faces of your clay gods when they look at you—that is to say, if you have clay gods. If you have not, I can only say that what you do have must needs be right in my opinion, since you are enlightened citizens of this great country while I am only a citizen of New York City, and not up to the average when there." Dan Emmonds is Crane's mock version of the "missionary" among the cannibals.[16]

The Reverend Dr. J. T. Crane believed in the necessity for missionaries because the Word must spread. However, he cautioned that the candidates for the post of missionary "should be strictly examined as to their motives in undertaking these duties. We hear grave reports of some who domineer and oppress these childish intellects committed to their care, and it cannot be doubted that some of our brethren seek to exalt their own station and that some are more interested to clothe the naked bodies of the heathen than to enlighten their minds." Missionary Dan Emmonds is indeed "a man of great liberality in religious matters," whereas Dr. Crane, "a strict Methodist of the old stamp," was said to be an austere bigot, more austere than the average reform clergyman of his day. "He leaves the impression of an unusually noble mind straightened by dogma and a narrow education," says the *Dictionary of American Biography* (1930). Even the Methodists' *Christian Advocate,* long edited by George Peck, D. D. (Mrs. Crane's father), permitted advertisements for novels.

Novel reading was the cursed vice of the age, said the elder Crane, whose *Popular Amusements* included: "Read your Bibles." In reading novels "If any harm results, Stop at once." He finally settled on a "rigid iron rule for the guidance of all, young and old, learned and unlearned: Total abstinence from novel reading henceforth and forever." Poor Stephen, cursed with the blight of all the sins damned by his father in print and in pulpit, not only read novels but wrote them. In defiance of his father's God, the wrathful Jehovah of the Old Testament, he set a God of human compassion:

> *A man went before a strange God—*
> *The God of many men, sadly wise.*
> *And the Deity thundered loudly,*
> *Fat with rage, and puffing,*

> *"Kneel, mortal, and cringe*
> *And grovel and do homage*
> *To My Particularly Sublime Majesty."*
>
> *The man fled.*
> *Then the man went to another God—*
> *The God of his inner thoughts.*
> *And this one looked at him*
> *With soft eyes*
> *Lit with infinite comprehension,*
> *And said, "My poor child!"*

In his *Black Riders and Other Lines* (1895) Crane castigated

> *Blustering God,*
> *Stamping across the sky*
> *With loud swagger,*
> *I fear You not.*
> *No, though from Your highest heaven*
> *You plunge Your spear at my heart,*
> *I fear You not.*
> *No, not if the blow*
> *Is as the lightning blasting a tree*
> *I fear You not, puffing braggart.*

In *War is Kind* (1899) he wrote: "You tell me this is God?/ I tell you this is a printed list,/ A burning candle, and an ass." Not even the angels can recognize the purpose of the church and the people congregated therein, he says in another poem: "Two or three angels/ Came near to the earth. / They saw a fat church. / Little black streams of people / Came and went in continually. / And the angels were puzzled / To know why the people went thus, / And why they stayed so long within." They went to church to hear Methodist clergymen like his father preach on the doctrine of spiritual growth and Christian perfection.

The Reverend Dr. Crane once noted that ministers were of two kinds: "One is a *son of thunder*, another a *son of consolation*." Both the thunder and the consolation appear in Stephen's poetry, but in his treatment of God and of religion (to quote Daniel G. Hoffman) there is "a progress from the utter denial of 'Well, then I hate Thee' to an affirmation of faith in the 'interior pitying God.' Crane goes even beyond proposing an alternative deity: in his best and most neglected poem there is an apocalyptic vision of the triumph of this God of love." That poem is "The Blue Battalions," written in 1897 after his return from the Greco-Turkish War.

> *Mistakes and virtues will be trampled deep.*
> *A church and a thief shall fall together.*
> *A sword will come at the bidding of the eyeless,*
> *The God-led, turning only to beckon,*
> > *Swinging a creed like a censer*

*At the head of the new battalions,*
  *Blue battalions,*
*March the tools of nature's impulse,*
*Men born of wrong, men born of right,*
*Men of the new battalions,*
  *The blue battalions.*

*The clang of swords is Thy wisdom,*
*The wounded make gestures like Thy Son's;*
*The feet of mad horses is one part—*
*Ay, another is the hand of a mother on the brow of a youth.*
  *Then, swift as they charge through a shadow,*
  *The men of the new battalions,*
    *Blue battalions—*
*God lead them high, God lead them far,*
*These new battalions,*
  *The blue battalions.*

In *Holiness* Dr. Crane urged the young Christian "not to rest content with the beginnings of the Christian life, but to go on unto perfection, to grow up into Christ in all things, and from a child become a man." The Wesleyan doctrine of spiritual growth is personified by Henry Fleming in *The Red Badge of Courage.* Untested by battle, young Henry progresses under stress and at the end of his battles he feels he has attained "a quiet manhood." The sense of guilt and isolation resulting from Stephen Crane's rebellion against his father's dogmas, which had been the original ground of his childhood security, found expression in all his writings, notably in the soul searching of Henry Fleming, that raw recruit in the Army of the Lord.

Dr. Crane, author of *The Right Way* (1853), had preached "the right way"; but his son took another way. In the later years of his brief life, when he was living in England, he wrote the Reverend Charles J. Little, who had taught him history at Syracuse, boasting of his literary successes. Dr. Little, in reply to his rather cocky letter, wrote him that "to know poison, one must have it in one's blood. Even then, the experimenter encounters a peculiar difficulty; the poison destroys his powers to perceive its effects." Crane knew the poison within him and perceived its effects. He was speaking of himself when he wrote in *The Black Riders* (1895): "In all drink / He detected the bitters."

His life, from the years of his publication of *Maggie* in 1893, was to be a concatenation of disillusionments. He somehow sensed that it was going to be that way. His curiosity-ridden mind impelled him to probe the warfare of life in the slums of New York and the battlefields of Greece and Cuba. But battlefields were to him no more the real thing than the Bowery. He tested the one and the other and found them equally metaphoric of the battle of life. To probe life's realities—that was to be for the son of the Reverend Dr. Crane "the right way."

# II

## ⊂⊅ Education

SOME months before Stephen introduced George Wheeler to the taste of beer and tobacco, he had been playing whist at Claverack College & Hudson River Institute, where at sixteen he signed the register on January 4, 1888. He wrote "Whist" at the top of a page in a notebook with the word "Autographs" imprinted on the cover, and signed: "Very Sincerely / Your Friend / S. T. Crane / New York City. Dated March 27, 1888, this inscription with the middle initial "T" is a still unriddled puzzle compounded by the fact that the New York City Directory for 1892–93 lists under Crane: "Stephen H. author, h(ouse) 1604 Av. A." Nowhere else is there any indication that Crane ever used a middle initial; he always signed himself as S. C. or Stephen Crane. (The New York City directory for the previous year, incidentally, lists Stephen Crane as a janitor living on W. 24th Street.)[1]

Before entering Claverack, Stephen had spent the previous fall semester at the Pennington Seminary in Pennington, New Jersey, where his father had served for a time as principal. At Claverack, a semi-military and co-educational school, he had "a bully time"—one of the happiest periods of his short life. He enjoyed the "tough devils who hang out in Sioux's room" and also the girls; in less than two years there he fell in love with two redheads and a tall dark-haired girl from Sioux City, Iowa. One of the tough devils was Earl T. Reeve of Rushville, Indiana, whom he nicknamed the Rushville Indian "Sioux." All his life Crane called his friends "Indians." beginning now as a term of affection but ending in later years as a term of contempt.

Another tough devil at the school on the Hudson was Odell Hathaway from Middletown, New York, near Port Jervis where Stephen's brother William had lived in a nice comfortable house on East Main Street since 1882. Crane's earliest known letters were written to Odell beginning with the one he wrote on Christmas morning (1888?): "Hello central: hello: Give me tough Hathaway, Middletown. Well, old man, I hope you are having a merry, merry X'mas. I expect to stop up and see you as I promised but cant tell you for sure yet. Johnnie wrote me that he was afraid he couldn't show up, but would try. I expect to go to P. J. in a few days and on my way back will stop and see you. . . .Write me here at A. P." (Asbury Park).

Mrs. Crane sent Stephen to a military school because she hoped the discipline would strengthen morally her brilliant but diffident son. As drillmaster he became a martinet although he never got to bed on time and "rose mornings at the last possible moment for drill, hurled himself into socks, shoes and trousers, and from the waist up wore usually only his uniform jacket." He managed to earn the reputation among the Claverack faculty that he would come to a bad end because he gambled, drank, and smoked. In his father's credo these were sins, but the Reverend Dr. Crane's boy could quote Scripture with the devil. He recalled the words of St. John which his father had quoted on the title page of his book, *Holiness:* "Whosoever is born of God doth not commit sin; for his seed remaineth in him, and he cannot sin because he is born of God."

Stephen was remembered by his classmates as a friendly boy, although moody and rebellious (as his sister Agnes had been); he was liked by all except those teachers whose classes he cut in preference for the baseball diamond. The only school sports in those days were baseball and lawn tennis, which he liked somewhat; but in baseball he starred as catcher. At first he caught the ball barehanded, but later in the season a buckskin glove saved him the iodine and witch hazel for hurt hands. As each player in those days outfitted himself in whatever clothes he pleased, the diamond "presented an appearance of Joseph in the Bible Days with his coat of many colors." An indifferent schoolboy in such studies as mathematics and science, he was far in advance of his colleagues in history and literature (thanks to Agnes' tutoring him as a youngster). By calling Tennyson's poetry "swill" he got into a fist fight which cost him part of a tooth sometime that spring. He endured the ordeal of memorizing and reciting "The Charge of the Light Brigade," an agony he recast in his English years into "Making an Orator," a Whilomville story. Abram Lincoln Travis, his fellow student at Claverack, where Travis later taught after graduating from Syracuse University in 1894, remembers him as a voracious reader of all 19th Century English writers and of the classics of Greece and Rome. Plutarch's *Lives* was his constant companion, and he could quote from Tennyson's "In Memoriam" and Bryant's "Thanatopsis" and was familiar with the English and American poets. And of course he knew the Bible well. That his readings all his life were miscellaneous and desultory is evidenced by the "List of Books / Brede Place." He was never literary or bookish.

Claverack College by Crane's day had deteriorated into the Hudson River Institute and was a mere boarding school for backward or semi-incorrigible offspring who found there in the long, crooked, uneven corridors a carefree spirit, free from discipline. The boys and girls "roamed as in a terrestrial paradise like packs of cheerful wolves out of bounds, out of hours and very much out of hand." No wonder Stephen was happy there; it was "simply pie."[2]

Harriet Mattison was his first "love". "I all but fell in love with her myself," said Crane's Claverack classmate Harvey Wickham. The malady of falling in love with Harriet was not uncommon. She was the best pianist in the so-called Music Conservatory at Claverack, and was very pretty, with her freckles and an adorable Irish nose; sad to relate, she died only a year later. Steve's chief infatuation, however, was for another redhead, Jennie Pierce. While he camped in the Summer of 1894 at Twin Lakes, Pennsylvania, a third redhead struck his fancy, but apparently he preferred blondes. If he ever found a woman with golden hair he would marry her, he said.[2]

As the school's leading tenor he accompanied choirmaster Harvey Wickham in the Methodist Church in Claverack, the tiny Dutch village across from the Catskills. Crane, says Wickham, had "a light pleasant voice, true in pitch, if of no great power or compass—Mr. [Thomas] Beer is mistaken in saying that it was a baritone—and though he pretended not to like to sing, the pretense was not convincing."

He also volunteered for the job of pumping the church organ at Claverack; it spared him from having to sit out front and listen to the sermons. Wickham had taken over the organist job from the Director of the Conservatory because that giant's boots clumsily brought two pedals down at a time.

In March 1890, when a prominent New York tenor, Albert G. Thies, sang at a Claverack recital, Stephen interviewed him and found that he had once given a performance before a Zulu chief in Africa. The incident appeared in a sketch he contributed the next year to the *University Herald* (May 1891) when he was flunking out at Syracuse University.

Harvey Wickham recalls answering a knock at the door of his dormitory room and opening to find two of his fellow students, one dressed in the height of collegiate fashion and the other in a dirty old sweater—that was "wistful" Stephen Crane. " 'We're taking up a collection of tobacco,' exclaimed the wistful one. Now, tobacco was a forbidden thing in these Methodist precincts, and for that reason I naturally had some. Why I parted with it was—to me—at the time a mystery; there was something about the wistful one that took me at once." Smoking was for Stephen part of his pose of rebellion. "I am smoking a cigar after a 10:00 A.M. breakfast of roast pigeon and gooseberries," he boasted to Odell Hathaway in June 1890, writing from Asbury Park about his longing for some of his old companions at Claverack, "yet I wish to God I was puffing on a cigarette butt after 7:00 A.M. breakfast of dried-beef and oat meal at H. R. I." A Claverack schoolmate wrote Stephen when he was a freshman at Lafayette College, and he replied: "So you are not having a hell of a time at C. C., eh? Well, you had better have it now because, mark my words, you will always regret the day you leave old C. C. The fellows here raise more hell than any college in the country, yet I have still left a big slice of my heart up among the pumpkin seeds and farmers of Columbia Co."

Wickham says that Crane all his life strove to win recognition as a regular fellow. To the contrary, he didn't give a damn whether one liked him or not. He knew he was no "regular fellow," and because he wasn't he was disliked, especially when he was a star reporter in Greece and in Cuba. Some time after his Claverack days but before he was famous, he spotted Harvey Wickham and hailed him—"Hello, Harvey!"—as he boarded a trolley between Middletown and Goshen, New York. "And immediately something perverse, absurd, took possession of me," Wickham says. "I had never been shocked by this man's profundities, not knowing that he had them, for one thing. But I was at the time an indifferently poor musician, with all an indifferently poor musician's horror of the impolite. Steve's sweater was still unwashed, and I was in that stage of culture which judges the world by its neckties. Here, evidently, was somebody to be put in his place. So I answered stiffly: 'How do you do, Mr. Crane?' Simply this, and nothing more." Which tells us more about Wickham than about Crane, whose bias was against merely polite persons.

Wickham, however, rightly detected the contradictions in Crane, "which puzzled so many. It was by no fortuitous circumstances that his chum [Earl Reeve] was the richest boy in the school. In the slums or among aristocrats he could breathe. With the middle class he was always a little David throwing unmannerly stones at the collective Goliath." He considered himself a real aristocrat by virtue of his heritage, as distinguished from the new rich middle class. "I swear by the aristocrat," he wrote Miss Nellie Crouse in early 1896. "The man whose forefathers were men of courage, sympathy and wisdom, is usually one who will stand the strain whatever it may be. He is like a thorough-bred horse. His nerves may be high and he will do a lot of jumping often, but in the crises he settles down and becomes the most reliable and enduring of created things." His example was the artist Hawker in his novel, *The Third Violet* (1897).

At Claverack Stephen was a first lieutenant when Wickham was a wretched private in Lieutenant Crane's squad on the parade ground, and he had a "hen-like attitude toward the rank and file." During a prize drill in the Drill Hall nervous Wickham dropped his gun and thereby ruined the hopes of Stephen's squad for the prize and his own for corporal stripes. " 'Idiot! Imbecile!' stormed Crane when it was over. 'You were fairly decent up to the last minute. And then to drop your gun!' Such a thing was never heard of. 'Do you think *order arms* means to drop your gun?' No, Stevie was not tender of other people's vanities. I even think he considered self-expression the exclusive privilege of the few." On the parade grounds, he wore a sheepish air and did not mingle with the students. He kept aloof and took himself very seriously.

He did not pick the locks of fellow students' chambers and turn their furniture upside down and fill his pillow-case with stolen apples. Nor did he think it funny when Wickham on finding the groceryman asleep tied his legs together, locked the grocery-store door, and then hammered on the window "as an experiment in behaviorism." He held aloof, too, when an indignant undergraduate mob hanged a certain unpopular student in effigy. He stayed away from the shoemaker Schram, who had an extensive repertoire of Rabelaisian tales, and his name was never read aloud in Sunday chapel with those "whose bearers were to lose a half-holiday for being caught mashing with co-eds in the romantic vicinity of Buttermilk Falls." Nor did he frequent Judd's pie-shop where it was possible to sit on a dark stairway with one of the girls. "Hudson, our neighboring and deliciously wicked city, where, according to rumor, initiation was to be had into the ultimate mysteries of life, seemed to hold no charms for the destined singer of the black ride of sin. He must as yet have been a theorist, for he never even jumped a freight train to cover the intervening three miles."

Stephen once told a youthful Don Juan: "I hear you're bad—I hear you're damn bad." He prophesied of a village belle what long after was fulfilled: "My God, what a lot of harm she is going to do before she dies!" His verdict upon the belle of another village: "A damn nice girl!" When Steve mingled with students, "it was frequently to deliver a pronunciamento, clothed, it might be, with profanity but of a distinctly ethical import." "Damns" were considered mighty naughty in those days, and a few years later he transposed his damns into print. "Damn you, Wickham," he said.

There was a colony of Cuban students at Claverack who qualified as social outcasts, and he learned to swear in Spanish and acquired from them a smattering of their language which afterward aided him during the Cuban War and in some of his Mexican experiences.

One of the Cubans whom he nicknamed Chick attempted to cut Wickham's throat with a razor because Wickham had stolen a postage stamp, and then he ran down the stairs shouting murder at the top of his voice in the Cuban manner while Wickham chased him with a chair. Lieutenant Crane did not bring Chick to trial for this onslaught, but he did insist upon a formal Queensbury investigation when the Cuban was charged with kicking a schoolmate in the shins during a fist fight. "He had, poor genius, the insane idea that the world might be regulated by justice."

Four years after leaving Claverack College Stephen met Wickham in Hagen's drugstore in Middletown and, ignoring the snubbing Wickham had given him because of his unwashed sweater a year or two previously, kidded him (without Wickham's being aware) by boasting that he was planning a camping expedition in a far country where women displayed a "very fetching zone" of nakedness by way of the waistline, with other attractions beyond the ordinary. Wickham, who probably impressed him as a fatuous ass, solemnly declares in his 1926 reminiscences of Crane at Claverack that this excursion never was achieved. (It took place at Camp Interlaken that summer of 1894. The girls were young innocent things, the camp was supervised by parents or wives, and no "fetching zone" was exposed.)

Stephen pretended that he did not like to drill, and Thomas Beer was of the opinion that he could not drill well, but his Company C under Captain Sutton won the 1890 prize drill (on Washington's birthday) and First Lieutenant Crane was promoted to Captain. His later interest in warfare was accelerated by the military drill at Claverack and by General John Bullock Van Petten's reminiscences of his Civil War experiences. Also, his brother William was a student of Chancellorsville, says Ripley Hitchcock in his Introduction to *The Red Badge of Courage* (1900). The battle is identified as Chancellorsville by the pontoon-bridges, the plank road, and the Rappahannock. But the unheroic flight of Fleming refashions what General Van Petten reminisced about in the dining hall at Claverack, the rout at Antietam. "He often recounted some of his war experiences while I was at his table," says a former Claverack woman student; "he became much excited as he lived over the old days." The Reverend General Van Petten, under whom Stephen studied history, personified, as true Christian and as brave soldier, the two strands of Crane's heredity. They are fused again in Jim Conklin of *The Red Badge of Courage*.

Crane's conception of an army as the "blue demonstration" in *The Red Badge* harks back to the four straggling companies of Claverack's student battalion. At one of their battalion drills the officers of the leading company startled the spectators by the colored ribbons tied to their swords; the ribbons by the time the third company passed in review were bows; last came Crane's men marching by—from his sword trailed an entire blue sash. Claverack figures in *The Red Badge* as the seminary where Henry Fleming bids "adieu to many schoolmates. They had thronged about him with wonder and admiration. He had felt the gulf between them and had swelled with calm pride. He and some of his fellows who had donned the blue were quite overwhelmed with privileges for all of one afternoon, and it had been a very delicious thing. They had strutted. A certain light-haired girl had made vivacious fun at his martial spirit, but there was another and darker girl whom he had gazed at steadfastly, and he thought she grew demure and sad at sight of his blue and brass." (The light-haired girl was redheaded Harriet Mattison, and the dark-haired girl was the "tall, dark girl from Sioux City" who was reported as Stephen's friend by natives of the town of Claverack fifty years later.)

Crane's first signed publication was an article on Henry M. Stanley's adventures in quest of the English missionary in Africa, David Livingstone, a well-written account appearing in Claverack's *Vidette* for February, 1890, which paper also referred to "Stephen Crane, non-grad." He did not graduate from Claverack; he transferred to Lafayette College, in Easton, Pennsylvania.

"I never learned anything there," said Crane of Claverack College. "American private schools are not as bad as our public schools, perhaps, but there is no great difference. . . . But heaven was sunny blue and no rain fell on the diamond when I was playing baseball. I was very happy there." The happiest times he was to know were at that school, his summers at Asbury Park, and his Western journey in 1895.

He registered at Lafayette on September 12, 1890, took a single room in East Hall that Friday, hiked it on Sunday with Delta Upsilon rushees to the summit Paxinosa, and pledged himself to D. U. six days after signing the register. On Thursday, September 18, the fraternity held a special meeting for the purpose of initiating brothers Stephen Crane '94, J. H. Smith '94, and F. Bretz '93. The bursar of Lafayette remembered the traditional mountain hike: Stephen, uncommunicative, difficult to know offhand, and smoking in silence.

In his locked room—Number 179, a rear room in dilapidated East Hall—Crane lived a couple of weeks in fright of a visit from the hazing squad of D. U. upperclassmen. "Steve tried to play possum by not answering a loud summons, and the usual practice followed by battering in the door. The sophomores crowded in, lighted a lamp. . . . Steve was petrified with fear and stood in a grotesque nightgown in one corner of the room with a revolver in his hand." One of the fraternity brothers who gained entrance to Crane's room, himself then a freshman, describes him as of medium height and of sallow complexion; but now in the oil lamp's light he seemed ghastly white and extremely nervous. "There was no time to escape what might have proved a real tragedy until Crane unexpectedly seemed to wilt limply in place, and the loaded revolver dropped harmlessly to the floor." That ended the hazing initiation of Crane, and he never again spoke of this incident.

He had prepared himself with a revolver after reading a newspaper item about the hazing episode that occurred in South College the week of his arrival at Lafayette; a freshman baseball player had used a bat to defend himself against a hazing squad of sophomores invading his room and had inflicted painful damage on several of his fraternity pranksters. The revolver had been given to Stephen by a Wyoming cowboy in exchange for the five dollars he had begged from his mother to start the cowboy back to Wyoming. That revolver, said the cowboy, had killed six Indians. When Crane himself went out West in 1895 he probably carried the same weapon with him. Later, in his English years, he would shoot a Mexican revolver from the hip in cowboy fashion to show off before novelist Ford Madox Hueffer. The hazing incident was long remembered by Stephen's Lafayette class-mates; "He could never be told, tamed, trained, or trammeled. He was to live his life his own way, in his own eccentric, bungling, nonconformist manner." His classmates, says Ralph Chamberlin, remembered him as a bit more sophisticated and cynical than average and very reticent. He preferred boxing, baseball, poker-playing, and beer to studying; it is a wonder that the faculty remembered him at all since he seldom attended classes. He impressed another schoolmate, Arthur Oliver, as an intellectual personality very old for his years with a keen sense of the real meaning of things that was not revealed by his somewhat diffident exterior. "He saw and felt deeply. Even as a boy, he had a richly developed vein of satire," Arthur Oliver recalls in "Jersey Memories—Stephen Crane" (1931).

At Lafayette he took part in the annual autumn combat between sopho-mores and freshmen, a tug-of-war which he long after described in his Greco-Turkish War novel *Active Service* (1899).

> The combat, waged in the desperation of proudest youth, waxed hot and hotter. The wedge had been instantly smitten into a kind of a block of men. It had crumpled into an irregular square, and on three sides it was now assailed with remarkable ferocity. It was a matter of wall meeting wall in terrific rushes during which lads could feel their very hearts leaving them in the compress of friends and foes. They on the outskirts upheld the honour of their classes, by squeezing into paper thickness the lungs of those of their fellows who formed the centre of the *melée*. In some way it resembled a panic at a theatre.[3] The first lance-like attack of the Sophomores had been formidable, but the Freshmen outnumbering their enemies and smarting from continual Sophomoric oppression had swarmed to the front like drilled collegians and given the arrogant foe the first serious check of the year. Therefore the tall Gothic windows which lined one side of the corridor looked down upon as incomprehensible and enjoyable a tumult as could mark the steps of advanced education.

The upperclassmen cheered the freshman on until an infuriated sopho-more swung an arm high and smote freshman Crane as he seized the sophomore banner. "It was no longer a festival, a game; it was a riot." Stephen kept as token of the freshman victory a piece of rag torn from that banner and sent it to Odell Hathaway. "It don't look like much does it? Only an old rag, ain't it? But you just remember I got a *black and blue* nose, a barked shin, skin off my hands and a lame shoulder, in the row; you can appreciate it. So, keep it, and when you look at it think of me scrapping about twice a week over some old rag that says 'Fresh '94' on it." That Lafayette College tug-of-war became the flag that is wrenched from the enemy in *The Red Badge*.

Crane played intramural baseball almost every afternoon that autumn in the hope of making the varsity team the next spring—when he wasn't playing pool badly against Porter Cheney in a poolroom behind a tobacco store in Easton. While he burned cigarettes between the fingers of his left hand or tried to balance a cue on his arched nose, he pronounced on books and authors to the young civil engineer. He declared that Count Tolstoy was the world's foremost writer, that a lesser fellow named Flaubert had written *Salammbô,* which he didn't like because it was too long, and that he didn't like Robert Louis Stevenson. He had read Tolstoy's *Sebastopol,* but he was bored by Henry James' *Reverberator* (1888), a study of journalism. Years later he became Henry James' close friend and, although forever detesting Stevenson, imitated him in his 1899 moustache and in his last novel.

He never did make the Lafayette varsity team. When the semester ended in December, 1890, he was advised to leave school because of scholastic "delinquencies." In three courses he drew a blank because of excessive absences: chemistry, drafting and Bible, in which he should have excelled as much as in theme-writing, for which he got zero. His grades were 60 in algebra, 92 in elocution, and 88 in French. "I tried to learn French," Crane said, "because my mother thought it important, but no foreign language will ever be my friend." The wife of General John Bullock Van Petten had attempted to teach him during his two and a half years at Claverack, and he later liked to show off what little French he knew. (When critic Edward Garnett in 1897 insisted that he must have read French authors, Crane replied: "I never read a word of French in my life." But he had read French authors—in translation.)

He returned to Lafayette College for a short visit after the Christmas holidays. He packed up quietly without saying much to anyone except to explain his departure by the excuse that family affairs would not permit him to remain in college. The truth was that he had flunked out.

His last try at a formal education was at Syracuse University, where again he lasted one semester. He entered the city of Syracuse the first week of January, 1891, by train—on the New York Central down Railroad Street (now East Washington)—and gazed at the women peering from the windows or porches of the eighteen "parlor houses" along the New York Central tracks while the engineer, perhaps deliberately, brought his train almost to a halt in front of them as though to declare what's what in Syracuse. It was impossible to enter the city in those days without being introduced to the parlor houses on either side of Railroad Street, though of course other houses of prostitution existed throughout the central area within walking distance of the downtown hotels.

"This is a dandy city at least," Stephen wrote Odell Hathaway at Claverack from the Delta Upsilon fraternity house on January 9, "and I expect to have some fun here." That day he enrolled at the registrar's office of the University and at night attended D. U.'s first meeting for the new semester. He reported that the fellows here *are* somewhat slow." What made the city dandy were the college girls, the prostitutes staring from the parlor houses six or seven blocks from his fraternity house on the top of Marshall Street hill, and the Putnam police court. At the police court he could find out what happened to prostitutes, and then he could investigate later the red-light district on Railroad Street. He reported to Hathaway on the 9th that he had spotted some damn pretty girls here ("praise be to God") and that not one of his Claverack friends had written him, not even Sioux (Earl Reeve). "I ate like a fiend as soon as I got away from Claverack and am eating like a devil now, every chance I get. . . ."

He arrived at Delta Upsilon house, said a friend, "in a cab and a cloud of tobacco smoke." It was a "dandy house valued at $20,000, situated on a high hill overlooking the entire city," he wrote Hathaway. Before moving into the fraternity house at the end of January, he stayed first with his great-aunt, the widow of his mother's uncle, Bishop Jesse Truesdell Peck, who had been the godfather of Syracuse University—if not its principal founder. His widow was living in the home Bishop Peck had left to the University, and Stephen's mother had made arrangements for his enrollment as belles lettres "special" student and for his domicile with the Widow Peck. But his great-aunt was not in sympathy with his ideas and way of living, and his stay under her roof was of short duration. He then lived for several weeks at a boardinghouse kept by a French-Canadian mother of six children. This delightful woman, Marie Branchards, later ran a rooming house in Greenwich Village, where Crane lived for a while. The rooming house at Number 61 on the south side of Washington Square became famous because he had stayed there, as had Willa Cather when she was writing her verses, and later Frank Norris, when he was working on the final draft of *McTeague.*

Crane never enjoyed being treated as a freshman and resented encroachments on his freshman dignity. One day a Delta Upsilon senior who served as steward at the house needed some carving knives sharpened and embarrassed Stephen by shouting at him across the crowded library: "I want a freshie to turn grindstone; come on, Crane!" With a red face Stephen retorted that he never would turn grindstone for anybody, a remark audacious for a freshman. Small, quiet and unprepossessing, he was always cool, never worried about anything, and took life as it came. He littered his room with tobacco cans and pipes, books and loose papers and newspaper clippings, canvas trousers and jackets, football shoes, baseball masks and bats, running trunks and other athletic and literary items. The walls were hung with trophies, signs and drawings and paintings—he was always an admirer of fine paintings. The room was furnished quite elegantly, however disorderly, and it had a deep bay window.

"I asked who lived there and was told: 'A new fellow from Lafayette, Steve Crane.' Later in the afternoon on the athletic field, I met the future novelist, then the new catcher of the 'Varsity Nine,' a wiry, slender youth under the average height, with a complexion almost yellow and very large and expressive eyes." So his classmate, Clarence Loomis Peaslee, remembers him. His face was long and sallow, his hair very light, and his eyes deeply set. When Crane was twenty-four he was interviewed by an editor of *Leslie's Weekly,* who wrote: "Physically, Stephen Crane is a slender young man of a little above medium height, with finely chiseled but rather delicate features and a large head covered with a luxuriant growth of light hair, which falls in careless disorder over a high forehead. The blue eyes which look out from beneath have a suggestion of weariness and even of sadness in them when the brain behind is passive, but when it is alert and active, as in interesting conversation, they light up and flash with sparkling animation. His eyes are a good index of his temperament."

Very early he impressed others as a boyish genius, a bohemian in dress, with untidy hair, but what struck almost everyone who wrote about him were his strange eyes. The man who pitched to him on the Syracuse Varsity said that he was of sallow complexion: "his skin, hair, and eyes appeared to be all of one dull and lifeless hue. That is, his eyeballs were of the same deep cream tint but the iris was of a cold, bluish-gray color." The pitcher was Mansfield French of the class of 1894, who wrote about Crane forty years later in the Syracuse University *Alumni News.* French, as Peaslee describes him, was a rather large man who threw a very swift ball. Steve disliked using the large catcher's mitt which had just then come into use and preferred the less awkward padded glove. According to French, "He had the habit of striking his bare, clenched fist three or four times into the palm of his gloved hand to express his approval of a 'strike' when missed by the batter. When we succeeded in striking out our man, an expression of diabolical glee would light up his face, and he always expressed to me his appreciation when our opponents were retired at the end of their inning."

The baseball team began training on February 2, and the *Syracusan* announced that day that Stephen Crane, the old catcher of the Lafayette College team, would make a good addition. He spent more time on the baseball field than in the classroom, except in February when the Syracuse *Herald* announced on the 16th that he had been quite ill the past week. Crane "plays a good game behind the bat, but he is weak in throwing to second," said the *Syracusan* for May, 1891. As the team lacked a shortstop, he was switched from catcher to shortstop. But he was back later that May as catcher and was applauded for his good work behind the bat by the Syracuse *Standard.* Peaslee remembers him as very gritty, standing up to the plate like a professional.

He was rated as the best infield man of his time and declined a post on a major baseball team after deciding to risk his future as a writer. Of quiet and taciturn mien off the diamond, on the ballfield he was constantly in motion, agile on his feet, a fast base runner, and a good batman although not a hard hitter. French describes Crane's body as slender, shoulders drooping, chest not robust, and knees inclining to knock together. He was about 5 feet 6 inches in height and did not weigh over 125 pounds. He played baseball with fiendish glee and was "free of speech, wantonly profane." He indulged in biting sarcasms when a teammate made a poor play but he was generous in praise of a good play. "Crane loved to talk baseball and took great delight in telling of his experiences on the ballfield and of his acquaintance, at least by newspaper reputation, with the leading professional players of those days. When on trips to play with other college teams he proved to be sociable and companionable. I remember to have seen his fingers deeply stained with nicotine but do not recall that he smoked during the baseball season, at least in public."

To pitcher French's swift ball, catcher Crane seemed to bound back with every catch, he was so light. He was the best player of the nine, says Peaslee, and one of the best catchers the University ever had. "Little did the motley crowd of students and onlookers that bright April afternoon think that the plucky boy behind the bat would so soon be a character of international interest."

When fame came to him with *The Red Badge of Courage,* he wrote his Appleton editor in early 1896: "I see also that they are beginning to charge me with having played baseball. I am rather more proud of my baseball ability than of some other things."

When he was not playing baseball Stephen was busy reporting college and Syracuse news for the New York *Tribune,* the assignment he had been given by the *Tribune's* day editor, Willis Fletcher Johnson, long a friend of his parents. He also spent a lot of time in the back room of a local restaurant impressing his classmates with his importance as newspaper reporter or as baseball player, and in the police court presided over by Police Justice Thomas Mulholland in the Putnam School building. A mighty character who let the law fall where it might, Mulholland administered justice to the prisoners being brought in on minor offenses. Prostitutes and criminals fascinated Crane, and his curiosity about the demi-world led him into interviewing the lower strata of Syracuse civilization—it was not much more than a mile from Delta Upsilon to the Putnam police court and nearby was the city's tenderloin.

"He gloried in talking with shambling figures who lurked in the dark doorways on deserted slum streets," says a Syracuse classmate, "and his love for adventure constantly kept his feet on the ill-lighted thoroughfares honeycombing the city." He maintained that art is "just a matter of treatment. The scene of Hamlet and his mother and the death of old Polonius behind the curtain is ugly, if you heard it in a police court." He thought the police court was the most interesting place in the city, and that he could get a better education than any university had to offer if he probed life itself.

When the president of the Women's Christian Temperance Union, Miss Frances Willard, came to the campus, he refused to meet her because he "considered Miss Willard a fool." He had met her some years earlier, when his mother attended a temperance meeting where Miss Willard lectured, and meeting her once was quite enough for him. (His own mother was national vice-president of the W. C. T. U. for New Jersey.) He climaxed his Syracuse career by disagreeing with his psychology professor about Saint Paul's theory of sin. "Tut, tut, what does Saint Paul say, Mr. Crane?" said the professor. "I know what Saint Paul says, but I disagree with him," said the student. It was the choir that drew Stephen to church. He and Frank Noxon sat in the rear pew and he told Noxon that "he had had such a dose of piety in his youth that the reaction was unfavorable to religious consecration in later years."

"Crane, you'll never amount to anything," another professor told him. "Why don't you let up on writing and pay a little more attention to conic sections?" An indifferent student, he flunked out in algebra, chemistry, physics, elocution, and German. The Dean of Syracuse University suggested that it would be inadvisable for him to return unless he underwent a change of intention, and that ended his college days.

Not that it mattered to Stephen. His dismissal worried his mother, who had several times written his Latin teacher, Frank Smalley, because she felt considerable anxiety about her son. "We looked upon him as an exceedingly bright young man of large capacity," Professor Smalley wrote Cora Crane in 1900 when she asked for reminiscences of Stephen for a biography she intended to write but never did. "He would not be cramped by following a course of study he did not care for. That is the secret of his few credits on the books."[4]

He had been classed as a special student, free to take whatever courses struck his fancy, but he had no natural taste for study and never tried to cultivate one. "He has a deep regard for true learning," says Peaslee, "but not for the rubbish that often passes under that name, and if he has not burned the midnight oil in search of 'school' knowledge, he has worked as but few men have in the field of observation and the study of mankind. In college Crane was an omnivorous reader and sat up late at night, diligently poring over the masterpieces of literature or trying to put upon paper his own peculiar views of man and life." His student days gave no promise of the talent he later displayed. But he had a purpose in view from the very first. "He wanted to produce something that would make men think, that would make men feel as he felt, and to do this he early realized that for him it must come through hard work."

His mother acquiesced in his determination to become a writer, and he proved himself by contributing "The King's Favor" to the Syracuse University *Herald* that May. He was writing tales but not getting them accepted. The editor of *St. Nicholas* praised his sketch of a dog named Jack but rejected it with the excuse that he had a backlog of dog stories. Crane's fraternity brother Frank Noxon read the sketch and got the impression that Stephen took his literary defeat with a note of pride.[5]

His literary hoax "Great Bugs at Onondaga" is the best thing he wrote for the New York *Tribune* (June 1, 1891) while he was at Syracuse. In deadpan style he reported that a locomotive hauling stone from the quarries off a branch track of the Lackawanna Railroad between Syracuse and Jamesville was brought to a stop by electric-light bugs swarming on the tracks; the rails were greased by the crushed bugs, who died "with a crackling sound like the successive explosions of toy torpedoes." Bigger than any electric-light bug, their turtlelike armor was "about the size and shape of half a shanghai-egg shell." An erudite recluse was of the opinion that these bugs were "the issue of a rare species of lithodome—a rock-boring mollusk—crossed with some kind of predatory insect." Nineteen-year-old Crane had read about an army of caterpillars stopping trains on the Milwaukee Railroad tracks at Mankato, Minnesota, as reported in the Syracuse *Sunday Herald* (May 24, 1891): "Millions of caterpillars came out on the track to sun themselves and were ground to grease. They have infested the locality for two weeks past, destroying many fruit trees." Stephen converted the caterpillars into the incredible Onondaga bugs, and his hoax was headlined in the Syracuse *Standard* (also June 1, 1891): "Huge Electric Light Bugs. What a wild-eyed Patriot from the Sand Hills Thought he saw." Biblical-minded Crane knew the verses in the Bible relating to locusts, beetles, grasshoppers, and he knew about the locusts-big-as-horses with crowns like gold on their heads and with "the teeth of lions," in The Revelation of St. John. "And they had breastplates, as it were breastplates of iron; and the sound of their wings was as the sound of chariots of many horses running to battle."[6]

Crane's bug story was the subject of a hilarious *Tribune* editorial the next day, unsigned but obviously written by Willis Johnson. In "The Syracuse Bugs" he remarks that it is seldom necessary to apologize for a newspaperman. "The stainless life, the high integrity, the nobleness of aim, the breadth of mind and the depth of scholarship of the journalist are so well known to the intelligent readers of the *Tribune* that it would be an impertinence to dwell upon them here. But sometimes, after all, the journalist will make a mistake; he is but human." Johnson tops Crane's jest. It was evident, he says, that the able correspondent had intended to produce a series of articles "beginning with ordinary bugs, running along through the summer with a gradual increase in size, and ending in October with these giant, mud-turtlelike bugs which stopped a railroad train and dumfounded the local scientists; but through some mistake the last account was sent first, and we shall probably hear nothing from the preliminary, cumulative bugs. It scarcely seems possible (though to genius nothing is impossible) that this could be the beginning of a series, and that October will find great bugs ten feet long and weighing half a ton galloping about Onondaga County, and in strange, unnatural cries voicing their horrid craving for human gore; but to this it might come after all." The electric-light bug superseded the old gas-light bug, "which took the place of the kerosene-lamp bug, which had itself driven out the tallow-candle bug. While not so large as the light-house bug or the bonfire bug, the electric-light bug is nevertheless a formidable bug, and has even been known, when suffering from hunger, to attack and kill the great oil-warehouse fire bug, which frequently comes out and chases the firemen around the corner and devours the hose."

The most important event of Stephen's semester at Syracuse was his writing the first draft of *Maggie: A Girl of the Streets*. With typical carelessness he left the sheets lying about in the front room he shared with Clarence Norton Goodwin, and some of these sheets were picked up and read by droppers-in. After lunch he would go up to the cupola, where on freezing days he wore earlaps, mittens and overshoes while smoking his beloved German waterpipe. Because the D. U. house's heating system carried smoke from one room to another, smoking was permitted only in the cupola, and there Crane, Goodwin and F. K. Congdon retreated to escape the protests of their nonsmoking brethren, most of them divinity students. He decorated the cupola as a kind of Turkish corner, and here he read an English translation of Flaubert's *Madame Bovary* and then began writing his Bowery version of that novel, substituting for the as-yet-unexplored demi-world of the Bowery his knowledge of Syracuse's red-light district.

The first draft of *Maggie* was wholly or partly written at the Delta Upsilon house, says Frank Noxon, who with other fraternity brothers read the manuscript and advised Crane about the plot. He put the plot into various lights and constructions, asking them "which was the more effective." Later he did the same with his manuscript of *The Red Badge* by turning it over to his friends at the Art Students' League for criticism and argument about changes.

Legend has it that in a fit of despondency he crammed one of his manuscripts into the D. U. chimney bricks, but no manuscript was ever found there. Of more tangible memory is the inscription he burned into the east wall of the Delta Upsilon cupola: "sunset 1891 May / Steph Crane."

## III

## ᴄᴈ *Sullivan County Tales and Sketches*

STEPHEN spent the summer of 1891 in Asbury Park—that "most American of towns"—working as a full-time reporter for Townley's news agency. He and reporter-friend Arthur Oliver combed an indefinite stretch of the Jersey coastline picking up resort news and gossip. Townley, the "shore fiend," was considered by hotel residents to be the incarnation of the *Tribune.* After playing at the faro table in Ohil Daly's emporium in Long Branch, he would rush over to Ocean Grove to write up the latest religious meeting at the Tabernacle—or let Stevie do it while he remained at the gaming table.

When not working, Stephen was lounging on the beach or playing ball or practicing target shooting with his revolver. He was a good shot, and a good swimmer. He was also busy with his stamp collection, which Townley had started for him and contributed largely to. Years later he wrote his brother William from London to try to retrieve his collection. "If Townley hasn't hocked it, it is now valuable."[1]

Willis Fletcher Johnson of the *Tribune,* who purchased Townley's shore "gabble" and for whom Stephen had reported from Syracuse, thought highly of his New Jersey coast news reporting. Crane later declared that from the start his "chiefest desire was to write plainly and unmistakably, so that all men (and some women) might read and understand. That to my mind is good writing. . . . I endeavored to express myself in the simplest and most concise way."

One day that summer Townley called on Johnson at the West End Hotel, where the Asbury Park newspaper reporters hung out, to tell him that Steve had some writings, and so Johnson sent for the youth. Somewhat shy and reticent, Crane appeared with a bundle of manuscripts clutched under his arm. It was his first draft of *Maggie.* Johnson, in a reminiscence he wrote in 1926, remembers having thought it crude, but powerful and impressive in its mastery of the speech and manners of Bowery characters, although, as he realized, the author had had as yet no opportunity for observing New York City slums. (Johnson earlier had found Stephen's Syracuse news items employing "words and phrases which indicated the posses-

*33*

sion of an imaginative and impressionistic mind.") He felt its chief fault was in that "exuberance and extravagance of adjectives which Stephen never was able wholly to outgrow."[2]

One of the most important events in Crane's life was his meeting Hamlin Garland at Avon that summer. Garland had arranged with the promoters of the Chautauqua-like assembly there, the Albertis, to lecture on American literature and the expressive arts. On August 17 he talked on novelist William Dean Howells, and Stephen wrote up the lecture so exceedingly well in the *Tribune*[3] the next day that Garland asked William Alberti the name of the reporter. "He is a mere boy," Alberti said, "and his name is Stephen Crane." The next evening they met, and then, because they had discussed sports, they pitched ball along the beach, and Garland recognized the youth as "a capital catcher of curved balls." They met several times after that to pitch ball and discuss theories of pitching in-shoots or outdrops to "confound the laws of astronomy by making a sphere alter its course in mid-air." When Garland said goodbye at the end of his Avon engagement, he had no expectations of ever seeing Crane again, but long after he remembered him as a reticent fellow, laconic in speech, sinewy and athletic although small.

In his Avon lecture Garland talked of his theory of realism—"veritism." Howells' "definition of realism cannot be improved upon: 'the truthful treatment of material,' " Stephen wrote in his *Tribune* report. "He does not insist upon any special material, but only that the novelist be true to himself and to things as he sees them. It is absurd to call him photographic. The photograph is false in perspective, in light and shade, in focus." The label "realism" has been applied to Crane and to Henry James and Joseph Conrad, but all three were impressionistic and symbolic artists whose best works went beyond mere realism. Crane advanced rapidly and within a year was writing the symbolic prose of *Maggie,* transcending Howells' theory of realism and Garland's theory of "veritism." He thus justified Howells' 1893 sobriquet: "Here is a writer who has sprung into life fully armed."

In this summer of 1891 Stephen fell in love with Helen Trent, but it was not until she left the resort for her home in New York City that he sent her a wire in which he lamented having failed to say goodbye. When she was packing things on September 10 for a journey to Switzerland her servant announced the arrival of Mr. Stephen Crane, and he was ushered into the gaudy drawing room of an old house on Twelfth Street where Miss Trent lived with an asthmatic old lady, Mrs. Potter.

Handsome he was that night, but shy and dull too. The nineteen-year-old aspiring novelist who had pitched ball with the successful author of *Main-Travelled Roads* (published that June) could talk only about Hamlin Garland, when he did talk, and he asked whether she had heard the new writer from the West lecturing at Avon. She hadn't, but she asked what he looked like. "Oh, like a nice Jesus Christ," Crane replied. Miss Trent, a European-trained contralto who sang charity concerts in the wicked slums and thought the Bowery not a "nice" place, was probably shocked.

The next morning he poured himself out in a twelve-page letter on the stationery of a Fifth Avenue hotel. Its contents were hardly literary. He told Miss Trent that William's daughter was named Helen (luckily, he did not mention that his mother's middle name was also Helen). He mentioned his other brothers, Wilbur and Townley, and his newspaper work. He asked her favorite color. Did she love flowers? Was she fond of dogs? Perhaps it was the Fifth Avenue stationery which improved his letter and impressed Miss Trent, for he was received at Mrs. Potter's house the next evening, and in his slow speech he told her about the curious people he had met on the Jersey coast and the camping trips he enjoyed in Sullivan County.

He kept coming back. She would play Chopin, while he hummed a tenor accompaniment, or she would sing songs in French, which he would not understand, or show him through the mansion. A flag of Ireland was in the colored tiles above the fireplace, the walls were hung with tapestries and great folds of cascading lace, a colossal chandelier hung "gleaming like a Siamese head-dress" (to quote Thomas Beer). Miss Trent showed off also the boudoir of her guardian, Mrs. Potter, and on seeing all that velvet and enamel Crane shrieked: "When will the stage hands take it away?" He seems to have followed up that tour by making inquiries about the old house, for on September 18 he wrote: "Dear Miss Trent: I have found out something that you should know at once and will be up this evening to tell you." Did Mrs. Potter realize that the house had belonged to a kind of Svengali who had commissioned an Italian to decorate it for an Irish chorus girl? And did Miss Trent realize that people might misinterpret her living there as working in a house of ill-fame?

Although young Stephen could tell Miss Trent to her face that her home was once a "house," he could also disapprove of women who smoked cigarettes and wore bathing suits cut to the daring style of the 1890's—at the same time he nervously lighted Helen's own cigarettes and suggested bathing naked at dawn. No less ambivalent was Helen, who was unconventional enough to smoke cigarettes in 1891 yet was disapproving of a man who frequented the slums. "Hully gee," Steve said, the Bowery was the only interesting place in New York.

He spent hours on the Bowery, watching and listening, and came to visit Helen one evening, boastful and bruised by a bottle flung in a barroom brawl. Miss Trent thought it improper of him to talk about using such nasty people in a novel, and Stephen, exasperated, walked out. His anger lasted until he boarded the ferry to Jersey City on the way home to brother Edmund's in Lake View. He wrote her a note on board: "I shall come back tomorrow night and we can start all over again. Yours sincerely, Stephen Crane." Although he was reconciled to her immediately, he did not forget the incident. Not long after, he revised *Maggie* to include a parody of Miss Trent's charitable concerts—a stage show with a "duet which is heard occasionaly at concerts under such auspices . . . supplemented . . . with a dance, which of course can never be seen at concerts under church auspices."

He loved to shock Helen with his outlandish opinions: that a Negro "could be handsome even without the 'classic profile' demanded by a world soaked in the art of Leighton and Poynter"; that "American religion was 'mildewed' "; that he "found Buddhism interesting"; that he still found bathing suits as repulsive as Robert Louis Stevenson's prose. And she, smoking another cigarette, would lament his going to the Bowery, and praise Stevenson. But what for Crane was fast becoming a serious infatuation remained for Helen a game; she was engaged to a young London surgeon who was studying at Guy's Hospital.

"Your window was lighted all last night but they said you were not in. I stood and looked at your window till a policeman came and made me go away. But I came back and looked until my head was just a sponge of lights. Please do not treat me like this. Nothing else counts but that," he wrote Helen on September 19 on a leaf from a yellow notebook when he came to the house and found her not at home. The next night they attended a play at Wallack's Theater, and it was perhaps on that evening after the play that Crane rented a hansom for a drive up Fifth Avenue. They rode in silence through the warm night and he was moved by the sight of her bare arms. "You have the most beautiful arms I ever saw," he wrote Helen. "You never should have to wear dresses with sleeves. If I could keep your arms nothing else would count. It would not matter if there was no more world. In dreams, don't you ever fall and fall but not be afraid of anything because somebody safe is with you? I shall be here tomorrow. I must get back to Ed's house now."

He returned to his attic study in Edmund's house in Lake View to transpose the contents of this love note into a poem—one of the earliest of the *Black Rider* series—in which he mentions his dreams of falling: "Should the wide world roll away / Leaving black terror, / Limitless night, / Nor God, nor man, nor place to stand / Would be to me essential, / If thou and thy white arms were there, / And the fall to doom a long way." Dreams were for Crane, throughout his life, the wellsprings of what he called his "poetic spout," from which would pour one poem after another in nearly flawless final draft.

He came back to the house on Twelfth Street the next day and Miss Trent—as Beer describes it—"strolled nervously into the florid drawing room to tell him that she was to be married in London, soon. Crane gave a quick gasp and lifted both hands to his face. Then he spun and walked out of the house, permanently," left, it seems, with nothing but an experience and a prototype for the jilted lover, Hawker, in his novel *The Third Violet.*

Helen soon became the wife of Dr. Charles Goodsall of London. When in January of 1900 the celebrated Stephen Crane was pointed out to her at a London theater, she looked across and recognized him without knowing why he was celebrated. And yet, for some reason, she preserved every note and letter of his and remembered as late as 1923, when Thomas Beer interviewed her, that she had once sewn a button on his coat and persuaded him to brush back his tousled bangs.

Judge William Howe Crane had opened a law office in Port Jervis in 1882, and in payment for his legal services to the Hartwood Club, of which he was President, he began acquiring land adjoining the Club's property; eventually he owned 3,500 acres. The Hartwood Club, syndicated by wealthy owners, possessed six thousand acres of mountain timber and lakes (with hunting rights on all but one thousand acres) and had a commodious clubhouse some few miles from the mill-pond and railroad station. Stephen became part of the history of the Minisink Valley, famous for its courageous Dutch and Huguenot settlers and its Revolutionary War patriots. His parents had vacationed there in 1879 when he was seven, and in the summers he swam in the Sullivan County ponds and fished for pickerel at Pond Eddy. He became a good swimmer, a good shot (he liked to hunt partridge), and an expert horseman. During his school years he spent winter vacations at Hartwood Park.

In the register of the newly formed Hartwood Park Association this entry may be found for September 30, 1891: "Shortly after dusk this evening a flock of Cranes flew up the property of the Association and alighted near the clubhouse. The mother bird had considerable difficulty in keeping her children quiet and in making them retire for the night. There were in the flock: Mrs. Helen Peck Crane . . . J. Townley Crane . . . William Howe Crane . . . E. B. Crane, Lake View, N. J., Stephen Crane, Asbury Park, N. J." Then on October 2 (Friday) "Mother Crane caught seven fine pickerel to her own satisfaction and the astonishment of her brood. The next day she caught three more fish in less than an hour."

Stephen, Ed, and William had in common the gift of striking language, says Judge E. J. Dimock in reminiscences of them from his childhood days at Hartwood.[4] And so did lawyer William's seven-year old daughter. "You are so fortunate in being able to live all the year round in this lovely country when we can only stay for a short vacation," said a lady to the youngster who was being entertained up at the Hartwood Club by the wife of one of the members. "Yes," replied the wide-eyed child, "but you know in midsummer Port Jervis is hotter than hell."

Seventeen years older than Stephen, William Howe Crane wore whiskers

like a horned owl and was always known as Judge Crane. While on one
of the Hartwood Park hunts, Judge Crane was standing on a runway for
deer when he encountered a herd of wild hogs. "Turning quickly, he caught
a glimpse of a brown body and fired. They carried home a wild hog weighing 200 pounds. The carcass was inspected, photographed and sketched.
A magnificent skin, with stuffed head, now hangs in the clubhouse at
Hartwood Park," said his twenty-year old brother Stephen in "Hunting
Wild Hogs."

In this New York *Tribune* hunting sketch for February 28, 1892, one
of six new Sullivan County sketches,[5] Crane reports that the hero of the
hog hunt was Lew Boyd, a famous bear-hunter, and with him was "a
young man with a bulldog . . . who said his dog would fight anything."
That was undoubtedly Stephen himself, whom we detect again in "The
Way in Sullivan County" as the city man listening awesomely to the
Sullivan natives telling their tall tales.

> One can buy sawlogs from a native and take his word that the bargain
> is square, but ask the same man how many deer he has killed in his
> life time and he will stop working, take a seat on the snake-fence and
> paralyze the questioner with a figure that would look better than most
> of the totals to the subscription lists for monuments to national heroes.
> The inhabitants grow up to regard each other with painful suspicion.
> So there is very little field for the expert liars among their fellows.
> They must keep to a certain percentage or they will lose their
> caste, but there is little pleasure in it for them because everybody
> knows everybody else. The only real enjoyment is when the unoffend-
> ing city man appears. They welcome him with joyful cries. After he
> recovers from a paroxysm of awe and astonishment he seizes his pen
> and with flashing eye and trembling, eager fingers, writes these brief
> but lurid sketches which fascinate and charm the reading public while
> the virtuous bushwhacker, whittling a stick near by, smiles in his own
> calm and sweet fashion.

As a spinner of hunting and camping yarns Crane himself is a skilled
Sullivan County "liar." In "The Last Panther" a man by the name of
Calvin Bush (according to an old authority on hunting, he was "the prince
of panther-killers") aimed a blow at a panther's head with a hatchet. "The
animal dodged and caught the handle in its teeth. It wrenched the imple-
ment from the hunter's hand with the utmost ease, and then dropped it to
fight the dog, which had begun a noisy attack in the rear. While the panther
was mutilating the dog, Bush loaded his gun and shot it through the head.
He always carried a crooked finger, which was made by the panther's teeth
when it grasped the hatchet-handle."

"My uncle," said Stephen's niece Edith, "was a good shot. He seemed to
enjoy target practice and tramped through the woods a great deal at Hart-

wood, but he was not as keen about hunting and fishing as my father [Edmund Crane]." Although he was to spend most of his life imagining battlefields or experiencing them, he had a deep respect for life and was opposed to hunting down animals wantonly. He admired the courage not of the hunter but of the hunted, and in several Sullivan County tales and sketches he exposes the cowardice of the hunter. Hunting is warfare, too. "Youths grew up with desire for fame and they took rifles and went to seek it in the woods. A hardy race of huntsmen made terrible war on the game," he says in "Sullivan County Bears." He spoofs at the hunters who, hiding in a cave, wait it out until a panther claws a bear to death: "the brilliant-minded and philosophical hunters dangled their heels and smiling looked on until the panther finished the bear. Then they shot the victor."

With this wry commentary Crane ends his sketch: "The Way in Sullivan County: A Study in the Evolution of the Hunting Yarn." Here he dwells on the gap between the hunter of fiction, the Sullivan County bushwhackers who thought themselves "very great men indeed," and the hunter of reality. Crane's sympathies are with the bear; his bias is against the hunter. He reminds us: "Not all men now are hunters. There are those surrounded by the best cover for game who never taste partridge or venison the year round." He concludes "Killing His Bear" with the little man gloating over a dying bear and waving his hat "as if he were leading the cheering of thousands. He ran up and kicked the ribs of the bear. Upon his face was the smile of the successful lover."

From "the old and weather-beaten inhabitants of the pines and boulders of Sullivan County" Crane picked up at the firesides of old homesteads the historical legends of that region and of the neighboring counties. Their fireside yarns he verified in certain books written by learned men who had "dived into piles of mouldy documents and dusty chronicles to establish their facts." One of these chronicles was J. E. Quinlan's *History of Sullivan County* (1873), which relates the hunting exploits of early settlers at the turn of the 19th Century and even previous to the War of the Revolution. Quinlan's *History* provided Crane some antecedents for his own hunting sketches, and from Quinlan's story of the murder of rich Hasbrouck he took the name Hasbrouck for a soldier in *The Red Badge of Courage:* "That young Hasbrouck, he makes a good off'cer. He ain't afraid 'a nothin'."

In "The Last of The Mohicans," in the *Tribune* for February 21, 1892,[6] Crane says: "This gives the great Sullivan County thunderbolt immense weight. And they hurl it at no less a head than that which once evolved from its inner recesses in the famous Leatherstocking Tales. When you tell them about the noble savage of Cooper's fiction, they shake 'metaphorical fists' at Cooper's *The Last of the Mohicans* and scornfully sneer. The old storytellers of Sullivan County insist that the original for Cooper's fictionalized bronze god Uncas ended his life there not as a noble warrior who had yearned after the blood of his enemies, but as a derelict begging from house to house a drink of the white man's rum. There was nothing noble about him. "He was a veritable 'poor Indian.' He dragged through his wretched life in helpless misery."

Crane's otherwise mysterious nickname "Indians" for his artist friends in New York City harks back to his familiarity with the legendary fallen Uncas of Sullivan County. His artist friends at the old Needham building on East 23rd Street, which housed the Art Students' League until October, 1892, were "Indians" because—like Uncas—they wore ragged garments and begged or borrowed their food, drink, and bed. So, too, did Crane himself. He declared in 1893 that he would sell his future for $23. He, too, was a veritable "poor Indian." London journalists who exploited Crane's hospitality during his English years by uninvited intrusions at Ravensbrook Villa in Surrey were cursed by his sobriquet "Indians." When seven men overstayed their visit Crane fled to a London hotel for two days to finish some work and wrote Acton Davies (on December 5, 1897) that "some of these Comanche braves seem to think I am running a free lunch-counter."

William wrote Stephen at Brede Manor in Sussex (on November 7, 1899) that a copy of Addison's *Spectator* should be sent to his daughter Helen, then at school in Lausanne (Switzerland), so as to edify her in moral conduct. "I do not know of any reading that inculcates a love of truth more effectively [than Addison's 18th Century essays in the *Spectator*], unless it may be *The Deerslayer*." Although Crane's list of books at Brede Place contains no book by James Fenimore Cooper, he obviously knew his Cooper. In "War Memories" (1899) he wrote that the Cuban pickets were "of the stuff of Fenimore Cooper's Indians, only they made no preposterous orations."

In "The Last of the Mohicans" Crane remarks that the pathos lies in the contrast between the warrior "with the eye of the eagle, the ear of the fox, the tread of the cat-like panther and the tongue of the wise serpent of fable," and the pathetic old tramp of Sullivan County. "The lover of the noble and fictional Uncas is overcome by great sadness," he writes. The sketch foreshadows his own life, itself built upon mountains which collapsed into banal troughs again and again, and the pathos lies in the contrast between his expectations and ideals and their collapse into disappointments, disillusionments, and grim ironies.

The cruel iconoclasm of "The Last of the Mohicans," the counterpointing of an ideal with its undercutting reality, initiated the debunked hero of Crane's later fiction. And the "little man" of his Sullivan County tales, the little man of less than heroic proportions who is deluded by his own vanity and conceit, becomes "the blustering man." He is in part the vain son in *George's Mother,* in part the seedy Bowery hero whose heroic act is Maggie's defloration. And he is the boastful Henry Fleming in *The Red Badge* who, like the story-telling historians of Sullivan County, shakes "metaphorical fists" in scorn and derision.

The contradictions in Crane's own life came to include a rich man with no money (always in debt), a Bohemian who in his manor house dressed for dinner in the English manner, and a husband with no married wife. When he was famous he wrote: "I saw the majestic forces which are arrayed against man's true success—not the world—the world is silly, changeable, any of its decisions can be reversed—but man's own colossal impulses more strong than chains, and I perceived that the fight was not going to be with the world but with myself." Crane's life (as one critic put it) "reminds us of his characteristic way of turning his irony against his own egotism and pride." His Uncas sketch anticipated what in Crane's fiction and poetry became their constant themes of disillusionment, debasement of illusionary and picturesque fronts by contradictory insights.

The Crane hero creates a flattering image of himself and of the world, whereas in the narrator's ironic viewpoint man is insignificant, "blind to his human weakness and the futility of his actions, pathetically incompetent in the large scheme of things. . . . Trapped within the confining circle of his swelling emotions of self," the hero sees himself "as god-like, dauntless, heroic, the master of his circumstances. The two images mark the extreme boundaries of Crane's imaginative scope—define, as it were, the limits of his vision of the world. For the Crane story again and again interprets the human situation in terms of the ironic tensions created in the contrast between man as he idealizes himself in his inner thought and emotion, *and* man as he actualizes himself in the stress of experience. In the meaning evoked by the ironic projection of the deflated man against the inflated man lies Crane's essential theme: the consequence of false pride, vanity, and blinding delusion."[7]

As *Maggie* and *The Red Badge* are designed by ironic contrasts of illusions undermined by crass realities, so too are his Sullivan County pieces with their little man of deflated bravado. They point to Crane's more mature writings. But he came into his literary maturity within a year of writing these sketches, tales, and fables; for he was simultaneously writing *Maggie* in 1891 and 1892, and in late 1892 he very likely began his Civil War novel. This fact rather contradicts the commonly held assumption that the Sullivan County writings anticipate *Maggie* and *The Red Badge,* since he evolved the grotesqueries of Maggie's ironic and metaphoric style at the same time, or nearly so.

Intrinsically, the Sullivan County pieces are slight things, and some of the tales are downright silly or pointless; namely "The Otcopush," "An Explosion of Seven Babies," and "The Cry of a Huckleberry Pudding." However, they have importance because they inaugurated his career as fiction writer and reveal clues to the evolution of his genius; also because they contain the very seeds of his later themes, of his impressionistic style with its addiction for color adjectives, his gift for intensity of psychological probing of character and scene, and his technique of paradox, metaphor, and symbolic realism.

In his portrayal of the little man's terror in "Killing His Bear" (*Tribune* for July 31), the first published Sullivan County tale (as distinguished from sketch), Crane practiced for his psychological portrayal of fear in Henry Fleming. Exactly like Henry Fleming, the little man in "Killing His Bear," which marks the beginning of Crane's fiction, indulges in inflated self-images. "Swift pictures of himself in a thousand attitudes under a thousand combinations of circumstances, killing a thousand bears, passed panoramically through him." John Berryman says that the Sullivan County sketches (he means, rather, the tales) have Poe as "their master" and yet "the most interesting parts of the stories are all Crane's." One feels a sense of terror from the dramatic impact of certain stories by Poe and Ambrose Bierce, but the gulf between them and Crane's tales is immense, for the latter are merely autobiographical incidents turned into spoofing tall tales. On the other hand, only Crane could have written—in "The Mesmeric Mountain"—that "the summit was a blaze of red wrath," which anticipates the red sun pasted in the sky like a wafer" (in *The Red Badge*), or, in "Across the Covered Pit,"[8] that the pit "would withhold its story of the tragedy until the Resurrection Morn," a phrase which initiates Crane's constant obsession throughout his fiction and poetry for Biblical and religious images and allusions.

His grotesque and pseudo-spooky horror tales hark back to Western tall tales and the Poe-like horror tales of Ambrose Bierce. Whereas Poe and Bierce aim to incite terror in the reader, Crane deflates the terror supposedly felt by his Sullivan County adventurers and thus debunks the genre of the horror story. Not at all in that category is his deadly serious sketch "The Snake," where for once the terror rendered has the impact of engaging the reader in the experienced thing. It is a little masterpiece of its kind, whereas Bierce's "The Man and the Snake"—a far-fetched Poe-like horror tale—is too artificial to be plausible.

In "The Mesmeric Mountain" the little man imagines that his ego has been challenged by an imperturbable mountain, and he vows to conquer this obstruction. He imagines that the mountain glowers at him, and he falls out of a tree in a fit of terror. Then he climbs the fierce mountain, only to find the world unchanged beneath him. It is clear that Crane intended the imperturbable mountain to be understood symbolically.

In "The Holler Tree" the little man is victorious over his pudgy companion by the chance falling of a dead and hollow tree onto the basket of eggs belonging to the latter. He had fallen into the hollow tree and crashed down inside it when it fell, and he was terrified; but when he crawls out of the trunk he resumes his pose of the boastful, wrathful hero. "He resumed his march down the forest pathway. His stride was that of a proud grenadier."

*Tribune* editor Willis Fletcher Johnson, to whom Crane showed two of his Sullivan County tales in the summer of 1891, thought "Four Men in a Cave" among the best pieces Crane ever wrote; but Crane himself thought otherwise. It is nothing more than an incident about a mad hermit encountered by the four men in a cave. He is standing with "what seemed to be a small volume" clasped in his hands before a great stone "cut squarely like an altar," and the terrified little man places three dollar-bills "upon the altar-like stone. The recluse looked at the little volume with reverence in his eyes. It was a pack of playing cards"—the bible of the gray-bearded "priest."

In August, 1892, shortly after completing these apprenticeship Sullivan County pieces, Crane "renounced the clever school in literature." "If I had kept to my clever Rudyard Kipling style, the road might have been shorter, but, ah, it wouldn't be the true road. The two years of fighting have been well spent. And now I am almost at the end of it. This winter fixes me firmly," Crane wrote Mrs. Lily Brandon Munroe (February 29, 1894). Whether or not he fashioned his Sullivan County tales (as distinguished from the sketches) on Kipling's stories, Crane's youthful *Tribune* tales were not so clever. He proposed them for a book in July 1895 to Copeland and Day, the Boston publishers of his *Black Riders* poems, as a "considerable work," and he wrote Mrs. Munroe to retrieve them from her: "Can you not send them to me? . . . There is no one in the world has any copies of them but you. Can you not send them to me?"[9] He had previously moaned: "How I wish I had dropped them into the wastebasket! They weren't good for anything, and I am heartily ashamed of them now, but every little while someone rakes them up and tells me how much pleasure he had from reading them—throws them in my face out of compliment."[10] However, he did not disparage his Sullivan County writings when in June, 1895 he proposed to Copeland and Day that they publish them: "I have considerable work that is not in the hands of publishers. My favorites are eight little grotesque tales of the woods which I wrote when I was clever. The trouble is that they only sum 10,000 words and I can make no more." In characteristic pose of diffidence he modestly added: "If you think you can make one of your swell little volumes of 10,000, the tales would gain considerably lengthy abuse no doubt." Nothing came of his book project.

The Sullivan County tales and fables derive from the little adventures Crane and three friends experienced (1891–1896) in Sullivan County. The Tall Man was Louis C. Senger, Jr., an artist who ended working for a railroad; the Pudgy Man was Frederic M. Lawrence, also of Port Jervis, with whom Crane shared a boarding-house on Avenue A in New York City after September 1892; the Little Man was Louis E. Carr, Jr. (as identified by Melvin Schoberlin). The Quiet Man in these tales was of course Stephen—he seldom spoke, but when he did his talk was as colorful as his prose. Often he was also the Little Man, however.

With the departure of vacationers from Asbury Park on Labor Day, Townley annually shut down his summer news agency. In early October 1891 Stephen's mother fell ill and was admitted to the hospital in Paterson, New Jersey, and there she died on December 7.[11] Of all her children only Townley was at her deathbed.

In a shirt never clean and in a borrowed gray ulster much too big, Stephen climbed Park Row stairs in hopes of a job at the New York *Tribune* or *Herald*. He took stoically his Park Row rebuffs, which in no way curbed his aspirations (said the *Bookman* in 1900). Finally, when he was on the verge of destitution and wearing shoes as well as a guilt that pinched, he took a job in a mercantile house for a very short while in the winter of 1892–1893.

Wilbur moved to Port Jervis in the hope of curing his asthma in the mountain air, and his daughter Helen says that Stephen wrote most of *Maggie* at her house "in two or three nights"; but this was the second draft, written after his mother's death on December 7 and before Christmas of 1891. He made a third and new version of *Maggie*, then an untitled manuscript, in March 1892 at Edmund's house on Cook Avenue in Lake View (at that time a suburb of Paterson). It was by no means the last re-drafting of *Maggie*.

The income left by the Reverend J. T. Crane to his wife was divided at her death among her surviving children, and lawyer William shrewdly bought up his brothers' inheritance—mainly stock in Pennsylvania coal mines—at a very low figure. Stephen sold his shares in order to publish *Maggie* in 1893. What cash he received as down payment on his inheritance he gambled away at poker tables as soon as he got it, according to Helen. He borrowed from his brothers, especially from William who could afford it and from Edmund who could not; he once told Ed not to lend him more than five cents at a time. Indifference to money countered by his desperate need for it patterned his life. Borrowing resulted in guilt, and guilt in the spending of more money. In the summer of 1899 Crane, while keeping up an English manor house at Brede Place which he could not afford, told Karl Harriman, a young admirer from Michigan: "I was foolishly proud back then. I hated to borrow money from my brothers who were not too well off. I borrowed too much which I never paid back. The sane thing would have been simply to have lived with Will or Ed constantly and trusted to fortune for some luck in paying them back. They have never asked me for a cent and that hurts like hellfire."

All his life Crane felt harassed by the need for money.

In April, 1893, when Hamlin Garland said to him: "You'll be rich and famous in a year or two. Successful authors always look back with a smile on their hard times," Crane replied: "You may be right. But it's no joke now. I'd trade my entire future for twenty-three dollars in cash." In a poem he wrote in Havana in 1898, he spoke of the same "lack of coin": "Your cross? / The real cross / Is made of pounds, / Dollars or francs. / Here I bare my palms for the silly nails / To teach the lack / The great pain of lack—/ Of coin."

After their mother's death, Wilbur and his brothers nagged at Stephen to stop wandering about the East Side with its flotsam of humanity and find a job. Wilbur admired Stephen's marvelous command of English and his sardonic humor. He was the kind of adolescent, says Helen, who would get a thrill out of being shot at sunrise. He would interrupt a dinner conversation about croup or hats "to inquire earnestly if any of the guests had ever seen a Chinaman wandering in Mott Street." Wilbur enjoyed talking with Stephen, but he felt that the boy was not going to make a success on the papers and suggested some other kind of work. Every time the unpleasant subject was broached Stephen would disappear. His brothers thought he was loafing but in fact he was tramping Park Row in hope that some editor would hire him.

He displeased his brothers by calling attention to his black eye and explaining that he got it in a grand fight in the Bowery. He shunned the dinner table gabble at his brothers' houses because he could not understand or tolerate their small talk. However, he could spend hours on the East Side with Mike Flanagan, a beer-truck driver, because, says Helen, "Mike's life was so foreign to his own world that all its details were colorful, and he could talk all night with Theodore Roosevelt [in 1896], Hamlin Garland, or William Dean Howells about the virtues of the Single-Tax or the genius of Flaubert; but when it came to the inanities of ordinary gossip, he was sunk." He could talk only if he was walking up and down with his hands in his pockets while he cocked his head sideways and half-smiled but never laughed. He kept his listeners laughing and urging him on to say more, because what he said was humorously bitter. And he was unpredictable and disconcerting in what he said, shocking "the nicely-laundered lives" of his relatives and of the best people of Port Jervis. He thought they were stupid, and he wilfully and painstakingly went out of his way to shock them.

With a cigarette always dangling from his lower lip (he endured a hacking cough even as early as 1892), his finely textured hands stained with cigarette yellow and his hair always sailing in the direction of the last wind, Stephen was obviously an embarrassment to lawyer William, member of the choir in the Drew Methodist Church. William's painfully respectable household was also embarrassed by the marriage of Wilbur to an Italian girl, Mattie, who had been a servant in William's house, and in after years their daughter, Helen, got her revenge by exposing in the *American Mercury* (1934) the smugness and hypocrisy of the Crane families.

Helen says her own father was "as indifferent and unconcerned about

Stephen as the others, Townley, Will, and Edmund." Yet even toward William, Port Jervis' penny-pinching lawyer, "obstructive, obstreperous, and tyrannical" (to quote Wilson Follett), Stephen felt, if not a love, at least a familiarity. He would think nothing of arriving at Will's house, on East Main Street in Port Jervis and battering on the door in the middle of the night expecting to be taken in hungry and penniless.

Edmund and his family were much attached to Stephen, after whom he named one of his twin sons. (It is interesting to note, by the way, that Edmund's wife's maiden name was Fleming, the same name that Stephen was to use for the hero of his *Red Badge of Courage*.) His brother Edmund was affluent only in the number of his children (three daughters and in 1900 the twin sons). He quit his railroad job and moved his family from Lake View to a house on the mill-pond at Hartwood, New York, in the Spring of 1893 to become caretaker and handyman for the Hartwood Club. Stephen later wrote his friend Willis B. Hawkins about Edmund, saying that he served as "postmaster, justice-of-the-peace, ice-man, farmer, millwright, blue-stone-man, lumberman, station agent on the P. J. M. and N. Y. R. R., and many other things I now forget."[12]

During Edmund's first winter at Hartwood in 1893, when his daughter Agnes was nine and her sister Edith seven, Uncle Stephen would plunge through the snow on a huge pair of skis with Agnes and Edith huddling behind him, riding along on his skis. Edith[13] says that her sisters "used to delight in watching him," especially when he'd come down the hills in a shower of snow "so that we could hardly see him. He was a delightful playfellow." They would attack him with snowballs, and Stephen on capturing them would march the girls (Alice, Edith, and Agnes) around the house with their arms up. Then little Edith would burst into tears (to her uncle's disgust), but when her mother would laugh, she would stop. On the other hand, he could never play too roughly for tomboy Agnes. She and her sisters used to battle with him with paper clubs and storm the fort he erected of two or three chairs. "Uncle Stephen would sit in a corner astride a chair in Napoleon style, and we three girls would attack him. Our weapons were newspapers rolled to make clubs. Many stinging blows we received, and we were delighted if we could get one in on Uncle Stephen. We three would keep him busy guarding and we would riddle our clubs striking him."

For Wilbur, life seemed rather anti-climactic after his career at Columbia University as canoeist and champion swimmer. He had dropped out of medical school after three years at the College of Physicians, and between asthma and children he never got anywhere in the world, says his bitter-tongued daughter, Helen. Another brother, Luther (Ludie) worked for the Erie Railroad until he got crushed between two freight cars. Townley, who remarried at forty-two, seems to have led the same kind of dissipated life that Stephen depicts in *George's Mother*.

## IV

### ⌘ Asbury Park

IN the summer of 1892 Crane was back at Asbury Park to service Townley's *Tribune* agency with shore news, but now he was a journalist in his own right instead of Townley's copy boy. He wandered between Ocean Grove and Asbury Park, the state's two most popular coastal resorts. The former was still the quiet, somber-hued resort home of lecturers, Methodists, and occasional bathers who attended Madame Alberti's School of Expression; the latter, a perpetual three-ring circus of tennis matches, tintype galleries and pool halls—with the merry-go-rounds and other mechanical amusements that sent showers of sparks and ashes against the wooden hotels, protested the Ocean Grove residents, and the "Observation Wheel," which tended to fog up "pious meditations on the evils of the world," to quote a delegation of Ocean Grove's vacationing clergymen. So Crane describes the situation in his unsigned *Tribune* sketch in Townley's column ("On the New Jersey Coast"), subtitled for July 24, 1892: "Summer Dwellers at Asbury Park and Their Doings."

Mrs. Lily Brandon Munroe, staying at the Lake Avenue Hotel while her husband was on a geology research trip, rode the merry-go-round at Asbury Park with Stephen, helped him to squander his meager income on ice cream at Day's, and strolled the boardwalk with him. Stephen had once said, we remember, that if he ever met a woman with golden hair he would marry her. Mrs. Munroe, bewitchingly lovely and well-to-do, was blond, as were two other women in his later life, Nellie Crouse and Cora Taylor. She lived in New York and Washington and was at Asbury Park with her mother-in-law, a suffragist, and Dottie, her younger sister whom Stephen was fond of teasing; he bet her a necklet that Townley would not remarry and two years later he wrote her that he had lost that bet.

Walking with Lily on the boardwalk, Stephen would rail against the smug, idle, gossiping hotel porch-sitters and delight in shocking them, or dance at Asbury Park, although he did not care for dancing, or discourage Lily from singing; although, as a fairly good tenor himself, he recognized that her good voice was at least in part the reason for her many admirers. Or he would reiterate his disapproval of women who smoked or wore "gay"

bathing suits and censor vehemently men who accepted a woman's prolonged fidelity without offering her marriage. He told Lily that he did
not expect to live long, that all he wanted was a few years of happiness. His
was a troubled spirit seeking a happiness, however, that was not within
his reach. It was "joy at a distance," the theme that weaves through *Maggie*
—into which he perhaps cast Lily as "the woman of brilliance and audacity." Abjectly poor and undernourished (he ate little and seemed to
resent others eating heartily), he smoked incessantly and had a hacking
cough. Lily did not think him handsome, but she always remembered his
remarkable almond-shaped eyes.

Reworking his *Maggie,* which he must have discussed with her, and writing sketches for the *Tribune,* Crane this summer saw with a keener perception than ever before. One of the main attractions was James A. Bradley,
noted for his wealth, his whiskers, and his creation of the resort at Asbury
Park. A sketch of him, undoubtedly by Crane, appeared on August 14
(1892) in the *Tribune:* "On the Boardwalk." A familiar figure, Bradley
carries a white sun-umbrella with a green lining as he strolls the ocean
front, and his rigidity is relieved by an occasional twinkle in his bright
Irish eyes. He has fierce and passionate whiskers, and he walks with bended
back and thoughtful brow, "continually in the depths of some great question
of finance involving, mayhap, a change in the lumber market or the price
of nails." A junk-collector at heart, Founder Bradley considers himself
a great seeker after the curious. "When he perceives it he buys it. Then
he takes it down to the beach and puts it on the boardwalk with a little
sign over it, informing the traveller of its history, its value and its virtues."
Consequently his boardwalk (if indeed one can manage to walk it) is a
museum for old boats, one ancient ship's bell, an antique hand fire-engine,
an iron anchor, and a marble bathtub.

It warms Founder Bradley's heart to watch people by the thousands
helter-skeltering in his sand or tramping his boardwalk or "diving into that
ocean of the Lord's which is adjacent to the beach of James A. Bradley.
He likes to edit signs and have them tacked up around. There is probably
no man in the world that can beat 'Founder' Bradley in writing signs. His
work has an air of philosophic thought about it which is very taking to
anyone of a literary turn of mind. He usually starts off with an abstract
truth, an axiom, not foreign nor irrelevant, but bearing somewhat upon a
hidden meaning in the sign—'Keep off the grass', or something of that
sort. Occasionally he waxes sarcastic. . . . He has made sign-painting a fine
art, and he is a master. His work, sprinkled over the boardwalk, delights
the critics and incidentally warns the unwary. Strangers need no guidebook
nor policemen. They have signs confronting them at all points 'Thou shalt
not' do this, nor that, nor the other. He also shows genius of an advanced
type and the qualities of authorship in his work. He is no mere bungler nor
trivial paint-slinger. He has the powers of condensation which are so much

admired at this day. For instance: 'Modesty of apparel is as becoming to a lady in a bathing suit as to a lady dressed in silks and satins.' There are some very sweet thoughts in that declaration. It is really a beautiful expression of sentiment. It is modest and delicate. Its author merely insinuates. There is nothing to shake vibratory senses in such gentle phraseology. Suppose he had said: 'Don't go in the water attired merely in a tranquil smile,' or 'Do not appear on the beach when only enwrapped in reverie.' A thoughtless man might have been guilty of some such unnecessary uncouthness. But to 'Founder' Bradley it would be impossible. He is not merely a man. He is an artist."

But the avalanche of pleasure seekers on the boardwalk at Asbury Park, if only by number and variation, outdid even James A. Bradley. Crane watched men and women as distinguished as Mr. and Mrs. Willis Fletcher Johnson, Mrs. Lily Brandon Munroe, and Hamlin Garland hobnobbing with James J. Corbett's trainer and with the boxer Jim himself, a big man making hosts of friends because of his "gentlemanly bearing and quiet manners. Even James A. Bradley came down momentarily from his pinnacle and conversed pleasantly with the boxer," says Crane in "Crowding into Asbury Park" (*Tribune,* July 3). In another unsigned article he wrote: "The thousands of summer visitors who have fled from the hot, stifling air of the cities to enjoy the cool sea breezes are not entirely forgetful of the unfortunates who have to stay in their crowded tenements. Jacob Riis, the author of *How the Other Half Lives* (1890)[1] gave an illustrated lecture on the same subject in the Beach Auditorium on Wednesday evening. The proceeds were given to the tenement-house work of the King's Daughters. Over $300 was cleared, which, at $2 each, will give 150 children a two-weeks outing in the country."

Hamlin Garland reported his own shore holiday in "Salt Water Day" in the *Cosmopolitan* later that year when William Dean Howells was briefly an editor of that magazine; Stephen made his first professional magazine appearance in the December issue with a Sullivan County sketch: "A Tent in Agony." As we know, he had brilliantly reported Garland's lecture on Howells' fiction the previous summer, and Howells repaid the apprentice reporter by promoting him in *Cosmopolitan* with profuse illustrations drawn by "Chip." In the sketch the men in the tent are terrified by an intruding bear, who is himself terrified—good vintage Crane—age 20.

Again and again Stephen filled in for Townley in the *Tribune*'s "On the New Jersey Coast," while Townley indulged in poker games or fishing for pickerel at Hartwood. Stephen took an obvious delight in competing with his brother. Warming to his assignments, he created grotesque *tableaux vivants* against garish, vulgar backdrops. Asbury Park had a grandstand with a restaurant, tennis courts, a baseball diamond, one of the best bicycle-tracks, a toboggan-slide, and in the process of construction a machine called a "razzle-dazzle." "Just what this will be is impossible to tell. It is, of course, a moral machine. Down by the lake an immense upright wheel has been erected. This will revolve, carrying little cars, to be filled evidently with desperate persons, around and around, up and down." He describes this scene again in "Joys of Seaside Life." He is as taken in as the rest of the vacationing middle-class America by certain new contrivances "to tumble-bumble the soul and gain possession of nickels": the "razzle-dazzle"—a sort of circular swing—and the merry-go-rounds, and the steam-organs making "weird music eternally"; and he is as excited by the boardwalk confusion: a frankfurter man who parades the avenues at all hours, "swinging his furnace and howling"; a sleight-of-hand Italian with "a courageous mustache and a clever nose" who mystifies indolent hotel guests on the verandas with a pack of playing cards; fakirs who sell silk handkerchiefs and embroidered petticoats; guitar players who sing and dance; and "a terrible creature in an impossible apparel, and with a tambourine. He, or she, wore orange stockings, with a bunch of muscle in the calf. The rest of his, or her, apparel was a chromatic delirium of red, black, green, pink, blue, yellow, purple, white and other shades and colors not known. There were accumulations of jewelry on different portions of his, or her, person. Beneath were those grotesque legs; above, was a face. The grin of the successful midnight assassin and the smile of the coquette were commingled upon it." He, or she, sang in an unknown tongue and danced on the hotel veranda with the airs and graces of the ballet. "And finally, he, or she, passed the tambourine about among the crowd, with a villainously-lovable smile upon his, or her, features. Since then he, or she, has become a well-known figure on the streets. People are beginning to get used to it, and he, or she, is not mobbed, as one might expect him, or her, to be."

There were numerous tintype galleries trundled about on wheels; even at Ocean Grove there was the camera obscura, a scientific curiosity of the Nineties. "People enter a small wooden building and stand in a darkened room, gazing at the surface of a small round table, on which appear reflections made through a lens in the top of the tower of all that is happening in the vicinity at the time. One gets a miniature of everything that occurs in the streets, on the boardwalk or on the hotel porches. One can watch the bathers gambolling in the surf or peer at the deck of a passing ship. A man stands with his hands on a lever and changes the scene at will"[2] to perhaps an image of "the sombre-hued gentlemen who congregate at this place in summer" and arrive "in solemn procession, with black valises in their hands and rebukes to frivolity in their eyes. They greet each other with quiet enthusiasm and immediately set about holding meetings. The cool, shaded Auditorium will soon begin to palpitate with the efforts of famous preachers delivering doctrines to thousands of worshippers. The tents, of which there are hundreds, are beginning to rear their white heads under the trees."[3]

This unsigned sketch again bears the unmistakable stamp of Crane's style. It has the characteristic color contrast (black valises and white tents);

it opens with what will soon become his device of epithet in the phrase "somber-hued gentlemen"; it marks a man aware enough of connotation to speak of "rebukes to frivolity" and "quiet enthusiasm"; and it is sardonic, ironic. Immediately following a listed directory of visiting clergymen, Crane tells us that the Gospel singers Mr. and Mrs. A. D. Sturgis will sing in the Auditorium, and that "a reformed convict named 'Big Frank' Carr addressed a large audience at the Bradley Beach surf meeting last Sunday night [June 26]. He went considerably into detail when describing the lives and methods of 'crooks.' "

The same ironic sense—one might call it less kindly, "smart-alecky"—pervades even the routine reporting of plays and piano recitals. In the same article which reviews a production of "My Lord in Livery" performed by a company of amateur actors from Philadelphia for the benefit of athletics,[4] Crane reports that Madame Alberti (she had known his parents) "was enthusiastically applauded for her pantomimic rendition of "Nearer, My God, to Thee," as was the Reverend John Peters who lectured that same week on "The Microscope and its Revelations." The conclusion of this article might be called a summation of Crane's feelings about educational resort areas. A passing question at this time was whether or not to make the Shark River into a harbor, thereby making it navigable by yachtsmen and increasing the potential of the resort. "Pirates used to anchor their vessels in the deep channels and go ashore to eat oysters and hang prisoners. It is said that Captain Kidd himself frequented the river in a villainous black-hulled schooner. But the sand bar at the inlet rose higher and higher until it poked its face out of the water, and still it grew until a huge wall of sand interposed between the waters of the ocean and the waters of the river. Then the river gradually became what it is now—a shallow stream, the resort of the crab and the crabber."

This streak of iconoclastic anti-intellectualism shows itself even more vividly in "Along the Shark River, The Pleasures of Biology and of Sketching from Nature,[5] in which Crane speaks of the summer youths and maidens from hotels and cottages at Avon and at adjoining resorts who compose an outdoor sketching class, seeking the browns and grays and greens of Shark River scenery. They perch "in rows on campstools and chatter and paint and paint and chatter. Sometimes they seem to do more of one than the other, but, notwithstanding this, when they arrive home they always contrive to produce for inspection a fair amount of work done. They sail on the river and picnic on its banks; they have clambakes in the pine woods and chase the blithesome crab among the sea weeds at the river's bottom." He speaks of the amateur biologists; if they seem to "prefer rare seaweeds to very scarce bottled beer, it is their privilege."

When he reported on a piano recital he would often bluff it if he could not spoof it. His report of Miss Ella Flock's performance of Beethoven's *Sonata Pathétique* is just such a bluff—"She plays with singular power and grace of expression, with the assured touch of a virtuoso," he wrote in the *Tribune* on August 21. The concert was given at the Lake Avenue Hotel where Mrs. Munroe was staying.

It was not so much the entertainments, but the entertained that infuriated Crane. He looks about at people participating in the "good life" and he sees the hypocrisy involved in it all. "The Seaside Hotel Hop"[6] is a sad montage. Skinny little girls with curls and short white dresses with blue ribbons "perform 'dancing in the barn' and other gems of the dancing school, to the delight of admiring parents." Nursemaids clear the floor of the small fry, and in from the veranda comes the sunbrowned summer girl in a ball dress "cut lower in the neck than her bathing suit, which makes her look like a doll with a bronze head on a porcelain body. She dances somewhat recklessly as one who is aware that the eyes of seventeen ancient and honorable spinsters in the front row are upon her and has determined to show her contempt for, and independence of, 'the horrid old things.' Her partner is a young man with tender, yearning eyes, a struggling mustache, a tennis shirt and russet shoes. He holds her—well, as if he were afraid of losing her." Only men in tennis clothes dance. The ones attired in evening wear only stand or flounce about. "The music varies with the character of the hotel, but is likely to consist of a wailing cornet and a piano which resembles a Christian who hath not charity in that it long ago became as sounding brass and tinkling cymbal. The music plays right along by the hour whether anybody is dancing or not. Occasionally the hotel proprietor looks in, rubbing his hands and beaming on the scene with an air that says, 'Enjoy yourselves, my people; these riotous festivities are given away with every package of twenty meal tickets.' "

These dancers are, after all only the children of their fathers, and their fathers form the composite of Asbury's typical summer visitor. He is a portly man with a gold watch-chain strung across the vest of a business suit, a wife, and three children, more or less. "He stands in his two shoes with American self-reliance and, playing casually with his watch-chain, looks at the world with a clear eye. He submits to the arrogant prices of some of the hotel proprietors with a calm indifference; he will pay fancy prices for things with a great unconcern. However, deliberately and baldly attempt to beat him out of fifteen cents and he will put his hands in his pockets, spread his legs apart and wrangle in a loud voice until sundown. All day he lies in the sand or sits on a bench, reading papers and smoking cigars, while his blessed babies are dabbling around throwing sand down his back and emptying their little pails of sea water in his boots. In the evening he puts on his best and takes his wife and the 'girls' down to the boardwalk. He enjoys himself in a very mild way and dribbles out a lot of money under the impression that he is proceeding cheaply."

If the young people are not the inheritors of this American dream, they are sad drudges and silly girls. "The amount of summer girl and golden youth business that goes on around this boardwalk is amazing. A young man comes here, mayhap, from a distant city. Everything is new to him, and in consequence he is a new young man. He is not the same steady and, perhaps, sensible lad who bended all winter over the ledger in the city office. There is a little more rose-tint and gilt-edge to him." He saunters forth in his false hues and finds on the beach a summer girl who just suits him. "She exactly fits his new environment. When he returns to the ledger he lays down his coat of strange colors and visions fade."

As for the summer girl, "a bit of interesting tinsel flashing near the sombre-hued waves, she gives the zest of life on the great boardwalk. Without her the men would perish from weariness or fall to fighting. Men usually fall to fighting if they are left alone long enough, and the crowd on the boardwalk would be a mob without the smile of the summer girl. She absent, the band would play charges and retreats and the soda-water fountains would run blood. Man is compelled by nature to be either a lover or a red-handed villain."[7]

While in mid-August 1892 Townley was away for a few days—probably off for Sullivan County to fish for pickerel—and more than likely telling the *Tribune* that he was attending a funeral in Newark—Stephen and beachcombing correspondent Arthur Oliver met on a Wednesday morning (August 17) and stopped in the pool parlor to have a cigar. When they came out they caught their first glimpse of "the parade that made Stevie Crane famous."

He was leaning against a door frame as he studied the procession with the half quizzical gaze of one who peers into a kaleidoscope, Oliver reports. "His cigar had gone out and was clenched tightly in his teeth. He stayed just that way until the last rank had passed. While he had been watching the parade, I had been watching him. He was a puzzle. Some inscrutable, internal influence was at work. 'Well, Stevie,' I said, 'how about it?' He took the cigar from his mouth and delivered himself of a few strong words. At this he was an artist, in the finer sense. Then he put back the unlighted cigar, clamped his teeth on it rather savagely, as I thought, and set off posthaste for his headquarters in the Lake Avenue Hotel to write his story before he lost his inspiration. Naturally, I wondered what the story would be. I was not prepared for what I read in the *Tribune* the next morning. It was just one sizzling roast. Not only at the parade did he hurl his glittering javelins of invective, but also at Asbury Park."

Stephen's sketch, "On the New Jersey Coast—Parades and Entertainments," headlined the feature section in the *Tribune* the following Sunday, August 21. His description of the most awkward, ungainly, uncut and uncarved procession ever to have raised clouds of dust on the sunbeaten streets of Asbury Park, stands as an early culmination of Crane the interpretive journalist, the stylist, and the chary observer of the "good life" in the United States in the 1890's.

The parade was a procession of bronzed, slope-shouldered and uncouth men begrimed with dust, and there were "enough brass bands to make furious discords." Members of the United American Mechanics, a political organization, they were ignorant of marching and were ill dressed. They plodded along, "not seeming quite to understand, stolid, unconcerned and, in a certain sense, dignified—a pace and a bearing emblematic of their lives. They smiled occasionally and from time to time greeted friends in the crowd on the sidewalk. Such an assemblage of the spraddle-legged men of the middle class, whose hands were bent and shoulders stooped from delving and constructing, had never appeared to an Asbury Park summer crowd, and the latter was vaguely amused."

As the sketch moves ahead, its writer becomes more and more angry; the anger fires his prose and becomes the vehicle for a blatant statement of what had so far been either half-concealed or mollified by humor. In contrast to the parading working men, Crane saw the throng of onlookers in summer gowns, lace parasols, tennis trousers, "straw hats and indifferent smiles," who stood on a fashionable street only a few miles from the factory where some of these union mechanics worked on the assembly line to produce night shirts. And in contrast to that factory, Asbury Park "creates nothing. It does not make; it merely amuses. . . . The bonafide Asbury Parker is a man to whom a dollar, when held close to his eye, often shuts out any impression he may have had that other people possess rights. He is apt to consider that men and women, especially city men and women, were created to be mulcted by him. Hence the tan-colored, sun-beaten honesty in the faces of the Junior Order of United American Mechanics is expected to have a very staggering effect upon them." Although Crane does not deny that the bona fide Asbury Parker "possesses principles," he also makes the effort to point out that he views the parade from the shady side of the street and consequently their "principles" and "honesty," like their faces, are not particularly "sun-beaten."

Even though Willis Johnson had admonished him that ordinary news reporting was not the place for subtle rhetorical devices, Crane stuck to his style in the parade sketch as he did throughout all his years as a newspaper reporter. He places one thing in contrast to its opposite; he phrases a thing, repeats the same phrasing, and then turns the phrase for ironic reversal. If style is indeed the "deference action pays to uncertainty" (to quote J. Robert Oppenheimer), then we may assume that Crane was in the process of forging a style which reflected technically how he looked at the world. At his best here in the "Parade Sketch," he seems unwilling to render a person or a scene without rendering its periphery as well and thereby implying far more than a liberal representation: the plodding march of the stolid working men was "emblematic of their lives."

As it happened the owner and editor of the *Tribune,* Whitelaw Reid, was running for the Vice-Presidency with the Republican presidential nominee, Benjamin Harrison. Newspapers opposed to Reid's candidacy seized upon and misrepresented Crane's ironic sketch of the American Day parade of workingmen by making it appear that it intended to make fun of and insult the parading laborers, and New Jersey members of the Junior Order of United Mechanics. The story snow-balled, until the original article was lost amidst the controversy about it. By this time everyone was certain that the United American Mechanics, an organization dedicated to restricting immigration and cheap labor, had paraded that day on behalf of the Republican candidates. Thomas Beer says that the paraders "lugged banners praising Harrison and Reid, and Crane—looking at the motion of the spectacle—forgot that Reid owned the New York *Tribune*. He merely saw a number of sweating persons who mostly worked with their hands, marching on behalf of capital, and the thing amused him." But Crane was not amused by the spectacle. (Beer had apparently never read "Parade Sketch," which was first reprinted in 1931 in the Newark *Sunday Call*.)

Then on August 24, a member of the Order of American Mechanics complained in an open letter to the *Tribune* that the unsigned article was an un-American criticism of a body of brothers bound together "to honor and protect our country and to vow allegiance to the Stars and Stripes." New York City papers ignored the incident, but not the Asbury Park journals. The *Daily Spray* reprinted the article and demanded an apology to the O. U. A. M. The Asbury Park *Journal* reported that "the *Tribune's* regular letter writer, J. Townley Crane, was engaged on something else last week, and delegated the task of writing the usual Sunday gabble to another. This young man has a hankering for razzledazzle style and has a great future before him if, unlike the good, he fails to die young. He thought it smart to sneer at the Juniors for their personal appearance and marching." The New York *Tribune,* itself in a state of turmoil, probably asked shore correspondent Billy Devereaux to answer the letter in an editorial. He wrote: "We regret deeply that a bit of random correspondence, passed inadvertently by the copy editor, should have put into our columns sentiments both foreign and repugnant to the *Tribune.* To those who know the principles and policy of this paper in both its earlier and later years, its devotion to American interests and its abhorrence of vain class distinctions, it can scarcely be necessary to say that we regard the Junior Order of United American Mechanics with high respect and hold its principles worthy of all emulation."

Although Devereaux, Oliver, Johnson and the rest of Crane's *Tribune* friends regretted that he had "toyed with a boomerang," and although even Hamlin Garland asked him what he expected by writing such a thing, Stephen himself revelled in the controversy. He posed as a righteous innocent: "I was so hot at the sight of those poor misshapen fools shouting for monopoly that I gave no thought to its effect upon my master [Whitelaw Reid]. I don't know that it would have made much difference if I had. I wanted to say those things anyway." Or he proudly called the entire matter an ironic error: "You see, I made a report of a labor parade the other day, which slipped in over the managing editor's fence," he told Garland.

Arthur Oliver, when Crane asked him what he had thought of the sketch, replied that it was clever and good for almost any purpose except publication, and Stephen replied with a grin: "Especially publication in the New York *Tribune*." "You see," he said, "I seemed to have forgotten for the moment that my boss on the *Tribune* was running for Vice-President. Those jolly paraders read my story and annoyed him with a telegram, informing him that his newspaper had better eat its words or he had better retire as a candidate, or something to that effect. So it was decided that the *Tribune* should eat its words; or so I understand."

Proud of the mess he had caused, he said: "You'd hardly think a little innocent chap like me could have stirred up such a row in American politics. It shows what innocence can do if it has the opportunity!" The self-dramatizing, contradictory Crane was bluffing, for he of course knew that the *Tribune's* Whitelaw Reid was a Vice-Presidential candidate, and he thought he would get fired and said so to shore-correspondents Arthur Oliver, Ralph Paine, and George P. (Post) Wheeler. "Have you heard the news?" Wheeler asked editor Wallace. "Townley was fired by mail and Stevie by wire! Stevie's out now and Townley goes at the end of the season." On being fired Stephen greeted Oliver "with a saintly smile he always had ready for every disaster."[8]

Willis Johnson of the *Tribune* denied that Stephen was fired, but he established this *Tribune* incident as the turning-point in Crane's career because it forced him from journalism for a while and back to fiction-writing. Whitelaw Reid was then out in the West and did not read the offensive article until Johnson showed it to him and explained the garbled exploitations of it in rival newspapers. Reid wasn't angry. However, Stephen was much agitated when he appeared before Johnson, in spite of his mask of levity, and when he asked Johnson what he should do and what would be done to him, Johnson replied: "Nothing." Despite Johnson's disclaimer, Stephen's family insisted that he was fired. His *Tribune* articles continued into mid-September, but thereafter its colmuns—at the rate of six dollars a column—were closed to him.[9]

The *Tribune* later remarked: "It does not appear to us that the modern era owes anything at all to Mr. Crane and his likes, anything save half-baked essays in work which it were idle to call either prose or verse, anything save weariness unspeakable." When Louis Senger sent Stephen this *Tribune* piece of vituperation, Crane wrote him: "Hope you will keep me posted on the *Tribune* acrobatics." Beneath his seeming indifference to being fired he was bitter. All of his shore-correspondent friends regretted the incident because they were fond of him and because he was an insurrectionist and liked battles with words. Founder Bradley was nettled by what the youth had said about his Asbury Park in that clever *Tribune* sketch, but he was generous enough to pass it off with a smile.

Asbury Park's radical American innocence filled a large gap in the young writer who had seen the workings of a Methodist ministry on the one hand and the degradation of the Bowery on the other. It completed his apprenticeship by allowing him to experience the rising class struggle between laborer and capitalist, and he went on to write about the poor and downtrodden in his Bowery and East Side sketches, in his Mexican sketches, and in his Cuban War dispatches. Asbury Park was a pleasure-resort of summer gowns, but it was also a manufacturing town with a factory producing nightshirts. This double view of Asbury's rich and poor never left Crane.

In spite of Willis Johnson's advice he was determined to stick to journalism (as well as to fiction writing). He wrote the Manager of the American Press Association on August 25 to ask for a job reporting on the far West: "I am going south and, also, west this fall and would like to know if I could open up a special article trade with you." Crane was bluffing. He ended doing a short spell on the Newark *Morning Times* for ten dollars per week, and then returned to New York City. How poor he was is suggested in his note to Acton Davies earlier that year, although perhaps written in jest: "Please send me $5 by this bearer whose name is only Smith. Am going to Ed's at Lake View and need some grub. Otherwise I shall eat the front door, his baby and the cat."

William Dean Howells turned his back on journalism because he disliked the sordid side of it, whereas Crane liked to study unvarnished human nature and to experience what he wrote about. One day that summer on the Asbury Park beach he told Arthur Oliver, who wanted to write but failed to get down "the real thing," that getting it down depended on your feeling it. "Forget what you think about it and tell how you feel about it." A few days later, when his unsigned "Parade Sketch" caused so much trouble, and Oliver asked him whether he would now revise what he had declared on the beach, Crane replied emphatically: "No! You've got to feel the things you write if you want to make an impact on the world." Oliver reminded him that his sketch of last Wednesday (August 17) had made just such an impact. " 'Well,' he replied in his mild, kindly way as he put his hand on my shoulder, 'that bears out just what I said.' "

The summer of 1892 saw the publication in the *Tribune* of the first of Crane's sketches of New York City: "The Broken-Down Van" (July 10, 1892). Although it is unsigned, it is unmistakably a city version of the same kind of sketch from life that Crane was writing at Asbury Park and Ocean Grove.[10] The writer sees "Two great red furniture vans painted with impossible landscapes" and drawn each by four horses plunging along the street, almost touching the roaring elevated road above, when a wheel on the rear van falls off and the axle goes down. The two men on the shelf half-way up the front of the stranded van begin to shout loudly to their brother cliff dwellers on the forward van. Behind them is a red horsecar with a red bull's-eye light, and a red-headed driver. "Then a car with a green light crept up behind the car with the red light; and the green driver blew his whistle and pounded on his dashboard; and the conductor of the red car seized his strap from his position on the rear platform and rung such a rattling tattoo on the gong over the red driver's head that the red driver became frantic and stood up on his toes and puffed out his cheeks as if he were playing the trombone in a German street band and blew his whistle till an imaginative person could see slivers flying from it, and pounded his red dashboard till the metal was dented in and the car-hook was bent."

Behind them comes a blue car, the driver blowing his whistle, and this drives the green driver mad enough to blow and pound, and this in turn makes the red driver yell and ki-yi and "whoop harder than the worst personal devil encountered by the sternest of Scotch Presbyterians." Meanwhile at the red car a six-year-old girl passes under the horse's neck with a pail of beer; another girl goes in front of the van horses with two pails of beer; a boy mounts the red car with the evening newspapers; another boy pokes his finger in the van wheel's greasy hub and writes his name in black grease on the van's red landscape; and still another studies "the white rings on the martingales of the van leaders with a view to stealing them in the confusion; a sixteen-year-old girl without any hat and with a roll of half-finished vests under her arm crossed the front platform of the green car. As she stepped up onto the sidewalk a barber from a ten-cent shop said 'Ah! there!' and she answered 'smarty!' with withering scorn and went down a side street. A few drops of warm summer rain began to fall"—the gas lamps have just been lit.

Each delayed car is full of passengers craning their necks and asking what the trouble is, while a dozen horsecars go down on the other track, and overhead thunder the elevated trains that make the whole street tremble. "Trucks, mail-wagons and evening paper carts crowded past. A jam was imminent. A Chatham Square cab fought its way along with a man inside wearing a diamond like an arc-light." The leader of the furniture vans light four candles to try to find the lost hub nut, but the wind blows out the candles, and the blue car driver suggests they get a fire-fly. A hand-organ man comes up and begins an overture, while the ten-cent barber eyes a Division Street girl, a millinery puller-in who is chewing gum with an almost fierce motion of her jaw. A policeman walks around the broken-down van, makes the hand-organ move on, and talks to the Division Street gum-chewing girl—"to the infinite disgust of the cheap barber. The trunk-strap man came out of a restaurant, with a sign of 'Breakfast 13 cents; Dinner 15 cents,' where he had been hidden and slunk into the liquor store next door with a sign of 'hot spiced rum, 6 cents; Sherry with a Big Egg in it, 5 cents.' At the door he almost stepped on a small boy with a pitcher of beer so big that he had to set it down, and rest every half block."

After much confusion and crowds of onlookers, the broken-down van is lifted onto a paving block and the wheel replaced. " 'Now, youse fellys move on!' said the policeman, and the crowd broke up. The cheap barber was talking to a girl with one black eye, but he retreated to his shop with the sign which promised 'bay rum and a clean towel to every customer.' Inside the liquor store the trunkstrap man was telling a man with his sleeves rolled up how two good men could have put their shoulders under the van and hoisted it up while a ten-year-old boy put on the wheel." But of course the man with his sleeves rolled up has already accomplished that very feat.

The irony, confusion, impressionism in shifts of scene and color, and the suggested squalor shape not only this New York City sketch but the novel of the Bowery, *Maggie,* which Crane was still revising in the fall. The millinery girl with a roll of tailored vests might well work at the collar-and-cuff factory where Maggie worked. Women influenced Crane's life at every turn, but as in "The Broken-Down Van," it is with rare exceptions a man's world that he portrays, and this is true even when he presents the point-of-view of a woman as in *George's Mother, The Third Violet,* and *Active Service.* Crane's fictional women are lifeless things; and his men are essentially men without women.

One exception is an Asbury Park tale—"The Pace of Youth"—about Lizzie Stimson's elopement with the impresario of her father's Mammoth Merry–Go–Round—that whirling circle of ornamental lions, giraffes, camels, ponies, goats, all "glittering with varnish and metal that caught swift reflections from windows high above them." The lovers elope, but Stephen and Lily Munroe merely rode in childlike sport these mechanical up-and-down animals that swept around in their never-ending race to whatever tune the steam-organ played. Sunlight "sprinkled its gold upon the garnet canopies carried by the tireless racers and upon all the devices of decoration that made Stimson's machine magnificent and famous. A host of laughing children bestrode the animals, bending forward like charging cavalrymen, and shaking reins and whooping in glee. At intervals they leaned out perilously to clutch at iron rings that were tendered to them by a long wooden arm." The young man who affixed the rings stood on a narrow platform erected like a pulpit, and from that risky position he flirted with the girl who sold tickets shyly behind a silvered netting. "Sometimes a little sign saying 'Cashier' in gold letters, and hanging upon the silvered netting got directly in range and interfered with the tender message." Frank conducts his silent courtship with the dark-eyed Lizzie not without despair, but finally he persuades her to elope and they run off in a buggy, while old man Stimson pursues them with a revolver in a rented hack. The race of real horses contrasts with the mechanized merry-go-round ponies.

Lizzie and Frank outdistance the pursuit of old man Stimson, and while his hack's horse lags in the race to overtake the buggy of the reckless lovers he senses the power of youth, "the power to fly strongly into the future and feel hope again." The irony is that anyone in conflict with John Stimson's "granite will usually end in quick and abject submission," but here his granite will is defied by the universe, by that other vehicle that is youth with youth's pace; "it was swift-flying with the hope of dreams." The old horse, spreading his aged legs "in quaint and ridiculous devices for speed," pursues "the eager spirit of a young and modern horse, while in the rear of the eloper's buggy there is a little glass eye of derision."

C. K. Linson in *My Stephen Crane* (1958) recalls that one morning in New York, some two years later, he found Stephen in his room at Avenue A near 22 East 57th Street, sitting by the window and writing on sheets of foolscap on his knees, with an ink-bottle on another chair beside him, and with a towel turban-like about his head. He handed Linson the manuscript of "The Pace of Youth" and stretched back wearily until his friend had read it. " 'Like it?' he asked laconically. Of course I liked it. That girl in a red dress—it would be red!" Linson liked the symbolism of the whole thing, how youth eludes age. Its "color emotion" was like that of a painter's, and its prose-poetry was deftly saved "from the sentimental by the comic contrast of people unable in the wind to hear the music but reassured by seeing 'the band with their lips glued to their instruments.' 'A bird of a story, Steve!' He warmed to my appreciation, while through his cigarette-smoke I studied his headgear. 'Yeh! the towel? This thing got me going and I couldn't sleep, so I got up. Been at it all night. A wet towel cools the machinery all right. And I work better at night. I'm all alone in the world. It's great!'" Linson wondered how Crane could keep the feel of those Asbury Park people months after he had last seen them. Steve smiled. "Can't you make sketches from memory? Of course. Well, haven't I known those types since I was a kid? Certainly."

Lizzie's elopement in "The Pace of Youth," was Crane's wish-fulfillment of what might have happened to him and Mrs. Lily Munroe but didn't. Lily was no Lizzie, and Crane was no impresario, but he tried to induce her to elope with him later when he was en route to Mexico. He arranged a meeting with Lily amid the noise of hammers in the chilly corridors of the Library of Congress, then under construction. She was moved by his passion ("the desperation of proud youth" was Crane's phrase for it), but she thought him too visionary. And after all he was going south for his health, he told her.[11] "The Pace of Youth" appeared in the New York *Press* for January 18 and 19 (1895), the very weekend he was trying to persuade her to quit her husband and the comforts of Washington for a romantic trip to the West and Mexico! Typically, it was after he had written his charming Asbury Park tale of Lizzie Stimson's elopement that he tried to experience the same thrilling adventure.

In a projected novel, *The Merry-Go-Round,* of which one chapter was to be his already published "The Pace of Youth," he hoped to salvage something of his happy times dancing with the beautiful Lily and strolling with her on the beach of Asbury Park in 1892. When they parted at the end of that 1892 summer, he told her she should think of him whenever she saw the sea. Neither of them realized then that their frustration was only a prelude to the course their love would take.

Stephen gave Lily, or perhaps her sister Dottie, a photograph of himself in the military uniform of the Claverack College or Hudson River Institute. One night some months after they parted at Asbury Park they met at Mrs. Brandon's home in New York City, and after leaving her he stood watching her window in hope of seeing her pass; a storm had come up, and she had turned out the light he had asked her to burn. He wrote her and sent a copy of the manuscript of *Maggie,* in 1893, which her jealous husband destroyed along with all letters but the four saved by Dorothy, who also preserved the photograph. One of his *Black Riders* poems, written about that time, declares his infatuation:[12]

> *And you love me*
> *I love you.*
> *You are, then, cold coward*
> *Ay; but, beloved,*
> *When I strive to come to you*
> *Man's opinions, a thousand thickets,*
> *My interwoven existence,*
> *My life,*
> *Caught in the stubble of the world*
> *Like a tender veil—*
> *This stays me.*
> *No strange move can I make*
> *Without noise of tearing.*
> *I dare not.*

In April, 1893 he wrote from New York City: "Dearest L. B. I am sure that you have not concluded that I have ceased to remember. The three months which have passed have been months of very hard work for S. Crane. I was trying to see if I was worthy to have you think of me. And I have waited to find out. Well, at least, I've done something. I wrote a book. Up to the present time, I think I can say I am glad I did it. I'm almost a success. And 'such a boy, too,' they say. I do not think, however, that I will get enough applause to turn my head. I don't see why I should. I merely did what I could in a simple way, and recognition from such men as Howells, Garland, Flower, and Shaw [Albert Shaw of the *Review of Reviews*] has shown me that I was not altogether reprehensible. Any particular vanity in my work is not possible to me. I merely write you these things to let you know why I was silent for so long. I thought if I could measure myself by the side of some of the great men I could find if I was of enough value to think of you, L. B. They tell me I did a horrible thing [in *Maggie*], but they say, 'it's great.' 'And its style,' said Garland to Howells, 'Egad, it has no style! Absolutely transparent! Wonderful—wonderful.'"

He wrote Lily that it seemed like a thousand years have passed "since we met and were comrades; I can readily see that, in that time, I have, perhaps, become a memory to you, a mere figure in a landscape of the past. . . . Yet you, to me, are still a daily vision, a dream that is part of my life, blending itself with my occupations each day. Your face is a torturing thing, appearing to me always, with the lines and the smile that I love,—before me always this indelible picture of you with its fragrance of past joys and its persistent utterance of the present griefs which are to me tragic because they say they are engraven for life. It is beyond me to free myself from the thrall of my love for you; it comes always between me and what I would enjoy for life—always—like an ominous sentence— the words of the parrot on the death-ship: 'We are all damned.' And yet, would I escape from it? Not I. It is the better part. . . . Besides, it is supremely true that I conceive those days with you well spent if they cost me years of discontent. It is better to have known you and suffered than never to have known you. I would not exchange one little detail of memory of you; I would not give up one small remembrance of our companionship. Yet, with it, I suffer and I wished you to know it because you are a woman and though you may value me as a straw, you will comprehend why I felt I must tell you of it. For, surely, it is a small thing. I ask nothing of you in return. Merely that I may tell you I adore you; that you are the shadow and the light of my life—the whole of it."

He persisted in his adoration of Lily until late in 1898 when he was possessed of her image in the "Intrigue" poems he wrote in Havana. He was with her briefly in Washington, D.C., at least once that year, and they met in January 1895 and probably again in 1896. "Don't forget me, dear, never, never, never," he wrote in his March 1894 letter. "For you are to me the only woman in life. I am doomed, I suppose, to a lonely existence of futile dreams. It has made me better, it has widened my comprehension of people and my sympathy with whatever they endure. And to it I owe whatever I have achieved and the hope of the future. In truth, this change in my life should prove of some value to me, for ye gods, I have paid a price for it."

There is no point in speculating how the course of his life would have been altered had she eloped with him, a proposal she seriously considered before declining, but she heeded the admonitions of her father, a colonel living in New York at the Carleton House; he was anxious that nothing serious should occur between them, and so after divorcing Mr. Munroe, the hot-tempered and jealous geologist, she settled down as Mrs. Smillie.

When Stephen first met Lily at Asbury Park in 1892, they went down to the docks and talked with the skipper of the catboat *Anna,* as he calls it in his charming little sketch "The Captain," which appeared in the *Tribune* on August 8. With them is a young woman from Baltimore who asks the Captain whether a squall is coming and, if so, from what direction? "The Captain looks up and studies the top of his mast. 'It's coming,' he says, with agonizing deliberation, 'from my house. My baby ain't missed a chance to squall in three months!' " The Captain is also a fireman and goes to fires in his yachting-dress with his fire-department badge of tin pinned to his left breast. A young woman from Philadelphia admires the badge and asks whether he has ever put any fires out. No, he always got there too late; and he never started a fire either. " 'How is that, Captain?' 'I mean never since I was married,' he replies. 'She—my wife—does that,' and a faint smile cracks his dry cheeks." The Baltimore girl suggests that she would like to go fishing and wonders what she will catch. " 'Well,' he answers in a low voice, but with ineffable scorn, 'you might catch some of those young men. Ain't any of 'em heavy enough to break your line.' "

The young man in Crane's sketch has already been "hooked." He has been caught hook, line, and sinker by the third woman in the party, the young woman from New York who is in all probability Lily herself. When the wind rises the catboat leaps like a racehorse and everyone gets wet. "The young woman from New York gets fairly drenched over the shoulders and head. Perhaps it is because she has pretty hair; perhaps it is because no woman likes to have her hair soaked in salt water; but, however that may be, she unfastens her hair and it tumbles about her shoulders, a mass of dark brown, with threads of it blown across her cheek and throat and drops glistening where the water in the dark curls is struck by the slanting sun." She tantalizes not the Captain but the young man: " 'How do I look, Captain,' she asks, putting her elbows on her knees and laying a hand on each cheek so that she can lean forward and look into his face with dark, flashing, and tantalizing eyes. 'Look like the gypsies that camp in the woods back of our house,' he says, carefully measuring his words. 'They're pretty, aren't they?' asks the 'smart young man.' 'Well,' answers the captain-fireman cautiously, 'They're wild, you know.' "

Sometime during that summer Crane saw two men who went bathing on the New Jersey coast and, in toying with a derelict raft, were carried out to sea. In "The Reluctant Voyagers," written in the Spring of 1893[13] but not published in his lifetime, Crane in this humorous tale has the two men rescued by a little coast schooner and deposited against their wishes in New York City—in their bathing suits. He took the manuscript to his artist friend Linson at his studio, then on West 22nd Street, some months after *Maggie* was published in March, 1893, when they had first met. Linson says it was late spring and the day was stewing with heat. Crane asked him to illustrate his tale, and posed for the tall man, while some friend posed for the fat man by stuffing a pillow inside his tightly-fitting bathing suit. Linson himself posed for the bath-ticket seller and grimaced at them from a mirror as he drew his sketch. They went down to the waterfront in hope of finding a schooner at the wharves and a sea Captain, but all they found were two men on the deck of an idling schooner. "The jays must be doing the Bowery," said Crane. "Anyway, these other bucks are ocean kings. Too high-toned for us. Just make him like a Sullivan County farmer with chin whiskers!" And so Linson, who knew as much about Sullivan County as Crane, drew the Captain just that way. Back in the studio Linson's "roof ladder became the one down which the captain—with chin whiskers—'brought a coffee pot from the sky.' Out of the expanse of red tin roof under the full sun Steve and I were snapped for the two men on the beach. 'Hurry up there!' he shouted to the camera. 'Gosh! You can brown wheats on this tin!' And for once he swore that absolute truth was not essential to a work of art." Crane sent his manuscript and Linson's illustrations to a magazine which had already printed one of his sketches—most likely James Ford's humorous *Truth*—and then reported "The Reluctant Voyagers" as accepted. He and Linson, who says that he never had more fun than when he drew these illustrations, rejoiced. But when Linson at the end of the summer returned from camping and painting in Ramapo, New Jersey, he learned that the magazine had rejected the tale and had lost his drawings.[14]

When Crane again wrote about Asbury Park in 1896, four years after his summer there with Lily, he was famous enough to obtain the New York *Journal's* headline: "ASBURY PARK AS SEEN BY STEPHEN CRANE."[15] It was the same confused scene, but now he renders it with a more mature and more experienced writer's contrapuntal imagery. Hacks and stages paraded to meet his train, and the voices of the hackmen clashed in a mellow chorus; but the passengers for the most part "dodged their appeals and proceeded across the square, yellow in the sunlight, to the waiting trolley cars. The breeze that came from the hidden sea bore merely a suggestion, a prophecy of coolness, and the baggagemen who toiled at the hill of trunks sweated like men condemned to New York. From the station Asbury Park presents a front of spruce business blocks, and one could guess himself in one of the spick Western cities. Afterward there is square after square of cottages, trees and little terraces, little terraces, trees and cottages, while the wide avenues funnel toward a distant gray sky, whereon from time to time may appear ships. Later still, a breeze cool as the foam of the waves slants across the town, and above the bass rumble of the surf clamor the shrill voices of the bathing multitude. The summer girls flaunt their flaming parasols and the young men in weird clothes walk with a confidence born of a knowledge of the fact that their fathers work.

"Coney Island is profane; Newport is proper, with a vehemence that is some degrees more tiresome than Coney's profanity. If a man should be goaded into defining Asbury Park he might state that the distinguishing feature of the town is its singular and elementary sanity." Here life is healthy and rational, but there are a number of restrictions "not sanctioned by nature's plan nor by any of creeds of men, save those which define virtue as a physical inertia and a mental death."

Of course Crane, a man with seven distinct thirsts in his throat, was irked by James A. Bradley's prohibition ordinance, and thirsty Crane is just as aware as he was in 1892 of the hypocrisy of Ocean Grove in Founder Bradley—"A heavy mist can vanquish gorgeous Orion and other kings of the heavens, but James A. Bradley continues to shine with industry"—and of the intense loneliness of being among the hordes of America's middle class. Except for those restrictions "not sanctioned by nature's plan" Asbury is no different from the Far West. Both "give the casual visitor the same deep feeling of isolation that comes to the heart of the lone sheep herder, who watches a regiment swing over the ridge or an express train line through the mesquite."

Meanwhile the wind snatches fragments of melody from the Asbury Park band pavilion "and hurls this musical debris afar," and as the sun sinks the incoming waves "are shot with copper beams and the sea becomes a green opalescence." It is a loneliness expressed through color, but otherwise it is the same loneliness as Crane felt when in the Far West and even when camping out in Sullivan County with three friends in 1892: "Suddenly it struck each that he was alone, separated from humanity by impassable gulfs." He felt himself always alone.

# V

## ⊂∃ *"Maggie"*

One of Stephen's fraternity brothers at Syracuse, George P. Wheeler (the boy he had introduced to beer and cigarettes back in 1888)—Post Wheeler as he came to be known more familiarly—claimed that he was the one who urged Crane to come to New York. His gambit for enticing Stephen was the mention of two uncorked bottles in his studio loft in the city. Crane replied: "You appal me by mentioning a couple of bottles. If I were sure you meant beer not one would reply with more fervent and fraternal joy. But I have a damnable suspicion you mean wine. Know then, my old companion, that I am living upon the glory of literature and not upon its emoluments. Nevertheless, we have gone too many leagues together to let the matter of beer or wine separate us." He must have taken Wheeler up on his invitation, for sometime in the autumn or winter of 1891 he bummed a bed in the studio loft.

Another fraternity brother, Frederick M. Lawrence, Stephen's friend from Port Jervis, suggested that he join him in New York. In the autumn of 1892 Crane moved into the boardinghouse at 1064 Eastern Boulevard (renamed Avenue A), where he shared the principal room on the second floor overlooking the East River and Brooklyn with Lawrence and another medical student, Lucius L. Button, later a physician in Rochester. Crane named this boardinghouse the Pendennis Club after Thackeray and here wrote his final draft of *Maggie,* which he tested by observations and adventures in the Bowery with Lawrence. Since he was a peripatetic writer borrowing the use of a bed now from one friend, now from another, and writing now in this house and now in that, it is no wonder that so many friends as well as members of his family claim that Stephen Crane slept in their homes and wrote *Maggie* there. He himself contributed to the confusion. "I wrote it in two days before Christmas,"[1] he boasted to Wallis McHarg about the December, 1891, draft.

In March of the following year, with a note of introduction from Townley, he had called on Richard Watson Gilder of the *Century* to show him the manuscript of *Maggie.* Crane had probably read Julian Ralph's "The Bowery" in the *Century* (December, 1891) while writing his second draft and thought it likely therefore that Gilder would publish his own

*66*

Bowery novel. Gilder was not exactly a stranger. He and Crane had met when Stephen was a boy; he knew all the Cranes. Stephen "was thin and his blue eyes seemed enormous," wrote Gilder. "He sat wrapped in a gray ulster much too big for him, talking very slowly about his family with whom I had lost touch. I saw that his manuscript was not long and gave him an appointment for the next day."

The manuscript gave Gilder quite a shock, as he admitted in 1904. "It seemed to him daring and filled with good touches but it was 'cruel.' There was no visible sentiment. These creatures of an environment had no tenderness and no restraint of action to excuse their callousness, and next day Gilder sat pointing out excessive adjectives and slaughtered infinitives to the shy boy, who finally cut him short with an untactful question: 'You mean that the story's too honest?' " (to quote Beer). Gentleman Gilder (then forty-eight) gave his courteous nod to the boy of twenty, and that ended Crane's prospects as of March 23, 1892.

It is difficult to decide what Gilder's reasons for the rejection were. He did not consider *Maggie* obscene, although perhaps too profane in its "damns" and too brutal in its honesty for publication in the *Century*. Possibly he may have considered it a breach of taste, although in 1904 Arthur Morrison's *Child of the Jago* did not offend him: "But Mr. Morrison's an Englishman!" However, when Englishman Robert Louis Stevenson had passed through New York City decades earlier Gilder refused to receive him because he did not consider him respectable (he'd heard rumors about his private life).

After his unpleasant interview with Gilder, Crane rewrote *Maggie* in March–April, and when the third draft failed to interest other magazines locked the manuscript up in a box at Edmund's house in Lake View and turned to reshaping his Sullivan County sketches to sell to the *Tribune,* where his reception was far more favorable.

In January, 1893 (?) Wallis McHarg, whom Stephen had pulled out of the surf in the summer of 1884, was visiting the city before sailing for Germany to study medicine and found Crane's address by calling at the New York *Herald*'s office. McHarg found him sharing a big bedroom on East 23rd, presumably in the Art Students' League building, with a young actor whom Beer identifies as probably William Riley Hatch. Together they walked through the Bowery while Stephen pointed out the sights: a notorious procurer and a girl who was supposed to be the daughter of a wealthy family and who came downtown "for the pleasure of attracting suitors and then making them quarrel while she went to refuge in the shadow of some policeman." Here was the dancehall a gang of sailors had wrecked for being wrongfully expelled, and there the saloon where he had got a black eye. Perhaps Stephen explained to McHarg that the Bowery got its name because it ran through the bowery or farm of Peter Stuyvesant and that the word *bouwerij* is Dutch for farm or country-seat.[2]

He surely pointed out the typical Bowery boy, a kind that began with the dandy who aimed to be a fireman and changed through the years to the ruffian who liked to punch other ruffians who were rude to the female sex. The Bowery boy of the nineteenth century dyed his moustache jet-black, wore perfume, oiled his hair profusely, and affected rough airs he considered exquisite. His trousers were very tight and needed no suspenders, he wore a silk hat and a huge black silk scarf under the collar of his flannel shirt, and instead of shoes wore well-polished boots. When Thackeray asked one of these East-Side Adonises: "Sir, can I get to Houston Street this way?" a Bowery boy replied: "Yes, I guess yer kin, sonny—if yer behave yerself." With a cigar tilted heavenward, the Bowery boy used to spread his elbows apart so that nobody could pass him, and then if someone jostled him he would immediately be insulted and fight with his fists. In a voice "modeled after that of a fire-trumpet," (to quote Julian Ralph) he spoke a language all his own. Crane caught that language in *Maggie:* "Deh moon looks like hell, don't it?" says Jimmie Johnson quite reverently. Wearing shoes of patent leather that "looked like weapons," Pete disdains to use any weapons but his fists. " 'Hully gee!' said he, 'dose mugs can't feaze me. Deh knows I kin wipe up d' street wid any t'ree of dem.' When he said, 'Ah, what d' hell!' his voice was burdened with disdain for the inevitable and contempt for anything that fate might compel him to endure. Maggie perceived that here was the ideal man."

In "Youse Want 'Petey,' Youse Do" the New York *Herald* for January 4 (1892) reported that three juvenile prisoners, two of them age seven and one thirteen, stood before the bar at the Jefferson Market Police Court with hardened faces. The leader of the gang—seven-year old Nathan Alstrumpt—said to Justice Divver: "Yer see, we was doin' notten but playen tag in der street when a blokie wat's called 'Petey' came along and says, 'Hi, fellers, let's go a swipen.' We went wid him—see? Youse wants 'Petey,' youse do. He did der swipen—not me nor de kids." Justice Divver asked, "Who's 'Petey?'" "Why, he's 'Petey' Larkin, a mug wot lives in Thompson Street." If Crane did not report this incident, he must at least have read it since it is that kind of juvenile delinquency which informs the opening scene of *Maggie.*

"Show you the Bowery for a dollar, mister?" Youths posted at Grand Central Station would escort mister anybody through the infamous Bowery on a tour that ended at Ahearn's saloon. After jostling through this Babylon of petty commerce, Crane and McHarg may have ended there or at the largest of the beer saloons—the Atlantic Gardens, the resort of sailors from German vessels and also of the Bowery Germans. The standard tipple at all these Bowery saloons was Lager, and on the morning after a busy Saturday night the air was weighted with the odor of soured beer.

While McHarg was staying in New York, Crane asked him to read the still untitled manuscript. McHarg read it at his room in the Gilsey House and decided that this thing was new, outlandish and strange: he had never before read anything this long in which the characters had no names. He was appalled and thrilled, but left for Germany doubting any publisher would accept the novel.

Stephen's brother William agreed with McHarg that the nameless characters would confuse his readers. In January, 1893, they were simply "the girl," "the girl's mother," etc. On January 19, Crane copyrighted his Bowery novel without the title *Maggie*,[3] and the following month he sent McHarg a note, undated and without an address, that William had titled the book *Maggie: A Girl of the Streets*. (Attached to his note was this postscript: "The Herald fired me last week."[4]) The characters now were named: the girl who "blossomed in a mud-puddle" became Maggie, her seducer became Peter, "the mere boy" became Freddie, and the "woman of brilliance and audacity" was christened Nell.

McHarg's judgment had been correct. Publishers one after the other refused the manuscript.[5] When Crane went to Willis Johnson for advice, the *Tribune*'s day editor warned him that it would be difficult to find a reputable publisher who would dare to bring it out and that if it were published, it would shock Mrs. Grundy and bring upon him a storm of condemnation. Stephen struck upon the idea of issuing it under an assumed name so as neither to compromise his future, nor to embarrass his brothers and especially their prudish wives. He discussed it with journalist George Wheeler and others. The outcome was that he renamed himself "Johnston Smith," which is about as anonymous as a name can get, the two names being the most numerous in the city directory. (He first made it "Johnson Smith" but finally inserted the "t.") Now nobody, not even Mrs. Grundy nor Mr. Podsnap, would suspect him of being the guilty author. Much later, he characteristically remarked about this *nom de plume* to Elbert Hubbard, editor of *The Philistine:* "You see, I was going to wait until the world was pyrotechnic about Johnston Smith's *Maggie* and then I was going to flop down like a trapeze performer from a wire, and coming forward with all the modest grace of a consumptive now, say, I am he, friends."

At last, under the pseudonym, the first printing of *Maggie* was issued in March, 1893, by a printing house that published medical books and religious tracts—a cheap paperbook with mustard-yellow cover minus the name of the publishing firm and Crane's own name, but printed at his expense. The publisher presented Crane with the outrageous bill of $869 for 1,100 copies, although the author himself had labored at typesetting the pages to hurry the book through the press.[6] Later his publisher Appleton told him that his printer must have made $700 out of him. "You may take this as proferred evidence of my imbecility. Will made me get the thing copyrighted. I had not even that much sense." For *Maggie* he sacrificed his inheritance from his father's coal-mine stock, and borrowed the rest from William (that he lent Stephen $1,000 is only legend).

Out $869, Crane was 1,100 copies of *Maggie* to the good but, of course, no newsstand would touch it, and no bookshop either, except Brentano's, which took a dozen copies and returned ten. Chambermaid Jennie Creegan at the Pendennis boardinghouse, who wore a feather that was a "quivering invitation," chewed gum "like a slim, reminiscing cow," told tales of the Bowery, and was called "Bunny" by the youths whose beds she made, is reputed to have used some copies from the pile in Crane's room to start a fire. No one ever witnessed that expensive kindling, however, and C. K. Linson contradicts Thomas Beer's legend by saying that "the books rested undisturbed except when used as a seat."[7]

So that elevated train passengers would think everyone in the metropolis was reading *Maggie,* it is said, Crane hired men to ride the trains and show off the book they were reading. But this report by Frank Noxon also seems more legend than fact since the author had not even money enough to pay his tobacco bill at Wortzmann's. For this debt of $1.30 he inscribed a copy of the 1893 *Maggie* to Wortzmann's daughter (it sold for $250 in 1922): "This story will not edify or improve you and may not even interest you."

By then Crane knew the cruel truth that his first novel was a failure, and so he gave away about a hundred copies. (By 1896 he had only one copy left.[8])

He was, as usual, destitute. One day in February he showed up at his brother's office in New York: "I'll trouble you for five cents, Ed"; he ate in a restaurant on Lexington Avenue where "the waiters wiped spoons in the leather pockets of fouled aprons," and the ancient eggs had "a snarling smell"; and one night he tramped it to Lake View because he did not have enough money for transportation. The hike however was not without its advantages. On the road he met a farmer, who joined him, shook hands when they parted, and may eventually have become the cheery man who guides the weary youth through the tangled forests in Chapter XII of *The Red Badge.*[9]

Crane was depressed as well as destitute: "I remember how I looked forward to publication and pictured the sensation I thought it would make. It fell flat. Nobody seemed to notice it or care for it," he wrote an editor of *Leslie's Weekly* in 1895. "Poor Maggie! She was one of my first loves."[10]

Nevertheless, a publication party was held at the Pendennis Club in the room Crane sometimes shared with Lawrence and Button. The stacks of unsold books lined the walls knee-deep and served as seats for the dozen young chaps intent upon the corpulent bowl of punch. Stephen thrummed a guitar while the "Indians" chanted to the rhythmic pounding of a war dance until the abused landlady protested that she rented rooms to gentlemen, not animals. "The animals apologize and will return to their cages at once," Stephen yelled down to her.

He still hoped to find a legitimate publisher for *Maggie.* Looking "like one who had been fed for months on crackers and milk," he visited publishing offices where desks were littered with sheets of copy and the floor with cigarette stubs. In one of these, a "dismal bell over an editor's desk jingled with the preemptory resonance of a call from the composing room beyond. Stephen Crane stood in the middle of that room as odd and plaintive appearing a specimen of eager humanity as had ever been there. He seemed to have withered so that all the vitality of his body was concentrated in his head. He was a slender, sad-eyed slip of a youth, looking around the room with yearning glances of his eyes as though he would like to find a place where he could deposit the manuscript."

In a voice of despair he said to a man of authority sitting behind a desk: " 'Well, I am going to chuck the whole thing,' and he pulled a listless hand out of his pocket and let it deliver an impulsive gesture, as though he was casting something away from him. 'What do you mean by that?' said the busy man. 'Oh, I have worked two years, living with tramps in the tenements on the East Side so that I could get to know those people as they are, and what is the use? In all that time I have received only $25 for my work. I can't starve even to carry on this work, and I'm going home to my brother in New Jersey and perhaps learn the boot and shoe trade.' "[11]

He left the office like a man in whose blood "there was not a particle of the vitality which comes from good beef or mutton," says E. J. Edwards. "He went out and strolled down Broadway, far more miserable than any of the sorry creatures whom he has been studying because he was conscious of his misery. He had failed in an ambition, whereas they had no ambition. A friendly hand was laid upon his shoulder and he started as though it was the clutch of a policeman. Then he saw that there was greeting in the touch and the smile. 'Crane,' said his friend, 'what do you think? William D. Howells has read your book, and he says it's great.' 'Eh?' said the youth, and it seemed to the friend as though a sort of blur came over his eyes. 'I say that Howells has read your book, and he compares you with Tolstoy, and he is going to say so in print.' It came upon that half-starved youth with such sudden force that he received it like a blow. If he had been told that Howells had condemned the book he might have heaved a sigh. He seemed dazed. He looked around like a man who did not know where he was. He gulped something down his throat, grinned like a woman in hysterics, and then went off to take up his vocation again." The friend was Curtis Brown of the New York *Press,* a colleague of E. J. Edwards, who later became a literary agent.

Crane had been depressed because he had not heard from Howells about *Maggie.* Hamlin Garland, while visiting Mr. and Mrs. Alberti, had received a copy by mail. The first paragraphs described a battle of street urchins, said Garland, "with so much insight and with such unusual and vivid use of English that I became very much excited about it. Next day I mailed the book to Mr. Howells in order that he might share the discovery with me. The author had the genius which makes an old world new. On that very afternoon Crane called upon me and confessed that he had written the book." Garland said to him: "I hardly dare tell you how good that story is. I have sent it to Mr. Howells as a 'find.' Go and see him when he has read it. I am sure he will like it." Garland and Howells had lunch together on March 22 and talked about *Maggie,* and then Howells wrote to Crane on the 29th to apologize for not yet having read the novel. At that time he invited him to dinner. Ill at ease in the borrowed best suit of John Northern Hilliard, Crane felt his situation little improved when Howells flattered him before his guests: "Mr. Crane can do things that Clemens can't." Howells read to him some verses of Emily Dickinson, unaware that his guest already fancied himself a poet. But Crane behaved well enough, and on April 8 Howells wrote him in praise of *Maggie* and mentioned also their pleasant interview at the dinner.

E. J. Edwards of the New York *Press* had read the manuscript of *Maggie* in the autumn of 1892 in his room on West 27th Street, where he had given Crane a place to sleep, and then in early March, 1893, he read the manuscript of *The Red Badge* (not yet completed) and was again impressed by the poetic force of the writing. He predicted the next year, on April 15, in the Philadelphia *Press,* that if the young author were careful of his powers and subjected them to thorough discipline he would surely make a name for himself in American literature. When *The Red Badge* began appearing in serial form in the Philadelphia *Press* in early December, 1894, Edwards, in his editorial column signed "Holland," praised Crane's power of imagination under the title "The Work of Stephen Crane," an article Crane liked well enough to make a handwritten copy. Edwards said the Civil War novel was "perhaps the most graphic and truthful in its suggestion of some of the phrases of that epoch which has ever appeared in print." However, in his notice about Crane earlier that year (April 22) he was critical of *Maggie.* "The realism of Mr. Crane as it is done in that book is certainly cold, awful, brutal realism, and it reveals a power which when the author has learned of experience and has disciplined his artistic sense may give us something that may be compared to Tolstoi with respect to art as well as realism. But it is possible to tell a story of realism quite as suggestive and not so shocking as that told in Mr. Crane's book."

That *Maggie* seemed shocking even to a journalist indicates the priggishness and hyprocrisy intrenched in that Age of Innocence. In the same issue of the New York *Press* a notice probably written by the Sunday editor, Edward Marshall, said that the author "has not failed to touch vice in his book where he has found it in real life; but he has not gilded it. He has painted it as it is; he has not made it clandestinely attractive. In this he rises far above such other Americans—Edgar Fawcett and Edgar Saltus, notably—as having endeavoured to gain recognition in somewhat similar fields." The truth in *Maggie* is unquestionable, but it is "the kind of truth that no American has ever had the courage (or is it bravado?) to put between book-covers before. It is a question if such brutalities are wholly acceptable in literature. Perhaps, as Mr. Howells says, they will be before long."

Howells' praise of *Maggie* was not surprising,[12] for here was the novel he had been asking for—the novel of social and moral intention which adjusts perspectives by portraying what Emerson had described as the familiar and the low, not "the great, the remote, the romantic." Crane insisted that he had "no other purpose in writing *Maggie* than to show people as they seemed to me. If that be evil, make the most of it." (He had, of course, another and deeper intention than that, as we shall see.) *Maggie* was Crane's Bowery version of Zola and Flaubert and, furthermore, it was his version of the American reformist writings—familiar to him since the days when his father preached and his mother took up crusading against vices.

Several of the most popular crusading books—Charles Loring Brace's *The Dangerous Classes of New York* (1872) and the Reverend Thomas de Witt Talmage's *Night Side of City Life* and "The Gates of Hell"—might very well have belonged to the Reverend Jonathan Townley Crane, who himself published moralistic tracts. Talmage's portrait of a girl of the streets—embodied in a familiar drawing of the time of a woman about to plunge into the East River in Brace's *Dangerous Classes*—deals with the wages of sin which is death. "What way out has one of these fallen souls but the sewing girl's garret, dingy, cold, hunger-blasted. But you say, 'Is there no other way for her to escape?' Oh, yes. Another way is the street that leads to East River, at midnight, the end of the city dock, the moon shining down on the water making it look so smooth she wonders if it is deep enough. It is. No boatman near enough to hear the plunge." And in *The Abominations of Modern Society* (1872) he sermonized: "And so the woman stands on the abutment of the bridge, on the moonlit night, wondering if, down under the water, there is not some quiet place for a broken heart. She takes one wild leap—and all is over." In "The Gates of Hell," the prostitute, who is also named Maggie, repents; she leaves the wicked city and returns to the country. She is greeted by her forgiving mother with the cry " 'Oh, Maggie!' The child threw her arms around her mother's neck, and said, 'Oh mother!' and while they were embraced a rugged form towered over them. It was the father. The severity all gone out of his face, he stooped and took her up tenderly and carried her to her mother's room, and laid her down on her mother's bed, for she was dying. Then the lost one, looking up into her mother's face, said, '*Wounded for our transgressions and bruised for our iniquities!* Mother, do you think that means me?' . . . . So the Lord took back one whom the world rejected." "Pink valentines"—that was Crane's damning slogan for the novels of his contemporaries, and the sentimental pap of the pulpit. *Maggie* is no pink valentine.

Crane may have taken his theme from moral tracts, but he got his story and tone from the French realists Flaubert and Zola. Perhaps that is what Gilder of the *Century* meant when he condemned *Maggie* as a novel of "no visible sentiment." Crane had read Flaubert and Zola in translation. Two translations of Zola's *L'Assommier* appeared shortly after its original French edition, and in an undated letter Crane discussed *Nana:* "This girl in Zola is a real streetwalker. I mean she does not fool around making excuses for her career. You must pardon me if I cannot agree that every painted woman on the streets of New York was brought there by some evil man. Nana, in the story, is honest. . . . Zola is a sincere writer but—is he much good? He hangs one thing to another and his story goes along but I find him pretty tiresome."

The Crane and Zola novels bear kinship in their philosophical outlook that we are all the victims of our environments. Trapped by the mud puddle of the Bowery in which she "blossomed," innocent Maggie "did not feel like a bad woman. To her knowledge she had never seen any better." She is permitted to see nothing better than the factory, the cheap sentiment-ridden theatres and bars, the tenement rooms of her drunken mother with their smashed furniture, and finally the street which ends where the East River begins. Limited to this closed world, she is as irrevocably destined by the Bowery as Eustacia Vye by Egdon Heath. The only non-Bowery segment of the world Maggie is permitted to know is the island with its ominous gray building where "a worm of yellow convicts" crawls along the river's bank; the prison is without as well as within.

The true villain is the environment that shapes the lives of the characters. Maggie is victimized not only by the collar-and-cuff factory where she works, but also by the saloon and theatre sanctuaries and by the Bowery missionary houses of soup and sentiment. "I have no opinion of missions," Crane told Catherine Harris in 1896. "That—to you—may not be a valid answer since perhaps you have been informed that I am not very friendly to Christianity as seen around town." A minister of the church bypasses Maggie on the street: he is "a stout gentleman in a silk hat and a chaste black coat, whose decorous row of buttons reached from his chin to his knees. The girl had heard of the grace of God and she decided to approach this man. His beaming, chubby face was a picture of benevolence and kind-heartedness. His eyes shone with good will. But as the girl timidly accosted him he made a convulsive movement and saved his respectability by a vigorous side-step. He did not risk it to save a soul. For how was he to know that there was a soul before him that needed saving?" His indifference to her plight prepares for her downfall. We next see Maggie several months later as a streetwalker, "a girl of the painted cohorts of the city," and one of the men she encounters mistakes young Maggie for her mother, a well-known prostitute. "Hi, there, Mary. I beg your pardon! Brace up old girl."

Pete, the destroyer of Maggie's virtue, swaggers with an air of "respecta-bility," and his eyes well with tears at the thought of the purity of his motives. Rejected by Pete, she is rejected also by her brother; Bowery pimp Jimmie Johnson regards himself as a virtuous fellow, although he has despoiled the women of his acquaintance even as Pete has despoiled Maggie. They view reality through "a mist of muddled sentiment." Maggie's down-fall, assured from the start, is mocked by the grim countenances of buildings along the final block to the East River and by the sound of streetcar bells jingling "with a sound of merriment. . . .The varied sounds of life, made joyous by distance and seeming unapproachableness, came faintly and died away to a silence." Joy at a distance becomes a recurrent theme in Crane.

One is reminded of the street girl's end depicted in Talmage's moralizing tracts when reading Crane's concluding scene in *Maggie*. It parodies pious sentiment as blatantly as any Bowery mission house. Maggie's mother weeping over the corpse of her nonrepentant daughter, whom she has brutalized and driven from home, wails in an orgy of self-pitying sentiment: "Oh, yes, I'll forgive her! I'll forgive her!" The grotesque buffoonery of this mock lamentation is comic enough, but underlying it is the tragic theme that all is false, even between mother and daughter. The voice of one of the mourners, who is Mary Johnson's friend, sounds like "a dirge on some forlorn pipe." She speaks for the whole Bowery world, and "her vocabulary was derived from mission churches." Crane thus ridicules both the cowardice of the Bowery people and the hypocrisy of the church.

By paired and contrasted images he reinforces his theme, and he quickens his characters into life by metaphor. His plot is a sentimental melodrama (like Frank Norris' *McTeague*), but in style Crane's *Maggie* is not sentimentalized. The irony by which he designs his forthright moral and social intent makes the crucial difference, and it is this difference that saves *Maggie* from the dustbin of outdated sociological novels.

"Sentiment is the devil," said Crane, echoing Flaubert. The confused Maggie, like the morally confused Emma Bovary, confounds dream and reality. Maggie's brother Jimmie, a bartender, fights with "the face of a sacrificial priest." Maggie's lover, Pete, his countenance shining with the true spirit of benevolence while drunk at the saloon, "was in the proper mood of missionaries." In a spasm of drunken adoration the swaggering Pete draws some dollar bills from his pocket in the barroom sanctuary where Jimmie officiates, and "with the trembling fingers of an offering priest," lays "them on the table before the woman." As a truck driver, Jimmie imagines himself a sun-charioteer and—seated on his throne—challenges the "god-driver" obstructing his path, who is no other than Pete, whom Maggie compares with "a golden sun." Jimmie disdains the stars, but at the same time is intimidated by a fire engine whose leaping horses strike sparks from the cobbles in their forward lunge and are "creatures to be ineffably admired." So at the mission house his mind confuses the "speaker with Christ." The Johnson tenement house is a perverse monastery presided over by a woman who "sat at a table eating like a fat monk in a picture." It is another church mission house of maudlin sentiment, and another theatre into which children venture and line up "as if they formed the front row" to ogle the main attraction: debased Maggie.[13] In naming Maggie's mother Mary, was Crane subconsciously thinking of his own mother, Mary Peck, and thus accusing her of abandoning her unwanted fourteenth child for mission house charity work and Methodist revivalist meetings? He was to recast her as George's mother in his Bowery novel of that title (1896).

The moral confusion of Maggie is reflected in the novel's action. Every scene is one of disorder and chaos. The book opens with a fight: Jimmie's defending the "honor" of Rum Alley against the gutter urchins of Devil's Row, his delusions of grandeur suffering degradation when his drunken father drags him home; and his deed of valor ends in confused reports, another "distorted version." Maggie's mother scraps with street urchins and defies "the universe to appear and do battle." She smashes all the furniture, as she and her son wrestle "like gladiators," while formidable tenement women "with uncombed hair and disordered dress" scream in frantic quarrels. These Bowery characters, disdaining the reality of their environment under the delusion that they are superior to it, contend not against it but against themselves. They seek release from their destiny in violence or, on the other hand, in illusions of happiness and grandeur derived from the theatre, the saloon (hilarious halls of "irregular shape," where Pete dispenses drunkenly his wealth from an "irregularly shaped pocket") and the mission house, where the preacher exhorts these sinners by sermons composed of "you's"—"You are damned," to which the starved sinners reply: "Where's our soup?" Their environment, the source of their mental and moral imprisonment, they ignore; their quarrel is with themselves.

The plot of *Maggie* is less impressive than its theme, and the theme is less impressive today than the metaphoric style. Appearing six years before Frank Norris' *McTeague,* Crane's was the first American novel to render urban slum life artistically. Even though the Denver *Republican* was convinced of Crane's "vivid realism"; the *Critic,* of his ability "to reproduce" Bowery life "with fidelity"; the New York *Advertiser,* of his success in drawing characters who, although they are "enough to give one the 'creeps,' . . . are absolutely true to life," no one seemed to see *Maggie* for what it was.

Athough Hamlin Garland had called it the "voice of the slums," it was not—and by his own definition. In *Crumbling Idols* Garland declared that the novel of the slums "must be written by one who has played there as a child and taken part in all its amusements; not out of curiosity but out of pleasure seeking. It cannot be done from above nor from the outside. It must be done out of a full heart and without seeking for effect."

If Crane had but one intention, it was the display of his effects. More than the story of a well-meaning Bowery girl doomed by an environment of drunkenness and grime, *Maggie* is a tone painting; it is the painter's novel, the poet's novel: the art novel. The characters are less individuals than types; they reflect the author's bent for aesthetic anonymity rather than sociological immediacy. Maggie is the "good prostitute," Maggie's mother the typical slum mother, albeit the worst of her kind, and Jimmie is the epitome of all truck drivers on the Bowery. But critics mistake if they suppose that generalized figures are less important and less difficult to create than individualized characters that may have no significance beyond themselves.

The artistic source of *Maggie* would seem not to be Zola—although the thematic resemblances are strikingly close—but Flaubert's *Madame Bovary*. The two novels are alike in the way their respective romantic escapes from reality are rendered. Maggie's dim thoughts were often searching for faraway lands where the little hills sing together in the morning. Under the trees of her dream gardens there always walked a lover. So, too, the personified landscape sings in accompaniment to Emma Bovary's dream of happiness: "the song of the postilion re-echoed by the mountains, along with the bells of goats and the muffled sound of a waterfall." Maggie's reverie of Pete as her ideal man collapses in the bathos of Pete's saying: "Say, Mag, I'm stuck on yer shape. It's outa sight," and Emma's imaginary voyage to distant lands is canceled out by the image of her dull husband: "But as the intimacy of their life became deeper, the greater became the gulf that separated her from him."

Maggie is like Emma Bovary, for whom "disappointment quickly gave way to a new hope." On returning to her sordid household from a meeting with Pete, she encounters grim reality in a clock in a splintered and battered box, an abomination because it suggests the real thing, time in its sordid frame: "She noted that it ticked raspingly. The almost vanished flowers in the carpet pattern, she conceived to be newly hideous. Some faint attempts which she had made with blue ribbons to freshen the appearance of a dingy curtain, she now saw to be piteous. She wondered what Pete dined on." She herself eventually becomes a faded flower, and her plight is suggested in the blue ribbons appearing on the dingy curtain as "violated flowers" and in the "almost vanished flowers in the carpet pattern."

In their despair, Emma and Maggie live out lives of succession rather than sequence. Crane once defined a novel as "a succession of sharply outlined pictures, which pass before the reader like a panorama, leaving each its definite impression." *Maggie* is divided into nineteen episodes that make up a panorama of impressionistic vignettes, disconnected scenes that reel off episode to episode with the same jerky, nervous effect that early motion pictures convey. Not logic, but mood, defines the relationship of image to image. Moods and romantic sentiment, illusion and hope, collapse in face of the contradictory moods of futility, disillusionment or despair: "She envied elegance and soft palms. She craved those adornments of person which she saw every day on the street, conceiving them to be allies of vast importance to women. Studying faces, she thought many of the women and girls she chanced to meet smiled with serenity as though for ever cherished and watched over by those they loved." Harsh reality immediately follows, however, and undercuts this mood of romantic sentiment: "The air in the collar-and-cuff establishment strangled her. She knew she was gradually and surely shrivelling in the hot, stuffy room." Crane never acknowledged his debt to Flaubert, although it seems obvious.

The lack of preaching in *Maggie* undoubtedly accounts for its neglect. Although it preceded Edward Waterman Townsend's *Chimmie Fadden* (1895) by two years, it was the latter, a sketched romance of the slums, and also Townsend's *A Daughter of the Tenements,* which became household familiars whose vivid language infected the nation.

"My good friend Edward Townsend—have you read his 'Daughter of the Tenements'?—has another opinion of the Bowery and it is certain to be better than mine," Crane generously remarked in writing to Catherine Harris in 1896. Both Crane and Townsend were driven as journalists to research the terrible problems of the city's slums, but Townsend, by regarding them "with alleviating humour," parted widely from Crane's grim irony. The *Bookman* for November, 1895, compared Crane and Townsend and concluded that *Maggie* is "among the saddest books in our language," failing to see that its grotesque irony makes it also deadly comic.

Rupert Hughes as "Chelifer" in *Godey's Magazine* called *Maggie* "probably the strongest piece of slum writing we have."[14] However, what keeps *Maggie* alive with such savage force today is the art by which it is constructed. Crane puts language to poetic uses, which is to use language reflexively (all things in an interrelationship) and symbolically.

On the copy of *Maggie* that Crane sent to Garland, he wrote across the paperback cover: "It is inevitable that you will be greatly shocked by this book, but continue please with all possible courage to the end. For it tries to show that environment is a tremendous thing in the world and frequently shapes lives regardless. If one proves that theory one makes room in Heaven for all sorts of souls (notably an occasional street girl) who are not confidently expected to be there by many excellent people. It is probable that the reader of this small thing may consider the author to be a bad man; but obviously that is a matter of small consequence."

Crane wrote the same legend on a batch of copies and sent them to a number of preachers who were fanatics for reform,[15] with perhaps the hope of finding a social market for his book. He still had such an inscribed copy with him in 1895 and sent it early that year to the Reverend Thomas Dixon, but the preachers all ignored his novel with its implied plea for reforming the Bowery in the inscription. "I knew they'd jump at first, but I hoped they were intelligent. You'd think the book came straight from hell and they smelled the smoke. Not one of them gave me a word!" These preachers were "icebergs," he told C. K. Linson.

William Dean Howells later sent a copy to the Reverend Dr. Charles Henry Parkhurst, who had led a spectacular crusade against vice in the city in 1892. Parkhurst was no psalm-singing, self-righteous reformist. From the pulpit of the Old Madison Square Presbyterian Church, and in the press as well, he had exposed the sanction that the police, Mayor Grant, and District Attorney Nicoll gave the vice that flourished in the Bowery. They were all linked, he preached, in an "administrative criminality that is filthifying our entire municipal life, making New York a very hotbed of knavery, debauchery and bestiality." When the matter was tried, the Grand Jury exonerated the city administration and discredited Dr. Parkhurst. His belligerence aroused, he disguised himself as a Bowery bum, and with a hired detective to serve him as guide began nocturnal guided tours of the city's dens of vice: Chinese opium dens; a Park Row five-cent lodging house with cots of naked men who became Tammany voters on election day; "tight houses" of prostitution, where all the girls wore tights; homosexual brothels, where all the painted men called each other by women's names and talked in high falsetto voices; and saloons that sold pint bottles of whiskey for ten cents to children ten years old. Thus collecting evidence through personal experience. Parkhurst told his Presbyterian congregation that the life of the church had lost touch with the life of things as they were, yet he refused to acknowledge Crane's book, which implied the same.

The seeming hypocrisy of reform preachers like Dixon and Parkhurst intensified Crane's rebellion against the traditions on which he had been reared: traditions that included the "vacuous, futile, psalm-singing that passed for worship" (to quote Wilbur's daughter Helen). And so in *Maggie* the mission house serves larger portions of maudlin sentiment than soup to Bowery bums. Crane detested pious sermons. "An artist has no business to preach." He told Linson: "You can't find any preaching in *Maggie*." Howells in "An Appreciation," which prefaced the 1896 edition of *Maggie,* compared it with a Greek tragedy.

The months that followed *Maggie*'s publication may have been lean, but they seem to have been relatively happy months as well. Answering an ad in the *Herald* just after losing his job there, Stephen became a clerk in a gentleman's furnishing shop on Bleecker Street. He recreated that experience in "Why Did the Young Clerk Swear?," one of the three sketches that appeared with his signature in 1893 in James L. Ford's humor magazine *Truth*. In this sketch the clerk with a "blond moustache" and "a dangling look" divides his time between observing pedestrians struggling along in the mud "with excited umbrellas," as he gazes gloomily through "the blurred panes of the windows," and secretly indulging himself in a French novel in between intrusions of customers. " 'Eloise!' Silvere was murmuring, hoarsely. He leaned toward her until his warm breath moved the curls on her neck." " 'Have you any nightshirts open front and back?' " " 'Say, young feller,' said a youth with a tilted cigar to the clerk with a blond mustache, 'where the 'ell is Billie Carcart's joint round here? Know?' 'Next corner,' said the clerk, fiercely." The heroine of the French romance at this moment screamed, wrenched herself from the young man's arms, locked the door of her room, and burst into tears as she flung herself on the bed. "She looked fresh, fair, innocent." The young clerk in disappointment hurled the novel to the floor, and standing up from his high stool, said "Damn!"

At night Crane returned to the old Needham building, which still housed a few artists after the Art Students' League moved out in October, 1892, to new quarters on 57th Street.[16] He was sharing its largest studio with Frederic Gordon, David Ericson and R. G. Vosburgh,[17] and although he could contribute nothing to its maintenance he added very little to its expenses. Crane and two others slept in a large old-fashioned double-bed, taking turns at sleeping in the middle; the fourth man occupied a cot. "For men struggling as they were against poverty and privation to force themselves into recognition, there was little incentive to go out except in search for work." On such occasions three colleagues contributed their clothing to the fourth man, and in that borrowed guise he went out in search of work on a stomach that had missed more than one meal, or was suffering from the ones it had consumed. The artists fed at the cheapest restaurants they could find, and Stephen obviously fed himself almost not at all. On rare occasions he and Gordon "would blow ourselves to a real 50 center, *with wine!* They could be had then. A favorite place for that was the Hotel Griffon on West 9th Street, the original of the Casa Napoleon of Thomas Janvier's stories [*At the Casa Napoleon, 1914*]. But we were not often enough at any of those 'expensive' places to be known there." One of the scandalously cheap eating places was an unsavory resort on Sixth Avenue, where on Saturday nights Crane, Linson and the Needham "Indians" gathered. At the Boeuf-a-la-Mode, the delicatessen very shortly nicknamed "The Buffalo-Mud," Crane could fill up on potato salad for breakfast; the guests, as he describes them in *The Third Violet*, "dined noisily and with great fire, discussing momentous problems furiously, making wide maniacal gestures through the cigarette smoke. . . . The little handful of waiters ran to and fro wildly."

Linson, who was an art student at the National Academy of Design and earned his way by doing illustrations for magazines, usually had a bit of cash in his pocket. " 'Hey! Steve!' " he said one day, " 'If you have fifty cents we'll eat together.' Steve halted, then in an apologetic voice said, 'Not a red, CK.' "

Linson preserved a yellow page dating from the Pendennis pow-wow to celebrate *Maggie*'s birth on which Stephen had written in his worst verse: "Ah, haggard purse, why ope thy mouth / Like a greedy urchin? / I have nought wherewith to feed thee. / Thy wan cheeks have ne'er been puffed, / Thou knowest not the fill of pride. / Why then gape at me / In fashion of a wronged one? / Thou smilest wanly / And reproachest me with thine empty stomach. / Thou knowest I'd sell my steps to the grave / If 'twere but honestie." In *The Third Violet* Crane wrote: "Poverty is everything to be ashamed of. A fellow isn't even a man and doesn't stand up straight unless he has some money." He was no doubt ashamed when occasional quarters and half-dollars passed from Linson's pocket into his.

"Congratulate yourselves if you have done something strange and extravagant and broken the monotony of a decorous age." That was a quotation from Emerson chalked in the topmost and remotest studio in the old Needham building on East 23rd, where Crane bummed his bed, and the quotation fit the building, its original architect, and its hundred subsequent remodelers as well as it fit the inhabitants. It had been remodeled and twisted about so much at various times, says Frederic Gordon, that it took an expert pilot to guide any stranger through its mysteries. There were three street entrances. "The upper floors were filled with artists, musicians and writers, young men and women, decent people all, who were glad of the low rents and really congenial atmosphere. The landlord was an artist and as considerate of our financial difficulties as he could be in reason. Our life there was free, gay, hard-working—and decent," wrote Crane. Gordon had one of the biggest studios, and "naturally people gathered there a good deal. Smoking, talking, and sometimes a little cards. There was no money going—no one had any—but I remember some game that required the loser to go out and fetch a can of beer. Once he failed to come back, and a search party with lamps (the hall-lights went out at 11) found him comfortable on a remote stairway, but the can was empty! He explained that he had lost himself in the labyrinth but was not worrying so long as the beer lasted. And there you see the sum of Crane's sins while he was with me—so far as I know."

Crane copied the Emerson motto in his pocket notebook fully aware of its implications, for he was writing at the time his first draft of "The Art Students' League Building."[18] He saw it through eyes different from those of Linson, Gordon or Vosburgh. To him it was a symbol of social change: formerly ringing "with the voices of a crowd of art students who in those days past built their ideals of art-schools upon the most approved Parisian models; it is a fact generally unknown to the public that this staid puritanical old building once contained about all that was real in the Bohemian quality of New York. The exterior belies the interior. . . . It is plastered with signs, and wears sedately the air of being what it is not." The interior, a place of slumberous corridors, rambled in puzzling turns and curves. "The large studios rear their brown rafters over scenes of lonely quiet. Gradually the tinkers, the tailors, and the plumbers who have captured the ground floor are creeping toward those dim ateliers above them. One by one the besieged artists give up the struggle and the time is not far distant when the conquest of the tinkers, the tailors and the plumbers will be complete." The symbolic idea of the essay which represents the encroachment of commercial forces upon the artist is almost too obvious a sequel to Crane's tour of duty as a haberdasher and his current economic plight.

In the less personal "A Mournful Old Building," Crane suggests through metaphor that the encroachment by new buildings upon the old one is that of youth upon old age. The mournful old building was "a sad thing; symbolizing a decrepit old man whose lean shoulders are jostled by sturdy youth."

He left the "antique rookery" of the Needham building in May, 1893, to move into a boardinghouse at 136 West 15th Street, run by the landlady of his former Avenue A Pendennis Club. Perhaps she invited him to accompany her, although their relationship at Avenue A had been less than cordial. As a matter of fact, he had written Lucius Button in 1892 from Lake View that he was glad to escape for a while their landlady, that "dragon." "But if she be vindictive, I will have my revenge." The revenge he proposed to inflict upon her was the little fox terrier someone had given him for Christmas—a dog with a pedigree "as long as your arm. It has a nose like a black head. It raises the devil on all occasions, mostly by tearing up gloves, and wading around in any butter plate, mince-pie, or cake which it may perceive at large. It also has a violent antipathy to larger dogs, cats, and all fowls of the air. Withal, it is a meek little thing when in human presence and keeps its black, white and tan coat spotlessly clean. If I can prevail upon our dear, domestic tyrant to let me pay its board, I shall certainly bring it down after Christmas. I adore dogs."[19]

One wonders why Crane rejoined his former Avenue A landlady at her new boardinghouse, but she is undoubtedly the landlady who had the beautiful daughter described in a splendid sketch which he never completed.[20] In "The Landlady's Daughter," a wolf in lamb's wool is looking for a room. Some boarders sitting on the steps measure him "from his umbrella to his necktie with all the curiosity and suspicion of New Yorkers who know no shame in these matters." In front of the other houses after-dinner groups were gathered; at the foot of the street was the river where "the tiny riggings of ships grew like grass." At one corner of the block streetcars moved past like links of a chain, and at the other corner a hand-organ man ground out melodies which were interrupted by the roar of an elevated train. The landlady's daughter escorts the newcomer into the house, and he dwells upon her graceful pose as she lights the gas. "It is a legend that at one time the mistresses of boarding houses welcomed their arriving prey with cordial words and smiles. It is not known that a prey of this period need expect cordial words and smiles. On the contrary, he might expect to go before a bar of judgment where he is scanned for his resemblance to men whose perfidy is engraven on the mind of the boarding house mistress, men who lied with skill and went away leaving an empty trunk in the house and a stone heart in the breast of the landlady. These men of sin leave thorns in the path of the virtue that comes afterward. 'In God we trust' is a motto often hung on boarding house walls. Here it expresses more than usual. It expresses a limit."

The newcomer rents a room for six dollars. It is on the third floor, "grim and grey like a cell." Alone there and saddened by his new environment he broods on the landlady's daughter, and the next morning awakens early to the thunder of the city's life. The wheels of the wagons rattle over the cobbles "with a noise like innumerable musketry volleys. Then at last a bell was rung and the tomb-like silence of the house itself was broken. Doors slammed." He covertly watches the landlady's daughter as she serves him breakfast in the basement floor of the house, while five young men and two old women consume their breakfasts, their faces fixed upon their plates. They are clerks: one of them a clerk in a Broadway flower shop, another in a famous shoe store. The boarder feels their aversion to him, and he is glad when one of them quits the breakfast room. His rival has "ogled the girl as she passed to and fro in a way that the new boarder considered exasperatingly confident." He is a trickster. But so is the new boarder. "He dallied with a second cup of coffee until nearly all the boarders had vanished from the table. He tried to note each move of the young girl. Still, he thought he contrived to do this without the young girl being aware. His instinct taught him that her too sudden knowledge of his interest would somehow shame him, for she certainly did not seem to recognize his existence in any way save as a boarder."

Leaving over three hundred copies of *Maggie* with Mrs. Armstrong for safekeeping, Crane in June joined Edmund and his family at Hartwood, where they had permanently moved in the spring. During the summer he worked on his war novel and although he read aloud portions of *The Red Badge* to his brother, he generally kept silent about his hard times in the city because he knew well that his brother had his own financial problems: the panic of 1893 had left most small businessmen destitute. In his pocket notebook Crane kept an account of the day's expenses: 25 cents, Breakfast, 5 shine, 10 cigarettes & tobacco, 5 elevated, 8 tin of pipe tobacco, 25 pillow case, 10 coffee cake / 88 cents, to which he added 12 for some unidentified item, probably beer and food. The summer was a quiet one and *The Red Badge* was nearing completion.

On returning to the city in October he took a little room near Frederic Gordon's studio in the Needham building. He had camped for three weeks in Sullivan County with some "bobcats" and felt rather "bully," but on arriving in the city he had a cold. He had written a large part of *The Red Badge* in the wilds of Sullivan County (as Gordon recalls in an unpublished letter) and he finished it in Gordon's studio this winter of 1893–94. He called on Edward Marshall, then Sunday editor of the New York *Press,* and later with Joseph Pulitzer's *World,* and showed him the manuscript of *The Red Badge* when it was about two-thirds done. Marshall, not much older than the author of *Maggie,* was much impressed by Crane's gift for vivid and colorful phrasing and had tried to persuade the *Press* to run the Bowery novel in serial. (In early 1894 Crane approached Marshall with his poems, but again with no luck.) Marshall sat on the corner of his desk and, swinging his watch chain, said: "No. I'll take all the special articles you can do, Steve, but you are made for better things. Don't waste your time."

Although that promise was no immediate consolation, Crane began writing in February his series of New York City sketches for the *Press* at five dollars per column; some also appeared in *Truth* and the *Arena.* He took heed of Marshall's criticisms of wrenched adjectives and coined adverbs: "The Reluctant Voyagers," which he wrote in Linson's studio in the spring or summer of 1893, and also *George's Mother,* as well as many of his New York City sketches, showed fewer epithets.

He had been wearing rubber boots without shoes, but to make his appearance before Marshall he bought a pair of shoes and tramped to the interview without the boots in a rainstorm, and afterward walked from the *Press* building in a cold downpour to Gordon's East 23rd Street studio, too proud to tell Marshall that he hadn't a nickel for carfare. Shaking and shivering, he appeared at Gordon's studio with no overcoat and he seemed ripe for pneumonia. "I got him into an extra bed I had, and in a week he was up, nearly as good as new. My shop was so big that he might just as well stay, and so he finished the *Red Badge* there and wrote a lot of other things" (namely, some of his "Midnight Sketches," which he rightly considered among his very best things). "The memory of that time is really precious to me," said Gordon in later years. "Crane was a delightful and stimulating companion."

Sometime early that year (1894) he met journalist John Northern Hilliard (later of the Rochester *Union and Advertiser*) from whom he borrowed the suit he wore to dinner at Howells' house in early April. Hilliard, telling stories of the West, would sit on a bench in Union Square with plump Acton Davies, drama critic of the New York *Sun.* Or Crane and Davies would walk there with Elbert Hubbard, who was visiting the city to take notes for his *Arena* article "The Rights of Tramps" (April, 1894). Crane recognized Hubbard as a professional 1890's bohemian of typical affectation, complete with flowing tie and long cloak, "a clever-looking duck"; and Hubbard recognized Crane as a genius. A former soap salesman of considerable success, Hubbard later published Crane's writings in his little magazine, *The Philistine,* which appealed to the very philistines it aimed to scandalize. When they first met, probably through B. O. Flower of the *Arena,* Hubbard thought Crane had "no sense of propriety" because he would often dash off, while they paraded through the Bowery, to talk with some stranger, tramp or whore. As Frank Noxon of the Boston *Herald* remarked, "Not even Crane, love him as most men did, was able to command from others that tolerance which he diffused so infinitely." He was tolerant of Hubbard, although he detested literary charlatans. "Fra Albertus," as Hubbard dubbed himself, persuaded Crane to read Twain's *Huckleberry Finn.* Crane subsequently dismissed it as a failure in formal composition simply by grunting his disgust over its absurd conclusion.

Before his artist friends in the Needham rookery, he pronounced Twain's *A Connecticut Yankee in King Arthur's Court* as "inappropriate as a drunken bride." For him Mark Twain was not even a writer, much less an artist—the artist-clown, not the artist-writer. Crane sensed the discrepancy between the "divine amateur" and Twain's flamboyant personality and reputation; "I only like one of his books," he said. It was *Life on the Mississippi.* Crane was with Holmes Bassett, an Englishman whom he had met by chance at Gordon's studio,[21] when he first saw Twain. Bassett had taken him to dinner at the Holland House and then to Madison Square Garden to watch the fights and an exhibition by Corbett. Samuel Clemens was in a box with Robert Reid and architect Stanford White, and there was some whistling and jeering in the crowd when they caught sight of Twain. He had gone bankrupt from his investment in a new-fangled printing press and the papers had just reported his plight.

Bassett was in his way, too, a "clever-looking duck." Wearing his monocle, he chanced into Gordon's studio, and was shocked at meeting Crane in an undershirt and hearing him call Mrs. Humphrey Ward, whom Bassett had met in London,[22] an idiot and her celebrated novel, *Robert Elsmere,* a lot of higgling rubbish.

Crane showed the Bowery to Bassett. One can imagine what a spectacle the Englishman must have been to the tramps, drunks and prostitutes as he paraded with his monocle and well-cut suit beside a man who could easily have been taken for a tramp himself.

Bassett often took Crane to dinner, where he drank white German wine because champagne made him dizzy; Crane reciprocated by telling his host all about horses, dogs, bears, sailing boats and marriage. "Marriage," Beer reports Crane to have told Bassett, "was a base trick on women, who were hunted animals anyhow. A wedding is a legal ceremony, if ceremony there must be." When Bassett left New York Crane's inscribed copy of *Maggie* reached him in Ottawa: "This work is a mud-puddle, I am told on the best authority. Wade in and have a swim." It was only then Bassett learned that his iconoclastic young New York companion was the author of a novel about the Bowery. What he could not have realized was that in this "mud-puddle" modern American fiction was born.

# VI

# ⏏ *Hamlin Garland*
# *—Crane's New York*

In December, 1893, Hamlin Garland took an apartment at 107
105th Street in Harlem with his brother Franklin, then an actor in Herne's
*Shore Acres* Company at Daly's Theatre near 29th Street, and Stephen
several times visited them there. On January 2, Garland sent him to S. S.
McClure with a personal note: "If you have any work for Mr. Crane, talk
things over with him and for mercy's sake! don't keep him *standing* for an
hour as he did before out in your pen for culprits."

By March, Crane was writing to Mrs. Munroe that he and Garland had
proved themselves too formidable for editors like McClure to mistreat them.
"They used to call me 'that terrible, young rascal,' but now they are beginning to hem and haw and smile—those very old coots who used to
adopt a condescending air toward me. There is an irony in the present situation that I enjoy, devil take them for a parcel of old, cringing, conven-
tionalized hens. In one magazine office once, the editor kept me waiting
for a good long hour and then made a cool apology in a careless manner
that I wouldn't have used upon a dog. I stopped in that office the other
day to see the manager and the editor caught sight of me through the
door of his office. 'Ah, Crane, my dear boy,' he said, 'come in and have
a cigar and a chat. I'm always glad to see you.' And he made haste to be
rid of an authoress of some kind who was haggling with him about a story.
The bare-faced old grey-headed diplomatist, I wondered if he considered
that I had lost my memory. 'No—thanks—I'm in a hurry.' He seemed
really grieved."

McClure finally recognized that he had a genuis on his hands and proposed to send him on various missions. Crane wrote Lily in Washington
that he was going to Europe in about two weeks and that if she would
write him he could then "take the memory of it with me. . . . Do this for
me, I can hardly go without it. Even though you can only consistently be
cold, do me this grace." He might leave for Europe sooner than expected,
"and in my infinitely lonely life it is better that I should have all the benefits you can say to me. Ever yours, S. C." In his next letter he recommends
that she go to the theatre if *Shore Acres* comes to Washington. "Young

Franklin Garland in the cast is a great friend and Herne himself is a great admirer of my work, they say; so really he must be a man of the most admirable perceptions, you know. I have accepted his invitation to see the play next Monday night. Those critics whose opinions are valuable say that Herne is the hope of the American stage; so study him."

Since Crane's literary godfathers, Howells and Garland, objected to the European trip and since Lily had not answered his two letters, Crane decided not to leave New York City until he had at least seen one more book into print. "I did not intend starting for Europe or anywhere else until I had given you sufficient opportunity to reply. It would have been a lonely business—to go so far without a word from you," he wrote Lily. However, Crane never went to Europe for McClure.

He had been writing five or six poems daily in January and February; one day he wrote nine and would have written more the next night, but the "Indians" in the Needham building blocked him by howling at his verses, while he took refuge on a divan which was secretly a coal box of fuel for the "fierce little stove" whose long pipe "wandered off in the wrong direction and then turned impulsively toward a hole in the wall." Amidst tumbled cots, crippled chairs, and tables supporting cartoons and drawings, ink bottles and unwashed cups, towels and various garments, he tried to write, but the "Indians" yowled like bobcats.

Late in January he attended a performance at Daly's Theatre of *Hannele,* in which Franklin Garland acted. After the performance he read Hamlin Garland one of his new poems, "The Reformer," which Garland liked well enough to try to get it published in Flower's *Arena.* In the meanwhile, however, Crane lost the poem and had to confess to Garland that he could not remember a word of it. He called on Edward Marshall of the New York *Press,* and handing him a package of poetry manuscript, said modestly: "I have written some verse." Marshall the next day left the package on an elevated train, but he recovered the manuscript (*The Black Riders,* then unnamed) twenty-four hours later from the Lost Property office of the Manhattan El. The *Press* did not publish the poems, however.

One February evening Crane rapped on the door of Linson's studio, shook off the snow from his derby and his tightly buttoned ulster, and hovered in the doorway with a sphinxlike smile as he drew from his coat some sheets of foolscap. Linson, in the flaring gaslight, was working at a drawing, and Crane covered it with the manuscript sheets of his poems.[1] "What do you think I have been doing, C. K.?" Linson had not known that he was also a poet, and he was not only surprised but profoundly moved by these short poems. "How did you think of them?" he asked, and Stephen put his finger to his forehead and said: "They came, and I wrote them, that's all." Linson marveled at his spontaneity much as did Garland and years later Joseph Conrad, when he watched Crane write prose effortlessly and without corrections at his desk in Villa Ravensbrook in England.

To Linson, the artist, the poems seemed done with a paintbrush: "There was a crimson clash of war. / Lands turned black and bare." Another poem was about a man who lived a life of fire: "This life glowed / A dire red stain, indelible; / Yet, when he was dead / He saw that he had not lived!" Crane's lines had neither rhyme nor the rhythm of blank verse, but they had a pungency and a "pastel of feeling that revealed a new and sometimes startling angle of vision that awakened some subconscious thought of my own," said Linson's friend Emile Stangé. Although painter Stangé was puzzled by their content and asked Crane what they meant, he too was struck by the use of color and texture, and—like Linson—was puzzled by their unconventional form.

If their form startled Linson, it did not annoy him. That was their value, he said. "I'm glad they're not Whitman. I thought at first they might be." Crane laughed and broke into a chant, a lilting chant that bespoke his joy.

But another man in the studio handed back the poems and dryly remarked: "I don't know much about poetry." Stephen then broke into another chant: "It takes nine tailors to make one man, / And a ninth of a man is he." Then he fled the studio in chagrin, and Linson caught him downstairs as he burst out: "I know everyone can't like them, but I hate to give a man a chance to hit me in the back of the neck with an axe!" Other times Crane was less resentful of the unappreciative "Indians" who made fun of his poems and pinned to the studio wall a squib with a graphic profile of the poet. " 'See what they do to me,' he said with a grin. 'They think I'm a joke, the Indians! They pin up these slams when I'm out. They make me ill.' "[2]

Crane reported his plight to Howells: "You see, we all live in a box together, and I've no place to write, except in the general squabble. They think my lines are funny. They make a circus of me." But he invited such treatment by reciting his verses as soon as he wrote them and taunting the struggling artists with his successes and perhaps their failures. Linson both confirms and denies that there was any conceit in Crane's attitude,[3] but as Beer put it, the always vacillating Crane was conceited by streaks. He declared that he would get his revenge on these studio artists who jeered at his verses by putting them into a novel, which he did later in *The Third Violet*. "The mutts yowl like bobcats when I try to write, but I'll get my innings. I'll put 'em in a book, the lobsters. They're a husky lot."

In late January or early February (1894) he took his poems to Hamlin Garland, and he appeared as embarrassed before the older man as he had been before Linson. He seemed to be concealing something. "Come now, out with it," said Garland, and Stephen with a sheepish look took out of his gray ulster a fat roll of legal cap-paper and handed it to him with "a careless, boyish gesture." Garland insisted: "There's another!" Stephen abruptly delivered himself of another but smaller parcel, handing it over with his habitual grim smile. The poems were written in blue ink without blot or erasure and almost without punctuation, and the first poem Garland read astonished him:

> *God fashioned the ship of the world carefully.*
> *With the infinite skill of an All-Master*
> *Made He the hull and the sails,*
> *Held He the rudder*
> *Ready for adjustment.*
> *Erect stood He scanning His Work proudly.*
> *Then—at fateful time—a wrong called,*
> *And God turned, heeding.*
> *Lo, the ship, at this opportunity, slipped slyly,*
> *Making cunning noiseless travel down the ways.*
> *So that, for ever rudderless, it went upon the seas*
> *Going ridiculous voyages,*
> *Making quaint progress,*
> *Turning as with serious purpose*
> *Before stupid winds.*
> *And there were many in the sky*
> *Who laughed at this thing.*
> (*Black Riders,* VI)

When Crane produced the second sheaf of poems on Garland's insistence he pointed to his temple and said: "I've got five or six all in a little row up here. That's the way they come—in little rows, all made up, ready to be put down on paper." Garland in another version of this same occasion[4] says that he was skeptical and asked for some proof: " 'Do you mean to say that these lines are arranged in your head, complete in every detail?' 'Yes, I could do one right now.' 'Very well. Take a seat at my desk and do one for me.' Thereupon with my pen he wrote steadily, composedly, without a moment's hesitation, one of his most powerful poems. It flowed from his pen like oil." Perhaps the poems came spontaneously because they were the dreams he had experienced the night before. Garland's theory was that Crane was the living agent of a sympathetic spirit of the ghost world who inhabited his mind and gave voice to the poems, which awaited only to be drawn off when the "poetic spout" was turned on. (Garland had presided at a meeting of the American Psychical Society in January, 1893, and later conducted sittings with a medium in Boston, a "psychic" he had met in California, to test him for "voices" and for "the movement of objects without contact.")

Crane's next chore was to find a publisher for his "lines," as he preferred to call them, and Garland urged B. O. Flower of the Arena Publishing Company in Boston to publish them. Stephen had written Lily in April, 1893, that his *Maggie* had made him "a powerful friend" in Flower, who "practically offered me the benefits of his publishing company for all that I may in future write." But Flower, whose *Arena* magazine issued Garland's review of *Maggie* that June, published neither the poems nor *Maggie,* as Crane hoped.

Garland wrote Richard Watson Gilder of the *Century Magazine* on March 23,[5] "I want you to read a great M.S. of Stephen Crane's making. I think him an astonishing fellow. And have advised him to bring the M.S. to you." Although Garland was referring to the manuscript of poems which Crane had shown him, Crane wrote in pencil a postscript across the bottom of Garland's letter: "This is not the MS spoken of. This is a different one." It is possible that Crane switched manuscripts, bringing Gilder *The Red Badge* instead of the intended poems because he feared the poems would shock Gilder even more than *Maggie* had unnerved him. But *The Red Badge* was not suitable for the *Century,* either.

Crane was in dread of his poems being misunderstood or treated with cold indifference; of all his writings they were his favorites. Invited to give an author's reading of his unpublished poems by the Uncut Leaves Society on Saturday evening, April 14, he said that "he would rather die than do it." They were read for him by John D. Barry of the *Forum* magazine, and for this reading Fred Lawrence and Louis Senger came all the way from Port Jervis, and medical student Lucius Button and Senger's cousin, C. K. Linson joined them. They all urged him to attend the reading. "Say, don't you want to hear Barry give 'em Stephen Crane, the new poet?" "Come on, Steve, they're lions; we want to hear them roar!" But he could not be induced; he would not be "dragged by the neck." And he snorted at their mentioning that the guest of honor was Mrs. Frances Hodgson Burnett, the creator of Little Lord Fauntleroy.

Sherry's ballroom was filled with brilliant company, and Stephen's friends who were not in evening dress sat in the rear. When Barry concluded his sympathetic reading of Crane's "lines" they raised "the first patter of hands to a polite clamor of applause—this was for Mr. Barry—and continued it vociferously for Steve, making the room resound again." Their guest-cards stated: "Evening dress, Ladies are requested not to wear bonnets. Beginning at half-past eight. Carriages at ten forty-five." Mrs. Burnett, doing a reading in New York for the first time, "was beautifully dressed in white silk, garnished with *mousseline-de-soie,* and a corsage bunch of violets," reported the *Tribune* on April 16. "Miss Kate Jordan read an unpublished story, 'Conrad Reuter of Second Avenue.' Gilbert Parker of London read one of his own stories called 'The Great Slave Lake' and John D. Barry read several unnamed poems from the pen of Stephen Crane, who, according to Mr. Barry, was too modest to read them himself."

While Barry was reading the poems, Stephen waited down the street until his friends joined him to report on how they had been received; they gave a glowing report. A press notice of the literary Uncut Leaves Society's last meeting for the season, appearing on May 1, was written by Elisha Jay Edwards, a journalist for the American Press Association. Although the cultured litterateurs asked, "Who is Stephen Crane?" the notice said, his poems were read "with delightful elocution, suggesting their perfect rhythmical quality, although they are not arranged in metrical form. If the opinion of those who heard the poems is a just one, they are likely to suggest high talent when they are published. Stephen Crane is a New York lad, for he is scarcely more than a lad, who plunged into the miseries of tenement life in New York and associated with the tramps and the outcasts for many months so that he might see them as they are and paint them thus. Mr. Howells has said that in the single book which Mr. Crane has written [*Maggie*] he has revealed a power of realism, a capacity to paint with almost brutal force and directness, which suggests much of the power of Tolstoy." Edwards claimed, and Crane hoped, that Howells would give his formal approval of the forthcoming volume of poems by writing an introductory note, but Howells dissociated himself from that kind of verse as "too orphic for me." He could no more understand Crane's verse than Maggie would have been able to understand William Dean Howells. He had written Crane that he wished he had given his poems "more form, for then things so striking would have found a public ready made for them; as it is you will have to make one." He could not persuade *Harper's* "to be of my thinking about your poems."

When Stephen visited Garland between April 18 and 22 with the manuscript of *The Red Badge* Garland at first thought it was more poetry. " 'What have you there,' I demanded, 'more lines?' 'No, it is a tale,' he said with that queer, self-derisive smile which was often on his lips at this time. 'Let me see it,' I said, knowing well that he had brought it for that purpose. He handed it over to me with seeming reluctance, and while he went out to watch my brother getting lunch I took my first glance at the manuscript." It was "a bit soiled from much handling. *It had not been typed.* It was in the clearly legible and rather handsome script of the author." (Crane always wrote legibly; as a newspaper reporter he kept in mind the compositor, "whose earnings depended upon the amount he could set, and this in turn upon the time it took to read the copy.")

While Stephen applied himself to a lunch of steak, Garland scrutinized the "sallow, yellow-fingered, small, and ugly" guest and was unable to relate him to the marvelous manuscript of images so keen and phrases so graphic and newly coined that Garland hardly dared express openly his admiration. He remembered his astonishment at the metaphor on the first page. (Crane later deleted the image, leaving it implied.[6]) "The first sentence fairly took me captive. It described a vast army in camp on one side of a river, confronting with its thousands of eyes a similar monster on the opposite bank. The finality which lay in every word, the epic breadth of vision, the splendor of the pictures presented—all indicated a most powerful and original imagination as well as a mature mastery of literary form. Each page presented pictures like those of a great poem, and I experienced the thrill of the editor who has fallen unexpectedly upon the work of genius. It was as if the youth in some mysterious way had secured the cooperation of a spirit, the spirit of an officer in the Civil War. How else could one account for the boy's knowledge of war? I spoke of this, and in his succinct, self-derisive way he candidly confessed that all his knowledge of battle had been gained on the football field."

We must get it published at once, said Garland. "But wait! Here's only part of the manuscript. Where's the rest of it?" Crane looked embarrassed and said it was in hock. " 'To whom?' 'To the typewriter.' We all laughed, but it was serious business to him. He could see the humor of the situation, but there was a bitter rebellion in his voice. 'How much is it "hung up" for?' 'Fifteen dollars.' I looked at my brother. 'I guess we can spare that, don't you think?' So Crane went away joyously and brought the last half of *The Red Badge of Courage,* still unnamed at the time. He told us that the coming of that story was just as mysterious as in the case of the verses, and I can believe it. It literally came of its own accord like sap flowing from a tree."

Stephen had got the first half of the manuscript back from the typist by borrowing fifteen dollars from his fraternity brother John Henry Dick, a writer for *Godey's Magazine:* "Dear Dicon: Beg, borrow or steal fifteen dollars. [McClure's] like the Red Badge and want to make a contract for it. It is in pawn at the typewriter's for fifteen."[7]

Garland lent Crane $15 to get out of hock the second half of the manuscript on proviso that " 'you'll bring me the remainder of the manuscript tomorrow.' 'I'll do it,' he said as if he were joining me in some heroic enterprise, and away he went in high spirits. He was as good as his word, and when I had read the entire story I set to work to let my editorial friends know of this youngster." He mailed two of Crane's sketches to B. O. Flower of the *Arena,* and he suggested to Crane that he call on Irving Bacheller. "Don't trouble yourself about the borrowing," Garland wrote on April 22; "we all have to do that sometimes. You'll soon be able to pay it back and more too. You're going to get on your feet mighty soon."

S. S. McClure, himself in financial difficulties, could not afford to risk a contract for *The Red Badge of Courage* just then, and this explains why he kept the typescript for at least six months. (Crane says it was eight months, but he also says it was six months; McClure was "a beast" about it.) While the typescript was still lagging in McClure's office, Crane brought the soiled manuscript to Irving Addison Bacheller of the Bacheller-Johnson newspaper syndicate—in desperation.

"Mr. Howells and Hamlin Garland have read this stuff and they think it's good," he told Bacheller, who had already heard about him from

Edward Marshall. "I wish you'd read it and, whether you wish to use the story or not, I'd be glad to have your frank opinion of it." Bacheller took the script home with him that evening, and he and his wife spent more than half the night reading it aloud to each other. "We got far along in the story, thrilled by its power and vividness." The next morning he sent for Crane and made an arrangement with him to use a shortened version— "fifty thousand of his magic words as a serial"—to be serialized in newspapers by the Bacheller Syndicate. He decided to take the chance of issuing it in installments far beyond the length permitted by his contracts with various newspapers as an experiment, hopeful that his judgment would persuade his editors.[8]

At the end of February there was a driving blizzard. Emile Stangé recalls that the next morning he drifted up to Gordon's studio and found Crane and another just arrived, "both in rags, no overcoat, clothes all holes, toes out of their shoes, no umbrellas (of course not), and soaked to the skin, water dripping in pools about them. I noticed Crane's rather flat chest was shaking every little while with spasms of a very hollow cough. His blond hair was matted over his eyes. A great wave of pity swept over me; I thought, 'My Lord! has it come to this?' Crane, as though sensing my unspoken thought, looked at me and grinned."

Stephen and an artist friend, an illustrator, had gone down to the Bowery to join one of the breadlines which formed regularly before certain bakeries that gave away stale bread, and then they had spent the night in a flophouse. Out of his breadline experience Crane wrote "Men in the Storm"; the flophouse produced "An Experiment in Misery."

Later that morning Linson and his brother arrived at Gordon's studio and found Stephen alone on a cot, looking haggard and almost ill. "Pulling a manuscript from under his pillow, he tossed it to me and settled back under the covers to watch," says Linson in *My Stephen Crane.*[9] It was that breadline classic, "Men in the Storm," which Hamlin Garland had urged him to write because the newspapers, during the hard times of 1894, were making much of bread distribution to the poor. Garland also persuaded Flower to aid Crane because the youth was hungry, and *Arena* magazine published it that October.

Linson, finding Crane exhausted, scolded him: "Why didn't you put on two or three more undershirts, Steve?" He replied: "How would I know how those poor devils felt if I was warm myself? Nit! Anyway, I didn't have the shirts, you mutt!" The studio was a topsy-turvy mess with papers and cartoons covering the tables and floor and with the bedclothes of three cots "all awry as if they were never made up." Crane had had no breakfast, and so Linson and his brother walked him over to Linson's studio on West 22nd Street, where the elevated trains roared by on Sixth Avenue and there they fed him a breakfast of fried smelts.

As they were walking to the studio Stephen said that when he first began to write he could hardly think of what to write about, "but now I have enough ideas to keep me busy the next two years." He was still wearing his Bowery outfit of a down-and-out bum, and the janitor of the studio building eyed him dubiously. This was the kind of adventure that pleased him most, he told artist Vosburgh; he liked to study human nature unmasked.

"I decided that the nearer a writer gets to life the greater he becomes as an artist, and most of my prose writings have been toward the goal partially described by the misunderstood and abused word *realism*," Crane declared in 1895. His "Men in the Storm," however, is far more than a photocopy of reality because it converts the actual experience into something larger than the thing itself. Even in his reporting Crane was a symbolist, an impressionist in prose.

The anonymity of the social outcasts in "Men in the Storm" is suggested by their pressing close to one another in the breadline "like sheep in a winter's gale, keeping one another warm by the heat of their bodies. The snow came down upon this compressed group of men until, directly from above, it might have appeared like a heap of snow-covered merchandise, if it were not for the fact that the crowd swayed gently with a unanimous rhythmical motion. It was wonderful to see how the snow lay upon the heads and shoulders of these men, in little ridges an inch thick perhaps in places, the flakes steadily adding drop and drop, precisely as they fall upon the unresisting grass of the fields."

These men of ill-fortune are meek and, like the field grass, unresisting. They see the world's progress leaving them behind and they try to perceive why they failed and what they lacked. Waiting for the door of the charity bakery to open, they surge heavily against it in a powerful wave of pushing shoulders, "jamming and wedging in a way that, it seemed, would crack bones." The door won't open because the men are crushed against it, and a dull roar of rage comes from the men on the outskirts of the breadline: "Yeh damn pigs, give 'em a chance t' open th' door!" Sometimes they made grim jokes "and no doubt very uncouth. Nevertheless, they were notable—one does not expect to find the quality of humor in a heap of old clothes under a snowdrift."

They are mocked by the figure of a man, rather stout and very well clothed, standing in the brilliantly lighted dry-goods shop window across the street. "His beard was fashioned charmingly after that of the Prince of Wales. He stood in an attitude of magnificent reflection. He slowly stroked his moustache with a certain grandeur of manner, and looked down at the snow-encrusted mob. From below, there was denoted a supreme complacence in him. It seemed that the sight operated inversely, and enabled him to more clearly regard his own delightful environment. One of the mob chanced to turn his head, and perceived the figure in the window. 'Hello, look-it 'is whiskers,' he said genially. Many of the men turned then, and a shout went up. They called to him in all strange keys. They addressed him in every manner, from familiar and cordial greetings to carefully worded advice concerning changes in his personal appearance. The man presently fled, and the mob chuckled ferociously, like ogres who had just devoured something. They turned then to serious business."

The men in the breadline battle among themselves "to get in out of the storm," which is rendered so as to suggest the storm of life itself. Boldly the drivers of streetcars stand erect against the wind and seem "models of grim philosophy," whereas in contrast these seekers of charity admit their defeat. While gusts of snow cut at them, they wait for the door of the charity house to open, and when it becomes known the door to be opened is the basement door at the foot of a steep flight of stars they jostle and heave "like laboring fiends" and stand there thus "upon the threshold of their hopes." On the curb a streetlamp seems struggling to illumine their plight, but it is "reduced to impotent blindness by the swift gusts of sleet crusting its panes."

In the *Arena* magazine version of "Men in the Storm" the opening phrase —never since reprinted—dates the occasion for February, 1894: "At about three o'clock of the February afternoon, the blizzard began to swirl great clouds of snow along the streets, sweeping it down from the roofs and up from the pavements until the faces of pedestrians tingled and burned as from a thousand needle-prickings." Crane in this sketch appears alone, but in "An Experiment in Misery" he is with some artist friend from the Needham building.

The opening passage of that sketch begins: "Two men stood regarding a tramp." They ponder the situation: " 'I wonder how he feels,' said one, reflectively. 'I suppose he is homeless, friendless, and has, at the most, only a few cents in his pocket. And if this is so, I wonder how he feels.' " The older man spoke with an air of authoritative wisdom: " 'You can tell nothing of it unless you are in that condition yourself. It is idle to speculate about it from this distance.' 'I suppose so,' said the younger man, and then he added as from an inspiration: 'I think I'll try it. Rags and tatters, you know, a couple of dimes, and hungry, too, if possible. Perhaps I could discover his point of view or something near it.' " And so Crane began his own experiment in misery.

"It was late at night, and a fine rain was swirling softly down, causing the pavement to glisten with hue of steel and blue and yellow in the rays of the innumerable lights. A youth was trudging slowly, without enthusiasm, with his hands buried deep in his trousers pockets, toward the downtown places where beds can be hired for coppers. He was clothed in an aged and tattered suit, and his derby was a marvel of dust-covered crown and torn rim." Stephen had borrowed that tattered suit and derby from an artist friend.[10]

The youth reaches Park Row and City Hall Park, where small boys plaster him with yells of bum and hobo, and he shuffles off down Park Row where the tatters of others match his own. He aligns himself with the aimless men strewn in front of saloons in Chatham Square, saloons shining with a golden radiance. Streetcars rumble softly, "as if going upon carpet stretched in the aisle made by the pillars of the elevated road. . . . The high buildings lurked a-back, shrouded in shadows. Down a side street there were mystic curtains of purple and black, on which lamps dully glittered like embroidered flowers. A saloon stood with a voracious air on a corner. A sign leaning against the front of the doorpost announced: 'Free hot soup to-night.' The swing doors, snapping to and fro like ravenous lips, made gratified smacks, as if the saloon were gorging itself with plump men. Caught by the delectable sign, the young man allowed himself to be swallowed. A bartender placed a schooner of dark and portentous beer on the bar. Its monumental form up-reared until the froth a-top was above the crown of the young man's brown derby." The youth and "a little yellow man in rags" grasp their schooners of beer and move over to the lunch counter where the free hot soup containing "little floating suggestions of chicken" is served, and where a man "with oily but imposing whiskers" presides, "like a priest behind an altar."

The youth encounters a reeling man who appears "like an assassin steeped in crimes performed awkwardly." His eyes peer with a guilty slant; he gestures "extravagantly" and takes "oath by strange gods." The "assassin" takes the youth to a cheap lodging house, a place of "unholy odors." On cots thickly littering the floor sprawl the forms of men "lying in deathlike silence or heaving and snoring with tremendous effort, like stabbed fish." The youth shivers on his leather-covered cot, a slab cold as melting snow, while his friend snores with incredible vigor. "His wet hair and beard dimly glistened and his inflamed nose shone with subdued luster like a red light in a fog." About the cots are lockers standing like tombstones. Sometimes limbs toss wildly "in fantastic nightmare gestures, accompanied by guttural cries, grunts, oaths. And there was one fellow off in a gloomy corner, who in his dreams was oppressed by some frightful calamity; for of a sudden he began to utter long wails that went almost like yells from a hound, echoing wailfully and weird through this chill place of tombstones, where men lay like the dead. The sound, in its high piercing beginnings that dwindled to final melancholy moans, expressed a red and grim tragedy of the unfathomable possibilities of man's dreams. But to the youth these were not merely the shrieks of a vision-pierced man. They were an utterance of the meaning of the room and its occupants. It was to him the protest of the wretch who feels the touch of the imperturbable granite wheels and who then cries with an impersonal eloquence, with a strength not from him, giving voice to the wail of a whole section, a class, a people." The youth does not sleep, but "lay carving biographies for these men from his meager experience."

A sign on a basement restaurant reads: "No mystery about our hash," and there he buys a bowl of coffee for two cents and a roll for one cent the next morning. His flophouse friend purchases the same at the youth's expense. The coffee bowls "were webbed with brown seams, and the tin spoons wore an air of having emerged from the first pyramid. Upon them were black, moss-like encrustations of age, and they were bent and scarred from the attacks of long forgotten teeth." Then they trudge slowly along Park Row, the "assassin" injecting into his limping step "a suggestion of lamblike gambols. His mouth was wreathed in a red grin." In City Hall Park the two wanderers sit down in the circle of benches "sanctified by traditions of their class," and the youth ponders on the infinite distance that the people who hurry by on important missions express to him: "Social position, comfort, the pleasures of living, were unconquerable kingdoms. He felt a sudden awe."

The New York *Press* version of "An Experiment in Misery" ends with a coda which returns us to the opening passage. In the coda the elder friend rejoins the youth and asks whether he has discovered the tramp's point of view. " 'I don't know that I did, 'replied the young man; 'but at any rate I think mine own has undergone a considerable alteration.' " In this sketch of sordid actuality Crane, says Linson, was making "his work touch life's deeper provocations, whereas the surface of things sufficed for most of his craft." The piece got Crane's name before the newspaper public for the first time. "A Wonderfully Vivid Picture of a Strange Phase of New York Life . . . by the Author of 'Maggie,' " proclaimed the *Press* (April 22, 1894).

Garland had been to Chicago and Crane had neglected him since his return to New York on March 10. Garland wrote him on April 17: "I'd like to know how things are going with you." The next day Stephen replied that he had not been up to see him "because of various strange conditions —notably, my toes are coming through one shoe and I have not been going out into society as much as I might. I hope you have heard about the Uncut Leaves affair. I tried to get tickets up to you but I couldn't succeed. I mail you last Sunday's *Press*. I've moved now—live in a flat. People can come to see me now. They come in schools and say that I am a great writer. Counting five that are sold, four that are unsold, and six that are mapped out, I have fifteen short stories in my head and out of it. They'll make a book. The *Press* people pied some of *Maggie* as you will note." The *Press* was in fact quite favorable except to ask whether such brutalities as Crane exposed in *Maggie* "are wholly acceptable in literature." Edward Marshall, in the same issue of the *Press,* published his interview with William Dean Howells, in which Crane came off very well.

The short stories Stephen boasts of were most likely the New York City sketches he was then writing, the "Midnight Sketches" he hoped to publish some day as a book. Garland's postal was addressed to him at the

Art Students' League and was forwarded to 111 West 33rd Street, where he had moved into his flat. He was used to bouncing in and out of one studio or rooming house to another—he could write no matter where or how strange the bed. He would write late into the night and often waited to crawl into bed until its occupant arose at dawn and quit the bed to accommodate that peripatetic bum.[11]

Crane said of his "Experiment in Misery" that he tried to make plain that the root of Bowery life is a sort of cowardice. "Perhaps I mean a lack of ambition or to willingly be knocked flat and accept the licking. The missions for children are another thing and if you will have Mr. Rockefeller give me a hundred street cars and some money I will load the babes off to some pink world where cows can lick their noses and they will never see their families any more."

No nineteenth century fiction writer knew New York City's demi-world more intimately. He actually found relief in the company of bums, says Linson; but like Mark Twain, he preferred wealth and social class to poverty. In "An Experiment in Luxury," the youth and a rich boy discuss their college days. There are those who have opportunities and there are those who are robbed of them, says Crane. It is a legend of comfort to the poor that "there are burrs under all rich cloaks and benefits in all ragged jackets, and the preaching of it seems wicked to me. . . . Theologians had for a long time told the poor man that riches did not bring happiness, and they solemnly repeated this phrase until it had come to mean that misery was commensurate with dollars, that each wealthy man was inwardly a miserable wretch. And when a wail of despair or rage had come from the night of the slums they had stuffed this epigram down the throat of him who cried out and told him that he was a lucky fellow. They did this because they feared."

Crane's scorn of the rich is epitomized in his observation that the butler, with mournful air, moves about the house "like a slow religious procession." The butler and the footman "of refined nose" are more atrociously aristocratic than the family they serve. They put the youth— as well as the wealthy boy's family—in their proper place, and the youth resents their social snobbery and detests himself for it. He imagines himself momentarily as the exemplar of social perfection returning to the pretentious household to "reduce this footman to ashes." The wealthy boy's father is "a great domestic Napoleon," and his mother is a statue of absolute despair, her face creased with the lines of cares and worriment like that of a common apple-woman. She wears the mask of terrible pride, "that kind of pride which, mistaking the form for the real thing, worships itself because of its devotion to the form."

In this house of gloom the three sisters of his host seem like flowers, but in certain places "no flower can flourish," and the youth meditates on the daughters of the rich compared to the daughters of the poor. Women who toil fade sooner than any millionaire's daughters because wealth is liberty.

In "An Experiment in Misery" Crane (in the manner of Flaubert) implied rather than stated his criticism of the social situation, but in "An Experiment in Luxury" he lectures about the rich and the poor, and he is not at his best on such occasions. His special gift is to portray a place or person ("women fade, shrivel, their bosoms flatten, their shoulders crook forward, in the heavy swelter and wrench of their toil"), or to evoke a significance from the place or person portrayed. The brownstone mansion, having an inanity of expression ("stolid like the face of a peasant"), lacked artistic strength, and yet "it symbolized something. It stood, a homely pile of stone, rugged, grimly self reliant, asserting its quality as a fine thing when in reality the beholder usually wondered why so much money had been spent to obtain a complete negation. Then from another point of view it was important and mighty because it stood as a fetish, formidable because of traditions of worship."

Life pulsed for Crane not on Fifth Avenue but in the Bowery and Chinatown and over on the East Side. But he chirped like a bird, says Garland, when he was served a chop. He was pale, thin and silent; but no sooner had he filled his "crop" with meat and coffee than he gave out an entirely different expression. He chortled and sang as he strolled about Garland's apartment "exactly like a well-fed hen. At such moments he talked freely and well, and always with precision and tang." He never offered to wash the dishes, but Garland was more amused than irritated by his indifference to such housekeeping courtesies and ascribed it not to laziness but rather to his remoteness from the practical business of living.

"An Experiment in Luxury," in the New York *Press* on April 29, links with "A Night at a Millionaire's Club" appearing in James Ford's *Truth* the same month.[12] Here the rich club members stare at the ceiling "where the decorations cost seventy-four dollars per square inch. An ecstatic murmur came from the remote corners of the apartment where each chair occupied two thousand dollars worth of floor. William C. Whitney was neatly arranged in a prominent seat to impart a suggestion of brains to the general effect. A clock had been chiming at intervals of ten minutes during the evening, and at each time of striking Mr. Depew had made a joke per agreement. The last one, however, had smashed a seventeen-thousand-dollar vase over by the window, and Mr. Depew was hesitating. He had some doubt whether, after all, his jokes were worth that much commercially."

In one of his *Journal* sketches (1898) Crane compares the streets of a squalid London slum with that part of Avenue A lying below 60th Street in New York City, which provided the street scene of "An Ominous Baby" (in *Arena:* May, 1894). Because he is a threat to the children of the rich, the slum child is an ominous baby. Nursery maids parade the children of the rich in perambulators and tell the slum child to go away because he is dirty. He seizes the toy fire engine from a pretty child, who has declared it is his property. " 'Well, can't I play wif it?' His voice was a sob. He stretched forth little covetous hands. 'No,' the pretty child continued to repeat. 'No, it's mine.' 'Well, I want to play wif it,' wailed the other. A sudden fierce frown mantled his baby face. He clenched his fat hands and advanced with a formidable gesture," his soiled dress showing the marks of many conflicts, "like the chain shirt of a warrior." The slum child wrenches the rope from the other's hands and runs down the street with the toy in his arms. Then, while the pretty child squalls lustily, the ominous baby weeps "with the air of a wronged one who has at last succeeded in achieving his rights."

The slum child is the Tommie of *Maggie,* the baby brother who is buried clutching a flower that Maggie has stolen from an Italian vendor. In "An Ominous Baby" (and in "A Great Mistake") he is not named, but on pink-lined pad sheets Crane wrote: "An Ominous Baby—Tommie's Home-coming." In this sketch of the slum child seizing the property of the rich child Crane epitomizes the social conflict between the poor and the rich during the hard times and labor troubles of 1893–1894. In "A Great Mistake" the unnamed urchin steals a lemon from the Italian vendor of a fruit stand under the elevated station at the corner of thronged streets. "He was fascinated by the tranquillity of the vendor, the majesty of power and possession." On the fruit stand, tumbled in luxurious heaps, were the sweets of the world; but all the child gets out of this "feast of gods" is a lemon.

In "A Dark Brown Dog," not published until 1901 in *Cosmopolitan* magazine but probably written in 1893–1894, an unnamed young urchin becomes friends with a dark brown dog, mainly by beating him with a stick. "On the way to his home the child turned many times and beat the dog, proclaiming with childish gestures that he held him in contempt as an unimportant dog, with no value save for a moment. For being this quality of animal the dog apologized and eloquently expressed regret, but he continued stealthily to follow the child. His manner grew so very guilty that he slunk like an assassin." The child drags his captive friend up the stairs to his tenement home, and there his parents molest the dog by throwing brooms or handfuls of coal at him. But this "small rug of a dog" prospers nevertheless, and his "devotion to the child grew until it was a sublime thing. He wagged at his approach; he sank down in despair at his departure."

One day the drunken father holds "carnival with the cooking utensils, the furniture and his wife." The child dives under the table, the dog mis-interprets it to mean a joyous gambol, and the father knocks the dog down with a heavy coffeepot, kicks him, then swings him hilariously above his head and flings him out the window. "The soaring dog created a surprise in the block. A woman watering plants in an opposite window gave an involuntary shout and dropped a flower pot. A man in another window leaned perilously out to watch the flight of the dog. A woman who had been hanging out clothes in a yard began to caper wildly. Her mouth was filled with clothespins, but her arms gave vent to a sort of exclamation. In appearance she was like a gagged prisoner. Children ran whooping. The dark brown body crashed in a heap on the roof of a shed five stories below. From thence it rolled to the pavement of an alleyway." It took the child a long time to toddle downstairs backwards, one step at a time, to reach that alley; but there he was found sitting by the body of his friend.

In the best of his New York City sketches, notably "Men in the Storm" and "An Experiment in Misery," and also in his poems, war dispatches, and short stories, Crane injects a double point of view: how the other fellow felt or thought as well as how he himself felt or thought about the situation. He felt pity for his characters, but he also recognized the irony of their plight. The note of irony and pity toolmarks Hemingway, who learned it from Crane. "Oh, give them Irony and give them Pity," says Bill Gorton in *The Sun Also Rises*.

Crane does not ask us to pity the "Men in the Storm," but neither does he spare us their agonies, said the *Commercial Advertiser*. He "gives you in vigorous Anglo-Saxon just what their position and condition is, and leaves your sympathy with them to be a matter between yourself and your human nature. He is a clever performer on the strings of pity, and his fingers are so firm in their arpeggios of the cruelty of destitution that you feel as if each stroke were a heartbeat." Technically, Crane was too advanced for his time, that Mauve Decade of sentimentality; it took a couple of decades before his unique combination of irony and pity—the ironic voice undercutting the sentiment—became acceptable.

The sketch "Sixth Avenue" was—like *Maggie*—"too honest," and so a *Press* editor cut it considerably because he thought that what Crane said was injurious to the *Press*'s Sixth Avenue advertising receipts and might involve it in libel suits. Curtis Brown says the editor expunged so much of this sketch that there was little left and that he then threw away the remainder "as not being exciting enough. So perished a manuscript for which a dealer in autograph letters would have given much a few years later." However, one single-sheet holograph of that manuscript exists,[13] and there is nothing alarming in what Crane says. "Sixth Avenue is a street that leads a dual existence. It typifies the man who walks very primly in the observing light of the sun but who, when in the shadows, cuts many strange pranks. The day finds it thronged with shoppers; the doors of the great shops clash to and fro in endless motion. Huge windows disclose masses of goods that have been dragged from all corners of the earth. Hosts of women crowd the sidewalks. The elevated trains and the street-cars unload battalions of them. The huge stores uprear their austere fronts to glance across the street at little saloons that in this white light of respectability remain subdued and silent. It is the time of the marching and counter-marching of the feminine buyers; it is the time when Sixth Avenue is profoundly busy but profoundly decorous."

Crane's fascination with Sixth Avenue is revealed in numerous sketches of 1894 and 1896. In his pocket notebook he wrote a first draft of "In a Park Row Restaurant" (New York *Press:* October 28, 1894) and a portion of his sketch of a Sixth Avenue bar fight between a Cuban and an Irishman whom the Cuban challenges to a duel with swords. A policeman breaks up their scuffle, and that ends "The Duel That Was Not Fought" (*Press:* December 9, 1894).

In this Park Row restaurant Crane met a Nevada sheriff who came there for excitement because the place suggested the Battle of Gettysburg. There he felt the kind of thrill he might have felt on the summit of Little Round Top. "I think if Pickett and his men charged on here they would be trampled under foot before they could get a biscuit," says the sheriff. "It is a frightful struggle. I have often wished to induce Detaille to come to this country and get a subject for a melee that would make his frenzied Franco-Prussian battle-scenes look innocent."[14] The restaurant reminds him of the fear and exhilaration of his life in the old days. Crowds of men swarm in from the streets and dash about in search of a vacant chair, while those already seated "were eating with terrible speed, or else casting impatient or tempestuous glances at the waiters."

In his pocket notebook version Crane wrote: " 'Hey! Did you forget those chops?' 'Waiter! Here! A napkin, please!' 'Hurry up that pie, will you, old man!' 'Got that mutton-stew yet?' 'Butter-cakes and coffee! Certainly! about ten minutes ago!' 'You needn't mind the pie! I can't wait!' 'Bring me a ham-omelet, a cup of coffee, and some corn muffins! What? Well, send the right waiter here then. I can't wait all day.' " The waiters carrying incredible masses of dishes and threading their swift ways with rare skill, dash about "as if something threatened them and they were trying to escape through the walls."

In the *Press* version Crane describes these waiters as scampering water bugs scattering across the surface of a brook broken by the splash of a pebble. "They served customers with such speed and violence that it often resembled a personal assault. The crumbs from the previous dinner were swept off with one fierce motion of a napkin. A waiter struck two blows at the table and left there a knife and fork." And the clatter of dishes was like the gallop of a thousand horses, and from the kitchen came "a continual roaring altercation, hoarse and vehement, like the cries of the officers of a regiment under attack. [In his notebook Crane originally phrased it: "Like the cries of the officers of a ship in a squall."] A mist of steam fluttered where the waiters crowded and jostled about the huge copper coffee urns." The stranger from Nevada remarks to Crane that a man with a very creditable stomach could easily get indigestion there. "It is astonishing how fast a man can eat when he tries. This air is surcharged with appetites. I have seen very orderly, slow moving men become possessed with the spirit of this rush"—they lose control of themselves and begin to dine like madmen.

Another restaurant Crane frequented was called A Little Bit of France and was located west of Broadway toward 30th Street. By 1894 he could afford to go regularly with Linson "to a seventy-five-cent French table d'hote with red juice in pint bottles. Louis Senger was never certain if this was claret or Burgundy or red ink, but 'it all goes' was his inclusive comment." Crane lived on and off for eighteen months during 1894 to 1896 with Charles J. Pike, an apprentice architect, in the third-floor studio of Pike and his brother at 281 Sixth Avenue (at the corner of 33rd Street), not more than a few blocks from a French restaurant which was probably the same Little Bit of France that Linson and his cousin Louis Senger frequented. Charles Pike and his brother, who like Linson had been to Paris, persuaded two French peasants to do the cooking for some artists who were homesick for the cuisine they had enjoyed in France, and the Pikes promised these two old ladies at least twelve customers nightly. The artists ate in the kitchen, which was one flight down from the street in the rear of a tenement, and their plates were shoved at them directly from the stove by the French cooks.

Crane and the Pike brothers sat at the head of the table, nearest the source of food. The conversation was not particularly outrageous, says Henry McBride in "Stephen Crane's Artist Friends." Once a cellist of some fame played a Bach fugue during an interval between dinner courses, and on another occasion the company was favored by the presence of Jesse Lynch Williams, a highly successful novelist of that day, but he turned out to be a stuffed shirt. As soon as the table was cleared of dishes Crane and the Pike boys invariably threw dice for unpretentious stakes, and once McBride after a few instructions from Stephen was persuaded to rattle the bones. "To my surprise I won. I continued to win. I had beginner's luck. I couldn't lose. After a while the thing became such a farce that Stephen suggested that we play 'double or quits,' and I agreed. I knew he could no longer pay and he knew he couldn't pay, but with 'double or quits' if he should accidentally win once, the whole indebtedness would be cancelled with one fell throw. It wasn't cricket, of course, but we did it and so the game ended. As we were laughing about it and saying good-night to the hostess, Stephen said: 'Just the same I think I do owe you something,' and with a flourish he produced from his pocket a very grand cigar, all wrapped in tin-foil and encased in a special box of its own. 'It's a dollar cigar,' he added, impressively."

The Pike brothers, both student architects, were built like professional football players; they became known through Charles Dana Gibson's drawings of Charles Pike for illustrations of art student life in Paris. The coterie of artists with whom Crane associated regularly included Edward S. Hamilton, an Academy exhibitor who seemed destined for fame until he was cut down by an early death; Gustave Verbeck, whose oils of prim ladies were considered avant-garde in 1900 and who almost flowered into fame in Paris and New York City only to end as a well-known cartoonist; and Henry McBride. Other artists, mainly illustrators, included Crane's friends whom we have already met: Frederic Gordon, David Ericson, R. G. Vosburgh, and C. K. Linson and his studio associates: John Willard Raught, Emile Stangé, and art editor A. F. Jaccaci.

One day there was a fire in McBride's studio, and he salvaged from that disaster the copy of the 1893 *Maggie* Crane had given him in his usual careless way ("without putting a *dédicace* on the title page, the vogue for that sort of thing not being so prevalent then as now"). The next day he told Stephen of the incident while they were riding up Broadway on the rear platform of the horse-drawn streetcar. Crane thought it all a great joke and, "assuming a caricatured posture of importance, said: 'Who knows, maybe in the years to come that may be considered the most valuable item to have been rescued from your fire.' "[15]

Another restaurant he sometimes visited was Pop Babcock's place in Minetta Lane, which in 1894 "shone with sin like a new headlight." Minetta Lane was then not a public thoroughfare, but a street set apart as a refuge for criminals. Two years later Crane researched the scene and interviewed some of the last relics of the days of slaughter still living there. Pop Babcock's restaurant had a dusty sign promising "Oysters in every style," but not an oyster could be found in the joint. In "Stephen Crane in Minetta Lane" he remarks sardonically: "As far as goes the management of Pop's restaurant, it differs from Sherry's. In the first place, the door is always kept locked" because objectionable guests brought investigations there by the wardmen of the Fifteenth Precinct of the Sixth Ward.

" 'Why, dis her Lane ain't nowhow like what it useter be—no, indeed, it ain't. No, sir! 'Deed it ain't! Why, I kin remember,' says Pop Babcock, 'when dey was a-cuttin' an' a-slashin long yere all night. 'Deed dey was! My—my, dem times was different! Dat dar Kent, he kep' de place at Green Gate Cou't—down yer of Mammy's—an' he was a hard baby—'deed he was—an' ol' Black-Cat an' ol' Bloodthirsty, dey was a'roamin' round yere a-cuttin' an' a-slashin' an' a-cuttin' an' a-slashin'. Didn't dar' say boo to a goose in dose days, dat you didn't, less'n you lookin' fer a scrap. No, sir!' " Of the three customers in Pop's restaurant at the time when Crane interviewed him one was asleep on the bench, one was asleep on the chairs, and one was asleep on the floor.

Sixth Avenue horsecars jingled by one end of that notorious alley, "a small and becobbled valley between hills of dingy brick" ending a block eastward in the darkness of MacDougal Street, while Minetta Street led southward from the Lane to Bleecker Street. Nearly all the nearby streets were unmistakably bad, but when Minetta Lane and Minetta Street started out "the other streets went away and hid. To gain a reputation in Minetta Lane, in those days, a man was obliged to commit a number of furious crimes, and no celebrity was more important than the man who had a good honest killing to his credit. The inhabitants, for the most part, were Negroes who represented the worst elements of their race. The razor habit clung to them with the tenacity of an epidemic, and every night the uneven cobbles felt blood."

It was the original Negro clan that made the trouble when there was trouble, but the Negro's most extraordinary quality "is his enormous capacity for happiness under most adverse circumstances. Minetta Lane is a place of poverty and sin, but these influences cannot destroy the broad smile of the Negro, a vain and simple child but happy. They all smile here, the most evil as well as the poorest." Even the laughter of that devil Pop Babcock was as fine and mellow as the sound of falling glass broken from the high windows of saints "in the silence of some great cathedral's hollow."

Minetta Lane boasted of such desperadoes as the Negro "Bloodthirsty," a large and very hideous man with a rolling eye that showed white at the wrong time and a neck "dreadfully scarred and pitted. Bloodthirsty was particularly eloquent when drunk, and in the wildness of a spree he would rave so graphically about gore that even the habituated wool of old timers would stand straight." He'd make lightning sweeps of his razor after an oration, and no one dared exchange epithets. A man in a boiler-iron suit would rather walk down to City Hall to look at the clock before he'd dare ask Bloodthirsty the time of day. Then there was No Toe Charley (so-called because his feet had no toes), who ended in the grim gray building up the river; and there was Black-Cat, another famous bandit who lived in Minetta Lane; and Guinea Johnson, not a great figure but just an ordinary little crook revisiting Minetta Lane's other little crooks. By 1896 the place was destitute of famous men whose industry in unlawfulness had earned them the dignity of a nickname. Italian families had come to occupy the MacDougal Street corner, and there were no more cutting affrays in the old Mulberry Bend fashion of life.

However, two years before his sketch appeared in the Philadelphia *Press* (December 20, 1896) Stephen had interviewed some of these notorious Minetta Lane characters with the probable intention of writing about them for his New York *Press* series of "Midnight Sketches." One of the derelicts he talked to lived across from Pop Babcock's restaurant in a tottering frame house with a flight of grimy stairs pasted on the outside and leading to "a hall blacker than a wolf's throat," and there at a kitchen fire sat old and fat Mammy Ross suffering from "de very las' dregs of de yaller fever." She breathed like a fish thrown on the bank, but when Crane mentioned the names of sublime figures of crime, she brightened at the invocation of the spirits of her memory. She had kept a sailor's boardinghouse near the Tombs Prison, and there a sailor got killed every day.

Sailors were welcomed to Minetta Lane with all proper ceremony if they appeared to have any money about them, but when they departed "they were fortunate if they still retained their teeth. It was the custom to leave very little else to them. There was every facility for the capture of coin, from trapdoors to plain ordinary knockout drops. And yet Minetta Lane is built on the grave of Minetta Brook, where, in olden times, lovers walked under the willows of the bank, and Minetta Lane, in later times, was the home of many of the best families of the town." Mammy Ross' face widened into a smile as she recalled her quarrel with Apple Mag, an "emphatic lady who used to argue with paving stones, carving knives and bricks." Mammy's recollections of past fights and murders served as the main food for her ancient brain.

When Stephen first entered her flat, the old Negress was taking a bath in a wash-boiler, and she called out: "Child, I'se all disdressed." He horrified Elbert Hubbard and his household when he related this experience during his visit to Hubbard's place at East Aurora in December, 1895. "That anecdote slew its thousands at Hubbard's and got me in much trouble," he recalled four years later. "I shall never know why. They acted as though I had read one of Zola's loudest roars. Over here [in England] I have told it in front of seven or eight mothers of families and I assure you nothing happened. Nothing at all."

Crane's "predominant hobby was to know life as it was," said Willis Brooks Hawkins; "and if he found it more freely expressed in those strata [of lower society] than in the more conventional circles, it is not for me to say that he approved all he saw. Indeed, after years of intimate association with him, I could truthfully testify that he was exceptionally clean in thought and deed."[16]

The *Press* reporters, trained to report factual news, thought young Crane a queer bird, but Stephen "was so gentle and wistful that everyone liked him." Marshall, who had come to the *Press* from a New York City press agency and was considered the most promising editor on Park Row, was a fair-haired and blue-eyed youth of about the same age as his assistant Curtis Brown, both of them not much older than Crane and each a remarkable man of fine character. Marshall saw young Crane as "merely the combination of clean, fine youth with genius. When one writes 'fine youth' of Stephen Crane, the expression must be qualified because he was never physically strong. His greatest eccentricity was his habit of all night work," said Marshall. "I never saw him wholly at bodily ease. He was not a persistent worker, because his body—a body which suffered from the constant drainings of an intensely active mind—was ever too weak to bear continuous labor. His brain never rested."

Crane once told Hawkins that his father's family had always looked upon him as "the black sheep of the flock." "This saddened him, in a way," said Hawkins, "though he bore it with fortitude; and if there was a streak of cynicism in him, as some critics of his writings have seemed to discover, it may have been due to this false estimate of him by those of whom he was really fond."

One of those "false" estimates was that of Hamlin Garland, who decided, after calumny attached to Crane's name in 1896, that his explorations of the seamy sides of life were just too daring and that he was "irresponsible as the wind." In February, 1894, when Crane explored the Bowery in the guise of a seedy outcast so as to test the life of Bowery bums, some "friend" pointed him out as the outcast son of a minister, an eccentric wasting his time in Bowery dives. Certainly his *Press* sketches did not render a flattering portrait of New York City, and this led to pressure in some quarters to get Marshall dismissed from his *Press* post, but he stuck by Crane and hung on.

"Keep me posted on New York affairs," Garland wrote from Chicago on May 9. Crane was too busy working on his stories for the *Press* to write him for almost six months, but the day before Garland's letter arrived he wrote him that he was "plodding along on the *Press* in a quiet and effective way. We now eat with charming regularity at least two times per day. I am content and am writing another novel which is a bird [*George's Mother*] . . . . When anything happens I'll keep you informed. I'm getting lots of free advertising. Everything is coming along nicely now. I have got the poetic spout so that I can turn it on or off. I wrote a decoration day thing for the *Press* which aroused them to enthusiasm. They said, in about a minute though, that I was firing over the heads of the soldiers. I am going to see your brother soon. Don't forget to return to New York soon for all the struggling talent miss you."

The Decoration Day piece ("The Gratitude of a Nation") was not published because it did not arouse any editorial enthusiasm. The *Press* had probably assigned Crane to write about the forthcoming parade of Civil War veterans, but as he was anxious to quit the city for "the blessed quiet hills of Hartwood" he wrote the sketch weeks in advance of the actual parade. His tribute to the wrinkled men in blue reads like an after-dinner speech at a banquet preceding tomorrow's parade. It limps along from platitudes to sentimentalisms. "Do not forget our heroes, our well-doers, until they have marched to where no little cheers of men can reach them. Remember them now, and if the men of the future forget, the sin is with them." These Civil War veterans are disappearing, and now they are on their last great march—"a march that ceases to be seen at the horizon and whose end is death." The characteristic irony of *The Red Badge of Courage* and "A Mystery of Heroism" is missing in Crane's patriotic tribute to these aged Civil War veterans. Indeed, no one would guess that he wrote the Decoration Day invocation, but extant is his manuscript to prove it.[17]

# VII

# ↩ *"Sunny Blue" Summer*

C. K. LINSON, who moved to a studio up at 112 West 40th Street, had been looking all over the city for Crane and couldn't find him because he, too, had moved—to the West 33rd Street flat. Then in late May, 1894, Linson reached him at William Crane's house on East Main Street in Port Jervis. Stephen was sitting on the porch exchanging jibes with Linson's cousin Louis Senger, who lived a block away. "Here he is!" Crane shouted at the sight of C. K. "Yes, I'm here," said Linson, not too happily, as he told Crane that McClure wanted him back in New York City. With a bang Steve's chair hit the floor. "The hell he does! What's up?" C. K. explained that McClure wanted Stephen to do a study of the coal mines at Scranton, Pennsylvania, for the August issue of *McClure's Magazine,* with Linson doing the illustrations.

For his link with S. S. McClure, who had a genius for getting the best writers "to put his ideas (or theirs) on paper," Crane was indebted to Hamlin Garland, as we have seen. Garland had written a muckraking exposé of the Andrew Carnegie steel mills with their tenement houses at Homestead, Pennsylvania. "The town was as squalid and unlovely as could well be imagined," wrote Garland, "and the people were mainly of the discouraged and sullen type to be found everywhere where labor passes into the brutalizing stage of severity. . . . Such towns are sown thickly over the hill-lands of Pennsylvania, but this was my first descent into one of them. They are American only in the sense in which they represent the American idea of business." Garland's "Homestead and Its Perilous Trades," appearing in *McClure's Magazine* in June, 1894, and Crane's "In the Depths of a Coal Mine," in August, share the same resentment against the American idea of business as represented by Carnegie's exploitation of the working class in his steel mills, and by the mine owners' exploiting of the Scranton coal miners. In Crane's sketch the coal-breaking machines are the black emblems of greed of the gods of "cruel and insensate" labor.

The gods paid a slate picker fifty-five cents per day, a miner three dollars, and his helper loading the coal cars not quite one-half that sum.

The slate pickers were boys still at the spanking period, and their hope was to become, first, door boys and then mule boys and finally real miners. They end with the " 'miner's asthma.' They are very ambitious." These urchins live in an infernal din with machinery thundering and dust clouds fouling the air, and yet they swagger.

An elevator drops Crane and Linson with extraordinary swiftness "straight into the earth. It was a plunge, a fall. The flames of the little lamps fluttered and flew and struggled like tied birds to release themselves from the wicks. 'Hang on,' bawled our guide above the tumult. The dead black walls slide swiftly by. They were a swirling dark chaos on which the mind tried vainly to locate some coherent thing, some intelligible spot." With a crash and jar the platform stops, and they enter "an inscrutable darkness, a soundless place of tangible loneliness. Into the nostrils came a subtly strong odor of powder-smoke, oil, wet earth. The alarmed lungs began to lengthen their respirations." Little points of coal shine like diamonds, and two sable-faced men crouch in a passage where the roof almost meets the floor, their eyeballs and teeth shining like bleached stones. The lamps in their hats tremble above these two grinning skulls in the shadows. Then in another tunnel Crane, Linson and their guide come upon a group of lounging miners who "upreared to gaze at us; it resembled a resurrection. They slowly uprose with ghoul-like movements, mysterious figures robed in enormous shadows."

Linson sketches a mule, "Molly Maguire," while a group of miners clutch her by tail, head and legs lest she change her position. Then Linson and Crane are guided through tunnels, tangled passages with roofs so low they have to crawl, and in the lightless stables they encounter the mule "China," who has been buried four years in this dark hell by which no one profits but the greedy coal-brokers. "Four times had the earth been ablaze with the decorations of brilliant autumns. But 'China' and his friends had remained in these dungeons from which daylight, if one could get a view up a shaft, would appear a tiny circle, a silver star aglow in a sable sky.

"Usually when brought to the surface, the mules tremble at the earth radiant in the sunshine. Later, they go almost mad with fantastic joy. The full splendor of the heavens, the grass, the trees, the breezes, breaks upon them suddenly. They caper and career with extravagant mulish glee. A miner told me of a mule that had spent some delirious months upon the surface after years of labor in the mines. Finally the time came when he was taken back. But the memory of a black existence was upon him; he knew that gaping mouth that threatened to swallow him. No cudgellings could induce him. The men held conventions and discussed plans to budge that mule. The celebrated quality of obstinacy in him won him liberty to gambol clumsily about the surface."

The mule in his obstinacy seemed to Crane wiser than the duped miners and also himself: "To those who have known the sunlight there may come the fragrant dream of a lost paradise. . . . Perhaps they despair and thirst for this bloomland that lies in an unknown direction and at impossible distances." Here again is Crane's insistent theme of joy at a distance. It is at a distance because man is in "the implacable grasp of nature. It has only to tighten slightly, and he is crushed like a bug." These thoughts have been prepared for by the opening passage of the sketch with its contrast between the sky stretching "incredibly far away from the sombre land," the mined hillsides and valleys where the coal-breakers squat "like enormous preying monsters, eating of the sunshine, the grass, the green leaves."

When Crane saw his coal mine sketch in print, he grunted in disgust because McClure had tampered with it: "The birds didn't want the truth after all. Why the hell did they send me up there then? So they want the public to think the coal-mines gilded ball-rooms with the miners eating ice-cream in boiled shirt-fronts?" McClure thought Crane's sketch too caustic of Big Business and expunged a passage excoriating coal-brokers, the men who make the profits by fiddling with the markets. Some of these gentlemen had recently visited the mine, and Crane in the passage that never saw print wrote: "I confess to a dark and sinful glee at the description of their pangs; a delight at for once finding coal-brokers associated in hardship and danger with the coal-miner. It seemed to me a partial and obscure vengeance. And yet this is not to say that they were not all completely virtuous and immaculate coal-brokers! If all men who stand uselessly and for their own extraordinary profit between the miner and the consumer were annually doomed to a certain period of danger and darkness in the mines, they might at last comprehend the misery and bitterness of men who toil for existence at these hopelessly grim tasks."[1]

Stephen wrote his sketch on the balcony of the Valley House, a Scranton hotel, and completed it at the house of artist John Raught in nearby Dunmore, after inspecting the mines there at Oxford. The foreman of the Dunmore mine, James Young, had arranged his inspection tour of Mine Number Five one May evening, and then Crane had his sketch in his head and Linson his drawings to illustrate "In the Depths of a Coal Mine."

Linson had lent Crane fifty dollars to get to Scranton as McClure's Syndicate paid no advance, but the money was never repaid. "Stephen never hesitated to borrow, but likewise this generosity never hesitated to meet another's need when the means were his"; Linson thought the debt was vicariously paid when Stephen gave fifty dollars to an ailing soldier to get him home from Florida in 1898 during the training-camp period of the war against Cuba. Generous-hearted Linson remembered Crane's sketch of the mines seven decades later as a painting—"a great canvas of a dramatic solemnity"—portraying the very genius of the Scranton coal region and life there. The painter John Raught, who shared Linson's studio, painted the same scene; but no one has pictured it better than Steve, said Linson.

While at Scranton they visited Stephen's Uncle Luther, a classical scholar and one of the three doctors of divinity linked with the Crane family. The old gentleman was interested in butterflies and queried Linson: " 'Ah, indeed! A painter? Yes? You know, butterflies are most colorful— I have studied them long—beautiful little creatures. But I have never been successful with their coloring—indescribable! And you are an artist? Can you paint butterflies, do you think?' Stephen gleefully nudged me behind while I shifted as best I could. 'Of course he can paint butterflies, sir. Can't you, C. K.? It would be quite a change from coal mines!' "

From Scranton they returned to Port Jervis, much to the delight of Stephen's nieces, his brother William's five daughters and Edmund's three. Stephen liked to make a game of chasing them; they were a band of law-breakers and he a "red-headed policeman." The neighbors thought it scandalous for a man in his twenties to disport himself thus and Stephen couldn't have cared less; his frolics with his nieces bore fruit later in his *Whilomville Stories*.

"A kid, when he wants to do a thing, is like an Indian after a scalp," he told Linson, "he fights and makes no excuse. If he gets into a scrap and gets a bloody nose, that's glory—until he gets home. Then he is up against Opinion, a Code of Ethics, a Mother. But his dad is satisfied if he licks the other boy. He may be forced into lace collars and curls, but he doesn't know a fried bean from a turnip about Ethics. If they were smashable he'd get a hammer. They are for grown-ups, anyway. What a kid wants to do he just does, and that's all there is to it. If we think of conduct all the time we are not sincere. We assume an intellectual attitude and use evasions and we call that good manners. Rank dishonesty: this goes through all one's work. If that is not sincere, it has no value as art. To know the truth and sidestep it by mental smartness is sheer hypocrisy. Better be sincerely mistaken. In matters of art, we are only responsible for what we see, eh, C. K.?"

Around the Port Jervis bandstand boys of fourteen watched the girls go by in two's and three's or hurled themselves at the girls walking arm in arm; then a boy and a girl would separate from their group and continue around the square together. These girls—William's daughters, and their neighborhood friends, and sometimes Edmund's daughters, visiting Port Jervis from nearby Hartwood—were an active and "healthy band of savages, keen as briars," says William's daughter Edna in her memoirs: "My Uncle, Stephen Crane, as I Knew Him."

But her uncle did not spend all his mornings chasing his nieces and locking them in the closet under the stairs. He sometimes donned white flannel trousers, a mark of sartorial elegance, played tennis and returned with trousers grass-stained, and the nieces were jealous of the vague young ladies "who kept our playmate from us." Or else he sat on William's front porch in a large wicker chair, almost screened from sight by a syringa bush, and wrote. Their mother gave the girls strict injunctions not to bother him, but Edna once sneaked by the bow window and said: "Ah, Uncle Stevie, come on and play." He told her to go away as he was busy. He never spoke that way except when he had on his white pants or when he was writing.

Young ladies played croquet on the front lawn and then the nieces retired to the porch to make lemonade for their beloved uncle lest he forget their existence. ' 'Uncle Stevie, here is some lemonade we made you.' 'Thanks,' he would say, tossing off the innocuous beverage. 'How was it?' I would ask hopefully, for we worked hard making it and thought it delicious. 'Out of sight,' he always answered, and I left perfectly satisfied. The rest of the children would be waiting for me around the corner of the house. 'How did he like it?' 'He said it was out of sight.' " Sometimes Stephen obliged his nieces by eating the bread they baked for him, and their mother would remark: " 'Stephen, how can you?' And he made answer, 'Why, I wouldn't hurt their feelings for the world.' Is it any wonder we loved him and haunted his footsteps?" Crane's nieces would have remembered their uncle well even if he had never become famous because they never had a more charming playmate. When Edna was told in 1895 that Uncle Stevie had written a book that was making him famous she laughed: "Uncle Stevie famous? It was a joke."

Life was "sunny blue" for Crane this summer, except for one unpleasant incident. A Port Jervis gossip accused him of corrupting a child of thirteen he had taken for a buggy ride, and Stephen in revenge pilloried this poor dried bean of a woman over and over again—where she fitted his fiction and where she didn't—in *The Third Violet,* even in *The O'Ruddy,* and as Martha Goodwin in "The Monster."

In late December, 1894, he wrote someone about this "feminine mule up here who has roused all the bloodthirst in me and I don't know when it will end. That damned woman grunted: 'You was drivin' Frances out yesterday.' " So, then, all the neighbors knew that Frances and Stephen Crane "should be hanged on twin gallows for red sins. No man is strong enough to attack this mummy because she is a nice woman." She criticized the new hat of William Crane's wife, Cornelia, because it had blue flowers on one side and a ribbon on the other, and so "we rustle in terror because this maggot goes to and fro grunting about. If this woman lived in Hester Street [on New York's East Side] some son or brother of a hat would go bulging up to her and say, 'Ah ,wot deh hell!' and she would have no teeth any more, right there. She is just like those hunks of women who squat on porches of hotels in summer and wherever their eye lights their blood rises." The big joke was that she accepted ruin at the hands of a farmer; she was "just the grave of a stale lust and every boy in town knows it." Her views of things belonged on the tablets of Moses. "No, by the legs of Jehovah! I will not insult any dog by comparing this damned woman to it." No man had power to contradict this maggot, but then "we are all cowards anyhow."

Linson, at Crane's invitation, rejoined him in August at Twin Lakes (back of Milford, Pennsylvania) to camp for a couple of weeks with a group of friends. He had returned to New York City to deliver some drawings, and S. S. McClure had asked him whether he'd like to go down in seadiver's rig with Stephen Crane. " 'I'll go to the North Pole with Steve if you send us, Mr. McClure,' I answered. With his quick smile he flashed back, 'Maybe we'll do that too!' " But neither of those ventures came off. Linson joined the campers at Twin Lakes instead. The place was called Camp Interlaken because it was on a narrow neck of land separating Twin Lakes. The campers were fine young men and women from Port Jervis and Middletown, and they were chaperoned by the wife of a Middletown doctor, Charles Lawrence, whose son Frederick had been Stephen's friend at Syracuse and whose room Stephen had shared at the Pendennis Club. As the Lawrence home was a center of young life in Port Jervis, Crane often stayed there instead of at his brothers' houses. He had known the nearby forests and streams since the early 1880's, had written about them a decade later in his sketches of Sullivan County, and in the autumn of 1895 he used the summer-resort life which flourished near Hartwood, perhaps at the little village of Rio in Sullivan County, in writing his novel *The Third Violet.*

The campers at Twin Lakes, then known as Brink Pond, were Crane and C. K. Linson, his cousin Louis Senger, and "Wicked Wickham" Young, a cousin of Crane's Claverack College classmate Harvey Wickham—and of course some girls. Stephen and Louis Senger wrote, edited and put into print through the *Gazette* newspaper printers of Port Jervis a mock newspaper called "The Pike County Puzzle." They edited it one hilarious night at Senger's Port Jervis home.[2] It is dated August 28, 1894, and its four pages report camp events in true reportorial style with clever hits at the campers in articles in mock telegraphic news style, in advertisements, in reviews of "concerts," etc. "Snakes Massacred. / Bradner Woods, Penn., August 28. L. C. Senger, Jr. and Stephen Crane when passing through this city late this afternoon killed a rattlesnake measuring over 93 ft. and with 362 rattles." Subscription rates for this Pike County "newspaper" were $9,000,000, but rattlesnakes or blue stones would be taken in exchange. "As Stephen Crane was traversing the little rope ladder that ascends the right hand side of the cloud-capped pinnacle of his thoughts, he fell and was grievously injured." In the inquiry column he asks the question: What can I do with my voice? He is answered thus: "In the Spring, Stephen, you can plough with it, but after corn ripens you will have to seek employment in the blue stone works. We have seen voices like yours used effectively as cider presses." "Fresh Details / New Facts Concerning the Late Terrible Riot in the Third Tent" reports that this dreadful affair of bloodshed "was caused by a dinnerhorn in the careless hands of Mr. S. Energetic Brinson of Port Jervis, N. Y. He has been arrested and is now suffering great agony with his feet tied together while jig-music is pumped automatically into his ears." S. Energetic Brinson and his sister Charlotte were Negro servants waiting on the twenty-five campers, who also shared in the camp work.

One morning Stephen was found stretched out on the ground near the embers of the campfire with his head in a wooden box, just in case of rain, and he was roused by a party of two from the nearby Wells camp who feared he might be trampled by some passing horse and wagon. He laughed and said he enjoyed sleeping outside the tents; he always heard horses on the stony road in ample time to roll out of danger, he said. He had simply passed out at the campfire after sipping one or another of the three quarts of "milk" Senger had brought back to camp.

Linson recalls that Steve was happy "as a colt let loose in pasture. The freedom of the woods and the youthful horseplay of the land and water sports were good medicine. Three times daily we fed at a long table, standing like the animals we were. In the orange light of a great campfire we gathered of evenings and perched on low branches and logs, Stephen with his back to a tree picking at a guitar. The campers jested at Crane's light tenor voice and also at his hair. No, S. C., don't make an asparagus bed in your hair; plant there poison-ivy and wild cucumbers."

Stephen killed a snake that summer. He had encountered what he thought was a snake during a previous camping excursion in Sullivan County with Frederic Lawrence and the Senger boys, Louis and Walter. He had reached through the cracks of the floor of their cabin to retrieve a mirror when suddenly he uttered a horrifying yell: "A snake bit me on the hand!" They laid him on a cot, cauterized his wound with a hot poker, and plied him with the cure-all for snakebite: whiskey. "It was of no avail. The patient was failing rapidly, as in faltering tones he gave them the last messages to his family. His friends stood around him gloomily; then one spoke up. 'Well, as we can't do anything more for poor old——, I, for one, want a wack at that snake.' 'Me, too!' chorused the others, their pale faces flushing with resolution. Arming themselves with suitable weapons, they lowered a lantern under the cabin and all gazed intently down the opening, clutching their weapons. Then one gave a yell. B'Gosh, it's a setting hen!' The others gave a look and then began to laugh hysterically. The pallid youth upon the couch, who had been giving a noble exhibition of how a brave man can die, suddenly became very drunk."

Crane recounted this tale and many others to Cornelia, brother William's wife, on the porch of his brother's Port Jervis house of a summer evening or at the sitting-room stove in the winter. Sometimes he told tales he had heard, sometimes it was tales he had invented, and sometimes it was tales recounting his own experiences. "My mother had as much faith in his literary ability as did my father and was always glad to see him in spite of the fact that he used to smoke in bed and burn holes in her sheets," says Edna Crane. Both Cornelia and Mrs. Edmund Crane of Hartwood were very fond of Stephen. As for his verse, however, Cornelia said: "Stephen, I can't make head nor tail of it." And Stephen replied: "Never mind, Cornelia. You're in lots of good company!"

(Cornelia said she never heard Stephen swear or use much slang in her house, but he remembered how he "used to sit around on her doorstep and think of swear words" for a dictionary of profanity.)

Crane feared snakes and expressed his terror of them in "The Snake," a Sullivan County sketch published in *Pocket Magazine* for August, 1896. The young man in this sketch has a dog named Rover, which was Stephen's Chesapeake Bay retriever Solomon. They encounter unexpectedly a shrill-whistling rattle—a snake had crossed their path. "The man and the snake confronted each other. In the man's eyes were hatred and fear. In the snake's eyes were hatred and fear. These enemies manoeuvered, each preparing to kill. It was to be a battle without mercy. In the man was all the wild strength of the terrors of his ancestors, of his race, of his kind. A deadly repulsion had been handed from man to man through long dim centuries. This was another detail of a war that had begun evidently when first there were men and snakes." Nature, in making a snake, reached her supreme point in the formation of devices, hideous and horrible, "so that priests who really paint hell well fill it with snakes instead of fire. These curving forms, these scintillant colourings create at once, upon sight, more relentless animosities than do shake barbaric tribes. To be born a snake is to be thrust into a place a-swarm with formidable foes." The snake's foe in this instance is the man making a preliminary feint with a stick and then striking the snake with it again and again until its last muscular quivers cause the rattles to sound their treble cry, "the shrill, ringing war chant and hymn of the grave of the thing that faces foes at once countless, implacable, and superior. 'Well, Rover,' said the man, turning to the dog with a grin of victory, 'we'll carry Mr. Snake home to show the girls.' "

The same year—1894—that Crane cast *The Red Badge* into final manuscript, and began in May[3] and completed by November his second Bowery novel, *George's Mother,* and composed "lines" early in the year and again in May and September, he was also writing his New York City sketches. "Some of my best work is contained in short things which I have written for various publications, principally the New York *Press* in 1893 or thereabouts" (actually 1894). "That should be your first care," he wrote William in late 1896, having in mind to get them collected into a book.[4]

Thirteen of these sketches were published in the *Press* in 1894, and began to appear in the summer while he was vacationing in Hartwood and camping at Twin Lakes.

New York City was Crane's inspiration, said Howells, and away from it he was not at home with any theme or any sort of character. His essential inspiration was the city of suffering and baffled and beaten life, of inarticulate or blasphemous life. "It was the pity of his fate that he must quit New York, first as a theme, and then as a habitat; for he rested nowhere else, and wrought with nothing else as with the lurid depths which he gave proof of knowing better than any one else." Crane in claiming that his New York City writings were amongst his best things thus echoed Howells' appraisal. The Edinburgh *Scotsman* did Howells one better by declaring that Crane's New York City sketches have extraordinary realistic power "with bits of dramatic dialogue as boldly true to life and nature as ever Shakespeare wrote."

In one of these—"Mr. Binks' Day Off"—a clerk trapped in the city longs to escape to the countryside. He sees the park at Madison Square, which was then "a radiant green. The grass, the leaves, had come swiftly, silently, as if a green light from the sky had shone suddenly upon the little desolate hued place." Nature calls to him, and Binks began to dream. When he sits down to dinner in his Harlem flat with an air of profound dejection, Mrs. Binks construes it as an insult to her cooking. They stare at each other as hostile as warring redskins. In her glance was "a jeer at the failures of his life. And Binks, filled with an inexpressible rebellion at what was to him a lack of womanly perception and sympathy in her, replied with a look that called his wife a drag, an uncomprehending thing of vain ambitions, the weight of his existence." He wants to get away into the country for a while, and when he comes home the next Saturday from the bank "his hat was far back on the back of his head from the speed he was in"—to get to New Jersey.

The Binkses—husband, wife and three children—get off the railroad at the little rural station and feel like a circus entering the village when confronted by the stares of citizens lounging on the porch of a battered grocery store. Two rows of austere and solemn trees line the street—"It was like parading between the plumes on an immense hearse. These trees, lowly sighing in a breath-like wind, oppressed one with a sense of melancholy and dreariness. Back from the road, behind flower beds, controlled by box-wood borders, the houses were asleep in the drowsy air. Between them one could get views of the fields lying in a splendor of gold and green. A monotonous humming song of insects came from the regions of sunshine, and from some hidden barnyard a hen suddenly burst forth in a sustained cackle of alarm." But "the tranquility of the scene contained a peace and virtue that was incredibly monotonous to the warriors from the metropolis. The sense of a city is battle." They had always thought of "the clash of the swords of commerce, as sin, crime." Now they "began to imagine something admirable in it. It was high wisdom. They put aside their favorite expressions: 'The curse of gold,' 'A mad passion to get rich,' 'The rush for the spoils.' In the light of their contempt for this stillness, the conflicts of the city were exalted." At the same time the Binkses are moved by nature's "song of the universal religion, the mighty and mystic hymn of nature, whose melody is in each landscape."

Crane as artist always recognizes both sides of the coin. Amidst nature and her song of universal religion the Binkses are brought to sudden meekness. "When a man hears it he usually remains silent. He understands then the sacrilege of speech." They think back upon their courtship days as they watch from the edge of a cliff the setting sun tumbling and heaving into crags, peaks and canyons, amidst "corn colored clouds" and purple hills standing "in motionless array. The valley lay wreathed in somber shadows. Slowly there went on the mystic process of the closing of the day. The corn colored clouds faded to yellow and finally to a faint luminous green, inexpressibly vague. The rim of the hills was then an edge of crimson. The mountains became a profound blue." As the green tints became blue, a faint yellow replaced the crimson. The sun was dead. The sigh arising from the pines in the still air "was filled with an infinite sorrow—a sorrow for birth, slavery, death. It was a wail telling the griefs, the pains of all ages. It was the symbol of agonies. It celebrated all suffering. Each man finds in this sound the expression of his own grief. It is the universal voice raised in lamentation."

The Broadway cable cars, yellow monsters prowling up and down in a "mystic search," provide a ride full of exciting action, wrote Crane in a later sketch—"In the Broadway Cars" (1894–1895). They head for the Battery with their janitors and porters who carry "the keys to set alive the great down-town. Later, they shower clerks. Later, they shower more clerks. And the thermometer which is attached to a conductor's temper is steadily rising, rising, and the blissful time arrives when everybody hangs to a strap and stands on his neighbor's toes. Ten o'clock comes, and the Broadway cars, as well as elevated cars, horse-cars, and ferry-boats innumerable, heave sighs of relief."

The conductor's pulse rises because he has come to the crisis in his day's agony, for now he is overwhelmed by feminine shoppers asking him to change a two-dollar bill. The car sweeps on its diagonal path through the Tenderloin (Tenth Avenue, from 43rd to 50th Streets), passes Madison Square, "and enters the gorge made by the towering walls of great shops. It sweeps around the double curve at Union Square and Fourteenth Street, and a life insurance agent falls in a fit as the car dashes over the crossing, narrowly missing three old ladies, two old gentlemen, a newly-married couple, a sandwich man, a newsboy, and a dog. At Grace Church the conductor has an altercation with a brave and reckless passenger who beards him in his own car, and at Canal Street he takes dire vengeance by tumbling a drunken man on to the pavement.

"Towards evening, when the tides of travel set northward, it is curious to see how the gripman and conductor reverse their tempers. Their dispositions flop over like patent signals. During the down-trip they had in mind always the advantages of being at Battery Park [at the bottom tip of Manhattan]. A perpetual picture of the blessings of Battery Park was before them, and every delay made them fume—made this picture all the more alluring. Now the delights of up-town appear to them. They have reversed the signs on their cars; they have reversed their aspirations. Battery Park has been gained and forgotten. There is a new goal."

Suppose you are in a cable car, clutching a strap overhead, and at your shoulder is a little dude in a very wide straw sailor hat with a red band. "If you were in your senses, you would recognize this flaming band as an omen of blood. But you are not in your senses; you are in a Broadway cable car. You are not supposed to have any senses. From the forward end you hear the gripman uttering shrill whoops and running over citizens. Suddenly the car comes to a curve. Making a swift running start, it turns three handsprings, throws a cart wheel for luck, bounds into the air, hurls six passengers over the nearest building, and comes down a-straddle of the track. That is the way in which we turn curves in New York. Meanwhile, during the car's gamboling, the corrugated rim of the dude's hat has swept naturally across your neck and has left nothing for your head to do but to quit your shoulders. As the car roars, your head falls into the waiting arms of the proper authorities. The dude is dead; everything is dead. The interior of the car resembles the scene of the battle of Wounded Knee, but this gives you small satisfaction. "

After the theater-goers depart, drunkards "emerge from the darker regions of Sixth Avenue and swing their arms solemnly at the gripman. If the Broadway cars run for the next 7000 years, this will be the only time when one New Yorker will address another in public without an excuse sent direct from heaven. The drunkard, trying to engage the passengers in conversation, tells everyone about the fun he has had. They listen, but they do not reply. He wrangles with the conductor "with an *abandon,* a ferocity, and a courage that do not come to us when we are sober."

It is a great ride, and "inexperienced persons who have been merely chased by Indians know little of the dramatic quality which life may hold for them. These jungles of men and vehicles, these canyons of streets, these lofty mountains of iron and cut stone—a ride through them affords plenty of excitement. And no lone panther's howl is more serious in intention than the howl of the truck driver when the cable car bumps one of his rear wheels."

In 'A Lovely Jag in a Crowded Car" (*Press*: January 6, 1895) a drunk boards a crosstown trolley and orders the conductor to serve nine Manhattan cocktails and a beer, and the conductor, who had aided this "wild, red demon of drunk and destruction" to board the car, says: "Say, lookahere, now, you've got t' quit this thing. Just close your face or I'll throw yeh out in th' street." The atmosphere of the car had been as decorous as a frigid drawing room until this drunk of benign amiability intruded, the women sitting in austere silence and regarding each other in furtive glances while "preserving their respectability with fierce vigilance." Once the trolley reaches the shopping district these women, whose faces had expressed dismay and disgust at the drunken man, make their exit and leave behind them only the jovial celebrator who "rejoiced that the world was to him one vast landscape of pure rose color. The humming of the wheels and the clatter of the horses' hoofs did not drown the sound of this high quavering voice that sang of the pearl-hued joys of life as seen through a pair of strange, oblique, temporary spectacles."

Toward the end of the Coney Island season Crane visited the acres of merry-go-rounds there and in his sketch—"Coney Island's Failing Days" (*Press:* October 14, 1894)—he interviews a stranger who would seem to be Crane himself speaking. Coney Island's merry-go-rounds are nothing but enlarged toys; but humanity needs to be provided with such toys because humanity needs to forget its misery. " 'I rejoice in these whirligigs,' continued the stranger, eloquently, 'and as I watch here and there a person going around and around or up and down, or over and over, I say to myself that whirligigs must be made in heaven.' "

In "The Silver Pageant," which Crane undoubtedly wrote at this time, he jests at C. K. Linson in the character of artist Gaunt. Gaunt has been to Europe, but once he returns "somebody told him that he must make his living." Like Linson, Gaunt cannot forget Paris—that silver pageant across the sea. Gaunt "never saw anything excepting that which transpired across a mystic wide sea. The shadow of his thoughts was in his eyes, a little grey mist, and, when what you said to him had passed out of your mind, he asked: 'Wha-a-at?' It was understood that Gaunt was very good to tolerate the presence of the universe, which was noisy and interested in itself." Younger artists declared that he "would one day be a great artist if he would move faster than a pyramid."

Crane depicts himself as Great Grief stretched out smoking on the bed, while Wrinkles and little Pennoyer work at their drawing boards tilted against the table, and then they go over to Gaunt's studio to criticize his drawings. Wrinkles has thought that Gaunt has "Pictures in his eyes," but he decides it is not so. Wrinkles is perhaps artist Emile Stangé; who visualized pictures out of Crane's impressionistic poems. Great Grief, Wrinkles and Pennoyer appear again in "Stories Told by an Artist" (*Press:* October 28, 1894). They reappear in the story of an artist and his model in *The Third Violet,* which Crane wrote a year later, and Pennoyer figures in that lost tale called "The Cat's March" which Cane wrote in Havana in late 1898.

In "Stories Told by an Artist" Crane is Warwickson (the wicked son at war with the world), but he is nicknamed Great Grief because he speaks in a dismal voice. Again the scene is the begrimed Art Students' League building of intricate corridors.

"Well, let's eat," says Great Grief. Corinson (Corwin Linson, who was wealthier than the others because he did crayon portraits at fifteen dollars per week) waits for the coffee Grief is boiling on the gas stove, which is balanced upon a chair, which in turn is balanced upon a trunk. While waiting for the water to boil for two eggs, Wrinkles plays serenades on a guitar. "When did you discover you couldn't draw?" Grief asks Corinson. " 'I haven't discovered it yet,' replied Corinson, with a serene air. 'I merely discovered that I would rather eat.' 'Oh!' said Grief. 'Hand me the eggs, Grief,' said Wrinkles. 'The water's boiling.' "

What is also boiling is Grief's temper. He is mad at Corinson for showing off his new overcoat that cost thirty dollars. "His egotism is so tranquil," says Grief of Corinson. Prosperous artist Corinson, although not invited to stay for supper of more eggs and bread, invites them to dine with him on Thanksgiving night. Pennoyer dances a ballet to Wrinkles' guitar serenade, but Grief disowns the invitation. "I hate that fellow," says Grief of Corinson, which is Crane's oblique way of saying that he loved Corwin Linson dearly. Crane shied from expressing personal sentiment, but he expressed it obversely—in his denial was his affirmation.

" 'Oh, fiddle,' said Wrinkles. 'You're an infernal crank. And, besides, where's your dinner coming from to-morrow night if you don't go? Tell me that.' " Pennoyer, on earning four dollars for six drawings, takes Grief and Wrinkles to a table d'hôte costing him $1.50. That left him $2.50, and he felt disheartened at the realization that his money was not going to last him forever. In fact he felt much worse than when he was penniless. As for Great Grief, when he received six dollars from comic weeklies "he dreamed of renting studios at $75 per month, and was likely to go out and buy five dollars' worth of second-hand curtains and plaster casts." Wrinkles, the older and wiser colleague, lectures Grief upon finances—but he listens not at all. Meanwhile, Crane and his artist colleagues in the old Needham building sustained themselves on rye bread and frankfurters and potato salad from Second Avenue, and it was as though these were the only foods available in the world.

In "When Man Falls a Crowd Gathers" (*Press:* December 2, 1894) an epileptic collapses on the street; we see his swaying form sliding limp to the sidewalk "as a body sinks in the sea." The crowd about him scarcely breathes. "They were contemplating a depth into which a human being had sunk, and the marvel of this mystery of life or death held them chained." The street leading to the night's East River ferries is crowded with laborers and shopkeepers, and they push savagely over the man's prone form. A policeman comes swiftly, "his helmet towering above the multitude of black derbys and shading that confident, self reliant police face. He charged the crowd as if he were a squadron of Irish lancers. The people fairly withered before this onslaught. He shouted: 'Come, make way there! Make way!' . . . . His was the rage of a placid cow, who wishes to lead a life of tranquility, but who is eternally beseieged by flies that hover in clouds. When he arrived at the center of the crowd he first demanded, threateningly: 'Well, what's th' matter here?' And then, when he saw that human bit of wreckage at the bottom of the sea of men, he said to it: 'Come, git up out a-that! Git out a-here!' Whereupon hands were raised in the crowd and a volley of decorated information was blazed at the officer. 'Ah, he's got a fit! Can't yeh see?' 'He's got a fit!' 'He's sick!' 'What yeh doin'? Leave 'm be.' "

Out of the golden haze made by lamps far up the street comes a black ambulance with red lights, its horses galloping. On the rear seat sits a young man as imperturbable "as if he were going to a picnic." The crowd feels disappointed when the ambulance removes the limp body of the fallen man. "It was as if they had been cheated. Their eyes expressed discontent at this curtain which had been rung down in the midst of the drama. And this impenetrable fabric, suddenly intervening between a suffering creature and their curiosity, seemed to appear to them as an injustice." It is the fallen man who has an army. The mob "with magnificent passions for abstract statistical information were questioning the boy. 'What's his name?' 'Where does he live?' " Their concern is not for the man himself, but Crane's sympathies are for the individual. Statistical information—"What's his name? Where does he live?"—seemed to him as a reporter irrelevant, and for not reporting such abstract data he was criticized by other reporters.[5]

In the *Press* of November 25, 1894, Crane reported on a Greenwich Village tenement fire: "When Every One Is Panic Stricken." In a side street west of Sixth Avenue, he wrote, a stranger was imparting to him "some grim midnight reflections" when they were startled by a woman's scream. The stranger dragged him excitedly down the dark street, and at Number 135 an old bakery in the basement of a four-story ancient structure was afire. (Crane did not give the name of the street or the name of the woman who had screamed.) They found the woman on the sidewalk fronting Number 135; she seemed dazed and was "fumbling mechanically with the buttons at the neck of her dress. Her features were lined in anguish; she seemed to be frantically searching her memory—her memory, that poor feeble contrivance that had deserted her at the first of the crisis, at the momentous time." A policeman grabbed her to prevent her reentering the burning structure after she rescued a little bamboo easel worth about thirty cents while leaving her baby in the flames. "The flames grew as if fanned by tempests, a sweeping inexorable appetite of a thing, shining with fierce, pitiless brilliancy, gleaming in the eyes of the crowd that were upturned to it in an ecstasy of awe, fear and, too, half barbaric admiration. They felt the human helplessness that comes when nature breaks forth in passion, overturning the obstacles, emerging at a leap from the position of a slave to that of a master, a giant. There became audible a humming noise, the buzzing of curious machinery. It was the voices of the demons of the flame.

"Then, from the direction of the avenue there suddenly came a tempestuous roar, a clattering, rolling rush and thunder, as from the headlong sweep of a battle of artillery. Wild and shrill, like a clangorous noise of war, arose the voice of a gong. . . . The roar grew and grew until it was as the sound of an army, charging. That policeman's hurried fingers sending the alarm from the box at the corner had aroused a tornado, a storm of horses, machinery, men. And now they were coming in clamor and riot of hoofs and wheels, while over all rang the piercing cry of the gong, tocsin-like, a noise of barbaric fights. It thrilled the blood, this thunder. The stranger jerked his shoulders nervously and kept up a swift muttering. 'Hear 'em come!' he said, breathlessly.

"Then in an instant a fire patrol wagon, as if apparitional, flashed into view at the corner. The lights of the avenue gleamed for an instant upon the red and brass of the wagon, the helmets of the crew and the glossy sides of the galloping horses. Then it swung into the dark street and thundered down upon its journey, with but a half-view of a driver making his reins to be steel ribbons over the backs of his horses, mad from the fervor of their business. The stranger's hand tightened convulsively upon my arm. His enthusiasm was like the ardor of one who looks upon the pageantry of battles. 'Ah, look at 'em! Look at 'em! Ain't that great?'"

Marshall called this sketch—subtitled "A Realistic Pen Picture of a Fire in a Tenement"—one of the best things Crane or any other man ever wrote. Howells spoke of it as a notable piece of realistic reporting; the hook-and-ladder truck of the Greenwich Village fire station Crane pictured was the only one in Manhattan with three white horses. (A photograph of this same fire engine appeared in *Collier's Weekly* in 1900.) He also describes the hosecart: "A hosecart swept around the corner and into the narrow lane, whose close walls made the reverberations like the crash of infantry volleys. There was shine of lanterns, of helmets, of rubber coats, of the bright, strong trappings of the horses. The driver had been confronted by a dreadful little problem in street cars and elevated railway pillars just as he was about to turn into the street, but there had been no pause, no hesitation. A clever dodge, a shrill grinding of the wheels in the street-car tracks, a miss of this and an escape of that by a beautifully narrow margin, and the hosecart went on its headlong way. When the gleam-white and gold of the cart stopped in the shadowy street it was but a moment before a stream of water, of a cold steel color, was plunging through a window into the yellow glare, into this house which was now a den of fire wolves, lashing, carousing, leaping, straining." Crane praises the beautiful might of the horses, and the drivers of the hook-and-ladder truck—"drivers in blood and fibre, charioteers incarnate."

It was all fiction. There was no fire, no hysterical mother, no baby, no brave policeman rescuing a child from a burning building.[6] Unlike *Tribune* editor Willis Fletcher Johnson, back in 1891, who knew that Crane's "Bugs at Onondaga" was pure fantasy, the New York *Press'* Ed Marshall never discovered he had been hoaxed.

Crane interviewed W. D. Howells sometime in October, 1894, for his New York *Times* article: "Howells Fears Realists Must Wait." "Have you observed a change in the literary pulse of the country within the last four months?" Crane asked. "Last winter, for instance, it seemed that realism was about to capture things, but then recently I have thought that I saw coming a sort of counter wave, a flood of the other—a reaction, in fact. Trivial, temporary, perhaps, but a reaction, certainly." Howells dropped his hand in a gesture of emphatic assent. "What you say is true. I have seen it coming. . . . I suppose we shall have to wait." However, they did not have to wait long; *The Red Badge of Courage* and *The Black Riders* were on the way.

By now it had been arranged that *The Black Riders* would be published by Copeland and Day of Boston, a youthful firm and one of the first American publishers to issue literary works in an attractive format. However, there were considerable problems. The publishers wanted the poet to write a few score more poems to fill in what they wanted expunged from the manuscript. Crane refused: "It is utterly impossible." He had already written Copeland and Day on September 4 in protest. "In the first place I should absolutely refuse to have my poems printed without many of those which you just as absolutely mark 'No.' It seems to me that you cut all the ethical sense out of the book. All the anarchy, perhaps. It is the anarchy which I particularly insist upon. From the poems which you keep you could produce what might be termed a 'nice little volume of verse by Stephen Crane,' but for me there would be no satisfaction. The ones which refer to God, I believe you condemn altogether. I am obliged to have them in when my book is printed." Copeland and Day replied on October 19 that they would publish Crane's book if he would permit the omission of seven poems and although he had objected to their expunging the poems which referred to God,[7] he finally consented.

Copeland and Day submitted to Crane several drawings explaining that one of these drawings would be "something illustrative, while the other would be symbolic in a wide sense. As to a title for the book, the one you suggest is acceptable if nothing better occurs to you. The omission of titles for separate poems is an idea we most heartily agree with." Crane proposed the title *The Black Riders,* although the manuscript when first submitted contained no such poem. He wrote it in Frederic Gordon's studio in the old Art Students' League, where he was then living: "Black riders came from the sea." Gordon designed the book, submitting an orchid design: "The orchid, with its strange habits, extraordinary forms and curious properties." That flower seemed to him the "most appropriate floral motive, an idea in which Mr. Crane concurred before he left New York." Gordon, who remembers Crane as "that brilliant young writer," was imitating Aubrey Beardsley with his orchids.[8] The *Bookman*'s reviewer, H. T. Peck, in May, 1895, called Stephen Crane the Aubrey Beardsley of poetry, no doubt influenced by the book's floral design.

Convinced that Crane was the unaccountable boy wonder and that America had produced in these poems another genius as singular as Edgar Allan Poe, Garland wanted to share his find with W. D. Howells. Good old Howells, who had introduced Crane to Emily Dickinson's poetry a year before, did not like Crane's "lines" because he did not understand them, but he read them with great interest and remarked: "They do not seem to relate directly to the work of any other writer. They seem to be the work of a singularly creative mind. Of course they reflect the author's reading and sympathies, but they are not imitations.[9] They are poems which couple tenderness and toughness in the same bed. Carve out a style, said James; "it is by style you are saved." This is what Crane did, not only in his poems but also in his Bowery novels. Linson later declared that the more he read Crane's poems "the less I can connect them with the personality of their author." However, they reflect Crane's religious heritage and are drawn from the very wellspring of his personality, his thoughts and dreams, and they are no less autobiographical than his fiction. "You say you are holy, / And that / Because I have not seen you sin. / Aye, but there are those / Who see you sin, my friend."

On December 10 Crane wrote his publishers that he was frightened by the idea of using old English type "since some of my recent encounters with it have made me think I was working out a puzzle." His publishers responded, and Crane on the 16th wrote that "The type, the page, the classic form of the sample suit me." (The poems were printed all in caps.) On the 22nd he wrote to ask how his book was coming along and said that he would not be able to get to Boston to meet Mr. Copeland and Mr. Day because he was about to go on a trip to the West for the Bacheller–Johnson Syndicate.[11] His letter from 33 East 22nd Street crossed their shipment of the proofsheets, which he corrected while spending the holidays with his brothers and their families.

He asked Copeland and Day whether they might print an announcement card about his forthcoming *Black Riders* to send to his friends: "I think it would benefit matters greatly," he wrote them on January 2. He sent some press notices of his works for quotation in advertisements, including a handwritten copy of the Philadelphia *Press* appraisal by his friend E. J. Edwards. He asked them specifically to quote Hamlin Garland's June, 1893, review of *Maggie* in the Boston *Arena,* and added, with some bravado, that most reviewers "call me a prominent youth." Copeland and Day complied by quoting Garland: "With such a technique already in command, with life mainly before him, Stephen Crane is to be henceforth reckoned with." He is a writer "who impresses the reader with a sense of almost unlimited resources." Although both Garland and Howells had admired Crane's "first love," *Maggie,* only Garland admired the poems too, and that is why Crane asked that *Black Riders* be dedicated "in just one line, no more, to Hamlin Garland." Years later Garland wrote on the dedication page: "I saw Crane set down some of these lines while sitting at my desk. Evidently they were composed subconsciously and (as he said) needed only to be drawn off [by] way of his pen's point."

Crane had neglected Garland all summer, but on November 15, 1894, he sent him a kind of progress report: "My dear friend. So much of my row with the world has to be silence and endurance that sometimes I wear the appearance of having forgotten my best friends, those to whom I am indebted for everything. As a matter of fact, I have just crawled out of the fifty-third ditch into which I have been cast and I now feel that I can write you a letter that won't make you ill . . . I have just completed a New York book that leaves *Maggie* at the post. It is my best thing. Since you are not here, I am going to see if Mr. Howells will read it. I am still working for the *Press.*" The new novel was *George's Mother.*

The Bacheller–Johnson Syndicate issued *The Red Badge of Courage* in early December, one month sooner than he had expected. It appeared in much shortened form (its 55,000 words reduced to 18,000) first in the Philadelphia *Press* for December 3–8 and then in a single issue of the New York *Press* for December 9, also in several hundred small city dailies and weekly papers across the country. Bacheller paid Crane ninety dollars.

"Who is this man Crane, anyhow?" someone asked James O. G. Duffy three days after the first chapters had appeared in the Philadelphia *Press.* "Well, if he keeps this up, we'll all know him in a few years." Literary editor Duffy seems to have forgotten that his *Press* had published an appraisal of Crane last April (by E. J. Edwards under the pen name "Holland"). Talcott Williams urged Irving Bacheller to bring the author to the (Philadelphia) *Press* offices, and so one afternoon in December, 1894, Irving and Stephen took the train to Philadelphia, and Stephen in his excitement sang Rudyard Kipling ballads. Bacheller remembers Crane reciting: "When you're wounded and left on Afghanistan's plains, / And the women come out to cut up what remains, / Jest roll to your rifle and blow out your brains / An' go to your Gawd like a soldier."

Bacheller and Crane presented themselves in Talcott Williams' sanctum.

"Word flew from cellar to roof that the great Stephen Crane was in the office. Editors, reporters, compositors, proofreaders crowded around him shaking his hand. It was a revelation of the commanding power of genius." Bacheller had been able to sell *The Red Badge* to the Philadelphia *Press* because Duffy's stock had run low on novels to fill daily installments of fiction (after the French fashion) and the demand had increased. The risk, however, was that the public had lost interest in Civil War fiction and the author was unknown.

His visit with the Philadelphia *Press* had a buoyant effect, and almost at once he took heart to approach Appleton and Company, one of the largest publishing houses in New York City. He left two short sketches with editor Ripley Hitchcock as examples of his New York *Press* writings. When Crane returned to learn his decision Hitchcock said: "Mr. Crane, I like your work very much. It has strength and originality; but these stories are too short for us. Haven't you got something we can make a book of?" Stephen answered hesitantly that he had a rather long thing which had just appeared in the Philadelphia *Press* and which "some of the boys around the office seemed to like." Hitchcock asked to see it, and Crane sent him on December 18 the *Press* clippings of the war novel with editorial comments by "Holland" and Talcott Williams:[10] "Dear Mr. Hitchcock: This is the war story in its syndicate form—that is to say, much smaller and to my mind worse than its original form."[11] On Sunday, December 9, the day his cut-down version appeared in the New York *Press* (pitilessly compressed into seven columns), Crane happened to meet Curtis Brown at the Potter building housing the *Press* on Park Row and Beekman Street. He was without an overcoat, "but his face—thin and white—lit up when he saw me. He threw his arms around me and said: 'Oh, *do* you think it was good?' Fortunately I could guess what he meant and said: 'It's great.' 'God bless you,' he said, and hurried on to anywhere in the sleet."

# VIII

## ❧ The West and Mexico

"ANY news of the war story will be grateful to me," Crane wrote Ripley Hitchcock from St. Louis on January 30, 1895. "If you had not read the story, I would wish you to hear the Philadelphia *Press* staff speak of it. When I was there some days ago [in December], I was amazed to hear the way in which they talked of it." Crane had already told Hitchcock of the ovation he had received from the Philadelphia *Press* staff, but he had yet to obtain a written contract from Appleton.[1] It finally reached him while he was in Lincoln, Nebraska. En route to the West, the South, and Mexico, he had taken train from St. Louis to Kansas City to Lincoln, where in early February he sauntered into the offices of the Nebraska *State Journal* in hope of finding a check from the Bacheller Syndicate.

As soon as he mentioned his name, Willa Cather knew who he was because she had proofread the *State Journal*'s syndicated version of *The Red Badge of Courage* in December. A junior at Nebraska State University, she was not impressed by Crane, the first author she had ever met. His shaggy hair hung low on his forehead and was unkempt and his face was gaunt and unshaven, and he was thin to the point of emaciation. Only her propensity for hero worship and her youthful enthusiasm could have made her see anything special in this somber young man whose triangular moustache gave him a certain resemblance to Edgar Allan Poe. "His gray clothes were much the worse for wear and fitted him so badly it seemed unlikely he had been measured for them. He wore a flannel shirt and a slovenly apology for a necktie, and his shoes were dusty and worn gray about the toes and were badly run over at the heel."

"I had seen many a tramp printer come up the *Journal* stairs to hunt a job," Willa Cather continues in her reminiscences of Crane, "but never one who presented such a disreputable appearance as this story-making man. He wore gloves which seemed rather a contradiction to the general slovenliness of his attire, but when he took them off to search his pockets for his credentials, I noticed that his hands were singularly fine: long, white, and delicately shaped, with thin, nervous fingers. I have seen pictures of Aubrey Beardsley's hands that recalled Crane's very vividly."

As she was just then fascinated by Maupassant, she tried to get Crane to express his opinion of "Le Bonheur," whereupon Crane, who knew some Maupassant in translation, said with a sarcastic grin: "Oh, you're moping, are you?" He continued to evade her questions, not taking seriously the young woman who was two years his junior. His talk was frivolous, absentminded; he seemed profoundly discouraged and moody. As he sat on the managing editor's desk with his soft felt hat low over his eyes, his shoulders drooping forward and his long fingers drumming on sheets of copy paper, he appeared to Willa Cather to be "as nervous as a race horse fretting to be on the track."

He was "like a man preparing for a sudden departure," she wrote years later. "Now that he is dead it occurs to me that all his life was a preparation for sudden departure. I remember once when he was writing a letter he stopped and asked me about the spelling of a word, saying carelessly, 'I haven't time to learn to spell.' Then, glancing down at his attire he added with an absentminded smile, 'I haven't time to dress either; it takes an awful slice out of a fellow's life.' " She sensed then that he was preoccupied and tense, with his burning eyes and self-centered air of desperate youth brooding upon some impending disaster. He slurred over less important things as if his time were short; spelling and grammar be damned. Let Miss Cather, a beginning journalist, correct his errors in *The Red Badge*. One of the *State Journal*'s reporters had savagely declared: "If I couldn't write better English than this, I'd quit."[2]

While waiting for his check to get him to Mexico, where he expected to get rid of his hacking cough, Crane lived from hand to mouth for several days. He borrowed money from the managing editor and ate in cheap restaurants on Tenth Street while living in the Hotel Lincoln. At the bar there on February 12 he tried to break up a fist-fight, and he later transposed this experience into the fight between the Swede and the hotel owner's son in "The Blue Hotel." Writing someone about that Lincoln hotel barroom fight in which he intruded between a tall man and the rather small fellow getting pounded, he declared that he had "offended a local custom" because "these men fought each other every night. Their friends expected it, and I was a darned nuisance with my Eastern scruples and all that. So first everybody cursed me fully and then they took me off to a judge who told me that I was an imbecile and let me go; it was very saddening. Whenever I try to do right, it don't." (Crane here echoes Huck Finn, whom he had first encountered the previous year.)

Willa Cather and Crane sat on the window ledge of the *State Journal* offices above the veranda of the Hotel Lincoln, where Negro waiters were serenading the guests, and listened to the twang of the banjos and the faint click-click of the telegraph sounder in the *Journal* office, where the drop-lights were dull under their green shades. White moonlight threw sharp blue shadows below them. They could hear the gurgle of the fountain in the Post Office square across the street on that oppressively warm February night when a dry wind—the curse of that country—was blowing up from Kansas. Crane recited some of his "lines" from *The Black Riders,* then in preparation for May, 1895, publication: "One man feared that he might find an assassin; / Another that he might find a victim. / One was more wise than the other." The poem has the same germinal situation as "The Blue Hotel."

Bitter about his double literary life as poet and journalist, he uttered tirades against journalism to apprentice journalist Cather: "What I can't do, I can't do at all, and I can't acquire it. I only hold one trump." That trump was his gift for rendering sense impressions much as a camera imprints images of reality. Almost all of his journalism is of that kind, from the vignettes of his New York City sketches and Mexican sketches to his war dispatches; the trend of present-day journalism is Crane's vignette style of impressionism. He was no police-court reporter, but when the correspondents gathered in Puerto Rico at the end of the Cuban War they voted him the best reporter covering the 1898 war against Spain. While denouncing journalism to Miss Cather he was carrying in his pocket a little volume of Poe.

In order to see more of him and trap him into conversation about literature and authors, Miss Cather cut her university classes. She began by asking him whether stories were constructed "by cabalistic formulae. At length he sighed wearily and shook his drooping shoulders, remarking: 'Where do you get all that rot? Yarns aren't done by mathematics. You can't do it by rule any more than you can dance by rule. You have to have the itch of the thing in your fingers, and if you haven't,—well, you're damned lucky, and you'll live long and prosper, that's all.'—And with that he yawned and went down the hall." Willa Cather never forgot what he told her about the need for details "to filter through my blood, and then it comes out like a native product, but it takes forever." Crane's imagination "pulled hard. After he got a notion for a story, months passed before he could get any sort of personal contact with it, or feel any potency to handle it."

The last night of his stopover in Lincoln, Miss Cather returned to the *State Journal* offices and found him wandering through the halls. She was going to write a notice of the play she had seen that night, and he was despondent and consequently more self-revelatory than usual. The night mail had not brought him the expected money from Irving Bacheller. He spoke slowly, monotonously, calmly, never raising his voice. "But I have never known so bitter a heart in any man as he revealed to me that night. It was an arraignment of the wages of life, an invocation to the ministers of hate." He confessed that he was bitterly despondent, and she was convinced that the young author "had a vague premonition of the shortness of his working day, and in the heart of the man there was that which said,

'That thou doest, do quickly.' " She suggested that in ten years he would probably laugh at his present bitterness, but Crane clenched his hands in strenuous tension and exclaimed: "I can't wait ten years, I haven't time."

What was it that had disillusioned the Proud Youth so early? And why did he pour out his soul thus to a stranger? "From the wise we hold back alike our folly and our wisdom," wrote Willa Cather, "and for the recipients of our deeper confidences we seldom select our equals. The soul has no message for the friends with whom we dine each week. It is silenced by custom and convention. . . . It selects its listeners willfully, and seemingly delights to waste its best upon the chance wayfarer who meets us in the highway at a fated hour."[3]

Crane had to appear in court Wednesday morning (February 13) after the barroom fight at the Hotel Lincoln, and then he headed west to interview farmers in Lincoln and Dawson counties, two hundred miles west of the capital city. He had taken notes in Lincoln on Governor Holcombe's optimistic doubletalk about the plight of Nebraskans who were suffering from the aftermath of the severe drought of the previous July, but he wanted to get his facts firsthand.

Out there it was wintry weather, quite a change from the warm nights he had experienced in Lincoln. While changing trains in Dawson County at some desolate junction town, he saw an unforgettable hotel that was painted a light blue, and this hotel became the setting for the Western short story he wrote in England in February, 1898: "The Blue Hotel." He reported the drought of July, 1894, as described by the farmers in Eddyville in Dawson County, amidst the February, 1895, snowstorm, in "Waiting for Spring." What the farmers were really waiting for was not spring but mercy shipments of food and coal. "The cry for aid was heard everywhere," said Crane in the *State Journal,* whose headline was mollified half-truth. Eastern newspapers, on the other hand, headlined the sketch with the grim titles of "A State's Hard Fight" (New York *Press*) and "Nebraskans' Bitter Fight for Life" (Philadelphia *Press*). During last summer's drought had come the scream of a wind as hot as an oven's fury and raging "like a pestilence. The leaves of the corn and of the trees turned yellow and sapless like leather. For a time they stood the blasts in the agony of a futile resistance. The farmers—helpless, with no weapon against this terrible and inscrutable wrath of nature—were spectators at the strangling of their hopes, their ambitions, all that they could look to from their labor. It was as if upon the massive altar of the earth, their homes and their families were being offered in sacrifice to the wrath of some blind and pitiless deity."

With a team of horses Crane and a driver covered some forty-five miles in a snowstorm that coated the horses with snow and ice. The horses became dull and stupid in the storm. Under the driver's flogging they barely stirred, holding their heads dejectedly, with an expression of patient weariness. The vehicle passed six men on the road. "They strode along silently with patches of ice upon their beards. The fields were, for the most part, swept bare of snow, and there appeared then the short stumps of the corn, where the hot winds of the summer had gnawed the stalks away." The farmers' hope was on next August's crop, and for money to buy seed when spring came. Otherwise they must journey to new lands, loading their families in wagons behind their hungry horses to conquer great distances. In their present crisis they depend "upon their endurance, their capacity to help each other, and their steadfast and unyielding courage." "I ain't had no aid!" said a Lincoln County farmer. "How did you get along?" Crane asked him. "Don't git along, stranger. Who the hell told you I did get along?"

Crane got back to Lincoln, took the Frisco Line to Kansas City, and then proceeded to New Orleans. From his boardinghouse there he wrote C. K. Linson on Tuesday, February 19 (having arrived on the 16th), "Je suis dans New Orleans. Cracked ice dans Nebraska, terra del fuego dans New Orleans. Table d'hôtes sur le balconies just like spring. A la mode whiskers on the citizens en masse, merci, of the vintage de 1712. . . . Sic semper tyrannis! . . . This boarding house est le terrible Français. I have learned to ask for vinegar at the table but otherwise I shall perhaps to Heaven go through starvation." Crane knew no more French than he exhibits in this jesting letter to Linson, who had lived in Paris, and perhaps for that reason he moved out of the French-speaking boardinghouse the next day to the Hotel Royal, where he wrote his sketch about the Nebraska drought. The Nebraska *State Journal* updated that sketch for February 22, by which time he had been in New Orleans for about six days. (Newspaper datelines are not reliable for dating where Crane was.)

In his letter to Linson he added: "Ce matin I write un article sur le railways due South which were all made in hell." His article about Southern trains got sidetracked, but years later he expressed his fascination with trains in after years in his study of a famous locomotive in "The Scotch Express." In "The Bride Comes to Yellow Sky," although Crane does not specify the train's speed, he creates the sense of it: a glance from the great Pullman's window "seemed simply to prove that the plains of Texas were pouring eastward."

"Mardi gras tres grand," he wrote Linson, "but it not does until next Tuesday begin"; it never has rained on Mardi Gras, and so it wouldn't rain this year, he said. Sunday, the 24th, was a springlike day: "decorations of purple and green and gold gently fluttered."[4] Tuesday brought out the gypsy hues of the maskers: boys arrayed in garments representing monkeys, gnomes, imps, parrots, etc. In the shine of electric lights "symbolistic initials appeared. The royal colors of green and purple and gold shone forth in bunting and silk and glass." Crane was in the stands reserved for

His Majesty, his queen and court. Beneath the stands were the maskers on the avenue where a streetcar "fought its irritatingly painful way through the throng." Adorned by a huge cossack beard, the king in royal robes lifted his sceptre and observed the crowd, while the ladies of his court chatted, their eyes shining. "With the vivid light upon this balcony the scene of violet and white had all the distinctiveness of a marvelous painting. The procession was delayed. Some of the court seemed petulant. If the king was bored, his weariness was hidden in his flowing beard," as he looked on his subjects, a waxen sea of faces amidst a purple haze.

High in the air on one of the vast confections in the parade of floats was the crown prince, gesturing and bowing amiably at the cheers, while girls leaned over balconies shouting: "Ah, there's Comus! There he is! Comus, Comus, look this way!" Crane found himself staring at the mask of the prince and thinking "not of the features, but of the emotion, and feeling exasperated at the baffling cover." While the glittering floats and shining and enormous emblems in wood-paper-and-cloth creaked slowly over the stoned street whose gutter contained two inches of water, ladies of temporary royalty in the balconies near the king and queen occasionally lifted a handkerchief and waved it. "A rocket went slantingly upward. There was some mild and good-natured jostling. A voice cried out: 'Ah, git off de cart an' give de grass a chanct t' grow.' A man with the shaven face and mobile lips of an actor immediately said: 'Great Scott! I know that breed! What's he doing away down here?' " The spectator was right out of the Bowery, and the man with the shaven face and the mobile lips of an actor was of course Crane himself.

The French Opera House on a narrow and gloomy street in the French quarter was the building possessing closest identification with New Orleans life. Its solemn gray-and-white pillars—leadened with age—appear suddenly among the low roofs on streets reminiscent of "the assassin-like gloom of some European cities," says Crane in "Grand Opera in New Orleans." (He knew nothing about the "assassin-like gloom" of European cities; he did not encounter Europe until 1897.) New Orleans opera was cheap at ten cents ($1.50 for the best seats). The cheap admittance fee "does not make a taste for grand opera to be thorns in the flesh of a small vendor of olives or matches. Perhaps these things adjust themselves. It may be that it is only when a public attains the cultivation of a New Orleans public that cheap opera can be given it. Perhaps it is necessary to charge a man the price of a schooner yacht in order to instruct him." In New Orleans—but not in New York City—opera was supported by the entire populace, and the stars of the opera were "the deities of the masses. Their adherents wrangle over their merits. There is a vast and elemental interest and enthusiasm." Soprano Madame Laville rendered her roles "with an impressive emotional sincerity." She sang, said Crane, "with a dramatic comprehension that is unusual."

In late February he quit New Orleans and took train to Hot Springs, Arkansas, to report in the New York *Press* the joys of invalidism at that picturesque winter resort, a sketch which the Philadelphia *Press* headlined as "The Merry Throng at Hot Springs" (March 3, 1895). An Indian legend attached to the Arkansas hot springs. Once when a terrible plague broke out among the Kanawagas, "they who had strode so proudly under the trees, crawled piteously on the pine-needles and called in beseeching voices toward the yellow sunset. After festivals, rites, avowals, sacrifices, the Spirit of the Wind heard the low clamor of his Indians and suddenly vapors began to emerge from the waters of what had been a cool mountain spring. The pool had turned hot. The wise men debated. At last, a courageous and inquisitive red man bathed. He liked it; others bathed. The scourge fled." Crane saw other connections: spring, supposedly the time when human emotion emerges from cynical darkness, is perpetual in Hot Springs, which displays its exuberance even in the dead of winter. "There is then proven that the human emotions are not at all guided by the calendar. It is merely a question of latitude. The other theory would confine a man to only one wild exuberant outbreak of feeling per year. It was invented in England."

Ripley Hitchcock had sent by express to New Orleans on February 25 the typescript of *The Red Badge of Courage* and Crane had returned it before making his excursion to Hot Springs. He wrote from the Hotel Tremont in Galveston, Texas, on March 9: "I am unable to see what to do with it unless the word 'Red' is cut out perhaps.—That would shorten it. . . . I made a great number of small corrections."[5]

While in Galveston he wrote "Galveston, Texas, 1895."[6] The town, he said, resembled not Texas but New England. "If a man comes to Galveston resolved to discover every curious thing possible, and to display every point where Galveston differed from other parts of the universe, he would have the usual difficulty in shutting his eyes to the similarities. Galveston is often original, full of distinctive characters. But it is not like a town in the moon." An illustration of Galveston streets could easily be obtained in Maine, and the Gulf of Mexico could be mistaken for the Atlantic Ocean. The city's two-storied frame houses reminded one of New England, except that the island of Galveston was as level as a floor. But the city, with its cosmopolitan character, did not represent Texas: here were men from everywhere. Cotton steamers, docks and sailors were a large element in the life of the city. Chuckling stevedores handled huge cotton bales amid a continual and foreign conversation, "the bales leaving little tufts of cotton all over their clothing." The city had some wealthy people, some typical Southern mansions with galleries, and some summer resorts. "In the heat of the season, life becomes sluggish in the streets. Men move about with an extraordinary caution as if they expected to be shot as they approached each corner." It was early March, however, and Crane, ignorant of Galveston summers, was drawing from what the natives there told him about the summers.

In "Apaché Crossing," an unpublished manuscript,[7] he spins a yarn which he probably heard from someone in San Antonio. The thriving town of "Blazer" is likely Wilcox, forty miles from Apache Pass, which is fifteen miles south of Bowie, Arizona. "Apaché Crossing" is probably Bowie, where in Crane's day there was the remains of old Fort Bowie, the scene of a great battle between the United States Army and the Apaches under Cochise.

Old man Miller in his Metropolitan Hotel at Apaché Crossing regards with cool dignity Spiteful Johnson and his card-table pals as he remarks: " 'Boys, I tell you what it is. We've got to hustle. Simerson Sumpkins was in from Blazer yesterday and afore he went, he up an' told me that Blazer's got more good men laid away in her cemetery than we've got in our hull blamed town. I hit up there,' and he pointed to a small round hole in the door a little higher up than a man's head." Spiteful Johnson observes that old Jim Miller couldn't hit a herd of six hosses at two rod. The inhabitants of Apaché Crossing are discouraged about their graveyard because it contains not more than twelve rotting shingles over no more than "twelve irregular and misshapen graves." Those rotting shingles speak eloquently of the affection the dead men inspired among the inhabitants of Apaché Crossing. Nevertheless, "the thriving town of Blazer, forty miles across the red, uneven plain, had a cemetery with thirty-three graves in it, a number of which contained some of the most noted fighters and desperados of Arizona. It also boasted a small marble shaft which had been transported to be erected over all that remained of old Jim Thompson, who had been buried with two revolvers and a wound in front as a good man should." In its competition with Blazer's graveyard Apaché Crossing has lost social status. Crane is of course spoofing the legends of the Wild West. He did the same, but more subtly, in his famous Western short stories "The Bride Comes to Yellow Sky" and "The Blue Hotel."

The legendary gun-toting Wild West provides the stage for his Texan tale "Twelve O'clock." Proprietor Placer is at his counter, which is painted a bright pink and surrounded by papier-mâché spittoons, when a cowboy enters to ask if a crowd of thirty can be grub-staked for dinner. "An' we want the best diner you kin raise an' scrape. Everything th' best. We don't care what it costs s'long as we git a good square meal." A cuckoo clock's doors fly open, and the wooden bird cries "Cuckoo!" Cowboy Jake wheels upon Placer and demands: "What in hell is that?" Placer reveals by his manner that he has been asked this question too many times. " 'It's a clock,' he answered shortly." Cowboy Jake brings over from the nearby saloon some men of his outfit who declare that this brown thing isn't a clock, for how could a wooden bird tell the time? Big Watson enters the saloon and quarrels with cowboy Jake; they glare murder while Placer with revolver in each hand aims at them from behind the pink counter. Cowboy Watson of Square-X outfit shoots him through the throat, cowboy Jake takes Watson, and another cowboy, about to gallop off from the saloon, slumps over his pony's neck and slides to the ground. The pony flees to the prairie. Inside the saloon the dead body of Placer is pitched over the dead body of Big Watson. "There was a curious grim silence, and then suddenly, in the death chamber, there sounded the loud whirring of the clock's works, little doors flew open, a tiny wooden bird appeared and cried 'Cuckoo'—twelve times."

The so-called Placer Hotel, the best within two hundred miles, was probably the Mahncke Hotel in San Antonio, where Crane was staying in mid-March, 1895. He later claimed that when he was twenty-three he wrote stories for English magazines, but he was boasting, for he wrote almost all of his Western stories during his English years and only five of them appeared in English magazines. He had written some Western tales before he went into the West, and while there he wrote the Civil War story "A Mystery of Heroism." The only Western tale he wrote in 1895 was the Mexican tale "One Dash—Horses!" and that was written in Philadelphia in September.[8] In Sussex at Brede Manor he wrote for the American magazine *Frank Leslie's Popular Monthly,* the Western tale "Moonlight on the Snow," a short sequel to his masterpiece "The Bride Comes to Yellow Sky." It is mainly for that reason that "Moonlight" has our interest.

To Warpost, in this tale, come Easterners, "both the sane and the insane with hope, with courage, with hoarded savings, humility and fear, with bland impudence. Most came with their own money; some came with money gained during a moment of inattention on the part of somebody in the East." The citizens decree that no man shall kill another man without being hanged for it, and Larpent—proprietor of the biggest gambling house in Warpost—kills a man who has accused him of cheating at a game. But there isn't a tree in Warpost to hang him on. Then into town come the famous marshal of Yellow Sky (now sheriff of the county) and a former desperado named Scratchy Wilson. Sheriff Jack Potter claims Tom Larpent his prisoner on a charge of grand larceny, and off to Yellow Sky the sheriff and Scratchy Wilson take Larpent, and thus save him. Scratchy Wilson, now reformed, aids the sheriff whom he tried to kill in "The Bride Comes to Yellow Sky."

The East impinges on the West in many of Crane's Western tales; he is juxtaposing two cultures, and while he is at it he is debunking both the tough Wild West and the Easterners' fixed idea about it. Crane himself could play the role of either the Easterner with Eastern scruples, as in "the Blue Hotel," or the Westerner with Western prejudices, like Sheriff Potter in "The Bride." In "London Impressions" (1897) he recalled a legend recited to him by the ex-Sheriff of "Tin Can," a town in Nevada. As he never got as far west as Nevada, he probably encountered this ex-sheriff or the tale of Tin Can, Nevada, in some barroom, possibly in San Antonio.

The tale is about the Western gun-fighter Cortright, who returns to Nevada with a top hat he has purchased in Chicago. To the Westerners that top hat symbolizes the sophisticated East, and that is why they shoot at it. Jim Cortright thereupon kills three Tin Can citizens and then a delegation requests him to bury the ill-fated top hat. Cortright refuses. When Spike Foster borrows the top hat, he gets killed for wearing it. Spike is in a supremely reckless mood, having drunk heavily at the Red Light saloon. "With the terrible gear hanging jauntily over his eye and his two guns drawn, he walked straight out into the middle of the square in front of the Palace Hotel, and drew the attention of all Tin Can by a blood-curdling imitation of the yowl of a mountain lion. This was when the long-suffering populace arose as one man. The top-hat had been flaunted once too often. When Spike Foster's friends came to carry him away they found nearly a hundred and fifty men shooting busily at a mark—and the mark was the hat."

That top hat, which seemed essential furniture to young Eastern dandies, was resented by the Westerner, but in fact it was the property of no select Eastern class. "It was the property of rogues, clerks, theatrical agents, damned seducers, poor men, nobles, and others. In fact, it was the universal rigging. It was the only hat; all other forms might as well be named ham, or chops, or oysters." It no longer was the mark of any class distinction, and Easterners wearing this headgear regarded it with indifference, a kind of ferocity of indifference. "Philosophy should always know that indifference is a militant thing. It batters down the walls of cities, and murders the women and children amid flames and the purloining of altar vessels. When it goes away it leaves smoking ruins, where lie citizens bayoneted through the throat. It is not a children's pastime like mere highway robbery." The threat of violence for Crane existed not only in the West but also in the East. (In *The Great Gatsby,* Scott Fitzgerald employs the same cross-identity of East and West.)

He spent mid-March in San Antonio, where he befriended a sixteen-year-old boy he found sobbing and penniless on the Alamo Plaza. He took the boy to a restaurant, fed him, and paid for his home-bound train fare. Young Edward Grover had run away from his Chicago home to become a cowboy. He had read Western magazines, like the Swede in "The Blue Hotel." The boy's uncle met him in St. Louis and wired Crane repayment of the railroad fare, and in early April Stephen wrote the would-be cowboy in Bowery lingo from Mexico City: "Dear Deadeye Dick: Thanks for sending back my money so fast. The hotel trun [turned] me out, as my friends of the Bowery say, and I was living in the Mex diggings with a push of sheep men till my boss in New York wired me money. Now, old man, take some advice from a tough jay from back East. You say your family is all right and nobody bothers you. Well, it struck me that you are too young a kid and too handsome to be free and easy around where a lot of bad boys and girls will take your pennies. So better stay home and grow a moustache before you rush out into the red universe any more."

Crane could parody himself as "a tough jay from back East," or as a cowboy—as in "Twelve O'Clock." A young chap dismounts and, clanking the huge spurs on his high-heeled boots as he enters a shop, asks for some tobacco and "a paper of fine cut, please." The very name Nantucket's Shop imposes the East upon the West, and the young fellow is obviously an Easterner imitating a Western cowboy. The Texas citizens contemplate him in silence. "He certainly did not look threatening. He appeared to be a young man of twenty-five years, with a tan from wind and sun, with a remarkably clear eye from perhaps a period of enforced temperance, a quiet young man who wanted to buy some tobacco. A six-shooter swung low on his hip, but at the moment it looked more decorative than warlike." His hair was watered down and brushed "until it lay as close to his head as the fur lies on a wet cat." (A self-portrait of Crane.)

From San Antonio's Mahncke Hotel on March 12 Crane wrote Lucius L. Button, a "Westerner" from Akron, Ohio, that he had "met a most intolerable duffer" back in New Orleans a month ago. The duffer was a Mr. Butler, a man of "ingenuous Akron spirit," who had no control over his emotions or prejudices. Butler "had fingers like lightning rods and on the street he continually pointed at various citizens with the exclamation: 'Look at that fellow!' People in New Orleans don't like that sort of thing you know." This duffer "let it be known that he was from Akron, O., although I do not see why he should. He told me that he knew your friends there or your friends who have escaped or are about to plan to escape from there. It is hard to feel kindly toward a man who makes you look like an unprecedented idiot and while I had only a general and humane objection to his making an ass of himself, I felt differently about myself. He enthusiastically requested me to stop off on my way home in the spring and visit him. I modestly replied that while I appreciated his generosity and courage, I had to die early in the spring and I feared that I would have to hurry home for the funeral but I had an open date in 1997 and would be happy to see him in hell upon that occasion. Well, at any rate, I lie, for I was considerate of him, treated him well at times, and was careful of his childish innocence. But there should be a tariff on that kind of an export from Akron, O."

Although he ribbed Button about his hometown, Crane felt quite otherwise about Miss Nellie Crouse, also of Akron, whom he had met in January at a tea given for her by Button at his house on 34th Street in New York. Later he wrote Miss Crouse seven letters within the period of three months, but he waited to write her until he had attained enough social status through recognition of his *Red Badge* to earn a response from her. Much given to the properties of social status and decorum, Miss Crouse responded more out of interest in Crane's being an Easterner than in fashioning a romance with an unkempt author. As with Willa Cather, he poured out his soul to a woman he knew not at all.

He emerged from his journey with changed ideas about the West—that is, the popular notion of its deriving from Frederic Remington's drawings and Western cowboy stories; he ended by admiring Westerners. He wrote Hawkins in late 1895: "I have always believed the western people to be much truer than the eastern people. We in the east are overcome a good deal by a detestable superficiality which I think is the real barbarism. Culture in its true sense, I take it, is a comprehension of the man at one's shoulder. It has nothing to do with an adoration for effete jugs and old kettles. This latter is merely an amusement and we live for amusement in the east. Damn the east! . . . I fell in love with the straight out-and-out, and sometimes hideous, often braggart westerners because I thought them to be the truer men and, by the living piper, we will see in the next fifty years what the west will do. They are serious, those fellows. When they are born they take one big gulp of wind and then they live. Of course, the east thinks them ridiculous. When they come to congress they display a child-like honesty which makes the old east laugh. And yet.

"Garland will wring every westerner by the hand and hail him as a frank honest man. I won't. No, sir. But what I contend for is the atmosphere of the west which really is frank and honest and is bound to make eleven honest men for one pessimistic thief. More glory be with them." Crane inscribed a copy of *George's Mother:* "To Hamlin Garland of the great honest West, from Stephen Crane of the false East" (New York City, July, 1896).

"I sent Crane to Mexico for new color," says Irving Bacheller (in *Stories from Memory,* 1933). "He wrote for me a number of vivid sketches of the life he saw there." He had no settled plans, Willa Cather says. "He was going to Mexico wholly uncertain of being able to do any successful work there, and he seemed to feel very insecure about the financial end of his venture." Crane wrote Lucius Button from San Antonio on March 12: "I am off to Mexico tonight." He took train from San Antonio to the border town of Laredo, and from there he reached Mexico City aboard the Aztec Limited.

En route to Laredo on the 17th he met a "Chicago capitalist," whom Beer identifies as Charles Gardner. In "Ancient Capital of Montezuma"[9] he describes his journey into Mexico, representing himself now as a Boston archaeologist telling a capitalist from Chicago that he knows no Spanish other than some swear words he has learned at school. At the station of Nuevo Laredo there is a throng of Mexican women in shawls and men wrapped in dark-hued serapes. "Over the heads of the men towered the peaked sombreros of fame. It was a preliminary picture painted in dark colors."

Crane and his fellow traveler have expected a radical change in the scenery once the train has crossed the bridge over the Rio Grande, the shallow and narrow river which connects the two nations; but it is only southern Texas repeated. From their train they see at dusk some square yellow huts with the crimson rays of household fires pouring through their doors. Crane draws the "black outline of a man upon one of these red canvasses. His legs were crossed, his arms were folded in his serape, his hat resembled a charlotte russe. He leaned negligently against the door post. This figure justified to them all their perceptions. He was more than a painting." Before Crane and his companion retire, they gaze from the train's platform at the Southern mountain range which rose like islands amid the black prairie heaving like a sea. In the West a star shines, and the capitalist remarks: "It is as large as a cheese."

Crane notices there has been a regular progression in color since Nuevo Laredo, where the prevailing tones in the dress of the people were brown, black and gray. Further south they become purple or crimson, the typical colors. "A horseman in a red serape and a tall sombrero of maroon or pearl or yellow was vivid as an individual, but a dozen or two of them reposeful in the shade of some desert railway station made a chromatic delirium. In Mexico the atmosphere seldom softens anything. It devotes its energy to making highlights, bringing everything forward, making colors fairly volcanic."

The two travelers the next morning discover that their train is high in the air, climbing mountains, while in plains of green and yellow fields, "spread out like a checkered cloth," are tiny villages, with white churches and haciendas. The peak of Nevada de Toluca is sun-smitten with gold, which makes it appear that it is staring "with a high serene eternal glance into the East at the approach of the endless suns. And no one feels like talking in the presence of these mountains that stand like gods on the world, for fear that they might hear." At sight of the two giant mountains (Popocatepetl and Iztaccihuatl), "clothed in snow that was like wool," "the capitalist nearly fell off the train." Crane wrote from Mexico City to Wickham Young on March 30 that he was about to ascend Popocatepetl, but that whether he would succeed was "a matter of speculation."

"When you first come to Mexico and you see a donkey so loaded that little of him but a furry nose and four short legs appears to the eye, you wonder at it," he wrote in "Old Mexico."[10] "Later, when you see a haystack approaching with nothing under it but a pair of thin human legs, you begin to understand the local point of view. The Indian probably reasons: 'Well, I can carry this load. The burro, then, he should carry many times this much.' The burro, born in slavery, dying in slavery, generation upon generation, he with his wobbly legs, sore back, and ridiculous little face, reasons not at all. He carries as much as he can, and when he can carry it no further, he falls down." Then the Indians club the fallen donkey, and they swear in Mexican—"a very capable language for the purposes of profanity. A good swearer here can bring rain in thirty minutes." The Indians, on realizing that the poor beast, having been hammered down as flat as a drumhead, cannot get up, remove his load. Then the burro struggles gratefully to his feet. Sometimes, however, one notices a man patting affectionately the soft nozzle of his donkey. It is the tender communion of two sympathetic spirits. "The donkey—ah, who can describe that air so sage, so profoundly reflective, and yet so kind, so forgiving, so unassuming. The countenance of a donkey expresses all manly virtues even as the sunlight expresses all colors."

In this same sketch Crane tells a story about an American lady who purchased two plum-colored birds from a Mexican shopkeeper in Mexico City. When the lady tried to induce one of the birds to perch upon her finger, the bird fell to the floor of her room "with a sound like that made by a water-soaked bean bag. The loving vendor had filled his birds full of shot. This accounted for their happy, restful countenances and their very apparent resolution never to desert the adored finger of their master. In an hour both the little birds died. You would die too if your stomach was full of shot."

Crane stayed several weeks in March and early April at the palatial Hotel Iturbide in Mexico City. He had access to the Mexican Athletic Club through a nonactive membership ticket belonging to E. Larrange.

In "City of Mexico"—three unpublished manuscripts[11]—he wrote that the city stirs into life at an early hour and after a noon siesta wakes up again at three-thirty. Carriages—with proud horses commanded by coachmen in sombreros—come from all directions, and young men crowd the curbs to watch the procession. At night "the blue quivering light of the modern electric lamp illuminates the fine old decorations of the buildings and, above all, rings the clatter of innumerable hoofs upon the concrete of the narrow streets." Every afternoon there is a shower for an hour or more, and each day is the counterpart of yesterday. "You could make picnic plans weeks in advance and be sure of your weather. It is precisely like late spring as we of the North know it." Some of the old houses have shaded courts "and simple stern decorations that must be echoes of the talent of the Aztecs. There is nothing of the modern in them. They are never incoherent, never over-done. The ornamentation is always part of the structure. It has not been plastered on from a distance."

Crane found the Mexican women frequently beautiful, but lacking the quality of bright quick eyes. "It has something to do with the mind, no doubt. Their black eyes are as beautiful as gems. The trouble with the gem, however, is that it cannot regard you with sudden intelligence, comprehension, sympathy. They have soft rounded cheeks which they powder with much skill, leaving it often in streaks. They take life easily, dreamily. They remind one of kittens asleep in the sunshine."

The bullfighters seemed to him the most impressive type of Mexicans, but in their faces there is "something cold, sinister, and merciless." In their faces there is also "a history of fiery action, of peril, of escape. Yet you would know without being told that you are gazing at an executioner, a kind of moral assassin. The faces of the priests are perhaps still more portentous, for the countenances of the bull-fighters are obvious but those of the priests are inscrutable."

It struck Crane as "the most extraordinary thing that the lower classes of Indians should insist upon existence at all. Their squalor, their ignorance seemed so absolute that death—no matter what it has in store— would appear as freedom, joy." On the other hand, he felt scorn for the stranger who finds their occupations trivial and inconsequent. The stranger "swells with a knowledge of his geographical experience. 'How futile are the lives of these people,' he remarks, 'and what incredible ignorance that they should not be aware of their futility.' This is the arrogance of the man who has not yet solved himself and discovered his own futility." The stranger writing about Mexico can be sure of two things, form and color; but he had better be wary of psychological speculation or judgment on the manner of a foreign people. Perhaps the most worthless literature of the world, Crane speculates, has been that written by the man of one nation concerning the men of another.

The submissive Indian works, worships and dies on less money than would buy a thoroughbred Newfoundland dog, "and who dares to enlighten him? Who dares cry out that there are plums, plums, plums in the world which belong to him? For my part, I think the apostle would take a formidable responsibility. I would remember that there really was no comfort in the plums after all as far as I had seen them and I would esteem no orations concerning the glitter of plums." Although the Indians are a most poverty-stricken class, they are not morally the lowest. "Indeed, as far as the mere form of religion goes, they are one of the highest. They are exceedingly devout, worshipping with a blind faith that counts a great deal among the theorists [of religion]. But according to my view this is not the measure of them. I measure their morality by what evidences of peace and contentment I can detect in the average countenance.

"If a man is not given a fair opportunity to be virtuous, if his environment chokes his moral aspirations, I say that he has got the one important cause of complaint and rebellion against society," Crane wrote. Yet, "I am of the opinion that poverty of itself is no cause, it is something above and beyond. For example, there is Collis P. Huntington and William [sic] D. Rockefeller—as virtuous as these gentlemen are, I would not say that their virtue is any ways superior to mine for instance. Their opportunities are no greater. They can give more, deny themselves more in quantity but not relatively. We can each give all that we possess and there I am at once their equal. As the rich are not capable of sacrifices possible to me I envy them nothing. Far from having a grievance against them, I feel that they will confront an ultimate crisis that I, through my opportunities, may altogether avoid. There is in fact no advantage of importance which I can perceive them possessing over me."

Crane foresees the coming struggle between American capitalists and the laboring class, which had already begun in the Populist movement of the 1890's, a crisis intensified by the financial panic of 1893, and he warns the capitalists that the vast army of the laboring class in our cities have faces cynical enough to fill one with awe and fear. "They have it in their power to become terrible. And their silence suggests everything." The people of the slums silently confront eternal defeat. "One listens for the first thunder of the rebellion, the moment when this silence shall be broken by a roar of war. Meanwhile one fears this class, their numbers, their wickedness, their might—even their laughter." The Mexican peasant—in contrast to the exploited American laborer—does not say "No" in thunder; he is singularly meek. In scant clothing he squats on pavements, sleeps in doorways, or carries bundles. But the faces of these peasants express a serene faith. "I can *feel* the superiority of their contentment." Crane envied them this. "I even refuse to pity them."

The first thing for the tourist in Mexico to sample is pulque, and the second thing is to cease drinking it. In "Jags of Pulque Down in Mexico,[12] Crane says that the native can get howling full for twelve centavos, which in American coinage is six cents. In New York City "many men of celebrated thirsts would consider this a profoundly ideal condition." But why should any man ever taste another drop of pulque "after having once collided with it?" One glass of pulque is enough to elevate the foreign visitor by the hair "and throw him violently to the ground. It resembles green milk. The average man has never seen green milk, but if he can imagine a handful of Paris green interpolated into a glass of cream, he will have a fair idea of the appearance of pulque. And it tastes like—it tastes like—some terrible concoction of bad yeast perhaps. Or maybe some calamity of eggs." The first encounter is a revelation comparable to the first taste of a sandwich made from doormats, but to the Mexicans pulque is a delirium of joy, and they line up at the pulque bars yelling thirsty appeals to the barkeepers. "These pulque shops are usually decorated both inside and out with the real old paintings done on the walls by the hand of some unknown criminal."

Haciendas have thousands of acres planted in nothing but maguey, from which is made the fermented pulque and the distilled mescal and tequila. "Mescal and tequila are two native rivals of pulque. Mescal is a sort of a cousin of whiskey, although to the eye it is as clear as water, and tequila is to mescal as brandy is to whiskey." The native prefers pulque, and filled with it, he "seldom wishes to fight. Usually he prefers to adore his friends. They will hang together in front of a bar, three or four of them, their legs bending, their arms about each other's necks, their faces lit with an expression of the most ideal affection and supreme brotherly regard. It would be difficult to make an impression on their feelings at these times with a club. Their whole souls are completely absorbed in this beatific fraternal tenderness." But at Santa Anita, on the Viga canal, the weekly ceremony was of the same order "as the regular Sunday night murder in the old days of Mulberry Bend. And it happened because the natives mixed their drinks" —pulque and tequila. Crane and an American tourist, who shared several sight-seeing excursions with him, enjoyed a pleasant sojourn on the Viga canal one cool afternoon when they viewed the floating gardens, which in fact turned out to be not floating gardens at all.[13] There was the clamor of the boatmen bargaining for passengers, beseeching, praying, appealing. "There could have been no more clamor around the feet of the ancient brown gods of Mexico. They almost shed tears; they wriggled in an ecstasy of commercial expectation. They smote their bare breasts and each swore himself to be the incomparable boatman of the Viga." Their assault was as fierce as a charge of desperate infantry, while above their howls tinkled streetcar bells as the driver lashed his mules toward the city. The boatmen poled madly and crashed into other boats, and then arose the fervor of Mexican oaths. Erect in the stern, they bent and swayed rhythmically, prodding the bottom of the canal with their long poles. Then suddenly appeared Popocatepetl towering to the sky, "a great cone of creamy hue in the glamor of the sunshine," and then later came Iztaccihuatl, "the white woman, of curious shape, more camel than woman, its peak confused with clouds."

At the little village of Santa Anita everybody disembarked. In front of the pulque shops was a great babbling crowd. Some policemen on horseback with dangling sabres-in-scabbards paraded; Indian girls sold flowers, and caballeros strutted with flowers in their sombreros. It was a colorful scene. But crouched in the narrow street leading away from the canal "a multitude of beggars, decrepit vendors of all kinds, raised unheeded cries. In the midst of the swarming pulque shops, resorts, and gardens, stood a little white church, stern, unapproving, representing the other fundamental aspiration of humanity, a reproach and a warning." A tottering caballero trying to kiss a waitress in a pulque shop is thwarted by a policeman, four men at a table roar with laughter at the tale of a fifth man and a boatman pursues some riotous youths who have neglected to pay him. Crane is in a pulque shop on whose earthen floor squat three old Indian women with wrinkled faces watching the crowd. Little beggars beseech the customers: *"Niña! Niña! Deme un centavo!"* When the little church's bell clangs harshly, people saunter back toward the canal, and Crane or his friend hires two native musicians—a guitarist and a violinist—to play "slumberously" along their canal voyage back to the City of Mexico.

In "Hats, Shirts, and Spurs in Mexico" he observes that the Mexican caballero "in his enormous sombrero and skin-tight trousers is top-heavy." The Mexican dude or gentleman of fashion expends fifty or even a hundred dollars on his gorgeous sombrero, "and these splendid masses of gold-braid and pearl-grey beaver surmount the average masculine head with the same artistic value as would a small tower of bricks." He wears spurs weighing a couple of pounds each—"immense things that look more like rhinoceros traps than spurs to urge on a horse. He may, too, when he rides in the country, have a pair of elegantly decorated pistol holsters at his pommel. A double row of little silver buttons extends down each leg of his tight trousers, and it is more than probable that his little jacket will be embroidered like mad." He is the true caballero: black moustache and vaguely sinister eye. Mounted upon a charger, he restrains his horse's gait down the avenue crowded with fashionable carriages. In the rural districts the caballero was then still supreme, but in the cities the men of greatest wealth dressed like American men of affairs, the younger men imitating the fashions of New York and London "with much diligence. Here begins the conflict between the holy London creed of what is correct and an innate love of vivid personal adornment. They clash, and the clash is sometimes to be heard for miles."

In contrast to the caballero, the Mexican Indian (in his serape and dusty sandals displaying bare toes) wears an old sombrero pulled down over his eyes. "Whether his blanket is purple or of some dull hue, he fits into the green grass, the low white walls, the blue sky as if his object was not so much to get possession of some centavos as to compose the picture." He is a fascinating character. "At night when he crouches in a doorway with his sombrero pulled still further over his eyes, and his mouth covered by a fold of his serape, you can imagine anything at all about him; for his true character is impenetrable. He is a mystic and silent figure of the darkness. He has two great creeds. One is that pulque as a beverage is finer than the melted blue of the sky. The other is that Americans are eternally wealthy and immortally stupid. If the world was really of the size that he believes it to be, you could put his hat over it." The Philadelphia *Press* (October 18, 1896) subheaded Crane's sketch: "Stephen Crane Says the Mexican's Chapeau Is the Blossom of Character."

In "The Wise Men" (not published until 1898) he describes the Café Colorado with a front of white and gold and, serving as doors, two wings of willow flip-flapping incessantly. The café is located in a building with marble floors and decorated ceilings reminiscent of the days "when the great building was a palace"; it is in the Hotel Iturbide. The wise men in this tale "were youths of subtle mind. They were very wicked, according to report, and yet they managed to have it reflect credit upon them. They often had the well-informed and the great talkers of the American colony engaged in reciting their misdeeds, and facts relating to their sins were usually told with a flourish of awe and fine admiration."

The American colony belonged to the American Club located in the Hotel Iturbide, and the two youths of subtle mind were Crane and the Chicago capitalist. One of the "Kids" had a "wild passion for salads, and the other did not care much. So at any hour of the day or night they might be seen ordering a salad." The Kids "were never apart in the City of Mexico."

A young chap called Freddie and old man Pop, the manager of the Café Colorado, compete at midnight in a foot race on the Paseo, a famous drive leading to the Castle of Chapultepec. Age against youth, the old man outruns youngster Freddie, and so the Kids, who had bet on the Old Man, are "The Wise Men." Apart from its autobiographical interest, it is scarcely worth mentioning; H. G. Wells, however, thought "The Wise Men" a perfect thing. "It tells of the race between two bartenders in the City of Mexico, and I cannot imagine how it could possibly have been better told," he said.

In "The Five White Mice,"[14] which Ford Madox Ford extravagantly praised while mistitling it "The Three White Mice," Freddie reappears as the bartender at Mexico City's Casa Verde. He talks scornfully of liquor while admiring those who drink, which ambivalence marks him as the ideal barkeeper. Freddie, "with the ironical glance of a man who is mixing a cocktail," surveys the dice-shaking brawlers at the bar: "a gambler, a millionaire, a railway conductor, and the agent of a vast American syndicate." The millionaire, who is referred to in this tale as the "San Francisco kid," might possibly be the very same person we have encountered as the "Chicago capitalist" and the American tourist. The agent of a vast American syndicate is of course Crane; he calls himself in this tale "the New York kid." These dice-shaking brawlers rail at the New York kid for his ill luck in the game of seven-up. "At each disaster, Freddie swore from behind the bar in a sort of affectionate contempt. 'Why, this kid has had no luck for two days. Did you ever see such throwin'?' " He is contending against a gambler holding "five queens," and the other gamblers assure him that he cannot beat that showing. The hoots of these guying noncombatants caused the New York Kid "to feel profoundly that it would be fine to beat the five queens. He addressed a gambler's slogan to the interior of the cup: 'Oh, five white mice of chance, / Shirts of wool and corduroy pants, / Gold and wine, women and sin, / All for you if you let me come in—/ Into the house of chance.' Flashing the dice sardonically out on the bar, he displayed three aces. From two dice in the next throw he achieved one more ace. For his last throw he rattled the single dice [die] for a long time. He already had four aces." If he now rolled another ace, the five queens were vanquished; and then he rolled the cup and planted it bottom up on the bar, with the one dice hidden under it.

"Oh, maybe it's an ace," he said with the boastful air of a conjurer or a cheat. "I'll bet fifty dollars it is an ace," but nobody dared accept his bet. He then turns the cup, lifting it in the manner of some mayor unveiling a statue, and it is but a ten-spot. "That was the greatest cold bluff I ever saw worked. He wouldn't know how to cheat with dice if he wanted to," says bartender Freddie. The gamblers jeer at the New York Kid and derisively quote the verse he had used to conjure his aces from his dicing cup. Then they go off to the circus at his expense and the Kid laughs at the comic "foolish-wise clown."

Afterwards the New York Kid encounters the San Francisco Kid and his friend Benson, both of them drunk, and the trio are stopped by some Mexican bandits in a street "as dark as a whale's throat at deep sea." One of the Mexicans, with sombrero drawn low over his eyes and a serape over his left shoulder, cuts a terrible figure. The New York Kid places his hand at his hip, gripping a revolver of robust size, and thinks as he faces the stout Mexican how his revolver's handle is stamped with "a hunting scene in which a sportsman in fine leggings and a peaked cap was taking aim at a stag less than one-eighth of an inch away." He withdraws his revolver until the hammer is free of the holster. "He waited immovable and watchful while the garrulous 'Frisco Kid expended two and a half lexicons on the middle Mexican. The Eastern lad suddenly decided that he was going to be killed. His mind leaped forward and studied the aftermath."

There would be a cablegram home, and then his "hard-mouthed old father" would come out here to Mexico City, and they'd tell him: " 'This is the place.' Then, very likely, each would remove his hat. They would stand quietly with their hats in their hands for a decent minute. He pitied his old financing father, unyielding and millioned, a man who commonly spoke twenty-two words a year to his beloved son. The Kid understood it at this time. If his fate was not impregnable, he might have turned out to be a man and have been liked by his father."

He is afraid, dismayed at the thought that his huge revolver might get entangled in his coattails as he pulls it out. "He feared that in his hands it would be as unwieldy as a sewing-machine for this quick work. . . . But at the supreme moment the revolver came forth as if it were greased and it arose like a feather. This somnolent machine, after months of repose, was finally looking at the breasts of men. Perhaps in this one series of movements the Kid had unconsciously used nervous force sufficient to raise a bale of hay." He takes aim first at one and then at another of the Mexicans, and they slink away. The tale ends with the remark "Nothing had happened."

Crane left the Hotel Iturbide in early April when the Bacheller–Johnson Syndicate wired him some money; he bought some expensive equipment and headed for the badlands with a servant and a horse. In some Mexican lodging house a Bowery fellow turned sheepherder told him that a band of Mexicans had tried to run him off his land and that he had shot them down. This germinal situation gave Crane "A Man and Some Others," but he reverses it by having the former Bowery saloon-bouncer shot down by the Mexicans.

The tale begins with a horseman approaching the campfire of sheepherder Bill on a shadowy sea of mesquite. Bill's hand drops to his revolver, but he sees that the stranger does not belong to the mesquite and plains, where the banging of a tin pan might make an iron-nerved man leap into the air. And so Bill releases his grip on his revolver. With that same revolver he has killed the foreman of a ranch where he has been a cowboy. It is his dearest possession. He loves that revolver because "its allegiance was more than that of man, horse, or dog. It questioned neither social nor moral positions; it obeyed alike the saint and the assassin."

The young horseman canters forward and says "Good evening" as he draws rein before Bowery Bill, who answers likewise—"without committing himself by too much courtesy. For a moment the two men scanned each other in a way that is not ill-mannered on the plains, where one is in danger of meeting horsethieves or tourists." Bill's eyes search the outfit of the horseman "for some sign of craft, but there was none. Even with his local regalia, it was clear that the strange young man was of a far, black Northern city. He had discarded the enormous stirrups of his Mexican saddle; he used the small English stirrup, and his feet were thrust forward until the steel tightly gripped his ankles. As Bill's eyes traveled over the stranger, they lighted suddenly upon the stirrups and the thrust feet, and immediately he smiled in a friendly way. No dark purpose could dwell in the innocent heart of a man who rode thus on the plains."

He forewarns the stranger of the danger he is in if he remains the night with him because he expects the Mexicans to rush his camp and chase him off the range. The stranger sticks with him, they are attacked, and Bill kills one of the eight Mexicans. At dawn the stranger utters a frightened cry when through the thicket he sees the dead face, a mask of dulled brass, and one arm clutching a cactus bush. They are attacked again and lie flat on the ground facing the thicket. "It is sometimes taught that men do the furious and desperate thing from an emotion that is as even and placid as the thoughts of a village clergyman on Sunday afternoon." The stranger suddenly screams in alarm, the guns roar, and Bill is killed.

"I am engaged at last on my personal troubles in Mexico," Crane wrote Willis Hawkins from Philadelphia in mid-September, 1895. His personal troubles included his encounter in April with a fat Mexican of "abominable egotism" who was a fashionable bandit named Ramón Colorado, and he was writing about this in a sketch entitled "Horses—One Dash!" In the Mexican badlands he had ridden his horse in fear of his life to outdistance a pursuing band of Mexican cutthroats, as does Richardson in the sketch. Richardson is equipped, as was Crane himself, with a sombrero, a blanket, a revolver and belt, enormous silver spurs, a servant and a horse. (Walking in Mexican spurs, says Crane, suggests a telegraphic lineman.) Richardson, when he walked, "sounded to himself like a pair of cymbals." With his Mexican servant from the Rio Grande country named José, he takes lodgings for the night at an adobe house, and a band of Mexicans plot to kill him for possession of his gun and spurs and money and saddle. At dawn Richardson and José sneak out and ride the wilderness of mesquite in fear of being pursued. They are chased, but are saved from the wild mob of drunken Mexican horsemen by a detachment of rurales, the cavalry corps of the Mexican Army policing the plains. Richardson remembers the many tales he had read about racing for your life, "and he thought them badly written." Crane wrote "One Dash—Horses!" (the title is variously given) with the intent of outstripping all other tales on the same subject. However, this sketch, like "The Wise Men," has little significance other than its autobiographical interest.

Crane's return from Mexico was precipitated by an incident which he related seven months later to Nellie Crouse. He had spent enough time in southern Mexico (about a month), he said, to get so very sunburned that his face turned "the color of a brick sidewalk. There was nothing American about me save a large Smith and Wesson revolver and I saw only Indians whom I suspected of loading their tamales with a dog. In this state of mind and this physical condition, I arrived one day in the city of Puebla and there I saw an American girl. There was a party of tourists in town and she was of their contingent. I only saw her four times—one in the hotel corridor and three in the street. I had been so long in the mountains and was such an outcast that the sight of this American girl in a new spring gown nearly caused me to drop dead. She of course never looked in my direction. I never met her."

But she reminded him of Nellie. "I have never achieved the enjoyment of seeing you in a new spring gown but this girl became to me not an individual but a sort of symbol and I have always thought of you with gratitude for the peculiar thrill you gave me in the town of Puebla, Mexico." Nellie's double gave him "one of those peculiar thrills which a man only acknowledges upon occasion. I ran to the railroad office. I cried: 'What is the shortest route to New York?' I left Mexico."

# IX

## ☞ "*The Black Riders*"

WHEN the *Bookman* for May, 1895, reported that Stephen Crane was in Mexico writing for the Bacheller Syndicate, he was actually on his way home. Before going on from New York to Hartwood he stopped in at Curtis Brown's desk at the *Press* and handed him a slim volume of verse with the inscription: "To Curtis Brown—not at all reluctantly but with enthusiasm—from Stephen Crane, May 16, 1895." The book was *The Black Riders,* which Copeland and Day had published just five days earlier.

He arrived in Hartwood on the 19th, the same day on which his "Mexican Sights and Street Scenes" appeared in the Philadelphia *Press.* On June 8, although he wrote to Copeland and Day that he was "not in very good health," he took the train to New York to attend a dinner honoring him at the Lantern Club, founded by newspaper men that May. The quaint house they dined in was an added story on the roof of a stable yard, in the middle of the Williams Street block between John and Fulton Streets, in a section known as Monkey Hill. It was approached by a "hanging stairway that climbed the side of a brick building occupied by an iron-monger." One of the two oldest houses on Manhattan Island, it was built in the early days of New Amsterdam and was once the inn and resort of Captain Kidd. Since the seven members of the club considered themselves literary lights, they used as their symbol a ship's lantern on a wrought-iron bracket at the door and for decoration hung ancient and medieval, Oriental and Colonial lanterns.

Irving Bacheller presided as perpetual president over the charter members: the New York *Press* editor, Edward Marshall; the managing editor of *Life,* Tom Masson; Charles W. Hooke, a writer of mystery tales; journalist George Wheeler, who later—as Post Wheeler—became Secretary of the American Embassy in London; Willis Brooks Hawkins and Crane, who arrived at the dinner wearing a Mexican necktie—an indigo whirl of silk striped red and green. For subsequent dinners, conceding to Masson's imploring, he gave it up.

He had many friends during these years, but none as close as Willis

Hawkins, editor of *Brains,* a periodical "devoted to the art of advertising."
Bacheller described Hawkins as "a most cheerful companion, a man
of playful whims and delightful fancies." He was the man who most often
helped Crane out of tight spots with cash, with the loan of an overcoat, or
with just good advice.[1] The other members of the club Bacheller called a
witty irresponsible lot of bohemians who knew the city and were skilled in
the art of poker, by which one friend separates another from his money.
They were good fellows but also able borrowers. Bacheller in fact warned
Crane not to play poker with them because they had mastered its "profound strategies," but he refused the advice. "What a guileless, gentle,
lovable country boy he was!" said guileless Irving Bacheller. "The Lan-
thornites were all fond of him. He was their hero," and, it would seem,
a source of ready cash. Crane was a wretched gambler and got trimmed
with some regularity, and out of some valuable objects. He had brought
back from Mexico half a dozen opals, "some with the lambent flame of the
sunset in their fiery depths," says C. K. Linson. "He freely gave me the
choice of the lot. I took a little one that flashed at me with the gleam of
the rainbow. Crane laughingly added a fine water opal to it. The next
morning he said: 'It's a good thing you came in for a deal yesterday, for
the newspaper Indians gave me a dinner last night and they got my pretty
pebbles.' "

During these months following the Mexican trip he amazed Linson
with stories of the West. Linson later read one of them in print, probably
"Horses—One Dash!" But Crane's vivid telling of it was far more colorful.
"That his luminous phrasing was not a trick was never more evident than
then," Linson says. "It was simply Crane. His speech was free from the
danger that his writing ran, of weakening with repetition. Each scintillation
eclipsed the last but left a complete impression of delight."

At the Lantern Club's Saturday dinners each member was assigned to
write a story to be read at the next week's dinner. Favorable appraisal and
encomium were prohibited, so the highest tribute a story could receive
was complete silence. After a member read his story, the others pounced
on it, "pointed out the flaws in it, and pooh-poohed it generally, if possible."
They read mainly sketches about the fading old-time color of the city,
and cherished hopes of winning literary fame. Crane stimulated their ambitions. Although criticism was sometimes vicious, they remained good
friends. Their spirit of friendship is indicated in an undated note to Crane
from Bacheller: "Go now and take a drink with O'Darrow to the health
of your friend Irving Bacheller."

It was a great day when Samuel Clemens was guest of the Lantern Club
and told yarns about his life on the Mississippi. As he smoked a long
Cuban cigar beside the fireplace, he remarked that he tried to shape his
tales with a double-snapper ending. Other visitors included Mrs. John
Langdon Heaton, for Crane the "most sensible woman in New York," and

Richard Harding Davis, with whom Crane shook hands for the first time. He was to become Crane's rival as star newspaper reporter both in Greece and in Cuba. When he appeared at the Lantern Club he was eight years older and far more famous than Crane. After his graduation from Swarthmore he had reported *The West from a Car Window* and had established himself with the New York *Sun*. But most important, he was author of the extremely popular *Van Bibber and Others* (1892), stories about a socialite who is kind to the poor and whose picaresque escapades involve him in hilarious situations. Other frequent visitors to the Lantern Club were William Dean Howells and Richard Watson Gilder, the old guard of the magazine world. Luncheons were also held for Rudyard Kipling, Booth Tarkington, Ethel Barrymore, Stanford White (the architect of Madison Square Garden) and Charles Dana Gibson, the creator of the Gibson girl, whose gentleman companion was modeled on Richard Harding Davis.

In his June 8 letter to Copeland and Day from Hartwood[2] Crane asked his publishers to write him about reviews of *The Black Riders:* "I hear they are making some stir." But he was embarrassed when he picked up the next day's Sunday *Tribune* at Linson's and read its review. The new poet Crane is "ludicrous," "a dabbler in mysteries which he is unworthy to approach," said the *Tribune*. "Does Mr. Crane really believe that he is writing of things from his heart? If so, why have not his 'lines' some poetic vitality, some obvious reason for being? In their futility and affectation they strike the impartial reader as so much trash."

While waiting for more reviews and for *The Red Badge* to come off the press, Crane spent the latter part of the summer in Pike County, Pennsylvania, as he had done the previous summer. He wrote Hawkins on August 9 that he was "cruising around the woods in corduroys and feeling great. I have lots of fun getting healthy." He asked Hawkins to let him know if any notices about his poems came out and invited him up some Sunday, while cautioning him that it was four deadly hours up the mountain. (Hawkins didn't visit.) The reason for Crane's good spirits was more than fresh country air: there were six girls in camp: "it is with the greatest difficulty that I think coherently on any other subject."

Writing to Hawkins put Crane in the mood to discuss anything but literature. He was more inclined to describe what happened while he was sailing a catboat on the pond at Hartwood or flirting with the camp girls, or to recount his experiences with a bicycle when he was at military school. Crane—like many writers—was given to expressing his literary ideas in creative writing rather than in personal letters or conversation. When he did mention his work at this time it was usually in his letters to Nellie Crouse.

He wrote Hawkins on August 19 from Pike County's Twin Lakes: "My remembrances to all the lanterns. I am getting mighty anxious to hear the

Apache Scalp Dance again," meaning the scalp dance of those Lantern Club "Indians" tomahawking his writings. He wrote Hitchcock of Appleton that the title-page proof of *The Red Badge* was all right, then he was off to Philadelphia in September for the *Press* post of dramatic critic, which he didn't get, and finally back in New York City at 165 West 23rd, writing Hawkins in October to bring over a poker contingent.

From Edmund's house at Hartwood Crane had written Hitchcock that *The Third Violet* was working out fine and that the first seven chapters in the rough gave him "the proper enormous interest in the theme." He could get more writing done here than in the city, he informed Wickham Young on October 23; the next day he was writing Hawkins that the brown October woods of Hartwood were simply great and said that he hadn't written a line and didn't intend to for some time (although this admission is contradicted by his report of progress on his new novel to Hitchcock on the 29th). He had heard that at Brentano's bookshop "the damned 'Red Badge' is having a very nice sale."[3] He went shooting and missed his first partridge: "Keh-plunk. Bad ground, though. Too many birch trees." (Not skilled as a hunter, he cared little for the sport.) "Lord, I do love a crazy horse with just a little pig-skin between him and me. You can push your lifeless old bicycles around the country but a slim-limbed thoroughbred's dauntless spirit is better. Some people take much trouble to break a horse of this or that. I don't. Let him fling himself to the other side of the road because a sumach tassel waves. If your knees are not self-acting enough for that sort of thing, get off and walk. Hartwood scenery is good when viewed swiftly."

Hawkins took issue with him on the horse versus bicycle topic, and Stephen responded on November 1 that he refused to listen to him on the question. At Claverack he had once ridden a wheel which an unsmiling young cadet had brought into the armory, only to have it taken away from him by senior officer Crane. "When I wished to dismount however I found I couldn't. So I rode around and around the armory. Shafer, who was champion of Pennsylvania in those old high-wheel days, watched me and said I did some things on that wheel which were impossible for him. A group of cadets gathered in a corner and yelled whenever I passed them. I abjured them at intervals to let me off that wheel but they only hollered. At last, I ran into a bench and fell neatly on my head. It broke the machine, too, praise God."

Bicycles had become the rage of New York City, with a new bicycle path in Brooklyn, and the next spring they took over the once quiet Western Avenue slanting from Central Park to the river. Here all Gotham comes together and rolls along in an endless, shimmering panorama, said the New York *Sun* under the headline "New York's Bicycle Speedway / By Stephen Crane" (July 3, 1896). "On these gorgeous spring days they appeared in thousands. All mankind is a-wheel apparently and a person on nothing but legs feels like a strange animal. A mighty army of wheels streams from the brick wilderness below Central Park and speeds over the asphalt. In the cool of the evening it returns with swaying and flashing of myriad lamps."

In the letter to Hawkins about hunting, he wrote that he had beaten his brother Edmund at the game of partridge shooting and that his fan mail had reached mighty proportions. If he answered all his correspondents he'd make the obscure little station at Hartwood a better class post office and that would make his brother Ed "a better class postmaster for you know he is a postmaster, justice-of-the-peace, ice-man, farmer, millwright, blue stone man, lumberman, station agent on the P. J. M. [Port Jervis, Midland] and N. Y. R. R. and many other things which I now forget."

Reviews of *The Black Riders* were now appearing frequently and would continue to appear for the next year or so. As Crane heard, his little poems made some stir; on both sides of the Atlantic opinions clashed over the matter of the author's genius and the merit of his "lines." The *Bookman* for May, 1895, said that Crane wrote his poems in a sudden fit of inspiration in less than three days and they were sent off polished and finished to the printer within a fortnight. (Karl Harriman after visiting Crane at Brede Manor reported in the *Literary Review* for April, 1900, the same legend, probably instigated by Stephen himself.[4]) Sudden inspiration or not, said the *Tribune,* "the visitation to which we owe Mr. Crane's 'lines' does not seem to have come from Parnassus."

Harry Thurston Peck of the *Bookman* declared *The Black Riders* to be "the most notable contribution to literature to which the present year has given birth." If Whitman when young had been caught by aesthetic influences he would likely have mellowed his "barbaric yawp" to some note such as Crane's. Stephen Crane, said Peck, is the Aubrey Beardsley of poetry. "When one first takes up his little book of verse and notes the quite too Beardsleyesque splash of black upon its staring white boards, and then on opening it discovers that the 'lines' are printed wholly in capitals, and that they are unrhymed and destitute of what most poets regard as rhythm, the general impression is of a writer who is bidding for renown wholly on the basis of his eccentricity." But Crane is a true poet whose verse fascinates long after the eccentricity of its form has worn off, and "even in the most fantastic of his conceits there are readily to be found a thought and a meaning." His work on the whole has "traces of *Entartung,* but he is by no means a decadent, but rather a bold—sometimes too bold—original and powerful writer of eccentric verse, skeptical, pessimistic, often cynical; and one who stimulates thought because he himself thinks."

"The spirit of the lines is generally rebellious and modern in the extreme," said the *Atlantic Monthly,* "occasionally blasphemous to a degree which even cleverness will not reconcile to a liberal taste." Some of the lines were intentionally amusing, the *Atlantic* thought, "and the satiric note sometimes serves to mollify the profanity."

The *Atlantic* reviewer noticed that Crane's poems were in parable form, that their freshness of conception set the reader to thinking, and that their audacity suggested a mind not without kinship to Emily Dickinson's. We recall that Howells, who had introduced Crane to Emily Dickinson's poetry in the spring of 1893, thought Crane's poems a little too orphic for him, but he changed his mind and declared *The Black Riders* the best book of the year 1895 (in *Harper's Weekly:* January 25, 1896). What is poetry? asked the Cincinnati *Commercial Tribune,* and answered that poetry was words with capital letters at the beginning of every line, but Crane had capital letters throughout the rest of the text, and that was about all the poetry in it.

Rupert Hughes in *Godey's Magazine* (September, 1896) was not bothered by the eccentricity of the poetry: "That it is neither rhymed nor metrical should not incite an admirer of Oriental poetry. That its 'lines' were uniformed with small caps, is a matter of little moment. This eccentricity was doubtless only a desire to get out from under the overshadowing mountain of Walt Whitman; and novelty is always a partial excuse. Some of these little chunks of sentiment are mere drivel; most of them are full of marrow." Much like what Peck had said, Hughes contended that ". . . Mr. Crane has been thinking—that is the main thing—and if in his thought-experiments he sometimes lands in a blind alley, so do the greatest scientists." The "work of the thinker that dares to be unconventional is always beer and skittles for the parodist."

The *Nation* (October 24, 1895) spoke in Crane's behalf also: "As formless, in the ordinary sense, as the productions of Walt Whitman, these 'lines' are in other respects the antipodes of his; while Whitman dilutes mercilessly, Crane condenses almost as formidably. . . . He grasps his thought as nakedly and simply as Emily Dickinson; gives you a glance at it, or, perhaps, two glances from different points of view, and leaves it there. If it be a paradox, as it commonly is, so much the better for him." The reviewer singled out No. XXXVII:

> *On the horizon the peaks assembled;*
> *And as I looked,*
> *The march of the mountains began.*
> *As they marched, they sang,*
> *"Ay! we come! we come!"*

Whether that is poetry, said the *Nation* reviewer, one must remember Thoreau's dictum that no matter how we define poetry the true poet will presently set the whole definition aside. "If it be further asked whether such a book gives promise, the reply must be that experience points the other way. So marked a new departure rarely leads to further growth. Neither Whitman nor Emily Dickinson ever stepped beyond the circle they first drew." "Is there room for a second Walt Whitman?" asked the *Literary Digest* (February 29, 1896). "Meantime the star of Mr. Stephen Crane is in the ascendant," and then the *Literary Digest* quoted the poem that later became the title poem of *War Is Kind* (1899), reprinting it from the *Bookman:* "Do not weep, maiden, for war is kind."

Although Crane's "lines" were brutally treated by some parodists and reviewers, his poetic genius was widely recognized.[5] *Munsey's* scoffed at Crane as one of our newly heralded geniuses who was merely a fad, and *Life* said: "We used to hear of the poetic ear; it has been superseded by the typographic eye." Quite favorable, however, was the San Francisco *Argonaut* (July 13, 1896), which stated that the author of *The Black Riders* had been an obscure reporter up to a few months ago, but "his extraordinary 'lines' drew attention to his originality." *The Black Riders* and his *Red Badge of Courage* set him among the new lights to be reckoned with. Crane wrote Hawkins in November, 1895, that the New York *Evening Post* had come out "very grandly in support of the *Black Riders*. And the Boston papers have said some fine things about the *Red Badge*." He conceded that some of the "pills are pretty darned dumb," but he thought his poetry more important than his fiction because in his poetry "I meant what I said."

The London *Academy* (January 16, 1897) remarked that "Crane's poems are essentially pessimistic, often cynical, but they strike a note of fearless novelty. He is . . . emphatically a young man with a future, and the new literature could ill afford to lose him." The London *Athenaeum* was more critical; it remarked that the poems hardly deserved the pretty get-up Heinemann (the British publisher) gave the book, binding it in black morocco with gilt letters, and the covers decorated with Frederick Gordon's orchid design. As for the poems, though occasionally forcible by sheer abruptness, they had no rhyme or rhythm, said the *Athenaeum*. Also: "Mr. Crane is too young in experience to write apologues and fables of destiny and man. The futility of human wisdom and the doctrine that every man is a law unto himself are themes so well worn as to need a master hand to illuminate them afresh, to which Mr. Crane, with all his promise, cannot pretend."

Amy Lowell, leader of the Imagist movement of free verse, whose progenitor was Stephen Crane, said in 1927 that he spoke in symbols far outdistancing his time and that his theme in *The Black Riders* was at once the cruelty of universal law and the futility of hope. "It is a creed of gall and aloes, and Crane believed it. It is the key to his life. A loathed and vengeful God broods over *The Black Riders*. Crane's soul was heaped with bitterness, and this bitterness he flung back at the theory of life which had betrayed him. His misery and his earnestness made the book, and the supreme irony of all is that it should have been issued as an aesthetic knick-knack and its author hailed as an 'affected ass.' "

"Personally I like my little book of poems, *The Black Riders*," Crane said, "better than I do *The Red Badge of Courage*. The reason is, I suppose, that the former is the more ambitious effort." Crane in this 1897 letter to his editor friend John Northern Hilliard of the Rochester *Union* (later managing editor of the Rochester *Post Express*) was strategically playing down his achievements and plumping for the poetry because it was less popular.

Yet he did have a higher opinion of his poetry than of his fiction. The poems "give my ideas of life as a whole, so far as I know it," he said. His poetic "lines" seemed to him more "sincere" and "honest" because they were spontaneous, whereas *Maggie* and *The Red Badge* were consciously designed. Inspired by Emily Dickinson's poetry but not modeled upon it, his poems derive their cadence and sometimes their framework from the Bible. Half the poems in *The Black Riders* are epigrammatic parables; several have close affinity with the parable poems of Ambrose Bierce. Hamlin Garland spotted another source. Olive Schreiner's *Dreams,* poetic parables of savage philosophy. *The Black Riders* and *War is Kind* have a family kinship with the free verse of W. E. Henley, Emily Dickinson, and Walt Whitman.

At their best the poems have the same structural design, and some of them even the same plot or mood as the short stories. "A youth in apparel that glittered" is a minature poetic version of *The Red Badge* (the would-be assassin of the youth meets an impasse). The conflict in the poem is between illusion and reality; but here it is reality—the assassin of dreams—that finds itself compromised.

> *A youth in apparel that glittered*
> *Went to walk in a grim forest.*
> *There he met an assassin*
> *Attired all in garb of old days;*
> *He, scowling through the thickets,*
> *And dagger poised quivering,*
> *Rushed upon the youth.*
>
> *"Sir," said this latter,*
> *"I am enchanted, believe me,*
> *To die, thus,*
> *In this medieval fashion,*
> *According to the best legends;*
> *"Ah, what joy!"*
> *Then took he the wound, smiling,*
> *And died, content.*

(XXVII)

In "The Bride Comes to Yellow Sky" the newly wedded sheriff—the dreamer—disarms his would-be assassin. As "A man adrift on a slim spar" reproduces the plight of the men in the dinghy in "The Open Boat," so the germinal situation Crane developed in "The Blue Hotel" was anticipated in this syllogistic three-line poem:

> *A man feared that he might find an assassin;*
> *Another that he might find a victim.*
> *One was more wise than the other.*
>                 (LVI)

The parable poem "I saw a man pursuing the horizon" recalls Henry Fleming and other Crane heroes who are busy "pursuing the horizon," as was Crane himself. *Black Riders* No. IX epitomizes Hawthorne's story "Young Goodman Brown." Here illusion is shattered by realities.

> *I stood upon a high place,*
> *And saw, below, many devils*
> *Running, leaping,*
> *And carousing in sin.*
> *One looked up, grinning,*
> *And said, "Comrade! Brother!"*

Amy Lowell said that Crane was no poet, but it was he who anticipated the program of Imagism she took over from T. E. Hulme and Ezra Pound; indeed, Crane fulfilled certain tenets of Imagism more truly than the Imagists themselves. They regarded his verse as experimental, but he did not deliberately experiment or pioneer, nor did he write according to program as they did.

Ezra Pound has spoken of Crane appreciatively, as did Carl Sandburg. In "Letters to Dead Imagists," in his *Chicago Poems* (1916), Sandburg acknowledged Crane's influence as a contemporary. By accidental resemblance to vers-librist and imagist verse, Crane thus heralded and in a way influenced the poetic renaissance of 1912 in America.

On November 8, 1895, the train from Port Jervis brought him some mail and fifty cents' worth of tobacco, and he wrote Hawkins for his advice about an "interesting communication" of November 5 from Elbert Hubbard of East Aurora, New York, and from the Committee for the Philistine Society: "Recognizing your merit as a man and your genius as a poet, and wishing that the world should know you better, the Society of the Philistines tender you a dinner to take place at the Iroquois Hotel in Buffalo in about one month. As soon as we receive your acceptance stating the date that suits you best we will send out invitations to 200 of the best known writers, publishers and newspaper men of the United States and England." The committee flattered Crane by adding that the dinner would be of very great value to his books and lead to "a wider recognition of your talents."

They did not mention *The Red Badge,* but Hubbard's covering letter took care of that: *"The Red Badge* is a strong work thoroughly well sustained. I congratulate you on it. Sincerely your friend, Elbert Hubbard. Send acceptance to me."

Crane by November 10 had not yet accepted, and so the committee wrote him again and said much the same thing as in their letter of the 5th but added more names to the list of newspaper editors sponsoring the dinner. Now the list included not only editors from Buffalo but also from Boston, Denver, New Orleans, Washington and Rochester. They would all cooperate to make the dinner a big success, said Hubbard. To accept their invitation, Crane wrote him on the 15th, would be a tacit admission of his worthiness, and that was the only obstacle. "Believe me, this sense of embarrassment that I should be at all considered as a fit person for such distinction is my solitary discomfort. But I have industriously blunted this sense and can say that it will deal me great pleasure to dine with the Society of the Philistines on Thursday evening, Dec. 19th."

Hawkins had insisted that he accept the invitation, even though Crane had asked him how to get out of the thing. He had no dress suit and no overcoat, but Hawkins assured him that he'd be togged properly for the occasion. "Send me your chest measurements and your length of leg (from your crotch to your heel—you remember Lincoln's answer when he asked how long an ideal soldier's leg should be) and I'll find some way." (A soldier's leg—said Lincoln—ought to be at least long enough to reach to the ground.)

"My chest, bad luck to it, measures 35 inches—scant—and my leg is 33—worse luck," Crane replied. "My foot—rot it—is a seven. There! It is over. I feel as if I have told you that I am a damned thief. Heaven send you rest, Willis, and in your old age may you remember how you befriended the greatest literary blockhead in America from himself. . . . What do you suppose made the Philistines do this dinner thing? Was it because I wrote for their magazine? You could have knocked me down with a gas-pipe when I got their bid. Until today [November 14] I was very miserable about it for I of course was resolved to refuse the offer. But, bad luck to me again, I was delighted with your letter and accepted it 'within-side' of thirty minutes. The woods up here are all dun and dusk and purple save where they are pines or white birches. The little lake is like blue crystal." There on what is now called "The Stephen Crane Pond" at Hartwood he sailed a boat that "leans like a shingle on a house—when she tacks—and the November winds are very strong . . . I am very contented here. For a while I felt incarcerated but not now. Good-bye. My remembrances always to your Greene Ave. castle. Your friend—ever."

Hartwood's pond and forests could have remained his sanctuary, but he was often tempted to sample the wide world, as now in this excursion to Buffalo. It portended an ordeal, this dinner scheme, he wrote, "but in the larger sense it overwhelms me in pride and arrogance to think that I have such friends. By the way, you ought to see the effect of such things upon my family. Aint they swelled up, though! Gee! I simply can't go around and see 'em near enough. It's great. I am no longer a black sheep but a star." Nevertheless, the prospective dinner worried him; he dreaded making any after-dinner speech.

Hubbard's stationery was watermarked with a colored drawing of his likeness large as half the sheet, and he also sent a photograph of himself, which Crane did not need for identifying the editor of *The Philistine*, since they had already met in New York. A year before Hubbard began publishing his magazine, he had lost on a train two of Crane's articles intended for *The Philistine:* an article expounding a social theory and a sketch about slum charities. Nearly every issue of the magazine in 1895 printed a Crane poem.

Hubbard called his magazine *The Philistine* because he was going after the "Chosen People" in literature: Howells of *Harper's,* Gilder of the *Century,* Edward Bok of *Ladies' Home Journal,* and McClure of *McClure's Magazine.* All these editors had turned down his manuscripts: so he declared war on the entire fashionable literary world and chose this epithet of contempt. He was also contemptuous of higher education because he had been let out of Harvard. He drolly named himself Fra Elbertus because he absorbed gluttonously from all whom he deeply admired. He used butcher-paper wrappers for his magazine, and when asked why, he retorted: "Because it has meat inside!" The brown butcher-paper became its emblem during the twenty years of its life. The *Philistine* survived all other little magazines and made Hubbard wealthy. Said the Boston *Herald:* "It is very handsome and sassy."

Sassy and flippant was Fra Elbertus and also serious and solemn and circumspect, irreverent and devout. He was a combination of Barnum, Buffalo Bill and Preacher Henry Ward Beecher. Like Barnum, he believed in ballyhoo; like Buffalo Bill, he wore his hair long and affected a loose, flowing Windsor tie. He made *The Philistine* his pulpit, but unlike hypocrite Beecher he was honest about his humbug. Fra Elbertus dramatized himself as a sort of composite of Ralph Waldo Emerson and William Morris, "but his chief claim to fame is that of being the father of Modern Advertising. He had a perfect genius for publicity," says Claude Bragdon in "The Purple Cow Period" (1928), "smoking up other people's talents and throwing them away like a daily newspaper, accomplishing a considerable amount of good in the process, for to his vast clientele he sustained something of the relation of Chautauqua, disseminating about as rich a brand of 'culturine' as the middle-class American stomach was able to stand." His *Philistine* was his speaking trumpet—"pungent, abusive, witty, knowing, vulgar." Its ugly brownish-green coarse cover and its typography had nothing of the beauty of other little magazines such as the *Chap Book,* edited by Bliss Carman, and *The Lark,* launched by Gelett Burgess, whose "Purple Cow" verse in the first number brought him fame and defined the Purple Cow period of American letters, which synchronized with *The Yellow Book* period in England. Hubbard and Harry Taber, a lithograph salesman for Cosack & Company, printed on a handpress the first three issues of *The Philistine: A Periodical of Protest,* beginning in June, 1895.

Crane was disappointed that Hawkins was not going by the Erie to Buffalo: "You were to be the moral reinforcement which I sought. I can't come to N.Y. because it requires 'dough.' I have mapped out my two or three shekels so that I will return home smiling but broke and in the smoking-car. I bought to-day one full dress shirt and what goes with it. I have a damn fine hat." He reminded Hawkins that he had "no overcoat save that little gauze one which you may remember. Nor no dress-suit." One of his brothers had a pair of patent-leathers, and Stephen slept with them under his pillow.

In the same letter to Hawkins, written during the week prior to December 15, when he took the rural train to Buffalo, he reports that other literary clubs were competing now with the Philistine Society to obtain his presence at dinners honoring him, and the Philistines were hot about it: "There is a peach of a row on in Buffalo." The Browning Club and the Saturn Club hoped to engage him there. "And now, Willis, old man, when I get in all this flumy-doodle business and see you behind there moving the scenes and knowing all the time what a damned fool I am and what a ridiculous hole I'm in, I get fair feeble-minded with dwelling upon it. I leave it all to you. For my part I wish the whole thing was in Ballyhoo because while I look forward to it as probably the greatest pleasure of my life, I feel as if I were astride your shoulders. And if I could stop the thing now I would." Hawkins responded that he was going by the New York Central to reach Buffalo by noon of Thursday, the 19th, and would go straight to the Genesee Hotel to look for him. He had sent him an overcoat by express on the 17th and promised to fix up the dress suit problem when in Buffalo. "We'll have a bully time."

The Philistine Society printed a banquet menu-folder presenting three dozen tributes to Crane with the regrets of authors and journalists unable to get to Buffalo. The affair originally was scheduled to be held in East Aurora, and then because that village was obscure and inconvenient the plan was revised for Buffalo, first at the Iroquois and finally the Genesee Hotel. East Aurora was the most unlikely place for any literary venture; although there was a Chautauqua reading circle, it was known mainly for its "World's Greatest Trotting Nursery" with trotting tracks, blacksmith and harness shops, a dozen barns, a covered track for year-round racing, and eight hundred horses. Crane bought one of them from Hubbard during his four-day visit with him after the Philistine banquet.

Poet Bliss Carman—as quoted in the menu folder—said it would give him "great pleasure to sit at a feast with Mr. Crane and the bold and worthy Philistines, but I cannot find East Aurora in my Railroad Guide." The menu printed Howells' tribute: "I am very glad to know that my prophecies are being realized and that Mr. Crane is receiving recognition at a time in life when he can enjoy it." Hamlin Garland said he took special interest in Mr. Crane, as he was one of the very first to know about *Maggie* and *The Red Badge*. Daniel Appleton, Crane's publisher, said much the same thing. Journalist Richard Harding Davis sent his respects.

There were notes from S. S. McClure, who the next year contracted Crane on a salary to write for *McClure's Magazine,* and from poetess Louise Imogen Guiney. There was a witty note from Twain's co-author of *The Gilded Age,* Charles Dudley Warner: "The Crane dinner, I hope, will encourage and strengthen the inner man without enlarging unduly that portion where our imagination is supposed to dwell." And from Hopper of the U. S. Treasury: "Mr. Crane certainly wears the Red Badge of Courage if he can face the Philistines in such an encounter as this." Someone wrote that the trade of literature contains the best fellows in the world—and some of the damnedest rogues, thus suggesting that Hubbard was exploiting Crane's rising fame. Hayden Carruth, editor and author of humorous writings, submitted a parody in verse: "I Saw a Man Reading an Invitation." Irving Bacheller and Hitchcock sent notes. A pert note came from the editor of the Albany *Express:* "I have a profound admiration for a man who, casting to the winds rhyme, reason, and metre, can still write poetry."

Ambrose Bierce out in California wrote Harry Taber to thank him for his kind invitation to the Crane dinner and expressed best wishes for the Society of the Philistines; in another letter Bierce wrote: "Were it not for the miles which separate us, I would be with you."

This collection of quoted tributes was headed by a line from John Dryden: "Fate Frowned upon Them and They Could Not Come." Then came the menu itself (from bluepoints to bonbons), and printed on the cover was a Beardsleyesque drawing of rocking horses somehow intended to suggest *The Black Riders,* while first lines of some of Crane's poems were quoted on the back of the menu. This menu-folder was reprinted in May, 1896, as *A Souvenir and a Medley*. It contained eight Crane poems (all but one reprinted from *The Philistine*), "A Great Mistake" (an East Side sketch published for the first time), and "A Prologue" (a kind of prose-poem).[6]

But the banquet intended to honor Crane ended as a farce, in an orgy of chaos and bickering among the thirty guests, many of them newspaper-men and drunk, who had assembled not so much to honor Crane as to enjoy the sport of ribald interruptions and pseudo-friendly guffaws. Hubbard had assured Stephen that the Philistine Society banquet would be perfect and complete in all its appointments and that it was not merely to be a pleasant meeting and dinner. Crane represented a cause, "and we wish in a dignified, public (and at the same time) elegant manner to recognize that cause." When Harry Taber of *The Philistine* and the Roycroft Printing Shop in East Aurora arose to give his after-dinner speech, he got as far as saying: "Probably the most unique—" That was as far as he got, for a voice called out "Can *unique* be compared?" That determined the tone of the festivities, said Frank Noxon of the Boston *Record,* who had come all the way from Boston—in borrowed clothes and on borrowed money—to pay homage to his Syracuse fraternity brother. "In the best Clover and Gridiron manner Taber and all the other speakers were guyed and ragged from start to finish."

Hubbard approved of the tongue-lashing Claude Fayette Bragdon gave his guests. When Crane sat down, up rose Bragdon: "I came here to do honor to Stephen Crane, not to ridicule him. I regret to take this step, but I cannot longer remain in the room." Hawkins blocked his way to the door, saying: "One moment. I am the oldest man in this room. I know Stephen Crane better than anyone else here. I have slept with him, eaten with him, starved with him, ridden with him, swum with him. I know him through and through, every mood. I have come here, like our friend, to do honor to Stephen Crane. I have taken part in all that has occurred, and he knows I love him and admire him. He knows that you all do. I assure you he feels more complimented by the spirit of this meeting than he would have been by all the solemn eulogies that could be pronounced." Crane nodded his head, and everyone applauded. Crane seemed to be having the time of his life, says Frank Noxon in "The Real Stephen Crane" (*Step Ladder*: January 1928). "I am sorry," said Bragdon, "if I have made a mistake. I ask your pardon." "The condition," said Hawkins, "is that you turn around and take your seat." And Bragdon did.

Elbert Hubbard's historic dinner for Stephen Crane, whose star was just then rising above the horizon, "provides a perfect example of his [Hubbard's] method of getting publicity for himself by means of others," says Bragdon in his *Bookman* article for July 1929 ("The Purple Cow Period"). "I do not impeach Hubbard's sincerity; he admired Crane's talent as sincerely as a lover the woman he desires; but that dinner, held in a private room of a Buffalo hotel, is still a distressing memory—like the sight of a young ox led to the slaughter." It was distressing to Crane, too, although he pretended not to have been disillusioned. Bragdon, who later designed costumes and scenes for theatrical productions and became known as the "the Beardsley of America" for his drawings in Hubbard's *Philistine* and in the Chicago *Chap-Book,* says that Crane made a deep impression on him: "A youth sincere and ardent, with an inward fire greater than that of other men—so great, indeed, that it was even then burning him up," says Bragdon in his *More Lives Than One,* 1938).

The noisy guests had much fun in forcing Crane to his feet for a speech in response to Taber's tribute to "the strong voice now heard in America, the voice of Stephen Crane." His speech scintillated with flashes of wit to the merriment of all, said the *Bookman*. It also reported that Taber "presided gracefully as toastmaster," whereas in fact he had a hard time of it. The Buffalo *News* the next morning reported that Mr. Crane responded modestly and gracefully, saying that he was "a working newspaper man trying to do what he could since he had recovered from college with the machinery he possessed—doing it sincerely, if clumsily, and simply setting forth in his own way his own impressions. He is a young fellow—twenty-four—with a smooth face and a keen eye and doesn't take himself over seriously." (He had shaved off the moustache that he wore while en route to Mexico.)

On New Year's Eve (1895) Crane wrote Willis Hawkins that he was returning the overcoat he had borrowed from him for the Philistine Society banquet and asked for his impression of that affair. "Hubbard and Taber think you are just the smoothest guy in the world. . . . I did not drink much but the excitement soon turned everything into a grey haze for me and I am not sure that I came off decently." On New Year's Eve he also wrote Nellie Crouse about the Philistine dinner, and he transcribed the committee's invitation and his November 15 reply. "I was very properly engaged at the word 'poet' which continually reminds me of long-hair and seems to me to be a most detestable form of insult but nevertheless I replied. . . . I went to Buffalo and this is not at all what happened." Here Crane attached a clipping of "The Philistines at Dinner" from the Buffalo *Evening News* of December 20: "Mr Crane is unquestionably a Philistine, according to the definition of the society, for he writes what pleases him, in his own way, and takes all the chances of its pleasing any one else. The purpose of the Philistines is to encourage just such independence and individuality in literature and other matters, and Mr. Crane was thus in the house of friends though personally known beforehand to none of the Philistines here." (Hubbard no doubt wrote that account for the *Evening News* as it says the same thing that he later said in his *Lotus* article.) Crane adds in his letter to Nellie that it is one man's idea of what happened and not altogether wrong, at least in proper names. "I had a good time and caused them considerable trouble in inventing nice things to say to me."

He no doubt had a good time, but he had thought the occasion was to be a tribute to him as a literary man, and it was hardly that. Now, in writing Hawkins and Nellie Crouse, he kept up the front, but something of his disillusionment lingered for months. Hubbard's Philistine banquet, although ostensibly intended to put him on the literary map, was really a bit of shrewd advertising for Hubbard himself. If Bragdon saw it that way, Crane could hardly fail to recognize what a fraud it had been.

On November 12, when he was working on a short story for McClure entitled "The Little Regiment," Crane wrote Hawkins: "It is awfully hard. I have invented the sum of my invention in regard to war and this story keeps me in eternal despair. However, I am coming on with it very comfortably after all." He was also finishing *The Third Violet*. Then after the Philistine affair he wrote Hawkins from Hubbard's house on the back of one of the dinner menu-folders that he was coming to New York City on Tuesday morning (December 24), but he didn't get there because his free railroad pass (obtained through station agent Edmund) was not good on the Central to New York but on the Erie to Port Jervis, and so he spent the Christmas holidays with Edmund's family at Hartwood instead. From there he sent the manuscript of his new story of country and city life, *The Third Violet,* and asked Ripley Hitchcock on the 27th for his opinion in haste, as he thought of starting "very shortly to some quarter of the world where mail is uncertain."

When *The Third Violet* had been two-thirds done in mid-November, he had given the first eighteen chapters to Edmund to read, and then had written Hawkins that Teddie (Edmund) "thinks my style wouldn't be used by the devil to patch his trousers with. I think he—Teddie—discovered the fellow and the girl in the story and read on to find out if they married. He hung around for a time asking for more chapters but I sent him away." Edmund was "an awful stuff in literature."

Curtis Brown sent a newspaper clipping about *The Red Badge* and some kind words, and Crane responded on December 31st: "I hear the damned book is doing very well in England. In the meantime I am plodding along. I have finished my new novel—'The Third Violet'—and sent it to Appleton and Co., as per request, but I've an idea it won't be accepted. It's pretty rotten work. I used myself up in the accursed 'Red Badge.' "

He had in mind writing a series of sketches of various Civil War battles, but he ended with imaginary war stories such as "The Little Regiment," "Three Miraculous Soldiers," and "A Mystery of Heroism," which Appleton published late the next year in *The Little Regiment* (a collection of six stories). He had thought he'd never again write about war, but Hitchcock and the Phillips-and-McClure Syndicate pressured him, and in despair about doing more war stories Crane poured out his plight to a neighbor at Hartwood while he was sitting on a rock near the pond below Edmund's house that December. From Hartwood he wrote John Phillips on the 13th: "Your project it seemed to me would require a great deal of study and a great deal of time. I would be required to give up many of my plans for this winter and this I am reluctant to do. I don't know how you would advise going about it but one of the first things I would want to do would be to visit the battle-field—which I was to describe—at the time of year when it was fought. The preliminary reading and the subsequent reading, and investigations of all kinds, would take much time. Moreover, if I did not place the original crown of pure gold on the heads of at least twelve generals they would arise and say: 'This damned young fool was not there. I was however. And this is how it happened.' I evaded them in the *Red Badge* because it was essential that I should make my battle a type and name no names but in your case, it would be very different." He preferred visiting the battlefields in the spring when "the anniversaries of the fights begin to occur, but he was pressured into going down to Virginia in late January to study the battlefields at Fredericksburg and Chancellorsville, which he had imagined as the battlefield for his *Red Badge of Courage* back in 1893.[7]

# X

## ☞ "*The Red Badge of Courage*"

"I WRITE what is in me, and it will be enough to follow with obedience the promptings of that inspiration, if it be worthy of so dignified a name," Crane had remarked at the Philistine Society banquet. To the *Book Buyer*'s reviewer, however, he said: "I don't believe in inspiration. I am one of those who believe that an enthusiasm of concentration in hard work is what a writer must depend on to bring him to the end he has in view." He had begun *The Red Badge of Courage,* he told the *Book Buyer* (April, 1895), as a short story for a newspaper and had selected a battle as his subject because warfare afforded plenty of color and range for the imagination. As he went on the story grew, and he determined to put the best work into it he was capable of.

He remarked to Louis Senger that his motive for tackling the job was a wager made during the heat of an argument with Acton Davies in William Dallgren's studio over Zola's *La Débâcle.* Crane declared that although he had never seen even a sham battle he could write a better book. "I deliberately started to do a pot-boiler, something that would take the boarding school element—you know the kind. Well, I got interested in the thing in spite of myself, and I couldn't, I couldn't! I *had* to do it my way." Crane made his boastful claim to Acton Davies shortly after he read a review of Zola's Prussian War novel in July, 1892, and so his Civil War novel may be said to have begun then; it emerged in first draft by early 1893. Thomas Beer says that Crane returned to Mrs. Armstrong (the Miss Brett who had spanked young Stephen for "burying" her little nephew in the ocean sands at Asbury Park) the Century's *Battles and Leaders of the Civil War* with a note of April 2 (1893): "Thank you very much for letting me keep these so long. I have spent ten nights writing a story of the war on my own responsibility but I am not sure that my facts are real and the books won't tell me what I want to know so I must do it all over again, I guess." Perhaps it was at this time he went to Fredericksburg, Virginia, and interviewed Confederate veterans; he was determined to write "a real story of the Civil War."

Crane would begin with a germinal idea and brood over it; then, he

168

said, "comes a longing for you don't know what: sorrow, too, and heart-hunger." Once the start was written, that determined the rest of the book; as each part progressed he discovered his next move, "never knowing the end, but forcing himself to follow 'that fearful logical conclusion.' " So it was with *The Red Badge of Courage*. Joseph Conrad describes how Crane in a prolonged creative spurt would go on writing whole chapters with no revisions other than a few words, and the evidence is in the manuscripts. He would sit down before a blank sheet of paper and write the first line at once, going on without haste and without pause for a couple of hours. It seemed to Conrad "always a perfect miracle in the way of mastery over material and expression." It is no wonder that Linson was awed by Crane's genius and felt in his presence "a power mysterious and unaccountable," or that Garland was amazed to see Crane "drawing off" poems spontaneously, "all without blot or erasure. Every letter stood out like the writing of a bank bill. . . . He wrote steadily in beautifully clear script with perfect alignment and spacing, precisely as if he were copying something already written and before his eyes." He wrote with astonishing facility: *The Third Violet* was written at the pace of twenty-five pages per week, and many of his sketches and stories were created in the same incandescent mood—in one night, sometimes in an hour. "Short stories are the easiest thing to write," he told Herbert Williams. He worked methodically and at the same time in spells, he explained to Karl Harriman, the young aspiring writer from Michigan who stayed at Brede Manor during the summer of 1899.

Writing *The Red Badge* was not the spontaneous, unpremeditated creative spurt Crane liked to say it was. Conrad speaks of Crane's unsophisticated inspiration and describes him as a writer "who in his art (as indeed in his private life) was the least 'contriving' of men," but he concedes that Crane contrived *The Red Badge,* every impression in it being preconceived and patterned, one image with another. His was not a studied technique, however, and he agreed with Linson that self-conscious work was bad as art. Vosburgh testifies that in *The Red Badge* "almost every impression was preconceived" and that Crane in the Needham studios studied with much care all his daring phrases and metaphors and then, after he had trimmed them to final form, he would repeat them aloud "and dwell on them lovingly."

He worked out the idea for *The Red Badge* first of all "not so much on paper as in his own mind. He spoke frequently of its hero as 'growing.' 'He's getting to be quite a character now,' he said one day. . . . The character was as clear and vital to him, in his mind, as a living person could have been; and it was such a conception and development of him that made him, when Stephen finally got him upon paper, appear so marvelously real" (to quote Willis Johnson of the *Tribune*).

*The Red Badge of Courage* begins with the army immobilized—with restless men waiting for orders to move, and Henry Fleming—the youth whose name is not given until halfway through the book—disillusioned by his first days as a raw recruit. There is a rumor that tomorrow, at last, the army will go into action. When the "tall soldier"—Jim Conklin—first announces it he waves a shirt, which he has just washed in a muddy brook, like a banner to summon the men around the flag of his colorful rumor. But his prophecy of hope meets with disbelief. "It's a lie!" shouts the "Loud Soldier." "I don't believe the derned old army's ever going to move." The skeptical soldier thinks Jim Conklin is just telling a tall tale; a furious altercation ensues. Meanwhile Henry in his hut engages in a spiritual debate with himself, whether to believe or disbelieve the word of his friend, whom he has known since childhood. It is the gospel truth, but Henry is one of the doubting apostles.

The opening scene thus sets the structural pattern of the whole book. Hope and faith shift to despair or disbelief. The countermovement of opposition begins with the small detail of the Negro teamster who stops his dancing when the men desert him to wrangle over Jim Conklin's rumor. "He sat mournfully down." This image of motion and change (the motion ceasing and the joy turning to gloom) presents the dominant leitmotif and the form of the whole book in miniature. In Chapter I the prologue ends in a coda with theme and anti-theme interjoined in the figure of the corporal. His uncertainties (whether to repair his house) and his shifting attitudes of trust and distrust (whether the army is going to move) parallel the skeptical outlook of the wrangling men. The same anti-theme of distrust is dramatized in the episode that follows this coda, and every subsequent episode in the sequence is designed similarly by one contrast pattern or another.

The army, which lies resting on the hills, is first revealed to us by "the retiring fogs," and as the weather changes the landscape changes, the brown hills turning to a new green; as nature stirs, the army stirs too. Nature and men are in psychic affinity; even the weather changes as though in sympathetic accord with man's plight. The "retiring fogs" in Crane's opening sentence anticipate Henry's mental awakening: "The cold passed reluctantly from the earth, and the retiring fogs revealed an army stretched out on the hills, resting." They are the fogs of Henry's own mind, and not until they are dispersed ("reluctantly") can the youth establish warm identity with life.

If the novel begins with motifs of change and deception, it ends with Henry's self-deception. It probes a state of mind under the incessant pinpricks and bombardments of life; the theme is that man's salvation lies in change, in spiritual growth. Only by immersion in the flux of experience does man become disciplined and develop in character, conscience or soul. Potentialities for change are at their greatest in battle since a battle represents life at its most intense flux. Crane's book is essentially not about the combat of armies; it is about the self-combat of a youth who fears and stubbornly resists change, and the actual battle is symbolic of this spiritual warfare against change and growth. Henry Fleming recognizes the necessity for change and development, but wars against it. He will not accept the truth that a man must lose his soul in order to save it.

In the paragraph that Crane first intended for the ending of *The Red Badge,* the rain, corresponding with the despondent mood of the soldiers, recalls the novel's opening image of the retiring fogs.

> The procession of weary soldiers became a bedraggled train, despondent and muttering, marching with churning effort in a trough of liquid brown mud under a low, wretched sky. Yet the youth smiled, for he saw that the world was a world for him, though many discovered it to be made of oaths and walking sticks.

Crane wrote "The End," but on second thought he added these words to the closing paragraph:

> He had rid himself of the red sickness of battle. The sultry nightmare was in the past. He had been an animal blistered and sweating in the heat and pain of war. He turned now with a lover's thirst to images of tranquil skies, fresh meadows, cool brooks—an existence of soft and eternal peace.

That this second ending was less effective he realized and therefore added a third ending which consists of a single image:

> Over the river a golden ray of sun came through the hosts of leaden rain clouds.

This final sentence does not appear in the manuscript. Crane added it in the typescript, which Appleton's office prepared from the final handwritten manuscript, and thus recapitulated the despair-hope contrasted mood initiated in the opening scene of Chapter I. The sun shines, but it pierces "hosts of leaden rain clouds." Henry sees himself as having attained manhood, a change of soul, an existence of eternal peace, but leaden rain clouds obscure the sunlight of his separate peace. He has sought redemption and thinks he has attained it, but the ambiguous imagery of sun-through-rain cloud both affirms and simultaneously undercuts that affirmation. His longing for "soft and eternal peace" is just as unrealistic as his earlier code of Greek heroics. Seen from Crane's ironic viewpoint, Henry Fleming has undergone no true spiritual change or redemption.

In the final scene the leaden rain clouds shine with "a golden ray" reflecting Henry's own tranquillity of mind, but at the beginning of *The Red Badge* (and throughout the book) his mind is in a "tumult of agony and despair." This psychological tumult begins when Henry hears the church bells announce that a great battle has been fought. The clanging bell and all the commotion arouse in him legendary visions of heroic selfhood. The noisy world clamors for Henry to become absorbed into the solidarity of self-forgetful comradeship, but he resists this challenge of the "mysterious fraternity born of the smoke and danger of death"; again and again he withdraws from the din of the affray to indulge in self-contemplative moods and magic reveries. The walls of the forest insulate him from the noise of battle.

In seeking retreat to absolve his shame and guilt, Henry, renouncing manhood, is "seeking dark and intricate places." It is as though he were seeking return to the womb. Nature, that "woman with a deep aversion to tragedy," is Mother Nature, and the human equation for the forest is of course his own mother. His flight from the forest sanctuary represents his momentary rejection of womblike innocence; periodically he rejects Mother Nature with her sheltering arms and her "religion of peace," and his flight is symbolic of his initiation into the truth of the world he must measure up to. He is the deceived youth, for death lurks even in the forest sanctuary. In the pond a gleaming fish is killed by one of the forest creatures, and in the forest he meets a rotted corpse, a man whose eyes stare like a dead fish, with ants scurrying over the face: the treachery of ideals—the illusions by which we are betrayed.

Throughout *The Red Badge* the young hero's longing to prove himself is frustrated: "The youth had been taught that a man becomes another thing in battle. He saw his salvation in such a change. Hence this waiting was an ordeal to him." In Chapter IX, where Crane struck off the phrase which he utilized as the final title of the novel, the youth "regarded the wounded soldiers in an envious way. He conceived persons with torn bodies to be peculiarly happy. He wished that he, too, had a wound, a red badge of courage."[1] But when Henry witnesses Jim Conklin's death he rejects the way of the battlefield—and therefore the way of salvation. He wants no red badge.

In his poem "The Blue Battalions" (1897) Crane calls God a War Lord:

> *The clang of swords is Thy wisdom,*
> *The wounded make gestures like Thy Son's.*

Mortally wounded, "the spectral soldier" tightens his lips as though to hold in check "the moan of great despair. There could be seen a certain stiffness in the movements of his body, as if he were taking infinite care not to arouse the passion of his wounds." When he turned his waxlike features toward Henry Fleming, the youth screams: " 'Gawd! Jim Conklin!' " The youth and the "tattered soldier" "began to have thoughts of a solemn ceremony. There was something ritelike in these movements of the doomed soldier. And there was a resemblance in him to a devotee [priest *canceled*] of a mad religion, blood-sucking, muscle-wrenching, bone-crushing. [They could not understand.*] They were awed and afraid. They hung back lest he have at command a dreadful weapon."

"His tall figure stretched itself to its full height. There was a slight rending sound. Then it began to swing forward, slow and straight, in the manner of a falling tree." His side "looked as if it had been chewed by wolves.

The youth turned, with sudden, livid rage, toward the battlefield. He shook his fist. He seemed about to deliver a philippic.
'Hell—'
The red sun was pasted in the sky like a wafer."

Crane first wrote the line: "The fierce [*canceled*] red sun was pasted in the sky like a fierce [*later canceled*] wafer." Although eliminated, the repeated word *fierce* underscores the fact that Crane intended the sun to personify the wrathful gods of Henry Fleming's insult and worship. In the final handwritten manuscript the youth shakes his fist at the sky and Crane spells out the philippic: "Promptly, then, his old rebellious feelings returned. He thought the powers of fate had combined to heap misfortune upon him. He was an innocent victim. He rebelled against the source of things, according to his law that the most powerful should receive the most blame." "War, he said bitterly to the sky, was a make-shift, created because ordinary processes didn't furnish deaths enough. To seduce her victims, nature had to formulate a beautiful excuse. She made glory. This made the men willing, anxious, in haste, to come and be killed. And, with heavy humor, he thought of how nature must smile when she saw the men come running. They regarded warfare and courage as holy things and did not see that nature had placed them in hearts because virtuous indignation would not last through a black struggle. Men would grow tired of it. They would go home. They must be inspired by some sentiment that they could call sacred and enshrine in their heart, something that would cause them to regard slaughter as fine and go at it cheerfully; something that could destroy all the binding of loves and places that tie men's hearts. She made glory. From his pinnacle of wisdom, he regarded the armies as large collections of dupes: Nature's dupes, who were killing each other to carry out some great scheme of life. They were under the impression that they were fighting for principles and honor and homes and various things. Well, to be sure, they were." Henry is enraged. "He turned in tuppenny fury upon the high, tranquil sky. He would have liked to have splashed it with a derisive paint. And he was bitter that among all men he should be the only one sufficiently wise to understand these things."[2]

At Jim Conklin's death the fiercely red sun assumes the color which

---

* This passage was expunged from the final manuscript, Manuscript LV, first published in *Stephen Crane: An Omnibus,* edited by R. W. Stallman (1952).

elsewhere in the novel symbolizes war, blood and violence. Henry Fleming blasphemes against the "wafer" of the sun in this climactic moment. The sun as "wafer" represents redemption and rebirth, but it is the emblem of salvation through death—in the Army of the Lord. Henry rebels against the God of War by shaking his fist at his bloody emblem.

In one of his *Black Riders* poems Crane had written:

> *Suppose that I should have the courage*
> *To let a red sword of virtue*
> *Plunge into my heart,*
> *Letting to the weeds of the ground*
> *My sinful blood,*
> *What can you offer me?*
> *A flowery kingdom?*
> *What? A hope?*
> *Then hence with your red sword of virtue.*

Red is the color of war ("the red animal, war, the blood-swollen god") but also red is the wine of the sacrament and the red wafer is the white wafer saturated by the blood of Christ.

It seems clear that Crane intended to suggest the sacrificial death celebrated in Communion and the Mass.[3] Henry Fleming curses the God of War, who offers redemption through bloodshed.

Jim Conklin's red badge of courage is the literal one, the wound of which he dies; Henry's is psychological, the wound of conscience. It is fitting that he should receive a head wound, a bump that jolts him with a severe headache. But what "salve" is there to ease the pain of his internal wound of dishonor? This is Henry's real "headache"! It is the ache of his conscience that he has been honored by the regiment he has dishonored. Just as Jim runs into the fields to hide his true wound from Henry, so Henry runs into the fields to hide his false wound, his false badge of courage, from the tattered man who asks him where he is wounded. "It might be inside mostly, an' them plays thunder. Where is it located?" The men, so Henry feels, are perpetually probing his guilt-wound, "ever upraising the ghost of shame on the stick of their curiosity." The unmistakable implication here is of a flag, and the actual flag that Henry carries in battle is the symbol of his conscience.

Conscience is also symbolized by the forest, the cathedral-forest where Henry retreats to nurse his guilt-wound and be consoled by the benedictions that nature sympathetically bestows upon him. Here in this forest chapel there is a churchlike silence as he bows his head in shame; the insects make a "devotional pause" while the trees chant a soft hymn to comfort him. But Henry is troubled; he cannot "conciliate the forest." Nor can he conciliate the flag. The flag registers the commotion of his mind, and it registers the restless movements of the nervous regiment—it flutters when the men expect battle. When the regiment runs from battle, the flag sinks down "as if dying. Its motion as it fell was a gesture of despair." Henry dishonors the flag not when he flees from battle but when he flees from himself, and he redeems the flag when he redeems his conscience.

Redemption begins in confession, in absolution—in a change of heart, in humility. Henry's example is the Loud Soldier, who becomes the humble soldier. The Loud Soldier admits the folly of his former ways. Henry comes nearest to spiritual change when he loses his soul in the flux of things, when he courageously deserts himself instead of his fellow men; then fearlessly plunging into battle, charging the enemy like "a pagan who defends his religion," he becomes swept up in a delirium of selflessness and feels himself "capable of profound sacrifices." But this new Henry, who has supposedly triumphed over the old is more conscious of himself than ever! Proud Henry still has no red badge of courage. Thinking that he is reborn he is self-deceived and has only a "salve" for his wounded conscience.

The conceit of man, says Crane in "The Blue Hotel," is "the very engine of life." The conceit of Henry Fleming links *The Red Badge* with "The Blue Hotel," where the arrogant Swede ends in ignoble defeat because of delusions of grandeur. It is the same ironic deflation of the conceit of man in "The Mesmeric Mountain," where the egocentric little man assaults an imperturbable mountain only to find when he swaggers with valor at its top that the mountain he assaulted is motionless and imperturbable. The little man of that fable has illusions which get undermined by realities, and so does Henry Fleming. The foil to Henry's conceit and vanity is the "tattered soldier." He had "loaned his last of strength and intellect for the 'Tall Soldier,' who, blind with weariness and pain, had been deserted in the field." And also the living reproof to Henry's vanity is the "Loud Soldier," Wilson, who after the first battle "seemed no more to be continually regarding the proportions of his personal prowess. He was not furious at small words that pricked his conceits. He was no more the loud soldier." He and the "Cheery Soldier" replace the "Tall Soldier," Conklin, who is virtually forgotten after his death. Henry, on the contrary, remains the conceited youth. In "The Little Regiment," a Civil War story Crane wrote in late 1895 after *The Red Badge of Courage,* the soldier Dan adopts "a fervid insubordination, an almost religious reluctance to obey the new corporal's orders." It is the same with Henry Fleming's religious reluctance to follow the example of Jim Conklin—Christ in the Army of the Lord.

In "The Little Regiment" Crane used a variation of the red sun image: "After the red round eye of the sun had stared long at the little plain and its burden, darkness, a sable mercy, came heavily upon it, and the wan hands of the dead were no longer seen in strange frozen gestures. . . . Suddenly, upon one dark spot, there was a resurrection." Here, too, as in *The Red Badge* the image of the red sun is fierce and wrathful—as opposed to darkness, "sable mercy," and the context carries religious overtones.

Crane's source for the notion of the red sun as wafer was Kipling's *The Light That Failed* (1891),[4] where the artist Dick Heldar—"suffering from swelled head"—speculates about his career as artist, much as Henry Fleming does about his career as soldier. Just then: "The fog was driven apart for a moment, and the sun shone, a blood-red wafer, on the water." The fog lifts at the moment when Dick Heldar has an insight, and his mood of defiance is imaged in the blood-red sun. It is the same situation in Henry Fleming's defiance of the red sun wafer appearing at Jim Conklin's grotesque ritual.

Although *The Red Badge of Courage* is not a sustained allegory or parable, considerable thematic counterpointing exists in Crane's inconsistently symbolic novel for interpreting it as a religious allegory. This interpretation has been much argued about, and Crane's ambiguities have confounded his readers. The image of the red sun pasted in the sky like a wafer has become the most celebrated metaphor in American literature. It has been praised—and roundly damned. Joseph Conrad, Willa Cather and Joseph Hergesheimer admired it (Hergesheimer didn't explain why), and others ridiculed it as a false, melodramatic, nonfunctional image or downright bad writing. The standard lantern-slide rerun of American literature by academic critics is a darkened spectacle when it comes to Crane. He obtained recognition in the 1920's solely through critics who were themselves artists in prose or verse. Mark Van Doren in 1925 said that the precise excellence of *The Red Badge of Courage* deserves analysis, but "it has never got it." And Willa Cather rightly remarked that Crane's image of the sun as a wafer—"that careless observation which Mr. Hergesheimer admires so much—isn't exceptional with Crane. He wrote like that when he was writing well."

Ernest Hemingway's statement that *The Red Badge of Courage* "is all as much one piece as a great poem is" is doubly revelatory because it defines not only Crane's novel but Hemingway's own *Farewell to Arms.* Hemingway's novel starts, as it were, where Crane's left off. Frederic Henry, who has for surname the same given name as Crane's hero, begins as the already maimed hero, the idealistic Henry Fleming turned cynic. Both are without father and are virtually nameless. Crane's hero is always simply the "youth." When, halfway through the book, the youth discloses what his name is, he is ashamed because he has fled the battlefield, and utters his name only to himself.

*A Farewell to Arms* is an inverted *Red Badge of Courage:* the one deals with disenchantment and withdrawal, the other with romantic illusion, quest and engagement. Both heroes undergo change and insight through wounds, but in opposite directions. Where Crane's hero progresses toward manhood and "moral triumph," Hemingway's Henry descends toward moral and spiritual degeneration. In both novels the education of the protagonist ends in self-deception. Frederic Henry renounces war, society and "the comforting stench" of comrades, to make a "separate peace." But his farewell to arms is as illusory as Henry Fleming's farewell to vain ideals and compromising illusions. Both heroes are deluded, the one believing he can turn his back upon the battle of life, the other believing that he has triumphed in facing up to it shorn of romantic notions and false sentiments. Both novels are ritualistic, mythic, symbolic. The alternating episodes in both concern withdrawal and return, the quest for self-identity, and insight or recognition through wound or suffering.

Frederic Henry's sanctuary of the lovers in *A Farewell to Arms,* whose central theme is that there is no sanctuary (everyone has to "get down off the mountains"), harks back through *The Red Badge* to *Huckleberry Finn.* Hemingway begins his novel exactly as Crane began his: on a change in the weather, on leitmotifs of change and deception. It is debatable whether Crane read *Huckleberry Finn* before writing his *Red Badge,* but both books have the same episodic structure (repetitions of ironic episodes), both deal with heroes in quest of selfhood, and both books have the themes of death and deception or betrayal. Neither book is merely the biography of a boy, a record of his adventures.

*The Red Badge of Courage* was the first nonromantic novel of the Civil War to attain widespread popularity. Appearing at a time when the war was still treated primarily as the subject for romance, it turned the tide of the prevailing convention and established a new if not unprecedented one. Ambrose Bierce and J. W. De Forest (in his *Miss Ravenel's Conversion,* 1867) had presented war from as unromantic a viewpoint as Crane did, but De Forest was never recognized and Bierce's war tales caused scarcely a ripple in 1891–1892. The American reading public—fed up with Civil War memoirs and novels—had escaped into the romantic world of George Du Maurier's *Trilby,* and yet that same public took to Crane's war novel, and he won a reputation greater than any other American as a realistic writer on war. Reviewers hailed *The Red Badge* as the most realistic war novel ever written, and critics since then have claimed that Crane initiated modern realism. But this ignores De Forest. Neither Crane nor Bierce rendered the actualities of recruits under fire with anything like the graphic realism of De Forest, yet what Crane wrote still passes—as it did even for Hemingway—as "real war literature."

In style and method he had no predecessors, but in viewing the war from the vantage point of the unromantic and commonplace conscript he was following the line of Walt Whitman's *Specimen Days.* Whitman's prediction that "the real war will never get in the books" was belied by his own *Specimen Days and Collect* (1882), by De Forest's graphic realism, and by Crane's psychological realism in *The Red Badge* and in "A Mystery of Heroism," one of his Civil War tales collected in *The Little Regiment.* Whitman actually had been at Chancellorsville, whereas Crane wrote about that battle imaginatively; his so-called unprecedented realism cannot compare with Whitman's report of that night battle, said the Manchester *Guardian* (March 26, 1898). We need a Stephen Crane, or an Ambrose Bierce, or a Rudyard Kipling in what is called military art, said the Glasgow *Sunday Times* (March 28, 1898), but in Crane's picture of warfare "we have not even a good follower of Detaille, still less of the realistic Vereshchagin." In a review of Whitman's *The Wound Dresser: A Series of Letters Written from the Hospitals in Washington During the War of the Rebellion,* the London *Daily Chronicle* (March 7, 1898) decided that Whitman's accounts of the horrors of war were more realistic than Tolstoy's, Zola's or Crane's. "The naked horror of the facts, or the sheer pity of them, far transcends anything which could be a 'literary' presentation."

It was realism that Crane himself aimed at, and his *Red Badge* has always been read as just that and nothing more: "Most of my prose writings have been toward the goal partially described by that misunderstood and abused word, realism," he said. Yet he is more than a realist in that the surface drama of his images conveys another significance. Truth in art consists not in fidelity to the observed or experienced facts of the actual world, but rather in the artist's fidelity to the felt truth in his vision. It is there (as Conrad intimated) that the honor of the artist lies: in fidelity to every part of the patterned whole:

*The Red Badge* is a literary exercise in language, in the patterning of words and the counterpointing of themes and tropes and colors. As the perceptive *Critic* noted, Crane's metaphors are employed purposefully, for thematic or structural pattern; they are not strung on for effect; they are as "living and actual as Homer's."

A tour de force of the imagination, *The Red Badge* is an impressionistic painting, not a realistic one like Vereshchagin's paintings of battlefields. Zola, not Crane, is the Vereshchagin of literature, said the New York *World* (February, 1896). An edition in French—*La Débâcle, par Emile Zola*—and an edition in English—*The Downfall*—were reviewed in the New York *Tribune* (July 10, 1892), and as Crane's sketch "The Broken-Down Van" appeared in that same Sunday issue he undoubtedly read there "M. Zola's War Story" and then the book itself, at least the opening chapters of *The Downfall.* He spoke of Tolstoy's *War and Peace* as "Peace and War," and that error he probably picked up from the *Tribune* review of Zola, where the same error occurs: "In making his witnesses private soldiers or noncommissioned officers, he [Zola] has clearly taken a leap from Tolstoy's *Peace and War,* though no suspicion of plagiarism attaches to him."

The opening situation in *The Red Badge* is much the same as in *The Downfall*: the army is at rest "in a sort of eternal camp" awaiting orders to move. And Crane's purpose is the same as Zola's: to show the experiences and sufferings of the rank-and-file as they really were. "It is Mr.

Crane's contention that any one can describe any sensation if he uses his experience, because suggestion creates so many sensations," wrote Herbert P. Williams of the Boston *Herald* in "Mr. Crane as a Literary Artist" (July 18, 1896).

"In spite of a vivid imagination that can conjure up almost anything, he does not think to trust the imagination of any one who reads. He puts everything so plainly that you can't help understanding it as he meant it. 'Trust their imaginations? Why, they haven't got any! They are used to having everything detailed for them. Our imaginations are defunct for lack of use, like our noses. So whether I say a thing or suggest it, I try to put it in the most forcible way.' Singular declaration this, for a man whose books appeal chiefly to men of powerful imagination. 'If what you write is worthy, somebody will find it out some time. Meanwhile that is not one of the problems that interest me.' He usually draws his pictures in four sentences like thumb-nail strokes. He has never tried to paint, which he says is fortunate because it would not have been a success. It is fortunate for another reason. Vereshchagin has painted the most wonderful pictures of war ever seen."

Vereshchagin lived everything he painted, but Crane wrote his war pictures in *The Red Badge* from the pure power of his imagination to conjure up the whole landscape by describing only a part of it and suggesting the rest. Swaying like a falling tree, soldier Conklin goes down against a sky that bleeds for the passion of his wounds, but nothing more than this is depicted of the terrain. As Williams remarks, Crane "merely states a problem in its barrenness, relying for effect on truth and vividness." Vereshchagin and Tolstoy, like Crane, portray things in their nakedness, and Vereshchagin and Crane "both have that feeling for the right kind of the right color (the right quality of sunlight, for instance). Mr. Crane is not inferior to either Russian in point of truth; but while he has accentuated the individual, Tolstoi and Vereshchagin continually preach the insignificance of the unit."

Vereshchagin painted a moral, and Tolstoy in his endless panorama of *War and Peace* sticks in lectures and stops to preach. Those sermons annoyed preacher's son Crane and he never finished reading *War and Peace,* which "goes on and on like Texas." He read enough of it, however, to transplant into *The Red Badge of Courage* the Tolstoy theory that battles are won by chance: "It can not be shown that God bends on us any definable stare, like a sergeant at muster, and his laughter would be bully to hear out in nothingness." The gods are indifferent to man's plight, but meanwhile the conscript must suffer the impersonal stupidity of General So-and-So.

It is ironical that the London *Academy* thought *The Red Badge* tiresome; that was Crane's own favorite epithet whenever he was asked to read Tolstoy, Zola, Mark Twain, or Henry James. He had no use for the old school of romance novelists such as Scott and Stevenson; he thought there was enough true romance in ordinary life. He liked Twain's Mississippi book because it was real life, but its four hundred pages (padded with humor) was "a little bit too much for me," he told C. K. Linson. And he criticized his own *Red Badge* for the same reason: it was too long. He knew that he was at his best in the short story or sketch.

In photographic realism Crane in *The Red Badge* only occasionally approaches Tolstoy, as in the image of a dead soldier leaning against a tree, with sodden eyes staring as from a dead fish. Or in the image of a corpse encountered in battle: "Once the line encountered the body of a dead soldier. He lay upon his back staring at the sky." To the youth, "it was as if fate had betrayed the soldier." He identifies himself with the corpse (he feels that he too is betrayed), and thus the detail is employed not merely for realism's sake but for a symbolic purpose. "The ranks opened covertly to avoid the corpse. The invulnerable dead man forced a way for himself. The youth looked keenly at the ashen face." The dead soldier who is metaphorically alive reappears in "The Upturned Face," which was written after Crane had encountered that weird experience in the Cuban War.

Henri Barbusse's *Under Fire* (1917), influenced by Crane, paints the very same picture, but one has only to compare it with Crane's to recognize the difference. Whereas Crane uses realistic detail metaphorically, Barbusse's details—facts in black and white—evoke neither symbolic intent nor theme. Crane's imagined painting of a battlefield seems somewhat synthetic and even theatrical when compared with the photocopy realism of Barbusse, Tolstoy and De Forest. But in *The Red Badge,* as Ford Madox Ford says, "we are provided with a map showing us our own hearts." Ford and other soldiers during lulls in gunnery read *The Red Badge* in the trenches of World War I—in English or in French and German translations.

"There is a clipping bureau in Boston which is said to send its bills once in three months, so when they wrote me the other day I took them up. I got forty-one new reviews of the *Red Badge*. And, oh, say, most of 'em were not only favorable but passionately enthusiastic. They didn't skirmish around and say maybe—perhaps—if—after a time—it is possible—under certain circumstances—but. No; they were cocksure." Crane was elated that almost all the reviewers seemed to have really read his book, and as he had no one to confide in at Hartwood he wrote Hawkins (November 19, 1895) and, sending him a fair sample of the batch, went on to admit that six reviews were "roasts. One is a copy of the *Tribune*'s grind.[5] New York, throughout, has treated me worse than any other city. Damn New York. Except the *Evening Post*. The *Evening Post* has just reviewed *The Black Riders* beautifully. There—I'm through talking about them but then you know there is nobody here whom one can talk to about them at all. It sounds sort of priggish, somehow. And it is I have no doubt."

The London *Saturday Review* and some other English commentators took it for granted that the author of *The Red Badge,* published in England in November, 1895,[6] must have seen real warfare. "The extreme vivid touches of detail convince us," says the *Review,* "that he has had personal experience of the scenes he depicts. Certainly, if his book were altogether a work of imagination, unbased on personal experience, his realism would be nothing short of a miracle."

Some Civil War veterans on reading *The Red Badge* felt certain that they had known the author. "I was with Crane at Antietam," Colonel John L. Burleigh told Elbert Hubbard (in 1895). In America the book had received higher praise than is usually bestowed with sincerity upon a living writer, said *Book Buyer* for April, 1896, and reproduced a note from Crane in his script: "I have never been in a battle, of course, and I believe that I got my sense of the rage of conflict on the football field. The psychology is the same. The opposing team is an enemy tribe." The *Book Buyer* quoted someone who gravely believed that the soul of some great soldier had gone into Stephen Crane at his birth, and that this theory of reincarnation explained how the author who had never seen battle was able to write descriptions in the guise of a seer's authority and compel the reader to accept his statement without question.

*The Red Badge* challenged criticism on both sides of the Atlantic. The London *Saturday Review* gushed over it; the *Atlantic Monthly* pronounced it "great enough to start a new fashion in literature"; and the *Critic,* while carping at the grammar, called it a little masterpiece. The English critics were not unanimous about its merit, but it was enthusiastically reviewed, except by the *Academy,* which said: "A serio-comic effect seems to be intended throughout, and Mr. Crane is no doubt highly gifted with that grotesqueness of fancy which is peculiarly a Transatlantic production; but the humor is scarcely of a sort to be appreciated by readers on this side, and not a few of them will lay the book down before getting half way through."

The *Spectator* (June 27, 1896), although agreeing that it was a remarkable book, pounced upon it as not a novel but rather a painful essay in pathology: "It presents the effects of physical danger upon the human nervous system in a youth who is morbid, hypersensitive, and over-conscious. It is believed that Mr. Crane has seen nothing of actual fighting.[7] As an achievement in imagination, in the art of placing one's self in the situation of another—of an exceptional other in exceptional surroundings— Mr. Crane's document can hardly be praised too much. It convinces; one feels that not otherwise than as he describes did such a man fall wounded and another lie in the grasp of corruption. But when we are asked to say that a specialized record of morbid introspection and an exact description of physical horrors is good art we demur; there *is* art in *The Red Badge of Courage*—an infelicitous title by the way—but the general effect which it leaves behind it is not artistic."

The Boston *Transcript* also saw *The Red Badge* as "more than merely an episode of the Civil War," but disagreed with the *Spectator*'s final evaluation. Said the *Transcript*: "It is a tremendous grasping of the glory and carnage of all war; it is the rendering, in phrases that reveal like lightning flashes, of the raw fighter's emotions, the blind magnificent courage and the cowardice equally blind of a youth first possessed by the red sickness of battle." An extraordinary bit of realism, said the *Outlook* (December 21, 1895): "The story is not pleasant by any means, but the author seems to lay bare the very nerves of his character; practically, the book is a minute study of one man's mind in the environment of war in all its horrible detail."

American newspapers gave *The Red Badge* almost universal eulogy, but not always the journals. Appleton's editor Hitchcock listed two dozen favorable reviews and claimed that our country—not England—was the first to recognize Crane's genius: "Our people have read his book so eagerly that it continues to be the most popular work of fiction in the market, and it has been the one most talked of and written about since October last." Hitchcock was replying to a soldier's bitter letter complaining that "respect for our own people should have prevented its issue in this country." On the same page of *The Dial* (May, 1896) on which Hitchcock addressed the soldier, a correspondent took up arms against that literary absurdity called *The Red Badge of Courage* for its general butchery of the language (vulgarisms, slipshod mannerisms, and split infinitives), for its affecting the absence of any gentleman in the Union Army, and for depicting not one agreeable character, not one praiseworthy sentiment, "and certainly not a new or original thought."

The bitter soldier the correspondent was defending and to whom Hitchcock responded was a General A. C. McClurg, who in the April *Dial* saw Crane's book as a vicious satire on American soldiers and armies. "The hero of the book, if such he can be called, was an ignorant and stupid country lad without a spark of patriotic feeling or soldierly ambition," wrote the general. "He is throughout an idiot or a maniac and betrays no trace of the reasoning being. No thrill of patriotic devotion to cause or country ever moves his breast, and not even an emotion of manly courage. Even a wound which he finally gets comes from a comrade who strikes him on the head with a musket to get rid of him; and this is the only 'Red Badge of Courage' (!) which we discover in the book." It is the work of a young man, and so of course it must be a mere work of "diseased imagination."

"Soldier Fleming is a coward, a Northerner who fled from the field," and that is why the English have praised *The Red Badge,* added the general; it could not be a book for Americans to read because the English have praised it. The *Dial* reviewer whom McClurg attacked happened to be an Englishman living in Chicago, and he replied on May 16 that apparently "it is a subtle insult for an Englishman to praise an American book." Other veterans, however, saw *The Red Badge* not as the grossest caricature but as absolutely faithful to facts. General Sir Evelyn Wood in the *Illustrated London News* expressed his opinion that Crane's work was quite the finest thing of its kind that had ever been done and that "the intentions of the boy who has never seen war are worth far more than the experiences of any writer known to him, even though he may have been in the thick of the fiercest battle."

Crane's description of battle, said the New York *Press* (October 13, 1895), is so vivid as to be almost suffocating. "The reader is right down in the midst of it where patriotism is dissolved into its elements and where only a dozen men can be seen, firing blindly and grotesquely into the smoke. This is war from a new point of view, and it seems more than when seen with an eye only for large movements and general effects. One should be forever slow in charging an author with genius, but it must be confessed that *The Red Badge of Courage* is open to the suspicion of having greater power and originality than can be girdled by the name of talent." The psychological realism of *The Red Badge* puzzled Howells, whose sympathy was for the social realism of *Maggie* and *George's Mother,* and he himself as critic floundered in saying that the novel floundered: "The narration repeats itself: the effort to imagine, to divine, and then to express ends often in a huddled and confused effect; there is no repose, such as agony itself assumes in the finest art, and there is no forward movement." Twain's co-author of *The Gilded Age,* Charles Dudley Warner had said the same thing in *Harper's Magazine* for May, 1896, in an unfavorable commentary on the lurid realism of an unnamed book which offended his genteel taste; it was obviously *The Red Badge of Courage.* "Great literature is always calm and produces its effect by less apparent effort," he remarked. (This puts into dry dock *Moby Dick* as well, not to mention Poe.) Howells in *Harper's Weekly* (November 26, 1895) had given *The Red Badge* faint praise; he wasn't for it, but neither was he against it. He said the author rendered the sense of deaf and blind turmoil, "but we might get that from fewer pages than Mr. Crane employs to impart it." His *Red Badge* was worthwhile "as earnest of the greater things that we may hope from a new talent working upon a high level, not quite clearly as yet, but strenuously."

Hubbard—while not naming Howells—attacked him in his tribute to Crane "As to the Man," in *A Souvenir and a Medley* (May, 1896): "There is a class of reviewers who always wind up their preachments by saying: 'This book gives much promise, and we shall look anxiously for Mr.

Scribbler's next.' Let us deal in no such case. A man's work is good or it is not. As for his 'next,' nobody can tell whether it will be good or not. There is a whole army of men about to do something great, but the years go by and they never do it." If Crane produced nothing more, he had already done enough "to save the fag-end of the century from literary disgrace; and look you, friends, that is no small matter!"

Although at first *The Red Badge* sold slowly, it did rather well for the first three months; by late March, 1896, it went into the fourth edition. For the English rights Heinemann Ltd. paid the author £20, but his real profit came from the Appleton edition. Crane remarked to H. P. Williams sometime after the Appleton edition appeared: "Oh, of course, I should be glad if everybody, Canadians, Feejees, Hottentots, wild men of Borneo, would buy *The Red Badge*—four copies of it—but they won't; so what's the use of thinking about the reader?"

The New York *Times* led the calvalcade of American reviews (October 19, 1895), praising *The Red Badge* as a remarkable book. The *Critic* counterblasted the *Daily News'* fable that the book had first been praised in England; it had been reviewed and discovered from Maine to California, the *Critic* said, before a single English reviewer had received the book, and it reminded the English editors that some half-dozen other authors had also been first discovered or boomed here in America. Said the London *Academy:* "Like so many American authors, he owes his success to British enthusiasm. It was not until *The Red Badge of Courage* was brought out in this country, in the autumn of 1895 [November], that America 'found' its author. Mr. Crane would be the first to acknowledge his indebtedness to the English critics and the English public, who, with one accord, forced his name into well-deserved prominence." Prior to his knowing about the *Academy* sketch of his career (January 16, 1896) Crane had already written the editor of the Rochester *Union and Advertiser* (January 2): "I have only one pride and that is that the English edition of *The Red Badge of Courage* has been received with great praise by the English reviewers. I am proud of this simply because the remoter people would seem more just and harder to win."

He was pleased that his *Red Badge* had been compared with Tolstoy's *War and Peace* and Zola's *Downfall* by the Undersecretary of State for War in the British Government, George Wyndham, in the London *New Review* (January, 1896). Crane staged the drama of war within the mind of one man, said Wyndham, and thus admits us as to a theatre, and "he confines his story to that single point of view, reporting only what the young soldier heard and saw and what thereby charged his emotions. Mr. Crane has thus hit upon a new literary device, while also portraying war under its new conditions. What he creates by this method cannot be found in the journals and letters of Civil War soldiers, nor in the pictures of battlefields by Tolstoi and Zola. This is unstinted praise, but I feel bound to give it after reading the book twice and comparing it with Zola's Sedan and Tolstoy's account of Rostow's squadron for the first time under fire [in *War and Peace*]. Indeed, I think that Mr. Crane's picture of war is more complete than Tolstoi's, more true than Zola's." The scene in *The Red Badge* where the lieutenant, the youth and his friend run forward to rally the regiment directly challenged comparison with Zola's scene in *La Débâcle* where the lieutenant and his girl expire together beneath a bullet-eaten flag. "Mr. Crane has probably read *La Débâcle* and wittingly threw down his glove. One can say only that he is justified of his courage." Not even Zola had surpassed the appalling realism of Jim Conklin's death. By his singleness of purpose Crane achieved a truer and completer picture of war than either Tolstoy, who portrayed the insignificance of heroes, or Zola, bent upon prophesying the regeneration of France. A great artist with something new to say, and consequently with a new way of saying it, Crane had surely contrived here a masterpiece, Wyndham said.

Years later Howells characterized *The Red Badge* as almost the best seller of its day "possibly because it was his worst book." He contended that Crane was valued by our critics long before he was known in England, as were also Harold Frederic and Walt Whitman. Everybody claimed he had discovered Crane, and Crane told the New York *World* (March 29, 1896) that while he was very much flattered by the kind reception of his *Red Badge,* he was getting a little weary of being told by every other man that he was the one who had discovered him. Crane "is no doubt glad that he was discovered, but he probably thinks that one Columbus could have done the work."

At home, derision and heated contention accompanied the praise, the American press taking offense at being told that Crane had been "first praised in England." After English praise, said the *Daily New*s, "the author's countrymen reconsidered their verdict." *Book News* (September, 1896) said that not until Mr. Wyndham's *New Review* eulogy of Crane as artist appeared, following upon innumerable English and Scottish reviews, did America awake "to the realization that a new literary force had come to the fore." Although Crane received splendid encomiums from the American press, the chief impetus for his American success followed upon his being heralded by Wyndham and later that month by the American novelist Harold Frederic, who dispatched to the New York *Times* from London (datelined January 15 and published on January 26, 1896): "Stephen Crane's triumph / London Curious about the Identity of America's New Writer."

Crane wrote Hitchcock about it: ". . . delighted with Frederic's letter in the Times." Frederic said it was evident that *The Red Badge* was to be more talked about than anything else in current literature. It seemed equally certain that it would be kept alive, "as one of those deathless books which must be read by everybody who desires to be, or to seem, a connoisseur of modern fiction. If there were in existence any books of a similar character, one could start confidently by saying that it was the best of its kind. But it has no fellows. It is a book outside of all classifications."

Frederic compared the tremendously effective battle scene with the best battle pictures from Tolstoi's *War and Peace,* Balzac's *Chouans,* Hugo's *Les Misérables,* and Zola's *La Débâcle;* he found them cold and ineffectual beside *The Red Badge* which "impels the feeling that the actual truth about a battle has never been guessed before." In construction and in its point of view the book was original and unique. It thrust aside all prescribed machinery of romance. We do not know anything about the soldiers, said Frederic, "except what, staring through the eyes of Henry Fleming, we are permitted to see. The regiment itself, the refugees from other regiments in the crowded flight, and the enemy on the other side of the fence are differentiated only as they wear blue or gray. We never get their color out of our mind's eye. This exhausts the dramatic personae of the book, and yet it is more vehemently alive and heaving with dramatic human action than any other book of our time. The people are all strangers to us, but the sight of them stirs the profoundest emotions of interest in our breasts. What they do appeals as vividly to our consciousness as if we had known them all our life." This is because we see it only through Henry Fleming's eyes, we think with his mind, we quail or thrill with his nerves.

One would suppose that the writer who had experienced a battlefield could write about it better than one who had never seen warfare, but it is just the opposite, Frederic maintained. To write about the Revolutionary War battle of Bloody Gulch at Oriskany, fought only a few miles from Utica, where Frederic was born, he read the narratives of the survivors and imaginative accounts by later writers, and he discovered the Mohawk Valley farmers who fought the French and Indians (in August, 1777) recorded much less vividly that desperate forest combat than did those later writers who had not experienced it. There is not a really moving story in all four volumes of the Century's *Battles and Leaders of the Civil War,* written by men who fought it. To put the reality into type baffled them, even though some had considerable literary talent. "It seems as if the actual sight of a battle has some dynamic quality in it which overwhelms and crushes the literary faculty in the observer. At best, he gives us a conventional account of what happened, but on analysis you find that this is not what he really saw but what all his reading has taught him that he must have seen. In the same way battle painters depict horses in motion, not as they actually move, but as it has been agreed by numberless generations of draughtsmen to say that they move. At last, along comes a Muybridge with his instantaneous camera, and shows that the real motion is entirely different. It is this effect of a photographic revelation which startles and fascinates one in *The Red Badge of Courage.*" Frederic's praise of Crane prepared for their meeting and friendship in England the next year.

Before writing his novel Crane had interviewed veterans of the Civil War only to find that they remembered very little that could be utilized in his imaginative rendering of battle. The old soldiers described the position of the troops and told how this regiment marched up here while another one marched down there; but as for their sensations in the fight, they seemed to have forgotten them. And yet, old soldiers say Crane has painted a most realistic picture, the *Critic* reported (March 7, 1896), and then when he is asked where he got his minute knowledge of battle scenes and sensations, he replies that he drew them from his imagination.

The Muse on Publisher's Hill showed prophetic wit in putting *The Red Badge* into Heinemann's "Pioneer Series of Modern Fiction" and in crowning the first American edition with a gilt top. The flash and blast the book made, the shock and excitement it produced, were unprecedented. It detonated on the public—to use Conrad's trope—with "the impact and force of a twelve-inch shell charged with a very high explosive." What caused the explosion was the style—Crane's own bombardment of similes and metaphors.

By September, 1896, *The Red Badge* had attained its ninth edition, and this popular success attracted critics to Crane's earlier work. Although *The Black Riders* (1895) was caviar to the general reader because of its form and tenor, it had gone into six editions with a steady sale through the author's fame arising from his war novel.

Even now, almost a year after the publication of *The Red Badge* (said *Book News* in September, 1896), the literary journals are still printing communications from readers who read a book like a proofreader to find how many grammatical errors Crane committed (the English reviewers ignored his deficiencies in grammar). *Book News* editor, E. St. Elmo Lewis interviewed Crane and recorded his impressions: "When assured of a real interest . . . . he is singularly frank, and at all times comfortably unconventional. His mental attitude towards all things in life is that of the man who is confident that the world holds few surprises for him, yet many things that are interesting. The man feels that he can 'do good work,' that there are greater things to come, and to the mystery of that future he turns eagerly. He seems at times to fail to realize the importance of his work, but when an amused twinkle gathers about his eyes as he reads the eulogies of those critics who at first welcomed him with Billingsgate, one is assured the man is observant of all things, even of himself.

"In the quiet of solitary rambles he 'gets close to things and thinks.' Then he goes home and writes, with the whole story in his head, always knowing the end from the beginning, playing no tricks as he goes with his characters, springing no surprises wantonly, but working out with relentless logic what to him is the inevitable ending of the tale. Once finished, there is no word added or subtracted, and then the story is put aside. Mr. Crane is of medium height, weighs not more than one hundred and thirty pounds, is a decided blonde with blue eyes that have that greenish tinge in them which Paul Bourget assures us is indicative of 'men of power and initiative.' " Lewis had contributed to the Philistine Society's dinner menu-folder: "To Stephen Crane we of the modern era owe much."

Elbert Hubbard wrote in May, 1896: "His intellect is as wide awake as the matin chimes, and his generosity is as ample as the double chin of Colonel Ingersoll. His handsome, boyish face and quiet, half-shy, modest manner make him a general favorite everywhere with women. And to me, it is rather curious that women flock around and pet this sort of man, who can read their inmost thought just as that Roentgen invention can photograph things inside of a box." Crane now had the ear of the world, publishers besieging him with checks in advance and bidding against each other for his latest manuscript, said Hubbard.

The *Critic* (March 7, 1896) in "The Author of 'The Red Badge' " published for the first time the photograph of Crane taken by F. H. King, which Crane himself regarded as a good likeness, and the reviewer found the young author small and slight—with a dark and sallow complexion and light hair, "which the camera, it seems, is not always truthful in picturing." He reported that Crane had just signed an agreement with McClure to write for *McClure's Magazine* on salary, but the *Critic* warned Crane that such a comfortable arrangement is not always the best thing for an author, particularly a young one. "Mr. Crane has made a splendid beginning, but he has not learned all there is to know of the art of writing. . . . The author's most ardent admirer is the [London] *Saturday Review*. Yet his book is not without honor in his own country, where we have known it to be read twice by one reader in a single week." The *Saturday Review* for January 11 gave a two-page synopsis of the story and compared its battle scenes with Tolstoy, Zola, Mérimée, and Kipling's *The Drums of the Fore and Aft,* adding that Zola's mass of studied knowledge in *La Débâcle* was too labored, not as convincing as Kipling's, and also certainly inferior to Crane's. His picture of "the effect of actual fighting on a raw regiment is simply unapproached in intimate knowledge and sustained imaginative strength." This was without forgetting Mérimée's celebrated account of the taking of the redoubt. "The writing of the French stylist is, no doubt, much superior in its uniform excellence; but Mr. Crane, in the supreme moments of the fight, is possessed by the fiery breath of battle, as a Pythian priestess by the breath of the God, and finds an inspired utterance that will reach the universal heart of man. . . . Mr. Crane's extraordinary book will appeal strongly to the insatiable desire, latently developed, to know the psychology of war—how the sights and sounds, the terrible details of the drama of battle, affect the senses and the soul of man."

# XI

## ⊂ *Nellie Crouse*

ONE night Crane was sitting in Moquin's restaurant with drama critic Acton Davies and playwright Clyde Fitch when a woman came up to ask him for the loan of fifty dollars. He borrowed a check from Fitch while Davies warned him that he would never be repaid. The woman, Doris Watts (later known as Mrs. Bowen), had let Crane into her rooms on West 48th Street in 1895. She was prosperous enough as a prostitute to keep a Negro maid, but she wrote Crane that she was destitute and wanted to reform. She finally threatened to come to Hartwood, whereupon he returned to New York City to have done with her.

"I leaned on the door and told her to drop this nonsense. There was one of those horrors called Turkish corners in the room with a shield stuck full of knives.[1] She lost her temper and grabbed a knife from the shield. It flew over my shoulder and stuck into the wood beside my ear and quivered so that I can still hear the noise." She swooned into the arms of her maid, and Crane fled hatless. He borrowed a cap from a friend and retired to Hartwood. It is not known whether Doris Watts reformed, but she managed to blackmail Crane for about $150 (according to Beer).[2]

"I live in Hartwood, Sullivan Co., N. Y., on an estate of 3500 acres belonging to my brother and am distinguished for corduroy trousers and briar-wood pipes," he wrote his friend John Hilliard of the Rochester *Union and Advertiser* on January 2, 1896. He had just finished his new novel, *The Third Violet*. "It is a story of life among the younger and poorer artists in New York." He had written with ease twenty-six chapters of that novel in November–December, 1895, and had sent the manuscript to Ripley Hitchcock on December 27, but he was dubious about it. "I am not sure that it is any good," he wrote Hawkins in November. "It is easy work. I can finish a chapter a day."[3]

Meanwhile, reviews of *The Red Badge* kept coming in the mail, which postmaster Edmund Crane collected at the Hartwood train stop and brought to his house on the millpond. Sitting at a window facing the pond, Crane wrote the *Tribune* on January 4: "I feel that it is perhaps unbecoming to feel immensely gratified at words concerning me in print but at the same time I cannot help from saying to you that of the notices of me which have appeared from time to time, the one in the *Tribune* of December 28 is the one I prefer above the others. I have friends who do not read many newspapers but who at the same time are interested in my prosperity and . . . I would like you to send . . . a few copies of the Dec. 28 issue of your paper."

One of the interested friends was Nellie Crouse, the girl from Akron, who advised Stephen to take advice from the reviewers. "Oh, heavens!" he replied. "Apparently you have not studied the wiles of the learned reviewer very much or you never would have allowed yourself to write that sentence. There is only one person in the world who knows less than the average reader. He is the average reviewer. I would already have been a literary corpse had I ever paid the slightest attention to the reviewers."

John Phillips of McClure had pressured Crane into writing a collection of war stories, and Crane wrote him that he ought to go to Virginia to explore battlefields and interview veterans. The only battlefield he could study at this time of the year (January, 1896) was Fredericksburg. "It was fought in December and no doubt the color of things there now would be the very same color of things of the days the battle was fought. I however could not arrange to go down there before the middle of February." But he did go in mid-January and had returned to Hartwood by the 26th, writing Nellie Crouse that Sunday: "I am just this moment back to the hills. I was obliged to go down to Virginia from New York and so the time of my little journey was unduly prolonged. I was impatient to get your letter and so had it forwarded to New York where I got it two days ago but was so badgered by silly engagements that I did not really own a minute in which I could reply."

One of his engagements was to see McClure about his projected *Little Regiment* collection of war stories, and another was to see Hitchcock of Appleton about it and also about his *Third Violet*. He also attended a dinner at the Lantern Club, where a toast was drunk to famous author Crane by Irving Bacheller and other friends, probably on Friday night, the 24th. When it came Stephen's turn to make a speech he was speecless except to declare them all "damned fools" and sit down again. At the Lantern Club he felt he was among friends, whereas at the Philistine banquet in Buffalo in December "everyone was strange. I was as cold as iced cucumbers when I arose and I said what I had to say very deliberately. The social crisis catches me sometimes and sometimes it doesn't," he wrote Nellie. "At Buffalo, however, I didn't talk as well as I could talk and to a woman I never talk as well as I can talk. Now that is exactly what I mean. And I never made a call, fought a tea, or sat on the sands by the mournful sea, that I didn't come away much discontented." To see those Lantern Club veterans arise and look solemnly at him "quite knocked the wind from me." The Lantern Club was to honor him on three more occasions that year.

Crane had "fought a tea" when he first met Nellie Crouse. "I saw in your eye once that the usual was rather tiresome to you," he confessed. "Your admission that many people find you charming leads me to be honest. So prepare. I called once in 34th St., when you were there, didn't I? Well, I was rather bored. I thought you very attractive but then I was bored, because I had always believed that when I made calls I was bored. However, to some sentence of mine you said: 'Yes, I know,' before I had quite finished. I don't remember what I had said but I always remembered your saying: 'Yes, I know.' I knew then that you had lived a long time. And so in some semi-conscious manner, you stood forth very distinctly in my memory." He recounts here his meeting that awful Akron chump who knew Nellie and said she was charming but a "rather queer girl." That "intolerable duffer" whom he had met in New Orleans did not understand Nellie, and to Stephen that was a very good sign—she wasn't a simple girl.

"You have been for me a curiously potential attraction. I tell it to you frankly, assured that no harm could come from any course so honest. I don't know what it is or why it is. I have never analyzed it. Couldn't. I am bound to let my egotism have swing here and tell you that I am an intensely practical and experienced person, in fear you might confuse the word 'poet' with various kinds of crazy sentiment." He'll bet on it that Nellie will feel embarrassed by his declaring that she is "a person of remarkably strong personality" and at his frankness, too. "Here is a young man who proclaims admiration of you from afar. . . . You don't care either way but then you feel a sort of moral responsibility. Great Scott! What a situation!"

He sent Nellie a newspaper clipping of "A Gray Sleeve," a Civil War story which had appeared in the Philadelphia *Press* in October, 1895, and he remarked in his letter of January 6: "It is not in any sense a good story and the intolerable pictures make it worse. In England, it comes out in a magazine and if I had a copy I would send you one, in order to make you think it was a better story but unfortunately I have not yet seen the English periodical." (It appeared in the *English Illustrated Magazine*[4] in January, 1896.) Nellie liked the story and Stephen replied that the Captain and the girl in their brief romance are "a pair of idiots. But yet there is something charming in their childish faith in each other."

He told Nellie he wasn't doing much newspaper writing now, "but in the spring I am wanting very much to go to Arizona to study the Apaches more. There is a man in Boston who has been unwise enough to ask me to write a play for his theatre and I wish to have some Apaches in it. For instance the music of their scalp dance is enough to set fire to a stone church." Nothing came of this plan. He hoped to see Nellie when he might get into the West again as the Erie Railroad to Arizona passed through her hometown Akron, but if he didn't go to Arizona he might get to Buffalo and from there make an afternoon or evening call on her. There were a lot of things Nellie wanted to know about him and he promised to confess them even "if it ruins my egotism for a fortnight. Anyhow, it is a very comfortable and manful occupation to trample upon one's own egotism. When I reached twenty-one years and first really scanned my personal egotism I was fairly dazzled by the size of it. The Matterhorn could be no more than a ten-pin to it. Perhaps I have succeeded in lowering it a trifle. So you will please keep in mind that there is a young corduroy-trousered, briar-wood-smoking young man—in Hartwood, N. Y. who is eagerly awaiting a letter from you."

"The lives of some people are one long apology. Mine was, once, but not now. I go through life unexplained." But with Nellie he was prepared to make "humble concession" and "to explain anything at all which I can find power to do. I have been told 84676 times that I am not of the cream of mankind but you make a sort of an inference that I might myself think I was of it, so I hasten to say that although I never line the walls or clutter the floors of ballrooms, my supreme detestation is dowdy women although they may be as intellectual as Mahomet. If you had seen me dashing through the back streets of Buffalo to escape the Browning Club, you would believe me."

Crane never saw Nellie Crouse again after their first meeting, as he did not go to Arizona nor to Buffalo. On January 12, he wrote her: "How dreadfully weary of everything you are. There are deeps of gloom in your letter which might have made me wonder but they did not, for by the same token, I knew of them long ago. As a matter of truth, I learn nothing new of you from your letters. They merely substantiate previous opinions. For my own part, I am minded to die in my thirty-fifth year." Life didn't seem to him, nor evidently to Nellie, "as particularly worth the trouble. The final wall of the wise man's thought however is Human Kindness of course. If the road of disappointment, grief, pessimism is followed far enough, it will arrive there. Pessimism itself is only a little, little way, and moreover it is ridiculously cheap. The cynical mind is an uneducated thing. Therefore do I strive to be as kind and as just as I may be to those about me and in my meagre success at it, I find the solitary pleasure of life."

During his weekend visit to the city on January 24–25 Crane had his photograph taken at the studio of Mr. King and then hied back to Hartwood to sail a catboat on the pond below Edmund's house and read his "armful of letters from people who declared *The Black Riders* was—etc, etc,—and then for the first time in my life I began to be afraid, afraid that I would grow content with myself, afraid that willy-nilly I would be satisfied with the little, little things I have done. For the first time I saw the majestic forces which are arrayed against man's true success—not the world—the world is silly, changeable, any of its decisions can be reversed —but man's own colossal impulses are more strong than chains, and I perceived that the fight was not going to be with the world but with myself.

I had fought the world and had not bended nor moved an inch but this other battle—it is to last on up through the years to my grave and only on that day am I to know if the word Victory will look well upon lips of mine." He felt sure that Nellie Crouse would understand. "When I speak of a battle I do not mean want, and those similar spectres. I mean myself and the inherent indolence and cowardice which is the lot of all men." He confessed that he liked her "wonderfully more, after confessing so unreservedly," and asked for her photograph as due to one who pays her "unconditional devotion."

"So you think I am successful?" he wrote on January 26. "Well, I don't know. Most people consider me successful. . . . But upon my soul I have lost all appetite for victory, as victory is defined by the mob. I will be glad if I can feel on my deathbed that my life has been just and kind according to my ability and that every particle of my little ridiculous stock of eloquence and wisdom has been applied for the benefit of my kind. From this moment to that deathbed may be a short time or a long time, but at any rate it means a life of labor and sorrow. I do not confront it blithely. I confront it with desperate resolution. There is not even much hope in my attitude. I do not even expect to be good. But I expect to make a sincere, desperate, lonely battle to remain true to my conception of my life and the way it should be lived, and if this plan can accomplish anything, it shall be accomplished. It is not a fine prospect. I only speak of it to people in whose opinions I have faith. No woman has heard it until now."

After the fabulous success of *The Red Badge* in England, Crane wrote S. S. McClure on January 27: "I feel I could do something to dwarf the *Red Badge*." He began now to play down his masterpiece. "People may just as well discover now that the high dramatic key of *The Red Badge* cannot be sustained," he wrote Hitchcock that same day. "You know what I mean. I don't think *The Red Badge* to be any great shakes, but then the very theme of it gives it an intensity that a writer can't reach every day. *The Third Violet* is a quiet little story, but then it is a serious work and I should say let it go. If my health and my balance remains to me, I think I will be capable of doing work that will dwarf both books."

He had just become habituated to the initial critical abuse over his book of poems "when this bit of a flurry about the *Red Badge* came upon me," Crane wrote Howells, also on January 27. "I am slightly rattled and think it best to cling to Hartwood where if I choose to shout triumphant shouts none can hear me. However, I have not elected to shout any shouts. I am, mostly, afraid. Afraid that some small degree of talk will turn me ever so slightly from what I believe to be the pursuit of truth, and that my blockhead will lose something of the resolution which carried me very comfortably through the ridicule. If they would only continue the abuse, I feel able to cope with that, but beyond I am in great doubt." In his letter to Hitchcock, too, he had said that he wouldn't venture into the city very soon again; too much praise had muddled him. "I had grown used to being called a damned ass but this sudden admiration of my friends has made a gibbering idiot of me. I shall stick to my hills."

In the same vein, he wrote to Dr. A. L. Mitchell on the 29th: "You delight me with your appreciation and yet it makes me afraid. I did not bend under the three hills of ridicule which were once upon my shoulders but I don't know that I am strong enough to withstand the kind things that are now sometimes said to me. I have a strong desire to sit down and look at myself."[5]

He was torn between that sanctuary of Hartwood's forests and that damned city which "tore my heart out by its roots and flung it under the heels of its noise. Indeed it did," he wrote Willis Hawkins the same day he wrote to McClure, Howells and Hitchcock. "I couldn't breathe in that accursed tumult. On Friday it had me keyed to a point where I was no more than a wild beast and I had to make a dash willy-nilly. It was a disgraceful retreat but I think you will understand me [he had neglected to visit Hawkins]. I feel myself perfectly capable of any sacrifice for you now with the sting of that retreat still upon me," and in remorse he sent the manuscripts of *The Red Badge,* a gift Hawkins prized so much that he had them bound with gold lettering on the cover.

The spurt of fame emboldened Crane to ask McClure for $25 against his account for manuscripts of his *Little Regiment* stories, which he liked to call a novel, to tide him over "until my February ship comes in; it would assist the Cranes of Sullivan County very greatly." He had just written "The Little Regiment," a story of Fredericksburg,[6] which he thought the most dramatic battle of the Civil War, and "Three Miraculous Soldiers" and "The Veteran," the only piece in the *Little Regiment* volume (1896) which is not a Civil War tale. In it, Henry Fleming is now an old man, and becomes a hero in trying to rescue some colts from a burning barn; he dies in the attempted rescue. All the stories in *The Little Regiment* are invented things; almost everything he subsequently wrote was devised from personal experience. For these invented stories he could use very little of the accounts told him by Southern veterans during his January visit to Fredericksburg and Chancellorsville, and it had been the same when he had interviewed Northern veterans while writing *The Red Badge* in 1893. Crane wrote the editor of the *Critic* that he was now finishing *The Little Regiment,* "which represents my work at its best I think and is positively my last thing dealing with battle." Jeanette Gilder, sister of Richard Gilder of the *Century,* declared in the *World*: "I am compelled to say that if Mr. Crane has turned his back upon the war story he has snubbed his best friend." Indeed, he spent the rest of his life with it, as the titles of five subsequent volumes indicate.[7]

"Whenever you have some article or other in mind," he wrote McClure in his letter of January 27, "let me know at once. Beware only how you catch me up here [Hartwood] without car-fare to N. Y. That is the spectre that perches on the back of the Crane 'child of promise.' I think it will be of a great advantage to me to have you invent subjects for me. By the way I would like to go to the scene of the next great street-car strike." He is perfectly satisfied with his end of the contract, but he worries about McClure's end, "for I am often inexpressibly dull and uncreative and these periods often last for days. I see by Sunday's *Times* that the Englishmen are mildly curious about me. Many of my friends—quite a number, I mean—are going to Europe on the 29th [28th] February. If you could think out some campaign for me I might go but I feel reluctant."

Knowing that C. K. Linson was leaving for Europe, Stephen had written him on January 4 to return by C. O. D. a lot of things he had left in Linson's studio, including the Appleton contract for *The Red Badge*. He was in Hartwood when Linson and C. C. Jaccaci, Scribner's art director, sailed for Europe February 5. But he was in the city on February 28 to see some other friends off for Europe, which voyage he himself had hoped to make. In "Sailing Day Scenes" (an undated New York *Press* sketch) he describes the departure of a big ocean liner, the huge pier thronging with stevedores and merchandise going up the gangplank, while the passengers standing in rows on the ship's white deck were "gazing fixedly at the shore as if they expected at any moment to see it vanish." They held extraordinary conversations with the people on the pier. And then—"A preliminary thrill went through the throng. The talk began to grow hurried, excited. People spoke wildly and with great speed, conscious that the last moments were upon them. . . . There were plentiful smiles, but they expressed always a great tender sorrow. It was surprising to see how full of expression the face of a blunt, every day American business man could become. They were suddenly angels. As for the women, they were sacred from stare through the purity of their grief. . . .

With the final farewell, there was "an undercurrent of despair of expression. The inadequacy of the goodbyes seemed suddenly apparent to the crowd. The forlorn pathos of the thing struck their minds anew and many of the women began to weep again in that vague way, as if overcome by a sadness that was subtly more than the tangible grief of parting. A pompous officer, obviously vain of his clothes, strode before the agitated faces upon the ship and looked complacently at the pier. It was an old story to him, and he thought it rather silly. He regarded all such moments with the contempt of a man of very strong nature." When the ship had passed out of shouting distance a woman sat weeping disconsolately, and another woman expressed a grief that had a quality of valor. She did not understand that tears were shameful things to be hidden in houses. Her veil was high upon her forehead. She paid no heed to the tears upon her eyelids. The weeping woman looked up as the beautiful woman who had stared imperturbably at the ship walked slowly by. "They exchanged a long, friendly glance. It was the freemasonry of two sorrows."

Stephen wrote Nellie Crouse on February 5 that McClure had requested him to go to London, but it was Crane himself who proposed the idea. McClure had no intention of sending him to London, and so Crane backtracked on his boast to Miss Crouse by explaining that "I've almost given up the plan. The publishers and things in London seem anxious for me to come," he bluffed, "and people on this side furnish me with unlimited introductions. So the journey seems so easy and simple that I am quite out of humor of it. I don't think I shall go until next fall." Miss Crouse was going to Europe, and so he joked about taking the same ship: "I wish you would tell me more about your European trip. By the way, if you forbid me going over on the same boat, it must be because you think I am not clever."

Would Nellie come East this summer? "I hope so. I never work in the summer. It is one long lazy time to fool away," he wrote amidst a snowstorm at Hartwood in the same February 5 letter. "Sometimes I am much agitated at the thought that perhaps the little train won't be able to struggle up the mountain and deliver my mail. As yet however nothing has happened to it. Did not you once ask me if Hartwood is out of the world? It is—very much. New York is only 104 miles but it is a terrible 104 miles, and the mail service is wretched. I have about four new books coming out.[8] Sometimes I feel like sitting and watching them appear. However, they are not good enough to delight me at all." Crane studied the photograph Nellie had sent him and decided that he was sure she was precisely the kind of woman he had judged her, but "the light of social experience in your eyes somewhat terrifies this poor outer pagan."

She had declared that she liked "the man of fashion," and that provoked her untidy correspondent on February 11 to send her his opinions about men who merely dress correctly, do the right things, sit with immovable legs on account of a teacup and twaddle. They are popularly supposed not to be worth much, he wrote, and though there are exceptions the general type of the correctly dressed and correctly speeched strike him as a kind of idiot. "There are men of very social habits who nevertheless know how to stand steady when they see cocked revolvers and death comes down and sits on the back of a chair and waits"; the social lion usually turns to a lamb and fails at precisely the moment when he should not fail. "In short they are precisely like the remainder of the race, only they devote their minds to riding smoothly. A slight jolt gives them the impression that a mountain has fallen upon them. . . .

"I strongly admire the social God even if I do despise many of his worshippers. As for the man with the high aims and things—which you say you like in your soul—but not in your heart—I don't know that he is to my mind any particular improvement on the society man. I shouldn't care to live in the same house with him if he was at all in the habit of talking about them. I get about two letters a day from people who have high literary aims and everywhere I go I seem to meet five or six. They strike me as about the worst and most penetrating kind of bore I know. Of course I, with my meagre successes, would feel like an awful duffer if I was anything but very, very considerate of them but it is getting to be a task. Of course that is not the kind you meant. Still they are certainly people of high aims and there is a ridiculous quality to me in all high ambitions, of men who mean to try to make themselves great because they think it would [be] so nice to be great, to be admired, to be stared at by the mob. 'Well,' you say, 'I didn't mean that kind of high aim either.' Tolstoy's aim is, I suppose—I believe—to make himself good. It is an incomparably quixotic task for any man to undertake. He will not succeed; but he will even succeed more than he can ever himself know, and so at his nearest point to success he will be proportionally blind. This is the pay of this kind of greatness."

Social form is truth, simplicity; but when people surround it with falsity "they become not society leaders but barbarians, savages, beating little silly tom-toms and flourishing little carved wooden goblins. They really defy every creed of this social god, the very deity which they worship." Crane recalls the society people he met following the reading of his poems by John Barry in April, 1894, at Sherry's. Nothing so serenely stupid had he ever witnessed as the woman who very graciously and confidently paid him compliments. "And the absolutely false tongue of her prattled away for ten minutes in more lies than are usually heard at one time. Of course it was nothing to me if she liked my stuff and it was nothing to her. She was merely being correct because she indifferently thought it to be correct at that moment, but how these old cats can stand up and lie until there is no breath left in them. Now, they think that is form, mind you, but, good heavens, it isn't. They think that a mere show of complacent idiocy is all that is necessary to a queen of society."

He had previously written Nellie (January 26), a few nights after he had been toasted by the Lantern Club: "It is awfully nice to be exhibited like a stuffed parrot. They say that [Richard Harding] Davis enjoys it. I should think he would. He has, I believe, the intelligence of the average saw-log and he can no doubt enjoy anything." Nellie probably defended Davis in raising the subject of the man of fashion and thus ignited Crane's chronicle of February 11: "For the hordes who hang upon the out-skirts of good society and chant 143 masses per day to the social gods and think because they have money they are well-bred—for such people I have a scorn which is very deep and very intense. These people think that polite life is something which is to be studied, a very peculiar science of which knowledge is only gained by long practice whereas what is called 'form' is merely a collection of the most rational and just of laws which any properly-born person understands from his cradle. In Hartwood I have a great chance to study the new-rich. The Hartwood Clubhouse is only three miles away [from Edmund's house] and there are some of the new rich in it. May the Lord deliver me from having social aspirations."

"I swear by the real aristocrat," he wrote. "The man whose fore-fathers were men of courage, sympathy and wisdom, is usually one who will stand the strain whatever it may be. He is like a thorough-bred horse. His nerves may be high and he will do a lot of jumping often but in the crisis he settles down and becomes the most reliable and enduring of created things."

"Many a duffer shines like a sun and many a brave man appears a duffer," Crane remarked in his January 26th letter to Nellie, no doubt having himself in mind.

No socialite and in appearance no gentleman, nor gifted in the social graces of small talk, he felt he had made a "chump" of himself before the fireplace of the Hartwood Club while drinking tea with people who wanted to meet the famous writer. "That disgraceful *Red Badge* is doing so very well that my importance has widened and everybody sits down and calmly waits to see me be a chump," he wrote Nellie on March 1. Depressed by that social gathering, he had fled to New York City only to find it worse there. "I am in despair. The storm-beaten little robin who has no place to lay his head does not feel so badly as I do. It is not that people want to meet me. When that happens I can endure it. But it is that mine own friends feel bitterly insulted if I do not see them twelve times a day—in short, they are all prepared to find me grown vain."

He had written Hitchcock at Appleton's from Hartwood that he didn't care much about money "up here save when I have a special need of it and just at this time there is a beautiful riding-mare for sale for a hundred dollars. The price will go up each week, almost, until spring and I am crazy to get her now. I don't want to strain your traditions, but if I am worth $100 in your office I would rather have it now." He had fallen in love with this horse while visiting Hubbard in East Aurora after the Society of the Philistines banquet in December. Hitchcock responded with prompt sympathy, and Crane wrote him on February 10 in thanks for the advance: "It is a luxury to feel that some of my pleasures are due to my little pen." However, Hubbard was asking $60 for the horse, so Crane netted $40 by his little deal. He held off paying Hubbard, writing him on the 13th: "I am going to pinch money this month from various places and will certainly be delighted to pay sixty bones for the mare. I will send you the check and you can board her out with some gentle people—if you will be so good—until I come after her in the spring. My business is boom-ing in great style."[9] Hubbard's son took care of the horse and trained him until Crane, instead of going to East Aurora, sent for the horse to be shipped to Port Jervis. The little brown horse, whose name was "Peanuts," was not a mare (Crane was mistaken); it was a gelding and a mustang.

He was now revising the paperback *Maggie* for Appleton's hard-cover edition, and in the same letter he had written Hitchcock to thank him for the advance, he said he would send him *Maggie* "by detail. I have carefully plugged at the words which hurt. Seems to me the book wears quite a new aspect from very slight omissions." Curse words such as "What deh hell's deh matter wid yeh?" offended the proper 1890's, and so Crane was obliged to appease Hitchcock by dispensing with "a goodly number of damns," converting "hell" into "h—ll," and politely saying "I'll paste yeh" instead of "I'll club hell outa yeh." He thought Hitchcock priggish and came to dislike him, although one would never guess it by the humble tone of his early letters. He resented Hitchcock's tampering with *Maggie,* as he had done before with *The Red Badge.*

Crane went to Washington, D. C., to prepare for a political novel for McClure, which he never wrote, and while there he finished the letter to Miss Crouse which he had begun on March 8 at 33 East 22nd Street. "Dear me," he had written, "how much I am getting to admire graveyards —the calm unfretting unhoping end of things—serene absence of passion— oblivious to sin—ignorant of the accursed golden hopes that flame at night and make a man run his legs off, and then in the daylight of experience turn out to be ingenious traps for the imagination." In this last of his known letters to Nellie, he expressed his bitterness: "If there is a joy of living I can't find it. The future is blue with obligations—new trials— conflicts." Now on the 18th he added a postscript: "Really, by this time I should have recovered enough to be able to write you a sane letter but I cannot—my pen is dead. I am simply a man struggling with a life that is no more than a mouthful of dust to him." It is no wonder that his correspondence with Nellie ended there, and that Miss Crouse quit her intellectual romance with the Hamlet of Hartwood.

His gloomy mood was provoked not by Nellie Crouse but by Mrs. Lily Brandon Munroe, whom he met (or perhaps failed to meet) at this time in Washington and had not seen since January of the previous year when he despaired of eloping with her. This mood, however, was contradicted by the lightheartedness of his March 15 (1896) letter from the Cosmos Club in Washington to Miss Viola Allen, whom he had known back in his Claverack days. She no doubt had written him for a copy of *The Red Badge,* for now he forwarded her a copy and wrote: "My years at Claverack are very vivid to me. They were, I believe, the happiest period of my life, although I was not then aware of it. Of course, you were joking when you inferred that I might not remember you. And Anna Roberts! And Eva Lacy! And Jennie Pierce! Alas, Jennie Pierce. You must remember that I was in love with her, madly, in the headlong way of seventeen. Jennie was clever. With only half an effort she made my life so very miserable. Men usually refuse to recognize their school-boy dreams. They blush. I don't. The emotion itself was probably higher, finer, than anything of my after-life, and so, often I like to think of it. I was an ass, such a complete ass—it does me good to recollect it."

Now that he had attained manhood he still saw himself sometimes as the same donkey he had been at Claverack. That double point of view about himself is seen in his 1896 fable "How the Donkey Lifted the Hills," which Irving Bacheller thought was the best thing Crane sent him.

"Years ago there was nobody quite so fine as the donkey. He was a great swell in those times. No one could express an opinion of anything without the donkey showing where he was in it. No one could mention the name of an important personage without the donkey declaring how well he knew him."

The donkey—a proud and aristocratic beast—converses with a party of animals. The ox expresses admiration for Atlas, that giant who could carry things. The donkey says that he knew Atlas well. The horse says: "It has always been a wonder to me how he could have carried the earth on his back," and the donkey replies: "Oh, my dear sir, nothing is more simple." The donkey boasts that he could carry a range of mountains on his back, and the horse wagers "my ears" that he couldn't. But who will shovel the mountains upon his back? True, some men could do it; but men are very sly, says the horse. "They will introduce some deviltry into the affair." No, says the donkey, "they are the most gentle, guileless creatures." So they ask the laborers who are digging ditches, felling trees, and building huts to shovel a range of mountains upon the donkey's back, and that is what the men do, only they load two ranges of mountains upon him when he had bargained for but one. The other animals protest against what these false, cowardly, and accursed men have done and the donkey begs them to remove some of the mountain peaks from his back. He promises to serve them in return, and this explains why the donkey forever toils as a slave to man. "Poor old foolish fellow," cries the horse; "he may keep his ears. He will need them to hear and count the blows that are now to fall upon him." The donkey's ears hang down "like the leaves of the plantain during the great rain. So, now when you see a donkey with a church, a palace, and three villages upon his back, and he goes with infinite slowness, moving but one leg at a time, do not think him lazy. It is his pride." What an ass is man to submit to his enslavement by village, palace, and church! To presume that he can carry the whole earth on his back, competing with Atlas himself! In his pride and ambition Crane, who toiled and never rested, saw himself as an ass.

"Many people suppose that the donkey is lazy. This is a great mistake. It is his pride." Looking back on what he had by then published, Crane wrote his old Syracuse classmate Clarence Loomis Peaslee, "It appears that I have worked, but as a matter of truth I am very lazy, hating work and only taking up a pen when circumstances drive me." There is no doubt that, like the donkey, he was "a proud and aristocratic beast."

Arrogant Crane alternates throughout his life with humble Crane. In a repentant mood he wrote Hitchcock from Washington to apologize for not having kept his appointment with him in New York City. "Of course eccentric people are admirably picturesque at a distance, but I suppose after your recent close-range experiences with me, you have the usual sense of annoyance. After all, I cannot help vanishing and disappearing and dissolving. It is my foremost trait. But I hope you will forgive me and treat me as if you still could think of me as a pretty decent sort of chap."

He had had a fling with some woman before going to Washington, and he owed Willis Hawkins, as well as Hitchcock, an apology. He wrote Hawkins on the 15th: "It was a woman! Don't you see? Nothing could so interfere but a woman. How sorry I am that I treated you so badly and yet how full how absolute is the explanation—a woman. I still want to know at once how angry you are. I am sure, of course, that you have been very much offended but it is a woman, I tell you, and I want you to forgive me." Hawkins forgave him, and Stephen wrote: "You are the only friend I ever had who possessed the decency to forgive me for being an ass and your value has doubled in my eyes."

The woman who had interfered with his meetings with Hitchcock and Hawkins was very likely Amy Leslie, a former actress and dramatic critic of the Chicago *Daily News,* well enough known to have been invited to the Philistine Society affair honoring Crane in December. Elbert Hubbard had printed her letter declining the invitation in the menu: "My most gentle thoughts are tinged with envy of you who are so lucky to meet Stephen Crane." That set the stage for their meeting in the early part of 1896. Amy Leslie, some twenty years Crane's senior, was obviously infatuated with the famous youth.

While waiting for the edited *Maggie* from Hitchcock, Crane wrote him from the Cosmos Club that he aimed to study the capital "in the manner of a stranger. . . . I am going to settle down to New York work in lazy Washington. I have had enough tea." He wrote him again on March 23 to ask whether the *Atlantic Monthly* might like to serialize *The Third Violet* and to say that yesterday he had met Horace Greeley, who told him that *The Red Badge of Courage* had been filed in the Archives of the War Department. "I am very well and am gradually learning things. I have been already in a number of the senatorial interiors. But I want to know all the congressmen in the shop. I want to know Quay of Pennsylvania, I want to know those long-whiskered devils from the west. So whenever you see a chance to send me headlong at one of them, do so."

The only piece he wrote about Washington for his projected book on political society was a news article about a session of Congress which was never published. Pennsylvania Avenue, he said, "displays more types of people than any other street in America. One suddenly becomes aware of the diversities of American life. It is a good education for a New Yorker who always considers that Union Square is the centre of the republic. You discover then the typical American—a thin-faced, shrewd-looking fellow walking at a slow pace and with eyes that see everything. If you stand on a corner and watch people board the cable-cars you can easily learn to distinguish between New Yorkers and Southerners. The Southerner signals the car to stop and then approaches it leisurely as if it were his private carriage. If his mind wavers between the choice of two seats he pauses on the asphalt and debates. The New York man comes out suddenly, waves a quick finger and, the moment the car stops, climbs aboard, meanwhile giving the grip-man a grateful look and as if it were his duty to be much obliged for being allowed to board the car at all. The police, the Broadway grip-man, the elevated railway guards have well-trained the average New Yorker.

"Owing to a curious dispensation of Providence visitors always arrive in the audience galleries when Congress is debating the erection and maintenance of a jetty at the mouth of some unheard-of harbor or a bill for the dredging of some unknown harbor. Of course everyone understands that the Congress does not meet solely for the purpose of surrounding itself with works of art and if it remains deaf to the orations of the artists and the art associations, one cannot altogether blame it. There are two sides to the question. A man may have a very good idea of how to adjust the annual appropriations and yet not know good from bad in statuary and it is to be supposed that he is performing his highest obligation when he knows all he can about taxation and appropriations. Still it is a great wonder—the quality of specimens of bad art generation after generation of congressmen have managed to get into the capitol."[10]

While in Washington Crane read in the Philadelphia *Press* (March 15, 1896) an article unsigned and titled "Rise to Fame of Stephen Crane," and on the 24th he wrote Irving Bacheller about it: "I saw the professor's article in the Philadelphia *Press* and I want to thank him through you for it. The tone of it was so generous and kindly throughout that it was a genuine pleasure to me. Moreover he didn't try to appear as wise as all-hell. I suppose the American critic's first anxiety is to impress the reader with the fact that he knows everything. No doubt there are many of them that do know everything but then the positive tone grows exasperating at last. There was so little—not any of that falsely-solemn judgment in the professor's article and so I think it was a great thing."[11]

The unsigned article was by Professor Charles Kelsey Gaines of St. Lawrence University, who had interviewed Crane at the Lantern Club. What gave Crane genuine pleasure in Gaines' tribute was his note that the author's work had received more general recognition in England than in this country, that any reader of Crane's work could detect the author to be a lover of horses, and that his *Black Riders* poems "are original in the highest degree and as full of 'reason' as they are lacking in rhyme and metre." Gaines remarked that Crane was one of the founders of "The Sign o' the Lanthorn," a unique literary club where the great attractions are "two old fireplaces and good company," and that among the many honors heaped upon him of late "none probably have been more acceptable than the invitation to be the guest of this club at a complimentary dinner to be given early in April." He was the first to point out that Crane on his mother's side "is descended from a long line of Methodist clergymen, of the order of the saddle-bag. Possibly this heredity, also, may be traced in his work: his style is curiously introspective and analytical. Is this a betrayal of confidence? I trust not. . . . Like Nathaniel Hawthorne, this author, whatever his theme, always treats 'the tragedy of a soul.' "

# XII

# ⊂ *"George's Mother"*

CRANE wrote Hitchcock on March 26, 1896, that he was now beset by many publishers to obtain his works, but "I have not considered at all the plan of playing one house against another but have held that the house of Appleton would allow me all the benefits I deserved. Without vanity I may say that I don't care a snap for money until I put my hand in my pocket and find none there. If I make ill terms now there may come a period of reflection and so I expect you to deal with me precisely as if I was going to write a GREAT book ten years from now and might wreak a terrible vengeance upon you by giving it to the other fellow. And so we understand each other."

The other fellow he was dickering with was Harry Thompson, a Claverack College schoolmate of ten years ago, now the American manager of Edward Arnold of New York City and London. Thompson "conducted such a campaign against me as is seldom seen. He appealed to my avarice and failing appealed to my humanity," Crane wrote Hitchcock. Thompson was about to sign Crane for his *Little Regiment* when Hitchcock took it, but Thompson snagged *George's Mother* for Edward Arnold. Crane admitted that in giving *George's Mother* to another publisher "I violated certain business courtesies. But, before God, when these people get their fingers in my hair, it is a wonder that I escape with all my clothes. My only chance is to keep away from them." This letter must have rubbed Hitchcock like sandpaper. At any rate, he did not risk publishing more Crane; it was not Appleton but Doubleday and McClure that published the next book (*The Open Boat,* 1898).[1]

Crane was back in New York by April 2, and that Thursday he wrote Hitchcock that he was engaged on a Preface to *Maggie* (it never saw print) and that the proofs of *Maggie* "make me ill. . . . I am too jaded with Maggie to be able to see it." He wrote Hawkins to bring the boys over for poker that night: "I am returned."[2] He had moved into an enormous room at the top of a house at 165 West 23rd and remained here until September, when he moved into a rooming house rented mostly to streetwalkers.

The Lantern Club gave Crane "a complimentary dinner" in early April and urged him to write a tale with a newspaperman as hero. (A year later Harold Frederic proposed the same idea, but it wasn't until 1899 that Crane completed his novel about a journalist, *Active Service*.) Meanwhile, sometime in March or April, he wrote an article about opium-smokers after buying the necessary ingredients to test the experience. He undoubtedly boasted about it, and then a certain Thomas McCumber with whom he had a nodding acquaintance spread the malicious gossip that he took morphine. Crane had won McCumber's enmity by not liking him. Very tall and handsome and very tipsy in the popular bars, McCumber was a clever talker whom James Huneker casually knew and whom O'Henry described as "an infernal nuisance." He lived at a boardinghouse on East 19th Street and for some months of 1896 at the old Gilsey House, where Crane probably met him.

Another authority for unpleasant tales about Crane—the opium story for one—was novelist Edgar Saltus, who caught the popular taste in such "diabolical" novels as *The Pace That Kills* (1899) and *The Imperial Purple* (1892), an exotic history of the Roman emperors. Vain and temperamental, he had a sharp wit not unlike the epigrammatic wit of Oscar Wilde.[3] As soon as Crane's success began ugly stories about his private life circulated, and when he died his friends had to issue denials that he took drugs. Although envious of Crane's fame and not liking him as a person, Richard Harding Davis chose to make himself spokesman of the younger man's reputation and declared that the yarn was absurd. Davis had heard Crane pronounce at various dinners his decided prejudice against drug-taking, but he looked the type and with heedless indifference to gossip-mongers fueled their calumny by carelessly remarking: "Oh, I'd have to get drunk to write that." The fiction of a successful man aided in his success by alcohol is very flattering to the less successful (as Beer puts it). Neurologist Weir Mitchell once speculated that the phenomena of envy "are very much more marked among artists than in any other profession. Invariably or nearly so, these take the form of gossiping stories about the person—or character—of a successful writer, and the stories always show the same trend: the successful man is given to heavy indulgence in alcohol or to irregular use of drugs. The point is most interesting when one considers that artists are perpetually demanding for themselves the license of conduct which they deplore in print."

Crane had simply reported in "Opium's Varied Dreams" (New York *Sun:* May 17, 1896) that there were 25,000 opium-smokers in New York City, most of them white men and women. "Chinatown furnishes the pipe, lamp, and yen-hock [variously spelled yen-nock], but let a man once possess a layout, and a common American drug-store furnishes him with the opium, and China is discernible only in the traditions that cling to the habit. . . . People who declare themselves able to pick out opium smokers on the street usually are deluded. An opium smoker may look like a deacon or a deacon may look like an opium smoker. The fiends usually conceal their vice. They get up from the layout, adjust their cravats, straighten their coat-tails, and march off like ordinary people, and the best kind of an expert would not be willing to bet that they were or were not addicted to the habit."

Each smoking layout consists of one pipe, one lamp and one cook. A pill is good for one long draw, and then the cook molds another. "A smoker would just as soon choose a gallows as an armchair for smoke purposes. He likes to curl down on a mattress placed on the floor in the quietest corner of a Tenderloin flat, and smoke there with no light but the tiny yellow spear from the layout lamp." The cook takes the opium from a box with a sort of sharpened darning-needle called the yen-hock and twirls it dexterously with his thumb and forefinger until enough of the gum substance adheres to the sharp point, and then he holds it over the flame of the layout lamp until the pill resembles boiling molasses. He then transfers the cooked pill from the yen-hock to the bowl of the pipe; etc.

"When a man arises from his first trial of the pipe, the nausea that clutches him is something that can give cards and spades and big casino to seasickness. If he had swallowed a live chimney-sweep he could not feel more like dying. The room and everything in it whirls like the inside of an electric plant. There comes a thirst, a great thirst, and this is so sinister and so misleading that if the novice drank spirits to satisfy it he would presently be much worse. The one thing that will make him feel again that life may be a joy is a cup of strong black coffee. If there is a sentiment in the pipe for him, he returns to it after this first unpleasant trial. Gradually the power of the drug sinks into his heart. It absorbs his thought. He begins to lie with more and more grace to cover the shortcomings and little failures of his life."

Crane's friend Edward E. Townsend described an opium den in *A Daughter of the Tenements,* which the *Bookman* compared with *Maggie* and preferred to *The Red Badge* but nobody but Crane would dare to incriminate himself by a circumstantial account of "Opium's Varied Dreams" and then follow it with sketches of the Tenderloin (including the story of Yen-Nock Bill). He also endured the ill-repute of being a heavy drinker, and this became gospel because he associated with playwright Clyde Fitch, "a curious and fantastic man who was always the subject of scandal." Men like Crane and Huneker and Fitch had an uncomfortable time because they were successful liberals in an illiberal era, "and an aura of gossip naturally followed them."[4] Clyde Fitch and Crane argued in Mouquin's restaurant about a play they intended to write but never did. In Crane's version the play would have no heroine, but Fitch objected that a play with no love interest would never do.

Chinatown, the Bowery, Harlem, the Tenderloin—all became part of his experiences, including the Western Boulevard, the great thoroughfare for bicyclists by the thousands. It was the Age of Bloomers along the city's bicycle speedway, and cafés and hotels were occupied mainly by people in bicycle clothes. Billboards advertised wheels and lamps and tires and saddles "with all the flaming vehemence of circus art," wrote Crane in "Transformed Boulevard" (*Sun:* July 5, 1896). Even when the billboards advertised a patent medicine, it was a lithograph of a young person in bloomers "who is saying in large type: 'Yes, George, I find that Willowrum always refreshes me after these long rides.'" To the truck driver the wheelman is a pest, some kind of new mosquito. Bicycle cops race to catch up with the speeding "scorcher," and a whole mob of wheelmen and wheelwomen—eager to see the race—chase after them.

In July, Crane spent some nights at two new roof gardens which had opened that season: Oscar Hammerstein's Olympia, ablaze on Broadway, and the Grand Central Palace's roof garden. The roof garden had probably been invented by some Arab or Moor in a long-gone century, but the American has only recently seized upon the idea, he wrote in "Evening on the Roof." The people who swarm to the Olympia are conveyed by two elevators "to where the cool and steady night wind insults the straw hat and the scene here during the popular part of the evening is perhaps more gaudy and dazzling than any other in New York." Oscar's garden was a feat. "It has an exuberance, which reminds one of the Union depot train-shed of some Western city. The steel arches of the roof make a wide and splendid sweep, and over in a corner there are real swans swimming in real water. The whole structure glares like a conflagration with the countless electric lights. Oscar has caused the execution of decorative paintings upon the walls. They appear to have been painted with a nozzle; if he had caused the execution of the decorative painters he'd have done much better.

"One of the main features of a roof-garden is the waiter, who stands directly in front of you whenever anything interesting transpires on the stage. This waiter is 300 feet high and 72 feet wide. His little finger can block your view of the golden-haired soubrette, and when he waves his arm the stage disappears as if by a miracle. . . . Some day there may be a wholesale massacre of roof-garden waiters, but they will die with astonished faces and with questions on their lips. Skulls so steadfastly opaque defy axes or any of the other methods which the populace occasionally use to cure colossal stupidity."

In "The Man from Duluth" Crane's title character complains to his companions that the big city is a dead-slow town, and one of the New Yorkers waves his hand mournfully. "'Well, you see, it is Sunday night, for one thing; and besides that, the town is about dead, anyhow.' 'That's what it is,' said the others. They began plaintively to deplore the ravages of reform. Their voices filled with pathos, they spoke of the days that had been. It was the wail of the Tenderloin, the lamentation of the 'rounders'

who have seen their idols of men and places taken from them." They walk
down the avenue to the criss-cross streets of Greenwich Village in search
of the little French concert hall, a private house with a mutilated hallway
and a little hall with a tiny stage. A youth in the corner thrummed the
piano, two score people sat babbling French at the tables, and papier-mâché
rocks and boulders decorated the dilapidated and dusty place. At intervals
one of the three men sitting near the youth at the piano would vanish
amidst the paper mountains and appear upon the little stage. "They relieved
each other with the regularity of sentries, and sang from the inexhaustible
store of French comic songs. One was wretched, one was fair, and one
was an artist. Even the man from Duluth, who comprehended less of
French than he did of Sanscrit, enjoyed this latter performer. It is not
always necessary to understand a language; sometimes one can be glad
that he does not. But the man from Duluth revelled in the songs of him
who was an artist. There were eloquent gestures and glances of the eyes
that were full of symbols."

When the audience laughs he leans forward and demands translation
from the painter who has studied in France. A one-eyed waiter and his
fellows clear the hall of chairs and tables, and then the pianist attacks his
instrument and the ball begins. "Couples emerged from all portions of the
hall to go whirling about in reckless fashion. There was nothing uniform
or sedate. It was all emotional. Each couple danced according to moods.
Some went solemnly, some affectionately, and at all times a man would
swirl his partner about the floor with a mad speed that would threaten to
send her head flying. They were having lots of fun; almost every one was
laughing. 'It's dead slow,' said the man from Duluth. Then, suddenly, in the
middle of the floor there was a fight. The music stopped with a crash; the
dancers scurried out of the way. The atmosphere of the place became
instantly tense, ominous, battleful." Two men hammer at each other with
their fists and lunge with their feet "in the manner of French infantry
soldiers. Their eyes flash tragic hatred. . . . But the men are about eight
feet apart. Their savage fists cut harmlessly through the air; the terrific
deadly lunges of their feet are mere demonstrations of some kind. The
man from Duluth climbs down from his chair. 'They're a pair of birds,'
he said with supreme contempt. He regarded them with eyes of reproach.
Apparently he considered that they had swindled him out of something,
and he was much injured."

But then everybody rushes forward gesticulating in tremendous excitement, men tussling, tugging, frenzied with rage. "The lightning-blooded
spirit of battle hovered over the swaying crowd." But even so it is all a
fake to the man from Duluth, a big fight in which nobody hits anybody else.
However, a fat, tipsy Frenchman intrudes and inaugurates a new turmoil,
and at last there is war, red war. A woman with arms outstretched like

the claws of an eagle attacks the tipsy Frenchman, who is a peril to her lover and has called her bad names. " 'Hurrah!' shouted the man from Duluth from on top of his chair. 'Hurrah! hurrah! for America and the star spangled banner! No man here dare call the lady anything.' 'What's that?' said the woman. She came ominously toward him. Her face was red and fierce. Her hands were held in the same peculiar clawlike manner. 'What's that yeh say?' 'Madam,' said the man from Duluth, suddenly sober and serious, 'I didn't mean to reflect upon you in any way.' " But she thinks he is jollying her and attacks his coattails as he flees the place. He bows out swiftly, "but with satirical ceremony," and makes a flying leap for the door. Like the Swede in "The Blue Hotel," the man from Duluth ends getting what he was asking for.

To succeed in life the youth of America have only to see an old man seated upon a railing and then to ask him for a match, says young Tom in "A Self-Made Man."[5] That is how Tom becomes Thomas G. Somebody. "His fame has spread through the land as a man who carved his way to fortune with no help but his undaunted pluck, his tireless energy, and his sterling integrity. Newspapers apply to him now, and he writes long signed articles to struggling young men, in which he gives the best possible advice as to how to become wealthy." But in fact it is sheer chance that brings him success.

"A Self-Made Man" is a parody of the Horatio Alger story. Strolling down Broadway, Tom meets an old man smoking a clay pipe who asks for a match. The old man asks if he can read, and then he hands over a letter having to do with the sale of land in Tin Can, Nevada. The old man realizes that "George" has double-crossed him. Tom proposes that he serve as lawyer to put the screws on George. The young impostor by assuming a highly legal air succeeds in scaring George into making good in the draft he has swindled the old man out of, and then old man Wilkins settles down in Tom's boardinghouse and lives happy ever after. He basks under the proprietress's smiles, which have a commercial value. The old man, with his quantities of sagebrush back in Nevada, is duped into thinking that Tom possesses "all the virtues mentioned in high-class literature" (such as Horatio Alger), and Tom's opinion, too, is of commercial value. "Also, he knew a man who knew another man who received an impetus which made him engage Thomas on terms that were highly satisfactory. Then it was that the latter learned he had not succeeded sooner because he did not know a man who knew another man." In sum, one succeeds not by integrity and tireless energy and pluck, but by bluff and luck. At the start, when Tom is down and out, his self-assurance is immense, and it increases in a proper ratio to the amount of his bills. He is used to stuffing his worn shoe with four aces, and when they become rain-soaked through the hole he feels he is walking on frozen dollars.

His luck changes when he runs out of aces and has to put up a better front. On the day he meets old Wilkins his replaced shoe-sole consists of king, queen, deuce and trey.

In May, *George's Mother* was published by Appleton and in mid-June by Heinemann Ltd. in London. Crane began it on the back of his manuscript of "The Holler Tree," a Sullivan County sketch written in 1892–1893, which never got published, perhaps because he misplaced the manuscript. He might readily have misplaced it because he used the back of the sheets to write first drafts not only of the novel but also of "The Reluctant Voyagers." C. K. Linson, who says he first met Crane just after *Maggie* was published (March, 1893), did illustrations for "The Reluctant Voyagers" in the summer of 1893, and so Crane most likely began the Bowery novel that year.[6] He put it aside until *The Red Badge* was completed, and then returned to it in May, 1894 and finished it by November 15. He wrote Garland on May 9: "I am content and am writing another novel which is a bird." And on November 15: "I have just completed a New York book that leaves Maggie at the post. It is my best thing." The *Bookman* for May, 1895 mentioned it as *A Woman Without Weapons,* the tentative title by which it was known until published in 1896 as *George's Mother.* To write another Bowery novel after the failure of *Maggie* took a certain amount of self-confidence, to say the least. William Dean Howells had *George's Mother* in mind when he said: "I like to see the novelists treating some of the other important things of life—the relation of mother and son." Crane in his first draft began the novel with the portrait of the mother, which appears in the printed version in Chapter II.

George Kelcey is his mother's ideal; her whole life is sacrificed to his well-being. She anticipates the time when her son will become "a white and looming king among men," and with the blind devotion of a religious fanatic she dies still believing in her son. She is a hard-working, psalm-singing old woman; like Crane's mother, she is a member of the W.C.T.U. Her great grief is that George refuses to attend prayer meetings. These conventicles are her shrine, as the "smiling saloon" is George's. Each has found a place of refuge from the world's harsh realities. In the saloon, as in the church, the chosen few congregate and are saved.

" 'George,' " Mrs. Kelcey says suddenly one evening at dinner, " 'come t' prayer-meetin' with me t'night.' The young man dropped his fork. 'Say, you must be crazy,' he said, in amazement. 'Yes, dear,' she continued rapidly, in a small pleading voice, 'I'd like t' have yeh go with me once in a while. Yeh never go with me any more, dear, an' I'd like t' have yeh go. Yeh ain't been anywheres at all with me in the longest while.' 'Well,' he said, 'well, but what the blazes—' 'Ah, comeon,' said the little old woman. She began to coax him with caresses. The young man grinned. 'Thunderation!' he said, 'what would I do at a prayer-meetin'?' " So she pleads in vain and goes alone to the prayer meeting, while George keeps an engagement at a blow-out in the room of one Bleecker. Some of the tenement women "concluded that the little old mother had a wild son. They came to condole with her. They sat in the kitchen for hours. She told them of his wit, his cleverness, his kind heart."

"Each morning his mother went to his room, and fought a battle to arouse him. She was like a soldier." George rebels against the injustice of rising every morning "with bitter regularity, before the sleep-gods had at all loosened their grasp. He hated that unknown force which directed his life. One morning he swore a tangled mass of oaths, aimed into the air, as if the injustice was poised there. His mother flinched at first; then her mouth set in the little straight line. She saw that the momentous occasion had come. It was the time of the critical battle. She turned upon him valorously. 'Stop your swearin', George Kelcey. I won't have yeh talk so before me!' " George's face "grew sour with passion and misery. He spoke in tones dark with dislike. 'Th' 'ell yeh won't! Whatter yeh goin' t' do 'bout it?' " Then for three days "they lived in silence. He brooded upon his mother's agony and felt a singular joy in it. As opportunity offered, he did little despicable things. He was going to make her abject. He was now uncontrolled, ungoverned; he wished to be an emperor. Her suffering was all a sort of compensation for his own dire pains. She went about with a gray, impassive face. It was as if she had survived a massacre in which all that she loved had been torn from her by the brutality of savages."

George announces that he has been fired from his job, while his mother goes on listlessly peeling potatoes. "It seemed to be the final blow. Her body gave a convulsive movement in the chair. When she finally lifted her eyes, horror possessed her face. Her underjaw had fallen. 'Fired? Outa work? Why—George?' He went over to the window and stood with his back to her. He could feel her gray stare upon him. 'Yep! Fired!' " Crane does not say so, but George is no doubt brooding upon the philosophy of these hoodlums who lived in a den on a vacant lot surrounded by high tenement houses and were all too clever to work. "Some of them had worked, but these used their experiences as stores from which to draw tales. They were like veterans with their wars. One lad in particular used to recount how he whipped his employer, the proprietor of a large grain and feed establishment," and in whipping him he felt "like a savage who had killed a great chief." These hoodlums felt contempt for life. Their philosophy taught them that "the whole thing was idle and a great bore. With fine scorn they sneered at the futility of it. Work was done by men who had not the courage to stand still and let the skies clap together if they willed. . . . They longed dimly for a time when they could run through decorous streets with crash and roar of war, an army of revenge for pleasures long possessed by others, a wild sweeping compensation for their years without crystal and gilt, women and wine. This thought slumbered in them, as the image of Rome might have lain small in the hearts of the barbarians. Kelcey respected these youths so much that he ordinarily used the other side of the street."

Once George has lost his job his friends forsake him. And that indefinite woman he has dreamt of, she with the fragrance of roses that comes from her hair, she too forsakes him. Broken and deranged, the forsaken mother is tormented by visions—"she was staring off at something sinister." The devils of sin she has warred against all her life have at last over-powered her. It is the demon world making final onslaught against that deluded hope she worshipped as her son. She has tried to save him, but on that one occasion when he entered the chapel after resentfully consent-ing to accompany her there, "he felt a sudden quaking. His knees shook. It was an awesome place to him." And in the chamber of death where his mother cries to him unheeded, there too he quakes and becomes so nervous "that he could not hear the chatter from the bed, but he was always conscious of the ticking of the little clock out on the kitchen shelf." That ticking clock—"emblematic of the life of the city"—signifies the realities: life dissipated and unconverted.

Where did Crane get the story of *George's Mother?* Harvey Wickham says that the incident of George's amazing lunch—a charlotte russe and a beer—was consumed in fact by a relative of his named Frank in a rather lurid resort on 14th Street directly opposite Tammany Hall. Frank was a handsome youth "much given to dress and to leisure; his mother was a most estimable lady and a devout follower of Mrs. Grundy. Crane transposed them to the slums, preserving only the characters—a plausible and worthless young man with an indulgent and credulous parent." Wick-ham's supposition that George is Frank and that Frank's mother is Mrs. Kelcey collapses under scrutiny. Crane told Edward Garnett that George's mother was an exaggerated portrait of his own mother's characteristics.

Mrs. Edmund Crane could detect no link between George's mother in the novel and Stephen's mother, who was a religious woman and never scolded or nagged. However, Mrs. Kelcey is also a religious woman; and as to her nagging her son, Crane by his own admission exaggerated his mother's characteristics in order to dramatize George Kelcey's plight. George is drawn mainly from brother Townley, the drunkard in the Crane family. Mrs. Kelcey is no common Bowery mother any more than George is the average Bowery workingman degraded by the bottle, or Maggie the typical streetwalker. They are all exaggerated for dramatic effect, with a heightened sense of life's promises.

The reviewers hacked away at *George's Mother.* The Brooklyn *Daily Eagle* (June 8) thought it a succession of uninteresting episodes; a good share of the book, said the *Eagle,* describes a booze session in a saloon and a debauch at old Bleecker's party. "Now, the idiosyncrasies of a 'drunk' participated in by a collection of 'tanks' in the back room of an east side gin-mill have some scientific interest for students of mental pathology, but it is pretty poor stuff to put into literature." Critic George Edward Woodbury rejected "the eccentric, the sensational, the abnormal, the brutal, and base," on the grounds that "life experience spiritualized is the formula for all great literature." Crane, like Henry James, saw "life indeed as ferocious and sinister" and portrayed it that way in his poetry and prose. Jeannette Gilder in the *World* saw *George's Mother* simply as the idea of the hopelessness of the lives of the working class, made hopeless by drink and debauchery (apparently the upper classes were exempt from drink and debauchery). The *Bookman* in 1900 thought *George's Mother* "too strained—too intense—it is all out of proportion." On the other hand, novelist Frank Norris in the San Francisco *Wave* (July 4, 1896) reviewed both of Crane's slum novels and judged *George's Mother* superior to *Maggie* because "it is less pretentious, has fewer characters and more unity, conveying one distinct impression."

John Barry, who had championed Crane's poems in April, 1894, by reading them at Sherry's, rightly recognized the construction of *George's Mother* as absolutely logical. "Taken as a whole, there is nothing insignificant, nothing that does not make for the completeness of the picture, for the consummation of the ghastly tragedy." The description of George and his mother going to prayer meeting, he thought, was a unique example of Impressionism in literature, as wonderful as a picture by Claude Monet. *George's Mother* justifies the use of utterly squalid material in literature, said Barry in the *Daily Tatler* (November 12, 1896). "It teaches us what the lesson of the life it depicts would teach us if we were to know it at first hand, the dreadful pity of it. I do not see how any one could resent or blame the characters in *George's Mother*; given the conditions surrounding them, and they had to be what they were." He thought it the most heart-rending picture of mother-love in literature, "and mother-love is a theme that ought to touch even critics. Yet the book is not for one instant either mawkish or morbid." One of the best scenes, said the *Literary Digest* (July 4, 1896), is the death scene of the old woman with her dazed mind wandering back to George's boyhood. "Mr. Crane's celebrity as a colorist is here well sustained, as in the image of drunken Kelcey falling with " 'a yellow crash.' "

*George's Mother* is a masterpiece, said the English critic Edward Garnett in the London *Academy*. "An ordinary artist would seek to dive into the mind of the old woman, to follow its workings hidden under the deceitful appearances of things, under the pressure of her surroundings. A great artist would so recreate her life that its griefs and joys became significant of the griefs and joys of all motherhood on earth. But Mr. Crane does neither. He simply reproduces the surfaces of the individual life in so marvelous a way that the manner in which the old woman washes up the crockery, for example, gives us her. To dive into the hidden life is, of course, for the artist a great temptation and a great danger—the values of the picture speedily get wrong, and the artist, seeking to interpret life, departs from the truth of nature. The rare thing about Mr. Crane's art is that he keeps closer to the surface than any living writer, and, like the great portrait-painters, to a great extent makes the surface betray the depths."

When the 1896 hard-cover edition of *Maggie* was published in early June, Crane sent out inscribed copies to friends as token payment of his debts to them. "It is indeed a brave new binding and I wish the inside were braver," he wrote a friend, DeWitt Miller, on July 3. Actually he was deeply aware that *Maggie* was one of the bravest things ever written about the Bowery. To H. P. Taber, editor of *The Philistine,* he presented his less humble side: "I wrote this book when I was very young; so if you don't like it, shut up."

Remembering his days "of suffering and trouble he sent E. J. Edwards a copy of *George's Mother* on June 14, and later that summer he wrote Herbert P. Williams when his supply of *George's Mother* had been exhausted by gift copies: "If you have any copies of George's Ma send one by boy, please. I am going today or in the morning at the latest [to Hartwood, where on August 23 he signed the register of the Hartwood Club]."

Williams of the Boston *Herald* had interviewed him in early July for his sketch "Mr. Crane as a Literary Artist," previously referred to. Describing Crane's studio at 165 West 23rd Street, he said the room seemed curiously typical of the man: "A tinted wall is relieved at intervals by war trophies and by impressionistic landscapes. . . . The small bookshelf contains batches of gray manuscript and potential literature in the form of stationery. One of the two chairs stands between the window and a writing-table at which a club might dine. An ink-bottle, a pen and a pad of paper occupy dots in the vast green expanse. A sofa stretches itself near the window and tries to fill space. No crowded comfort is here—no luxury of ornament—no literature, classic or periodical: nothing but the man and his mind."

Williams says that Crane wrote only what he pleased, that is, "what seems to him true; you are privileged to like it; he is your good friend if you don't. It has been said that he describes everything in terms of color; perhaps he would call his position 'red independence.' After five minutes in his company you will see colors everywhere, even if you did not see them before." In his long interview Williams got the impression of a man frank and devoid of affectation, a man who "sees things flat" because he knows his mind without being self-conscious. "He is hampered by nothing: the traditions of the past—the sensationalism and the subjectivity of the present he neither imitates nor criticises." Crane had collected the war trophies which decorated his room during his visit to the battlefield of

Fredericksburg in late January, 1896, and the Impressionistic paintings had been with him since his college days.[7]

He wrote Williams on July 6: "You are at liberty to write what you think best. As to the pictures, however, it will take some weeks to provide them. If you care to wait, let me know at once." (Williams used an early photograph of Crane with the triangular moustache.)

"I want you to dine tonight with me at the Lantern Club," Crane wrote Garland on a postal which he left at Garland's hotel[8] with an inscribed copy of *George's Mother.* "Sure!! Roosevelt expects to be there. He wants to meet you. Don't fail. I will call here at six—again."

Having helped the young Crane formulate the principles by which *Maggie* and *The Red Badge* were revised, Garland ended by echoing him in his unpublished *Chicago Studies.* The more Crane influenced Garland, the cooler Garland became. First, he avoided their association because of what he called "the shady side of [Crane's] Bohemian life." In the 1930's he reread *George's Mother* and wrote in it, "As I read this book now it appears an unimportant youthful venture. It is a heightened, artificially colored transcript of life. It is Crane, the boy telling of things he has seen but putting his own psychology into his observations. His English is admirable, concise, vivid and unfaltering. It will live only as a literary phase of a brilliant young literary man, whose later phases were not much more important. Crane never quite grew up in any sense. Disease came in to weaken his work and death cut it short. His marvelous command of simple English words is his chief claim to distinction to me now as it was in the days when I first knew him."

"If we insist on sincerity," Garland had written in *Idols,* "the question of dignity will take care of itself. Truth is a fine preparation for dignity, and for beauty as well." And Howells had told Crane (probably in 1893), "a writer of skill cannot be defeated because he remains true to his conscience." Conscience (honesty and sincerity of purpose) was Crane's criterion of judgment; "I write what is in me," he said. "A man is born into the world with his own pair of eyes and he is not at all responsible for his vision—he is merely responsible for his quality of personal honesty." His infrequent comments on literary art amount to no more than the canon which Howells and Conrad and Henry James promulgated. Their art, however, transcended their theory, but Hamlin Garland's seldom did, and this may explain Garland's envy of young Crane's fantastic success.

"What a boom Crane has had!" Howells wrote Garland on July 22. "Have you read *George's Mother?* Mrs. Howells thinks it the best of all— he's a good boy, with lots of sense." Crane also thought at the time that this book was his best. Howells, grounding his verdict on his own literary theory of realism, thought *George's Mother* and *Maggie*—"as pieces of art"—superior to *The Red Badge of Courage;* Garland stood at odds with this verdict. The business of the novel is to picture daily life as exactly as possible and "with a clear sense of proportion," Howells said when Crane interviewed him in October, 1894, for the New York *Times.* "That is the important matter—the proportion. . . . It is a perspective made for the benefit of people who have no true use of their eyes. The novel, in its real meaning, adjusts the proportions. It preserves the balance. It is in this way that lessons are to be taught and reforms to be won."

In "New York Low Life in Fiction" (in the *World* for July 26) Howells praised the honesty of *Maggie* and *George's Mother* for what we would today call social realism: the pathos of the underprivileged. "Mr. Crane has the skill to show how evil is greatly the effect of ignorance and imperfect civilization." The wonder of *George's Mother* is "the courage which deals with persons so absolutely average and the art that graces them with the beauty of the author's compassion for everything that errs and suffers. Without this feeling, the effects of his mastery would be impossible, and if it went further or put itself into the pitying phrases it would annul the effects. But it never does this. . . . He never shows his characters or his situations in any sort of sentimental glamour; if you will be moved by the sadness of common fates you will feel his intention, but he does not flatter his portraits of people or conditions to take your fancy." He renders them "without one maudlin touch."

Crane wrote on August 14 to thank Howells for his New York *World* appraisal. "It is of course the best word that has been said of me, and I am grateful in a way that is hard for me to say. In truth you have always been so generous with me that grace departs at once from my pen when I attempt to tell you of my appreciation. When I speak of it to others however I am mighty fluent and use the best terms every time. I always thank God that I can have the strongest admiration for the work of a man who has been so much to me personally for I can imagine the terrors of being indelibly indebted to the Chump in Art or even to the Semi-Chump in Art."

In Howells' *World* sketch Crane is linked with Abraham Cahan for having written "The truest picture of East Side life," and Cahan is hailed in a subheadline as "A new star of realism."[9] Abraham Cahan, editor of the *Jewish Daily Forward,* was author of *Yekl: A Tale of the New York Ghetto.* Crane was then reading the book and wondering how in the name of heaven Cahan learned how to write it, he remarked in his letter to Howells. "I am going tomorrow on a business journey and shall be gone until Wednesday. Upon my return I shall call at Far Rockaway and I hope then you will tell me where to find him [Cahan]. I have a delicious feeling of being some months ahead of him in the recognition, critically, and I would like to take some trouble in looking him up at his home."

Howells replied the next day, Saturday, the 15th: "Come a week from the time you mention—that is, come Wednesday the 25th [he meant the 26th], and spend the night and the next day with us, so as to get two sea baths. . . . Cahan lives at 213 East 6th St. He will be glad to see you, and is a fine fellow—a school teacher and editor of the Yiddish socialist paper. We all join in regards to you." Crane visited Howells on August 26 at Far Rockaway, Long Island, having sent him on the 17th a copy of *The Red Badge of Courage*. As his letter was written on the stationery of *McClure's Magazine*,[10] it is likely that the "business journey" he mentions was McClure's assignment to visit the prison at Sing Sing (now Ossining, New York).

Accompanied by a *World* artist whose sketches illustrated the study, "The Devil's Acre," Crane inspected the death chamber at Sing Sing and the convicts' graveyard on the hill overlooking the Hudson. An odor of oiled wood pervaded the death chamber. It was of course empty except for a chair of polished wood, a broom near the steel door, and a bit of sky showing through a window small enough to have been made by a canister shot. The doomed men end in the convicts' graveyard underneath white boards whose inscriptions are abrupt: "Here lies Wong Kee, died June 1, 1890." Cows chewing grass on the hillside trample down the wood markers, and the rains destroy the boards also. There is none to plant them upright again, and as these graves hold men whom the world wishes to forget, "there is no objection raised to the assault of nature. And so it comes to pass that the dates on the boards are recent. These white boards have marched like soldiers from the southward end of the field to the northward," while the boards in the south field rotted and fell. "It is a fine short road to oblivion. In the middle of the graveyard there is a dim but still defiant board upon which there is rudely carved a cross. Some singular chance has caused this board to be split through the middle, cleaving the cross in two parts, as if it had been done by the demoniac shape weaved in the clouds, but the aged board is still upright and the cross expresses its form as if it had merely expanded and become transparent. It is a place for the chanting of monks. At night one could assuredly hear at this place the laugh of the devil. One could see here the clutching, demoniac fingers. It is the fiend's own acre, this hillside."[11]

# ꭢ *The Dora Clark Affair*

CRANE sent a signed copy of *George's Mother* to Theodore
Roosevelt, President of the Board of Police Commissioners of New York,
and Roosevelt wrote back that he'd also like his *Red Badge of Courage*
inscribed, "for much though I like your other books, I think I like that book
the best." The author of *The Winning of the West* thought of himself as a
literary man. When William Dean Howells was editor of the *Cosmopolitan*
he used to assign articles to Roosevelt, but Howells' so-called realistic
fiction alarmed Roosevelt; he was inclined to associate "morbid" realism
with the political left and considered their association "not an uncommon
development of the reform spirit."

Police Commissioner Roosevelt's "beat" was the Bowery, where he
liked to walk in evening dress after a late party. Disguised by a cape and
a sombrero, he would sneak up on a delinquent policeman whom he found
boozing or taking bribes in a dark alley. In spite of his disguise he could
be readily recognized because of his spectacles and big gleaming teeth. One
newspaperman covering the same Bowery beat impersonated T. R. by
wearing a sombrero, and he frightened policemen by chattering his teeth
at them. Reporters called the commissioner "Haroun al Roosevelt."[1]

On reading *Maggie,* Roosevelt asked the author to call upon him because
"I have much to discuss with you about Madge." In mid-August, 1896,
Crane evidently tangled with the police at Madison Square Garden and
notified Roosevelt in criticism of his policemen. Roosevelt replied on
August 18: "This evening I shall be around at the Madison Square Garden
to see exactly what the Police do. They have a very difficult task with a
crowd like that, because they have to be exceedingly good humored with
the crowd, and they also have to please the Managers of the meeting who
know nothing about crowds, and yet they have to control twenty thousand
people. I will say one thing for them at the Bryan meeting; we have not
had a single complaint of clubbing or brutality from any man claiming
to have suffered; the Managers of the meeting and the Manager of the
Garden have both written us in the warmest terms. I hope to see you
again." He regretted that he didn't get to the Lantern Club to meet Hamlin

Garland. He had read Garland's *Crumbling Idols* (1894) but found it "rough riding."

In the same letter Roosevelt said he wanted Crane to write someday "another story of the frontiersman and the Mexican Greaser in which the frontiersman shall come out on top; it is more normal that way!" The Mexican story was "A Man and Some Others," previously mentioned, in which a gunfight occurs between a band of Mexicans and a frontiersman who had once been a Bowery saloon bouncer. Crane must have sent Roosevelt a copy of his typescript because it was not published in the *Century* until February, 1897; Richard Watson Gilder postponed its publication because Crane got himself involved with the police and thereby damaged his reputation. It brought Gilder to ask indignantly of Stephen's literary agent, Paul Revere Reynolds, just what Crane meant by getting himself into such a mess when he had sold a story to the highly respectable *Century Magazine*. He also objected to Crane's use of swear words. "You may think me over anxious, but I am particularly sorry he did not change that 'B' Gawd.' It is difficult to know what to do with swearing in fiction. When it appears in print it has an offensiveness beyond that of the actual word; and it is never true or 'realistic' because, if the actual oaths were printed just as the swearer swears it would be as unendurable among men as among gods. I am a sincere well-wisher of the author, and I am anxious that his story should not attract unfavorable criticism in any details; so I particularly ask him through yourself to omit that expression, for his sake as well as yours."

"I am truly obliged to Mr. Crane for getting out of that hackneyed 'crown of thorns,' " Gilder added. The "crown of thorns" cliché had become hackneyed in 1896 through William Jennings Bryan's crusading speech at the Democratic Presidential Convention, where Bryan won the nomination on his platform of devaluating gold for a silver standard. His famous speech ended with Biblical incantation: "You shall not press down upon the brow of labor this crown of thorns, you shall not crucify mankind upon a cross of gold."

William Randolph Hearst's *Journal* for September 20 announced that the author of *The Red Badge of Courage*, which "everybody has read," had arranged to write for the New York *Journal* "a series of life in New York. He chose the police courts as his first subject." The *Book News* also announced that Mr. Crane "will publish a new series of stories, or a long story, he has not definitely decided which, in which will be presented the life of the metropolitan policeman. This apart from a volume of stories that may appear just prior to Christmas (*The Little Regiment*)." A certain H. R. Huxton had spoken to Hearst on September 10 about Stephen Crane's doing some studies of "real incidents of New York life." Hearst said to go ahead, and Huxton reported it that day to Crane.[2]

Out of this arrangement came "Adventures of a Novelist (in the *Journal* for September 20), but nothing came of Crane's projected studies of "the life of the metropolitan policeman." On September 14 he scrutinized "the machinery of justice" at the Jefferson Market Police Court in Greenwich Village. He decided that in order to learn more about the throngs of unfortunates who passed in kaleidoscopic view before the magistrate's judicial gaze he must first study these "victims of injustice" in their haunts. And so by appointment Crane on the night of September 15–16 met some "chorus girls" at the Turkish Smoking Parlors on West 29th Street.

From the Turkish Smoking Parlors he walked with them to the Broadway Garden, where another "chorus girl" introduced herself as Dora Clark and joined the group. Unknown to Crane, Dora Clark—also known as Ruby Young—was a streetwalker who had several times been arraigned for soliciting. Crane did not care who they were; it was enough that he had found their types. After he had interviewed them at the Broadway Garden, a resort of ill-repute, he escorted one of the women across the street to catch an uptown cable car, leaving the other and Dora Clark on the corner of Broadway and 31st Street. While they stood there conversing, two men walked swiftly by, as though in a hurry to get home, and neither they nor the two women took notice of each other. However, the women were just then spotted by a policeman, not in uniform, from the vestibule of the Grand Hotel. It was 2 A.M.

Walking back to them from the cable-car, Crane suddenly realized that they were being arrested. "Come to the station house. You are under arrest for soliciting two men!" Crane and the two women protested: "What two men?" The officer pointed to the men who had just walked by. The women, hysterical, tried to free themselves from the policeman's grip. The chorus girl "seemed nearly insane with fright and fury. Finally she screamed: 'Well, he's my husband.' And with her finger she indicated the reluctant witness," as Crane calls himself in his *Journal* report. The reluctant witness at once replied "to the swift, questioning glance of the officer, 'Yes, I am.' If it is necessary to avow a marriage to save a girl who is not a prostitute from being arrested as a prostitute, it must be done, though the man suffer eternally." "But I have got this other one," boasted Detective Becker ("as picturesque as a wolf"); and so Dora Clark spent the night in a prison cell, while Crane debated whether he dared afford to damage his reputation by defending a girl of the streets.

He asked himself: Do reputable citizens interfere? "Suppose I were a clerk and I interfered in this sort of a case. When it became known to my employers they would say to me: 'We are sorry, but we cannot have men in our employ who stay out until 2:30 in the morning in the company of chorus girls.' Suppose, for instance, I had a wife and seven children in Harlem. As soon as my wife read the papers she would say: 'Ha! You told me you had a business engagement! Half-past two in the morning with questionable company!' Suppose, for instance, I were engaged to the beautiful Countess of Kalamazoo. If she were to hear it, she would write: 'All is over between us. My future husband cannot rescue prostitutes at 2:30 in the morning.' These, then, must be three small illustrations of why men of character say nothing if they happen to witness some possible affair of this sort. . . . I possess nothing so tangible as a clerkship, as a wife and seven children in Harlem, as an engagement to the beautiful Countess of Kalamazoo; but all that I value may be chanced in this affair. Shall I take this risk for the benefit of a girl of the streets?"

Sergeant McDermott gave Crane fatherly advice to withdraw his defense of the woman known to the police as a solicitor. " 'If you monkey with this case, you are pretty sure to come out with mud all over you.' 'I suppose so,' said the reluctant witness. 'I haven't a doubt of it. But I don't see how I can, in honesty, stay away from court in the morning.' "[3] A reporter at 8:30 that morning advised Crane: "Go home; your own participation in the affair doesn't look very respectable. Go home."

"The sense of a city is war," Crane had once remarked to Emile Stangé on seeing a painting, and now he was about to battle the entrenched police force of the city for the sake of saving a prostitute. He was well aware of the corrupt power of New York City's policemen, who tolerated can-can and peep shows and houses of prostitution so long as they remained within a restricted area in the West Thirties, alien to conventional society. He was aware also of the hypocritical prudery of the public and the risk to his reputation, but he nevertheless appeared in court the next morning. Captain Chapman, "a special protégé of Commissioner Roosevelt," believed Policeman Charles Becker's version of the Dora Clark case, and Crane never succeeded in bringing Commissioner Roosevelt to believe his testimony against Becker.

He sent Roosevelt a telegram saying that he was going to prefer charges against Policeman Charles Becker for threatening to arrest him when he protested the innocence of Dora Clark and the woman he had interviewed at the Broadway Garden. Frederic Lawrence, who was with Crane the morning he sent the telegram, says the result was that "an aroused and resentful police department bent all its unscrupulous energies to discrediting him and making New York too hot for him to live in." Even as late as 1898 he was almost arrested on a trumped-up charge while emerging from a theatre with a priest, whose presence saved Crane from arrest.) Commissioner Roosevelt ignored Crane's telegram and whitewashed his policemen. He kept aloof from Crane thereafter, holding a grudge against him that persisted into 1898 when they were together at San Juan battlefield; he makes no mention of Crane in his *Rough Riders*.

Roosevelt discussed the Dora Clark case with Hamlin Garland and said: "I tried to save Crane from press comment, but as he insisted on testifying, I could only let the law take its course." Garland evidently intervened on Crane's behalf; but while he sympathized with him in his loyalty to a woman unjustly accused of soliciting, he felt that Stephen's stubborn resolve to go on the stand in her defense was quixotic. With the resulting scandalous exposé of Crane's life not only Roosevelt but also Garland turned a cold shoulder to him. Garland saw him several times during his troubles with the police and on meeting him one day in McClure's office he very earnestly advised him: " 'Crane, why don't you cut loose from your associations here? Go to your brother's farm in Sullivan County and get back your tone. You don't look well. Settle down to the writing of a single big book up there, and take your time to do it.' Impulsively thrusting out his hand to me, he said, 'I'll do it.' Alas! He did not."

Dora Clark denied Becker's charge of soliciting and told Magistrate Cornell that she had been persecuted by the police of the Nineteenth Precinct for the last three weeks. She said that Policeman Rosenberg of the 30th Street station had arrested her three weeks ago because she had refused his advances and that he had threatened to arrest her for spite afterward and had done just that two weeks later on a false charge. The New York *Sun* for September 17 related details about her arrest by Policeman Rosenberg on Sunday, August 23, when she was walking along a poorly lighted section of Broadway. "I told him to go along about his business, adding that I wanted nothing to do with Negroes. The man is very dark, and I really supposed him to be a Negro. He arrested me, and then I recognized my mistake." There was a titter in the courtroom at her misidentification of Rosenberg as a Negro; and when she left, Rosenberg—extremely angry—swore that he would get even with her even if he had to arrest her every night.

"He made good his threat two nights later and got his side partner Conway to arrest me on a side street while I was on my way home," Dora Clark testified. "A short time before I had been warned by two cabmen in Twenty-third street that Rosenberg and his partner, Conway, were looking for me. I was fined $5 by the Judge who was then sitting here. I have been arrested twice since then on sight. This morning two friends, a man and woman and myself came out of the Broadway Garden and walked to the corner of Thirty-first Street. While the man was handing the other woman into a cable-car I stood on the corner. I spoke to no one. In fact, I noticed no one until this policeman came up to me, took hold of my arm, and said: 'Aha! I've caught you at it again! You come along to the station house.' 'But you do not deny that you frequent the Tenderloin, do you?' asked the Magistrate. 'There would be no use in making such a denial,' was the answer. 'Well—'

" 'Just a word, your Honor!'

"The interruption came from a slender young man of medium height, with very long, tawny hair, parted in the middle and falling in great masses over his temples. It was Mr. Stephen Crane, the writer. With the 'red badge of courage' flaming on his breast, Mr. Crane stepped up to the bar and said: 'I was the man whom this woman spoke of as being with her and a companion when they came out of the Broadway Garden this morning. I am studying the life of the Tenderloin for the purpose of getting material for some sketches.' " He maintained that the woman had been constantly in his sight and had not spoken to any other man and that he had never seen her before.

The New York *Tribune* on the 17th quoted much the same account. " 'The testimony of this gentleman, whom I know, causes me to discharge you this time,' said the Magistrate. 'But, your Honor,' replied the prisoner, 'I will be arrested on sight the next time I show my face in the precinct.' 'I will look out for that,' " he said.

After the girl left the courtroom Crane told newspaper reporters that her arrest was an outrage. "There was absolutely no occasion for it. I was astounded when I saw the woman being lugged to the station house. Although I had never seen her before until last night, I made up my mind to find out what she was arrested for, and to see her through. The Sergeant at the desk in the West Thirtieth Street station told me the woman was just an ordinary streetwalker, and that I had better not get mixed up in the case, adding that it might do me a deal of harm if I did. But what did I care for such talk? I'd do the same thing again, if I thought it necessary. By heaven, I'd do it, even if I lost any little reputation I may have and strived to get. It would be well if others would follow my example." And so the Red Badge of Courage flamed with a new brightness, said the *Sun,* as Mr. Crane walked away.

The New York *Journal* on the 17th reported that Crane "was as brave as his hero" in the police court: " 'Your Honor, I know this girl to be innocent.' He was pale and nervous, 'but his voice had a ring of vibrant strength. He was plainly dressed in a dark blue suit and blue striped shirt. Even the look of thoughtful intelligence on his face could hardly have prepared an observer for the news that he was Stephen Crane, the youngest, latest and most successful of American novelists. He had been on the bridge in Jefferson Market Police Court since the opening hour, and had been watching the tide of human misery flow past. A very pretty girl was led from the prisoner's box and gruffly ordered to the bar. Sobbing violently, there she stood flushed and downcast, ringed in by rows of pitiless eyes. She was charged with that most degrading of all offenses, soliciting. Policeman Becker, who had made the arrest while in civilian clothes, said airily that she was an old offender. At that a flash of anger nerved the girl to speak. She grasped the rail with both her small hands and looked straight up into the Judge's face. 'Yes, Judge, it's true,' she said bitterly, 'that I have been arrested before.' She then explained that she had repelled a policeman who had spoken insultingly to her. Policeman

Rosenberg arrested her and told other policemen that she was bad and asked them to keep on arresting her.

"The Magistrate, annoyed because he had often listened to baseless charges against policemen, hesitated: 'Is there any doubt in this case, officer?' 'None at all,' said Becker. 'She's an old hand and always lies about it.' 'Young woman,' said the Magistrate, 'I have listened patiently because it is a terrible thing to judge a girl on such a charge unheard. But the officer's testimony and your past record!'" Then up spoke Crane, holding himself "with an air that was curiously like that of the girl; for he, like her, knew that he was surrounded by condemnatory eyes. The girl, in uncomprehending wonder, gazed at him. She could hardly understand how it was that he dared to defend her."

When interviewed at his rooming house by a New York *Journal* reporter he said: "As to the girl's character I know nothing. I only know that while with me she acted respectably, and that the policeman's charge was false. She certainly did not look dissipated, and she was very neatly and prettily dressed. I noticed, too, that she was still neat in court, even after the hours of imprisonment. The policeman roughly threatened to arrest me, when I told him that the girl had done no wrong. He arrested the other girl, too, but let her go when she went into hysterics at the police station. I was strongly advised by Sergeant McDermott not to try to help her, for I seemed a respectable sort of man, he said, and it would injure me. I well knew I was risking a reputation that I have worked hard to build." However, "she was a woman and unjustly accused, and I did what was my duty as a man. I realized that if a man should stand tamely by, in such a case, our wives and sisters would be at the mercy of any ruffian who disgraces the uniform. The policeman flatly lied, and if the girl will have him prosecuted for perjury I will gladly support her." The *Journal* reporter asked Crane: " 'While waiting to speak in the court-room, and to thus openly dare the censure of the public, did you not feel like your own hero in *The Red Badge of Courage* before his first battle?' "

"He smiled. 'Yes, I did. I was badly frightened, I admit, and would gladly have run away, could I have done so with honor.'

" 'And now that it is over, I presume you are also like your hero, in being ready to face a sword ordeal without a tremor?'

" 'No, no!' Mr. Crane exclaimed. 'I differ from my own hero, for I would be just as frightened the next time!'

" 'Just how would you describe the girl, Mr. Crane?'

" 'Why,' he said, 'she was really handsome, you know, and she had hair—red hair—dark red'—

" 'Yes!'—

" 'And she was dressed, I am pretty sure, in some kind of shirt waist,' he concluded, desperately.

"At the Nineteenth Precinct Police station it was learned last evening that the girl's fears of re-arrest were well founded. 'I only hope she'll be out to-night and be run in here!' said Sergeant Daly, chuckling gleefully at the thought. Captain Chapman said he fully believed Becker's story. 'Does it make no difference that a man of world-wide reputation states that she committed no offense?' he was asked. 'Who is this Crane? An actor?' 'No. An author.' 'Never heard of him before.' Captain Chapman admitted that Becker had recently made a similar arrest and that a number of reporters had alleged that the girl was innocent."

The New York *Journal* on October 8 disclosed the fact that Policeman Becker and another officer had recently shot at a young burglar named O'Brien and killed him. "Both officers were placed under detention and ordered to merely report at their station house and remain there during their hours of duty." When the Reverend Dr. Parkhurst and a young parishioner explored the lower depths of the city in 1892, the detective Dr. Parkhurst engaged to serve them as guide spotted Captain Chapman speaking to the proprietor of Paresis Hall, a house of prostitution for homosexuals which was obviously under police protection. In the Becker–Dora Clark case this same Captain Chapman protested with self-righteous indignation as though his character could not be impugned. He could count on his defense by the naive or duped Commissioner of Police, T. R. Roosevelt.

Some newspapers slanted the story so as to make Crane appear in the ridiculous figure of a knight-at-arms or Don Quixote. Here seems to be a novelette all ready made, said the Boston *Herald* on the 18th; novelist Crane distinguishes himself "in a manner that does credit to his heart, if not to his head." The same paper on the 21st remarked that Crane was still writing up his experiences with that doubtful chorus girl whom he met in the Bowery. "She bids fair to become almost as famous as Trilby." (Dora Clark was not a chorus girl.) Stephen Crane had gotten himself into warm water by his valiant defense of a young woman in police court in New York City, said the Boston *Traveler* for October 2. "The chances are that the youthful literary prodigy was on a genuine 'lark,' and, when his companion was apprehended, invented the tale about searching for book material. That is the way it looks to a cold and unprejudiced world."

Crane wrote some friend that most streetwalkers "would be 'demi-mondianes' [sic] if they had money. Lots of women are just naturally unchaste, and all you jays know it." He was not speaking from hearsay. Association with women in scarlet, said the Chicago *Dispatch,* was not necessarily any "Red Badge of Courage."

Dora Clark had preferred charges against Policemen Charles Becker and Martin Conway of the Tenderloin precinct for persecuting her and unwarrantably arresting her for soliciting. (Crane decided not to prefer charges against Becker, said the *Journal* on October 8.) She then preferred *new* charges against Becker on the claim that he had brutally assaulted her the previous Sunday—October 4—at three o'clock in the morning. (Miss Clark thus unwittingly incriminated herself as a night-time prowler.) In her new charge she claimed that when she was standing on the corner of Sixth Avenue and 28th Street talking to some cabmen, Becker walked up to her and said: " 'So, you made charges against me, did you?' at the same time using profane language. 'You're a loafer to talk that way,' I replied, whereupon he seized me by the throat, kicked me and knocked me down. I got up and he threw me down again. The bystanders then interfered and Becker went away." The cabmen said they recognized the girl's assailant as Becker, but he declared that at that time he was in the station house.

The trial was set for October 15, after being twice postponed. Meanwhile *Harper's Weekly* on the 10th reported that Commissioner Roosevelt and other high police authorities were skeptical of Crane's accuracy in reporting the Dora Clark affair. "All the reports of the case give the reader the impression that a tendency to light conduct actually existed in the young woman and that the only question was whether the policeman had observed this tendency at one of the moments of its acute development or not."

Chief Conlin had asked Crane to call at his office to make a statement about Dora Clark's charges, but Crane made no reply and, said the *Tribune* on September 29, he deliberately remained silent and withdrawn. Had the police frightened him from his determination to appear at the trial as witness against Becker? The *Tribune* reported the rumor that the police at the Thirtieth Street station had warned him that they would prosecute him if he testified on Dora Clark's behalf; they were prepared to swear that he led a fast life among women of the Tenderloin and that they would prosecute him on the charge of maintaining an opium joint.

Crane told the *Journal* reporter: "There is not an atom of truth in any report that I shall fail to appear against Becker. I have not tried to avoid subpoena servers, and I have not left town. My address is with a lawyer, who will notify me when the time arrives to appear. I have not received any intimations from the police that I would be 'shown up' if I appeared against Becker, either. It wouldn't make the slightest difference to me if I had. I have never, since I testified in the police court, had any idea of refusing to proceed further in the case.' When asked about his opium joint, Crane laughed. 'I have got an opium lay-out in my room,' he said, 'but it is tacked to a plaque hung on the wall. I consider it my duty,' he said, 'having witnessed an outrage such as Becker's arrest of this girl, to do my utmost to have him punished. The fact that I was in her company, and had just left what the detectives called a resort for thieves, prostitutes and crooks, does not bear on the matter in the least. I had a perfect right to be there, or in any other public resort anywhere else in the city where I choose to go.' "

The hearing on charges preferred by Dora Clark against Becker and

Conway began at 9 P.M. on October 15 and didn't end until 2:38 A.M. the next morning; it was the longest trial-session ever held in New York's Police Headquarters. The *Journal* reported that Crane's subpoena called him to appear at 3 P.M., and he waited in the corridor for ten hours before being called to the stand, dining off a sandwich and a glass of beer while hack-drivers, winking at each other, pointed at him, and women with artificial complexions and manners sneered at him. At 1:55 A.M. lawyer David M. Neuberger opened the court door and talked with Crane there, while a fellow who had not lost sight of Crane for ten hours slipped into the trial room and whispered to lawyer Louis Grant,[4] who jumped up intensely indignant: "This is an outrage, unjust to all concerned. This witness, Crane, has heard everything within ear-shot."

Policeman Becker was well-supported by Captain Chapman and his wardens. They anxiously regarded Crane with a fixed determination as he was sworn in, said the *Journal*, "but he in turn cared nothing for them. He was perfectly controlled, cold as ice. Thin and pale, with a large nose and prominent teeth, with straight hair plastered down on a curiously shaped head and with a poorly nourished moustache, he is a young man who does not look brainy but has proved that he has brains. Bending far over on the edge of his witness chair and looking at the floor until it came to answering questions, he then raised his head for a moment and, looking straight into the eyes of his questioner, snapped out his answers like the crack of a whip: 'Yes.' 'No.' 'If you want it so.' His explanation that he interviewed two chorus girls at the Broadway Garden so as to weave them into stories of the Tenderloin he was then writing amused the police immensely. They joked that he could find these types in a composing room or a printing office."

The police had found an opium layout in Crane's rooms, but in fact "it was merely part of the bric-a-brac there," said the *Journal* on October 17. Lawyer Grant made it appear that Crane's mind "was stupefied by opium that night at the Broadway Garden and Dora Clark seemed to him an angel." " 'Dopey,' said the policeman, the women and the hack drivers. But it came to the direct question: 'Do you smoke opium?' Mr. Crane raised his head, as always, in answering, looked straight into Mr. Grant's eyes, smiled as if to say, 'Really, really, I have a type before me,' and snapped out: 'No.' " Mr. Crane admitted that he had lived in a house on West 22nd, and Mr. Grant sneeringly queried: "With what woman did you live there?" Lawyer Neuburger (variously spelled Newberger and Neuberger) advised Crane not to answer that question, and so Crane refused to answer. Said Crane wearily: "I refuse to answer." Said Lawyer Grant triumphantly: "On what ground?" Said Crane: "Because it would tend to degrade me." Lawyer Grant replied: "Perhaps you think to answer this will tend to disgrace you. With whom did you live at such and such a place?"

Grant tried to get Crane to admit that he had smoked opium in a house on 27th Street, but he refused to answer. He asked Crane, reported the New York *Sun,* if it was not true that he lived on money given him by women of the street. "This Mr. Crane denied." Captain Chapman had a card up his sleeve by bringing as witness the janitor of the house at 121 West 27th Street, where Crane had visited that summer. Crane refused to say how many times he had visited there and whether he was acquainted with Sadie and Amy Huntington of that house; he denied having smoked opium there. Janitor O'Connor testified that Crane had lived there with a woman as husband and wife for six weeks. He said that "some of the women in the house took men to their rooms and robbed them," and mentioned in particular Effie Ward.

"Miss Ward was one of a row of half a dozen women who were listening to the trial, and the reflection on her character evidently hurt her feelings. She nursed her wrath and joined the party that filed down stairs. As the witnesses and their friends reached the steps, O'Connor walked out on the top step. Miss Ward had waited for him, and she gave him a vigorous punch on the end of his nose. He nearly lost his balance and ran down the steps. She called him a vile name and screamed: 'I'll teach you to call me a thief.' Then Miss Ward turned upon a woman who had testified in Policeman Becker's behalf and made an energetic effort to tear out all her hair, while the woman retaliated by trying to scratch out Miss Ward's eyes." They were separated and led away. What novelist Crane learned, said the *Sun,* is that a police trial is not the most pleasant thing in the world.

Witnesses vouching for Becker included two sisters who swore that Dora Clark had left the Broadway Garden alone. They spoke of her as "that woman" until Lawyer Neuburger interrupted them: "In what does she differ from you? Why do you call her 'that woman'? What enmity have you against her?" These unnamed sisters were probably Amy and Sadie Huntington of the West 27th Street house of prostitution where Crane visited. In some newspaper accounts he admitted knowing them.

Another witness for Becker was "Big Chicago May," who testified that Dora Clark had offered her twenty-five dollars if she would swear falsely against him. "We must protect ourselves," she stated Dora Clark had said to her. "Becker is persecuting us. We must break him. Then I'm going to Europe." Big Chicago May (May Kane) was a huge blonde with diamond earrings as big as hickory nuts and as familiar on Sixth Avenue at 23rd Street as the Masonic Temple. Neuberger queried her as to her occupation. "I'm a typewriter," she retorted. "On what machine do you typewrite?" She did not know. "Name one typewriting machine." She could not. "Did you earn those diamonds with your wages as a typewriter?"

Big Chicago May lied, and so had Stephen Crane. He was exposed as having lied in claiming that the "chorus girl" whom Becker threatened to arrest in his presence was his wife. Lawyer Louis Grant asked him: " 'She is not your wife?' 'No.' 'Why did you say she was?' 'Because I know she was guiltless. It was impossible that she solicited, because she was under my protection; because I felt bound to protect her.' The policemen smiled at each other. The women were puzzled. Being of the Tenderloin, it was utterly impossible for them to understand the motive Mr. Crane expressed."

Neuberger asked Becker what he understood by the term "soliciting," and Becker replied that any woman who talks to a man late at night on the street is a prostitute. As Crane had to admit that he frequented a house of ill-repute, so Dora Clark was exposed as a streetwalker and forced to admit that she was a kept woman. She was the mistress of a wealthy man living at the Waldorf. Well-mannered and obviously above the level of her kind, she was an extremely handsome redhead of twenty-one years. She said she lived on East 81st Street. She wore a large black hat adorned with black feathers, a black dress trimmed with purple velvet, and she was veiled and gloved. Her only jewelry was a diamond star at the throat. Her arrest had brought such publicity that her landlady forced her to leave her room in fear that the rooming house would be raided by the police, and sure enough Captain Chapman called to inspect the room Miss Clark had occupied. By then she had moved elsewhere, and then her new landlady placed a note under her door one morning stating that her room was needed for another tenant. "Why, this girl has been so hounded by the police that two charitable associations have retained me to defend her," Neuburger exclaimed.

Dora Clark was arrested again on Sunday, November 1, charged with disorderly conduct. She said that she was struck on the head by Big Chicago May. When she went to the 30th Street police station as complainant against May Kane, the sergeant directed that Miss Clark be locked up on the Kane woman's complaint of assault. Both women were fined $5 each, which they paid (New York *Times:* November 2, 1896). A young well-dressed man forced his way in front of Magistrate Mott, who demanded: " 'Do you know anything about this case?' The man said he did. His name was Smith, he said, and he had just arrived from Philadelphia. He was walking along Sixth Avenue when he saw May Kane run up to Dora Clark and strike her. Then a lively fight ensued. . . . Dora Clark turned to the Bench, saying: 'Your Honor, may I'— 'Get out of this court at once. I won't listen to you.' The girl left the room immediately. "This is the second occasion within a comparatively short period of time that strangers have appeared in court in behalf of the girl, who seems to have incurred the animosity of the police," said the Rochester *Times* on November 3.

"Stephen Crane, poet and novelist, was tried yesterday by a New York police commissioner," the Brooklyn *Daily Eagle* reported on October 17. Police commissioners, as the *Daily Eagle* pointed out, have no legal authority to try citizens. They have authority only to try offending policemen charged with neglect of duty, insubordination, drunkenness, blackmail, collusion with thieves and prostitutes, and brutality—the offenses they most often commit. But in this case the victim of police censure and revenge was a citizen who had not violated any laws. If Policeman Becker's statement that any lone woman seen on the street at night is a prostitute be taken as a rule to guide the police in the future, well, then all women must refrain—if they value their good names—from asking the way to a hotel or station, etc. "And the remarkable thing about it all is that before a board that has the public welfare in its keeping, the reputation of private citizens is permitted to be assailed without comment or protest, while so much is done to shield one of a body of men that, collectively, was lately shown to be one of the most corrupt, brutal, incompetent organizations in the world."

Crane had written in "Notes about Prostitutes," as first draft of his *Journal* sketch of the Becker trial, this note of indignation: "Prostitutes walk the street. Hence it is a distinction of our municipal civilization that blockheads shall be licenced to deprecate upon the sensibilities of all who are out late at night. 'Imprison them. Hang them! Brain them! Burn them! Do anything but try to drive them into the air like toy balloons, because,' said the philosopher, 'you can't do it.' He also said that a man who possessed a sense of justice was a dolt, a simpleton, and double-dyed idiot for finally his sense of justice would get him into a corner and, if he obeyed it, make him infamous. There is such a thing as a moral obligation arriving inopportunely. The inopportune arrival of a moral obligation can bring just as much personal humiliation as can the sudden impulse to steal or any of the other mental suggestions which we account calamitous."

In another piece, "A Blackguard as a Police Officer," Crane wrote that the right of arrest "is one of the most dangerous powers which organized society can give to the individual. It is a power so formidable in its reaches that there is rarely a situation confronting the people which calls for more caution. A blackguard as a private citizen is lamentable; a blackguard as a police officer is an abomination. Theoretically the first result of government is to put control into the hands of honest men and nullify as far as may be the ambitions of criminals. When government places power in the hands of a criminal it of course violates this principle and becomes absurd." Crane used neither of these passages, but what he finally wrote in "Adventures of a Novelist" was almost as sharply critical. Of Becker he said: "This officer has dishonored his obligation as a public servant . . . has it become a distinction of our municipal civilization that men of this character shall be licensed to deprecate in such a manner upon those who are completely at their mercy?"

The Lexow Committee's report of 1895 that the police of New York City engaged in unlawful avocations and in the commission of licensed crime had shocked the nation, but police power—in spite of indictments of some policemen for graft or brutality—continued to prevail for more than a decade. Witnesses were scarce because they dared not testify lest the police persecute them. Those in humble ranks of life, said the report, were subjected to appalling outrages: "They are abused, clubbed and imprisoned, and even convicted of crime on false testimony by policemen and their accomplices."

Distortion of Mr. Crane's private history was an unpardonable, outrageous assault upon an honorable gentleman who had the courage to protect an unfortunate woman, said the Hearst editorial for October 18. If Dora Clark (or Ruby Young) was guilty of soliciting, policeman Becker's act was justifiable; but "if she was innocent, his act was an offense against his uniform and deserved punishment. The testimony of eye witnesses was required, and testimony to the effect that she was innocent was offered by a reputable man, who in the pursuit of his calling as a novelist was engaged in the study of life in New York's darkest centre and was in the company of the woman for that purpose. Mr. Stephen Crane acted the part of a man in declining to abandon Dora Clark to the tender mercies of the police out of fear that his own reputation might be besmirched. He confessed that he expected to be assailed, and his expectation was well founded. . . . Whether Mr. Crane had previously known Dora Clark, whether he had ever been acquainted with other women of the 'Tenderloin' district, had nothing to do with the case, because such acquaintance does not necessarily make a man a liar. The assault upon Mr. Crane's private life was part of a deliberate and despicable scheme of police intimidation of which any voluntary witness in a trial for police outrage may become a victim." The *Journal* that same day published a wonderful parody of the whole affair by James L. Ford, editor of *Truth,* in which four of Crane's city sketches had appeared in 1893–1894. In Ford's parody it is the trial of "Officer Nightstick" before Police Commissioners "Guff and Stuff."[5]

Hearst's *Journal* was not alone in praising Crane's courage in persevering to the end. It was a miserable time for him, however, and the damaging scandal injured him more than any other incident in his life. He took it on as a soldier might when assigned to guard duty, said Edward Marshall; he took it like a man and accepted the exceedingly unpleasant notoriety with no comment except that which he made in court. He told a reporter: "It may be against my interest to act as I did, but by Heaven I'd do it every time, though I have some little reputation which I have starved myself to acquire, and though I should lose it by my action."

Everybody who knows the novelist, said the New York *Press* on October 24, "believes that he told the truth under circumstances where many a man of the world would have deemed it discretion to have slipped away from the scene and left the girl to her fate—since what does one arrest, more or less, matter to an exile of society? But Mr. Crane, well aware that the affair might bring him a large amount of unsavory advertisement, did not shrink from doing an act of justice to a pariah. The whole world loves justice and takes high delight in a man. It may be divided in its opinions about this author's literary value, but it has no doubt about the essential worth of his nature."

The story does not end here; years later Becker, then a lieutenant and head of the Gambling Squad, became a partner of the gambler Herman Rosenthal, whose establishment was located in West 45th Street near Broadway. In March, 1912, Rosenthal incurred the enmity of Becker by refusing to pay five hundred dollars for the defense of the policeman's press agent, who had been charged with killing a man during a raid on a dice game. Lieutenant Becker retaliated by raiding Rosenthal's gambling house on April 15, and Rosenthal publicly threatened to reveal to the District Attorney, Charles S. Whitman, the extensive ramifications of the system under which the gamblers obtained protection. Rosenthal then made an affidavit which was published in the *World,* in which he swore that Lieutenant Becker was his partner and had received twenty percent of the profits of his gambling house. These disclosures caused a tremendous sensation, and District Attorney Whitman promptly summoned Rosenthal to the Criminal Courts buildings. The gambler agreed to make his long-delayed revelations, and then at midnight on July 15 he was shot down just outside the Hotel Metropole on West 43rd Street east of Broadway. The gunmen escaped but were captured within the next few weeks, and Lieutenant Becker was subsequently arrested. The four gunmen were convicted, and in April, 1914, they went to the electric chair. Convicted twice for murder, Lieutenant Becker lost his appeal to the higher courts and was electrocuted in July of the following year. He was the first New York City policeman to be sentenced to death. The Becker–Rosenthal case —prolonged and sensational—swept the nation and brought about investigations into police department corruption throughout the country.[6]

When Crane began his *Journal* assignment in September to study the life of the metropolitan policeman and the Tenderloin life in New York, he witnessed at the Jefferson Market Police Court on September 14 the case against a Negro girl accused of stealing fifty dollars' worth of silk clothing from the house where she had been a servant. Her full lips turned quite white when the lawyer asked her some questions "with the air of a man throwing flowerpots at a stone house." She wept constantly, but none of the curious in that courtroom noticed "the devastation which tears bring upon some complexions. Her tears seemed to burn like acid, and they left fierce pink marks on her face. Occasionally the girl looked across the room, where two well-dressed young women and a man stood waiting with the serenity of people who are not concerned as to the interior fittings of a jail." Her employers showed her no mercy, and the judge said that he would have to commit her to trial. Then it was, Crane wrote, that a

THE DORA CLARK AFFAIR 233

great cry rang through the courtroom, the cry of this girl who believed that she was lost as she was led toward a door with an austere arch leading into a stone-paved passage. The courtroom loungers "underwent a spasmodic movement as if they had been knifed. The court officers rallied quickly. The girl fell back opportunely for the arms of one of them, and her wild heels clicked twice on the floor. 'I am innocent! Oh, I am innocent.'

"People pity those who need none, and the guilty sob alone; but, innocent or guilty, this girl's scream described such a profound depth of woe, it was so graphic of grief, that it slit with a dagger's sweep the curtain of the commonplace, and disclosed the gloom-shrouded spectre that sat in the young girl's heart so plainly, in so universal a tone of mind, that a man heard expressed some far-off midnight terror of his own thought." The courtroom loungers who had come solely out of curiosity wore an air of being in wait for just such a cry of anguish, "some loud painful protestation that would bring the proper thrill to their jaded, world-weary nerves—wires that refused to vibrate for ordinary affairs."

After the cries of the Negro girl died away, an aged and toothless wanderer tottered to the bench and grinned: " 'Plase, yer honor,' said the old man as the time arrived for him to speak, 'if ye'll lave me go this time, I've niver been dhrunk befoor, sir.' A court officer lifted his hand to hide a smile."

The courthouse in this sketch, which Crane titled "An Eloquence of Grief," was the same Jefferson Market Courthouse where he had defended Dora Clark.

The sketch begins with a description of the courthouse: "The windows were high and saintly, of the shape that is found in churches. From time to time a policeman at the door spoke sharply to some incoming person. 'Take your hat off!' He displayed in his voice the horror of a priest when the sanctity of a chapel is defied or forgotten."

In the Tenderloin district of Madison Square to 48th Street between Fifth and Ninth Avenues there were pleasure sanctuaries of theatres and saloons, dance halls with prostitutes, cheap lodging houses (by the hour or the night), gambling resorts, and brothels whose customers included socially prominent pleasure-seekers. All these places had to pay tribute money to the police, except for one house—that of influential Georgiana Hastings. When the Lexow Committee served a bench warrant on her, the warrant was not executed because city officials were in her house, one of them a judge of the criminal courts.

The Lexow Committee in December, 1894, interrogated policeman Alexander Williams, then a captain and later an inspector, and recorded his explanation as to how the notorious 29th district came to be known as the Tenderloin. Captain Williams had been transferred from the 4th district to the 29th in 1876 after long toil in outlying districts, and a friend meeting him on Broadway a few days later asked him why he was so happy there. Well, said Williams, "I've been transferred. I've had nothing but chuck steak for a long time, and now I'm to get a little of the Tenderloin." In testifying before the Lexow Committee he identified this friend as a newspaper reporter for the New York *Sun* who used to call on him at his 4th precinct and asked him how he liked being transferred to the 29th.[7]

An old-line newspaperman recalls that the first night he took a walk up Sixth Avenue in the Tenderloin girls grabbed his arm. "They were young and heavily made up, but still some looked a lot like my sister back home. They wore big hats and swung large bags, just the way they were supposed to. They were insistent, hanging on my arm and saying: 'Come on dearie. It's only a dollar and I got the room.' Some had pat stories about starving mothers or putting kid brothers through college. It was all sad and exciting, fascinating and frightening, to a youth just in from the sticks."[8]

Crane studied the Tenderloin district by interviewing that summer (1896) some dissipated, gay old boys of "the Silurian period" on the corner of Broadway and 28th Street. The wonders of that prehistoric time filled the mind of the youth with poignant regret, he wrote. These old gentlemen with convivial records sang requiems to the memory of the Tenderloin and, as it were, burned candles over its corpse. They remembered the glories of the old Haymarket in the days when everything was wide open, my boy. " 'You should have seen it. No sneaking in side doors. Everything plain as day. Ah, those were the times! Reubs from the West used to have their bundles lifted every night before your eyes. Always somebody blowing champagne for the house. Great! Great! Diamonds, girls, lights, music. Well, maybe it wasn't smooth. Fights all over Sixth Avenue. Wasn't room enough. Used to hold over-flow fights in the side streets. Say it was great!' Then the type heaves a sigh and murmurs: 'But now? Dead—dead as a mackerel. The Tenderloin is a graveyard. Quiet as a tomb. Say, you ought to have been around here when the old Haymarket was running."

The scene in "The 'Tenderloin' as It Really Is" is a dance hall on Seventh Avenue. Billie Maconnigle, whom Crane ironically describes as a celebrated cavalier and "probably one of the greatest society leaders that the world has produced," dances with Flossie until her fellow, Johnnie, interrupts them. " 'Here!' he said, grabbing Maconnigle by the arm. 'Dis is me own private snap! Youse gitaway f'm here an' leggo d' loidy!' 'A couple a nits,' rejoined Maconnigle swinging his arm clear of his partner. 'Youse go chase yerself. I'm spieling wit' dis loidy when I likes, an' if youse gits gay, I'll knock yer block off—and dat's no dream!' 'Youse'll knock nuttin' off.' 'Won't I?' 'Nit. An' if yeh say much I'll make yeh look like a lobster, you fresh mug. Leggo me loidy!' " Two well-dressed youths, drinking bottled beer at one of the tables, nudge each other as they watch the fight in ecstatic delight.

The orchestra stops playing, and the waiters toss Maconnigle through the door and trample upon Johnnie, but the tall waiter about to kick Johnnie in the head for the fourth time gets a beer mug in the ear, and Flossie's fingernails make a ribbon of blood down the face of another waiter "as neatly as if a sign painter had put it there with a brush. This cohort of waiters was, however, well-drilled. Their leader was prone, but they rallied gallantly, and flung Johnnie and Flossie into the street, thinking no doubt that these representatives of the lower classes could get their harmless pleasure just as well outside. The crowd at the door favored the vanquished. 'Sherry!' said a voice. 'Sherry! Here comes a cop!' Johnnie and Flossie sherry with all the promptitude allowed to a wounded man and a girl whose sole anxiety is her man. They end their flight in a little dark alley," where Flossie sobs over her wounded hero, "weeping with the deep and impressive grief of gravesides, when he swore because his head ached. 'Dat's all right,' said Johnnie. 'Nex time youse need'nt be so fresh wit' every guy what comes up.' 'Well, I was only kiddin', Johnnie,' she cried, forlornly. 'Well, yeh see what yeh done t' me wit' cher kiddin','" replied Johnnie."[9]

In another Tenderloin tale, "A Duel Between an Alarm Clock and a Suicidal Purpose," Crane says that a tenement air shaft is a grim thing conveying to everyone in the tenement the tragedy next door: the sobbing girl, and the bursts of a man's hoarse bitterness and rage roaring with deadly menace up and down the air shaft in quarrel with the sobbing girl. " 'Lied to me didn't you?' he cried. 'Told me a lie and thought I wouldn't get onto you. Lied to me! Lied to me! There's where I get crazy. If you hadn't lied to me in one thing, and I hadn't collared you flat in it, I might believe all the rest, but now—how do I know you ever tell the truth? How do I know I ain't always getting a game? Hey? How do I know?' " Black as a storm-god he said with ferocity: " 'Come! Get up out of that. Get up and look at me and let me see you lie!' " There was a flurry of white in the darkness, and then the gas glared out and she stood before him: "a wondrous white figure in her vestal-like robe. She resembled the priestess in paintings of long-gone Mediterranean religions. Her hair fell wildly on her shoulder. She threw out her arms and cried to Swift Doyer: 'Oh, oh, my heart is broken! My heart is broken!' But Swift knew as well as the rest of mankind that these girls have no hearts to be broken, and this acting filled him with a new rage. He grabbed an alarm clock from the dresser and banged her heroically on the head with it. Then she arose, and, calm and dry-eyed, walked to the mirror. Swift thought she was taking an account of the bruises but when he resumed his cyclonic tirade, she said: 'I've taken morphine, Swift!' Swift leaped at the little red pill box. It was empty. Eight quarter-grain pills make two grains. The Suicidal Purpose was distinctly ahead of the Alarm Clock."

Swift drags the girl to the sideboard and forces her to drink whiskey, and then she sinks into the depths of an infinite drowsiness, "sliding limply in her chair like a cloth figure. He dealt her furious blows, and our decorous philosophy knows little of the love and despair that was in those caresses. With his voice he called the light into her eyes, called her from the sinister slumber which her senses welcomed, called her soul back from the verge. He propped the girl in a chair and ran to the kitchen to make coffee. . . . When the steel-blue dawn came and distant chimneys were black against a rose sky, the girl sat at the dining room table chattering insanely and gesturing." She babbles to a little fly as she holds it close to the flame; she herself is like the injured fly. Swift Doyer has been told that dying people behave in a certain manner, but this scene defies his preconceptions. Why does she occupy herself with an accursed fly?

"What was wrong with this death scene? At one time he thought that his sense of propriety was so scandalized that he was upon the point of interrupting the girl's babble. But here a new thought struck him. The girl was not going to die. How could she under these circumstances? The form was not correct. All this was not relevant to the man's love and despair, but, behold, my friend, at the tragic, the terrible point in life there comes an irrelevancy to the human heart direct from the Wise God. And this is why Swift Doyer thought these peculiar thoughts." The girl chatters to the fly until finally she collapses in sleep with her fingers stretching across the table where they touched the locks of slumbering Swift Doyer. "They were asleep, and this after all is a human action, which may safely be done by characters in the fiction of our time."

Crane was scoffing at the priggishness of such fiction with its fixed ideas of propriety. This sketch, which appeared in *Town Topics* (October 1, 1896), begins with the statement that everybody knows all about the Tenderloin because the clergy and police forces have collected a great amount of truth about it.

Professor Bliss Perry remembered sitting at the Lantern Club one night probably in late 1896 with Frank Stockton, a now forgotten short-story writer who was then a gentleman of sixty-two. "Who was that young fellow who went up and came down like a rocket?" asked Stockton. Perry replied that it was Stephen Crane, and noted the whimsical smile on Stockton's tired face as though to hint that all our little rockets will come down in time.

Crane's rocket, after ascending to meteoric heights in early 1896, fell to earth during the scandal of his trial with the police, but his reputation bounced upwards once more with the publication of his great short-story "The Open Boat" in *Scribner's Magazine* for June, 1897, and again the following year with his war dispatches from Cuba.

# XIV

# ☞ *Jacksonville and Cora—*
# The Commodore *Disaster*

CRANE was in Cambridge, Massachusetts, on Saturday, October 31, 1896, to report the football game between Harvard University and the great Carlisle Indian School team, which everyone thought would defeat the Harvard white men. At the end the Indians with seventeen minutes to go made a last desperate play. They took a drink of water all round and then began a ferocious series of mass attacks. "They banged away as coolly as a lot of blacksmiths. Slowly and steadily the Harvard line was forced back. A touchdown seemed inevitable and the vast crowd went mad. The thundering Harvard cheers roared over the field like a storm, and the men who fought for the Crimson heard five thousand of their friends call upon them to be steadfast. Still the impassive Indians bucked and bucked, and the Harvards went slowly backward. It was a matter of ten yards; it was a matter of eight yards; it was a matter of five yards; it was a matter of less than five yards. The crowd at the side line turned into a howling mob of maniacs and ran and shrieked at their team. It was a dark and tense moment for the Crimson. But here it was that the Crimson showed at its best and greatest. The Harvard men played like fiends." After the game the Indians moved off the field through the dusk with their characteristic impassiveness.

Crane had interviewed the red men at their hotel and found them quietly shy and modest, like well-behaved children. On the football field their sweaters of flaming red seemed like campfires on a Western reservation. The crowd of fifteen thousand were there "to observe how the red man could come from his prairies with a memory of four centuries of oppression and humiliation as his inheritance, with dark years, perhaps utter extinction before him, and yet make a show of the white warriors at their favorite sport."

The paleface Harvard team won by a score of four to nothing, and so there is sorrow in Lone Wolf, who played center, and despair upon the brow of Cayou, who played left half-back. How old Geronimo would have enjoyed this battle on Soldier's Field between these red men and these paleface Harvard eleven! "The point of view of the warriors was terse but plain: 'They have stolen a continent from us, a wide, wide continent, which was ours, and lately they have stolen various touchdowns that were also ours. The umpire, on several occasions, has made monkeys of us. It is too much. Let us, then, brothers, be revenged. Here is an opportunity. The white men line up in their pride. If sacrifice of bone and sinew can square the thing, let us sacrifice, and perhaps the smoke of our wigwam campfire will blow softly against the dangling scalp of our enemies.' " The red men lost here again, but "Lone Wolf won a crown of laurels and the great Apache Kid will henceforth have to look twice to his own bloody laurels, wrote Crane in "Harvard University Against the Carlisle Indians" (*Journal:* November 1, 1896).

The *Journal* for Sunday, November 8, 1896, celebrated the newspaper's first birthday party by boasting that no other newspaper ever gave its readers the work of so many famous men in a single year. William Randolph Hearst had bought the *Journal* in 1895 and transformed it into a flamboyant morning and evening paper, rival mainly of the *World,* which Joseph Pulitzer had acquired in 1883. Among the notable contributors to the *Journal*'s birthday party edition was Stephen Crane with a letter in facsimile headed "A Birthday Word from Novelist Stephen Crane."[1] "It is a condition of most of us who are in journalism that we do not know how to define it because your newspaper seems to change and advance each day," he wrote. The same birthday issue of the *Journal* carried Crane's account of the football match between Harvard and Princeton on Saturday, November 7. At the start fate seemed inclined for Harvard, "if fate was anywhere." But Harvard University's team ended in defeat, and Princeton's three hundred maniacal chrysanthemums danced "with weird joy in the gloom." It was probably that weekend that Crane made his last appearance in New York City "as a star attraction at the late French ball in New York, which was reported to be so 'deadly respectable' that the women who attended could only while away the time by sliding down the bannisters."

"Mr. Stephen Crane, ex-'94, left New York for Cuba on Friday, November 13, to report the Cuban War news for the New York *Journal,*" said the Syracuse University *Herald.* "He postponed his journey a week in order to defy superstition by starting on a so-called unlucky day." He had been fooling around in New York for over a month expecting to go to Jacksonville and Cuba at any time, and then suddenly he received orders to skip and he left for Jacksonville that very night. That is how Crane explained to his brother William why he failed to notify him that he had left without a word to the family; actually, he had been in Jacksonville two weeks before writing William his letter of apology on November 29. Now he was waiting for some filibustering ship to take him to Cuba, and in that vain hope he was stuck in Jacksonville from mid-November until mid-March.

"The town looks like soiled pasteboard that some lunatic babies have been playing with," he wrote someone (perhaps music critic James Huneker). "The same old women are sitting on the hotel porches saying how well the climate suits them and hurling the same lances with their eyes to begin bloodshed. . . . I went down the shore some distance yesterday and watched the combers come counting in. Sometimes their addition changes to multiplication and the music is confounded, like a war of drummerboys." His theory that the basis of music was mathematical interested Huneker, who remembered Crane in afteryears as an intuitive natural philosopher.

What made the city of 28,000 lively just then was the conspicuous presence of top New York City officials of the Cuban Junta, a propaganda and fund-raising organization campaigning to break the hold of Spanish rule on the island, with their Jacksonville headquarters in a cigar store owned by J. A. Huau (pronounced "wow"). Their head man, called "Delegate," was Estrada Palma; the chief of the expeditionary department was Colonel Emilio Nuñez, and their general counsel was Horatio Rubens. They were Crane's prospective employers.

Thomas Beer says that "complete darkness" covers Crane until December 29, that Jacksonville bored him, and that "he was alone who liked to have people always around him." But in fact he couldn't possibly have been alone because the city was filled with adventurers and correspondents aiming to get to Cuba. They congregated at hotel bars, at gambling rooms such as Duval's across from the Duval Hotel, at Huau's cigar store to get the so-called "news," which was deliberately slanted so as to deceive the Spanish consul; they attended operas and such plays as *A Bowery Girl* and *Monte Carlo* at the Park Opera House; or they visited brothels such as Lydia de Camp's place on "the line" (Ward Street).

Among the reporters Crane met was young Charles Michelson, who described him as haunting the dark backrooms of waterfront saloons, chainsmoking and drinking countless bottles of beer, listening more than he talked and always ready for poker or dice (at small stakes). Other reporters Crane met were E. W. McCready of the Philadelphia *Press* and the New York *Herald* and his old friend Ralph Delahaye Paine of Hearst's *Journal*.

He had no sooner arrived in Jacksonville than he went to a "fashionable night club, the Hotel de Dream, where he met the golden-haired hostess, Cora Taylor (Cora E. Stewart). They discussed literature. He said he was a writer, and then and there she fell in love with the author of *Maggie* and *The Red Badge*. He gave her a copy of Kipling's *The Seven Seas* (1896), and in later years Cora wrote in it: "The first thing my mouse ever gave me was this book / 1896."[2] On that same Saturday night of November 14 he inscribed to her *George's Mother:* "To an unnamed sweetheart." And this note: "Jacksonville, Fla. / Nov. 1896. To C. E. S. [Cora E. Stewart] Brevity is an element that enters importantly into all pleasures of life, and this is what makes pleasure sad; and so there is no pleasure but only sadness." Crane misdated both of these inscriptions for November 4 instead of November 14.[3]

Although no girls boarded on Cora's premises,[4] a nightclub in the Victorian era (and in the heyday of Carry Nation) was synonymous with haunts of sin. Her house of joy was proclaimed by a semicircular sign over the door bearing in great gold letters the inviting legend HOTEL DE DREAM. To her girls and guests Cora went by the name of Cora Taylor or "Miss Cora." She had bought the Hotel de Dream in March, 1895 (bought the business and leased the house) from Ethel Dreme, and that establishment—sometimes spelled Hotel de Dreme—reflects in its very name Cora's own romanticism and sense of humor. She was hostess—in the later euphemism—says Ernest McCready, who was with Crane and Cora in November. "The non-coms & privates numbered some 12 to 15—of unusual comeliness and youth."

He remembers Cora as handsome, of some real refinement, and aloof to all. Born in 1865, she was then five or six years older than Stephen, who had passed his twenty-fifth birthday on November 1, 1896. It "pierced the lady's very liver," says McCready, when Cora was shocked into recognition that the young reporter was also the author of *George's Mother, Maggie* and *The Red Badge,* not to mention *The Black Riders.* She had "class," although she was quite dowdy, and was cultured enough to have possibly read the *Godey's Magazine* review of Crane's four books in September 1896. On meeting him she seemed to know at once that writing was her true profession and that author Crane was her salvation, her knight-at-arms here to rescue her tarnished soul from that sordid castle of false dreams. "Stephen took her in his stride—and, as it turned out, in some very solid respects the gray mare proved to be the best horse." Not to offend his unnamed sweetheart, Crane discreetly gave her an inscribed copy of *George's Mother,* whereas when he visited Lydia de Camp's sporting house in February, 1897, he inscribed a copy of *Maggie: A Girl of the Streets.*[5]

Cora was born Cora Howorth in Boston at 26 Kneeland Street. Her grandfather had an art gallery there. Her father John Howorth was a painter. He died when Cora was six years old, and her mother remarried within a year. Cora's marriage while still very young to Thomas Vinton Murphy in New York City lasted but a few months. Two and a half years later in London she married Captain Donald William Stewart, the younger son of an English baronet, and this marriage too was unsuccessful. Because Captain—later K. C. M. G.—refused to give her a divorce she and Crane could not marry, although Crane bluffed it that they were married. As hostess and proprietor of the Hotel de Dream she took the name of Taylor for business reasons. Crane became the sole passion of her banal life.

Cora, said Ernest McCready, had poise and surety of command of herself and of others. "If she had any false notes I was then all too unskilled in recognizing authentic 'class,' or lack of it, to detect any. She was a cut above us in several ways. Managing a nightclub involved her in certain unpleasant and rowdy situations, and one can only guess why Crane asked a Jacksonville attorney 'to give me a paper to protect this lady.' " The attorney waved him away, saying that he was too busy.

Loafing into March at Cora's house and at the St. James Hotel, Crane played cards with Cora and with some guest named Camille. Crane kept score on the empty portion of an unpublished page of *The Red Badge of Courage* manuscript. Imprinted on it is the half-ring mark of a large beer mug. (Camille is likely Camillus S. l'Engle, a member of one of the most prominent families in Jacksonville; if this identification is correct, he was paying a call at Cora's house of joy while on a visit from Atlanta, Georgia, to see his Jacksonville relatives.)

Jacksonville's best hotel was the St. James, where Crane stayed after his arrival with a moneybelt containing $700 in gold given him by Irving Bacheller. The St. James Hotel was run by a charming strait-laced old gentleman named Jerry Campbell; nevertheless, it was one of the most ribald, free-and-easy hostelries of that gaudy era. For the benefit of guests the night clerk, Morton, had a list of the better houses of ill-fame, and Cora's establishment was given a "Class A" rating. It was the smartest house of joy in the vicinity of Jacksonville, out near the Sub-Tropical Gardens. Richmond Barrett of Newport, Rhode Island, whose parents wintered at the old St. James Hotel, reports by the recollections of his parents that Cora was a figure of distinction and authority, the resourceful type who could adapt herself with equal skill "to the most nefarious practises and the most reputable career." A figure of distinction and authority, she played hostess to the "right" people. She was very much in the grand manner, "a sort of Tannhauser Venus among Madams."

Sometime in November, 1896, Ralph Paine, between sessions at the roulette wheel, discovered that Miss Cora had been reading *George's Mother*. He and Ernest McCready returned some nights later and the next day he sat at the "family" board, carving a turkey. That was surely on Thanksgiving Day.[6]

On November 29 Crane made out his last will and testament because of the chance that he might not survive the hazardous expedition to Cuba. He wrote his brother William, granting him one-third of his estate and appointing him executor. Edmund was to receive another third, and his two other brothers—Townley and Wilbur—were to divide the remainder. (Nothing was said about brother George, who worked in the post office in Jersey City.) Stephen wished his saddle horse Peanuts should not be sold but kept in easy service at Hartwood. Do "have him cared for as much as possible by Ed himself or by somebody whom it is absolutely certain would not maltreat him." Edmund used Stephen's horse—his riding horse—for hauling ice from the Hartwood pond.

In his letter to William, Stephen also expressed the hope that his stories would be collected: "There are some of them which I would hate to see lost. Some of my best work is contained in short things which I have written for various publications, principally the New York *Press* in 1893 [1894] or thereabouts. There are some 15 or 20 short sketches of New York street life and so on which I intended to have published in book form under the title of 'Midnight Sketches.' That should be your first care."

He wrote Willis Brooks Hawkins the same day asking him to serve with Howells, Hamlin Garland, and editor Ripley Hitchcock as his literary executors in the event he encountered some disaster en route to Cuba, and he added that he was feeling very good in Jacksonville. In case Hawkins saw Amy Leslie would he "encourage her in every sensible way."

Some tragedy, perhaps the loss of her four-year-old son, had occurred in Amy's life about the time she met Crane which made her emotionally unstable; also her marriage to a member of a light opera company had failed. At any rate, Crane explained to Hawkins: "Of course feminine nature is mighty peculiar and she might have that singular ability to get rid of mournful emotions which is possessed by a great many of her sex, but I was positively frightened for the girl at the moment of parting and I am afraid and worried now. I feel that no one hardly could need a friendly word more than this poor child, and I know you are just the man to do it in a right way if the chance presents itself. . . . It broke my heart to leave the girl but I could feel comparatively easy now if I could feel that she had good friends. There is not one man in three thousand who can be a real counsellor and guide for a girl so pretty as Amy, and this will present itself to your mind no doubt as a reason for supposing that Charley would not be very capable in the position."[7] Charley—Charles W. Hooke—wrote Crane, "fastens his intellect so securely to some damned molecule that he loses sight of a broad question and I do not think he is very efficient as a bracer."

Amy lived on West 25th Street with her sister, Mrs. O'Brien, who although a good-hearted sort of creature was of no help to her. As Crane explained it, she "is weak, very weak, and so I am sure that she would be of no help to Amy in what is now really a great trouble. I do not want to bore you with any of my affairs but I am obliged to feel that you are about the only man who could possibly help me and do it in the way that would count for some good, so just remember this and when you think some times of your friend remember that he left behind him one to whom he would count favors done as favors done to himself."

But he wasn't doing Hawkins any favor in instructing him to pay out periodically sums from the $500 he deposited with him. The *Tribune* (January 4, 1898) reported the civil suit Amy Leslie brought in the Supreme Court to recover $550 from Stephen Crane. According to the plaintiff, she gave him $800 on November 1, 1896. "Instead of depositing it in her name, she says, he placed it to his own credit. Since then he has paid her $250. She sues to recover the remainder. Crane at present lives in London." Hawkins all in all paid out $352.95 to Amy and $151.05 to Crane and was himself out of pocket in these transactions $4.00. To the distressed Amy it seemed a case of embezzlement, and her attorney, George Mabon, wrote Hawkins, who replied on December 28, 1897, that more than a year ago he had received a certain sum from a friend "who wished me to pay it out in certain prescribed manners. I paid it all out in those manners, and I hold receipts for all the items. When that sum was paid out my connection with the matter ceased. For your information, I will say that a long time afterward, I did receive another sum of money from the same friend, but I returned it to him and declined to make any further disembursements for him. I hold a receipt for this sum. I presume you will agree with me that I do not have to receive and disburse money for my friends if I do not wish to." Attorney Mabon proceeded next to obtain on January 3, 1898, from the Supreme Court of the State of New York a warrant of attachment in the sum of $550 against Crane as damages for "a breach of contract, express or implied, other than a contract to marry." The newspapers the next day broke the story.

As for Amy Leslie's suit against Crane, there is no record of further proceedings beyond the warrant of attachment issued on January 3, 1898. The date of November 1, 1896, she set as the day of Crane's embezzlement was a Sunday, an improbable day for depositing funds as banks are not open then. Also, Crane had then no need to borrow $800 as he wore in his money belt Bacheller's $700 in gold for his expedition to Cuba. And he now had royalties coming in from *The Red Badge* (fourteen printings in 1896) and 15 percent royalties on *Maggie* (issued in June, 1896). He could look forward to royalties from *The Little Regiment* (December, 1896), *The Third Violet* (May, 1896), and perhaps something from *The Black Riders* (November, 1896). All in all, this was the one period in Crane's lifetime that he was truly affluent.

On Christmas Eve—just a week before he sailed on the *Commodore*—Crane wired Hawkins: "Leave soon. Telegraph frankly Amy's mental condition. Also send fifty if possible.[8] Will arrange payments from Appleton. Troubled over Amy."

During his restless days of November–December, awaiting orders for getting to Cuba, Crane read Lousie de Ramée's two volume illustrated edition of *Under Two Flags* (1896), and the January, 1897, *Book Buyer* published Crane's review, the only book review he ever wrote other than his appraisal of Harold Frederic's works in March, 1898. Miss Ramée was famous under the pen name "Ouida," and Crane confesses to a youthful admiration for her earlier works, but here was "Ouida's masterpiece." Most of us, says Crane, forget Ouida. "Childhood and childhood's different ideal is often required to make us rise properly to her height of sentiment.

The poetic corner in the human head becomes too soon like some old dusty niche in a forgotten church. For my part I had concluded that I had outgrown Ouida. I thought that I recognized the fact that her tears were carefully moulded globules of the best Cornish tin and that her splendors were really of the substance of shadows on a garden wall." But he succumbed to her sentimental Love versus Honor plot, which harks back to seventeenth-century heroic drama. Personal integrity—the code of Crane—is the code of Ouida's hero in this romance amid warfare in Algiers. The hero risks the firing squad by breaking the military code for the sake of personal integrity, honor, conscience. Her characters "abandon themselves to virtue and heroism as the martyrs abandoned themselves to flames. Sacrifice appears to them as the natural course. Pain, death, dishonor is counted of no moment so long as the quality of personal integrity is defended and preserved. Certainly we may get good from a book of this kind." Her romance—"a song of the brave"—had for Crane "a fine ring in the gospel of life it preaches."

His own literary code, he said, wanted art straight: "I happen to be a preacher's son, but that heredity does not preclude—in me—a liking for sermons unmixed with other material. . . . I have been very careful not to let any theories or pet ideas of my own creep into my work. Preaching is fatal to art in literature." Nevertheless, he liked Ouida's "imperfect creation" because it voiced "the old spirit of dauntless deed and sacrifice which is the soul of literature in every age." (This sounds more like the critic George Woodberry than the Stephen Crane whose works undercut all heroic poses.)

Cuba was now the storm center of the Western Hemisphere. Some seventy expeditions had been fitted out in the United States to aid the insurrectionists, and several vessels, including the revenue cutter *Boutwell*, patrolled the Florida coast to thwart violation of American neutrality laws. Twenty-seven expeditions had successfully reached Cuban shores, including the *Commodore*'s filibustering expeditions. Revenue cutters had stopped the *Commodore* in September, 1895, and released her and again in October, 1896; on two other occasions she had evaded them.

When Crane boarded the ill-fated *Commodore* she was making her fifth attempt. A year before, the steamer *J. W. Hawkins* was shipwrecked in a storm in January, 1896, and lost nine of her crew of sixteen. Her filibustering party was under General Calixto García, leader of the Cuban insurrection against Spain. In "the rough sea a leak started in the engine room, which was soon flooded. The water gained on the pumps and the steamer sank." This is what happened also to the *Commodore*.[9]

Almost prophetically Crane had several times written about ship and raft wrecks[10] long before he heard the foreboding last whistle of the sinking *Commodore*: "this cry on the sea at night," when "if there ever was a voice of despair and death, it was in the voice of this whistle." At the start of her doomed voyage, "as she turned her bow toward the distant sea the Cubans ashore cheered and cheered. In response the *Commodore*"— as Crane reports it—"gave three long blasts of her whistle, which even to this time impressed me with their sadness. Somehow, they sounded as wails."

In going down the St. Johns River out to sea on New Year's Eve the *Commodore* struck a sandbar off Commodore's Point, less than two miles from Jacksonville. The pilot—blinded by fog—rammed her bow "hard upon the mud, and in this ignominious position we were compelled to stay until daybreak," said Crane in the New York *Press* ("Stephen Crane's Own Story"). The mate of the *Commodore* went on board the revenue cutter *George S. Boutwell* at 2:30 A.M. (as recorded in Revenue Cutter Service, 1897), and stated that "his vessel had gone ashore while on her way down the river during a dense fog"; he requested assistance to float her. At daylight the *Boutwell* got under way and on reaching the steamer took a line and towed her off some distance toward sea.[11] However, no examination was made of the *Commodore*'s damaged hull. When she got to sea, water was coming in. Her seams had been opened by the heavy thumping she received in crossing the bar, and that caused her fatal leak. But other questions were raised as to the cause of her disaster.

"Was it treachery,[12] do you think?" asked the Florida *Times-Union* reporter. Captain Edward Murphy replied: "It was neglect, more than anything else." Engineer Redigan had reported to him about midnight that water was gaining in the *Commodore*'s hold and that "the pumps would not heave the water. The pipe was evidently choked or the suction gone. It is customary to keep the water clear of the hold. . . . If the water is allowed to get into the coal, the coal is washed down and chokes the pumps," said Murphy in the *Herald*. Captain Murphy, with previous filibustering experience on the *Bermuda* and *Laurada,* and with British and American sailing master's licenses, was new to the *Commodore*.

Was the vessel overloaded? the *World* asked Captain Murphy. (If so, he was to blame.) "We couldn't have had a better boat till this trouble," he said. Crane's account—in the same New York *World* for January 5— consistently tallies with the Captain's: "The *Commodore* was a fine boat. She carried her load like a cork and breasted the waves like a duck, and she was buoyant and did not seem to strain at all. It is rather queer, to say the least, that such a leak occurred."

Supercargo Paul Rojo impugned Chief Engineer Redigan: "When I went into the room and found water on the floor the engineer seemed either drunk or so confused that he couldn't understand my orders. At any rate, he didn't seem to understand the machinery." Crane says Redigan had no whiskey, and with that Steward Montgomery agreed: "Engineer Redigan is a noble old man. He was not drunk. He retired at eight o'clock to his bunk. He was called at ten o'clock and informed that the water was rising in the hold. He cried like a baby and exclaimed: 'Nobody told me of it. When I went to bed all was well. If they had but told me, even at nine o'clock, I would have saved the ship, but now it's too late! too late! Too late!' " (*Herald*: January 5.)

After the engine room was flooded and the pumps failed, Captain Murphy gave the order to use the buckets and to pile into the furnace some wood, oil and alcohol so as to get up sufficient steam to run into Mosquito Inlet, about eighteen miles due west of the ship. The men used the buckets with a will, said Captain Murphy. None stood back. But to their chagrin "the water gained upon us slowly and surely, and we had not proceeded three miles when the fires were quenched. There was no hope then of saving the ship. I let go the rudder to get her head to the sea and told the men to quietly proceed to man the boats. We got two of the boats off. They contained all the Cubans."

Crane had heard talk of lowering the boats when he came up from the fireroom. There, he first met the oiler Billy Higgins. In character always, the oiler "was sloshing around this inferno filling buckets with water and passing them to a chain of men that extended up the ship's side. Afterwards we got orders to change our point of attack on water and to operate through a little door on the windward side of the ship that led into the engine room. During this time there was much talk of pumps out of order and many statements of a mechanical kind, which I did not altogether comprehend but understood to mean that there was a general and a sudden ruin in the engine room."[13]

Also on deck, Crane overheard Mate Frank Grain—a German married to a Cuban lady and engaged in the strife of his adopted country from the beginning—talking with a man near the corner of the galley. " 'Why don't you send up a rocket?' said this unknown man. And the Mate replied: 'What the hell do we want to send up a rocket for? The ship is all right.' " (But Grain did not survive.) The engine room at this moment "represented a scene taken from the middle kitchen of Hades. In the first place, it was insufferably warm, and the lights burned faintly in a way to cause mystic and gruesome shadows. There was a quantity of soapish sea water swirling and sweeping and swishing among machinery that roared and banged and clattered and steamed, and, in the second place, it was a devil of a ways down below."

Crane claimed there was "no particular agitation at this time, and that even later there was never a panic on board the *Commodore*." But, said the Florida *Times-Union*, the swashing water in the hold and the vessel rolling from side to side "alarmed everyone on board. A panic ensued; but Captain Murphy, Stephen Crane, R. A. Delgado and one or two others soon quieted the excitement and put everybody to work at the pumps and with buckets."

In the *World,* January 4, a big coal heaver was reported to have come up from the hold with a package of dynamite "and told the captain that they might as well let that off at once. The dynamite was carefully taken from him, and then Captain Murphy's fist did the rest. 'Lie there, you cowardly dog!' shouted Captain Murphy. Obey orders, and we'll all get off.' " One of the sailors went out of his mind and ran up the rigging and tried to stand on his head on the yards. And one of the Cubans tried to jump overboard, but Mate Rios hauled him back on board. "Another was so thoroughly demoralized that he knelt down at the Captain's feet and prayed to be thrown overboard." Contrary to Crane's statement, plainly there was some agitation on board.

The New York *Press* account for January 4 quoted Steward Montgomery: "One of the Cubans got rattled and tried to run out one of the boats before time, and Crane let him have it right from the shoulder, and the man rolled down the leeway, stunned for the moment." Crane omitted this incident in his January 7 *Press* interview. Although Montgomery is not always a reliable witness, he had no reason for inventing the story; the evidence indicates that there was much agitation—if not panic—both before and after the ship sank. Montgomery, who could not swim, was of "a portly and noble exterior," but judging by his inwards he was a nervous wreck. (Crane calls him ironically "the cheerful cook" in his short story about the *Commodore* disaster.) Montgomery anticipated disaster, and when it came he exaggerated it. At the start he told Crane: "God, I don't feel right about this ship, somehow. It strikes me that something is going to happen to us. I don't know what it is, but the old ship is going to get it in the neck, I think." "Well," said Crane, "are any of us going to get out, prophet?" The *World* quoted Captain Murphy: "I want to say that Crane is a man every inch of him, and he acted throughout with true grit."

" 'That man Crane is the spunkiest fellow out,' said Captain Murphy to-night to the *Press* correspondent. 'The sea was so rough that even old sailors got seasick when we struck the open sea after leaving the bar, but Crane behaved like a born sailor. He and I were about the only ones not affected by the big seas which tossed us about. As we went south he sat in the pilot-house with me, smoking and telling yarns. When the leak was discovered, he was the first man to volunteer aid.

" 'His shoes, new ones, were slippery on the deck, and he took them off and tossed them overboard, saying with a laugh: "Well, Captain, I guess I won't need them if we have to swim." He stood on the deck by me all the while, smoking his cigarette, and aiding me greatly while the boats were getting off. When in the dinghy he suggested putting up the overcoat for a sail, and he took his turn at the oars or holding up the oar mast. . . . He's a thoroughbred,' concluded the Captain."

When the first lifeboat was about to be lowered, Crane said, "a certain man [Paul Rojo] was the first person in the first boat, and they were

handing him in a valise about as large as a hotel. I had not entirely recovered from astonishment and pleasure in witnessing this noble deed
when I saw another valise go to him. This valise was not perhaps as large
as a hotel, but it was a big valise anyhow." Next, Crane and Higgins, two
colored stokers and First Mate Grain wrestled to loosen from the deckhouse another lifeboat, which "I am willing to swear weighed as much
as a Broadway cable-car," said Crane. "She might have been spiked to
the deck. We could have pushed a little brick schoolhouse along a corduroy road as easily as we moved this boat. . . . It was now the First Mate
who showed signs of losing his grip. To us who were trying in all stages
of competence and experience to launch the lifeboat he raged in all terms
of fiery satire and hammerlike abuse. But the boat moved at last and
swung down toward the water." Although the Captain rarely lost his
temper, he cursed at a colored stoker "done up in life-preservers until he
looked like a feather-bed."

As the first boat was putting off—loaded with twelve Cubans and their
baggage—Rojo called out to his Cuban colleague Major Baz: "Come on!"
Major Baz replied: "My duty is on this ship." He remained at his post for
a half hour. Then he and his party—the remainder of the Cubans—quit
the *Commodore* in the second lifeboat but remained nearby to render
assistance should it be required. "This conduct was in sharp contrast to
that of Rojo, who immediately put off for shore, fifteen miles away, landed
on the beach, hired a sailboat, and instead of using that sailboat to come
to our rescue, carried his men to New Smyrna." Steward Montgomery
claimed the crew of the first boat did not attempt to send assistance to
their comrades. But in fact Rojo and Delgado did at least wire their
Jacksonville agent to send aid to the shipwrecked *Commodore*. The first
boat reached the shore at ten o'clock Saturday morning (January 2) and
the second about noon that same day.[14]

"That newspaper feller was a nervy man," said the Cook. "He didn't
seem to know what fear was." Signed on as an able seaman at twenty
dollars a month, Crane "insisted upon doing a seaman's work, and he did
it well, too. When aroused Saturday morning he never quailed when he
came on deck and saw the foaming and raging billows and knew that the
vessel was sinking and that it was only a question of time when we would
be at the mercy of the terrible sea in a small ten-foot dinghy. He stood
on the bridge with glasses in hand, sweeping the horizon in an effort to get
a glimpse of land. . . . I thought sure that he would be swept off as the
vessel rolled from side to side, her yards almost touching the water as she
rolled. . . ."

Crane's fearlessness and gallantry distinguished him from the others,
excepting oiler Higgins and Captain Murphy. When the ship's lifeboat was
launched, the Captain told all those to go in her who desired to do so.
The ship's boat was launched with seven men in charge of Mate Grain

(variously spelled Grane or Graines). "All went except Mr. Crane, a brave little gentleman, Steward Montgomery, and William Higgins"—and the Captain himself. (Reported by the Captain in the Florida *Times-Union*.) These four then took the only remaining boat, a dinghy (an English style of lifeboat much smaller than any of the *Commodore*'s three boats.) "The strange possibility must be mentioned here that there were not four men in this dinghy, but five," John Berryman suggests in his *Stephen Crane* (1950). But such a conjecture cannot be pressed this way without evidence, for it impugns Crane as journalist.[15]

Although Montgomery said that Crane was the last one to get into a boat, he was actually the first in the dinghy. The others put him over the side of the ship to fend the dinghy off with an oar. Higgins was the last one in. When the dinghy had quit the *Commodore* and proceeded a few yards away a cry was heard from the ship. The ship's boat, with seven men, had been stoved in when Mate Grain returned to the *Commodore* in an attempt to get some article he had forgotten. So all seven men climbed back onto the *Commodore*'s decks and flew a distress flag, and then Captain Murphy, already in the dinghy, reapproached the sinking ship and "told the men to construct a raft. They made three and got on these.[16] Meanwhile our little boat was remaining distant about 200 yards," Murphy reports.

Crane's own story in the *Press* squares with Captain Murphy's account of the disembarkation from the shipwreck: "The first mate cried out from the ship that the third boat had floundered alongside. He cried that they had made rafts, and wished us to tow them. The Captain said, 'All right.' Their rafts were floating astern. 'Jump in!' cried the Captain, but there was a singular and most harrowing hesitation. There were five white men and two Negroes. This scene in the grey light of morning impressed one as would a view into some place where ghosts move slowly. These seven on the stern of the sinking *Commodore* were silent." (Steward Montgomery says they were "screaming with fear.")

When the Captain cried "Jump," the Chief Engineer landed on one of the rafts. Said Crane: "He obeyed as promptly and as docilely as a scholar in riding school." Then a stoker followed him, "and then the First Mate threw his hands over his head and plunged into the sea. He had no lifebelt and for my part, even when he did this horrible thing, I somehow felt that I could see in the expression of his hands, and in the very toss of his head, as he leaped thus to death, that it was rage, rage, rage unspeakable that was in his heart at the time." Mate Grain seems deliberately to have plunged into the sea. He knew his plight was helpless, and he resented the Captain's sitting "safely" in the nearby dinghy. By the code of the sea the Captain should have been the last to quit the sinking ship. But once in the dinghy he could not get back onto the ship's deck because his arm had been broken when a wave crashed into the deckhouse and now he had his arm in a sling. It would have been a pointless risk to return to the ship.

Crane in his extraordinary short story "The Open Boat" says that "the mind of the master of a vessel is rooted deep in the timbers of her, though he command for a day or a decade." The injured Captain in the dinghy could not forget those "seven turned faces" on the stern of the sinking ship. "Thereafter there was something strange in his voice. Although steady, it was deep with mourning, and of a quality beyond oration or tears." Those faces "turned toward us" haunted the Captain's conscience, if not also the cook's because he let go the towline to the Negro on the raft. One of those seven faces was Tom Smith's, "the man who was going to quit filibustering after this expedition."

Crane wrote in his *Press* sketch: "I saw Tom Smith . . . jump to a raft and turn his face toward us." Were not the faces of those seven doomed men before they plunged onto flimsy rafts or into the sea turned toward the Captain in accusation of his dereliction of duty? It is probably these seven to whom Crane refers in "The Open Boat" as "the seven mad gods who rule the sea" in the reiterated burden patterning the story: "As for the reflections of the men [in the dinghy], there was a great deal of rage in them. Perchance they might be formulated thus: 'If I am going to be drowned— if I am going to be drowned, why in the name of the seven mad gods who rule the sea, was I allowed to come thus far and contemplate sand and trees?'" Fate took retribution against the men in the dinghy through the death of oiler Higgins, that "wily surfman" who was killed in the surf.

Not all the seven men on the *Commodore*'s deck plunged onto the makeshift rafts. Three of them remained on deck and one of them "had his arms folded and was leaning against the deckhouse. His feet were crossed, so that the toe of his left foot pointed downward. There they stood gazing at us, and neither from the deck nor from the rafts was a voice heard. Still there was this silence," says Crane in the *Press*. Contemptuous of the Captain in the dinghy, they resigned themselves to their death because they knew that the rafts could not possibly save them. The men on the rafts begged the men in the dinghy to take them in tow, said Captain Murphy, and they made a towline fast. But the sea "nearly filled our boat, and we were compelled to let her go and bail our craft dry. We went back again and once more made fast, but the first sea parted the rafts and broke over our towline. The rafts all parted and were scattered."

"I was at the oar and so faced the rafts," Crane reported. "The cook controlled the line. Suddenly the boat began to go backward and then we saw this Negro on the first raft pulling on the line hand over hand and drawing us to him.

"He had turned into a demon. He was wild—wild as a tiger. He was crouched on this raft and ready to spring. Every muscle of him seemed to be turned into an elastic spring. His eyes were almost white. His face was the face of a lost man reaching upward, and we knew that the weight of his hand on the gunwale doomed us."

When the Cook let go of the line, the men in the dinghy rowed around to see if they could get a line from the Chief Engineer, "and all this time, mind you, there were no shrieks, no groans, but silence, silence and silence, and then the *Commodore* sank." The three men on the stern of the sinking *Commodore* went down with the ship, says Crane, "like heroes with no cry of despair, not a murmur. I remained by the rafts twenty minutes longer, but as the boat was being filled by almost every wave and the wind was constantly increasing in force we allowed our boat to go whither the elements carried her." In conflict with Crane's report, there may be reason to believe Montgomery's report not of silence, but of "heart-rending cries" —uttered by the raft survivors perhaps. Were the men in the dinghy conscience-troubled, and did not Crane slant his *Press* dispatch somewhat so as to shield Captain Murphy from any accusation of dereliction of duty? That he felt a measure of guilt can perhaps be inferred from the disingenuousness of "Stephen Crane's Own Story."

While the dinghy had tried to tow the rafts, it was an "absolute impossibility" because the dinghy "was within six inches of the water's edge" and "there was an enormous sea running, and I knew that under the circumstances a tugboat would have no light task in moving these rafts." "The waves were tremendous," said Captain Murphy in the *World* for January 5, "as high as I have ever seen them hereabouts. They rolled in on us, threatening to dash us against the sinking tug, and we expected every moment to be overthrown. But good luck favored us, and we got off." The *Herald* for January 4 reported Captain Murphy: "The sea was running big hills, and a cold northeast gale swept over the party." In the Florida *Times-Union* he said: "heavy sea and wind all that afternoon and all that night [January 2]."[17]

Although the Cubans in their lifeboats made it through the surf by noon on Saturday, January 2, the dinghy contended with rough seas for twenty-seven to thirty hours on through the night. Why didn't Captain Murphy take the dinghy through the surf much sooner? Several factors were against the four men: the Captain had a broken arm, the cook (Montgomery) could not swim a stroke, the dinghy was a frail thing compared to the lifeboats, and the undertow and the sharks threatened. The surf was so dangerous by the time they got there Saturday night, and it was so dark that "we couldn't see our way in. Early Sunday morning we put in, but I could see that we would go over," Captain Murphy said.[18]

Montgomery in the *Journal* stated: "We found the surf so high that we were afraid to trust ourselves in the seething breakers. So we laid there where we were all the rest of the night and worked for our lives until the sun rose this morning, in the effort to keep our boat from filling. Then at 7 o'clock we determined to brave the surf and sturdily rowed our little vessel into the combing rollers. In the twinkling of an eye we were struggling in the water, our dinghy having gone under before the first big wave.

Although I cannot swim a stroke, I was fortunate enough to be swept high onto the beach before I had swallowed enough salt water to kill me, and was actually the first man to get to shore." In the Boston *Evening Transcript,* Montgomery added: "For almost an hour we battled for life, and then managed to crawl out on the sands, almost dead. Captain Murphy saved Mr. Crane by helping him when a cramp caught him. Higgins was struck on the head by floating timbers and he died soon after landing. He was a good sailor and a brave man. He worked to save his comrades."

By other accounts Higgins was hit by the overturned dinghy. Crane held up Higgins (an expert swimmer) when Higgins got terribly tired, and endeavored to bring him in, but he was so far gone that he could hardly help himself, said Captain Murphy in the *Press.* In "The Open Boat," the correspondent, who is Crane, is knocked into a heap by every wave, "and the undertow pulled at him." It was probably at this moment when Crane, sensing that he might not make it to shore, jettisoned his chamois-skin belt containing the $700 in Spanish gold he had hoped to expend in Cuba to report on the insurrection for the Bacheller–Johnson Syndicate.[19]

Montgomery reported in the *Journal* that Captain Murphy finally rescued Crane as he was about to go under the dinghy. It was previous to this that Higgins must have been struck by the overturned boat or by one of the loose oars. When the surf upset the dinghy Captain Murphy "grabbed it and got on the bottom, but she was rolled over again. Higgins tried to swim, but sank. I tried to encourage him, and he made another attempt," said Crane in the New York *Press.* "The boat went over again, and I saw no more of him until his corpse came up on the beach." Captain Murphy "gave orders amid the wilderness of the breakers as clearly as if he had been on the quarter deck of a battleship."

On the afternoon of January 2, when the boat was close to shore but dared not breach the heavy surf, Captain Murphy had seen people on the shore and flew a flag of distress and repeatedly fired his pistol to attract their attention. "I do not see how they could have failed to see us and appreciate our perilous position, for we were only a half mile from shore." By a bath towel tied to a stick he signaled to two men on the beach, one of them on a bicycle. The men in the dinghy saw something on the beach that they thought was either a lifeboat or a hotel omnibus, and they argued about its identity, and then on the beach a third fellow appeared, or so it seemed. Captain Murphy felt certain that a surf-boat would be sent out, and so "we waited at the spot, pulling like Trojans against the heavy sea and wind all that afternoon and all that night. I do not see now, looking back upon it, how human strength could have successfully contended against the fierce odds of nature," said the Captain in the Florida *Times-Union.* Their only comforts were cigars and a little store of brandy. One of the men who saw them from the shore was Fred Niver, and he recollected sixty-four years later (in a 1961 interview): "Sure, we saw them, but we didn't know they were in trouble."

On the morning of January 3 there was no one on the beach when they resolved to reach shore through the breakers. Captain Murphy gave one life belt to Steward Montgomery and one to Crane. Although the Captain had a badly injured arm and shoulder, he took no life belt for himself. When the dinghy was overturned in the surf that morning, a man on the beach "saw our dreadful predicament." He was John Kitchell, whom Captain Murphy misnamed Getchell. "He stripped to the skin and plunged into the surf and helped the steward and Mr. Crane in. I was safe in shallow water. I then saw Higgins' body on the wet sand. We rolled him and made every effort to bring him to life, but unfortunately failed. Poor fellow, he was brave and did his duty faithfully." (Murphy in *Times-Union* for January 5.)

Crane in his *Press* account, but not in his short story, says that John Kitchell of Daytona Beach "came running down the beach and as he ran the air was filled with clothes. If he had pulled a single lever and undressed, even as the fire horses harness, he could not seem to me to have stripped with more speed. He dashed into the water and dragged the Cook. Then he went after the Captain, but the Captain sent him to me, and then it was that he saw Billy Higgins lying with his forehead on sand that was clear of the water, and that he was dead."

Kitchell bounded into the surf, running and undressing as he ran, Crane says in his short story, "naked as a tree in winter; but a halo was about his head, and he shone like a saint." That was probably the only occasion on which John Kitchell was elevated to sainthood. He managed a boatyard on the Halifax near Main Street and a ferry to the mainland. Captain Murphy called him "one of nature's noblemen."

The three survivors had not been on the beach long before the women of the town brought them coffee and "all kinds of restoratives. Their attention warmed a man's heart to the appreciation of charity," said Crane in his *Press* report, while in his short story he said: "It seemed that instantly the beach was populated with men, with blankets, clothes, and flasks, and women with coffee-pots and all the remedies sacred to their minds." One of these women was Pearl Spalding (later Mrs. Albert Strange), who prepared food for the survivors in her Surf Crest cottage on the dunes, where Montgomery and Murphy spent the night. Crane made his Sunday overnight stay with Lawrence Thompson at his house near the Halifax River on the peninsula, and later in gratitude he sent the Thompsons a copy of *The Red Badge of Courage.* The Daytona citizens buried William Higgins, and legend has it that he is still buried there in Pinewood Cemetery, but he was buried a second time by his relatives, who ordered his body shipped home to Salem, Massachusetts.

Crane wired the *World:* "I am unable to write a thing yet, but will later." Cora Taylor telegraphed him to come to Jacksonville by special train that day—"never mind overcharges answer and come surely. C. T." Only the extravagant and romantic Cora would have thought of hiring a special locomotive to bring Stephen from Daytona (no regular train ran on Sunday). Crane balked; it cost too much. After spending the night with the Thompsons, on Monday (January 4) he took John Kitchell's ferry across the Halifax and met Cora in the Daytona railroad station; she had wired him that she would be there by the noon train. There the telegraph operator, Fred J. Niver, eavesdropped on the lovers. "They sat in a corner of the waiting room with their arms around one another, kissing and hugging like love birds, until time for the afternoon northbound train. That's the last I saw of them."[20]

Several Saturday afternoon papers had reported that Stephen Crane had drowned, and night clerk Morton at the St. James Hotel in Jacksonville sent Cora Taylor a note that Saturday night (January 2) about an empty boat being washed ashore. "The operator at New Smyrna tells me that he has it pretty straight that it came in bottom up. God save Crane if he is still alive." When Crane was saved the next morning, Cora wired him: "Telegram received Thank God your safe have been almost crazy / C. T." And the *World* reported: "Stephen Crane Safe."

# XV

# ⊂⋑ *"The Open Boat"*

In his seaman's shirt and dungarees, now shrunken to half their size, Crane appeared in the lobby of the St. James Hotel in the late afternoon of Monday, January 4, with his excited escort, Cora Taylor. He was greeted by a little girl who looked up at him as though he were "the divinely appointed Saviour of the Island" (Cuba). She wanted him to sign her autograph album, but he was too exhausted. They met again a week later after he had regained strength enough to get out of bed, and he called out: "Where's that album?" The little girl, the precocious nine-year-old daughter of the Barrett family, grabbed her album from the hotel desk, where she kept it, and presented it to Crane. He wrote on the page facing William Jennings Bryan's signature: "Stephen Crane, able seaman S. S. Commodore."

Later that month, or in February, little Miss Barrett and her parents bicycled out toward the Sub-Tropical Gardens and saw Crane as he passed them in Cora Taylor's carriage, the same carriage that was usually transporting the girls of Cora's Hotel de Dream. He waved his hat gaily, and the Barrett child responded with enthusiasm, but Mrs. Barrett acknowledged his salute with a very chilly bow. Her daughter was chagrined and disappointed by her mother's lack of cordiality. She later learned why Mrs. Barrett had stiffened so perceptibly on that long-ago day in Jacksonville.

No sooner had Crane reached Jacksonville than Hawkins sent him money, and Crane responded on the 7th: "Thanks awfully old man greeting to club" (the Lantern Club). Edward Marshall, now Sunday editor of Hearst's *Journal,* wired him: "Congratulations on plucky and successful fight for life. . . . Will wire you money."

Crane wrote, on a long piece of paper pasted onto an envelope postmarked January 26, 1897, these words (Cora preserved the note): "Love comes like the tall swift shadow of a ship at night. There is for a moment the music of water's turmoil, a bell, perhaps, a man's shout, a row of gleaming yellow lights. Then the slow sinking of this mystic shape. Then silence and a bitter silence—the silence of the sea at night." The sunken *Commodore* was his metaphor of the ship of love, threatened by the seas of life.

He dedicated his *Open Boat and Other Tales of Adventure* (1898) to "the memory of the late William Higgins and to Captain Edward Murphy and Steward C. B. Montgomery of the sunk steamer *Commodore.*" He had in mind Higgins, who had met his death in the surf, or one of the men on the flimsy raft, when he wrote a poem sometime after the shipwreck, very likely in January or February, 1897. (It was not published until April, 1929.) The opening and final stanzas comprise a unit in themselves:

> *A man adrift on a slim spar*
> *A horizon smaller than the rim of a bottle*
> *Tented waves rearing lashy dark points*
> *The near whine of froth in circles.*
> *God is cold.*

> *The incessant raise and swing of the sea*
> *And growl after growl of crest*
> *The sinkings, green, seething, endless*
> *The upheaval half-completed.*
> *God is cold.*

In the closing stanza the drowning man confronts a cold deity in the waters, the one being equated with the other:

> *A horizon smaller than a doomed assassin's cap,*
> *Inky, surging tumults*
> *A reeling, drunken sky and no sky*
> *A pale hand sliding from a polished spar.*
> *God is cold.*

> *The puff of a coat imprisoning air:*
> *A face kissing the water-death*
> *A weary slow sway of a lost hand*
> *And the sea, the moving sea, the sea.*
> *God is cold.*

Elbert Hubbard reported that Crane had drowned. *"He died trying to save others,"* said *The Philistine* for February, 1897. In flamboyant sentiment Hubbard wrote: "How he faced death the records do not say; but I know, for I knew the soul of the lad. Within the breast of that pale youth there dwelt a lion's heart. He held his own life and reputation lightly. He sided with the weak, the ignorant, the unfortunate, and his strength and influence were ever given lavishly to those in need. . . . So here's to you, Steve Crane, wherever you may be! You were not so very good, but you were as good as I am—and better, in many ways—our faults were different, that's all. I don't know where you are, Stevie, but when I die I hope I will face Death as manfully as you did; and I hope, too, that I shall then go where you are now. And so, Stevie, good-bye and good-bye!"

When he had stayed with the Hubbards at East Aurora following the Philistine Society banquet in December, 1895, some woman—probably Hubbard's wife—had remarked: "Stevie is not quite at home here—he'll not remain so very long." But when Hubbard's *Philistine* announced Crane drowned, he was on dry land or wading the swamps of Florida. It was Hubbard himself who went to the bottom of the sea when the *Lusitania* sank on May 6, 1915. He went down manfully with his wife Alice, their arms linked when last seen by a survivor.

In the same number of the *Philistine* in which Hubbard announced Crane's death, he corrected himself with a simple note about his resurrection: "Thanks to providence and a hen-coop Steve Crane was not drowned after all. He swam ashore." Where Hubbard got that hen-coop is a mystery.

Crane wrote "The Open Boat" in waterfront cafés, at the St. James Hotel, and at the Hotel de Dream, where in order to find out whether he had his facts right he read his story aloud to Captain Edward Murphy. He was overheard by Ralph Paine and Ernest McCready, who were having dinner in one of the private dining rooms, and Paine recorded their conversation in his *Roads of Adventure:*

" 'Listen, Ed. I want to have this *right,* from your point of view. How does it sound so far?' 'You've got it, Steve'—said the other man, 'That is just how it happened, and how we felt. Read me some more of it.' "

The difference between what Crane reported in his *Press* dispatch and what he recreated as fiction, adhering to the facts of his experience in the *Commodore* disaster, is that in "The Open Boat" every detail or image is patterned, one thing linked to another, and thus designed, the short story evokes a significance transcending the literal, experienced, event. For instance, the Oiler (Higgins) at the beginning of the dinghy's voyage is represented by the thin little oar he steers, and this detail prepares for the final incident, the death of that "wily surfman"; at the start his thin oar "seemed often ready to snap."

Also, the death of Higgins is foreshadowed and epitomized in the song the Correspondent recites during a moment of reveries of his childhood: "A soldier of the Legion lay dying in Algiers." This verse had meant nothing to him as a child; he never regarded then the death of this soldier as important or meaningful, nor felt any sympathy for him because he himself had not experienced it: "It was less to him than the breaking of a pencil's point." That fragile pencil point correlates with the delicate oar of Higgins; the death of the Oiler is foretold in the death of the Soldier of the Legion.

When the dinghy, in "The Open Boat" version of the *Commodore* disaster, heads for the beach through the treacherous surf, the Correspondent sees a tall white windmill in the distance. He wonders if anyone ever ascends it and looks seaward. "The tower was a giant, standing with its back to the plight of the ants." It represents to a degree "the serenity of nature amid the struggles of the individual—nature in the wind, and nature in the vision of men. She did not seem cruel to him then, nor beneficent, nor treacherous, nor wise. But she was indifferent, flatly indifferent. It is, perhaps, plausible that a man in this situation, impressed with the unconcern of the universe, should see the innumerable flaws of his life, and have them taste wickedly in his mind, and wish for another chance." All's by chance; "willy-nilly, the firm fails, the army loses, the ship goes down."[1] What the men who survive their ordeal through the surf learn is that man must not be indifferent to his fellow men. As he cannot trust nature, he must count on his fellows.

To the three survivors the wind brings "the sound of the great sea's voice," and "they felt that they could then be interpreters." Now they understand what the sea says—what life means—because they have suffered. They have suffered the worst that the grim sea can exact from them, including the loss of one of their brotherhood. "None of them knew the color of the sky," but now they know it.

The story ends on the same contrast motif as at the start, and thus the ending—hope / despair—returns us to the beginning to form the whole in circular design. At the end "the white waves paced to and fro in the moonlight," but those waves are deceptive. The violence of the sea—or nature's threat to man—remains only temporarily abated. The serenity of the survivors has its parallel in those quieted waves, once "most wrongfully and barbarously abrupt and tall." At the start "there was a terrible grace in the move of the waves," and at the end when all seems serenity the corpse of the Oiler reminds them of the sea's terrible grace. Their serenity is thus negated, their affirmation thus denied.

One of Crane's gifts that delighted Conrad was "an inspired audacity of epithet." His epithets are at their most audacious in his "cold, comfortable sea-water," an image fusing contradictory emotions. The Correspondent, nestling in the cold water of the dinghy, falls asleep. "His head, pillowed on a thwart, was within an inch of the swirl of a wave-crest, and sometimes a particularly obstreperous sea came inboard and drenched him once more." Not literally is he comfortable, for "his teeth played all the popular airs." Thus "cold, comfortable sea-water" is an intended paradox, the seawater being comfortable only in an ironic sense. "It is almost certain that if the boat had capsized he would have tumbled *comfortably* out upon the ocean as if he felt sure that it was a great soft mattress." But the ocean obviously is anything but a mattress. The Correspondent struggles in the raging surf to reach the Captain and the boat in the final scene of the story, and he reflects "that when one gets properly wearied drowning must really be a comfortable arrangement—a cessation of hostilities accompanied by a large degree of relief." What is readily recognizable is the irony of opposites which formed the personality of the man who wrote it;[2] Crane is a master of the contradictory effect.

His ironic point of view is again expressed in the seagulls hovering over the dinghy: the gull's "black eyes were wistfully fixed upon the Captain's head." But it is the Captain—not the gull—who is wistful, and he envies these birds who can sit "comfortably in groups" because the men in the dinghy can't. These seagulls exemplify nature's indifference to their plight. Things viewed by the men at sea are seen as though they were on land, and these land images impinge upon their plight to mock it. The land is their hope, but it eludes them. They are mocked also by their domestic thoughts: the ocean is their mattress, the bottom of the dinghy is the Oiler's "sea-water couch," and their grotesque domicile is furnished also with a stove—in the stovelike shape of the Cook in his life belt.

The cynical Correspondent and the Cook and the injured Captain are given to illusions; the Oiler is spokesman for the hard cruel facts and is the only one without hope. The Correspondent, although he has been "taught to be cynical of men," learns in this ordeal of the dinghy a comradeship, a "subtle brotherhood of men that was here established on the seas." The people on the shore do not share it; they share only the usual social formulae of polite conversation, and as soon as the Correspondent touches land he reverts to the code of the land. "The correspondent, schooled in the minor formulae, said, 'Thanks, old man.'" He thanks the man who undressed and bounded into the surf and dragged ashore the Cook, the man who "shone like a saint" with "a halo about his head."

Conrad, himself a symbolic artist, said that Crane's story by its "deep and simple humanity of presentation seems somehow to illustrate the essentials of life itself, like a symbolic tale." The Correspondent comes to recognize that every man is, as it were, in the same boat—a dinghy tossed by treacherous sea and surf, trying to get to shore. "The Open Boat" is symbolic not only in this overall sense, but also in its minute particulars. Its meaning transcends the personal.

"None of them knew the color of the sky"—the opening line of Crane's splendid story—was remembered by Conrad in 1899. Crane was visiting Conrad at his home. He was lying on a couch and Conrad, sitting in a chair opposite, "said suddenly across the width of the mantelpiece: 'None of them knew the color of the sky' . . . Truth to say, it was a time when neither he nor I had the leisure to look up idly at the sky. The waves just then were too 'barbarously abrupt.' I do not mean to say that it was always so. Now and then we were permitted to snatch a glance at the color of the sky." Conrad was always telling Crane that one thing or another "was 'barbarously abrupt,' or begging him not to be so 'barbarously abrupt' himself."

Harold Frederic, London editor of the New York *Times,* wrote an adulatory review of the London edition of *The Open Boat and Other Stories* in the New York *Times* (May 1, 1898): "No living English prose writer of his years approaches his wonderful gift of original and penetrating observation, while no writer of English is today prouder of being an American. Possibly this steady, unswerving loyalty to his native land helped to make him so many friends among Englishmen, who, even when men of letters, are sportsmen enough to like that man who stands up for his own regiment. Maybe Crane little knows himself what a powerful factor he has been of late in drawing England Westward." England, that nation of sailors, appreciated the great sea story, and H. G. Wells was right in calling it a perfection.³ Wells considered it the crown of all Crane's work.

Stephen wrote William at Hartwood on March 11 from Jacksonville: "I have been for over a month among the swamps further South wading miserably to and fro in an attempt to avoid our derned U. S. Navy. And it can't be done. I am through trying. I have changed all my plans and am going to Crete. I expect to sail from NY one week from next Saturday. Expect me in P. J. [Port Jervis] on Thursday. Give my love to all and assure them of my remembrances."⁴ He also wrote someone: "I am going to Greece for the *Journal* and if *The Red Badge* is not all right I shall sell out my claim in literature and take up orange growing." He had tried to find some ship to take him to Cuba, but the revenue cutters were by then rigidly enforcing the neutrality laws. Unable to get to Cuba, he was going to Greece—and so was Cora. She would be with Stephen at any cost. While she remained in Jacksonville to dispose of her Hotel de Dream, Stephen took the train to New York to join the *Journal* as one of their war correspondents.

How did Stephen get back to New York from Jacksonville? Thomas Beer asked the Crane family. He was told that Crane came by way of New Orleans, but Stephen never saw New Orleans after his 1895 expedition to the West. He wired William on March 11: "Expect me in P. J. on Thursday." Edmund's daughter Edith says that "we did not see him after the shipwreck on the coast of Florida. I'm sure he didn't come. "Father and Uncle Will got a hurry call to go N.Y.C. to bid him goodbye just before he sailed." The last time the children of any of his brothers' families saw him could not have been later than 1898 [actually 1896] when he left for the filibustering expeditions. But Crane did go to Port Jervis to see William, if not to Hartwood to see Edmund; according to Corwin Linson's memoirs, he recited "The Open Boat" to William's wife, Cornelia.

In New York he surprised Linson one evening in late March at his studio, and Linson gave him a riotous welcome. "It was a new Stephen, almost, who confronted me, by contrast a rather dandified Steve. His hair was precisely brushed, his lip covering was much more than a mere shading, a well-fitting suit showed a trim, well-set figure. He was now a bit over twenty-six. Yes, another Stephen." (In March, 1897, Crane was twenty-five, not twenty-six.) Linson contrasted him with the youth who four years ago had sat on the same studio couch. "Life had become more worthwhile to both of us. He was full of a forthcoming trip to Greece. I knew all about that feeling. I had been [there] only a year ahead of him." Hearst was sending him for the *Journal,* and Crane asked what the Greeks were like: " 'How did you chin their lingo?' Why, here was the same Steve, after all."

They both wanted the Greeks to win, but maybe the war would fizzle out before Crane got there to see his first battle. "The Greeks were like hounds crazy for the hunt. If only they had competent commanders!" Stephen was yet to learn "how Greeks can talk, as though a dozen tongues are let loose in their mouths at once and the words like water rippling over stones, smooth running, and bewilderingly rapid to the stranger's ear." In his Greco–Turkish War novel, *Active Service,* he said the Greeks made "noise much like a coal-breaker."

They left the studio to have dinner together in a restaurant at Fourth Avenue and 23rd Street and overheard two men at the next table talking not very intelligently about Sullivan County. Crane grinned and leaned toward Linson: "If they knew it as we do, they couldn't make such brilliant asses of themselves before old inhabitants!" They reminisced about Port Jervis and Linson's cousin Louis Senger, who was now a writer, and Frederic Lawrence and Lucius Button, both M.D.'s now. Their world was looking up. Then Stephen, with a reserve characteristic of him when speaking of women, told about the woman he was about to marry: Cora Taylor. "She would sail on the same steamer and be married in England. But there were tongues. 'The weasels would draw blood anyhow.' He hated to leave her alone, but his job was to go on to Greece and come back when the stew was over. 'What would you do, C.K.?' Just that. It could not last long. Prussian-officered Turks would do the business of Europe's rotten politics, and all he would have to do would be to see the Parthenon and come home and get his wife! It did not turn out that way."

Late that night Crane and Linson parted, not knowing that it was their final farewell. When Stephen was in New York in 1898, Linson was in Palestine.

While waiting for his ship to sail Crane encountered a new *Journal* reporter who had recently come from San Francisco, Robert H. Davis. He had been born on the Nebraska prairies, where his father was an Episcopal missionary, and he knew all about Crane through Ed Marshall. Davis wanted to meet him to tell him what Ambrose Bierce in San Francisco had said about his war novel. He had heard that Crane had signed with the *Journal*'s managing editor (Sam Chamberlain) and made an appointment that same day to meet him at the Hoffman House to discuss matters of transportation and of cabling the news from Greece. Crane broke the appointment; but by chance they met that night opposite the Imperial Hotel on Broadway. Davis remarked that Crane would be covering a war in that country "for which the poet Lord Byron was prepared to shed his blood."

"No man should be called upon to report a war in a country that he loves. I shall do a better job than Byron could have done," Crane said. "Greece means nothing to me, nor does Turkey. After Cuba it will be cold over there, I imagine. By the way, this is a hell of a town. I never come here without feeling the necessity for taking immediate steps to go elsewhere."

"Hardly the place for a minister's son," said Davis.

"Well, for that matter, is there any place exactly suited to a minister's son?"

"We are not understood," Davis said.

"You too?" said Crane.

In spite of Davis' reportorial training he found it hard to get anything out of Crane about himself, but the fact that they were both ministers' sons seemed to open him up.

"Have you ever observed how the envious laity exult when we are over-taken by misfortune?" Crane said. Davis made no reply; he watched the cigarette hanging from Crane's lips, performing like "a baton to the tempo of his speech." Crane, obviously feeling himself cursed by being a minister's son, according to Davis, posed this fable: A bartender's boy falls from the Waldorf roof, and a minister's son falls from a park bench. "They both hit the earth with the same velocity, mutilated beyond recognition."

Noticing the lack of sparkle in his manner, Davis invited him for a drink: " 'Would you mind trying a novelty? It is a combination of one part *amer picon* and three parts of ginger ale.' 'Sure, I'll try it,' replied Crane—'with your belly.' Crane led a loud explosion of laughter and seemed quite delighted with his flash of humor." At that moment he noticed a girl emerging from the shadows of the Sixth Avenue Elevated and, tossing his cigarette into Greeley Square, he "placed his left hand upon his heart, removed his hat, and made a most gallant bow. I have never seen a more exquisite gesture of chivalry than this youth sweeping the pavement with his black felt." Crane asked the streetwalker with the utmost delicacy, as though addressing one lost in the city: "A stranger here?" "Well," said the girl, "suppose I am a stranger. Can you show me anything?" "Yes, I can show you the way out, but if you prefer to remain—" "You shouldn't hang out here, kid," said the streetwalker as she sauntered off under the Sixth Avenue Elevated.

"This is a long canyon. I wonder if there is a way out," said Crane. He had met his own Maggie.

Davis says that under the flickering shadows of the arc lights which illuminated Broadway, "I got for the first time a blinding flash of the romantic Crane. A lock of soft hair lay upon his high, white, and shapely forehead. There was a fullness about the temples and over the eyes; the modelling exquisite. Crowning the cheek-bones was a tone of light coral accentuated against the sallow dominant tone. . . . Around the mouth hovered an elusive smile, while the whole posture of the body suggested the dancing master about to begin a minuet. I was not a hero-worshipper. My whole newspaper training had been toward the development of composure. Nevertheless, at that moment I discerned an almost indescribable luminous beauty in the eyes of this modern Villon. They were large, the iris seemingly out of proportion to the pupil, blue in general tone, brilliant, flashing." Davis in spite of himself sentimentalized Crane: "But from that forehead and those eyes quivered an aurora."[5]

Steven's friend Frederic Lawrence thought him "incurably romantic about women, and this extended even to the girl of the streets. Many unkind things said about him were justifiable, for he was absolutely irresponsible in money matters; but whatever the stories about women, you can always find in Crane's behavior a curious trace of chivalry." Another fraternity brother, Frank Noxon, reports that Crane in the company of girls showed respect and deference; when he wrote about scarlet sisters his dominant impulse was "a desire to serve the helpless." Others ascribed his interest in unfortunate women to an instinct other than sympathy and compassion. Frederic Gordon said that he never saw Crane intoxicated when he returned to the studio and that whatever his conduct may have been at times "his ideals were fine, his sense of honor high, and his faith in mankind unshaken. He was all that we used to mean by the word *gentleman.*"

Crane drank and smoked and had a hankering for women. There is nothing unusual about that. What is unusual is Beer's slanted notion that Crane was so sensitive to women and men older than himself that "the trait lends itself to psychiatric description." There seems to be an insinuation of homosexual tendencies in Beer's assertion that Crane would turn from the prettiest girl in a crowded room to chat with an elderly lady. But we know from several sources that Crane, as John Northern Hilliard put it, again and again brought a lady of the streets to his room. When he lived in a boardinghouse of ill-repute in the summer of 1896, he had no need to bring a lady in from the streets—she was right down the hall. All the women in his life—except Helen Trent and Nellie Crouse—were experienced, older women like Lily Munroe, childless and later separated from her husband; actress Amy Leslie; hostess Cora Taylor; or prostitutes.

He could afford to court innocent young girls only in his fiction. Meanwhile, he "took up with many a drab and was not overly particular as to her age, race or color," according to Ernest McCready. This rather upsets the legend of "romantic Crane." He liked people for obscure reasons, says Beer, "and his open dislikes were so few that inevitably he collected both bores and boors." In Havana in late 1898 he began a novel about a boy prostitute—*Flowers in Asphalt*—which he aimed to make longer than anything he had done, according to James Huneker, but he destroyed what he wrote. (His erotic verse shared the same fate.)

Everything Crane said about women was admirable, says Linson. "His was a fine nature, and his appreciation of the charm and frankness of true womanhood and the innocence of young girlhood was chivalry itself." He was also sometimes a smart-aleck and an irresponsible heel.[6] However, one must keep in mind how very young was this conceited youth. "I used sometimes to think that Steve was perhaps the most complete example of a self-absorbed ego that was ever carried on two feet," says Linson, "and as irresponsible—sometimes—as a goat, yet these shortcomings would no sooner be apparent than they would be wiped off the slate by his very charm of personality and sturdy honesty of intent. And as to all the rest, there is plenty of petty meanness in the world to account for it."

Crane never tried to hide his relations with women of the underworld any more than an animal would, says Hilliard. He lived his own, free and untrammeled life; in the slums he got what he was looking for—the real, naked facts of life. In seeking them, he was tolerant and absolutely unashamed. He had contempt for conventional hypocrisy. Never mincing the truth, he spoke out as nakedly as he wrote *Black Riders*. Always he "had a gay spirit, even when, as often happened in those days, we sat together in Union Square and speculated on the flapjacks and coffee we would eat and drink if we had two-bits between us. And then, when the gods were kind and a newspaper editor gave us a check, it was ho! for the fleshpots and an all-night session at poker." Hilliard warms to his hero: "Crane was a big man as well as a big writer—the biggest writer, to my mind, this country has produced." Of course, he must have shocked his relatives, adds Hilliard.

At the Imperial's walnut bar stout Robert Davis and lean Stephen Crane conversed at the brass rail, Crane gliding his glass up and down the bar while shifting his mind to the topic Davis had broached when they met on Broadway outside the hotel. The topic was Ambrose Bierce and "An Occurrence at Owl Creek Bridge." "Nothing better exists," said Crane. "That story contains everything."[7] "Move your foot over," Davis said. "He will not be appreciated until long after he is dead," Crane said. "Has he plenty of enemies?" "More than he needs," Davis said. "Good," remarked Crane. "Then he will become an immortal."

Davis reported Bierce's praise: "This young man has the power to feel. He knows nothing of war, yet he is drenched in blood. Most beginners who deal with this subject spatter themselves merely with ink." Bierce admired *The Red Badge of Courage*, but as a veteran of the Civil War he was irked by the chorus of inflamed acclamation over a novel by a youth who had not experienced warfare. The London *Athenaeum* spoke of young Crane as a "somewhat neglected author," but not one of the reviewers of *The Red Badge* mentioned Bierce's *Tales of Soldiers and Civilians,* and this neglect provoked one of his admirers—Percival Pollard—to explode in the New York *Journal* (May 22, 1896) that both books were practically the same in subject, the gruesomeness of battle carnage and the feelings of men exposed to it, and that "Mr. Crane has merely done crudely what Mr. Bierce did most admirably." Three days after Pollard's "In the Matter of a Badge" appeared in the *Journal* Bierce wrote him from Washington, D.C., that he valued the article "more for its just censure of the Crane freak than for its too kindly praise of me. I have been hoping some one still in the business of reading (I have not myself looked into a book for months) would take the trouble to say something of that kind about that Crane person's work."

As a writer Ambrose Bierce, said the New York *Press,* "is a rare compound of vitriol and velvet, fierceness and facetiousness." On the Pacific coast no writer's reputation had currency until Bierce pronounced his appraisal. His single-line book review is a classic: "The covers of this book are too far apart." Of an actress who had died he wrote: "Always famous for her composed manner, she is now quite decomposed." Not so funny was the quatrain he wrote when Governor-elect William Goebel was shot dead in an election quarrel in Kentucky: "The bullet that pierced Goebel's breast / Can not be found in all the West, / Good reason, it is speeding here / To stretch McKinley on his bier." Twenty months after the New York *Journal* printed Bierce's verse (February 4, 1900) President McKinley was assassinated.

Both Bierce and Crane were now writing for Hearst's *Journal.* Hearst admired Bierce, who had written for his San Francisco *Examiner* at $100 a week. In early 1897 Bierce was in New Jersey making a successful invasion of the East. Said the *Atlanta Constitution:* "Bierce is hot on the track of Stephen Crane. There is no doubt about one thing, however: Everything that Crane writes is red."[8] (But also the color blue had a curious effect on Crane and plays a conspicuous part in his color scheme. Parodist Carolyn Wells wrote: "C is for colorful Crane, / Who has a phenomenal brain. / His language amazes, / He writes in blue blazes, / And his verses are really insane.")

Cora had two hopes: to be with Stephen at any cost and to become the first woman war correspondent. From Jacksonville she wrote: "Only a line that you may know I am thinking of you and to say that I should indeed be happy if you were with me, or even if I had sufficient time to sit down and write you a long letter, for whilst writing it I might delude myself with the happy thought that you were by my side and I was talking to you. But fate wills otherwise and I can only add goodnight—be good and *I love you.*"

Cora took train from Jacksonville after Crane's arrival in Port Jervis on March 14. They made separate journeys to the ship that was to carry them to England.[9] Edmund came from Hartwood to see Stephen off to Liverpool on the *Etruria* on March 20, and the *Etruria* arrived in Liverpool the next Saturday (March 27). Cora took the same ship, but Stephen did not introduce her to Edmund at the dock. She shared her cabin not with Stephen, but with Mrs. Charlotte Ruedy from the Hotel de Dream, whose expenses she paid all the way to Greece. Mrs. Ruedy, known as Mathilde, remained with Cora and Stephen at Ravensbrook, after the end of the Greco–Turkish War, and she was with Cora when Crane was in Cuba in 1898.

Crane in *Active Service* undoubtedly cast into fictive form what had actually occurred on the voyage of the *Etruria* to Liverpool. Actress Nora Black (Cora) confronts the seemingly surprised Rufus Coleman, a reporter for the New York "Eclipse," aboard a ship bound for Liverpool, and Coleman (Crane) pretends he did not know that she was a passenger on the same ship. Like Rufus Coleman, Crane himself hid out in the smoking room playing poker. In the novel the ship is off the coast of Ireland when Coleman apologizes to Nora Black: " 'Been playing poker in the smoking room all voyage. Didn't have a look at the passenger-list until just now. Why didn't you send me word?' These lies were told so modestly and sincerely that when the girl flashed her brilliant eyes full upon their author, there was a mixture of admiration in the indignation." Rufus Coleman has been playing poker with a millionaire, and Crane met a millionaire either on the *Etruria* for Liverpool or later on the *Guadiana* out of Marseilles for Crete, for he scribbled on a scrap of paper "Sharefe millionaire." On this same scrap he noted some numbers, possibly stateroom numbers: "New York 290 / 261. Took up collection 43 dollars / Captains own money pd to Paris. / In Paris, 100 police, commissioner of minister of interior. / Arrested in Marseilles No tickets. / Sharefe millionaire."[10]

Everything about this note resists unriddling. It would seem that Crane took up a collection of $43 from the passengers, at the Captain's suggestion, and what sum the Captain contributed was paid by a note against a Paris bank. Then in Paris, what? Police on parade? Or perhaps Crane had to appear before the Commissioner for the Minister of Interior, about some passport difficulty. The stateroom numbers, as that's what they seem to be, put Cora on the same ship with Stephen, but not in the same room. "Arrested in Marseilles" tells us that he got there to catch the *Guadiana* for Crete and Athens.

He reached London from Liverpool on Monday morning—March 29—

and left it on Thursday afternoon, said Arthur Waugh in his "London Letter" of April 2 (in the *Critic*: April 17, 1897). "Mr. Stephen Crane has flitted through London this week on his way to the scene of insurrection in Crete, but his visit was of the briefest. Indeed, it was characterized by extreme and refreshing modesty, being conspicuously free of the tendency to self-advertisement which is so often characteristic of the Novelist's progress." Within a few hours of his arrival he called on his publisher, Heinemann, "who has worked so hard to push his books in this country. He seemed much pleased with the reception of his work in England and jokingly remarked that he was off to Crete because, having written so much about war, he thought it high time he should see a little fighting. Which proves him a man of humor—an excellent thing in letters."

Editor Sidney Pawling of Heinemann Ltd. had written Crane in December: "We think so highly of your work—of its virility, actuality and literary distinction that we have been pleased to place it prominently before the British public." He generously arranged for Crane to represent the London *Westminster Gazette* in reporting the war, and some of his best sketches appeared there in May, 1897. Crane asked to meet Joseph Conrad and the American novelist Harold Frederic, who were Heinemann authors, but he did not get to meet Conrad until October, when Pawling—something of an officious bore—took them to lunch.

These four days gave Crane the premature impression that "London is simply alive with bounders"—vulgar upstarts, ill-mannered. (But when he next saw the city, on his return from Greece, everyone was charming—even the porters.) At the clubs "the topic is solely bounders. On the street one can go no distance without hearing of a recent achievement of some bounder. The bounders have taken London by assault." Crane tries to define what a bounder is, but he's more fascinated by the word itself. "This word is an axe that has an edge like a Damascus. It can be used like a rapier, and yet it falls on your victim with the enthusiasm of a brick chimney." He ends this silly sketch—"New Invasion of Britain"—by noting that one man calls another "a bounder and afterwards you hear the other man call the man a bounder, and ultimately appears a man who calls both the man and the other a bounder. You begin to reflect upon elasticity and point of view. This infernal word ends by making one quake." He must have written this sketch during his trip to Marseilles and Crete from London; it was published on May 9 (in the Omaha *Daily Bee,* unsigned) when he was in Greece.

Richard Harding Davis had sailed on the *Germanic* on March 17 to cover the war for the London *Times* and was in London prior to Crane's arrival. At the Savoy (founded in 1895) he gave a luncheon for Crane on Wednesday, March 31,[11] and Harold Frederic was present. Davis wrote to his mother on March 31, just after the luncheon, that Crane "is very modest, sturdy and shy. Quiet, unlike I had imagined." He had been curious to meet Crane, he tells his mother, but he did not expect to meet Cora also, "a bi-roxide blonde who seemed to be attending to his luggage for him and whom I did not meet." Which means that Davis snubbed Cora. He had known since December, 1896, when he was in Key West, who Cora was (by the journalists' grapevine of gossip), and he did not approve of women of that kind. Later in Greece, he wrote home just before the war ended: "I left Athens with John Bass and Crane accompanied by a Lady Stuart who has run away from her husband to follow Crane. She is a commonplace dull woman old enough to have been his mother and with dyed yellow hair." However, her sunny hair was not artificial, and she wasn't dull and commonplace. She was plump and dowdy, but as she was only five years older than Stephen she wasn't exactly old enough to be his mother.

Davis ("Richard the Lion-Hearted") had acknowledged Stephen Crane a genius when in September, 1896, he said that Crane "seems to have written the last word, as far as battles or fighting is concerned, in *The Red Badge of Courage.*" Crane with less chivalry had spoken of Davis the previous year as a stuffed parrot and an old saw-log, but now he was Davis's guest at the Savoy. Perhaps their rivalry was inevitable. Davis represented the ideal of the American male, a keeper of the code of good manners and noble conduct who nevertheless gave the impression of being a fraud. Yet he was honest and courageous, but so was Crane. When Hearst's *Journal* slanted one of Davis' Cuban War dispatches in 1898, Davis exposed that fact in Hearst's rival paper, Pulitzer's *World,* and lost his job and joined the *World.* When Pulitzer's *World* cheated Crane, he walked out and joined Hearst's *Journal.*

At the Savoy, Crane was presented to Anthony Hope, known for his *Prisoner of Zenda,* James Barrie of *The Little Minister,* and Justin McCarthy, who had already been to Greece and had published a novel about it. Harold Frederic urged Crane to utilize his war experiences in Greece by writing a novel about the war, which he did, in *Active Service.*

More important to Crane than Davis' Savoy Club luncheon was the Savoy Club luncheon given him on his arrival on March 29 by Harold Frederic. A big man (both bulky and generous), Frederic intimidated everyone and presided over young Crane as though he had invented him. He was fifteen years older than Stephen, who responded rather meekly at first to the bushy-moustached giant. They had much in common. Frederic's *Damnation of Theron Ware* (1896) and his tales of the Mohawk Valley undermined the saccharine conventions dominating American literature in the 1890's, and Crane debunked or "parodied" those conventions again and again. (What also had prepared for their mutual friendship, of course, was Frederic's rave notice of the *Red Badge* in the New York *Times* in January, 1896.)

Harold Frederic went with Crane and Davis to Dover to see them off to

Paris on April 1 (Cora and Mrs. Ruedy were in a separate compartment), and Davis parted with Crane in Paris. He was going to Greece by a different route; he was traveling first to Florence to visit his brother, the American Consul there. At Dover, Frederic introduced Crane to Arnold Henry Sanford Bennett, and in Paris in early April Henry Bennett—he dropped the name Arnold after the notoriety of Arnold Bennett began—guided Crane through the city. Stephen sympathized with shy and luckless Bennett. A French Canadian, he married a French woman in 1896 who died of puerperal fever three years later. His first wife had killed herself. His first son was killed in battle in 1918, and Bennett himself spent his last years blind and bedridden. Crane remarked of him: "Destiny sets an alarm clock so as to be up early and strew banana peels in front of him. If he trusts a friend, he is betrayed. If he starts a journey, he breaks an ankle. If he loves, death comes to her without a smile."

Crane took not the slightest interest in any of the showplaces in Paris except the Luxembourg Gardens, and there Bennett had to help him while talking with some French children. He watched a review of cavalry, possibly that parade of one hundred policemen he mentioned in his enigmatic scrap-note, and he got Bennett to query in French one of the troopers as to whether he'd been at Gravelotte in 1870. Their horses elicited Crane's interest, but not Notre Dame and its colorful procession to the altar. While watching this ceremony he pulled Bennett away and exclaimed: "I can't stand that nonsense!"

Sometime after he left London, probably while in Paris, he wrote: "I now know that I am an imbecile of rank. If nobody shoots me and I get back alive through those Indians in London I will stay home until there is a nice war in Mexico where it does not matter when you talk so long as you can curse immoderately. Willie Hearst has made a bad bargain." Beer says that he wrote this from Basel, Switzerland, but it is possible that Cora mailed it there for him, when Crane left her in Paris to get to Marseille. The French steamer *Guadiana,* having left London on March 30, sailed from Marseilles on April 3 for Greece, Turkey, and the Black Sea via Piraeus, Smyrna, the Dardanelles, Constantinople, and finally Batum (Batumi).

By April 8 Crane was off Crete in the Bay of Suda. His dispatch in the New York *Sun* (May 9, 1897), "Half a Day in Suda Bay," is datelined "On board French steamer *Guadiana,* April 22."[12] A phrase in this sketch —"supported the war"—indicates that he wrote it shortly after Turkey declared war on Greece on April 17. Cora and Mrs. Ruedy took the Orient Express from Paris (its western terminal) to Vienna,[13] and thence to Varna on the Black Sea; and then by sea to Constantinople on the *Danae*—"a terrible old tub," said Cora. "The journey is supposed to be seven hours —it took the *Danae* on that memorable trip from Sunday at 6 P.M. till Wednesday night to reach Constantinople." Cora had picked the longest and the most difficult way to get to Greece. Richard Harding Davis got there by the same route taken by Rufus Coleman, the newspaper reporter and hero of Crane's *Active Service*. Davis' journey was from Calais to Brindisi on the Adriatic, and "from wretched Brindisi to charming Corfu, from Corfu to the little war-bitten city of Patras, and from Patras by rail at the speed of an ox-cart to Athens."[14]

# XVI

## ⊂⋑ *The Greco-Turkish War*

"I have changed all my plans and am going to Crete," Crane had written William on March 11. But the French steamer *Guadiana,* which left Marseilles on April 3, brought Crane to Crete only by chance five days later (April 8) when the ship changed course. "Leaving Marseilles, the passengers of this ship had no expectation of anything more than a tedious voyage to Athens without pause, but circumstances furnished us with a mild digression. In the early morning of the fourth day a ponderous headland appeared to the north, and we knew it to be the expected glimpse of Greece." All the way from Marseilles the thin wail of a baby had objected without pause to the roll and heave of the ship, but then came the excitement of headlands appearing first to the north and then some hours later another one to the south. "We could not arrange our geographical prejudices to suit this phenomenon until a man excitedly told every one that we had changed our course, that we were not bound for Piraeus, but for the Bay of Suda, in Crete."

The Greeks in the bow of the *Guadiana* excitedly chanted or crooned at sight of the island, but as Crane could see nothing but some blockhouses and a village, there seemed no point in going ashore. It looked about as thrilling as a goat pasture. The Greek passengers stared at a tiny blood-red banner, the Turkish flag over a redoubt, and the hills of Crete "slid aside, and impressively, like the scenes in a melodrama before the final tableau," wrote Crane. "Crete spread high and wide precisely like a painting from that absurd period when the painters each tried to reproduce the universe in one canvas." But the picture "lacked the boat with a triangular sail and a pie-faced crew occupying the attention in the foreground. It was lonely and desolate like a Land of Despair."[1]

Comically short in duration, the war had been long in coming about. Greece had demanded the independence of Crete from Turkish rule, but the Congress of Berlin in 1878 had ignored the situation, and so for almost twenty years Crete was rent by revolt and bloodshed. The years that followed saw a reign of "stupid and cruel mismanagement." The revolt of

*271*

Christian Cretans in 1895 was aided by the Greek nationalist society Ethnike Hetairia, and public opinion called for war against Turkey; but the Concert of Europe stepped in to restore an uneasy peace. By January, 1897, however, Crete was once more in turmoil.[2]

Two weeks before Crane was off the coast of Crete on the *Guadiana*, the Powers of Europe had proclaimed Cretan autonomy and on March 21 inaugurated a blockade of the island. In support of Crete's autonomy the Crown Prince had sent a torpedo-flotilla there on February 10, and three days later Colonel Vassos landed with 2,000 men to proclaim "the annexation of Crete to Greece." The Cretan insurgents flushed out the Turks defending the Akrotisi blockhouses and occupied them on March 26, but the next day the combined fleet of the Powers of Europe opened fire, and the Cretans fled. Their flight foretold the outcome of the Greeks in this not so splendid war.

Crane knew nothing about the March 27 defeat of the Cretan insurgents, humiliated by the punitive gunfire of the Powers' fleet. A formidable collection of ships—English, Russian, German, French—patrolled these waters. Crane described them as "great steel animals . . . menacing with their terrible glances a village of three rows of houses and a dock and vast stretches of hillside, whereon there was not even a tree to shoot at for fun." It might be a joke, but they represented the Concert of Europe. "Colossi never smile."

Prince Konstantinos (Constantine) had left Athens on March 27, amidst much cheering, for the Thessalian frontier. The act needed for hostilities to commence was committed when the Greek irregulars crossed into Thessaly and Macedonia (Turkish territory), but Greece was totally unprepared for the war she had provoked. Greece, said the *Fortnightly Review*, "plunged into the campaign without an intelligence department, without maps, without field glasses, without sufficient provisions for signalling, and with the most incompetent body of officers that ever troops had set over them." American and English war correspondents with the Greek Army favored Greece to win, the London *Chronicle* going "hysterically mad about this Greek business."

Crane, arriving in Athens by April 12, was possessed by the same fixed idea that the Greeks were invincible. They were brave and patriotic; the Crown Prince was heralded as a hero and King George of Greece became a legendary mixture of Ulysses and Agamemnon. But the Crown Prince was in fact a military nincompoop.

The war began in Epirus, the southwestern province of Turkey at the time, and ended in Thessaly. In both campaigns the Greeks were defeated mainly because they were gravely mismanaged. The day after Turkey declared war Edhem Pasha on April 18 ordered an advance of the Turks. The same day Crane left Athens to pursue the Greek Army's campaign toward Yannina (Ioannina), the principal town in Epirus. On April 18 the Turks began a three-day bombardment of Arta (south of Yannina), but they failed to take the bridge over the Arta river and retreated. The Greeks advanced. But their position was attacked on April 28 and 29, and although they made a good defense they had to retreat. Their retreat degenerated into panic-stricken flight across the Arta.

"I was with the Greek Army in the campaign toward Yannina," Crane says in his New York *Journal* report filed in Athens on April 29. "The journey from Arta overland to Thessaly requires a longer time than it does to go by way of Athens, and so I have been fortunate enough to arrive in the capital in time to witness another popular outburst of the Athenians." On hearing rumors of the sharp fighting over in Thessaly he had gone south from Arta to Athens and filed on the 22nd his sketch about Crete ("Half a Day in Suda Bay") and on the 29th an article about Greeks who couldn't be curbed. His bias for the Cretans and the Greeks stands in contrast to the point of view expressed by correspondents with the Turkish Army.

Young George Steevens[3]—who reported the war with the Turkish Army—describes the battle of Melouna in Thessaly "as if a battle were a Jubilee procession. Some grey-bearded sons of the Prophet went so far as to put up sunshades. The fighting became Oriental or Balkanic—no attempt to gain ground and break the enemy, but a dogged firing from behind cover till a man dropped." The Greeks had seized a dominating mountain west of Melouna and thus put the Turks in danger of being outflanked and separated from their main force at Elassona (in Thessaly). When the Turks charged with fixed bayonets the Greeks stood their ground, but then they gave way. "They had had enough; the Turks had outstayed them. The battle of Melouna was over. Everybody was dog-tired, famished for sleep. But the Turks had won the gate to Thessaly." At a critical moment for Field Marshal Edhem Pasha's forces, the opposing Greek Army was ordered by the Crown Prince to cease fire and retreat back to their side of the frontier, reported Englishman Bennett Burleigh.

The Greeks had been aroused from sleep to fall to and thought they were going to deliver a surprise attack. But it was just the opposite. Then mad panic seized the marching army. "Cavalry and artillery, to escape from an imaginary danger, charged through their own infantry and galloped towards Larissa. Rifles were fired, blows were struck, men and animals were thrown down, and vehicles were overturned and smashed. The army broke into pieces and became a furious rabble, which fled by road and fields south as hard as most could run. Arms and ammunition and baggage were cast aside wholesale. The Greek officers, as a rule, behaved worse than the men, for they led the fleeing mob, and many of them never stopped until they reached Pharsala or Volo. Shamefaced pretense was made that a stand would be made at Larissa, but no serious attempt was made to stop the fugitives"—they fled twenty-five miles to

Larissa and beyond to Pharsala.[4] The Turks, on finding the Greek Army nonexistent, did not pursue because they feared a trap.

Not that they feared death, these Turks. They exhibited "some of the most sterling qualities of the ideal soldier," says another English reporter. He speculates that the Turks have probably few, if any, superiors as rank-and-file in Europe, and they have a special relish for fighting non-Moslems, unbelievers or Christians, namely the Giaour—to demolish him for the glory of Allah and his Prophet. The Turks do not fear death because, even if worsted in the fray, they "look forward with complacency to Al Jannat, the garden before Paradise, where, among other amenities, the liberal allowance of seventy-two dark-eyed houris awaits and welcomes the arrival of each true believer."[5]

In his April 29 dispatch, Crane stated that Greece was armed to fight for her life. To this dispatch the New York *Journal* attached this soul-stirring headline: "Stephen Crane Says Greeks Cannot Be Curbed." He reported a popular outburst of the Athenians, all excited patriots anxious to get to the front. In his hotel—the Grand Hotel D'Angleterre—there was a scarcity of waiters and porters because they had gone to the front. "Crowds broke into the gun shops yesterday to obtain weapons, and a battalion used for uniforms the stable clothes of a cavalry squadron already gone to the front. In fact, this is not a king's war, not a parliament's war, but a people's war. It is absurd to say that the Greeks undertook this contest because they believed they would take Constantinople in a fortnight. No nation ever had a truer sense of the odds. The Concert of Europe had calmly informed them of possible consequences; there had been a general movement to impress Greece with her danger, but the Greeks said: 'Well, we must fight, anyhow.' "

Crane in his Greco–Turkish War novel remembers the dragomen preserving an ardor for their glorious traditions; and his hero Coleman was almost intoxicated with it, as indeed was Crane. The white dust lifting from the plaza floated across the old-ivory face of the Athens palace, and it was as if in that white dust there were "the souls of the capable soldiers of the past." He wanted to believe in the legendary heroism of the Greeks, but even in his sketch of Crete he had some misgivings because the Cretans had celebrated the terrors of a collision of boats before there was any probability of a collision, and if there were some small crash, their cries were heart-rending. "The twirling of their fingers as they waved their hands tragically over their heads . . . made a sight not to be seen in the West. This action seemed to stand out in their minds as being more likely to carry them safely through the crisis than a sudden and skillful application of the oars."

In this comic-opera war unearned Greek sentiment anticipated again and again the unearned victory. It had its serious moments, however. Nobody has yet invented a war without its solemn moments, but Prince Konstantinos came near to doing just that. The object appeared to be not to destroy the enemy's army. To English reporters with the Turkish Army, such as George W. Steevens, the war looked more like a benevolent conspiracy between two opposing generals plotting to spare innocent blood. The Greeks hurried away as soon as it was necessary to start shooting the Turks in earnest, and then the Turks accommodated the Greeks by holding back for a week as though apprehensive lest they might forget themselves and do irreparable damage to the Greeks.[6]

Cora, who had reached Athens with Mrs. Reudy on the Orient Express from Paris, had been hired by the New York *Journal* as their so-called first and only woman war correspondent.[7] Signing herself "Imogene Carter," she filed her dispatch in Athens on April 26 "War Seen Through a Woman's Eyes." She had seen the Greek volunteers start for the front in Epirus (sometime after mid-April) "amid flowers and tears and seen afterward the tears when the flowers were forgotten." Crane quoted an Athenian amidst his family's farewell to him: "tears and flowers added to a Spartan injunction from my mother." Although his dispatch appeared later than Cora's, the phrasing suggests that Crane wrote or recast "War Seen Through a Woman's Eyes." "I have seen the crowds rave before the palace of the King, appealing to him for permission to sacrifice, as if death was a wine." Here, too, is a Cranesque phrasing ("as if death was a wine"). Cora adds that she has seen the wounded come in "hastily and clumsily bandaged, unwashed and wan, with rolling eyes that expressed that vague desire of the human mind in pain for an impossible meadow wherein rest and sleep and peace come suddenly when one lies in the grass. In Athens this is war—the tears of mothers, the cheers of the throng and later the rolling eyes of the wounded." Cora's iterated "I have seen" bears the signature of Crane in that his dispatches locate the point of view in that irritating "I," for which obsession he was parodied.[8] The telltale phrase "an impossible meadow" could have been written only by Crane. One of his 1895 poems ends: —"gardens / Lying at impossible distances."

An Athenian complained to war correspondent "Imogene Carter" that this kind of American journalism was very strange to Greek minds. " 'Why don't they send a man?' 'They have sent many men,' I reply, 'but now they want to know what a woman thinks of a battle.' The Greeks solemnly shake their heads." But said Cora in the *Journal:* "I do not altogether believe in the point of view of the women of Athens, and, at any rate, I am going"—to the front. Nothing could stop that Amazon. Richard Harding Davis, like the Greek women, did not approve. He wrote his mother from Athens (on April 28) that Stephen Crane had been "searching for me all over Albania and to my satisfaction told me he had been in Crete all this time that I have been in Florence. So that he is not a day ahead of me as we start from here together. . . . He has not seen as much as I have."

"But then when a man can describe battles as well as he can without seeing them why should he care," he adds. (Despite what he told Davis, Crane had not been in Crete all that while.)

Crane's sentimentalized version about the Athenians breaking into gunshops to obtain guns against the Turks, in "Greeks Cannot Be Curbed," stands at odds with the London *Saturday Review*'s claim that crowds of men and their wives and mothers clamored before the Ministries of War and Marine to obtain release of their men from duty at the front. "Hundreds, nay thousands of able-bodied men drawn for service, evaded their military duty. The officers were like the men, men like the officers. Cowardice was a virtue; patriotism, when put to the test of physical danger, a crime. In Constantinople the Greeks showed themselves even worse than in Athens. Thousands changed their nationality rather than run the risk of war, many becoming Turkish subjects in preference to facing Turkish bullets." To English people such cowardice seems impossible; "to Greeks it seems but natural."

Contrary to Crane, the Athenians were plainly not clamoring to be sent to the front. Rather, they attempted to assassinate King George, who had professed that he didn't want war and who had also professed—from the balcony of his palace—that "if war should come, he himself would lead them into Thessaly." But he didn't. A weak man playing the role of king badly, George was carried beyond his depths by the too easily moved Greek people. When on April 21–22 they had stampeded from Mati and then fled on the 23rd to Pharsala, the Athenians protested that their army had been betrayed, and the soldiers believed that they had been deceived by the King at the demands of the Powers and that the Crown Prince Constantine, their commander in chief, had received orders not to give battle but to retreat continually. Richard Harding Davis reported that this feeling "was strong among the people in the towns and cities as it was among the soldiers in the fields, and portraits and photographs of the royal family were defaced and thrown out into the street, and in Athens a mob led by a Deputy marched upon the palace to assassinate the King, after having helped itself to arms and ammunition in the different gunshops."

A certain deputy and editor of an Athenian journal stirred up a demonstration before the palace and called the King a traitor. Crane reports this attempt to assassinate King George in "The Man in the White Hat" (in the London *Westminster Gazette*). Whereas John Bass, who headed Hearst's *Journal* staff in Greece, identifies the rebel deputy by name (Gennadius), Crane simply calls him a man with white hair and a tall hat. "He had the mobile mouth of a poet and the glance of surpassing vanity. He wore a tall hat, grey in scheme, moulded in a curious form. . . . It was the hat of violence. It was the hat of insurrection. It proclaimed terror.

In New York this hat would foreshadow the cessation of the cable-car, the disappearance of the postman, the subterranean concealment of the cook, the supreme elevation of the price of beer—all the horrors of municipal war. No one could wear this terrible and revolutionary hat unless he was a deputy of the Two-Miles-Beyond-the-Extreme-Edge of the Radicals. Where this hat of anarchy and inhumanity appears, there comes change." The wearer of the hat gives an oration to the mob and then goes to the palace door, before which an evzone on guard paces back and forth, and the hero of the minute is met by an old palace servitor.

Crane treats the incident in mock tone, first the grandeur of the hero and then the ridicule of him. "I wish to see the King," says the hero, and the old servitor replies to him tranquilly: "The King does not receive today." "The servitor stood waiting. 'Oh-um!' said the statesman at last. 'Well!'—he went away." The crowd cheered him as he took his seat in a landau. "As he passed through the streets his trooping followers cheered and cheered the victor, and from time to time he modestly lifted in recognition his tall, white hat."[9]

Crane, Davis of the London *Times,* John Bass, heading the *Journal* staff, probably several other correspondents, and Cora left Athens at 9 P.M. on April 29 by steamer for Stylis and arrived there the next evening about 6 P.M. (Another Cora note says: "left Athens 30 April 1897.") They stopped at noon at Chalkis, where the other correspondents left Cora and Crane behind, but the *Journal's* dispatch boat "took us on board, caught up our steamer and were transferred," as Cora's scrambled notes tell us. From Stylis "went ashore sail boat. Got carriage—drove to Lamia which was reached midnight. Bunked on floor, weird hotel. Café. Soldiers. Drove to Domokos. Started 7 A.M. Arrived 5 P.M." (May 1.) Along the way: "Stopped to lunch by spring.

"Shepherds and goatherds driving flocks along route. Entire population of villages fleeing away to the frontier. The coming Turk." Greeks "moving household goods on camels, in carts, some modern Greek and some old Turkish with huge wooden disks for wheels—children piled on top. Constantly meeting volunteers with guns on shoulders and cartridge belts. . . ." Domokos (as Cora spells it) is "situated on top mountain" and is a "grim old tumbled down place—cobbled, narrow streets very Turkish." With some human "figures on top houses" and "guns saved from Larissa—old fortifications top mountain—crowds curious people. Greek officer. Left Domokos about 7 P.M. Drove to Pharsala. More fleeing villagers, flocks etc. in great numbers, some camped along route. Halted by outposts"— Greek sentries of the Pharsala army. She saw a "fallen soldier," and that night she slept on a billiards table in a coffee house and experienced a "miserable morning. Room overlooking plain—curious officers. Mass desertion."[10]

With a peasant girl as maid, Cora slept in a coffee house, "dimly lighted by two oil lamps." Coffee, native cognac, and mastika were available, but the furniture was comprised of an ancient pool table and a few old filthy benches. At first Cora intended to roll up the rugs and sleep on the floor, but it was too dirty. "My maid, who had grumbled constantly at everything and who cried over our dinner of black bread (which is sweet and good) and chicken" flatly refused to sleep there, "and I paid her and sent her to the diligence by which she returned to Lamia. And so I was alone, the only woman in Pharsala or within miles of it." So Cora slept on the pool table, while the coffee-house proprietor, who "seemed to have the general Greek admiration for Americans," stood guard.

Every few moments some soldiers wanting a drink would knock at the door. The old man had secured it by stacking against it a table and a few chairs, but these were several times pushed away by the entering soldiers. "When the knocks came, he would mutter in Greek and shake his fist at the door, then look towards me, and if he caught me peeking out from a corner of my blanket," then the old man "would lay his head on his hand, then pat the rifle—trying to tell me to go to sleep, he would protect me. Toward day I fell asleep. It did not seem but an instant when a loud knocking awakened me to the fact it was daylight. A voice demanded to be admitted, and the scuffling of feet on the stone porch again had caused the landlord to shake his fist and mutter. Finally, someone said 'The Gendarmes command you to open.' "

The place was filled with officers loudly calling for coffee. Cora finally sat up, put on her hat, and climbed on a chair to the floor. "It was embarrassing, but I tried to look as if it was my usual manner of sleeping and awakening. I must have expressed my admiration for the manners of these Greek officers. They also tried to appear unconscious, and when one did look at me it was in a respectful manner. As new officers entered and saw a woman, they would for an instant gaze in astonishment and then pass on."

Cora then went to the Greek headquarters to interview the Prince, but he slept until nine or ten in the morning, and so she had to wait in a deserted house. Prince Constantine would have been unnerved by the energetic American woman correspondent had they met. It wasn't her fault that they never met. She waited in one of the best houses in the village. "It was high on the hills and the view from balcony was superb. The entire plain of Pharsala—where Caesar defeated Pompey in 48 B.C.— lay before me covered with waving grain. On each side of the road, which crossed it towards Velestino, soldiers, troops were camped. They were far out and looked like the tin soldiers children play with. I could see them moving about in long lines and in squads of about fifty, and some on tiny horses. Occasionally a cavalryman with orders perhaps would gallop up the road toward Pharsala, growing larger and larger as he approached.

Infantry soldiers were also constantly coming and going on this road, increasing or diminishing in size as they came and went. On the opposite mountain a flash attracted my attention. It was messages being sent by the mirror system of field telephoning. . . . Just below me to the left was the jail, queerly constructed, with the roof covered with storks' nests. The storks were flying about making queer noises and flapping their wings. The only inhabitants of Pharsala who were not afraid of the coming Turks and did not desert the home nest." Then Cora went on to Volo and was "picked up by carriage." In Volo she "met French officer from *Guadiana*—breakfasted with us in Volo." She was with Stephen Crane, and the French officer breakfasted with them because he had known Crane aboard the *Guadiana*.

Crane in his "Pen Pictures of the Powers' Fleet Off Crete" had expressed his admiration of French seamen on their ships amongst the Powers' fleet and he cleverly compared them with the Russian seamen there off Crete. The French were by far the proudest and most conscious that the eyes of the world were upon them, but "they wanted to do everything with such heaven-born accuracy that they lost their minds at times." They made light fun of it when a launch from the *Guadiana* bumped into a launch from the Russian flagship and scraped "three yards of paint from her side. The Russian seamen looked at the Frenchmen, and the Frenchmen laughed and nodded and chattered and apparently pointed out the incident as a bit of friendly wit. Whereupon the Russians smiled, faintly smiled. Indeed at any time when a Russian boat was near a French one, the Frenchmen smiled with bright friendliness. And the echoing amiability of these men of the Czar was faint, certainly, merely like a shadow passing softly across the face of a stone figure, and to the onlooker there was something grim and strange in it."

Volo, as Cora describes it, was surrounded by "humpy-looking mountains with patches brown, red-brown, yellow, different greens, black rocks and shadows. House, shops—closed." In the seaport: "Greek fleet, one English, one French"—the *Guadiana* on her return from the Black Sea port of Batum (Batumi), stopping now at Volo en route back to Marseilles. Crane at Volo had a toothache that kept him in bed (so he told Richard Harding Davis), but also he had dysentery, and so he missed out on the First Battle of Velestino. "Word has just come the Greeks have killed 2,000 Turks Cavalrymen," Cora wrote in her travel notes, adding, "mouse ill—8 P.M."

At Velestino the Turkish Army had assailed General Smolenski's center on April 30 but had failed to dislodge it. They made three attacks on three different days, with heavy losses on both sides, the Turks being repulsed each time. The Greeks claimed—with some justification—a victory. But they were premature in their enthusiasm. The Crown Prince had made the mistake of sending only a brigade from Pharsala to Velestino. He betrayed his military ignorance by splitting his forces. On May 5 the Greeks were driven from Pharsala and retreated to Domoko. Edhem Pasha did not attack Domoko until the 17th, and the Greek trenches in the center repulsed him. Colonel Smolenski arrived from Velestino on the 18th with directions to hold the pass of Thermopylae, but the Greek Army had abandoned the whole position during the night of May 17. By the 20th an armistice was arranged through the intervention of the Czar of Russia, who sent a personal appeal to the Sultan of Turkey.

Crane witnessed only the Second Battle of Velestino, coming there twelve miles from Volo on May 5. That same day the Greek Army withdrew to Domoko from Pharsala,[11] but they were thereby forced to fall back to the seacoast town of Volo. The train to Volo was shelled, and Cora wrote that shells screamed about her as she went to the station. "I had a narrow escape. The soldiers were amazed at the presence of a woman during the fighting." She had been with Battery No. 2 under actual fire at Velestino. The *Journal* published her account as "Imogene Carter's Pen Picture of the Fighting at Velestino." However, she provides no picture of the battle, as Crane did in "Crane at Velestino."

While he was bedridden in a hotel in Volo, Richard Harding Davis and John Bass on May 3 found a deserted house, climbed into the front window to discover inside a treasure trove of a cake of soap or a tin of coffee—it was the house of the mayor of the village. Davis and Bass tried on his fluted petticoats "and found them very heavy. We could not discover what he did for pockets. All of these things, and the house itself, were burned to ashes, we were told, a few hours after we retreated, and we feel less troubled now at having made such free use of them than we did at the time of our occupation." On the morning of the 4th, they were awakened by the firing of cannon from a hillside over their heads, and they got up to shake hands because they were the only correspondents on the spot. There was to be a battle, and they alone saw the whole thing.[12]

"Crane came up for fifteen minutes and wrote a 1300 word story on that," said Davis in his letter home. "He was never near the front, but don't say I said so. He would have come but he had a toothache which kept him in bed. It was hard luck but on the other hand if he had not had that woman with him he would have been with us and not at Volo and could have seen the show toothache or no toothache." Davis, rather spitefully, was much pleased that he had beaten Crane; for his part, Crane admitted in his dispatch that in the first two days' combat "some other correspondents saw more than I did." "I was rather laid up and had hurried on from Pharsala when I learned of the strong attacks on Velestino. I knew the taking of Velestino practically uncovered the base of supplies of the army at Volo, and so came immediately"—from Volo, not from Pharsala. "I arrived at noon of the second day. I had been in skirmishes and small fights, but this was the first big battle"—the first he had ever seen. He remained with the Greek forces that night, and then "in the gray early morning the musketry fire was resumed."

At Velestino John Bass directed the firing of the Greek soldiers from the shelter of a trench, and Davis took a photograph of Bass there. Of Crane, Davis wrote in an 1898 letter: "I don't like him myself." Although Crane never said so flatly, he disliked Davis, who later wrote home: "There is nothing to be said about what Crane did on the battlefield of Velestino."

Bass was more generous and found something interesting to say in "How Novelist Crane Acts on the Battlefield" (*Journal:* May 23, 1897): "Your correspondent sought shelter in a trench and cautiously watched the pale, thin face of the novelist as the latter seated himself on an ammunition box amid the shower of shells and casually lighted a cigarette. Stephen Crane did not appear surprised, but watched with a quiet expression the quick work of the artillerymen as they loaded, fired, and jumped to replace the small cannon overturned by the recoil. I was curious to know what was passing in his mind, and said: 'Crane, what impresses you most in this affair?' The author of *The Red Badge of Courage* lighted another cigarette, pushed back his long hair out of his eyes with his hat and answered quietly: 'Between two great armies battling each other the interesting thing is the mental attitude of the men. The Greeks I can see and understand, but the Turks seem unreal. They are shadows on the plain— vague figures in black, indications of a mysterious force.' " By then the Greek Army was in full retreat. "As the last mountain gun was loaded on the mules Stephen Crane quietly walked down the hill. The Turkish artillery had drawn nearer, and amid the singing bullets and smashing shells the novelist stopped, picked up a fat waddling puppy and immediately christened it VELESTINO, the *Journal* dog." Ignoring the fact that Bass witnessed Crane's finding that puppy and that Crane described it in his "Dogs of War" *Journal* sketch, Cora wrote on a photograph of the dog that she had picked him up at Velestino, competitive even in this little incident.

Bass' *Journal* report of Crane's indifference to Turkish bullets was filed at Athens on May 21, but somehow got scooped by the *Tribune* for May 20: "Stephen Crane when last seen was calmly rolling a cigarette, a splendid symbolistic phrase on his tongue. He was standing amid an 'avalanche of thunder.' The downward rush of this vast mass of noise did not overwhelm him, but he was observed to pick up a few chunks and put them in his pocket for future use. He complains that he cannot understand the Turks. . . . A little thing like that ought not to stand in the way. Mr. Crane and the Turks should be introduced to each other, as the acquaintance would be of mutual advantage."

Richard Harding Davis wrote home that Crane "ought to be ashamed of himself," but at Velestino Stephen had nothing to be ashamed of, for Davis had missed out on this or that battle, as had Bass, and not Crane alone. Although booked by Hearst as a star reporter, he wasn't as competent as John Bass and Julian Ralph, and he was plagued by illness and bad luck. He nevertheless wrote several masterpieces of journalism on the conflict. Davis sums up the war in comparing the opposing armies to two football teams lined up for a scrimmage, a point of comparison which Crane had long ago made when he said that he learned about warfare on the football field. When the war began, says Davis, "the Greeks had possession of the ball, and they rushed it into Turkish territory, where they lost it almost immediately on a fumble, and after that the Turks drove them rapidly down the field, going around their ends and breaking through their centre very much as they pleased." The Turks fought for the glory of Allah, says Davis, and the Greek—although he fought to extend the frontiers of Greece—was at his noblest when defending his homeland.

The town of Velestino had "a great number of fine trees, which in Greece is very unusual. Many of the houses were quite buried in foliage, and it was impossible to see the Turks toward Larissa owing to the many strips of forest on the plain," says Crane in "A Fragment of Velestino" (from "With Greek and Turk"). "It was a deserted village. One walked the streets wondering of the life that had been, and if it would ever return. It is a human thing to think of a community that has been, and here was one with all its important loves, hates, friendships; all its games, spites, its wonderful complexity of relation and intercourse, suddenly smitten by the sledge of chance and rendered nothing—nothing but a few vacant staring houses. The spectator notes then that some villager had carefully repaired his front gate, and the chance-comer's sense of the futility of repairing that front gate causes him to know more of life for a moment than he had known before."

Cora wrote in her Notes: "rode to Velestino—warned to turn back, but kept on. Went on mountain, Battery No. 2—under actual fire. Shells over head." This matches what Crane described in "A Fragment of Velestino." "There was a battery of howitzers on a hill above the mosque and the bullet-swept square." The Captain of the battery addressed his men. "His chest was well out, and his manner was gorgeous. If one could have judged by the tone, it was one of the finest speeches of the age. It was Demosthenes returned and in command of a battery of howitzers. There was in it a quality of the best kind of sentiment. One waited for the answering cheers of the men. The poor devils of men are always obliged to give answering cheers to the patriotic orations on the field. But what was the Captain saying? He was merely ordering the gunners to elevate their pieces for a range of sixteen hundred meters."

Crane had fashioned in his *Red Badge* the very same kind of bathos— the collapse of grandiose illusions—that now he witnessed on the battlefield of Velestino. What happened there reads like *The Red Badge*. The Captain of the battery "sent a man to the rear for another pair of field glasses. His first pair had suffered a rifle-ball wound. The man misunderstood the order, and he came with a bottle of wine. . . . There was a look of pious satisfaction on his face at having concluded his errand with wisdom and celerity. Suddenly the Captain reached for his field-glasses and got instead a bottle of wine." Again the puncture of the serious by the trivial.

"Astonishment and incredulity mingled on his face. He looked sternly at the soldier and harangued him on the necessity of not being an idiot during the battle. His gestures were wild and rapid. Nevertheless he did not relinquish his fast grip on the bottle of wine. Presently he went along the lines giving an order, and sometimes he absent-mindedly waved the bottle towards the Turks. He looked down at last and saw that he still grasped the bottle. He went then and gave it into the care of the trusty corporal who commanded the horse and mule squad below the hill. When the actors are under fire, small dramas of this kind may be interesting to the spectator."

Velestino will surely be famous as one of the greatest battles of this war, said Crane in "Stephen Crane at Velestino" (*Journal*: May 11)[13] "The Greek reverse began at Larissa, and the world expected a quick conclusion, but Velestino proved that the Greek soldiers could, when well led, successfully cope with the overwhelming numbers of Turks. It proved them good fighters and long fighters and stayers. . . . To be sure, the army retreated from Velestino, but it was not the fault of this army. The Commander bit his fingers and cursed when the order came to retreat. He was at that time perfectly confident of success." General Smolenski, the Macedonian who had achieved fame early in this thirty days' war by his defense of Ravenni, knew that to retreat from Velestino meant the sacrifice of Volo.[14] "The troops were jubilant, their commander confident"—because he had defeated the Turks in the First Battle of Velestino, which was the only defeat the Turks suffered in the entire war.

The Greeks had whipped this vastly superior number of Turks in three days, and they wanted to do it again, but then the Crown Prince ordered the retreat, an extraordinary order at which Smolenski wept. Crane and Cora joined the retreat, a shell just missing her head. They caught the last train to Volo, while a regiment of kilted evzones covered the army's retreat. The engineer talked to Crane in wild Greek. "He was a daisy."

Volo in peacetime was the summer resort for wealthy Greeks. "The houses are gay with awnings and the situation high on the mountain side overlooking the harbor is charming. Every available ship in the harbor was employed to transport fugitives—except one, which above all others should have been employed in the work. This was the English Red Cross ship, and its non-employment was due to a particular and splendid ass, the surgeon in charge. He had some rules—God knows what they were— and he was the kind of fool to whom a rule is a holy thing."

Just as the advance guard of the Turks reached the hilltops of Volo, Stephen and Cora managed to get aboard a ship packed with women and children "in heaps on the decks. They have no food, and they will be landed where they can." It was a miserable voyage. He went ashore at the small fishing village of Oreci (Areos, as Crane names it) "with a great crowd. . . . This town consists of six houses already crowded. The refugees came ashore carrying their household goods. They camped on the fields by great bonfires. These peasant women are patient, suffering in curious silence, while the babies wail on all sides. This is war—but it is another picture from what we got at the front. The Greek naval officers, with their eyes full of tears, swore to me the Turks would pay for all this misery. But the Turks probably will not; nobody pays for these things in war."

The ship rounded the northwest peninsula of Euboea sailing for Chalkis through the narrow Gulf of Euboea, and here he had the luck to find the puppy "Velestino" which he'd lost in crowded Volo. Your correspondent, Crane wrote in "The Dogs of War," was in a restaurant "when he observed a peasant come in and walk toward the rear of the place. This man had a pup inside his shirt, and the woolly head projected. The correspondent said to his dragoman: 'That is my dog.' The dragoman laughed. 'There are a million dogs like that in Greece, sir.'" Crane and his dragoman pursued the peasant into the courtyard to reclaim the pup, which the peasant said he got in Volo. Well, said Crane, I got him in Velestino, and he belongs to the New York *Journal*. Crane bought him back for two drachmas, and on his way to Athens "Velestino" received constant ovations. "He was such a wee thing that the correspondent was not sure whether he was going to grow to be a cow or a caterpillar, but the kilted mountaineers that studied him said he was of the famous shepherd dog breed of the Greeks and was destined to be a big dog." Crane lunched at Thebes, getting there by carriage across a drawbridge over the narrow Strait of Euripos. The boys of the village congregated around the puppy, who became "easily the most famous dog in Greece. In Athens itself he was put up at the best hotel, and the honors he received befitted his social position. . . . He has a personal attendant engaged at a fabulous salary. He is well-known here already, and his appearance on the street causes popular demonstration. But he don't care." The *Journal*'s dog got to England at Crane's expense, and when the dog died, Stephen buried "Velestino" in the garden at Ravensbrook with the dog collar which Sylvester Scovel of the *World* had bought for him in Athens.

Meanwhile the Greek Army had reached Halmyro en route to Domoko. Crane's "Blue Badge of Cowardice," which was filed in Athens on May

11 by courier from Chalkis, told the *Journal* readers that the army was more afraid of an order from Prince Constantine to retreat once more than it was afraid of the Turks. "While I write, the glad news has come that the Crown Prince will not retreat further while the army lives. Everybody believes it. If it is true, the big ridge back of Domoko will be drenched with blood." Domoko was by nature a stronghold. Steevens thought that no firmer stronghold than Domoko could be found in the whole world and that it was a bungle for Edhem Pasha to attack it; for the Furka Pass is nearly 3,000 feet high and hills commanded the roads by which the Turks advanced. "It was one more attempt to surround the Greek Army—to destroy or capture it. And once more the attempt failed."

The Turks lost the Greek Army because Prince Constantine ordered Domoko and the Furka Pass abandoned: he was retreating to Thermopylae. So the Army fell back from Halmyro to Lamia. Crane with the Greek Army in Domoko interviewed a member of the Foreign Legion, who was filling his canteen at a spring and saying: "The deuce! It is a great bore— all these retreats." "Whom do you blame?" Crane asked, and the soldier said: "I am inclined to think it is the Crown Prince." "Is he not a good soldier?" said Crane, to which the soldier replied: "The Prince, he is a duffer."[15] (What he actually said was probably unprintable.)

At Lamia, Crane interviewed a kilted mountaineer with "a small rakishly piratical scarlet fez. He sat alone because, in the first place, he was a man of the hills, and, in the second place, the other soldiers in the place were town-bred, and knew him as we know a 'hay-seed.' And, in the third place, he sat alone because he considered the evzone had done the best fighting." The Greek Army was at its best always in defensive actions, and the best of the Greek Army was comprised of evzones—they always saved the situation by defensive rear-guard engagements, aided by soldiers of the Foreign Legion. At Stylis there were clouds of dust on the road "over which Smolenski's division is retreating toward Thermopylae. The movement completely uncovers this place, and the Turks are advancing from Halmyro."

Crane had sailed north from Athens to report on the evacuation of the wounded, the New York *Journal* steamer taking him to St. Marina to land some hospital stores there. He commandeered a schooner to get to Stylis to retrieve some bread left there by the commissary department of General Smolenski's division. The Captain of the schooner refused to go, and so Crane and seven bluejackets stormed the schooner, took it by assault, and "towed the protesting schooner back to Stylis, with the Captain on the bow gesticulating violently throughout the voyage. Incidentally we never found the bread." What towed the schooner was the *Journal*'s boat, which steamed back to St. Marina to take aboard some wounded men and Red Cross nurses of the hospital there. Then on to Chalkis.

On May 18, Crane was aboard the boat *St. Marina,* which left Chalkis to return to Athens with the soldiers wounded at Domoko and with the women and children and household goods. On the *St. Marina* were eight hundred bleeding soldiers and some dead "jammed together in an insufferably hot hole"; and the light in that ship's hold was so faint that "we cannot distinguish the living from the dead. Near the hatch where I can see them is a man shot through the mouth. The bullet passed through both cheeks." Wounded at the battle of Domoko on May 17, he was now asleep with "his head pillowed on the bosom of a dead comrade," wrote Crane in "War's Horrors and Turkey's Bold Plan."[16]

"Still backward fall the Greek soldiers. First it was Velestino, then Domoko, next it will be Thermopylae," he says in the dispatch he sent from Lamia (*Journal,* May 22): "Greeks Waiting at Thermopylae." The armistice had been signed on May 20, and Crane hoped it would last long enough "to give the Greek infantry some rest. They need it. Plans for truces are nice things, but I really don't know that they are always possible of fulfillment. There is a strong possibility that the next fight will be begun by Turkish irregulars. These men from the wild mountains of Albania are in the war business exclusively. They don't know an armistice from a pie or a truce from a trilobite, and the shooting will surely go on with them in the game."

The Greek Army's advance to a new position at historic Thermopylae was protected at Lamia by the Greek evzones. "They were always last when the Greek army retreats and first when it advances. Here they are in their old position, the rest of the Greek Army miles away, and the Turks so near that their advance is plainly visible from the top of the old Acropolis, about four miles away. As they come closer I recognize them as Circassian cavalry. There are the elements of a first-class scrap right here in the range of my field-glasses."

He reports what the Greek Army at Lamia told him about Thermopylae, that the new position there is very strong. "Although the pass has been widened and much changed since Leonida's fight, it is still an ideal place to hold an enemy in check and here, if the war goes according to the rules of the game and the supreme authority lets the Greek army do what is in it to do, the advance of the Turks be damned. I would like to write a dispatch telling of a full blown Greek victory for a change." But the Greek Army never gave him the opportunity.

Although Crane missed out at Thermopylae, Steevens with the Turkish Army there watched "the black columns of the Greek main body heading across the plain for the snow-crested wall of Oeta opposite us; we could see the broad miles of sea-lapped flat which they absurdly call the Pass of Thermopylae. The Greeks' rear-guard was on the last slope—the Ghegas [Albanians] were driving it down; the one mountain battery had come forward and was shelling it merrily; the cavalry was just behind us on the winding road; it was only two o'clock." At last, says Steevens, "we could get at the Greeks retreating along the level, with four hours of good daylight to cut them up in. And then, of course, up came the white flag"— the flag of truce from Lamia on May 20. "The guns sank into sulky silence. With difficulty they silenced even the Ghegas. . . . And that was the end of the Turko-Grecian war."

The whole thirty days' war consisted of a series of retreats and rearguard or defense actions: at Pharsala, at Velestino, at Domoko; and at the start of the war the retreat of the arrogant Greeks in Epirus after provoking hostilities by crossing into Turkish territory. Crane saw the landscape at Velestino as religious in "Stephen Crane at Velestino." "A tall lean shepherd was necessary to it. Furthermore, the rocks were gray, save when a reddish tinge of lurking ores appeared on their rough surfaces." A column of infantry had its prayers interrupted while marching to support troops on a hill. Here was a stone shrine with "a little holy picture of a saint, a little chromo in red and green, with a frame of gilt paper. Under this picture was a little lamp, wherein oil was sometimes burned. It was the common wayside shrine of the Greek church." The column of infantry cross themselves and pray before it. They are three hundred yards from the firing-line, and then suddenly a great hooting shell struck the shrine and lifted the structure into the air. "Then men in the rear of the column, finding no shrine, prayed quietly facing its ruins."

The correspondents debated about what the sound of bullets was like. "The roll of musketry-fire was tremendous. In the distance it sounded like the tearing of cloth," says Crane. Richard Harding Davis described the sound of bullets as humming-birds or rustling silk. Crane says that the nearer it came it sounded like rain on a resonant roof, and close by the musketry-fire was just long crash after crash. It "was a beautiful sound; beautiful as had never been dreamed. It was more impressive than the roar of Niagara and finer than thunder or an avalanche, because it had the wonder of human tragedy in it. It was the most beautiful sound of my experience, barring no symphony. The crash of it was ideal.

"This is from one point of view. The other might be taken from the men who died there. The slaughter of Turks was great, the fire of the Greeks fierce, the Turkish soldiers while charging often shielded their eyes with their hands. The Turks made eight charges this day and were repulsed each time. Desperate Turkish cavalry even attacked a steep rocky hill. The insane and almost wicked squadrons were practically annihilated, and their scattered fragments slid slowly back, leaving the plain black with wounded and dead men and horses. From a distance it was like a game. No blood, no expressions of horror were to be seen; there were simply the movements of tiny doll tragedy." A lieutenant standing up with his back to the trench was rolling a cigarette, "his lips wide apart, and in a careless attitude," when he was shot through the neck. "His servant came from the trench, kneeled over the body, regardless of the battle, and wept. Men had to drag him in by the legs."

"Stephen Crane at Velestino" says that he "learned to curse the German officers who directed the fire of the Turkish batteries." He was so biased for the Greeks that he seems to have thought the Turks could not possibly have won had they not been led by German officers. "I think they are a normal outgrowth of German civilization, which teaches that a man should be first of all a soldier. As a consequence, he ultimately becomes simply a soldier, and not a man at all. I consider these German officers hired assassins. One has strong feelings under the circumstances." He was repeating what the Greeks wanted him to report, but in fact the legendary Germans managing the Turks did not exist. How many German officers were there really with the Turks? friends asked George Steevens when he returned to London. "And I answered confidently: Not one," he said.

Crane went to Greece to see if his *Red Badge* "is not all right," and he found warfare there as he had imagined it. The irony was that as Henry Fleming dreamed of heroic deeds, Greeklike struggles in grandiose Homeric style, and "despaired of witnessing a Greeklike struggle," so too did Crane. He and the Greek soldiers had entertained—like Henry Fleming —"impossible pictures." And Fleming had been quite right: "Greeklike struggles would be no more." George Steevens, whom the flamboyant H. L. Mencken thought "the greatest newspaper reporter who ever lived," claimed that the Greek Army fought well the first day of the war at Melouna Pass but "never once afterwards." This ignores, however, the success of the Greeks in the first battle of Velestino.

Steevens was a member of London's National Liberal Club and had perhaps met Crane there through Harold Frederic, but now they were reporting the war from opposite points of view. Steevens with the conquering Turks said that he had seen more rioting at a supper bar in the National Liberal Club than he saw during the Turkish Army's occupation of Larissa.[17]

Crane finally realized how impossible it had been for the Greeks to win: "I never was within two miles of the fighting line," he told Edwin Pugh. "But I was mostly two miles closer to the Turks than the Greek army was. Bekase they ran like rabbits." His witty remark ignores the fact that he was in the trenches at Velestino. He characteristically either belittled himself or—just the opposite—he boasted. He shared nothing in common with the Greeks, whom he erroneously idealized, for the Greek with restless deference was one who seemed too obviously anxious to please and conciliate, whereas the Turk—always polite and self-contained—held himself one's equal if not one's superior.

In Crane's Greco–Turkish War story "Death and the Child" an Italian correspondent named Peza gets to the battlefield of Velestino from the white town of Volo. The men in the trenches view him with the curiosity of café gossipers, and Peza feels ridiculous and aghast that these soldiers can turn their faces from the ominous trenches to gossip about him, about his clothes and his business there on their battlefield. They gossip with the hum of a tea party. All this contradicts his theory of war. "He thought that if he was killed there at that time, it would be as romantic to the old standards as death by a bit of falling iron in a factory."

Peza—like Henry Fleming in *The Red Badge*—discovers that his theory of war gets exploded by the realities, and like Fleming, he flees from the battlefield. Some say he's a coward. One bearded Greek soldier, fat and greasy, munching hard bread and sitting "like an idol made of tallow," scoffs at the runaway Peza. But other soldiers do not bawl out curses at him because they sense that he's been wounded in the neck. Here again—as in his fiction so in his newspaper sketches—Crane presents two points of view.

A child, deserted by his parents (or perhaps they've been killed), weeps beside his flocks and dogs on the mountainous battlefield. "If the men struggling on the plain had had time, and greater vision, they could have seen this strange, tiny figure seated on a boulder, surveying them while the tears streamed. It was as simple as some powerful symbol." In contrast to the weeping child is Peza, who lies there on the crest of the hill, breathing "as if life was about to leave his body" and rolling "his eye glassily at the child." Peza does not answer the child's question: "Are you a man?" He has noticed when he first approached the battery of mountain guns that the Greek soldiers accepted "the conditions of war as easily as an old sailor accepts the chair behind the counter of a tobacco shop. Or it was merely that the farm boy had gone to sea, and he had adjusted himself to the circumstances immediately, and with only the usual first misadventures in conduct. Peza was proud and ashamed that he was not one of them—these stupid peasants." But in death he is at one with them, and the peasant child will no doubt repeat Peza's fate in one war or another.

In the story the child is deserted and Peza dies. "Peza gasped in the manner of a fish. Palsied, windless, and abject, he confronted the primitive courage, the sovereign child, the brother of the mountains, the sky, and the sea, and he knew that the definition of his misery could be written on a wee grass blade." Crane says it is the peasants who, "throughout the world hold potentates on their thrones, make statemen illustrious, provide generals with lasting victories, all with ignorance, indifference, or half-witted hatred, moving the world with the strength of their arms, and getting their heads knocked together in the name of God, the king, or the stock-exchange—immortal, dreaming, hopeless asses who surrender their reason to the care of a shining puppet, and persuade some toy to carry their lives in his purse."

H. G. Wells in 1900 detected in "Death and the Child" a new ingredient that was absent from Crane's earlier stories. "The new ingredient is the encroachment of journalism on Crane's later fiction, an underlining of the intended meaning: there is just that touch of insistence that prevails so painfully at times in Victor Hugo's work, as of a writer not sure of his reader, not happy in his reader, and seeking to drive his implication (of which also he is not quite sure) home."[18]

In Crane's novel of the war, *Active Service,* the hero—Rufus Coleman —is a correspondent sent by the New York "Eclipse" to rescue a group of Americans trapped in Turkey. The Americans are Professor and Mrs. Wainwright, his students, and the Wainwright daughter Marjory, who has jilted Coleman back in New York City because her father disliked him. Professor Wainwright has taken his daughter to Europe in order to break up that romance, and now here is Coleman as hero rescuing them when they get lost in Turkey—in Epirus. They are north of the Arta River near Yannina, and then the Turks drive the Greek Army across the Arta.

By collating the events given as fiction with the historical facts of the Greek Army's campaign in Epirus, it becomes obvious that *Active Service* is a faithful record of Crane's experience there. He was with the Greek Army near Yannina when the Turkish Army put its enemy to flight across the Arta on April 18 (or a day or so later). He observed that the Greeks wore heavy overcoats even in the heat of mid-day because the dews became very destructive to the lungs—an item which interested him because of his own lung trouble. At Athens—which he quit on April 18—the American minister warned him about trying to get to Epirus. The American minister was Eben Alexander, who invited the dying Crane in 1900 to come back to America and live in his house in North Carolina because the air there would improve his lungs. Crane dedicated *Active Service* (1899) to Eben Alexander for kindness rendered him in Athens.

In the novel the American minister tells Coleman that he cannot get to Nikopolis because the Turkish and Greek armies "are looking at each other from the sides of the river at Arta"—the river is the frontier; Nikopolis is on the wrong side. "You can't reach them." But Coleman would not be a hero if he did not reach the stranded party, and reach them he does; he gets there by the same route Crane himself took from Athens, by train to Patras, where the opposing armies engage in an artillery duel while the Greek fleet bombards Prevesa.

The situation Crane imagined in his *Red Badge of Courage*—two armies opposing each other across a river—is identical with the situation he later witnessed and reported on in his Greco-Turkish War novel. He took the title *Active Service* from Tolstoy's *War and Peace.* Zherkof answers an officer's question as to how he came there: "Active service, gentlemen." His colleagues mock him: "Active service! active service! give him a bottle, for bringing such news!—but how come you here?" That is the same question Professor Wainwright in Crane's *Active Service* presumably asks Coleman, and vice versa. How come you here? A voice hails Professor Wainwright in the darkness: "Halt! Who's there?" The professor from Washurst College, whose Greek does him no good in Greece, asks, "Do you speak English?" And thus Coleman knows that he has found the Wainwright party.

Located in a war that was called a comic opera the novel is itself a comic opera with the usual triangle plot of present-day soap operas. Coleman "was on active service, an active service of the heart, and he felt that he was a strong man ready to conquer difficulty even as heroes of old conquered difficulty. He imagined himself in a way like them; he too had come out to fight for love with giants, dragons, and witches." He rescues Marjory, a Smith College student of Greek who is an emotional dud not worth rescuing. The romantic Coleman, however, envisions his lady-love as might a young knight in medieval poetry and takes his rescue-journey to be a sentimental and shining affair. As Marjory has jilted Coleman, so Coleman has jilted his old flame Nora Black, who is now at the battlefront as woman war correspondent for the New York "Daylight." Nora Black of the *Daylight* competes with Coleman of the *Eclipse,* and she is "eclipsed" as reporter just as Cora Crane was eclipsed by Stephen when he wrote or recast her New York *Journal* sketches.[19] It is no compliment to Cora that he calls her Nora Black. As Nora is a variant on the French *noir,* Nora Black is doubly black. This is Crane's jest at Cora. The name Rufus Coleman he probably knew from the name of a Civil War drummer boy at Manassas.

Nora surprises the Wainwright party on the road south to Arta, and Coleman's eyes bulge at the sight of that audacious woman sitting on a fat and glossy horse and dressed "in probably one of the most correct riding-habits which had ever been seen in the East." He explains to Nora that the *Eclipse* has sent him to Greece to rescue the Wainwrights. "But why are you here?" he asks her. " 'I am here,' she said, giving him the most defiant of glances, 'principally to look for you! . . . Coleman looked at her with a steely eye. 'Nora, you can certainly be a devil when you choose.' 'Why can't you present me to your friends? Miss Nora Black, special correspondent of the *New York Daylight,* if you please. I belong to your opposition. I am your rival, Rufus, and I draw a bigger salary— see?' " Coleman's "bloom of innocence" sets him apart from Crane but links him with Richard Harding Davis, who was virtuous and dignified. Davis wouldn't think of carting "a notorious woman about the world with him," and he snorted at Crane for doing so. But like Coleman, Ivy League Davis would settle for a naive sorority sister like Marjory Wainwright, and in fact in late life he finally married a woman of that kind. Here is Cora Taylor as Nora: "She raised her finely-pencilled eyebrows and looked at him with the baby stare." Or again, when insulted by Coleman, she asks: "Do you mean that I am not a respectable woman?"

Mrs. Wainwright is shocked on learning that this woman is Nora Black the actress, queen of comic opera, and much later she confides to her husband that Nora is a hussy. "Her conversation in the carriage on the way down to Agrinium sickened me. . . . The vicious thing!" Coleman calls Nora "the tigress" who cajoles him with "velvet purrings." Like Cora, she has azure eyes, sometimes seemingly purple or even black—"a pair of eyes that had made many an honest man's heart jump if he thought they were looking at him."

The curious thing about Nora's balconied room, where Coleman has dinner with her over champagne, is that it has once been part of a harem, which for Nora—or Cora—is appropriate. "Seems curious, doesn't it? A harem. Fancy that." She knew that she was conquering him, but she flirts without betraying any elation. "With the most exquisite art she aided his contemplation, baring, for instance, the glories of a statuesque neck, doing it all with the manner of a splendid and fabulous virgin who knew not that there was such a thing as shame." And how naughty of her to wear stockings of black silk. Rufus Coleman was tempted to go to the devil with Nora Black and thought that "to go to the devil with this girl was not a bad fate—not a bad fate." Crane thought the same. To someone critical of Cora he wrote: "For some funny woman's reason, she likes me. Mind this."

"I attack anew my infamous business of making a novel finished before March 30," Crane wrote Mrs. Moreton Frewen in 1899. He ended it with a love scene to round out his potboiler, a ridiculous love scene echoing a comic opera. Rufus Coleman and Marjory Wainwright announce their enagement and then leave Athens by carriage to visit the seashore—with Marjory's parents! The lovers, while the Wainwrights hover nearby, recline in a cove, "in which sea-maids once had played no doubt," and he looks up at her as she looks not at him but at the sea. Here Crane injects a Conradian note on the Mystery of Womanhood: "She was staring at the sea with woman's mystic gaze, a gaze which men at once reverence and fear, since it seems to look into the deep simple heart of nature, and men begin to feel that their petty wisdoms are futile to control these strange spirits, as wayward as nature and as pure as nature, wild as the play of waves, sometimes as unalterable as the mountain amid the winds; and to measure them, man must perforce use a mathematical formula." It is doubtful if Marjory can be measured by any formula, for there is nothing in her to measure. Nor is she "wild as the play of waves"—the wildest thing she does is to play her fingers "in his hair near the forehead." Even then "with woman's mystic gaze" she is staring out to sea. And the wildest thing he does is to wonder whether he dare "lay his head softly against her knee." No, he dare not (Professor and Mrs. Wainwright might be peeking round the bend of the lovers' seacove). Coleman "looked up suddenly, lifting his arms. He breathed out a cry which was laden with a kind of diffident ferocity." And with this diffident ferocity the novel ends: "I haven't kissed you yet."

Crane admitted the failure of this novel in saying that "a reporter is no hero for a novel." The only nonwooden character making any impact is Nora Black, and that is because she is drawn after the eccentric and energetic Cora.[20] That Crane had a good time writing *Active Service* is apparent to anyone who reads it as autobiography; only then does it come to life. Beer says that some of Crane's friends "were indignant for the contemptuous portrait of a newspaperman," and those friends included readers of *Active Service* who recognized Rufus Coleman as a portrait of Richard Harding Davis. As Davis had snubbed Cora Taylor in London when she and Stephen were about to leave for Greece, so in the novel Coleman jilts Nora by quitting her in London without saying goodbye. A reviewer of Davis' *A Derelict* (1901) detected a resemblance between Crane and the reporter Channing in the novel. Davis denied there was any connection, but Channing talks in Crane's style, whimsical, witty, sardonic. When Davis recited a portion of his novel to test the character before an actor, he described himself playing it "as a sort of drunken Stephen Crane."[21]

*Active Service* is not Crane at his worst, but it is Crane downhill. He apologized for it in writing Moreton Frewen, owner of the ancient manor house where he completed the novel which Harold Frederic had urged him to write. "I fear that in later years people who wish the house well will be saying that Stephen Crane did not write *Active Service* in the room over the porch at Brede Place."

In March, 1899, when he had written 48,000 words of *Active Service,* he said: "I wish it were a better novel." And Cora probably wished it were a different thing altogether. The London *Academy* thought it a little below Crane's best. "It is mannered, and the mannerisms of a writer with methods so audacious and novel as Mr. Crane's are apt to irritate. But it quite deserves to be called a remarkable book." However, the prose is as starched as an 1890 collar-and-cuff, while structurally the novel is limp. The only remarkable thing about *Active Service* is that the author of *The Red Badge of Courage* wrote it.

# XVII

## ⊊ *Ravensbrook*

STEPHEN and Cora were in Athens for at least three days after the May 19 armistice, and then Cora and Mrs. Ruedy took train to Venice to meet him later in Paris; Stephen, suffering from dysentery, remained in Athens. He took a stroll with Julian Ralph of the New York *Journal,* who was surprised to find that Crane knew nothing about Greek architecture and could not distinguish one type of column from another on the Acropolis. He had no curiosity about historical treasures.

He argued with the older and more knowledgeable Ralph about Henry James' *Portrait of a Lady,* which he thought a masterpiece, and read Tolstoy's *Anna Karenina,* which seemed to him too long because Tolstoy had to stop and preach but "it's a bully book." He wrote Cora[1] and she responded that his letter was "plain and sincere; therefore beautiful and it fills my soul with perfect delight. It contents me to think that for the present you love me, and for me the morning of hope is born." Of all the sweet letters he had written her, none was so sweet as the one she had just received, "and that is why I am light-hearted tonight. My heart swells with gratitude and love, and peace and charity for the world, and is as clean and pure of all doubt, hate, envy . . . as the heart of the penitent when he leaves the confessional."

In an undated note, probably written when she was still in Jacksonville before going to Greece, she had said: "A month will pass by without our touching hands. . . . Ah, but how little, in some respects, do you understand the heart of a woman such as I am! The trouble is, you have met so many and formed your opinion from their standard, and measure me accordingly."

Crane took ship to Marseilles and a train to Paris, bringing with him the Ptolemy twin brothers from Greece and the dog Velestino. In England, he and Cora must have smuggled the dog somehow through Customs. As for the Greeks, Stephen had overreached his pocketbook; only one of them, Adoni Ptolemy, was kept to serve the Cranes at Ravensbrook.

"Mr. Stephen Crane was seen on the Strand yesterday afternoon," said

Arthur Waugh in the London *Critic* for June 26, 1897, and Mr. Richard
Harding Davis was also in London. "Of Mr. Crane's next move there is
no certainty, but he will probably 'conclude' as you say, that nothing pays
him like fiction. The unanimity of his reviewers, indeed, must sometimes
suggest to him that he merits the envy of the gods. In England nothing
succeeds like success. Mr. Crane, one would think, would be the first to
confess that his last little book, *The Third Violet,* is an absolutely unpretentious piece of work, thrown off as a parergon, and yet his critics
have been proclaiming it these three weeks as a masterpiece. There must
be something rather disconcerting about this bellwether school of eulogy,
and one wishes Mr. Richard Harding Davis better luck." Davis' new book
—*Soldiers of Fortune*—was one of the most widely discussed of the
season, and he had been retained by the *Times* to report the Jubilee
celebration, said the *Critic.*

What could be more pleasant than to arrive in London with your book
being talked about in all the English reviews? Some copies of *The Third
Violet,* bound in buckram and selling for six shillings, were displayed
in the windows of the publisher, William Heinemann. The London *Academy* proclaimed that the impression of the author as a genius was confirmed; for psychological insight, dramatic intensity, and potency of phrase
he was already in the front rank of English and American writers of fiction.
He possessed "a certain separate quality which places him apart. It is a
short story and slender; but taking it in conjunction with what he has
previously given us, there remains, in our judgment, no room for doubt."
The London *Athenaeum* thought *The Third Violet* made Crane more the
rival of Henry James than of Kipling; he was intensely American, the
*Athenaeum* said. That the English learned a good deal about America
from the book may explain why the critics liked *The Third Violet.* The
*Athenaeum* complained that its American slang was unintelligible to
readers of the King's English: "snickered" for "sniggered," and "so long"
as a goodbye were intelligible only among certain classes. How horrible
of Mr. Crane to phrase it "mucilaged to their seats" instead of glued.

Most American reviewers, said the *Literary Digest,* dismissed *The Third
Violet* in decidedly contemptuous fashion. It was lightly praised in Scotland and England, the London *Literary World* calling it a pleasing and
passable story. The *Spectator* for May 29 singled out the dog of artist
Hawker as "one of the most delightful animals we have encountered in
recent fiction." That must have pleased Crane when he read it in Heinemann's office files. The dog Stanley is sketched from his brother Edmund's
setter Chester.[2] The *Lady's Pictorial* said the dog was the only interesting
character in the book, while the American *Critic* remarked that the author
"not only shows no grasp of character, but omits to present any characters
to grasp." Crane, said the *Book News,* had succeeded in getting published
a story without action and without interest, and that was the best one

could say. The author himself was dubious about that novel and inscribed a copy to Frank Harris, to whom he had been introduced by Harold Frederic: "Dear Mr. Harris: This book is even worse than any of the others."

On the back of an 1896 letter Crane wrote this note: "The Third Violet is really the history of the love of one of the younger and brilliant American artists for an heiress of the ancient New York family kind." He had written the novel in October, 1895, as a demonstration that he could write a charming love story, but it was not a successful demonstration. As H. G. Wells noticed, the emotions of the lovers go on behind the curtain of Crane's style, "and all the enrichments of imaginative appeal that make love beautiful are omitted."

In revolt against his *Red Badge* and writing about war, Crane dwells on an artist's frustrated love for a wealthy girl staying at Hemlock Inn, a summer resort not far from Hartwood: "A great bustle ensued on the platform of the little mountain station. The idlers and philosophers from the village were present to examine the consignment of people from the city." Hawker with his paintbox and easel greeting the dog Stanley is probably Corwin Linson: " 'Hello, Stanley, old man!' cried Hawker. The ardor for battle was instantly smitten from the dog, and his barking swallowed in a gurgle of delight. He was a large orange-and-white setter, and he partly expressed his emotion by twisting his body into a fantastic curve, and then dancing over the ground with his head and his tail very near to each other. He gave vent to little sobs in a wild attempt to vocally describe his gladness."

Before the summer's end Hawker is back in the city at the Art Students' League talking with other painters about art and hopefully waiting for the girl to visit him at his studio. His romance does not succeed, and neither does the novel, although it has many interesting things to say about the author and about art. Hollenden, who is Crane himself, explains why Hawker seems ill-mannered—"he gets so absorbed in a beastly smudge of paint that I really suppose he cares nothing for anything else in the world. Men who are really artists—I don't believe they are capable of deep human affections. So much of them is occupied by art. There's not much left over, you see." Hollenden is criticized by one of the girls at the inn: "And yet you—really, Hollie, there is something unnatural in you. You are so stupidly keen in looking at people that you do not possess common loyalty to your friends. It is because you are a writer, I suppose. That has to explain so many things. Some of your traits are very disagreeable." It is mainly as a chapter in autobiography that *The Third Violet* has any value today.

"The meaning of the title is not quite clear to us," said the London *Literary World;* "but as the three violets mark three stages in the process of Hawker's wooing we may let it pass." Violets represent faithfulness.[3]

Grace Fanhall (the young heiress) purposely drops the first violet on the tennis court, and Hawker picks it up and thereby plunges into love. He is faithful, but Miss Fanhall is unfaithful both to him and his rival. Oglethorpe or poor Hawker, which one is the heroine's choice? Hawker cannot afford to send her bunches of violets. "Suddenly she drew a violet from a cluster of them upon her gown, and thrust it out to him as she turned toward the approaching Oglethorpe." Thus once more she taunts him. Then at the end she thrusts a violet towards him. "Here's a third one." "Please don't pity me," Hawker says. " 'I don't,' she replied. She gave the violet a little fling."

Her giving Hawker the third violet—said the *Literary Digest*—leads to mutual understanding. Perhaps so, but the ending is rather ambiguous. In "sudden tearfulness" Miss Fanhall says: "Oh, do go!" "Go! Please! I want you to go!" He is going away for a long time, and he says: " 'I have the three violets now, you know, and you must remember that I took the third one even when you flung it at my head. That will remind you how submissive I was in my devotion. I feel as if this third one was pelted at me, but I shall keep it. You are rather a cruel person, but, Heaven guard us! that only fastens a man's love the more upon a woman.' She laughed."

At Asbury Park Crane had twice endured the role of the jilted lover, once in 1891 with Helen Trent and then, since 1892, with Mrs. Lily Brandon Munroe, and something of his own love-entanglements pierces the distraught and tantalized Hawker. In *The Third Violet* Crane transposed the personal plight of his Asbury Park love-affairs to the countryside of Sullivan County's summer-resort romances.[4]

*The Third Violet* was something of a success, but artistically it seemed a distinct blot on Crane's reputation. "Imagine the panting sentences of *The Red Badge of Courage* thus degraded, and you have the result," said *Book News*. "We give it review notice," said the *Queen*, "only because it is written by the author of that formidable *Red Badge of Courage*. There is scarcely a story in *The Third Violet;* but then, Mr. Crane's strong point is never plot. We hope that *The Third Violet,* which is a hopelessly scentless one, will be the last of its kind, and that instead of violets Mr. Crane will give us war—war—war." To the very end he was doomed to write about war—about man's war against man and his war against God, against the social injustices by which the common man is trapped, against nature indifferent to his plight.

In *The Third Violet* he lifts a scene right out of *The Red Badge* with the artist Hawker putting brush to canvas to paint a landscape of heavy blue, "as if seen through powder-smoke, and all the skies burned red. There was in these notes a sinister quality of hopelessness, eloquent of a defeat, as if the scene represented the last hour on a field of disastrous battle." Other scenes in the book recast the characters—artists Grief,

Wrinkles and Pennoyer—in his New York City sketches of artists in the Art Students' League building; it also echoes "The Silver Pageant" and "Stories Told by an Artist."

Crane was already repeating himself by casting anew previously published materials. There is no reason for assuming that had he lived beyond his twenty-eight years he might have reversed this trend and created masterpieces wholly different from anything he had yet written. Those who contend that he probably would have created works comparable in stature to *The Red Badge of Courage* ignore the hard fact that he couldn't possibly afford to write anything but potboilers in his last years—with now and then time out for exceptional short pieces such as "The Upturned Face" and "An Episode of War"; he had to write for money to pay his constant and mounting debts.

Stephen and Cora settled in England, first at Limpsfield Chart, in some furnished rooms in Millhouse with Cora's travel companion Mrs. Ruedy in the same boardinghouse. While there in June (before moving to Ravensbrook at Oxted-Limpsfield later that month) Stephen was invited by his Fabian Society neighbors to give a lecture. In the drawing room of a Fabianite he stood on an improvised platform to deliver the one and only lecture of his life; he detested public speaking. Socialism was the Fabian Society's dish, but Crane lectured on flag-wagging, as he called it. He had learned how to use flags to send messages during his stint in the Greco-Turkish War. His lecture was enthusiastically received, but Ford Hueffer, who later changed his name to Ford Madox Ford, thought him arrogant because of the harshness of his voice and the precision of his language as lecturer, and so he avoided being introduced to him.[5]

In after years Ford spoke of him as "an Apollo with starry eyes," a man who "did not seem to have the motives of common clay" and whose writings had "something of the supernatural. He comes back to me always as joyous." There are few men whom "I have liked—nay, indeed, revered —more than Crane. He was so frail and so courageous, so preyed upon and so generous, so weighted down by misfortunes and so erect in his carriage. And he was such a beautiful genius." Ford did not read *The Red Badge of Courage* until he was a soldier with the English Army in France in World War I. He read it by the light of a candle stuck above his campbed and became so engrossed that on emerging from his tent at dawn he was shocked to find that the men preparing breakfast tea were dressed in khaki. "The hallucination of Crane's book had been so strong on me that I had expected to see them dressed in Federal blue."

Edward Garnett recalls that on Crane's first visit to his home in Limpsfield in June, 1897, Stephen's strange eyes, with their intensely concentrated gaze, seemed the eyes of genius, and he was so struck "by the exquisite symmetry of his brow and temples that I failed to note, what a lady pointed out when he left, the looseness of his mouth." Ford seems to have been there when Crane visited, for he reports that when Garnett remarked to Crane that he must have read a great deal of French literature, he said defiantly that he'd never read a word of French in his life. He would insist with expletives that he had never heard of those fellows Maupassant and Zola, but in the next moment he'd display a considerable acquaintance with their work. "Indeed, he said that it was after dipping into Zola's novel about the Franco-Prussian War that he determined to write a real war novel, and so sat down to *The Red Badge of Courage.*" When Garnett persisted and pointed out the great resemblance of his handling of a story to Maupassant's, he said: "Oh, well, I've read ol' man James' . . . ." He confessed to having read one of James' French critical studies.

As reader for T. Fisher Unwin, Garnett had discovered not only Conrad but dozens of authors, and almost all of them called on him at The Cearne, his small house on the border of Surrey and Kent. His hospitality was as boundless as that of his father in the Museum courtyard when Richard Garnett was the Principal Librarian of the British Museum. Edward Garnett and his wife Constance, renowned now as the translator of Russian novelists, built their small house in a hidden pasture and named it The Cearne because it was encearned (encircled) by forest and was approachable only by a cart track through the woods. The Cearne in its isolation was symbolic of Edward's awareness that he did not fit into the Victorian social hierarchy and did not wish to belong to a community. (It was just the opposite with Stephen and Cora, who tried to fit into the English social life—the more highbrow the better for Cora.) As Garnett was advocating the very kind of prose impressionism that Stephen had already practiced in *Maggie* and *The Red Badge,* they had that much in common at their first meetings. He recognized that Crane's style was wholly intuitive, not fostered by any study, and that his genius was unique.

When Garnett brought Stephen Crane to Ford's cottage in Limpsfield in June, Ford at first took a jealous dislike to the famous author of *The Red Badge of Courage.* Then twenty-four (two years younger than Crane), he had published in 1892—before he was twenty—his first novel, *The Shifting of the Fire,* and in 1896 a biography of Ford Madox Brown, his famous grandfather. With the sardonic attention that Englishmen bestow upon foreigners, he watched Stephen plant a rose tree at the door of his (Ford's) cottage, which Crane mistook for a baronial ruin, "bully baronic ruin." Surrey inhabitants and Ford, who had just moved into Surrey from Essex, did not credit writers with much practical skill, especially American journalists. "But Crane was all right. He could use a spade or an axe," Ford conceded. Henry Sanford Bennett, whose French wife Ford had somehow offended, complained to Crane about Ford's arrogance, and he replied: "You must not mind Hueffer; that is his way. He patronises me, he patronises Mr. Conrad, he patronises Mr. James. When he goes to Heaven he will patronise God Almighty. But God Almighty will get used to it, for Hueffer is all right."[6]

At Limpsfield—as Ford reports in *Thus to Revisit*—flourished the Fabian Society: elite and affluent highbrows like the Sidney Webbs, some Russian revolutionists and some stockbrokers, the Peases and other socialists like George Bernard Shaw. The Fabians held meetings to define the Society's rules of conduct, including the sanctioning of the marriages of their members (often with wealthy American women); Shaw's marriage was sanctioned there. An ardent deputation of Fabian members, for instance, requested Ford Hueffer—a confirmed golfer—newly arrived from Pent Farm—not to wear his golfer's cap in Limpsfield; no wonder he detested the Fabians. "These things may seem trivial but they have made England what she is today," he says in *Return to Yesterday*. And with characteristic humor he adds that Shaw, Olivier, and Webb wore beards and homespuns and Stetson hats; and now they govern England! Local residents were requested to imitate them. Ford and his Limpsfield neighbors all dressed in the medieval style of the disciples of William Morris' school of socialism, and they drank mead out of cups of bullock's horn. In spite of their attire, the Fabians were advanced socialists and tolerated unmarried couples such as the Cranes, who settled at Oxted-Limpsfield knowing they would not be ostracized there.

Ravensbrook, which Stephen and Cora occupied in June, was a sordidly pretentious type of suburban architecture. It was a four-square brick and tile "villa" with a drive-in and a lodge at the gate. There was a culvert over a little brook, a damp bottom, and a garden. Beyond was a chalk cliff, a pit which had been dug into the chalk hills that run through Kent and Surrey east and west. A similar residential villa was on the other side of the brook toward the railway station. (This house became the laundry for Oxted village in the 1920's, and on the paddock a dozen small houses were erected at that time. One of them—named the Cranes—was occupied by the English poet W. H. Davies.)

Ford said he was trepanned at Ravensbrook, and so was Stephen, who rapidly came to detest the house that Edward Garnett had selected for him in that banal suburb of London, located just inside Oxted and just outside Limpsfield. He was trepanned there by the local merchants who began dunning him for his bills in October, which was one reason he detested the place. Most people see dunning tradesmen as fiends, says Ford, but Crane saw them as the starving fathers of families and would say: "'Do you suppose Simpson, the butcher, will be bankrupted if I don't pay him?' Or: 'Oving the saddlemaker's children are said to be without shoes. Damn it! I owe him £50 for harness.'"

Ford speculates that Crane might have lived longer had he stayed on at Limpsfield Chart's "breezy, uplifting hilltop" instead of moving into

Villa Ravensbrook down in a damp Surrey valley.[7] A spring flowed through the basement of that "hideous and disastrous villa," and Crane was to end his days in still another damp house, windy Brede Manor. He knew that Hartwood's mountain air—devoid of humidity—was a rest cure for the lungs, and that if he stayed at Hartwood at his brother Edmund's house he might live longer. He deliberately risked his health instead of trying to preserve it.

Ford says that Crane was not fortunate in those who chose his residences for him, yet claims that he himself introduced him to Brede Manor, an ancient and enormous place requiring servants "and someone like a rich stockbroker to run it."[8] He calls it "that doomed place that cursed the world by murdering so great a talent," which is of course nonsense. If Ford had anything at all to do with bringing Brede Manor to the attention of the Cranes, it must have been through Cora, not Stephen, for he was then in Cuba. And Harold Frederic had as much to do with selecting Ravensbrook for the Cranes as did Edward Garnett.

Novelist Robert Barr with his wife and daughters lived at Hillhead in nearby Woldingham. Barr in 1900, a few days after Crane died on June 5, wrote another admirer of Crane, Karl Harriman, that from his window at Hillhead he could see down in the valley Ravensbrook Villa where he and Crane and Harold Frederic had many a merry night together. "When the Romans occupied Britain, some of their legions, parched with thirst, were wandering about these dry hills with the chance of finding water or perishing. They watched the ravens, and so came to the stream which rises under my place and flows past Stephen's former home; hence the name, Ravensbrook. It seems a strange coincidence that the greatest modern writer on war should set himself down where the greatest ancient warrior, Caesar, probably stopped to quench his thirst." And Brede Place in Sussex is located in the region where William the Conqueror landed in 1066.

At the hamlet of Kenley, seven miles from Crane's Ravensbrook at Oxted-Limpsfield, Harold Frederic lived with his common-law wife Kate Lyon and their children at "Homefield" in Caterham valley. On weekends he visited his first wife, Grace, and her children at Brook Green, Hammersmith, and relaxed at his hobby of bookbinding. Kate endorsed what Grace endured: a double household.

Crane's affinities with Frederic are striking. Frederic also began his career as novelist in the trade of journalism; he came from a family of Methodists and had a common-law wife. He spent his last years in financial panic and died young and in debt. The author of *The Damnation of Theron Ware* (1896), for which the *Bookman* hailed him as a great novelist, he had been acclaimed more in England than in America, and, again like Crane, when he died he was for decades utterly forgotten.

He, too, was ambitious and overtaxed himself; his strength was not equal to his ambition, and he wore himself out because he never thought of taking care of himself. He never busied himself about cultivating friendships; he made enemies or friends with equal indifference. Self-taught in many fields, he scoffed at college-bred airs and had no patience with the notion that "literary pussons" are somehow superior to their neighbors. In setting down his profession on the income-tax returns he filled out in London, he wrote on the line headed Occupation: "a Paper Stainer."

In "Harold Frederic" (Chicago *Chap Book:* March 15, 1898) Crane wrote that Frederic had spent his early boyhood in the Mohawk Valley and there studied the alphabet on a soapbox while delivering milk on snow sleds at dawn in a land of lightless windows, where tables were set for three instead of for five—the missing all being the Civil War dead. He complained that American critics had not given Frederic's *In the Valley* (1890) its due, whereas it is "easily the best historical novel that our country has borne. Perhaps it is the only good one." Crane was repaying the older author for his having trumpeted *The Red Badge,* and Frederic in turn wrote in his review of *The Open Boat* in the New York *Times* (May 1, 1898): "The genius of this young son of America is being keenly felt here [in London] and there is a quickening touch in this volume of stories which will put a new face on British appreciation. . . . No living English prose-writer of his years approaches his wonderful gift of original and penetrating observation, while no writer of English is today prouder of being an American." Said the *Critic,* it is pleasant to see such an exchange of courtesies between authors.

But Frederic and Crane were not indulging in the literary game of scratching each other's back. They were both the uncompromising enemy of flattery and sham. Big-hearted and without envy, the generous Frederic liked Crane at once, and the feeling was reciprocated. They dined together at the Savage Club, and Crane wrote: "There was a tall, heavy man, moustached and straight-glanced, seated in a leather chair in the smoking-room of a club, telling a story to a circle of intent people with all the skill of one trained in an American newspaper school. At a distance he might have been even the editor of the Albany *Journal.* The sane man does not live amid another people without seeking to adopt whatever he recognizes as better: without seeking to choose from the new material some advantage, even if it be only a trick of grilling oysters. Accordingly, Frederic was to be to me a cosmopolitan figure, representing many ways of many peoples; and, behold, he was still the familiar figure, with no gilding, no varnish, a great reminiscent panorama of Mohawk Valley!" Born in Utica in 1856, Frederic drew upon the scenes of his youth in the Mohawk Valley for his best work, but the critics did not recognize his presence, said Crane. "All this goes to show that there are some painful elements in the art of creating an American literature-by what may be called the tattlety-bang method. The important figures, the greater men, rise silently, un-

spurred, undriven. To be sure, they have come in for magnificent cudgel-
ings later, but their approach is noiseless, invincible, and they are upon
us like ghosts before the critics have time to begin their clatter."

Sometime this summer of 1897 the Cranes had luncheon with Edmund
Gosse, translator of Ibsen and author of *A History of Modern English
Literature* (1897). Their meeting came about through Edward Garnett,
whose father was a friend of Gosse. He remembered Cora as a small
plump woman visibly older than Stephen. She was most entertaining at
this luncheon when an American became long-winded on reporting a
quarrel between some exalted personage and his mistress. The rupture
was discussed exhaustively, "and we were all close on madness when
Mrs. Crane said, 'Well, if the Prince *has* left her, I suppose we must all
just grin and bear it.' This ended the matter." Gosse thought Cora "rather
suggested Réjane in appearance, although blonde. I saw her very seldom.
She was supposed to have had a 'past.' But she seemed to me very vivid
and agreeable. . . ."

So she seemed also to a fifteen-year-old girl boarding in Oxted with her
conventional Victorian cousins, who called on the Cranes and were
shocked. The girl was named Vere and later as Mrs. Charles Sidmore
she recalled that she was approached on the train from London by a
smartly dressed woman with American shoes, who told her how to cure
her cold. And then the next day Cora sent her a bottle of some American
cold cure with a nice note about using it, and the cure worked, and the
conventional Victorian cousins were very grateful. And so Vere was put
into her best frock and taken to call on the Cranes to say thank you, but
the visit ended badly when Stephen said something about will power being
the cure for most ailments. Whereupon Cora, parodying his slow voice,
said: "Yes—I—know—a—young—man—named—Crane—who—got—
out—of—bed—to—go—to—a—dinner—party—in    Athens—and—I—
know—what—happened—to—him." What happened to him in Athens?
asked one of the cousins, and Cora blandly replied that he had had dysentery. Vere's cousins decided that the Cranes were really very nice, but try
to imagine the effect of the word "dysentery" on sedate Victorians. A
servant in the kitchen at their house was a friend of somebody in the
kitchen at Ravensbrook, and so Vere heard the gossip that the Cranes
consumed champagne on ice and truffled pheasants for lunch. Then, too,
on first meeting Cora on the train from London, Vere had noticed that she
was adorned with a bower of orchids and "some costly white flower; no
English family in the same circumstances would have spent three or four
pounds on flowers even for a small dinner party."

But young Miss Vere adored Mr. Crane, who assured her that all
Yankee girls were named Sunset and Orange and Praline. He was jesting
at her being named Vere, the heroine of Ouida's novel *Moths*. (Vere's

mother was a warm friend of Ouida.) Stephen found out the girl's secret sorrow, probably some boy she pined for, and he was, she remembered, so consoling. One day when Cora was being dressed in a hurry by Mrs. Ruedy for luncheon at Robert Barr's house at Hillhead, she called Vere into her bedroom, "and I sat about while her clothes were put on, *seriatim*. It was not what an Englishwoman would have done. I can not conceive that she had ever been a beautiful woman. But she had lovely arms and feet. Shortly after that I was very suddenly told that I must not go to see Mrs. Crane again." One of Vere's uncles had picked up the gossip about Cora. If her past was known to Vere's uncle, it probably was known also among some of Crane's close friends, but not one of them ever divulged the secret. They all took Stephen at his word that he had married Cora in Athens earlier that year, and they always spoke of her as Mrs. Crane.

The Cranes were so nice and gay, Vere recalled years later. Cora was very smartly dressed, and it surprised Vere to learn that others regarded her as badly dressed. "She seemed the apogee of smartness to me, especially her American shoes. I do not know how she lived and do not care. She was 'on the level.' She was plucky and gay and kind."

War correspondent Sylvester Scovel was entertained at Ravensbrook in July, on his return from Greece. Scovel knew the secret of Crane's nonmarriage to Cora, and he wrote in a letter about it on May 19 from Greece that even if Stephen wished to "he can't marry her" because Cora's husband refused to grant her a divorce.[9]

Mark Barr, an American chemist in London, who considered Cora a woman of education, "an ample 'Negro mammy' sort of person," quoted Crane as saying: "I brought Cora back." Instead of his usual explanation that he brought Cora back from Greece after marrying her there, he told Barr that he had married her in England in the presence of H. G. Wells and one or two others. However, no legal wedding could possibly have taken place.[10] Barr sympathized with their plight. They kept the secret from others; Conrad, for instance, thought they were married. Crane wrote Henry Sanford Bennett that Harold Frederic and William Heinemann "have been urging me to stay in England for a time. So my wife—after practicing nine days I can write that without a jump—and I will be hunting a house or an attic in London pretty soon."

Crane's note was a ruse to comfort the conventional-minded Bennett. He never mentioned any "marriage" in letters home to his brother until March, 1899; William first learned of Cora when she cabled him in desperation to locate Stephen's whereabouts at the end of the Cuban War (September, 1898).

In Athens, she had been known as Mrs. Stewart, and thus Eben Alexander referred to her in his letter of July 14, 1897: "My dear Crane, It would be altogether lovely to drop in and see you and Mrs. Stewart. My kindest remembrances to Mrs. Stewart. I am not likely to forget either of you." On July 2 Stephen had invited Alexander to Ravensbrook, and he replied on the 14th that he thought he'd get there. But he was replaced in his consulate post and enroute to America he had no stopover in London. He became a professor in Chapel Hill, North Carolina, and in 1900 he invited Stephen to stay with him for a possible cure of his lung trouble. England is a decent country to live in, he wrote in July, 1897, "but the clear sky of Greece is lacking. Also the infernal heat."

The Pease family in Limpsfield became intimate friends of the Cranes, and their son, Nicolas A. Pease, remembers from his childhood days Cora's beautiful and striking shock of golden hair; Mrs. Ruedy quiet and unobtrusive; Crane looking like Robert Louis Stevenson, ill and worried; and the grown-ups perpetually urging the Pease children to play quietly so as not to disturb him when he was in his study writing. A photograph of the time shows Stephen at his desk—with a tobacco jar and a decanter of water and a framed photograph of Cora in the togs she wore in Greece. At the fireplace is his guitar, and on the desk is an oil lamp atop a Grecian-like stone pilaster and covered by a fantastic lampshade.

Stephen was waited on by Adoni, one of the two Ptolemy brothers he had brought with him from Greece, but he liked to be shaved by Adoni's twin brother, who had been taken into the Pease household at Limpsfield, and so he visited there regularly. He called Adoni "a butler in shirt sleeves," and Mrs. Pease thought the young Greek lazy because when he should have been cleaning the silver he was playing with Michael Pease and his younger brother. Michael's father, the austere Quaker Edward Pease, disapproved of Stephen's self-indulgence in not shaving himself, a defection from English middle-class standards.[11]

From his desk at Ravensbrook Crane reported his impressions of London. Like any American tourist who passes Buckingham Palace, he did not dream of the existence of the beautiful garden inside its grimy walls. "There is no spot so lovely, and those who enter here leave all smoke and dirt and hurrying humanity behind. These royal precincts are not by any means vast, yet so cleverly have the landscape gardeners done their work that in whichever direction one turns groves, sweet-smelling nooks, green swards and woodland shrubs greet one, and over all reigns the peace of the country, interrupted only by the happy twittering of the birds. . . . Then pretty rowing boats flit about the large lake, propelled by the Queen's watermen, each in his gorgeous red and gold livery. The main front of the palace faces this lake, beyond which is a mound dividing the royal stables from the grounds. Numbers of stately peacocks sun themselves and spread their tails on the lawns, adding bits of brighter color to the scene."

Instead of reporting Queen Victoria's Diamond Jubilee of 1897, Crane in this same sketch—"Fresh Bits of Gossip on European Affairs" (New York *Press:* (August 15, 1897)[12]—jested about the Queen's 1887 jubilee celebrating her fiftieth year on the throne. Two Scots women gossip:

> "Can ye tell me wumman, what it is they ca' a jubilee?" "Weel it's this," said her neighbor. "When folks has been married twenty-five years, that's a silver weddin', and when they have been married fifty year, that's a gowden weddin', but if the man's dead, then it's a jubilee."

For decades after Albert's death Victoria had preserved his suite of rooms just as they had been before he died: Albert's clothing was laid out fresh each day upon his bed, and the basin filled with water fresh as if he were still alive. The common people, however, sensibly reduced Albert's death to the common denominator of the joke Crane reported.

In "London Impressions," appearing in Frank Harris' *Saturday Review* in July and August, he contrasts London with New York City. In these humorous impressions he drops his earlier fixed ideas about Londoners. There is a porter with the most charming manners in the world, and that is quite a shock to a New Yorker. Both the porter and a cabman with a supreme intelligence observe "my profound ignorance without contempt or humour of any kind observable in their manners." Crane is unnerved because they know the details of their business, "whereas I was confronting the inscrutable."

"The cab finally rolled out of the gas-lit vault into a vast expanse of gloom. This changed to the shadowy lines of a street that was like a passage in a monstrous cave. The lamps winking here and there resembled the little gleams at the caps of the miners. . . . It was evident that the paving was very greasy, but all the cabs that passed through my cylinder were going at a round trot, while the wheels, shod in rubber, whirred merely like bicycles. The hoofs of the animals themselves did not make that wild clatter which I knew so well. New York, in fact, roars always like ten thousand devils. We have ingenuous and simple ways of making a din in New York that cause the stranger to conclude that each citizen is obliged by statute to provide himself with a pair of cymbals and a drum. If anything by chance can be turned into a noise it is promptly turned. We are engaged in the development of a human creature with very large, sturdy, and doubly fortified ears." New York City day and night "cries its loud, fierce, aspiring cry, a noise of men beating upon barrels, a noise of men beating upon tin, a terrific racket that assails the abject skies." Its noise is a consequence of bad pavements. "Any brigade of artillery in Europe that would love to assemble its batteries, and then go on a gallop over the land, thundering and thundering, would give up the idea of thunder at once if it could hear Tom Mulligan drive a beer wagon along one of the side streets of cobbled New York." Crane listened for the noise of London and found only a silence, "a low drone," with everything moving "with the decorum and caution of an undertaker.

"Finally a great thing came to pass. The cab horse, proceeding at a sharp trot, found himself suddenly at the top of an incline, where through the rain the pavement shone like an expanse of ice. It looked to me as if there was going to be a tumble. In an accident of such a kind a hansom becomes really a cannon in which a man finds that he has paid shillings for the privilege of serving as a projectile." He marvels at the skill of this cab horse: "He tranquilly braced his four feet like a bundle of skates, and then, with a gentle gaiety of demeanor, he slid swiftly and gracefully to the bottom of the hill as if he had been a toboggan. When the incline ended he caught his gait again with great dexterity, and went pattering off through another tunnel." And then there was a great omnibus whose dignified horses, "bidden to halt their trot, did not waste time in wild and unseemly spasms. They, too, braced their legs and slid gravely to the end of their momentum." It reminded Crane of "skating parties on moonlit lakes, with laughter ringing over the ice, and a great red bonfire on the shore among the hemlocks."

In another of his "London Impressions" he pressed an electric button before a grim portal marked "Lift," "and heard an answering tinkle in the heavens. There was an upholstered settle near at hand, and I discovered the reason. A deer-stalking peace drooped upon everything, and in it a man could invoke the passing of a lazy pageant of twenty years of his life. The dignity of a coffin being lowered into a grave surrounded the ultimate appearance of the lift. The expert we in America call the elevator-boy stepped from the car, took three paces forward, faced to attention, and saluted. This elevator boy could not have been less than sixty years of age; a great white beard streamed toward his belt. I saw that the lift had been longer on its voyage than I had expected. Later in our upward progress a natural event would have been an establishment of social relations. Two enemies imprisoned together during the still hours of a balloon journey would, I believe, suffer a mental amalgamation. The overhang of a common fate, a great principal fact, can make an equality and a truce between any pair."

Frank Norris remarked that Crane spoke of a lift at his hotel that ran so slowly "that the elevator boy grew to be an old man between trips. Mr. Crane has started in with his descriptions at the railway depot. The best that I can wish for him is that he may live long enough to reach his hotel." Norris, one and a half years younger than Crane and not yet a novelist in print, sniped at the "London Impressions" in the San Francisco *Wave* (September 18, 1897) under the pen name of Justin Sturgis: "Mr. Crane in London." Perhaps irked by Crane's fame and envious of *The Red Badge of Courage,* he scoffed at his reporting of London. He says that Crane was like a locust in a grain elevator carrying off one grain of corn at a time. What a little world does this Mr. Crane live in! He never soars—"a bird's eye view would smite him blind. Mr. Crane observes and observes and observes—always through a microscope; to him life is a play seen through reversed opera glasses. On his wonderful way from the depot a horse falls down. This is an event, a horrible formless catastrophe. Out with the microscope; everything stops; what else matters now?"

# XVIII

# ⊂⊃ *Early Days in England*

THE London *Bookman* (August 19, 1897) stated that "Mr. Stephen Crane has settled down in this country for an indefinite period. He has taken a house in Oxted and is turning his attention chiefly to short stories, one of which, 'Flanagan and his Filibustering Adventure,' will appear in the *Illustrated London News* and *McClure's Magazine*." The London *News* published "Flanagan" on August 28, and the Boston *Globe* reviewed it as strong in parts, "strong almost to brutality, but taken as a whole, we consider it as falling grievously below the level of 'The Red Badge of Courage.' When Mr. Crane wrote that book he was beginning; he had his name to make. He wrote carefully, patiently, humbly. In this new story of Flanagan he is cocksure, dogmatic, self-conscious. He offers us exaggerations of Mr. Kipling's least admirable traits. This is a great pity, for Mr. Crane is a very clever writer, well able to do sound genuine work off his own bat. 'Flanagan' is bluster, not literature."[1]

The year 1897 was one of Crane's most productive. After his war dispatches, during his first half-year of English residence he wrote "London Impressions," "Irish Notes," "The Scotch Express," "The Monster," "Death and the Child," "The Bride Comes to Yellow Sky," and "The Blue Hotel"—an astonishing succession of first-rate works, and proof enough that he had nothing to fear from British admiration, which he had been warned against lest he become an exile and suffer the fate of Bret Harte. Expatriates Frederic, Whistler, James and Conrad prospered under British admiration; so did Crane, who was received and flattered by the most exclusive London circles. His social success was instantaneous, reported the London *Bookman*.

"Mr. Thomas Beer said that Crane did not have a very tumultuous reception in England. He was wrong," said Ford Madox Ford, "for that was exactly the type of reception that poor Crane did get once he was settled first in Oxted and afterwards in Brede. Before that he had the reception that any serious man of letters should have wanted at that date to have in England. He was, that is to say, accepted at once, on his achievements and personality, as a serious and distinguished human being by practically all the serious people in England."

Crane was indifferent not to social success but to English culture and society, of which the closest segment was right next door at Limpsfield in the Fabian cult. Unlike Whistler and James, he became an exile for personal—rather than cultural—reasons. He took up residence in England, said the American *Bookman* in 1900, because of the success of his books there. This is only partly true, for what the *Bookman* did not say was that he had no choice. He could write in either America or England un-hampered by his celebrity, but the Cora situation blocked him. "Over here in England they say that 'The Open Boat' was my best thing," he wrote his brother William on October 29. He makes no mention of living with Cora Taylor at Ravensbrook and gives as his return address his publisher's office at 21 Bedford Street. He has Cora in mind, however, in saying: "There seem so many of them in America who want to kill, bury and forget me purely out of unkindness and envy and—my unworthiness, if you choose." His sense of "unworthiness" could have been a self-confessed guilt about his relationship with Cora, although William might have read his declaration of "unworthiness" as humility. "All the hard things they say of me [in American reviews] affect me principally be-cause I think of mine own people—you and Teddie [Edmund] and the families. It is nothing, bless you. Now Dick Davis [Richard Harding Davis] for instance has come to like the abuse. He accepts it as a tribute to his excellence. But he is a fool. Now I want you to promise to never pay any attention to it, even in your thought. It is too immaterial and foolish. Your little brother is neither braggart or a silent egotist but he knows that he is going on steadily to make his simple little place and he can't be stopped, he can't even be retarded. He is coming." However, his career might be retarded if his envious critics should somehow get wind of Cora. Scandal was always a possibility.

To Sylvester Scovel he wrote on August 1: "Tonight Cora and I want to speak to you because you are the only one will understand. . . ." He would understand their grief over the death of the dog Velestino, which had occurred an hour earlier. Smuggled into England from Greece, Velestino had died in Cora's bedroom at Ravensbrook "with all the pillows under him which our poverty could supply." For eleven days they had tried to save the life of this hardy mountain shepherd-bred dog, but the English climate was too much for him. "He made a fine manly fight, with only little grateful laps of his tongue on Cora's hands. . . . We are burying him tomorrow in the rhododendron bed in the garden," Crane wrote Scovel, whose gift in Athens of a dog collar was buried with Velestino.

To celebrate Harold Frederic's birthday the Cranes rented a horse and carriage to get to Homefield, but the carriage overturned, and Stephen was laid up for a week at Homefield. Cora, who was also hurt, sought without success to obtain damages from the job-master of the improperly harnessed carriage, and a year later she wrote Moreton Frewen of Brede Place that she wanted never "to see another lawyer if I can avoid it." She lost that legal squabble; all her life she was frustrated by legal and social codes. She wrote Scovel on October 17 about the carriage accident and added that the Frederics, "dear people, took us in and cured us and carted us off to Ireland where we had a delightful three weeks in the wilds"—until September 9 or so. From Schill (County Cork) in Ireland, Crane wrote Edmund on September 9 that he had finished a novelette of 20,000 words— "The Monster."

When he wrote William on October 29 he said he was then working on a big novel. "It will be much longer than *The Red Badge*. My next short thing after the novelette (The Monster) was *The Bride Comes to Yellow Sky*. All my friends who come here say it is my very best thing. I am so delighted when I am told by competent people that I have made an advance." That was true, but he was not yet writing the "big novel" about the Greco–Turkish War which Harold Frederic had urged him to do. That was *Active Service,* of which he wrote Reynolds in December that it was "not yet begun." He did not write it until late the next year when he was hiding out in Havana after the close of the Cuban War. Acton Davies says that Crane "finished" it there and then "threw the last chapters aside and wrote them afresh." He recast the whole thing at Brede Manor in March, 1899.

In August—en route to visit the Frederics in Ireland—the Cranes took the Scotch Express from Euston Station, Stephen riding in the engine cab and Cora in the coach. Writing about his trip to Scotland in "The Scotch Express" for *McClure's Magazine* (1899), Crane says that you catch the train in a railway station whose entrance does not resemble a railway station; its front resembles the front of some banking house. It imitates "the front of the temple of Nike Apteros, with a recollection of the Egyptians proclaimed at the flanks." (If Crane knew nothing about Greek architecture, how did he know about Egyptian architecture? Perhaps from Kate Frederic.) The Euston Grove station looked like the temple of Nike Apteros, except that "the frieze, where of old would prance an exuberant processional of gods, is, in this case, bare of decoration, but upon the epistyle is written in simple, stern letters the word 'Euston.' The legend reared high by the bloomy Pelagic columns stares down a wide avenue." Four-wheeler hansoms dash back and forth "between the legs of the solemn temple," the gate to Scotland. At this gate, "in August particularly, one must note the number of men with gun-cases, the number of women who surely have Tam-o'-Shanters and plaids concealed within their luggage, ready for the moors. There is, during the latter part of that month, a wholesale flight from London to Scotland which recalls the July throngs leaving New York for the shore or the mountain."[2]

The vermilion engine of the Scotch Express (with Crane in the engine-cab) awaits the sign from the signal house before pulling out from the curve-roofed Euston railway station. In the signal house are many levers resembling a church organ except that here "these rows of numbered and indexed handles typify something more acutely human than does a key-board. It requires four men to play this organ-like thing, and the strains never cease. Night and day, day and night, these four men are walking to and fro from this lever to that lever, and under their hands the great machine raises its endless hymn of a world at work, the fall and rise of signals and the clicking swing of switches." The monster now moves "along the platform at the pace of a mouse. To those in the tranquil carriages this starting was probably as easy as the sliding of one's hand over a greased surface, but in the engine there was more to it. The monster roared suddenly and loudly, and sprang forward impetuously. A wrong-headed or maddened draught-horse will plunge in its collar sometimes when going up a hill. But this load of burdened carriages followed imperturbably at the gait of turtles."

He compares the English engine-cab with the Scottish and with the American. "The engine-cabs of England, as of all Europe, are seldom made for the comfort of the men. One finds very often this apparent disregard for the man who does the work—this indifference to the man who occupies a position which, for the exercise of temperance, of courage, of honesty, has no equal at the altitude of prime ministers.

"The American engineer is the gilded occupant of a salon in comparison with his brother in Europe. The man who was guiding this five-hundred-ton bolt, aimed by the officials of the railway of Scotland, could not have been as comfortable as a shrill gibbering boatman of the Orient. The narrow and bare bench at his side of the cab was not directly intended for his use, because it was so low that he would be prevented by it from looking out of the ship's port-hold which served him as a window. The fireman, on his side, had other difficulties. His legs would have to straggle over some pipes at the only spot where there was a prospect, and the builders had also strategically placed a large steel bolt. Of course it is plain that the companies consistently believe that the men will do their work better if they are kept standing." The cabs on trains in Scotland, however, are much larger and have seats located so that the men can see "through the round windows without dislocating their necks."

The English roadbeds, "made in the pattern by which the Romans built their highways," are superior to the American, and there are very few grade-crossings but instead bridges or tunnels. "Once train met train in a tunnel. Upon the painting in the perfectly circular frame formed by the mouth there appeared a black square with sparks bursting from it. This square expanded until it hid everything, and a moment later came the crash of the passing. It was enough to make a man lose his sense of balance. It was a momentary inferno when the fireman opened the furnace door and was bathed in blood-red light as he fed the flames. The effect of a tunnel varied when there was a curve in it. One was merely whirling then heels over head, apparently in the dark, echoing bowels of the earth. There was no needlepoint of light to which one's eyes clung as to a star."

Crane captures his excitement in being hurled through space at "sixty-five miles an hour" (the Scotch Express made 49.9 miles an hour on the average), thundering past stations "at thrilling speed" while people on the platform rivet their eyes upon this projectile, "and to be on the engine was to feel their interest and admiration in the terror and grandeur of this sweep. A boy allowed to ride with the driver of the band-wagon as a circus parade winds through one of our village streets could not exceed for egotism the temper of a new man in the cab of a train like this one. This valkyric journey on the back of the vermilion engine, with the shouting of the wind, the deep, mighty panting of the steed, the grey blur at the track-side, the flowing quicksilver ribbon of the other rails, the sudden clash as a switch intersects, all the din and fury of this ride, was of a splendour that caused one to look around at the quiet green landscape and believe that it was of a phlegm quite beyond patience."

He thinks the engineer "altogether more worthy than the soldier" and better than the sailor. "There is surely no engine-driver who does not feel the beauty of the business, but the emotion lies deep, and mainly inarticulate, as it does in the mind of a man who has experienced a good and beautiful wife for many years." (Which may, perhaps, be taken as a tribute to Cora. His emotion for her was deep but not inarticulate. They seem never to have had a quarrel, Cora always acquiescing to Stephen's wishes. Many of his friends—including Ernest McCready and Ralph D. Paine—had a very high opinion of Cora, and Richard Harding Davis wrote Mrs. Charles Sidmore: "Any decent man will tell you that she was a loyal wife to Crane as long as he lived.")

From Glasgow the Cranes took the River Clyde steamer—which made daily sailings to the major Ireland ports—to Queenstown, described in the first of the "Irish Notes."[3] He saw Queenstown as a terraced city tilting sharply toward the bay and disclosing herself through clouds of rain. "Cork was weeping like a widow. The rain would have gone through any top-coat but a sentry box. The passengers looked like specimens of a new kind of sponge as they separated to gloomy ways." At the bay's edge was Her Majesty's ship the *Howe,* and her white pennant of the English navy strikes Crane as the "emblem of the man who can play one game at a time."

The Irishman is modern: "He is akin to the steam-engine, the telephone, the electric lamp." His agile mind "moves with the rapidity of light from the past to the future, here, there, and everywhere. It is the type that can in the same breath imagine a radiant idol out of a pewter mug, and subtract ten shillings from half-a-crown. When it fails, it fails because it has eyes at the back and at the sides of its head, and thus merges twenty scenes in a confusing one. It would attempt forty games of chess at one time, and play them all passably well."

These Queenstown Irishmen possess "a strange broad quality, a kind of egotism of vision as if from their hills they could comprehend the gestures of a man in Denver." And because of their pinnacled position they assimilate with newcomers "like lightning." The stranger need not explain himself, and the Queenstown citizen "never says 'It is not customary.' He does not at once flee to this loft and pull the ladder of speech up after him. He is capable of making excursions into the domain of another man's habits. In short, he is a citizen of the world, a philosopher, an intelligence." The Englishman, on the contrary, is provinical, solipsistic and smug about it. He lacks the Irishman's "egotism of vision."

Of Ballydehob, an obscure village northeast of Schull on Roaringwater Bay, Crane writes: "Nobody lives here that has money. The average English tradesman with his back-breaking respect for this class, his reflex contempt for that class, his reverence for the tin gods, could here be a commercial lord and bully the people in one or two ways, until they were thrown back upon the defence which is always near them, the ability to cut his skin into strips with a wit that would be a foreign tongue to him. For amid his wrongs and his rights and his failures—his colossal failures—the Irishman retains this delicate blade for his enemies, for his friends, for himself, the ancestral dagger of fast sharp speaking from fast sharp seeing—an inheritance which could move the world."

Ballydehob has three hundred Irish and four constables. Crane sardonically remarks that male innkeepers die young: "Apparently they succumb to conviviality when it is presented to them in the guise of a business duty." Hard-drinking innkeepers "invariably leave behind them capable widows, women who do not recognize conviviality as a business obligation. And so all through Ireland one finds these brisk widows keeping hotels with a precision that is almost military." In Mrs. Kearney's pub sits a yellow-bearded Irish farmer, "a man to whom a sudden two shillings would appear as a miracle, a ragged, unkempt peasant, whose mind roamed the world like the soul of a lost diplomat." This farmer in tattered clothes discusses with Crane the Armenian massacres, the political aim of Russia versus China, the situation in Cuba, etc. "His pipe glowed comfortably from his corner; waving the tuppenny glass of stout in the air, he discoursed on the business of the remote ends of the earth with the glibness of a fourth secretary of Legation. . . . And yet, when the talk had turned another corner, he confidently assured the assembled company that a hair from a horse's tail when thrown into a brook would turn shortly to an eel.

"The national custom of meeting stranger and friend alike on the road with a cheery greeting like 'God save you!' is too kindly and human a habit not to be missed. But all through the south of Ireland one sees the peasant turn his eyes to the side of the road at the passing of the constable.

"It seemed to be generally understood that to note the presence of a constable was to make a conventional error. None looked, nodded, or gave a sign. There was a line drawn so sternly that it reared like a fence. . . . One hears often of the ostracism or other punishment that befell some girl who was caught flirting with a constable."[4]

The constables fish for trout when they are not strolling in pairs over country roads or putting down a village crisis consisting of occasional drunken men "who were unable to understand the local geography on Saturday nights." There was a certain sergeant who "fished more than any twelve men in Cork County. Some people had never seen him in any other posture than that of crowding forward on his stomach to peer into a pool. They did not believe the rumor that he sometimes stood or walked like a human being."

"A Fishing Village" is the best of Crane's "Irish Notes." "Innocent and white, the brook curved down over the rocks, until it faced a little strand of smooth gravel and flat stones.[5] It turned then to the left, and thereafter its guilty current was tinged with the pink of diluted blood. Boulders standing neck-deep in the water were rimmed with red; they wore bloody collars whose tops marked the supreme instant of some tragic movement of the stream. In the pale green shallows of the bay's edge, the outward flow from the criminal little brook was as eloquently marked as if a long crimson carpet had been laid upon the waters. The scene of the carnage was the strand of smooth gravel and flat stones, and the fruit of the carnage was the cleaned mackerel."

This opening section prepares the reader for the contrast between the optimistic youth and the old melancholy fisherman: "The young man is the type that America procures from Ireland, and the old man is one of the home types, bent, pallid, hungry, disheartened, with a vision that magnifies with a glance any fly-wing future. Usually the thing that remains to one of this last type is a sympathy as quick and acute for others as is pity for himself." The young man is confident of catching fish, whereas the old man complains: " 'There will be no more big kills here. No more. No more.' At last his voice was only a dismal croak. 'Come along outa that now, Mickey,' cried the youth impatiently. 'Come away wid you.' " The old man "groaned as Mordecai groaned for his people."

Yet the village has just brought in the first respectable catch of the year, and now they are preparing—at the point where the brook changed its colors—the mackerel for the market. Beautiful "as fire-etched salvers," the mackerel are cleaned by "two motions of the knife. Then the washers, men who stood over the troughs filled with running water from the brook, soused the fish until the outlet became a sinister element that in an instant changed the brook from a happy thing of the gorse and heather of the hills to an evil stream, sullen and reddened. . . . A vast tree hung its branches over the place. The leaves made a shadow that was religious in its effect, as if the spot were a chapel consecrated to labor. There was a hush upon the devotees." (Crane here echoes the forest chapel in *The Red Badge of Courage*.)

Cora reprinted "A Fishing Village" and "An Old Man Goes Wooing" in Crane's *Last Words* (1902).[6] In the latter sketch a giantess of a girl, who approaches "the fiery stove in the manner of a boxer," greets an old man to whom the kitchen of the inn is a paradise. Nora, "with her towering figure and bare brawny arms, was like a feminine blacksmith at a forge. The old man, pallid, emaciated, watched her from the shadows of the other side of the room. The lines from the sides of his nose to the corners of his mouth sank low to an expression of despair deeper than any moans. He should have been painted upon the door of a tomb with weeping willows etched above him and men in grey robes slowly booming the drums of death. Finally he spoke. 'I would be likin' a bottle o'stout, Nora, mr girrl,' he said." She demands money, and the old man brings forth two coppers, laying them "sadly, reproachfully, and yet defiantly on the table. 'There now,' cried Nora, stupefied. They brought him a bottle of black brew, and Nora poured it out for him with her own red hand, which looked to be as broad as his chest." Some pig-buyers are dining in the next room, and she waits on them. "When Nora returned, the strapping grenadier of a girl was blushing and giggling. The pig-buyers had been humorous. 'I moind the toime—' began the man sorrowfully, 'I moind the toime whin yez was a wee bit of a girrl, Nora, an' wouldn't be havin' words wid min loike thim buyers.' 'I moind the toime whin yez could attind to your affairs, ye ould skileton,' said the girl, promptly. He made a gesture which may have expressed his stirring grief at the levity of the new generation, and then lapsed into another stillness."

The new generation betrays the old. When the old man falls asleep, Nora "marched to him and put both hands to his collar. Despite his feeble and dreamy protestations, she dragged him out from behind the table and across the floor. She opened the door and thrust him into the night."

If Crane was charmed by the Irish folk, he held no high opinion of the Irish writers of the Nineties except the poet Yeats. He mistook George Bernard Shaw, whom he probably met amongst his Fabian neighbors at Limpsfield, for a clerical person. He considered Oscar Wilde "a mildewed chump. He has a disease and they all gas about him as though there was a hell and he came up out of it. . . . Mr. Yeats is the only man I have met who talks of Wilde with any sense. The others talk like a lot of little girls at a Sunday School party when a kid says a wicked word in a corner."

Henry Harland, a former editor of the *Yellow Book,* told Crane in 1897 that "terrible things might be expected to happen if the collapsed dandy found a publisher for his book of memories." Crane liked some passages of Wilde's dramas but he thought Wilde as a poet was "just a sentimental neurotic who should be shipped for treatment to S. Weir Mitchell,[7] or some other doctor who knows all about that kind of thing. He would later be shocked and nauseated," Beer reports, "by the sight of Wilde's blotched and powdered face bleating compliments at him in the smoke of the Café Procope [in Paris], but now his refusal to discuss Oscar as a splendid sinner irritated Harland sharply."

During the summer of 1897 Crane earned close to $2,000, "but the sum actually paid in to me has been only £20. 17 s. 3 d.—about 120 dollars. In consequence I have to borrow [from literary agent Pinker] and feel very miserable indeed. I am not sure that I am not in trouble over it." he wrote William. "McClures with security of over 1000 dollars against my liability of four hundred, refuse to advance me any money. And yet they think they are going to be my American publishers." The New York *Journal* claimed he had overdrawn his account; he felt they were in error, not he, and so there was a big misunderstanding with them.

In October he wrote literary agent Paul Reynolds in New York: "Good: Now we can do something. I will allow you ten percent on the sales and refer everything to you, giving you the clear field which is your right. You will have the whole management as in the theatrical business. Now one of the reasons of this is to get me out of the ardent grasp of the S. S. McClure Co. I owe them about $500, I think, and they seem to calculate on controlling my entire out-put. They have in their possession 'The Monster' (21,000 words) and 'The Bride Comes to Yellow Sky' (4500) both for the American rights alone. The American rights alone of 'The Monster' ought to pay them easily, minus your commission. No; perhaps it wouldn't pay them fully but it would pay a decent amount of it. Then the American rights of 'The Bride'—I judge to be worth $175. As for my existing contracts there are only two. I. To write an article on an engine ride from London to Glasgow for the McClures. II. To give them my next book."

Later that month Crane wrote William: "I am just thinking how easy it would be in my present financial extremity to cable you for a hundred dollars but then by the time this reaches you I will probably be all right again. I believe the sum I usually borrowed was fifteen dollars, wasn't it? Fifteen dollars—fifteen dollars—fifteen dollars. I can remember an interminable row of fifteen dollar requests."

Crane had met Paul Revere Reynolds in early 1896 at a luncheon given by Irving Bacheller after *The Red Badge of Courage* had swept the English and American public. He had arranged then for Reynolds to become his literary agent, but this did not materialize until October, 1897. Thus he was still trying to handle his American rights himself when he wrote E. Leslie Gilliams, on September 19: "Dear Sir: My terms for a story of between five and ten thousand words is $500. This does not include the English rights. I would be willing to submit to you a story to be paid for on these terms."[8] His English rights were handled by his London agent, James B. Pinker, without whom the writers of that day might not have survived; neither Crane, nor Conrad, nor many lesser lights. That little man (to quote Ford) "with spectacles and a singular accent at the bottom of Arundel Street in London" would take long odds in backing a writer.

Literary London was filled to capacity with literary bums, and no sooner did the word go around that there was at Oxford a shining young American of genius ready to entertain than these leeches from Limehouse, Bedford Park, and the Savage Club descended upon Villa Ravensbrook, and Crane would sit up all night with them dispensing hampers of caviar, foie gras, champagne, and oysters in season. These London "Indians," as he said, scalped him—at Pinker's expense. He never objected to Cora's extravagances, only to Pinker's lagging in paying advances against works not yet written.

Pinker guaranteed Crane £20 per thousand words (ten cents per word), says Ford in *Thus to Revisit,* and that sum squares with Crane's terms in his letter to Gilliams. Ford reduced it to £10 in his sketch "Stevie" appearing in the New York *Evening Post* (July 12, 1924), and Thomas Beer corrected him a week later in the *Post* by producing Pinker's signed statement: "I had no control of poor Mr. Crane's American sales, and if he had been obliged to live on what I paid him he would have starved. We had an agreement of forty pounds per thousand words." But all the evidence contradicts that claim, including some thirty unpublished Pinker letters. Cora boasted that Stephen got high prices for his work: five cents per word "at least," and occasionally even fifteen cents. But in fact few famous American writers have received fifteen cents per word, and Crane was not one of them.[9]

Before going to Greece Crane had promised Clyde Fitch, author of *Beau Brummell* (1890), to collaborate on a play, but expenses at Ravensbrook trapped him and nothing came of that risky project. In December he asked McClure to advance him £200 by the first of January for the book rights on his Greco–Turkish War novel—"not yet begun." If McClure advanced him £200 on *Active Service,*[10] he might want to hold back payment on his Greco–Turkish War story "Death and the Child," about which he apologized when sending it to Reynolds in December. "I wouldn't have done it if I was not broke. For heaven's sake raise all the money you can and *cable* it, *cable* it sure between Xmas and New Year's. Sell 'The Monster'! Don't forget that—cable me some money this month." McClure should give $300 for the child story, and get the *Herald* and *World* to up their price per article, he urged Reynolds, while admitting that these articles are "a big graft to play as long as I am here in Europe."

He and Cora were writing newsletters from London every Sunday under the name "Imogene Carter," half a dozen or more appearing in the New York *Press*. He had sent an installment of his "Irish Notes" and of "London Impressions" to the *Journal*, hoping they might appear on the editorial page at $25 per article, and some of them did. He wrote William in late October to excuse himself from sending home descriptions of what he was seeing in England and Ireland and Scotland because "I write myself so completely out in articles that an attempt of the sort would be absurd."

# XIX

## ✑ *Friendship with Conrad*

In his *Notes on Life and Letters* (1921), Joseph Conrad says that in June of 1897 Heinemann's editor Sidney S. Pawling wrote him that Stephen Crane had arrived in England and, on being asked if there was anyone he wished to meet, had mentioned two names. "One of them was yours." Crane said he wanted to meet the author of *The Nigger of the "Narcissus,"* but since he could have known that book only through the installments that began appearing in W. E. Henley's *New Review* in August, he must have mentioned the subject of meeting Conrad later than June. They did not meet until October.

At the luncheon William Heinemann and Pawling gave for Crane's first meeting with Conrad, Crane quite tactlessly declared that Stevenson bored him, and it irked Heinemann that this young American should criticize the most attractive and beloved writer of the age. How presumptuous of this young man of twenty-five to offend the prevailing Stevenson cult! "What I discovered very early in our acquaintance was that Crane had not the face of a lucky man,"[1] wrote Conrad. "That certitude came to me at our first meeting while I sat opposite him listening to his simple tales of Greece." Pawling did not leave until four o'clock, and then Conrad and Crane tramped the streets from Green Park to Kensington Gardens and, after tea, resumed their stroll through unchartered mazes of streets.

Conrad remarked that Crane had seen no war before he went to Greece, and Crane answered: " 'No. But the *Red Badge* is all right.' I assured him that I never had doubted it; and, since the title of the work had been pronounced for the first time, feeling I must do something to show I had read it, I said shly: 'I like your General.' He knew at once what I was alluding to, but said not a word. Nothing could have been more tramp-like than our silent pacing, elbow to elbow, till, after we had left Hyde Park Corner behind us, Crane uttered with his quiet earnestness the words 'I like your young man—I can just see him [Jim Waite].' Nothing could have been more characteristic of the depth of our three-hour-old intimacy than that each of us should have selected for praise the merest by-the-way vignette of a minor

*320*

character. This was positively the only allusion we made that afternoon to our immortal works."

They talked little until they had tea at an A.B.C. shop and got to Tottenham Court when Crane queried Conrad about Balzac. "How he came in I have no idea. Crane was not given to literary curiosities of that kind. Somebody he knew, or something he had read, must have attracted lately his attention to Balzac. And now suddenly at ten o'clock in the evening he demanded insistently to be told in particular detail all about the *Comédie Humaine,* its contents, its scope, its plan, and its general significance, together with a critical description of Balzac's style." Over the remnants of a meal at Monico's, amidst clattering crockery and rushing waiters, Conrad continued his discourse about Balzac, and then at eleven o'clock at the Pavilion they parted "with just a handshake and a goodnight—no more—without making arrangements for meeting again, as though we had lived in the same town from childhood and were surely to run across each other next day. It struck me directly I left him that we had not even exchanged addresses; but I was not uneasy. Sure enough, before the month was out there arrived a postcard [from Ravensbrook] asking whether he might come to see us."[2]

When Crane visited the Conrads in late November, he was the first American Jessie (Mrs. Conrad) had ever met; he seemed to her "little more than a boy." Conrad himself later remarked: "You are the greatest of the boys—and you are as good as I want you so you needn't trouble to apologize." Though he was the older, Crane was his senior as author, and now and then Conrad jestingly reminded him of this reversal of situation, and Stephen would smile. "He had a quiet smile that charmed and frightened one. It made you pause by something revelatory it cast over his whole physiognomy, not like a ray but like a shadow. I often asked what it could be, that quality that checked one's carefree mood, and now I think I have my answer. It was the smile of a man who knows that his time will not be long on this earth."

On November 9, Conrad sent Crane a copy of *Almayer's Folly* inscribed: "To Stephen Crane with the greatest regards and most sincere admiration from Jph Conrad." Two days later Crane wrote him in care of Heinemann, since he had lost his address. "Did we not have a good pow-wow in London?" Conrad then had grave doubts about his prospects as a writer in spite of H. G. Wells' review of his *Outcast of the Islands* in 1896, which Wells thought was "perhaps the finest piece of fiction that has been published this year, as *Almayer's Folly* was one of the finest that was published in 1895." In May–June, 1897, Conrad wrote his splendid story "Youth" and began as a short story what ended as the novel *Lord Jim,* but he failed at his start of what years later became *The Rescue.* In despair and doubt he went to Glasgow in September, 1897, in search of a ship sailing anywhere. All summer he had been too nervously depressed to take comfort in the periodical publication of *The Nigger of the "Narcissus"*; but that is the way Conrad was all his life, an irascible hypochondriac not given to silent suffering, although one would never surmise this from his fictional works. He lived at Stanford-le-hope in a house called Ivy Walls in the Essex mud flat edging the Thames estuary, and from that dreary hamlet could hear the sound of the tides and of steamer sirens. He detested Ivy Walls as much as Crane detested Ravensbrook.

When Stephen met him in October, 1897, he saw a short, round-shouldered man whose head seemed shrunken into his body. "He had a dark retreating face with a very carefully trimmed and pointed beard, a trouble-wrinkled forehead and very troubled dark eyes, and the gestures of his hands were very Oriental indeed"—to quote H. G. Wells, whose first impression of him was "of a swarthy face peering out and up through the little window panes." Conrad once nearly came to blows with Bernard Shaw, for whom he conceived an intense dislike, but Wells tactfully intervened and drew him away. On another occasion, when Wells criticized as undignified an article Ford Hueffer had written about Hall Caine, Conrad in his role of Polish aristocrat urged Ford to challenge Wells to a duel. Ford tried to explain that in England duelling wasn't done. He described Conrad as dark in complexion with black hair and clipped black beard, very broad in the shoulder and long in the arm. "He had the gestures of a Frenchman who shrugs his shoulders frequently. When you had really secured his attention he would insert a monocle into his right eye and scrutinise your face from very near as a watchmaker looks into the works of a watch. He entered a room with his head held high, rather stiffly and with a haughty manner, moving his head once semicircularly. In this one movement he had expressed to himself the room and its contents; his haughtiness was due to his determination to master that room, not to dominate its occupants, his chief passion being the realisation of aspects to himself." He was infinitely reserved, said Virginia Woolf. "His humour is aristocratic—ironic, sardonic, never broad and free like the Common English humour which descends from Falstaff." His figure was astonishingly thin, with a suggestion of great nervous force (to quote R. L. Megroz). His voice "was like a fervent whisper, suave, dulcet, urgently restful as the foam-surface of a maelstrom."

He talked with great rapidity, said Arthur Symons. "He had at times the same convulsive chuckle as Verlaine's; his laughter when he was most excited reminded me of Whistler's sharp crackle of laughter, which was as if a rattlesnake had suddenly leapt out; which was in fact a crackling of thorns under the pot, but of flaming thorns, setting the pot in a fury of boiling." His penetrating dark brown eyes—as variable as opals—changed as his moods and nerves changed, "and under his black brows they had that terrible fixity of vision which, like a cat's, is inexorable; eyes, that having in their deep sorcerous depths something of the sea's glamour, had never forgotten the sea." His curious Oriental spirit of courtiership, said Ford Hueffer, led Conrad "to greet the humblest of human beings with gestures of servility, with strokings of the hand, with bendings of the back, and with verbal eulogia that would have added glory to a czar on his throne." He told Symons: "I've never looked into myself. There was no time in these years to turn my head away from the table. There are whole days when I did not know whether the sun shone or not."

A few days after his happy first encounter with Conrad, Crane wrote on October 12: "I believe in ghosts. Mr. Stevenson has not passed away far enough. He is all around town." Stevenson had died in Samoa in 1894, but the charm of his genius was still the talk of London in 1897. "Everyone tells me that Mr. Stevenson was a fine fellow," Crane wrote, "but nothing on earth could move me to change my belief that most of his work was insincere." But Stevenson did not regard himself as a fine fellow. In abandoning Kate Drummond—a girl of low origins—when his parents threatened to cut him off financially if he married her, his behavior in his own eyes was not heroic, only prudent. His later relations were with older women of the maternal type, the very kind that Crane pursued or was pursued by. Both shied from sex in their writings. Stevenson finally went to California in pursuit of Mrs. Osbourne, whose husband courteously obliged the lovers. She was his mistress until she obtained a divorce a year later and married him.

In 1897 she wrote C. M. Maurice: "Many thanks for the photograph of Stephen Crane. Several people have spoken to me of his resemblances, but I should imagine the likeness is simply one of photography." The likeness was in the face—oval and with identical moustache, with the difference that Stevenson's eyes were large and brown—Crane's large and gray-blue. Crane's hair was matted and bowl-shaped, whereas Stevenson wore his hair long—long enough to be done up in a bun. "I hear that he married a newspaper lady in Athens and that they are living in Surrey," Mrs. Stevenson added. "She is nine or ten years older than Mr. Crane and 'all the tongues are wagging.' Mr. Gosse says that she is very amusing. . . ." Fanny Stevenson was herself eleven years older than R. L. S.

Like Crane, Stevenson traveled in constant search of some promised land. Both were rebels against social conformity, but in their art they differed radically in that Stevenson romanticized life. Crane despised him as a fake esthete, Bohemian, literary poseur; yet he had read at best but a fraction of Stevenson's works.[3]

If Crane scorned R. L. S., he in turn was scorned by George Meredith, who snubbed him on the steps of a London club. Why Meredith, forty-five years older and a literary demigod, should flip his nose at a young American author is puzzling. His friend Algernon Swinburne, however, entertained Crane for tea at Putney by reading him translations of sixteenth-century manuscripts—what a bore! That same evening, Stephen—on the rebound from his cultural session with Swinburne—tramped Limehouse, the slum section of London, with Robert Barr. In his Irish romance, *The O'Ruddy*, he describes the London version of New York City's Tenderloin:

"We passed into another street, where each well-lighted window framed one or more painted hussies who called out in jocular obscenity, but when we marched stiffly on without replying their manner changed, and they delivered us volley after volley of language incredibly foul. There were only two of these creatures who paid no heed, and their indifference to us was due to the fact that they were deeply engaged in a duel of words, exchanging the most frightful, blood-curdling epithets. Confident drunken men jostled us from time to time, and frequently I could see small, ashy-faced, ancient-eyed youths dodging here and there with food and wine."

Crane found London taverns more interesting than the fashionable drawing rooms where "everybody knows everybody else's business in the superlative degree and everybody reads everybody's books mainly—unless I'm blind—to be at once able to tell everybody else how bad they are. Politics and literature have got wonderfully boiled into a kind of chowder. I feel like a clam."

He wrote James Gibbons Huneker, whom he had known in New York the previous year, that Englishmen believe "anything wild or impossible you tell them and then if you say your brother has a bathtub in his house they—ever so politely—call you a perjured falsifier of facts. I told a seemingly sane man at Mrs. Garnett's that I got my artistic education on the Bowery and he said, 'Oh, really? So they have a school of fine arts there?' I had, you see, just told Mrs. Garnett while this mummy listened all about the Bowery—in so far as I could tell a woman about the Bowery—but that made no difference to this John Bull. Now I'm going to wave the starry flag of freedom a little even if you condemn the practice of one who knows not Balzac and Dostoywhat's his name."[4]

He reminded Huneker, who had praised Englishmen for their fine manners: "You Indians have been wasting wind in telling me how 'unintrusive' and 'delicate' I would find English manners. I don't. It has not been the habit of people to meet at Mr. Howells or Mr. Phillips or Mrs. Sonntages [Sonntag] to let fall my hand and begin to quickly ask me how much money I make and from which French realist I shall steal my next book. For it has been proven to me fully and carefully by authority that all my books are stolen from the French. They stand me against the walls with a teacup in my hand and tell me how I have stolen all my things from De Maupassant, Zola, Loti and the bloke who wrote—I forget the book. I find nothing 'unintrusive' or 'delicate' in these goings on. The simple rustic villagers of Port Jervis have as good manners as some of the flower of England's literary set." For instance, Lady Cardigan at a tea given by Ambassador

John Hay broke into laughter offensive to Hay and to Crane, who later wrote someone that Lady Cardigan had no more manners than a street-walker. A few days later at the house of Lafayette Hoyt De Friese (some-time after late November, 1897), he told a lady dining beside him that his father had been a Presbyterian Cardinal, and she said: "Oh, do Dis-senters have Cardinals in the States?"

When the American Ambassador, John Hay, congratulated him on his success, Crane replied: "I wish success paid me a salary, sir." He wrote John Northern Hilliard earlier in the summer that he was disappointed with success and was tired of American abuse, whereas over here they give everyone "an honest measure of praise or blame. There are no disgusting personalities." He came to think differently later on, as we have seen. "Now that I have reached a goal, I suppose that I ought to be contented; but I am not," he wrote. "I was happier in the old days when I was always dreaming of the thing I have now attained."

In late October Irving Bacheller's syndicate invited him to go to the Klondike. Maybe his brother Edmund would quit Hartwood to join him. "I do not believe there is exactly too much money in it for me but there will be enough to clear all heavy expenses and so I have accepted the offer in the hope that I may be able to do some small service to Ted"—if his brother Edmund (Ted) was serious about joining him in the trip to the Klondike. Then, on October 29, he wrote William: "I go to the Soudan in about a month. The English forces are surely going to Khartoum. Perhaps I may be able to write you from there. That would be nice. I wanted badly to go to India to see the frontier row there but English papers discouraged me. They said it would be all over before I could get there. That was eight weeks ago and the war is still in full blast. The Afridis have thrashed the life out of the Englishmen on one of two occasions but we don't hear about it. That is the Englishman's strong point. However I hope there will be some good fighting in the Soudan before long."[5]

But he went neither to the Klondike nor to Khartoum. In July he had written Edmund: "Expect to hear from me in the Soudan. The S. A. fight is off."[6] In his October letter to William declaring that he was going to the Soudan in about a month, he looks forward to settling down in Port Jervis or Hartwood, a prospect which he knew was an impossibility.[7] He felt himself lucky in having surmounted the "social hedges" of English literary society with no one probing into Cora's past, whereas the proper citizens of Judge William Howe Crane's hometown would regard Cora's eccentric mannerisms as suspiciously improper.

That autumn he wrote his short masterpiece of the American West, "The Bride Comes to Yellow Sky," and then in utter contrast to it his sentimental Grecian War story: "Death and the Child." He hoped that his debt to

McClure would be paid off by "The Monster" or else by "The Bride"—"it is a daisy and don't let them talk funny about it," he wrote Reynolds in October.

"The Bride" is the story of Sheriff Jack Potter, who has sneaked off to San Antonio to bring his bride to Yellow Sky, and of Scratchy Wilson, who is possessed by the fixed idea that the West is still a lawless region where one shoots it out with the town sheriff. The gun-toting Wilson confronts a sheriff who has no gun and he is thus unnerved, disarmed. The story turns on a single ironic moment. Wilson feels "like a creature allowed a glimpse of another world." With the shock of recognition that his enemy has dared to enter Yellow Sky gunless, he gets a glimpse of that new world Sheriff Potter brings home. Potter—married—is a new man now, and his new world saves him—his weapon is a spiritual one. It is an hourglass turnabout beginning with Sheriff Potter in the power of Scratchy Wilson. Wilson is "trapped" by the unexpected. At the crisis Potter recalls the train which had seemed to him to represent his new world, "all the glory of the marriage, the environment of the new estate." His bride—wearing velvet patches in her blue cashmere dress with steel buttons abounding—is identified for him with the train's dazzling fittings of "sea-green figured velvet and shining silver." The train stops at Yellow Sky to take on water; Potter, like the train, has "a constricted throat." And Scratchy Wilson's throat, when he confronts the gunless sheriff, "worked like a pump." Wilson is thus identified with Potter, his opposite. Both share a fear of changed worlds. The frontier code, which Sheriff Potter has betrayed by getting married and going gunless, collapses for Wilson, whose despair and abasement is symbolized by the funnel-shaped tracks his feet make in the heavy sand. A married sheriff is to him, "a simple child of the earlier plains," a foreign condition in the code he lives by. It may herald a new era for Yellow Sky, but it is the end of the old era for Scratchy Wilson and his fixed idea about the West. The East has overtaken the West—even Wilson is not an oldtime Westerner, not the real thing. We know him by his clothes. He wears not what the old Westerners wore but "a maroon-colored flannel shirt, which had been purchased for purposes of decoration, and made principally by some Jewish women on the East side of New York," and "his boots had red tops with gilded imprints, of the kind beloved in winter by little sledding boys on the hillsides of New England."

Did Crane see his own situation in the Sheriff's? Potter has been "spurred by his sharp impulse" into marriage; he has "gone headlong over all the social hedges." He has thought of telling his friends in Yellow Sky about it by telegraph, but "a new cowardice had been upon him. He feared to do it." He feels his friends "would never forgive him."

Potter's bride looks at him anxiously: " 'What's worrying you, Jack?' He laughed again. 'I'm not worrying, girl; I'm only thinking of Yellow Sky!' She flushed in comprehension. A sense of mutual guilt invaded their minds and developed a finer tenderness." Stephen and Cora must have felt this "sense of mutual guilt" in their bluffing at Ravensbrook that they were married, and a "finer tenderness" because of it. Potter knew "full well that his marriage was an important thing to this town. It could not be exceeded by the burning of the new hotel."

Crane liked to entertain his guests by imitating Scratchy Wilson. When drunk Scratchy was a terror, but when sober he "wouldn't hurt a fly," he said. At Ravensbrook Stephen would hold in his hand a Smith & Wesson and wait until a fly approached the piece of sugar he'd placed on the table. "When the fly was by the sugar, he would twist the gun round his wrist. The fly would die, killed by the bead sight of the revolver. That is much more difficult than it sounds," says Ford Madox Ford in his *Return to Yesterday*. "I can see him sitting in the singularly ugly drawing room of the singularly hideous villa he lived in for a time at Oxted. Then he wore— I dare say to shock me—cowboy breeches and no coat, and all the time he was talking he wagged in his hand an immense thing that he called a gun and that we should call a revolver. From time to time he would attempt to slay with the bead-sight of this Colt such flies as settled on the table, and a good deal of his conversation would be taken up with fantastic boasts about what can be done with these lethal instruments. I don't know that he celebrated his own prowess, but he boasted about what heroes in the Far West were capable of. I did not much believe him then and I believe him still less now. I don't believe any one is capable of anything with a revolver." But neither did Crane. Scratchy Wilson "is a wonder with a gun—a perfect wonder," but the point of the story is that no man "is capable of anything with a revolver."

When Ford was asked if he didn't think Conrad's "Youth" the finest story ever written, he replied: "What about 'The Bride Comes to Yellow Sky'?" He hadn't read the story for many years, but he saw at that moment "quite vividly even the pages of the magazine in which 'The Bride' was serialized . . . and I had the odd conviction that the story had 'influenced' me more than anything else I ever read." Ford—given to distortions of facts and faulty memory—is here again amusing. "The Bride" could not possibly appear serialized as it is a short story of only 5000 words. It appeared in *Chapman's Magazine* and in *McClure's* in February, 1898, and in *The Open Boat* collection in June. But then Ford also claimed that the Crane work which influenced him most was "Five White Mice," which he misnamed "Four White Mice" and elsewhere "Three White Mice."

Conrad wrote Crane about *The Open Boat and Other Stories* when the author presented him a copy. "But my great excitement was reading your stories. Garnett's right. 'A Man and Some Others' is immense." It is curious how he failed to recognize that "The Bride" was a masterpiece. He misquoted Garnett's praise that in "The Bride" Crane's "art is immense" by applying these words to "A Man and Some Others," which Western tale

Garnett mentioned not at all in his London *Academy* appreciation of Crane for December, 1898. The only thing immense about "A Man and Some Others" is its length—its beginning and ending are too far apart. Its ending is melodramatic and its middle is false.

Conrad, then, perversely ignored "The Bride" and praised "A Man and Some Others"! He admired it "without reserve. It is an amazing bit of biography . . . The boat thing is immensely interesting. I don't use the word in its common sense. It is fundamentally interesting to me. Your temperament makes old things new and new things amazing. I want to swear at you, to bless you—perhaps to shoot you—but I prefer to be your friend. You are an everlasting surprise to one. You shock—and the next moment you give the perfect artistic satisfaction. Your method is fascinating. You are a complete impressionist. The illusions of life come out of your hand without a flaw. It is not life—which nobody wants—it is art—art for which everyone—the abject and the great—hanker—mostly without knowing it."

Conrad declared that there were "profound similitudes in our temperaments." There were profound similitudes in their artistry, in their aesthetic code of impressionism and symbolism, and in their probing of psychological conditions of heroes or non-heroes in stories of conflict and action, placing trapped or baited characters in paradoxical situations seen from a double and therefore ironic point of view. In Crane any affirmation is contradicted by some denial of that affirmation, and in Conrad it is the same reversal or double mood. As persons, however, their temperaments differed radically. Crane is forthright and hasty, not prudent; Conrad is crafty. Crane shared nothing of the Slav's cautious and withdrawing, skeptical and secretive moods. Conrad winced at his ailments, while Crane complained of his not once in all his life. Conrad is shrewdly deceptive and often deliberately misleading.

Crane claimed that the average reader has no imagination, and Conrad admonished Norman Douglas: "You must realize the inconceivable stupidity of the common reader—the man who forks out the half crown." He protested that he was a much simpler person than he appeared in Arthur Symons' pen portrait of him, but like Stephen, he was crafty, cryptographic in his speech and in his literary works.

Conrad sent Crane the page proofs of the book version of *The Nigger of the "Narcissus"* and Stephen on November 11 responded: "I have read the proof sheets which you so kindly sent me and the book is simply great. The simple treatment of the death of Waite is too good, too terrible. I wanted to forget it at once. It caught me very hard. I felt ill over that red thread lining from the corner of the man's mouth to his chin. It was frightful with the weight of a real and present death. By such small means does the real writer flash out in the sky above those who are always well."

On the 16th Conrad replied: "I must write to you before I write a single word for a living to-day. I was anxious to know what you think of the end.

If I've hit you with the death of Jimmy I don't care if I don't hit another man. I think however that artistically the end of the book is somewhat lame. I mean after the death. All that rigmarole about the burial and the ship's coming home seems to run away into a rat's tail—thin at the end. Well! It's too late now to bite my thumbs and tear my hair. When I feel depressed about it I say to myself 'Crane likes the damned thing'—and am greatly consoled. What your appreciation is to me I renounce to explain. The world looks different to me now, since our long pow-wow. It was good. The memory of it is good. And now and then (human nature *is* a vile thing) I ask myself whether you meant half of what you said!"

But Crane of course meant what he said, and he was so impressed by the book that he wrote Hamlin Garland to ask Irving Bacheller to reissue it in America. "Get his Nigger of the Narcissus. It is a crackerjack. Conrad knows your work. You should meet him when you come to England." Garland on November 29 replied from New York: "I was very glad to hear from you and from Mr. Conrad. I wish you had written another page to tell me how you are getting on and what you intended to do. I heard you were to make your home in England but this I take to be somebody's lie. I shall not believe it till you write and tell me so. Mr. Conrad's work is not known to me, I am sorry to say, but I shall be all the more delighted to have a copy of the book you speak of."

Conrad's book, published on December 4–5, was reviewed by W. L. Courtney in the London *Daily Telegraph* on December 8,[8] and his claim of Crane's influence on Conrad was echoed in the London *Speaker*'s remark that *The Nigger of the "Narcissus"* is a "worthy pendant" to Crane's *Red Badge of Courage*. This irked Conrad, who wrote Crane on the 24th that the criticism by "that ass Courtney" was "the most mean-minded criticism I've read in my life. . . . Do you think I tried to imitate you? No sir! I may be a little fool but I know better than to try to imitate the inimitable."

He had read *The Red Badge of Courage* sometime after its publication in London by Heinemann, and Crane's story did influence him—notwithstanding his disclaimer. Crane's impact on Conrad may be seen also in the story "Youth" (1898) where—much as in "The Open Boat"—a subtle bond unites the men who endure their ordeal and trial by sea when the *Judea* catches fire and seems doomed. The desperation of Crane's "proud youth" sums up the substance of Conrad's story with its cry of "O Youth!" Crane's influence extends beyond "Youth" and *The Nigger of the "Narcissus"* to *Lord Jim*.

The Conrads could not visit Stephen and Cora at Ravensbrook because Jessie was pregnant and unable to undertake even a short journey ("not presentable just now"), and so Stephen visited them on November 28 and was received as an old friend by Jessie, whose sympathy was "as undemonstrative and sincere as his own quiet friendliness." Joseph had prepared her to meet an unusual youth with a charm peculiarly his own, and he appeared to Jessie's material mind as very slight and delicate. She saw at once that the two men were on the easy terms of complete understanding. Stephen was "conceited by streaks" (as Beer puts it), but never before his elders. More often than not he was modest, and always he was quite unpredictable. He had about him "a great deal of the defiant mistrust that the French call *méfiance*," says Ford in "Stevie," (New York *Post:* July 12, 1924), and he never uttered moral platitudes.

Jessie remembered Stephen balancing himself on a tilted chair and discoursing gravely on the merit of the three dogs he'd brought to Ravensbrook from Ireland: Sponge, Flannel and Ruby. They also discussed Crane's poetry. Conrad had suggested that he write to Henri D. Davray of the *Mercure de France* in Paris to ask him to translate *The Black Riders* into French, and Crane on November 11 had sent Davray the book. "Perchance, there would be a publisher who would print it," he wrote. "What I wish is the distinction." His dearest wish is to see it translated. He says that some of his books have received German and Russian translations, "but, let alone translations, the British public nor even my own American public will not look at *The Black Riders*."[9]

Conrad wrote Edward Garnett about Crane's visit and said that they talked and smoked half the night. "He is strangely hopeless about himself. I like him. . . . His eye is very individual and his expression satisfies me artistically. He certainly is *the* impressionist and his temperament is curiously unique. His thought is concise, connected, never very deep—yet often startling. He is *the only* impressionist and *only* an impressionist. Why is he not immensely popular? With his strength, with his rapidity of action, with that amazing faculty of vision—why is he not? He has outline, he has colour, he has movement, with that he ought to go very far. But—will he? I sometimes think he won't. It is not an opinion—it is a feeling. I could not explain why he disappoints me—why my enthusiasm withers as soon as I close the book. While one reads, of course, he is not to be questioned. He is the master of his reader to the very last line—then—apparently for no reason at all—he seems to let go his hold." He gets his hold on his reader, but then it is "as if he had gripped you with greased fingers. . . . It just occurs to me that it is perhaps my own self that is slippery. I don't know."

Crane's impressionism of phrase "went really deeper than the surface," said Conrad. "In his writing he was very sure of his effects. I don't think he was ever in doubt about what he could do. Yet it often seemed to me that he was but half aware of the exceptional quality of his achievement." He seemed "almost childlike in the impulsive movements of his untutored genius. The most simple-minded of verbal impressionists, using his great gifts of straight feeling and right expression with a fine sincerity and a strong if, perhaps, not fully conscious conviction. His art did not obtain, I fear, all the credit its unsophisticated inspiration deserved."[10]

Conrad wrote this in the first decade after Crane's death, when his name had sunk almost into oblivion. But the fact is that Crane was not an "un-tutored genius"; and while he sometimes may have seemed childish he was anything but unsophisticated.

Crane, said Ford in 1935, had a passion for elisions, for economy of words, and he never tired of declaring that his ambition was "to make every damned word do the work of six." Crane, Conrad and Henry James were the English protagonists of literary impressionism, but it was perhaps Crane of all that school (which included W. H. Hudson, Robert Cunningham Graham, and Ford himself) who most observed the canon of literary impressionism: " 'You must render: never report.' You must never, that is to say, write: 'He saw a man aim a gat at him!'; you must put it: 'He saw a steel ring directed at him.' Later you must get in that, in his subconsciousness, he recognized that the steel ring was the polished muzzle of a revolver. So Crane rendered it in *Three White Mice,* which is one of the major short stories of the world. That is Impressionism."[11] ("Five White Mice," which Ford hadn't read since its publication in 1898, is neither one of Crane's major stories nor one of the major short stories of the world.)

After his all-night session with Conrad Crane was in need of sleep the next day, but he was disturbed by the visit of a literary boy living in the neighborhood, who imposed himself on the Cranes from nine to four. Cora, in an exasperated mood that Monday morning, replied to Henry Sanford Bennett's telegram announcing his arrival from Paris: "As Stephen is asleep I have taken the liberty of opening your telegram. Will you do a distracted wife a favour? I know that Stephen wants to see you as soon as possible. But we have been overwhelmed with callers all [last] week. He is desperately trying to finish a story ["Death and the Child"] . . . . So I am not going to tell Stephen that Mrs. Bennett and you have arrived in London. Please telegraph or write again, day after tomorrow. I know this is rude."

The following day Harold Frederic, now living in Robert Barr's house at Woldingham while Barr was in Algeria, walked over to Ravensbrook with five of his friends and embarrassed Cora at lunchtime. Another uninvited guest on the 30th was Lafayette Hoyt de Friese, a partner in a law firm in London, who came with a note of introduction from John S. Stokes, a cousin of the Duke of Norfolk. Cora invited him to lunch and Stephen, although in no welcoming mood for visitors, was very pleasant in his quiet and boyish way. The American lawyer De Friese was surprised that Stephen was so young and that he used little slang, although his books are full of it. He thought Mrs. Crane was a Southerner and had reddish hair (she was born in Boston and was blonde). He reported to his wife that Harold Frederic was not at all agreeable. "He is funny in a sarcastic way about politics and people but he kept interrupting everybody else and was downright rude to Mr. Crane several times."

What Frederic was rude about was "The Monster," and a few days later he quarreled with Stephen about it. Crane was not at all in any pleasant boyish mood; Frederic was urging him to throw away "The Monster," and Stephen, in passionate defense, beat the butt of his Mexican revolver upon the furniture. Perhaps Frederic felt he was giving him fatherly advice lest the story prove too awful for public taste. Always hot for an argument, he switched his attack from "The Monster" to Conrad's *The Nigger of the "Narcissus."* Crane—already enraged—crashed a dessert plate with his huge Mexican revolver and shouted: "You and I and Kipling couldn't have written The Nigger!" (Privately he thought Frederic's *The Damnation of Theron Ware* "could have been written a darned lot better.")

Bennett sat listening as the argument blazed all through lunch, and ended in an explosion (to quote Beer). Too humble to intrude into the argument, he was horrified by Frederic's damnation of "The Monster." He was also horrified by the story itself, and on rereading it years later he discovered that what had troubled him in 1897 had been Crane's statement that the Negro "hasn't any face."

After the trying lunch, Crane's guests asked him to shoot his revolver, and some children came over from the next house to watch. This must have calmed his nerves. Frederic, too, calmed down, for it was not long before he repaired the rift in his friendship with Crane. This big, brusque fellow was not so fierce as he seemed. At the Savage Club they said of him: "He has the heart of a babe and the hide of a rhinoceros." After you got to know him passing well, "you knew that there were two Frederics—the Frederic of the books and *The Times* letters, and the high voiced, careless, over generous, pugnacious, gentle-hearted, hard-working, dogmatic Frederic of Fleet Street and the smoking room. You had your choice." Oddly enough, he wrote a script "like the handiwork of a girl who has learned copperplate engraving," and you'd never suspect that the writer of this exquisite penmanship "was something of a giant with the grip of a vise and the voice of a liner's siren."

Crane quit Ravensbrook the night of the quarrel over "The Monster," or the next morning, to hole up in a room at the Brown Hotel in London so as to finish "Death and the Child." Here he met with Conrad for their third session together. Conrad was in London at the beginning of December to dine with the Scotsman Cunninghame Graham, who had returned from his captivity among the Moors. He was a picturesque figure with pointed beard and shining moustache—like a Velásquez come to life. A kind of Don Quixote, El Conquistador of lost causes, Cunninghame Graham, with the blood of hidalgos and of Scottish kings in his veins, wrote of gauchos on the South American pampas, and was united to Conrad and W. H. Hudson by memories of an adventurous past in strange and faraway places. Conrad early the next year urged him to read *The Red Badge of Courage.* "It won't hurt you—or only very little. Crane-ibn-Crane[12] el Yankee is all right."

In Crane's story "The Monster," a Negro rescues a white boy from a burning house and survives the flames as a faceless idiot. The original for the Negro Henry Johnson was Levi Hume, who hauled ashes in Port Jervis. His face had been eaten by cancer. He was an object of horror to the children there, says one of Crane's nieces, "for it could truthfully be said of him 'He had no face.' "

Henry Johnson enters the burning house and gets to the head of the stairs. "As he opened the door great billows of smoke poured out, but, gripping Jimmie closer, he plunged down through them. All manner of odors assailed him during this flight. They seemed to be alive with envy, hatred, and malice. At the entrance to the laboratory he confronted a strange spectacle. The room was like a garden in the region where might be burning flowers. Flames of violet, crimson, green, blue, orange, and purple were blooming everywhere. There was one blaze that was precisely the hue of a delicate coral. In another place was a mass that lay merely in phosphorescent inaction like a pile of emeralds. But all these marvels were to be seen dimly through clouds of heaving, turning, deadly smoke.

"Johnson halted for a moment on the threshold. He cried out again in the Negro wail that had in it the sadness of the swamps. Then he rushed across the room. An orange-colored flame leaped into Johnson. There was an explosion at one side, and suddenly before him there reared a delicate, trembling sapphire shape like him and Jimmie. Johnson shrieked, and then ducked in the manner of his race in fights. He aimed to pass under the left guard of the sapphire lady. But she was swifter than eagles, and her talons caught in him as he plunged past her. Bowing his head as if his neck had been struck, Johnson lurched forward, twisting this way and that way. He fell on his back. The still form in the blanket flung from his arms, rolled to the edge of the floor and beneath the window.

"Johnson had fallen with his head at the base of an old-fashioned desk. There was a row of jars upon the top of this desk. For the most part, they were silent amid this rioting, but there was one which seemed to hold a scintillant and writhing serpent." Then suddenly the glass splintered, "and a ruby-red snake-like thing poured its thick length out upon the top of the old desk. It coiled and hesitated, and then began to swim a langorous way down the mahogany slant. At the angle it waved its sizzling molten head to and fro over the closed eyes of the man beneath it. Then, in a moment, with a mystic impulse, it moved again, and the snake flowed directly down into Johnson's upturned face.

"Afterward the trail of this creature seemed to reek, and amid flames and low explosions drops like red-hot jewels pattered softly down it at leisurely intervals."

In gratitude for saving his son's life Dr. Trescott lodges the faceless Negro in a hut, but he escapes and terrifies the townsfolk, and so Dr. Trescott keeps him on his own premises. The doctor's former patients shun him, and his wife on her reception day is left with fifteen untouched cups and saucers—the townsfolk shun her society.

Henry Johnson is no longer acclaimed a hero. He is tabooed as a monster by the townsfolk and also by the Negroes, even by his former mistress in "Whilomville" (Port Jervis). Stephen later, when there was gossip in Port Jervis about "The Monster," wrote his brother William: "I suppose that Port Jervis entered my head while I was writing it but I particularly don't wish them to think so because people get very sensitive and I would not scold away freely if I thought the eye of your glorious public was upon me."[13]

"The Monster" was an appeal for brotherhood between white and black.[14] The *Century,* however, did not see it that way when its editor rejected it in 1897 as simply a horrible thing: "We couldn't publish that thing with half the expectant mothers in America on our subscription list." Rupert Hughes saw it as "an incursion into the realms of the horrible without once losing sight of realism or plausibility. There is no strain on credulity, no mysticism of any sort." The sickening qualities in the situation are "mitigated by the indirectness of their suggestion; its trivialities are redeemed by the psychological dignity of the physician's problem. The characters are all discriminately and vividly drawn," Hughes wrote in "The Genius of Stephen Crane," in *The Criterion* (January 6, 1900). This parable is Mr. Crane's Aeschylean method of telling us how silly we are, said reviewer Harry Thurston Peck, while Howells considered it the greatest short story ever written by an American.

Julian Hawthorne's petulant disclaimer that Crane was no artist[15] is readily refuted by quoting the rescue scene, the best thing in the story. However, it is as a social parable that "The Monster" retains its impact today. The Negro Henry Johnson is disfigured literally but also allegorically: physically by the literal fire and then by the allegoric fire which consumes the moral face of the community. Crane's social irony is that the white man's face is also disfigured—by white society's cruelty to the Negro. Henry is stoned. "Of course nobody really wanted to hit him," explains the chief of police in Whilomville, "but you know how a crowd gets. It's like—it's like—." Dr. Trescott recognizes in the face of the mob "an utterly new challenge in the night of the jungle."

No white American author had pictured a Negro performing a truly heroic act before Crane did it in "The Monster." Ralph Ellison, whose *Invisible Man* (1952) is a variant on Crane's theme that the American Negro has "no face," points out that between Twain and Faulkner "no artist of Crane's caliber looked so steadily at the wholeness of American life and discovered such far-reaching symbolic equivalents for its unceasing state of civil war. Crane's work remains fresh today because he was a great artist, but perhaps he became a great artist because under conditions of pressure and panic he stuck to his guns."[16] However, important as Crane's story is as a social parable, it is artistically flawed because its ending drags on and on. Cora, no doubt echoing Stephen's intended meaning in "The

1. Stephen Crane as a student at Hudson River Institute (Claverack, N. Y., 1888)

2. Drew Methodist Church in Port Jervis, N. Y., where Stephen's father, the Reverend Dr. Jonathan Townley Crane, was the minister, 1879-1880

3. Home of Judge William Howe Crane, Stephen's brother, on East Main Street in Port Jervis

4. Edmund Crane's house on the millpond at Hartwood, N. Y., showing the then Hartwood railway station at left

5. The house at Twin Lakes, near Milford, Pennsvania, where Crane stayed as a guest of the Watsfamily when camping with Port Jervis friends in tnearby woods

Stephen Crane (right) with L. Button on the roof of Corwin Knapp Linson's studio on West 30th Street, New York City, 1893

STEPHEN CRANE Aged 22 1894

7. Portrait of Crane painted by Corwin Knapp Linson and inscribed "Stephen Crane, Aged 22/1894/Author/"The Red Badge of Courage."

8. Crane in 1896, taken by "Mr. King, the artist . . . It is a picture that has never been used for publication and is I think a very good portrait." (Crane to the editor of *The Critic*, February 15, 1896)

Hartwood, N. Y.
January 1st.

Dear Mr Howells: Every little time I hear from some friend a kind thing you have said of me, an interest which you have shown in my work. I have been so long conscious of this, that I am grown uncomfortable in not being able to express to you my gratitude and so I seize the New Year's Day as an opportunity to thank you and tell you how often I think of your kind benevolent life.
Sincerely yours
Stephen Crane

9. Letter to William Dean Howells, January 1, 1896

The Red Badge of Courage.
An Episode of the American Civil War.
By Stephen Crane.

~~[scribbled out]~~

The cold passed reluctantly from the earth and
the retiring fogs, revealed an army stretched out on the hills,
resting. As the landscape changed from brown to
green the army awakened and began to tremble
with eagerness at the noise of rumors. It cast
its eyes upon the roads which were growing
from long ~~[crossed out]~~ troughs of liquid mud to
proper thoroughfares. A river, amber-tinted in
the shadow of its banks, purled at the army's
feet and at night when the stream had become
of a sorrowful blackness one could see across,
the red eye-like gleam of hostile camp-fires
set in the low brows of distant hills.

Once, ~~Jim Conklin~~ a certain soldier developed virtues and
went resolutely to wash a shirt. He came fly-
ing back from a brook waving his garment, ban-
ner-like. He was swelled with a tale he had
heard from a reliable friend who had heard it
from a ~~reliable~~ truthful cavalryman who had heard
it from his trust-worthy brother, one of the orderlies
at division head-quarters. ~~He~~ He adopted the important air of a herald in red and gold.

"We're goin' t' move t' morrah - sure", he said

11. Lily Brandon Munroe

12. Nellie Janes Crouse
(Akron, Ohio, winter of 1896)

**CRANE RISKED ALL TO SAVE A WOMAN.**

His Bohemian Life in New York Laid Bare for the Sake of Dora Clark.

For Ten Long Hours He Waited, Determined to Testify Against Policeman Becker.

Cold as Icicles the Novelist's Answers Came, Short, Snappy, and to the Point.

WOMEN AND CABBIES AS WITNESSES.

They Swear, as the Police of the Tenderloin Swear—Dora Clark Directly Accuses Captain Chapman and He Demands a Hearing.

Here are a few hard facts:

POLICEMAN BECKER

DORA CLARK

STEPHEN CRANE TESTIFYING

CHARACTERS AT THE TRIAL OF POLICEMAN BECKER.

13. The Dora Clark affair:
Clipping from the *New York Journal,* October 17, 1896

14. Cora Crane

15. Crane in Athens, May 1897

16. Crane and John Bass of the *New York Journal*, war correspondents in Greece, 1897

17. Crane in his "den" at Ravensbrook Villa, Oxted, Surrey, 1897. (The Mexican blanket and spurs date from his trip to the West and Mexico for the Bacheller Syndicate in 1895.)

RAVENSBROOK,
OXTED,
SURREY.

Nov 11 [1897]

y dear Conrad: My first feat has
een to lose your note and so I
n obliged to send this through
ineman. I have read the proof
eets which you so kindly sent
e and the book is simply great.
e simple treatment of the death of
aite is too good, too terrible. I
anted to forget it at once. It
ught me very hard. I felt ill
er that red thread hung from
e corner of the man's mouth to
s chin. It was frightful with
e weight of a real and present
ath. By such small means does
e real writer suddenly flash out
the sky above those who are
ways doing rather well. In the

meantime I have written to Bach-
-eller and told him to be valiant
in the matter of "The Nigger" —
I have also written some other
little notes to America.

I am afraid you must write
to me soon so that I can finally
nail your address and put it away
in my little book. I was very
stupid. Are you quite sure you
could not come down for a
Sunday luncheon with Mrs
Conrad? Say your own date,
barring this next one. We could
then keep you as long as you
would stay.

Did not we have a good
pow-wow in London?

Faithfully yours
Stephen Crane

18. Letter to Joseph Conrad, November 11, 1897

19. The *Commodore* disaster, as featured in the *New York Journal*, January 3, 1897

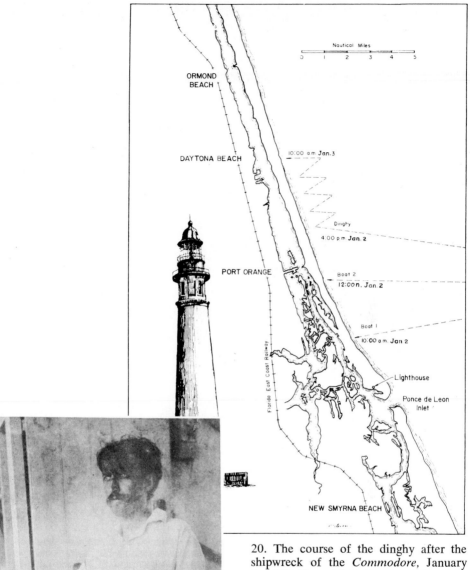

Nautical Miles

ORMOND BEACH

DAYTONA BEACH

10:00 a m Jan. 3

PORT ORANGE

Dinghy
4:00 p m Jan. 2

Boat 2
12:00 n. Jan. 2

Boat 1
10:00 a m Jan. 2

Florida East Coast Railway

Lighthouse

Ponce de Leon Inlet

NEW SMYRNA BEACH

20. The course of the dinghy after the shipwreck of the *Commodore,* January 1, 1897. From U. S. Coast and Geodetic Survey Charts 1244 and 1245

21. Crane after his ordeal in the dinghy following the sinking of the *Commodore*

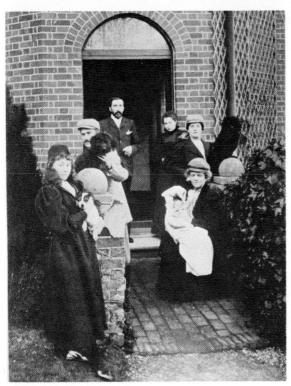

22. The Conrads visit the Cranes at Villa Ravensbrook in early February, 1898. Cora, in cap matching Crane's, is holding the Conrads' infant son, Borys. Behind her is Mathilda Ruedy, formerly of Cora's Hotel de Dream in Jacksonville, and on the step beside Joseph Conrad is probably Jessie, his wife. Up front to the left is Jessie's sister, Dollie.

23. Harold Frederic. From Helen Crane's sketchbook.

24. Crane on the *Three Friends,*
off Cuba, 1898

5. Stephen Crane in 1899. Photo
y Elliott and Fry

26. Brede Manor, Brede, Sussex

27. Crane at Brede Place, 1899

28. Crane in his study over the porch at Brede Place, September 1899

29. Stephen and Cora at the bazaar, flower show and garden party held in the Rectory Gardens, Brede, Sussex, August 23, 1899

30. Cora and Henry James at the same garden party

31. Mr. James enjoys one of Cora's doughnuts at the party.

32. Villa Eberhardt, where Crane died, June 5, 1900

33. The grave of Stephen Crane at Hillside, New Jersey

34. The plaque which marked the location of the house at 17 Mulberry Place, Newark, N. J. where Crane was born

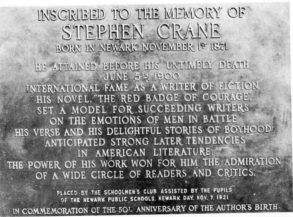

INSCRIBED TO THE MEMORY OF
STEPHEN CRANE
BORN IN NEWARK, NOVEMBER 1ST 1871

HE ATTAINED BEFORE HIS UNTIMELY DEATH
JUNE 5TH 1900
INTERNATIONAL FAME AS A WRITER OF FICTION
HIS NOVEL "THE RED BADGE OF COURAGE"
SET A MODEL FOR SUCCEEDING WRITERS
ON THE EMOTIONS OF MEN IN BATTLE
HIS VERSE AND HIS DELIGHTFUL STORIES OF BOYHOOD
ANTICIPATED STRONG LATER TENDENCIES
IN AMERICAN LITERATURE.
THE POWER OF HIS WORK WON FOR HIM THE ADMIRATION
OF A WIDE CIRCLE OF READERS AND CRITICS.

PLACED BY THE SCHOOLMEN'S CLUB ASSISTED BY THE PUPILS
OF THE NEWARK PUBLIC SCHOOLS. NEWARK DAY, NOV. 7, 1921
IN COMMEMORATION OF THE 50TH ANNIVERSARY OF THE AUTHOR'S BIRTH

Monster," declared in the *Academy* (March 2, 1901) that Henry Johnson "was a hero only as he was a horror."

In "The Veteran," written at Hartwood in 1896 as a sequel to *The Red Badge,* old man Fleming—Henry Fleming grown old—rescues the drunken hired hand whose lantern set the barn afire, and then returning to rescue some forgotten colts is himself trapped in the burning barn. As with the Negro in "The Monster," the old man's face "ceased instantly to be a face; it becomes a mask, a gray thing, with horror written about the mouth and eyes." Thus the hero is dehumanized, exactly as in "The Monster," written at Ravensbrook in 1897. When the barn roof falls in on old man Fleming, "a great funnel of smoke swarmed toward the sky, as if the old man's spirit, released from its body a little bottle . . . like the genie of fable. The smoke was tinted rose-hue from the flames, and perhaps the unutterable midnights of the universe will have no power to daunt the color of this soul."

Old man Fleming's admission of fear in "The Veteran" upsets the fixed idea of the villagers about his heroism and unnerves his grandson Jim. He reminisces about his youth as a raw recruit in battle, and to the villagers' query he replies: "Why, in my first battle I thought the sky was falling down. I thought the world was coming to an end. You bet I was scared." His admission of fear sobers their laughter and strikes terror in the heart of his grandson Jim.

Heroism is not a predictable possession, but rather an impersonal gift thrust by chance upon a man at the wrong moment. In "A Mystery of Heroism" Fred Collins is taunted by his comrades to risk his life by running under shellfire to get water at a well, and so he has no choice but to become a hero, "an intruder in the land of fine deeds." "He had blindly been led by quaint emotions, and laid himself under an obligation to walk squarely up to the face of death." Once at the well, his canteens fill up with maddening slowness, and he is smitten with terror. "The stupid water derided him." He returns not with the canteens but with the well's bucket filled, and as he offers the bucket to a wounded officer "his shaking hands caused the water to splash all over the face of the dying man." Then he runs on "in the manner of a farmer chased out of a dairy by a bull." The regiment gives him a welcoming roar. Soldier Collins has done an heroic deed, but as in Kipling it is the heroism of moral fortitude on the edge of a nervous collapse (the phrase is Edmund Wilson's). His vainglorious triumph is symbolized by the indifference of two jesting lieutenants who jostle the bucket until the water spills and the bucket "lay on the ground empty." The empty bucket suggests the emptiness of his heroism. Challenged, he had undertaken a foolhardy venture, and because he felt no fear at the start he figured: "He was, then, a hero." But if so, then, "after all, heroes were not much."

# XX

# ꧂ *Money Troubles*

CRANE hid out two days at the Brown Hotel in London until Cora wired him that she had got rid of the seven guests boarding there three days. On Sunday, December 5, he wrote Acton Davies to see if Davies could collect the sums he had lent to newspaper cronies while in Greece. "I took X's note for $300 and Y owes me about $250. I hate to press nice fellows, but it costs me more to live here than I was led to believe and some of these Comanche braves seem to think I am running a free lunch counter." Davies collected nothing.

The Cranes gave the impression of affluence, serving their guests game pies and claret, which had not been paid for. Cora to the very end counted on Stephen to solve their money problems by writing; surely prosperity was just around the corner. Both Stephen and Cora seemed to have been psychologically compelled to over-spend. Crane's debts drained his health and his last writings: "the dollars damned him" (as A. J. Liebling said). From October 1897 on, Stephen and Cora were in deep financial trouble, due to their living above their means. By June 1900 he owed agent James B. Pinker one thousand pounds ($5000). As Hemingway says in *The Green Hills of Africa,* "It is only by hazard that a writer makes money, although good books always make money eventually. Then our writers when they have made some money increase their standard of living and they are caught. They have to write to keep up their establishments, their wives, and so on, and they write slop. It is not slop on purpose but because it is hurried. Because they write when there is nothing to say or no water in the well."

During the week after Stephen returned from London, Henry Sanford Bennett brought his young French wife to Ravensbrook when Hueffer was visiting the Cranes, and Cora cut Ford short so as to avoid another squabble. With his usual arrogance, Ford undertook to instruct Bennett's wife on the subject of Seurat. "He talked to her in very bad French," says Bennett, whose wife had known Seurat as a family friend for years. "When she tried to correct Mr. Hueffer's ideas of the artist and his paintings a considerable tension developed, and then Stephen got rather nervous and we were all rather uncomfortable. Mrs. Crane suddenly broke into the conversation and in a 'dangerous' voice said: 'Mr. Hueffer, Mrs. Bennett speaks English very well. Let's change languages—*and the subject.*' The subject was changed. . . . After they were all gone, she relapsed into silence and seemed half asleep."

Bennett says that his first impression of Cora "was awful. She looked like a dance-hall girl in the morning. I must say that the effect, in part, was accidental. She had a profusion of brilliant yellow hair. Its color was perfectly natural, but certain colors made it seem artificial." With her yellow hair in disorder, she lounged into the room in a loose garment. She did not care much about clothes, according to Bennett.

Speaking of Cora and clothes, Ford tells an amusing story. Cora thought she wanted to learn about medieval costumes and dressmaking, about which Ford knew quite a lot. He was a disciple of the William Morris school of arts and crafts, in which his wife Elsie excelled. Cora got her interest in medievalism from Mrs. Marjory Pease of Limpsfield, who knew that one of the ladies in Ford's family wore a close-fitting bodice and very full skirt "and a sort of yellow surcoat with dangling pointed sleeves which got into the baby's milk." At Cora's urging, Mrs. Pease came to Ford's cottage one evening to announce that his presence was urgently needed at the Cranes. Ford says that it was his knowledge of the dress of "the ladies of the Courts of Love" that occasioned his first visit to Ravensbrook, but as we have already encountered him there on the occasion of his offending Bennett's wife in early December, this was in fact his second visit to Ravensbrook—on December 15.[1] Mrs. Pease, a boyish figure with springy gait, wearing a bonnet with strings and knee breeches, delivered her urgent message from Cora, and then Ford set out immediately to nearby Ravensbrook only to find that Stephen was not there.

"Mrs. Crane was almost as puzzled by my English-English accent as by my errand and we finally did talk about medieval dress. It was perhaps the beginning of poor Crane's undoing. For it was, I think, Mrs. Crane's amiable romanticism which led her and poor Crane into various fantasies and ended with their lodging themselves in Brede Place. There, truly, Mrs. Crane wore hanging sleeves, hennins and pointed shoes. Beneath the refectory tables were rushes where the dogs lay and fought for the bones that were dropped to them. I did, of course, know a little more of how the ladies of the Courts of Love garbed themselves than she did."

But Ford had difficulty in getting Mrs. Crane of Jacksonville, Florida, to understand what medieval clothes were like. The long hanging sleeves of fourteenth-century ladies were cut on the cross, but Cora was of the opinion that Ford ought to have said "on the bias." Cora—large, fair and placid—and her attendant, Mrs. Ruedy—dark, thin, and vivacious but quite shy—would no doubt have looked admirable in hennin, as Ford says. But Cora had no idea of abandoning coats and skirts. She did not want to lesson in dressmaking of the medieval variety. She may have wanted to make amends for having told Ford off curtly when he offended Mrs. Bennett and she wanted him there to welcome Stephen back from his London visit with agent Pinker. She had tricked Ford and involved Mrs. Pease in her scheme, which little incident tells us much about her.

She begged him to await Stephen's return because she expected that he would be nervous and distracted, and Ford's presence would jolly him into good humor. Stephen came back from London laden with packages at eleven o'clock that night (says Ford in one account) or else on the last train at half past twelve (says Ford in another account); but no matter. He held a whispered colloquy in the doorway with Cora. They leaned against the doorposts, Stephen with his hat tilted over his eyes while he told Cora the good news he'd brought from Pinker. Then there were explosions of joy. "I have never seen such gladness as was displayed on that Oxted night by that great and elf-like writer." Pinker had guaranteed Crane £20 per thousand words; that was the great good news. And so, bearing purchases of foie gras, caviar, champagne and claret, Crane returned from his triumphal session with the little gentleman of Arundel Street, and there was jovial Ford to share in his good fortune—exactly as Cora had planned it. However, when Stephen had first entered the house he was puzzled to discover Ford there and mistook him to be the bailiff. The local tradesmen had cut off his groceries, and the Cranes were short of food. They purchased everything on credit now at Villa Ravensbrook and later at Brede Manor—piano, horse, typewriter, Kodak, groceries, wine, and firewood. At Brede, when Ford last visited Crane (January 2, 1900), Stephen once more mistook him to be the bailiff.

He kept Ford up all that night at Ravensbrook, talking until breakfast about his glorious future. He ascribed to his visitor certain theories which he then demolished in "the manner and voice of a Bowery tough hammering an Irish scavenger. He was immensely happy." He told Ford that he couldn't write and never would know how to write, and then "pausing to denounce me and my family" proceeded to tell him how to write.

Crane proposed to Conrad that they write a play, and Conrad wrote him in early January, 1898: "You want no help. I have a perfect confidence in your power—and why should you share with me what there may be of profit and fame in the accomplished task?" He asks for a sketch of his idea, and "if you should really, honestly, artistically think I could be of some use—then my dear Crane I would be only too glad to work by your side and with your lead. And quién sabe? Something perhaps would get itself shaped to be mangled by the scorn or the praise of the Philistines."

Crane wanted him "to share in a certain success—'a dead-sure thing,' he said. His was an unrestrainedly generous temperament." It was to be a Western drama in which a man, in the hope of winning a girl, impersonates her lover who has died. Conrad recalls that the scenes were to include a ranch at the foot of the Rocky Mountains, and the action was to be "frankly melodramatic. Crane insisted that one of the situations should present the man and the girl on a boundless plain standing by their dead ponies after a furious ride (a truly Crane touch). I made some objections. A boundless plain in the light of a sunset could be got into a back cloth, I admitted; but I doubted whether we could induce the management of any London theatre to deposit two stuffed horses on its stage."

Stephen Crane, Conrad wrote a friend, "is worrying me to write a play with him. He won't believe me when I swear by all the gods and all the muses that I have no dramatic gift. Probably something will be attempted, but I would bet nothing shall be done." In collaborating, Conrad wrote Crane, "I'd be either cheating or deceiving you. In any case disappointing you. I have no dramatic gift. . . . You have all—and I have only the accursed faculty of dreaming." Crane meanwhile wrote someone (probably drama critic Acton Davies) that "Mr. Conrad and I are writing a new kind of play." Nothing came of the intended collaboration; nothing by Crane ever reached the stage except "The Ghost," which was intended to be a charade. Conrad himself became a dramatist with two plays drawn from his short stories and with *The Secret Agent: A Drama in Four Acts* (1924), based on his novel of that title (1907). As for Crane's idea for "The Predecessor," Conrad made use of its primary idea thirteen years later in one of his short stories.[2]

Conrad wrote Stephen a few days before his first son was born that as he would soon become a father any day now he wasn't in "a decent frame of mind" to write anything and what with one trouble or another he was having a hell of a time. A few days after Borys was born Jessie Conrad was deeply moved on receiving from the Cranes a box of flowers and a warm invitation to spend a week at Ravensbrook as soon as the baby "was old enough to travel. Conrad, writing his cousin Mme. Angèle Zagórska said that Borys was born "on the 17th of this month. [He was born on the 14th.] He has dark hair, huge eyes and resembles a monkey. What pains me is that my wife pretends that he also resembles me. Enfin!" He wrote Cora that he wanted Stephen to give the child (here he calls him "it") "his artistic benediction and—call upon its head the spirit—the magnificent spirit that is his familiar—the genius of his work. And then when our writing days are over he who is a child today may write good prose—may toss a few pearls before the Philistines." He thanked Cora for the flowers and hoped that Jessie would be able to travel by February 19, when Borys would be exactly five weeks old. Borys was as yet "absolutely callous to the honor awaiting him of his very first visit," he wrote Cora on January 25. He said he talked himself hoarse trying to explain the greatness of that occasion to the baby and added that because of Borys' ferocity they might have to bring him in a strong iron cage.

He had written Stephen (January 16) to ask about "The Monster" because that "damned story has been haunting me ever since. It's a subject for you." Crane wrote his New York agent on January 14 that he'd sent "The Monster" to McClure, where he owed money but now had paid up, so Robert McClure in London agreed to release it. But the affair got bungled back in the New York office. "McClure's claim on the story was one which I gave him through courtesy and honor—no other," Crane wrote Reynolds. "Your final manipulation of the novelette I consider very brilliant and I am sorry to see it handicapped by that Scotch ass. In all the months I have been in England I have never received a cent from America which has not been borrowed. Just read that over twice! The consequences of this have lately been that I have been obliged to make arrangments here with English agents of American houses but in all cases your commission will be protected. This is the best I could do. My English expenses have chased me to the wall. Even now I am waiting for you to cable me my share of the Monster money, and if there is a fluke I am lost. Don't kick so conspicuously about the over-charge on the damned manuscripts. If I was a business man, I would not need a business man to conduct my affairs for me. I will try to do better, but if I shouldn't, don't harangue me." Crane was in fact a very shrewd businessman in his dealings with agents and editors, even if he was not at all shrewd in managing his own household expenses.

Conrad, also in debt, worried about Crane's money troubles during his visit with Edward Garnett at The Cearne on February 3–4. Himself in despair, he wrote Cunninghame Graham on January 31: "Last night a heavy gale was blowing and I lay awake thinking that I would give ever so much (the most flattering criticism) for being at sea, the soul of some patient faithful ship standing up to it, under lower topsails and no land anywhere within a thousand miles. Wouldn't I jump at a command, if some literary ship-owner suddenly offered it to me!"

Before visiting the Garnetts, he sent Crane a copy of *The Nigger of the "Narcissus"* inscribed on February 2, 1898, "To Stephen and M³[rs. Crane] with the author's affectionate regard," and then on the 5th he wrote Crane: "We got home last night. Ever since I've left you I am wondering how you have passed through your crisis. I would like to hear all is well; it hurts me to think you are worried. It is bad for you and it is bad for your art."

As a means of solving his money problems, Crane thought up a potboiler celebrating *The Great Battles of the World*, and Kate Frederic started digging for data at the British Museum to aid him—first on "The Brief Campaign Against New Orleans." Harold Frederic also aided the Great Battles project, writing Crane: "I ran across a little book on Naval Names yesterday which impressed me at once as having been made expressly for you—and it leaves by this same post for Ravensbrook." In fatherly tone he addresses his letter "My Dear Boy," and he proposes that the Crane household settle at Ahakista with the Frederic household now that Mrs. Rice—a wealthy admirer of Harold—had lent him that mansion in Ireland. "The scheme of moving the family to Dunmanus Bay in March or the earliest April has reached the point where I have the house. It is a mansion on the sea itself—two boats (one with a lug sail), etc., etc. Seven bedrooms, bath, hot & cold water, etc. We think of it solely with reference to your sharing it with us. The expenses will be very light. I am going to finish my book there! We can work as well as loaf."

Frederic called on the Cranes on Saturday, February 5, the same day that Conrad wrote about the worry he shared with Edward Garnett over Stephen's finances, and he had an altercation with Cora over his proposed joint-household sojourn in Ireland. Cora the next day wrote him about their flare-up, and Frederic called her letter "characteristically kind and straight-forward." He wrote on February 8: "I left Ravensbrook on Saturday dismayed at the proportions of the mistake I had made in opening up the Irish business at all. My error arose from my taking as my guide the very delightful memories we both have and cherish of the Irish trip last autumn. I had not at all realized—up to the time of our discussions last week—that so much had changed since then. You see, you and Stephen then were still in the chrysalis stage, so to speak, of housekeeping, and you were both relatively fresh from the haphazard, bohemian life of the champaign in Thessaly. It was comparatively easy for you both, therefore, to fall in with the general views of the organizer of the picnic. How charmingly you both did so we shall never forget. And you were both ill, too, and that contributed its very sweetening effect, in our minds, to what we look back upon as one of the happiest times of our life."

But now all's changed. Frederic is vexed about his stupidity in not recognizing that since last autumn the Ravensbrook household has defined for itself "a system and routine of its own—quite distinct, as is natural, from the system of Homefield—and that an effort to put these two side by side under one roof would necessarily come to grief. There would be the common bond of great and deep personal attachment between the two households, of course—but when it came to a test of strength between that and the divergent impetus of two wholly different sets of habits, I have seen too much of the world to doubt that the bond would be injured much more easily than the habits would be harmonized. And God forbid that that should happen."

The idea of the Cranes living with the Frederics on a permanent basis wasn't feasible, but Frederic persisted. "If we were all off on a holiday, with no necessity of work for either Stephen or me, we could probably take a sufficient number of differences by the scruff of the neck, and thrust them back where they belong. But with the necessity of work weighing upon us both, I am frankly afraid of the experiment." And so he proposed an alternative because he had built "so fondly on the project of having some long, good fishing days alone with Stephen. . . . Do you and Stephen and Mrs. Ruedy carve out of your spring a three weeks of entire leisure (and I will make that period free for myself, or nearly free) and come over and visit us at Ahakista. Everything then will be perfectly simple, and I surely need not waste words in saying how warmly you would be welcome. Bring Adoni with you. Kate is going to write you tomorrow. Meanwhile I beg you both to read into my letter all the regret and affection which your hearts will tell you I wanted it to contain." However, they did not get together in Ireland after all because Frederic fell ill of a cardiac embolism.

While Frederic was proposing a joint household with the Cranes, Conrad in his letter of February 5 was writing Stephen with the same idea: "We must take a house together—say in Brittany for three months or so. It would work smoothly—I am sure." Fortunately nothing came of that notion; such arrangements are seldom successful.

That Saturday of February 5 Crane and Frederic went to London to dine with Charles Gary Griswold at his hotel. It turned out to be a hilarious occasion. A nobleman and his mistress, Madame Zipango, were guests of Griswold's supper party, and Henry James arrived to pay his compatriots a call. Madame Zipango, whose lover had by then passed out from too much imbibing, poured champagne into James' top hat. Very funny thought Harold Frederic, especially since James just then was cross-questioning Crane about literary style. Bearded and slightly magisterial, he was "obviously of the *grande monde* and of the daily habit of rubbing on equal terms with the great." Stephen did not find the incident amusing. James no doubt registered his own dismay in his characteristic stutter. Crane, "coldly tactful," got the handsome Madame Zipango out of the hotel and then returned to aid James in the restoration of the abused hat.

He liked "Old Man" James, "Old Man" Conrad, "Old Man" Frederic, and even that patronizing youngster Ford, whom neither Cora nor Jessie liked. They all liked Stephen—even Ford Hueffer finally, who had misgivings about all of them at the start and then changed his mind. Conrad at the start of his relationship with Ford disliked him, but he mellowed in recognition of Ford's considerable aid in refining his use of the English language and he ended—at least formally—as his good friend. He never liked Harold Frederic, though, and Frederic in turn detested Henry James. He had written someone in late 1895 that James "is an effeminate old donkey who lives with a herd of other donkeys around him and insists on being treated as if he were the Pope. He has licked dust from the floor of every third-rate hostess in England . . . Mr. James recommended Mr. Crane's novel[4] before me in the house of our mutual acquaintance [at Heinemann's in the fall of 1895] and I was deterred from reading it for some days for that reason. With his usual lack of sense or generosity he described the book as an imitation of Zola's 'The Downfall,' which it resembles as much as I do Ellen Terry."

Shortly after Griswold's unfortunate supper party, Crane defended Henry James, the master of them all. "I agree with you that Mr. James has ridiculous traits and lately I have seen him make a holy show of himself in a situation that—on my honour—would have been simple to an ordinary man. But it seems impossible to dislike him. He is so kind to everybody."

On February 8 Crane sent Reynolds by the steamship *Majestic* (sailing on the 9th) his story "The Blue Hotel," which he said was "a daisy." Reynolds did not sell it to *Harper's Magazine;* it was published in *Collier's Weekly.*

Reynolds had sold *Harper's Weekly* "Death and the Child," and it appeared there in March, and "The Five White Mice" to the New York *World,* where it appeared on April 10, and then he placed "The Monster" in *Harper's Magazine* for August, 1898. He placed "The Blue Hotel" in *Collier's Weekly* for November and December, 1898, after having submited it to *Scribner's* and then to *Atlantic Monthly,* whose editor, Walter Hines Page, wrote him: "When you had one or two longer stories which have a book value as well as a serial value, you took them to Harper's. . . . But after you have taken the really valuable part of Mr. Crane's work to another magazine and another publisher, it hardly seems to me worthwhile for the *Atlantic* to step in and buy the remnant." So "The Blue Hotel" ended in a ten-cent weekly, not in a quality magazine. Crane thought he should get $500 (five cents per word) for this story of ten thousand words, but he got $300. Doubleday and McClure had now in preparation *The Open Boat and Other Tales of Adventure,* published in April that year, and Crane protested against including "The Monster" on the grounds that it didn't fit with "Death and the Child." That combination "would be rotten." And so he proposed to Reynolds another volume to contain "The Blue Hotel" conjoined with "The Monster," which go neatly together because together they make 32,000 words. "Very little more is needed for a respectably sized $1.00 book, and that can be readily submitted within the next six weeks." What Crane wrote to complete *The Monster and Other Stories* (1899) was "His New Mittens," but he didn't write it until April. All three tales are stories of social criticism with the protagonist pitted against conventions.

Crane praised Reynolds for managing his affairs handsomely; otherwise, "I would have been stumped absolutely. As you see, I am buckling down and turning out stuff like a man. If you hold your fine gait it will only be a short time before we are throwing out our chests." How boyish of him to boast that he is turning out stuff like a man, and yet how shrewdly he jockeys Reynolds around the race track of his desperate plight: "I shall need every sou for the next two months. . . . A ten pound note even fills me with awe. You must understand as my confidential agent that my settlement in England cost me in the neighborhood of $2000 worth of debts. Your payments from the Harpers knocked a comfortable hole in them but I must have about $1200 more. This would have been simple if it were not for that blackmail at Appleton's. [His royalties at Appleton were legally tied up through the lawsuit Amy Leslie had brought against him in January.] I have got big matters to attend to this month. Get me through this and I am prepared to smile." And of course once Reynolds sold "The Blue Hotel," he should cable the money instantly.

Conrad wrote Crane that he had been rather seedy lately—"all worry, I think. But I'm going to put my worries aside and have a real good time with you. I shall wire you on Sat. by what train we are coming . . . I shall bring a lot of paper and you shall find a pen. I am anxious to know what you have done with your idea of a play. A play to write is no play. I believe you can do anything. Ever Yours. J. Conrad. Our kindest regards to Mrs. Crane. Baby sends a friendly howl." Conrad—then absorbed in writing *Lord Jim*—referred to his son as "The Ominous Baby"—after the title of Crane's New York City sketch, which he probably had read in the page proofs of Heinemann's edition of *The Open Boat*.

David Meldrum of Heinemann had asked him to arrange for a luncheon in London so that Blackwood could meet Stephen Crane during the week of February 14, but they did not meet until late the following month. William Blackwood of Blackwood & Sons in Edinburgh, for whom Meldrum was literary consultant in London, was a good old Scotchman to whom Stephen became indebted for a loan he never fully repaid. "If you like the idea [of meeting Blackwood] drop me a line to name the day," Conrad wrote Crane. "It is left to you. Your whiskey, old man, has effected a cure and I feel quite fit for work. How long that disposition will last only the devil in charge of my affairs knows. I miss you horribly." (Stephen had brought a bottle of whiskey when visiting him in November.)

The Conrads, accompanied by Jessie's sixteen-year-old sister Dolly, arrived at Villa Ravensbrook on February 19 and remained four days. Conrad claims that he never heard Crane laugh except in connection with his five-week-old son, for whom Stephen declared he had "some distinct claim." Adoni Ptolemy, butler in shirt-sleeves, caused a great deal of amusement by persisting in treating the baby as a person of importance. He set him in a big easy chair at the dining table close to Jessie's side. When Jack Stokes dropped in, butler Adoni announced: "Mr. Conrad, Mr. Stokes he come, he want you, Mr. Crane." Conrad's visit was commemorated by a group photograph taken by an artist who was "summoned with his engine (regardless of expense) to Ravensbrook." Cora, as she herself admitted, was "a spendthrift in every way." What money she had obtained from the sale of her Jacksonville nightclub had long ago been spent on her travels with Mrs. Ruedy to Greece and on such unnecessary expenditures as the purchase of a fur coat for a theological student named Ferris, an utter stranger she had met on the Orient Express to Constantinople; she had been as reckless with her own money as she was now with

Crane's. "Stephen and 1," she said, "are the same person. We have no sense about money at all."

Conrad jested that the best things in that costly photograph were the dogs. These outlandish poodles—Sponge, Flannel and Ruby—were "amazingly sedate and yet the most restless animals" he ever met. He thought Stephen was like his dogs: sedate and yet restless. Crane later on insisted that Conrad look for a dog for Borys, and he made "quite a scene about it. He seemed to imply I should drop everything and go look for a dog. I sat under the storm and said nothing. At last he cried: 'Hang it all, a boy ought to have a dog.'" (Later at Brede Manor in 1899 Crane gave one to Borys.)

Jack Stokes invited Conrad and Crane for dinner at the Savage Club on March 19, but Conrad, because of "nervous trouble," wrote Cora that he did not feel up to it and begged off. "I am so glad Stephen is writing; it consoles me for my own inability to work. I haven't written three pages since I left you. I simply *can't*. I am like a man under a fiendish spell cast over the power of thinking." Stephen replied to Conrad's March 15 letter two days later: "Cannot you endure it? . . . You *must* accept, says Cora and I, our invitation to come home with me on Sat. night." He enclosed a bit of original manuscript "under the supposition that you might like to keep it in remembrance of my warm and endless friendship for you."[5] Then Conrad, always fussing about what mood he was in, changed his mind and decided to attend the Savage Club dinner. On that occasion Crane talked with the Honorable George Wyndham, M. P., Parliamentary Undersecretary of State for War, a young and very handsome man with turned-up moustache, German style. They discussed Crane's forthcoming *Pictures of War*, which Heinemann was publishing in July with George Wyndham's "An Appreciation," a reprint of his 1896 appraisal of *The Red Badge* in the London *New Review*. Wyndham had singled out the young American as "a great artist with something new to say and consequently with a new way of saying it." They talked about the likelihood of America's entry into war against Spain, a topic on which Wyndham was well informed, and also they no doubt discussed the mystery of the explosion of the battleship *Maine* with the loss of 260 of her crew a month before. That disaster had enraged Americans into popular patriotic fervor; but Crane was not enraged, and Jack Stokes reproached him for his indifference.[6]

The next day (March 20) he wrote someone that the notion of "no such thing as the U.S. Navy" had been clearly proven to him last night at the Savage Club "by a Mr. Wyndham who once met General Grant." Some derogatory remark about the United States Navy must have irked Crane into downgrading Wyndham to the anonymity of "a Mr. Wyndham." He found Englishmen ignorant of America's military might, also of geography. "I have vainly tried to tell some good men and true that Cuba is not on friendly terms with California, but they will have it that one gets on a tug at San Francisco to go to Havana."[7] In the same Sunday letter he observed that this war "will be fought in English. I can at least swear in Spanish and it will be more comfortable all around. But I have not decided on going yet." He had not yet spoken to Cora of the idea; he was almost afraid to mention it.

Conrad asked Crane on March 24 to meet him at Heinemann's before going to luncheon at the Garrick Club the next day, Friday, "to feed at old Blackwood's expense." He had to get home that Saturday night, but perhaps they took in a theater. Then, or on some earlier occasion, Crane was amused to find that the queue while waiting at the theatre for the doors to open was entertained by some begging actors, and he wrote it up in "At the Pit Door," a companion piece to his 1897 "London Impressions." The theatre queue was entertained by a girl with a guitar, an acrobat, a boy whistler, and a minstrel with tambourine. The acrobat reminds the queue of people two abreast "that a man's got his livin' to make, altho p'raps we may 'ave different ways of doing it. Can you oblige, miss, by starting the subscription list with a copper?"

Having given up the idea of writing "The Predecessor" in collaboration with Conrad, Crane wrote "The Blood of the Martyr," a closet-drama which the New York *Press* thought enough of to publish in its Sunday magazine for April 3. He wrote it very likely after the sinking of the *Maine* in mid-February provoked rumors of the possibility of America's declaring war against Spain. Crane's comic drama has to do with German imperialism in China, but it transposes readily enough into a satire of imperialism anywhere, including the American brand. He was as critical of British imperialism at the end of his writing days as he had been at the start when in 1891 he ribbed it in his satiric sketch: "A Foreign Policy in Three Glimpses."[8] He was always alert to the potential military and political triggers of war. In "The Eastern Question" (1897) he scorched Turkey's political maneuvers, and his dispatches from Greece reported that country's plight from political, economic and military points of view. He attacked social injustices in the Transvaal in his splendid study "The Great Boer Trek" (*Cosmopolitan:* June, 1900), and speculated about the Boer War in "Some Lessons from the Transvaal" (*Journal:* January 7, 1900). In his "Talk of London" (*Journal:* March 11, 1900) he gave a bird's-eye view of the world powers' chessboard: the Russians on the move in Persia, and France in the Barbary States.

In "The Blood of the Martyr" he says that the Emperor of Germany, "devotes himself at this time to declaring to his people that the plight in England is an object lesson which teaches that the German Empire should have a largely increased navy." This is the only advantage he sees, says Crane, and "the excitement among his people against the English is greater even than it is in France." Crane thus early, in his trivial sketch, scratched a match, as it were, to illumine German imperial ambitions.

Sometime shortly after April 11 Conrad again met Crane in London on a cloudy afternoon. The United States Congress, after debating President McKinley's message of April 11, passed resolutions recognizing Cuba's independence from Spain, and this amounted to a declaration of war. (The formal declaration of war against Spain occurred on April 25). Crane had no money, and his problem was how to get to Cuba, and so Conrad's problem on that cloudy afternoon was how to find sixty pounds "before the sun set, before dinner, before the 'six forty' train to Oxted, at once that instant—lest peace should be declared and the opportunity of seeing a war be missed. I had not sixty pounds to lend him. Sixty shillings was nearer my mark." They tried various offices without success, Conrad recalls, and "Crane's white-faced excitement frightened me. Finally it occurred to me to take him to Messrs. William Blackwood & Sons' London office. There he was received in a most friendly way. Presently I escorted him to Charing Cross, where he took the train for home with the assurance that he would have the means to start 'for the war' next day." Conrad pledged his own work as security, and Sanford Bennett supplied an additional £10. (Stephen repaid Conrad in early 1899 but never did pay Blackwood in full, and Blackwood washed his hands of him.) Conrad felt as though he were leading Crane to his doom that afternoon in April, 1898, but then, characteristically, reversed himself in saying: "But, indeed—I was only the blind agent of the fate that had him in her grip! Nothing could have held him back. HE WAS READY TO SWIM THE OCEAN."

He was right, though, in thinking that Crane's going to Cuba was the beginning of the end.

At Sanford Bennett's rooms Stephen left a note: "Sorry not to have seen you. I have raised the wind and sail tomorrow. Nothing I can do for Harold [Frederic]. Barr will look after him. Write me at Hartwood, N. Y., care of Edmund Crane. Shall get myself taken in the Navy if possible." He was so swiftly out of England (to quote Beer) that guests came down to Oxted and were surprised to find him gone. Conrad wrote Cora on April 19 that "the dear fellow" had wired him from Queenstown just before boarding the ship. "We imagine how lonely you must have felt after Stephen's departure." They thought it a good thing for Cora to join the Frederics in Ireland "as solitude after separation is sometimes very hard to bear," and invited her and Mrs. Ruedy "to undertake the risky experiment of coming to us" on her return from her visit with the Frederics. "Moreover I fancy Stephen's absence won't be very prolonged and we may have the felicity of seeing you all here together. I trust you will let me know how he fares whenever you hear from him. He is not very likely to write anyone else—if I know the man."

Throughout the nine months of Stephen's absence Conrad kept in touch with Cora. "Oh, happy is the human being who has never yet had occasion to cry: 'I cannot bear it!' But we bear things," Cora wrote in her journal. "Somehow we bear them, though that endurance leaves us forever after with a mark upon us." My uncle, said Helen Crane, had "many romances, for he appealed much to women; but a great love eluded him."

His going to the war in Cuba was the beginning of the end; in all probability he was already afflicted with tuberculosis.[9] Now he was off to war again, not because he thought his fame as journalist demanded his presence in Cuba, but simply in the hope that he could enlist as a seaman in the United States Navy and thus satisfy his obsession to witness war. He must have known that he was not fit for service, but he gambled on the odds. After he had sailed from Queenstown (now Cobh, Ireland), Pulitzer's *World* cabled him an offer and Cora cabled him that news.

Poor Cora had twice been separated from Stephen, but now she felt deserted. He had left her and their Ravensbrook debts to join the Navy! The Frederics comforted her by taking into their borrowed mansion Ahakista on the Irish coast the Ravensbrook household—not only Cora, but Mrs. Charlotte (Mathilde) Ruedy, butler Adoni, and the three poodles. They returned sometime in May. When Frederic in August had a severe stroke Cora, to free Kate for nursing him, took her children to Ravensbrook. Stephen had left Cora without funds, and of course she felt lonely and abandoned. Nothing could cheer her but the prospect of his returning home, and to this end Edward Garnett proposed a new home at Brede Place owned by Mr. Moreton Frewen—Brede Manor, for which the Frewens of London just then had no need. Frewen would lend the Cranes his manor house for a nominal rental, and they in turn would make certain restorations to the house and gardens. Cora on June 4 wrote Clara and Morton Frewen about the architect's report on the cost of repairs to make habitable an almost uninhabitable and ghost-ridden manor house. That fabulous house was to cost Stephen for its upkeep in servants and firewood far more than he could afford. He couldn't afford even modest Villa Ravensbrook, and after he went to Cuba the butcher and grocer at Oxted, anticipating that they might be bilked, stopped Cora's credit and obtained court summonses. To escape them she shut up Villa Ravensbrook and lived in London in rooms at 6 Milborne Grove.

Fabulous Brede Manor, which she had not yet seen, would provide Cora the proper social status, and Stephen succumbed to her dream of possessing an English estate, boasting aboard a tugboat that at the war's end he would settle in England as lord of a famous manor house. He, too, liked the prospect of the life of an English gentleman, whether or not he could afford it. In spite of near bankruptcy at Ravensbrook, Cora negotiated with the Frewens about restorations, not simply repairs but additional structures to the manor house. "Then I would like the privilege of building a small conservatory. You see it will mean over £120 a year rent. The remarkable old house will be a delight to us. . . . I am sure it will prove an atmosphere where good work must be done. P.S. The architect has neglected to send estimate of stable, but of course this will be put in order." On June 8 Stephen cabled her from Jamaica saying he hadn't heard from her. On the 10th Cora wrote Frewen: "Letters were delayed, but I expect to hear from him any day now that he is satisfied with my arrangements for Brede. I can, however, safely say that he will take it on the terms named in my letter and as soon as I hear from Mr. Crane I will write you a formal letter to that effect." She is pleased that no lawyer is required for these negotiations.

After writing Frewen for literature about historic Brede Place and permission to utilize it in an article she intended to write, Cora took a four days' driving trip with friends to Tunbridge Wells, Brede, Rye, and Battle, falling "quite in love with that part of England." On her return she found waiting for her two letters from Frewen, and she responded on the 16th to assure him that "Mr. Crane will be delighted at the idea of camping in your old house." Brede Manor is one of the landmarks in English history; only an American would describe it simply as an old house or suggest camping in it. It was begun in 1370 during the reign of Edward III. The Frewens invited the Cranes, once Stephen had returned from Cuba, to visit them at Innishannon in Cork County, Ireland. But Cora thought it would be October before "this war business is settled so that Mr. Crane will return." In her letter she said that she had that Thursday morning received a cable from Stephen at Port Antonio, Jamaica, "that he has been fighting. To see what it is really like I suppose. But it's very distressing to me." When he returns, "I shall go to Queenstown with an American lady [Mrs. Ruedy], who is stopping with me, to meet Mr. Crane." (He did not return until January.) He had been away from her only two months, but Cora was already anticipating his imminent homecoming and planning his future: "A good book should be written while we are at Brede Place, which may please you as adding a wee bit more history to the place."

Stephen cabled Cora that he hadn't received any of her letters, and so she wrote someone at the New York *World* or at the Key West Hotel to forward them, but then on June 27 Conrad wrote her: "I was delighted to hear good news of dear Stephen. The life on board that tug of his will set him up in strength and appetite for years. Have you heard from him since you wrote? I suppose he landed with the army and is in the thick of everything that's going. . . . It looks as though the war would drag after all."

# XXI

# ☞ *The Splendid Little War Begins*

CRANE sailed from Queenstown to New York on the *Germanic* on Thursday, April 14, and while aboard that small and elderly ship he wrote a sketch about destroyers and torpedo boats from notes he had taken at the Yarrow shipyards on the Isle of Dogs. He probably also began the first of his Whilomville stories—"His New Mittens"—which he was writing three weeks later aboard the tug the *Three Friends*. When the *Germanic* docked at Manhattan's Pier 45 on April 21, he had been absent from New York thirteen months almost to the day.

The next day he received the cable from Cora that Joseph Pulitzer of the New York *World* wanted to commission him as war correspondent for the Cuban War. But on the day following, after he had deposited a dispatch at the Hearst office,[1] he applied hopefully as a volunteer with the U. S. Navy in response to President McKinley's first call for volunteers. He was rejected by the Navy because the physical requirements were too rigid for him, and he had no alternative but to settle for the post with the *World*. He signed up that same day (April 23) at Pulitzer's building on Park Row. His fee was $3,000, but he probably collected only half that amount since he quit the *World* halfway through the war. And so it was Saturday and he had to obtain a passport,[2] then dash to Washington to see his beloved Lily Brandon Munroe. It was to be the last time he saw her. His visit was cut short on his receiving notice from the *World* "that there was to be a big fight off Havana and I was to go there instantly. I flew," he explained to Lily's sister Dorothy a month later.

Crane told photographer James H. Hare of *Collier's*[3] that he had joined the *World* so as to get a military pass in order to write a book about the war. He was fortunate to have Sylvester Scovel, his friend in Greece the previous year, as head of the *World* staff. The "buoyant irrepressible" Scovel had already been inside Cuba, and he had bounced back there again and again, even taking with him once his young bride to visit rebel leader General Maximo Gómez. The *insurrectos* admired him as much as the Spaniards hated him. A reward of $10,000 was placed on his head; he became the best-known name in Cuba. The Spaniards finally captured him;

*350*

by order of Captain General Ramón Blanco y Arenas he was sentenced to be shot as a spy, but the United States demanded and obtained his release.

One of Scovel's missions was to tell Gómez that the United States had declared war against Spain. President McKinley had proclaimed the blockade of Cuba on April 22. On April 24, Spain declared war against the United States. And on April 25 the U. S., not to be outdone, declared that a state of war against Spain had existed since the 21st. Key West, Florida, now became "the storm center of the map of the United States."

Crane got to Key West by the 26th and the next day filed his *World* report about a captured Spanish ship, the *Panama,* a prize of war brought into Key West harbor. In "The Terrible Captain of the Captured *Panama"* he depicted the Spanish captain as a frightened humbug, a blustering, hollow man.

The war was to be won or lost at sea. Until control of the seaways was obtained, the Army could not prudently cross the Straits of Florida. And so for a month—"the rocking-chair period of the war"—the generals and their staffs waited it out on the porch of the Tampa Bay Hotel in the Port of Tampa until Admiral William T. Sampson's fleet eventually succeeded in locating and then blockading the fleet of Rear Admiral Pascual Cervera y Topete. Cubans in Tampa and in Key West complained about the heat, claiming that the Cuban hills were much cooler. Along with its tropical flora, Key West had its mosquitoes and prostitutes, its busy harbor and bustling hotel—the bedlam headquarters of war correspondents and naval officers on shore duty. More than a hundred correspondents had gathered at Key West and at the Port of Tampa, headquarters of the soldiers destined to invade Cuba: the Fifth Army commanded by Brigadier General William R. Shafter. Because Scovel had obliged Admiral Sampson by carrying messages to the Cuban insurgents and, with photographer Jimmie Hare, making photographs of the Cuban coast, the Admiral repaid him by permitting Ralph D. Paine aboard the flagship *New York.* Scovel's deal was that Paine would submit his dispatches to the *World* as well as to his own New York *Journal* and Philadelphia *Press.* By that deal he gained a double point of view: his own, while he carried out missions along the Cuban coast; and Paine's by his reporting actions viewed from the flagship.

On April 27 Admiral Sampson's fleet bombarded the earthworks at Matanzas for eighteen minutes. Richard Harding Davis was aboard the flagship and wrote his dispatch about the bombardment, and then he dropped his manuscript into a weighted envelope from the *New York's* deck onto the *Herald's* tugboat. No other newspaper tugboat was in sight, and so Davis scored an exclusive scoop for James Bennett's *Herald.*

Meanwhile, Scovel through his friendship with Admiral Sampson arranged for Crane to replace Ralph Paine, on the *New York,* which left Havana on the morning of April 29 on an inspection trip to the west of Havana toward Mariel (spelled Muriel in our newspapers). On the New

York *World*'s tugboat *Triton,* Crane caught up with the *New York* thirty-five miles west of Havana, two days after she had bombarded Matanzas. He reported this incident in "Sampson Inspects the Harbor at Muriel," his first dispatch from the war zone. But there was nothing at Muriel "worthy of the flagship's attention" and Sampson headed for Cabañas, thirteen miles away. At Cabañas—the second naval engagement of the war—the big guns shelled the shore and put to flight a troop of Spanish cavalry who had only rifles to fire at the steel-clad ship.

Having witnessed the shelling, Crane quit the deck to take coffee in the junior officers' mess, where an ensign banged out a popular tune on the ship's piano. Richard Harding Davis in the senior officers' mess (which Crane probably avoided because Davis hung out there) was entertained twice daily by a *Meistersinger* and the goldfish song from the *Geisha.* "This is not a touch of fiction, but of reporting in cold coincidence," Davis wrote someone and smugly added, "for war as it is conducted at this end of the century is civilized." To Davis it apparently seemed a merry war between American Boy Scouts and Spanish gentlemen. But then, as John Hay wrote Teddy Roosevelt, "it has been a splendid little war—begun with the highest motives, carried on with magnificent intelligence and spirit, favored by that fortune which loves the brave."

A splendid little war indeed! One week after General Shafter's army landed, American soldiers in Cuba began to sicken with fevers, and three weeks later not more than one-quarter of Colonel Roosevelt's Rough Riders were fit for duty, half of his command having fallen out of ranks from exhaustion a few days before. Five thousand soldiers in the Fifth Army Corps were ill with Cuban fever by July 22.

Scovel controlled a dispatch boat, the hallmark of the Grade A reporter. The *World* in fact had rented three dispatch boats: the *Triton,* the *Somers N. Smith,* and the Jacksonville tugboat the *Three Friends,* familiar to Crane from his filibustering *Commodore* disaster. William Randolph Hearst's *Journal* had ten such boats slinging around Cuba; the Associated Press and James Gordon Bennett's *Herald* had five each; other newspapers could afford only one. Arthur Brisbane declared that the major New York papers would have ended in bankruptcy had the war lasted for two years because expenditures for boats to carry the correspondents to cable stations and for cabling their dispatches were exorbitant. The *Herald* spent $5,000 on cable fees for one dispatch from Jamaica, and the Associated Press $8,000 for a single story. Scovel shared the *Triton* with a trio of ministers' sons: Crane of the *World;* the flamboyant Ernest McCready of Jacksonville, now with Bennett's *Herald;* and Ralph D. Paine, the Presbyterian minister's son whom Crane had known at Asbury Park and years later at Jacksonville.

After the *New York* had shelled Cabañas, the flagship returned to Key West by midnight of May 1, and the newsmen were ordered off. They included Crane, Fred Remington, illustrator for Hearst's *Journal,* the artist

Rufus Zogbaum, and Stephen Bonsal. Rival newspapers had protested favoritism, and the Navy Department had issued an edict banishing correspondents from the ship (but Richard Harding Davis managed to stay aboard until May 10).

Scovel had taken the *World* tugboat *Triton* to the Cuban coast to rescue Charles B. Thrall, an American who was spying on military activity. But Scovel failed to catch Thrall's signals on the appointed date of April 22. They were recognized by the warship *Wilmington,* and a boat was lowered to rescue him. The next day Thrall was transported to the flagship *New York* so that Admiral Sampson could interview him. He had information about Havana's fortifications and the severe distress of that city's inhabitants.

Aboard the *Triton* as she hovered alongside the *Wilmington* on the morning of May 4 Crane queried Thrall in a ship-to-ship interview and reported back at Key West's cable office on the 7th: "Stephen Crane's Pen Picture of C. H. Thrall." In describing Thrall he might have been talking of himself: "The striking thing about him now is his eyes . . . they are peculiarly wide open as if strained with watching. They stare at you and do not seem to think, and at the corners the lids are wrinkled as if from long pain. This is the impress of his hazardous situation still upon him. As for his own deeds, he talks as little and wants to talk as little as most intrepid men." So closely did Crane identify himself with Thrall that he recast him as "Johnnie"—an American spy in Havana—in "This Majestic Lie." Johnnie's life is a majestic lie not only because as a spy he conceals his identity, but also because he risks his life for an ideal that fails him. The very title of "The Ideal and the Real," an unpublished manuscript not yet known in Crane's canon, pinpoints the conflict within Crane himself— the same conflict of ironic selfhood he saw in Thrall: "Somewhere in him there was a sentimental tenderness, but it was like a light seen afar at night. . . . And if his sentimental tenderness was a light, the darkness in which it puzzled you was *his irony of soul.* This irony was directed first at himself; then at you; then at the nation and the flag; then at God." Like Thrall, Crane was "a young man of great energy, ready to accomplish a colossal thing for the basic reason that he was ignorant of its magnitude. In fact he attacked all obstacles in life in a spirit of contempt, seeing them smaller than they were until he had actually surmounted them—when he was likely to be immensely pleased with himself."

The two men met again in October, 1898, in Havana when Thrall returned there to resume his post as manager of a sugar manufacturing company in Piñar del Río. Crane admired him, as he did Admiral Sampson, whose indifferent and apathetic manner appealed to him. Men cheered for Sampson, "and he said: 'Who are they yelling for?' Men behaved badly to him, and he said nothing. Men thought of glory, and he considered the management of ships. All without a sound. . . . No bunting, no arches, no fireworks; nothing but the perfect management of a big fleet. That is a record for you. No trumpets, no cheers of the populace. Just plain, pure unsauced accomplishment."

On April 29 the Spanish Admiral Pascual Cervera y Topete sailed for Martinique in the Windward Islands from the Cape Verde Islands off the coast of West Africa with four armored cruisers and three torpedo boat destroyers. Two days later Admiral Sampson—the Dewey of the Atlantic, as he was later nicknamed—countered by sending three fast cruisers to the Windward Islands and another fleet under his command to San Juan, Puerto Rico. Sampson didn't reach that city until May 12, because one of his ships, the *Indiana,* was disabled by faulty boilers and two monitors had to be towed. The Atlantic fleet, with Sampson aboard the battleship *Iowa,* bombarded San Juan for three hours. But Cervera wasn't there. The news of Sampson's arrival in San Juan had leaked out in the American papers, and Cervera had read those papers in Martinique.[4]

The *World's* managing editor cabled Scovel: "Take tug; go find Cervera's fleet." So on a cloudless May day Crane and Scovel, with novelist Frank Norris as their guest, cleared the dock at Key West aboard the *Three Friends* and drifted out over the torpedo beds and submarine mines, while Sampson's *New York* cleared Sand Point Lighthouse that same Wednesday (May 4) on a wild-goose chase after the Spanish fleet at Puerto Rico. Norris described Crane as the "Young Personage, celebrated the world round by reason of his novel of battle and sudden death." He "approached more nearly to the ideal type of war correspondent than any I had yet seen," said Norris, a novice reporter for *McClure's Magazine* and not yet a Personage. Handsome and talented, he was envious of that "Young Personage" who was only twenty months older than himself.

As it was impossible to write while sitting in a chair aboard the plunging *Three Friends,* Crane and Scovel wrote their dispatches in their bunks. "Both men were tanned to the color of well-worn saddles, and upon the bridge of their noses was the little calloused spot that comes with long use of the field glasses." The Young Personage wore a pair of duck trousers "grimed and fouled with all manner of pitch and grease and oil. His shirt was guiltless of collar or scarf and was unbuttoned at the throat. His hair hung in ragged fringes over his eyes. His dress suitcase was across his lap and answered him for a desk. Between his heels he held a bottle of beer against the rolling of the boat, and when he drank was royally independent of a glass. While he was composing his descriptive dispatches which some ten thousand people would read in the morning from the bulletins in New York, I wondered what the fifty thousand who have read his war novel and have held him, no doubt rightly, to be a great genius, would have said and thought could they have seen him at the moment." Crane could not have cared less what they thought. Let Benjamin Franklin Norris, his hair parted carefully down the middle and a scarf tied around his neck, perform the role of war correspondent as gentleman.

From the *Three Friends* the trio boarded the flagship *New York,* heading for Havana. In "With the Blockade on the Cuban Coast" (datelined May 7) Crane described the despair of the jack-tars over the improbability of an immediate fight. "The officers were at breakfast; a piano rattled away. With immense dignity the *New York* steamed six miles off the Havana fortifications. Morro Castle, low to the water, looked exactly as it did in photographs of it. On the hillsides to its right were two long, straight yellow scars, modern batteries. Everybody thought those batteries would open on the flagship. Everybody on board the flagship hoped so. The newspaper boats pounded eagerly along in the rear. But Havana remained silent, enigmatical. The only fun was allowing the imagination to dwell upon the emotions, gestures, orations which were hidden behind the six miles which separated the ships from Havana."

When the *New York* swung to the northeast, the houses of the blockaded city could be counted, and the ship's bugle sounded the call-to-quarters. After inspection the bluejackets "took their trot about the deck in perfect rhythm to the music of the band, which played a rollicking, fascinating melody. It was a peaceful scene. In fact it was more peaceful than peace, since one's sights were adjusted for war."

Meanwhile, Cervera managed to elude the Atlantic fleet. So back to Key West Hotel went Crane, Norris and Scovel with no news to report. Norris disapproved of the seaport's resort atmosphere; he considered it undignified for the war correspondents, idling on the verandah in straw hats and clean creased flannels, to be paying court to smartly dressed summer girls, while out there the grim gray ships pursued their blockade. "But the quiet is deceptive and the calm makes one forget the possibility of storm."

The Key West Hotel was a bedlam. For diversion you could stroll over to the resort known as the Eagle Bird, where the roulette wheel was spun by a certain Jack Oakhurst, a "jay" who was "straight out of a dime novel, moustache and all, with bunches of diamonds like cheap chandeliers on each hand."[5] There, says Ralph Paine, you'd be most apt to find Stephen Crane, "a genius who burned the candle at both ends." Stephen won $300 off Jack Oakhurst's roulette wheel, and it was a straight wheel—not crooked, says McCready.

He made a one-day visit from Key West to Tampa, probably during the last week of May, and there he picked up the gossip that Richard Harding Davis had declined a Captaincy offered him by President McKinley. Davis felt sure he had made the wrong decision, but Crane didn't. "It is the fashion of all hotel porches at Tampa and Key West to run Davis down because he has declined a captaincy in the army in order to keep his contract with his paper. The tea party has to have a topic." He knew that he also was a topic of the tea party that "buzzed waspishly" at the Key West Hotel. At the bar one day, after listening to some gentlemen of the press, he asked quietly: "Did any of you Indians try to enlist?" Again at Tampa he affronted a group of volunteers: "Didn't the militia take an oath to defend the country anyhow?" This unprovoked criticism of the volunteers, who were doing their duty without complaint, suggests that Crane had a chip on his shoulder. Typically he gave a discharged soldier fifty dollars for his fare back to Wisconsin.

Tampa was nothing but sand and sunshine and quinine pills. At the rococo hotel strode Richard Harding Davis in impeccable khaki costume,[6] while at Tampa's sandy camping place General Shafter, who weighed 300 pounds and suffered from gout, pondered how to review his troops without torturing himself by mounting a horse. (He never thought what a torture he was to the horse, who sagged under his weight.) Platforms were built so that he could mount, but most of the time he got around in a buckboard with his foot wrapped in burlap, or else he lay prostrate in his tent. He was a Gilbert and Sullivan figure. His bullfrog jowls pulsed like bellows, and his immense abdomen actually hung down between his legs. T. R. Roosevelt remarked bitingly that "not since the campaign of Crassus against the Parthians has there been so criminally incompetent a general as Shafter." He was the constant butt of cartoonists and reporters. Never was an army more unready, says Ralph Paine. "It could not be said that the high command changed its mind, for the reason that it had no mind to change. Confusion was its middle name."

On May 14 Harry Brown (dean of the New York *Herald*'s war staff), Ralph Paine, Ernest McCready and Crane made their first visit to Haiti aboard the *Three Friends*. To cut down expenses the *World*'s managers no longer rented the *Triton*. Scovel and Crane now rented cheaper boats such as the *Three Friends* and the *Somers N. Smith* when needed, and other newspapers shared the expense. "We had sailed from Key West on a mission that had nothing to do with the coast of Cuba," says Crane in "Narrow Escape of the *Three Friends*," and that night, "steaming due east and some thirty-five miles from the coast, we did not think we were liable to an affair with any of the fierce American cruisers. Suddenly a familiar signal of red and white lights flashed like a brooch of jewels on the pall that covered the sea. Answering lanterns sprang at once to the masthead of the *Three Friends*." The USS *Machias* with every gun on her port side was bearing down on her and threatened to smash her into smithereens. At the last moment the gunboat *Machias* veered off and left the tug trembling from head to foot. The miracle was that she wasn't cut in two "as neatly as if she had been cheese." Paine tells about the narrow escape of the *Three Friends* in his *Roads of Adventure* (1922), and Crane wrote about it in his "War Memories" (1899). There he says that the tug had nothing but two lanterns for signals, and the quartet of correspondents scrambled wildly to utilize them. "It amounted to a slowness of speech. I remember a story of an army sentry who upon hearing a noise in his front one dark night called his usual sharp query. 'Halt—who's there? Halt or I'll fire!' And getting no immediate response he fired even as he had said, killing a man with a hare-lip who unfortunately could not arrange his vocal machinery to reply in season. We were something like a boat with a hare-lip. And sometimes it was very trying to the nerves."

The gunboat and the tug had met previously late one afternoon off Cárdenas' harbor, when the *Machias* begged of the *Three Friends:* "Have you any onions, potatoes or eggs?" As the *Machias* had starved for three weeks during blockade duty, the tug patriotically gave up its last spud. But now the ungrateful *Machias* came at the *Three Friends* "with such dangerous fury. We wanted to demand the return of our potatoes." Crane called the mistake of the *Machias* an "onion," his private code word for any adventure that missed its mark.

The *Three Friends* on her voyage to Haiti in mid-May stole beneath the dark heights of Haiti mountains and, with moonlight guiding her, anchored in the bay at Cap Haïtien. When the four correspondents advanced into town to find the French cable service at Mole St. Nicholas, they were challenged by sentries: "*Qui vive?*" In this difficult situation, McCready challenged Crane: "It is your move, Crane. Fiction is your long suit. Here it is. Things like this don't happen in real life. Let us have a few remarks from the well-known author of *The Red Badge of Courage.*" Crane, as Ralph Paine reports it, grinned in reply: "If I caught myself hatching a plot like this, I wouldn't write another line until I had sobered up. Steady, boys, the night is still young, and I have a good hunch that there'll be lots more of it. This opening is good."

Harry Brown despaired of locating the French cable office: " 'Stick around, Harry,' advised Crane. 'Age has dulled your feeling for romance. We can beat this game yet.' " But it was a young deckhand, Bill, who beat the game by boldly pronouncing the password: " 'I am the Boss! Salute, you black sons-of-guns.' At his heels marched the four correspondents, chanting in unison: 'I am the Boss! Salute, you black sons-of-guns.' The effect was as magical as the astute deckhand had foretold. The slouching sentinels rolled their eyes and bobbed their heads in recognition of the password." Said Crane: " 'Bill, you are a wonder. But, darn you, you are too impossible for fiction. I shall have to get good and drunk to do you justice. And you told them you were the boss and got away with it?' 'Come along and see,' said Bill. 'I'll show you. And listen, I met an awful pretty girl, and there was mighty little tar baby about her, I could see that, an octoroon, mebbe, and I made a date with her.' "

Negro fires were winking in the black hills, and the drums gave out "that woodeny sound which some likened to the music produced by a bevy of folk thumping distantly on a flock of wooden piss-pots," says McCready.[7]

He says that Crane managed to seduce a native girl—to change his luck. "Steve went adventuring on this occasion in his bare feet, clothed only in exceedingly soiled blue-striped pajamas, an equally soiled brown beard of a week's well-fertilized herbage—and his circumambient breath. This last was protection enough for all ordinary purposes."

The next day (May 15) Crane filed at Porto Plata, San Domingo, his dispatch: "Hayti and San Domingo Favor the United States." Here he says that the French cable company at Cap Haïtien was issuing daily bulletins quite pro-Spanish, and the colony of French and German merchants were all openly rooting for Spain. They did not like the United States and said that the Spanish squadrons would surely down Admiral Sampson's ships. One venerable French merchant, says Crane, refused to believe even that Dewey had been victorious at Manila. (Commodore Dewey's Asiatic Squadron had destroyed the Spanish fleet in Manila Bay on May 1.) "All lies!" said the venerable French merchant. "All lies by this—what you call?—damn telegraph." The Haitian Army considered the Americans a menace to their country, but a Negro merchant told Crane: "The history of Spain is the history of cruelty."

As the *Three Friends* steamed into Porto Plata's anchorage on the morning of the 15th, "a crowd of people gathered on the green headland that shields the little cove and cheered the famous tug as if she were really the *Campania*. Flags and handkerchiefs fluttered away from every fist. There is a considerable Cuban colony here, and only the requirements of journalism prevent us from being feted tonight by an enthusiastic populace, with a band and a dinner and all other modern excitements."

The "requirements of journalism" forced the quartet to leave Porto Plata late that night. They went to Puerto Rico, and then—homeward bound and "Off Havana: May 19"—Stephen wrote Lilly Brandon Munroe's sister Dorothy that he was returning to Key West from Puerto Rico: "I have not changed in the least, and you may be sure that the S. Crane you knew so well long ago would not seem thoughtless if he could help it. I am going to England as soon as the war is over. My address will be Key West Hotel, Key West. Adiós." He wrote Dorothy on the stationery of the Titchfield Hotel in Jamaica's Port Antonio, where he had visited earlier. Actually Crane did not return to England until early January. He toyed with the idea of going around the world as soon as the war would end: "A Polish friend of mine who is an unancient mariner [Joseph Conrad] says I would be dippy over Polynesia."

He got back to Key West on May 20 and that day filed his *World* dispatch: "Narrow Escape of the *Three Friends*." On board they had nothing to do but play poker, write letters, or swap yarns. There had been nothing to report thus far but Navy skirmishes. Paine says Crane refused to take the responsibilities of daily journalism seriously. But what news there was to report was but a mouse exaggerated by managing editors of the yellow press into a front-page elephant. The title of Crane's tale "This Majestic Lie" sums up what the yellow press of Hearst, Pulitzer and Bennett drugged the American people with, and the correspondents—says Crane—"lulled them. We told them this and we told them that, and I warrant you our screaming sounded like the noise of a lot of sea birds settling for the night among the black crags."

If a cruiser (formerly a towboat) fired a single shot from her turret, "the world heard of it, you bet. We were not idle men. We had come to report the war and we did it. Our good names and our salaries depended on it." The managing editors demanded hair-raising dispatches, bombastic scoops on heroism, and urged the correspondents to remember "that the American people were a collection of super-nervous idiots who would immediately have convulsions if we did not throw them some news—any news. It was not true, at all."

The correspondents, says Crane, solved the war in a "babble of tongues," saying ironically to one another as they drank iced tea: "War is hell." "The papers should have sent playwrights to the first part of the war. Playwrights are allowed to lower the curtain from time to time and say to the crowd: 'Mark, ye now! Three or four months are supposed to elapse.' But the poor devils at Key West were obliged to keep the curtain up all the time. 'This isn't a continuous performance.' 'Yes, it is; it's *got* to be a continuous performance. The welfare of the paper demands it. The people want news.'" Bored with it all, he told McCready of the *Herald* "vehemently, imperatively, loftily, sarcastically" how to write any story. "He told me, also, with equal force, variety, and even seeming interest, that he knew I wouldn't grasp the notion, and that he was wasting his time. He was right, of course, as to that last; but I couldn't see why he need be so damned triumphant about it."

No sooner had the *Three Friends* docked at Key West on May 20 than Crane with Scovel and photographer Jimmie Hare chartered the *Somers N. Smith* to go to the Windward Islands—once again in hope of locating Cervera's fleet. This long-distance adventure was "ultra-hazardous, almost suicidal," says Crane, because their harbor tug had "no architectural intention of parading the high seas." It could do only eleven knots. Elsewhere, in "God Rest Ye," he says that they "tossed themselves in their cockleshell even as far as Martinique; they knew many faces and many flags, but they did not find Cervera's fleet. If they had found that elusive squadron this timid story would never have been written; there would probably have been a lyric."

Cervera had quit Martinique on May 23; but en route westward the trio in their cockleshell encountered off the southeast coast of Cuba the USS *St. Paul*. They knew that Cervera was not in Havana harbor, nor in Puerto Rico, and they figured that he therefore must be in Santiago de

Cuba (on the southeastern belly of that island). But here was the Captain of the *St. Paul* reporting by megaphone that Cervera was not in Santiago de Cuba. The *St. Paul* by heaving a shell over the unknown *Somers N. Smith* forced her to heave to, and then the all-knowing Captain Sigsbee—hero of the sunken *Maine*—shouted: "I advise you to make yourself scarce, as Cervera may show up at any minute. You are in a very dangerous position." However, when they later docked at Key West the newspaper headlines were proclaiming that the Spanish fleet was in Santiago. Thanks to Captain Sigsbee and the *St. Paul,* they had lost out on a journalistic scoop.

On May 29 Crane and six reporters were off the coast of Santiago en route to Jamaica aboard the *Somers N. Smith,* hired jointly by the New York *World* and *Herald* to circumnavigate the island of Cuba to discover the whereabouts of Cervera's fleet, but by June 2 they were back at Key West with nothing to report. The *Smith* had sailed from Key West on the 24th and the next day "the wind blew half a hurricane. The dispatch boat . . . made very bad weather, but wallowed and pitched safely through while the fine fruit steamer *Belvedere* was piling upon the rocks to the south of Cape Maysi." So Scovel reported to the *World,* while Crane also reported in the *World* that under the awning in the stern of their dispatch boat the seven correspondents—attired in pajamas and sometimes less than that—lamented their tobacco famine "as if it were the central fact in the universe." The blue mountains of the eastern Cuban coast and the ocean composed "one vast silence. The grimy stokers frequently emerged from a hatch and soused themselves with buckets of sea-water under the tropic sun." The Captain came aft and casually remarked to the correspond-ents that the smoke of a steamer was within sight, and sure enough they saw through Jimmie Hare's glasses a trail of tawny smoke heading straight for their ship.

Crane reported this "hair-raising experience" in his *World* dispatch: "Chased by a Big Spanish Man-O-War" (not published until July 3). The Spanish warship ate the distance between them, and the correspondents made mournful preparations for capture and Spanish prisons—even gar-roting, for newspapermen would be treated as spies. If only a British flag could be found aboard so as to deceive the enemy. But Crane's hopeful notion was crushed by the despairing thought that "the enemy would not believe it anyhow!" In this sketch he uses the device of juxtaposing now a mood of hope and then a mood of despair. He speculates hopefully that the dispatch boat speeds toward paradise, paradise being Jamaica: "Oh, happy isle, dream harbor, heart's ease, asylum, refuge, sanctuary, peace place, resting place, vast chamber of safety, paradise of the pursued, you are popular." He then undercuts his dream by flatly noting that Jamaica was "160 miles to the southward of a certain newspaper despatch-boat." "On swept the pursuing steamer—inexorable, certain as a natural law. She had fired no gun. She was a terrible water sphinx in her silence. Presently her wheel swung her to starboard, and to the eyes of the speechless and immovable crowd on the despatch-boat was presented the whole beautiful length of the American auxiliary cruiser *St. Paul.*"

In addition to his dispatches, Crane found time to tinker with a projected novel called "The Merry-Go-Round" (it survives only as a title), and to work on his Greco–Turkish War novel, *Active Service*. He abominated the drudgery of grinding out news stories, and seldom could he be coaxed to turning his hand to it, says Ralph Paine. "His was the soul of the artist—slowly, carefully fashioning his phrases, sensitive to the time, the place, and the mood." Photographer Jimmie Hare remembers Crane as a "charming fellow, fond of a drink and not too fond of work." But his mind was as busy as Hare's camera. His war dispatches( to quote one historian[8]) give us more of "the real feel of the war than all the gaudy paragraphs of the gorgeous Dick Davis and all the romantic drawings of the popular Remington." Or even the photographs of Jimmie Hare. Not all of Crane's dispatches were eye-witness reporting, however, nor did he always report the stories he picked up from eye-witnesses. Scovel, heading the *World's* staff, found it "very difficult to get Crane's copy."

From officers of the blockading ships which the tug encountered, he gathered such stories as the *Dupont's* exchange of fire with the Spanish shore batteries at Cárdenas, where five sailors and one officer were killed by Spanish shells when the *Winslow* rashly entered the harbor on May 8. Or again the story of the flagship *New York's* bombardment of San Juan on May 12, when one sailor (Frank Widemark) was killed and others were wounded. "What? the battles? Yes, I saw something of all of them," Crane declared in his later "War Memories." He missed out on several naval engagements, however.

Admiral Sampson first reached Santiago on June 1; the Flying Squadron under Commodore William S. Schley got there by May 26, steaming from the Atlantic coast, which it had patrolled to protect our shores from possible attack. However, Sampson ascertained that the Spanish fleet had all the while been inside Santiago harbor, a fact which his rival Schley had failed to investigate. Because of Schley's "dilatory and stupid tactics," says Ralph Paine, no effective blockade of the Santiago harbor had yet been established. With Sampson's arrival our naval force finally bottled up the enemy fleet and by our searchlights made it impossible for Cervera to escape by night. That situation prevailed all June. But when on July 3 the Spanish fleet tried to get out of Santiago harbor and the fight began which won the war, Sampson's fleet was bound eastward. Sampson returned to Santiago only in time to see his rival Schley signaling from the *Brooklyn* that victory had just been won. The triumphant Schley immediately dispatched a boat to Guantánamo to file the first official bulletin of his victory over the Spanish fleet of Rear Admiral Pascual Cervera y Topete.[9]

The first invasion of any foreign soil by an American military force and the first amphibious attack by American Marines occurred on June 7 when Commander Bowman H. McCalla's cruisers invaded Guantánamo, drove off a Spanish gunboat, immobilized a blockhouse offering no resistance, and landed a hundred Marines. More—towed in cutters by steam launches to the beach—landed three days later from the *Panther*.

Cooped up since Tampa, they were crazy to get at the Spanish, and they went ashore singing "There'll Be a Hot Time in the Old Town Tonight." They burned the blockhouse as a preventive against yellow fever, ran up the American flag, and on a ridge over the bay raised their tents and called it Camp McCalla. However, they neglected to dig trenches. Crane was sick, but he was determined to stick it out. He had landed with Ernest McCready and Ralph Paine, along with the Marines. There was no enemy firing the first night. "We thought it rather comic," says Crane in "War Memories." But the next night there was some firing: "We lay on our bellies; it was no longer comic. On the third night the alarm came early; I went in search of Gibbs [Surgeon John Blair Gibbs], but I soon gave over an active search for the more congenial occupation of lying flat and feeling the hot hiss of the bullets trying to cut my hair. For the moment I was no longer a cynic. I was a child who, in a fit of ignorance, had jumped into the vat of war."

Surgeon Gibbs had given Crane some quinine, and he remained with the Marines because "he foresaw much personal enjoyment. A hawser could not have dragged him away from the show," says Paine. McCready and Paine, on seeing that there was no enemy resistance that first night (June 7), steamed to Haiti's French cable station—a run of 110 miles—to cable their reports of the landing of the Marines. At the first enemy fire on the second night Sergeant Smith on picket duty was killed, and two privates (Dumphy and McColgan from Massachusetts) were shot in the head. The Spaniards stripped these two soldiers of their shoes, hats and cartridges; it was erroneously reported that they mutilated the bodies.

An insurgent officer, General Mario García Menocal, later told Crane that the "Marinos Americanos" confronted the most formidable corps in the Spanish Army, and reporter Henry James Whigham of the Chicago *Tribune* realized that the Spaniards were strong enough to massacre the Marines. "But they were too cowardly to make the attempt. They have been content to lie in ambush and try to pick off our men."[10] On Thursday, June 9 (the third night), Crane and Whigham and two other Chicago reporters (Beach and Billman) carried supplies from the coast to Camp McCalla on the hilltop and also aided the Marines in lugging a couple of field guns up there. Under enemy fire, they sought the trenches which had been newly dug by the Marines, and just then a Spanish Mauser bullet whistled between Beach and Billman and ended its course by stopping the life of Marine surgeon John Blair Gibbs. Three Spaniards had sneaked to the edge of the camp, shot Gibbs, and then run helter-skelter down the hills when our Cuban guide—Colonel José Campiná—fired upon them. (So Crane reported it in a dispatch he directed to McCready a few days later.)

While the Marines were firing all around him, he was trying to sleep in a shallow trench. In "War Memories"[11] he says that he heard somebody "dying near me. He was dying hard. Hard. It took him a long time to die. He breathed as all noble machinery breathes when it is making its gallant strife against breaking, breaking. But he was going to break. He was going to break. It seemed to me, this breathing, the noise of a heroic pump which strives to subdue a mud which comes upon it in tons. The darkness was impenetrable. The man was lying in some depression within seven feet of me. Every wave, vibration, of his anguish beat upon my senses. He was long past groaning. . . . I thought this man would never die. I wanted him to die. Ultimately he died. At that moment the adjutant came bustling along erect amid the spitting bullets. I knew him by his voice. 'Where's the doctor? There's some wounded men over there. Where's the doctor?' A man answered briskly: 'Just died this minute, sir!' It was as if he had said: 'Just gone around the corner this minute, sir.' " Thomas Steep of *Leslie's* wrote that assistant surgeon Gibbs had remarked as he walked to the doorway of the hospital tent: "Well, I don't want to die in this place." Just then he was shot in the forehead. "When the doctor was gasping his last, a private with a bleeding hand ran up crying, 'Where's the doctor? Where's the doctor?' The doctor must have heard it." The next morning Crane awoke to find a group of exhausted men sleeping beside the body of Gibbs "so closely and in such abandoned attitudes that one saw that a certain head had beneath it a great dark pool."

During the last months of his English years Crane recreated in his story "The Upturned Face" the burial of Surgeon Gibbs at Guantánamo amidst enemy fire. Timothy Lean and an officer wearing sword and revolver bury their friend "old Bill" amid "a windy sound of bullets, and on top of the hill." Crane begins the story with a question: " 'What will we do now?' said the adjutant, troubled and excited." The adjutant is Lean's superior officer, and yet he asks the question and Lean has the answer: "Bury him." That seems simple enough, but unexpected events occur which upset that simple fixed idea. Two privates begin to dig the hole "amid the swift snap of close bullets," but they are as much frightened by the body of their comrade as they are by the bullets. The situation they confront presents a contradiction of Lean's simple formula: "Bury him." And even after they've buried him they remain in doubt as to whether they've properly buried old Bill, and so they look down on him in "curious abstraction." The Marine Adjutant was First Lieutenant Herbert Draper, a graduate of the U.S. Naval Academy, 1887.

Before that first shovel of earth is poised above the corpse, Lean recites a portion of the service: " 'O Father, our friend has sunk in the deep waters of death, but his spirit has leaped toward Thee as the bubble arises from the lips of the drowning. Perceive, we beseech, O Father, the little flying bubble, and—' Lean, although husky and ashamed, had suffered no hesitation up to this point, but he stopped with a hopeless feeling and looked at the corpse." He seems to realize that his words are inadequate for the occasion, that the grim reality contradicts the fixed idea of "bury him." The service ends as a maimed ritual, for while they honor their friend by burying him, they must dishonor him by shoveling dirt on his face. Similarly, the words Timothy Lean recites as appropriate are not, for they come from the burial service for the dead at sea.[12] Crane's theme is that our fixed ideas get contradicted by unpredictable and trivial realities; our intentions get contradicted in the very act of our carrying them out. The story ends with Lean swinging the shovel in a pendulum-curve: "When the earth landed it made a sound—plop."[13]

The great majority of our men, said Crane in his dispatch "In the First Land Fight 4 of Our Men Are Killed," had never before been under fire, "and though a night attack is especially trying, not one of them flinched." Nothing seems to have happened on Friday, but on Saturday (June 11) the enemy began firing at three o'clock that afternoon from the cover of tropical thicket and kept up the firing until Sunday morning. At midnight of June 11 they charged the hilltop Camp McCalla and came so close that revolvers were used. Crane with four Marine signalmen had been lying belly down in a shallow trench, taking turns with them to stand up and signal messages by lanterns to our ships in the bay beneath Camp McCalla. He describes that Saturday night attack in "Marines Signalling Under Fire at Guantánamo," which Richard Harding Davis called the best piece of descriptive writing during the Spanish–American War. "When one of the signalmen stood up to wave his lantern," writes Crane, "I, lying in the trench, invariably rolled a little to the right or left, in order that, when he was shot, he might not fall on me." He does not mention that he also took turns standing up to expose the lantern lights amid the rifle fire of Spanish guerrillas. At midnight Colonel Robert Huntington came himself to signal an important message to the *Marblehead* down in the Bay, and at sight of the lantern's yellow gleams the Spaniards drove enough bullets to kill the whole Marine Corps. He stood up beside the signalman, and when Adjutant Draper urged him to step down, the gray old veteran said: "I am in no more danger than the men." A few minutes after the moon rose at 12:45 A.M. the enemy attacked in force, and an hour later Huntington signaled for a doctor.

Meanwhile a thousand rifles were rattling, "the diabolic Colt automatics clacking," and field guns boomed. The *Marblehead*'s guns roared from the Bay, and Spanish Mauser bullets were "sneering always in the air a few inches over one's head," says Crane. The wonder was that the four signalmen and Crane and Howbert Billman were not "riddled from head to foot and sent home more as repositories of Spanish ammunition than as

Marines. . . . The noise; the impenetrable darkness; the knowledge from the sound of bullets that the enemy was on three sides of the camp; the infrequent bloody stumbling and death of some man with whom, perhaps, one had messed two hours previous; the weariness of the body, and the more terrible weariness of the mind, at the endlessness of the thing, made it wonderful that at least some of the men did not come out of it with their nerves hopelessly in shreds." Lt. Colonel Henry Cochrane later declared that he could never forget the calmness of Crane and Billman of the Chicago *Record* "on the night of the 11th of June on top of that red gravel hill. I have a mental photograph of the several scenes and tableaux that can be produced at will and with endless interest."[14]

Probably no man who was there at Guantánamo that night had ever before understood "the true eloquence of the breaking of the day," says Crane in "Marines Signalling Under Fire." The Marines were ravenous for the dawn, and they argued in the trenches whether daybreak had yet begun. To Stephen it seemed that the patch of eastern sky "whitened in about the speed of a man's accomplishment if he should be in the way of painting Madison Square Garden with a camel's-hair brush." But finally the night was done with, and Crane was "furious with this wretched sunrise. I thought I could have walked around the world in the time required for the old thing to get up above the horizon."

On Sunday morning Ernest McCready, having returned from Haiti with Ralph Paine on the *Three Friends,* searched for Crane in the war zone and found him sitting on a rock. "The shells from the cruisers were still going over our heads, the Marines were still going up the ravines and extending on less rugged but more heavily bushed ground, and the Spanish rifle-fire was evidently slackening," says McCready. He ignored Crane's gruff greetings and proposed: "Let's hustle like hell down to the boat." Crane, dirty and exhausted from the night attack, was disgusted with life. He seemed "somehow gloomily elated over the scenery and the prospect that presently it would be a whole lot worse." He wouldn't stir from the rock. " 'Gimme a cigarette!' he commanded. 'Do you think, for God's sake, that I'm going away now on your damned boat and leave all this?'—and he waved a hand in a sweeping gesture covering the battle picture. I knew what he meant." He had shared the adventure of the Marines in holding the hill against three thousand crack riflemen of the Spanish irregular forces, and he wanted to see the end of this first infantry encounter.

McCready urged him to remember that he, McCready, was the only reporter who had means of getting to a cable station and that to get there at once was the right newspaper tactic, but Crane was not interested. No matter when it reached the *World* what he reported would still be news because he wrote it. His business was to gather impressions and write them as the spirit moved. He was not just a newspaperman, says McCready. "He was an artist from crown to heel, temperamental, undisciplined in the narrow sense of the word, careless of any interest that did not match with his own private ones, contemptuous of mere news getting or news reporting, thinking of his *World* connection as a convenient aid rather than as one imposing sharp and instant responsibility upon him."

McCready's temper was short and explosive, but he wanted to obtain the casualty list from Crane, so he played a little "poker" by telling him that there were women at the cable station. " 'Have you got a drink on the damned boat? Or did you and the Armored Cruiser [Ralph Paine] lap it all up?' That was better. It was surrender—or half surrender—disguised as something else." So Crane was coming. He had been frowning at the brush up ahead where the shells still pitched, singly now or again by salvos, but now his eyes flickered in uncertainty. McCready was scared, "whenever I had time to think about it; but Crane wasn't. There was no fear in him so far as battle, murder, or sudden death was concerned— in the observation of any one who saw him in places where the average man feels a chill wind momentarily, or is afraid he's about to get the wind up."

" 'What the hell's the rush?' he asked. 'Do you realize that I've not had a damned wink of sleep for 48 hours? Besides all this mess last night— that was a real mess compared with this.' And now in contempt of me and my fears, my haste, and perhaps in disgust, too, that in part he had seemed to allow himself to be persuaded from his purpose, he waved briefly toward the front where the skirmishers had disappeared. The popping of rifle fire & the crash of shell fire were becoming less intrusive. Contrariwise, we were moving toward the Bay, and the cruisers were talking more plainly. That irascible old man McCalla on the *Marblehead* seemed to be particularly irritated, judging by the volume of his fire as compared with that of his consorts."[15]

His clothes full of red mud, Crane startled the chief engineer of the *Three Friends,* John Dunn, when he came aboard. "We all had quite a laugh at his red appearance," Dunn later wrote Cora. "I inquired how he got painted up so, and he said that he was lying on his stomach dodging bullets all night. There was no sleep for anybody near the hill."[16] Dirty and heavy-eyed, it was all Crane could do to drag himself into the boat's galley to gulp down food and coffee. Then he sprawled on deck and talked (to quote Paine now) "in a slow, unemotional manner as was his wont; but the thin, pallid face kindled, and the somber, weary eyes brightened when he told us how he had fared with the battalion of Marines. And as he went on, he used words as though they were colors to be laid on a canvas with a vigorous and daring brush."

Paine and McCready urged him to duck into the cabin and write his sketch of the first land engagement with the Spaniards, but he paid no attention and continued to talk about the Marines. McCready's bribery of bottles of ale and bananas and cigarettes finally persuaded him to dictate a dispatch while pacing the quarter deck with a bottle of ale in his hand. "You may fire when ready, Gridley!" said McCready, quoting Admiral Dewey's remark to his gunner Gridley aboard the flagship at Manila. So Crane fired away with his account, meanwhile kidding McCready about his journalistic wordiness by mocking Joseph Pulitzer's motto: "Accuracy! Terseness! Accuracy!"

"It was a ridiculous scene," Paine says. "McCready, the conscientious reporter, waiting with pencil and paper—Crane, the artist, deliberating over this phrase or that, finicky about a word, insisting upon frequent changes and erasures, and growing more and more suspicious. Finally he exclaimed: 'Read it aloud, Mac, as far as it goes. I believe you are murdering my stuff.' 'I dropped out a few adjectives here and there, Steve. This has to be *news,* sent at cable rates [$3.25 per word]. You can save your flub-dub and shoot it to New York by mail. What I want is the straight story of the fight.' " Paine left them wrangling bitterly, with small hope of a satisfactory adjustment, and later McCready went off on the tugboat *Triton* to file the dispatch at Porto Antonio, Jamaica, on June 12.[17]

Wearing a Panama hat lent him by engineer John Dunn, Crane went ashore again. The hat protected him from the sun blazing down on the barren Camp McCalla hilltop, where the prostrate Marines were "red and sweating like ship's stokers." Paine, having quit the *Three Friends,* was taking Sunday breakfast with the Marines during a lull in the fighting while the Spaniards themselves indulged in breakfast. There Crane found him on the brow of the hill with a bottle of whiskey, "which I took from him violently." But he got only a swig of it because Paine passed the bottle down the line of Marines in their shallow trench. Each man sparingly took a drink and then passed the precious bottle to his comrade.

Some of the Marines had gone down to the ocean and were bathing naked when suddenly the staccato of a Spanish machine gun broke the lull; whereupon these naked Marines scampered ashore and clothed themselves with cartridge belts. "Raked, enfiladed, flanked, surrounded, and overwhelmed, what hope was there for William B. Perkins of the Minnesota *Herald?*" says Crane in his fictionalized version of this incident, "The Lone Charge of William B. Perkins." Perkins is Paine of the New York *Journal.* He spotted an old steam boiler in the bushes on the beach and crept into it—emerging only when the enemy ceased fire. Crane in this sketch was pinning a leather medal on his old friend Ralph Paine of Asbury Park days.[18] Just before the firing began, he had gone down to the beach to poultice his sore feet in wet clay. He sat on the little rickety pier near the corrugated-iron cable station, while some Marines were poking with sticks into the smoking ruins of the fishing hamlet in search of mementos. "Down in the shallow water," says Crane in "War Memories," "crabs were meandering among the weeds, and little fishes moved slowly in schools." Then the Spanish guerrillas volleyed, and their firing interrupted his interlude on the beach.[19] The guerrilla forces, severely mauled and convinced that they could not dislodge the battalion, finally retired inland, and the harbor became safe for Admiral Sampson's ships.

A friend of Van Wyck Brooks recalls Crane's bravery at Guantánamo when our troops were huddled against an earthwork at which the Spaniards directed an unusually vicious fire. "Suddenly Crane, who was incapable of bravado, let himself quietly over the redoubt, lighted a cigarette, stood for a few moments with his arms at his sides, while the bullets hissed past him into the mud, then as quietly climbed back over the redoubt and strolled away. It was impossible . . . to question the insouciance of this act: Crane's bearing was that of a somnambulist. He appeared to be, as it were, detached from himself, possessed by an irresistible impulse to register, in his body, and without regard to the safety of his body, certain sensations."

Richard Harding Davis appraised Crane in Cuba as "the coolest man, whether army officer or civilian, that I saw under fire at any time during the war."

# XXII

## ᴄᴈ *The Cuban War*

"THE next day [Monday, June 13] we went shooting," says Crane in "War Memories." "It was exactly like quail shooting. I'll tell you. These guerrillas who so cursed our lives had a well some five miles away, and it was the only water supply within about twelve miles of the Marine camp. Captain Elliott, of C. Company, was to take his men with Captain Spicer's company, D, out to the well, beat the enemy away, and destroy everything. He was to start at the next daybreak. He asked me if I cared to go, and of course I accepted with glee; but all that night I was afraid. Bitterly afraid. . . . But if I was frightened I was also very cold. It was a chill night, and I wanted a heavy topcoat almost as much as I wanted a certificate of immunity from rifle bullets. These two feelings were of equal importance to my mind. They were twins."

The fight at Cuzco, which Crane prized as "really the tightest, best fight of the war," lasted four days and nights. It began at daybreak of June 14 and ended Friday night or Saturday morning June 18. Captain George F. Elliott was short of officers and therefore declined to take with him any adjutant from Camp McCalla, "but having been notified that a Mr. Stephen Crane would be allowed to accompany the expedition, I requested him to act as an aide if one should be needed. He accepted the duty and was of material aid during the action, carrying messages to fire volleys, etc., to the different company commanders." So Captain Elliott reported to Lieutenant Colonel Huntington. They took the narrow path skirting the shore for seven miles around the outer slope of the mountain in the enemy's left and rear. Captain William Spicer meanwhile led a smaller force along an inland trail through thick underbrush.

The brown line of Elliott's Marines followed some sailor-clad Cuban guides in single file and climbed a chalky cliff to make camp on a hill which Crane describes as "steep as a Swiss roof." They passed a stone house that had been demolished by a Yankee gunboat because it sheltered a Spanish garrison. "Tall gaunt ridges covered with chaparral and cactus shouldered down to the sea, and on the spaces of bottom-land were palms and dry yellow grass. From the cliffs, around Windward Point they could see the gunboat *Dolphin* steering a course parallel to them. "I was as glad to see her as if she had called out my name."

A halt was made to give the Cuban scouts more time; the Cuban Colonel, revolver in one hand, machete in the other, waited their report before advancing. Crane does not identify him, but he was Lieutenant Colonel Enrique Tomás, who had urged McCalla and Huntington (in a conference aboard the *Marblehead* on the night of the 13th) to destroy the well at Cuzco. He posed like a statue of liberty, and boasted afterwards to Crane that he alone had been responsible for winning the fight at Cuzco. Elliott's men met the enemy's Mauser bullets as they reached the crest of the 350-foot hill at eleven o'clock. The fighting "banged away with a roar like a forest fire. Suddenly a Marine wriggled out of the firing line and came frantically to me," says Crane in "War Memories." The Marine offered him five dollars for a drink of whiskey and tried to force into his hand a goldpiece. " 'Go to the devil,' said I, deeply scandalized. 'Besides, I haven't got any whiskey.' " A Cuban Negro soldier was shot through the heart, and one man took the body on his back and another took it by the feet, and they trundled his body off as though they were a wheelbarrow. Another man—shot through the ankle—nursed his wound as though he were pleased with it. "It seemed to suit him. I don't know why."

The Spaniards had raced to contain the hill and lost. Spicer's men arrived in the vicinity and bullets "sang in the air until one thought that a good hand with a lacrosse stick could have bagged many." Elliott sent Crane to find out who occupied a hill some six hundred yards away. (Lieutenant Lewis Lucas and his men had not arrived as expected. He was in fact on the next ridge.)

Crane went off on his mission "as jaunty as a real soldier, while all the time my heart was in my boots and I was cursing the day that saw me landed on the shores of the tragic isle." It "proved to me that I had inherited histrionic abilities." But he admits, "I was afraid," even though other men about him did not seem that day to be afraid at all. "Men with quiet, composed faces who went about this business as if they proceeded from a sense of habit. They were not old soldiers; they were mainly recruits, but many of them betrayed all the emotion and merely the emotion that one sees in the face of a man earnestly at work." They were "terribly hard at work; red-faced, sweating, gasping toilers."

He found Lieutenant Lucas' men and their Cuban guides on the summit of a ridge overlooking a small valley where there was a house, a well and a thicket of shrub with broad oily leaves. "It was a blazing, bitter hot day on top of the ridge with its shrivelled chaparral and its straight, tall cactus-plants. The sky was bare and blue, and hurt like brass." The *Dolphin* shelled a hill where Lieutenant Magill and forty Marines were covering the left flank of the two fighting companies; it was necessary to stop the *Dolphin's* fire at once. Captain Elliott called for a signalman, and Sergeant

John H. Quick responded with "a blue polka-dot neckerchief as large as a quilt. He tied it on a long, crooked stick. Then he went to the top of the ridge and, turning his back to the Spanish fire, began to signal to the *Dolphin*. Again we gave a man sole possession of a particular part of the ridge. We didn't want it. He could have it and welcome. If the young sergeant had had the smallpox, the cholera, and the yellow fever, we could not have slid out with more alacrity.

"As men have often said, it seemed as if there was in this war a God of Battles who held His mighty hand before the Americans. As I looked at Sergeant Quick wigwagging there against the sky, I would not have given a tin tobacco tag for his life. Escape seemed for him impossible. It seemed absurd to hope that he would not be hit; I only hoped that he would be hit just a little, in the arm, the shoulder, or the leg. I watched his face, and it was as grave and serene as that of a man writing in his own library. He was the very embodiment of tranquility in occupation. He stood there amid the animal-like babble of the Cubans, the crack of rifles, and the whistling snarl of the bullets, and wigwagged whatever he had to wigwag without heeding anything but his business." Crane called it a great feat. Just before Quick signaled the *Dolphin,* he had watched another man doing the same thing. He calls him Clancy, a redheaded mick. It was no doubt private John Fitzgerald, who for gallantry at Cuzco was awarded the Congressional Medal of Honor, as was also Sergeant John Quick. Crane never mentioned in print his own heroism at Cuzco.

A company was surrounded by Spaniards, and Crane was close enough to see that the soldiers had run out of water. The temperature was about 108 degrees, and there was the high, steep hill which had to be climbed to bring water to the men. "Yet Stephen Crane never hesitated. Collecting about a dozen big bottles, he retired to the rear, filled them, and turned to climb the hill again—'his little person festooned with bottles,' as one who saw the incident described it afterwards. When he reached the fighting-line he dropped exhausted, and this gave rise to the report that he had been shot. Happily it was not true. The soldiers were too busy to cheer him at the moment, but they repaid him afterwards with the warmest admiration. That was only one of several occasions on which he showed his genuine pluck." This incident was witnessed by a correspondent for the London *Daily Chronicle* who was present at the Cuzco skirmishes, although he did not report it until after Crane's death (in an obituary of June 6, 1900). He says that Crane in 1898 looked more like a boy of eighteen than a young man of twenty-six. "With his fragile physique and shy and sensitive disposition, he was the last man who might be expected to figure in the storm and stress of battle. Yet 'Little Stevey'—as his friends and colleagues delighted to call him—was possessed of the highest and truest courage, the courage of the man of keen imagination, and he proved it on more than one stricken field."

In "A Mystery of Heroism" Crane had already anticipated in 1895 what he was to experience in the Cuzco skirmishes: a well, a house and a hill. As Fred Collins in that Civil War story carries water from a well and rightly thinks himself a hero, so Crane at Cuzco carried up the steep hill casks of water sent ashore by the *Dolphin,* while "the dripping Marines looked with despair at their empty canteens." And what he saw on the trail to Cuzco was what he had depicted in *The Red Badge of Courage:* the body of a dead soldier who "lay upon his back, staring at the sky."

Spanish guerrilla scouts called back into the hills warning of their enemy's approach by imitating the voice of doves. Crane says he never heard "such a horrible sound as the beautiful cooing of the wood dove when I was certain that it came from the yellow throat of a guerrilla." The Marines on the ridge of their hill had some fine open-field shooting at the Spaniards who swarmed up the slope from their thicket. It was like trap-shooting. Crane calls the shells from the *Dolphin* the "dogs who went in and stirred out the game. The Marines were suddenly gentlemen in leggings, alive with the sharp instinct which marks the hunter. The Spaniards were the birds. Yes, they were the birds, but I doubt if they would sympathize with my metaphors."

The fight at Cuzco ended with the Spaniards running away; once they ran from the valley's thickets, Crane says, his courage increased. The Marines destroyed the enemy's camp, the house and the well, and the *Dolphin* gave them water—"and we filled our canteens." Major Charles McCawley wrote Crane the next year: "I, in company with all my brother officers, have always looked back with pleasure and pride upon your service with us in Cuba, for you were the only outsider who saw it all, and we regard you as an honorary member of the Corps and hope you will always have the same affection for us as we have for you. I shall never forget the night I offered you half of my tent which sadly enough we were only able to occupy for about 5 minutes as the firing began before we had closed our eyes. I read with much satisfaction your stories of the signalling at Cuzco & with the lanterns at night & only wish that you had written the whole story of those four days & nights."[1]

The Cuzco Hill skirmish dislodged the Spaniards from their place of harassing the Marines at Camp McCalla and gave the Americans control of Guantánamo Bay.

After the Marines had accomplished their mission at Cuzco, Crane returned to Camp McCalla and then left Guantánamo Bay with his *World* colleagues, Sylvester Scovel and Alexander Kenealy, on Friday, June 17. They boarded the *Triton* and disembarked at Cuero, thirteen miles west of Santiago. Almost under the guns of Santiago's forts they set up the first newspaper headquarters on Cuban soil, daringly raising the Cuban flag and the New York *World* banner. Scovel and Crane swam two Jamaica ponies ashore from the *Triton,* while Kenealy and his attendants landed with signaling apparatus. A third horse was purchased from a native. Scovel's plan was to proceed from Cuero, opposite a Cuban camp he knew of, to sneak through the Spanish lines to some place from which to view the Spanish squadron down in Santiago's harbor. There was a rumor that the *Vizcaya* had escaped the harbor and Sampson needed to know the truth.

While Kenealy took the *Triton* to Haiti to file his dispatch,[2] Scovel and Crane started up into the mountains with an escort of Cuban soldiers and found, at the first ridge they mounted, "a simple illumination as to why the insurgents if they had food and ammunition could hold out for years. There is no getting men out of such hills if they choose to stay in them." In his "War Memories" Crane says that in the evening he and Scovel "reached the camp of a major who commanded the outposts. It was high in the hills. The stars were as big as coconuts. We lay in borrowed hammocks and watched the firelight gleam blood-red on the trees. I remember an utterly naked Negro squatting, crimson by the fire and cleaning an iron-pot. Some voices were singing an Afric wail of forsaken love and death." At daybreak, leaving their horses with the Cuban pickets, they climbed hills and crawled through fields on their hands and knees, up and down hills for nine miles—until the final hill. On ascending it, they lay on the ground exhausted, while their Cuban guides chopped a hole in the foliage with their machetes. When they got up and peered through the hole, they could see Santiago and the harbor, with Cervera's fleet in it— the whole show.[3] There, tranquil at anchor, lay the *Oquendo,* the *María Theresa,* the *Cristóbal Colón,* the *Viscaya,* the *Pluton,* the *Furor.* "The bay was white in the sun and the great blacked-hull armored cruisers were impressive in a dignity massive yet graceful. We did not know that they were all doomed ships, soon to go out to a swift death."

Scovel drew maps of the position of each enemy ship, while Crane rested, "blinking lazily at the Spanish squadron. We did not know that we were the last Americans to view them alive and unhurt and at peace. Then we retraced our way, at the same noiseless canter. I did not understand my condition until I considered that we were well through the Spanish lines and practically out of danger. Then I discovered that I was a dead man. The nervous force having evaporated, I was a mere corpse. My limbs were of dough, and my spinal cord burned within me as if it were red-hot wire. But just at this time we were discovered by a Spanish patrol, and I ascertained that I was not dead at all. We ultimately reached the foot of the other mountain on whose shoulders were the Cuban pickets, and here I was so sure of safety that I could not resist the temptation to die again. I think I passed into eleven distinct stupors during the ascent of that mountain while the escort stood leaning on their Remingtons. We had done twenty-five miles at a sort of man-gallop, never once using a beaten track, but always going promiscuously through the jungle and over the rocks. And many of the hills stood straight on end, so that it was as hard to come down as it was to go up."

Crane and Scovel were more exhausted than their Cuban guides even though these men had lived on nothing but mangoes and the carcass of a small lean pony. One of these Cuban pickets when at the foot of a precipitous hill asked Crane's permission to cling to the horse's tail, "and then the Jamaica pony would snake him to the summit so swiftly that only his toes seemed to touch the rocks. And for this assistance the man was grateful. When we crowned the last great ridge we saw our squadron to the eastward spread in its patient semicircular about the mouth of the harbor. But as we wound towards the beach we saw a more dramatic thing—our own despatch-boat leaving the rendezvous and putting off to sea. Evidently we were late. Behind me were fifteen stomachs, empty. It was a frightful situation. My friend and I charged for the beach, and those fifteen fools began to run. It was no use. The despatch-boat went gaily away, trailing black smoke behind her. We turned in distress, wondering what we could say to that abused escort."

The men had been promised a reward of supplies from the *Three Friends*. Not at all indignant, the Cubans "simply smiled and made a gesture which denied the existence of everything but mangoes and pony." Crane vowed to get them their promised reward, but he never saw them again. The Cuban insurgents put Crane and Scovel into their boat, a dugout, with two black boys, and they waved a hearty goodbye from the shore. The *Three Friends* rescued the dugout, and Crane and Scovel relieved their feelings of debt to the Cubans by over-rewarding the two black boys. "They were two rascals." As for the Cuban guides, Crane saw them from his usual double viewpoint. They were heroic insurgents, liberators of their country; but also they were rascals exploiting the situation. "I hope they are all on the police-force in the new Santiago," he wrote a year later in his "War Memories."

The *Three Friends* took Crane and Scovel to Admiral Sampson's *New York,* and they reported the position of Cervera's fleet as drawn by Scovel in his sketches of Santiago de Cuba's harbor. This was precisely the information Sampson needed. Officers on the flagship entertained them at cards in the insufferable, steamy wet-heat below deck, and then the *Three Friends* picked them up to take them to a cable station. "I think it was Jamaica." (Crane could not remember because he was then ill with malarial fever.)

Returning from Jamaica to the Cuban coast, they found "the sea alive with transports." The American army of invasion had set out on June 12 from Tampa for Cuban shores via Key West, where the fleet of thirty-two transports was to be joined by a convoy of twelve naval vessels—but the transports stayed in Tampa harbor until the 14th; Secretary of War Russell Alger—frightened by the false alarm that some Spanish ships had been sighted—had wired General W. R. Shafter: "Wait until you get further orders before you sail." And so Shafter called back the transports while the Navy tried to locate the nonexistent Spanish enemy. The second embarkation duplicated the chaos of the first, and once out to sea the transports lost themselves and each other while torpedo boats—like "keen-eyed, intelligent collies rounding up a herd of bungling sheep"—desperately rounded them up and tried to keep them in line.

Crane boarded one of the transports commanded by a Scandinavian "who was afraid of the shadows of his own topmasts." Officers in the convoying warships loathed him. This skipper had in his hold "a great quantity of military stores as successfully secreted as if they had been buried in a copper box in the cornerstone of a new public building in Boston. He had had his master's certificate for twenty-one years, and those people couldn't tell a marlin-spoke from the starboard of the ship."

The transports and convoying warships arrived off the Cuban coast near Santiago on June 19 with about 17,000 officers and men, but they waited there for several days while their leaders made up their minds what to do next. Noncommittal Shafter duped Admiral Sampson into believing that his plan for the landing point of the troops coincided with the Navy's plan, but then General Shafter ordered the landings at points not figuring in the Navy's plan: at Daiquirí, with its unusable MacWilliams' pier and at Siboney, a coral shore with heavy surf and no docking facilities. Shafter's courage in his years as a soldier fighting the Confederates and later in patrolling the Indians did not at all prepare him for the job of organizing the Santiago campaign. In his bungling, however, he was assisted by other obtuse administrators. The regulars arrived in wool uniforms suitable for a campaign in Alaska, and their medical supplies as well as food were equally unsuitable to the climate. "What put my command in its present condition," Shafter wrote President McKinley (August 8, 1898), "was the twenty days of the campaign when they had nothing but meat [fat bacon], bread and coffee, without change of clothes and without any shelter whatsoever."

The Marines, ten weeks after landing at Guantánamo, had not lost a single man from disease. They drank water only after it had been boiled, whereas Shafter's soldiers drank from brooks contaminated by fecal matter. The Marines had surgeons, medicines (quinine) and the full Navy ration—not just hardtack and fat bacon. They also had intelligent administrators. Colonel Huntington had destroyed by fire all buildings at Guantánamo so as to prevent yellow-fever infection, but Shafter ignored his chief surgeon's advice to burn the buildings at Siboney and instead utilized them for hospitals and offices. Hospital cots were off Siboney on one of the transports, but the question was which one. Where were the medical supplies, on which transport? And then, how get them ashore? It wasn't written in the contracts of the transport commanders to deliver their cargoes ashore, and to safeguard their shipowners' interests they stayed out beyond the danger zone. On the third day after arriving at Siboney, the commander of an ambulance company obtained a rowboat to reach a cargo ship containing medical supplies, but the rowboat was taken away from him—says Dr. Edward Munson—"by direct order of General Shafter, who wished to assign it to other duty." Several transports returned to the United States with unloaded cargo intended for Shafter's Fifth Corps. Later at Las Guásimas, Colonel Leonard Wood sent Lieutenant Kilbourne back to Siboney to obtain ammunition for their Hotchkiss rapid-fire guns, but General Shafter declared he had no idea where the ammunition could be found, nor had Chief Quartermaster Jacobs at Daiquirí; so Kilbourne returned to Colonel Wood after a march of twenty miles to report that it could not be had because nobody knew where it was.[4] The Army had been only two weeks in Cuba when General Shafter reported: "Sickness was increasing very rapidly, and the weakness of the troops was becoming so apparent that I was anxious to bring the siege to an end."

Disembarkation at Daiquirí began on the 22nd and Crane landed there that Wednesday at 5 P.M. It ended at nearby Siboney, but not until June 25 was the whole army ashore. Aboard one of the steamships used as a transport to land troops at Siboney was a Captain of Company D in the New York 71st Volunteers. He was busy unloading the transport *Vigiliancia* when up the ladder came two war correspondents from a small tugboat. The tugboat was no doubt the *Three Friends* with Sylvester Scovel aboard. The other correspondent was Stephen Crane, and the Captain was Corwin Knapp Linson's brother,[5] who had met Stephen in Corwin's studio in New York City and had thought him rather somber. But now when Corwin's brother introduced himself, Crane seemed entirely of the opposite disposition: animated and jolly, "the spirit of the fighter in him." He was full of anticipation of what was before him and immediately inquired about C. K., who was then in Palestine. Later they met again near Santiago, probably at San Juan hills as Crane never got into that city (so far as we know), and C. K.'s brother reported: "I met your friend Stephen Crane at Santiago. He's going to Manila, he says, He's a hustler, isn't he?" (After the Santiago campaign Crane was lucky to get to Puerto Rico, not to mention far-off Manila.)

Shafter's order that no newspaper reporter should disembark with the first landing troops at Daiquirí enraged Richard Harding Davis into protesting to the General that he deserved to go ashore in Boat Number One because he was no ordinary reporter. A star reporter, Davis was then aboard the *Sequranca* with Shafter. "I don't care a damn what you are," the General said. "I'll treat all of you alike." Davis didn't get to land until June 23, whereas Crane had been on Cuban soil since the 7th. On Wednesday afternoon of the 22nd he wrote his "Story of the Disembarkment" in sight of troops landing at Daiquirí from transports. "Ten minutes ago the great crowd of soldiers working at the landing—the troops filing off through the scrub, the white duck jack tars in the speeding launches and cutters, the ragged Cuban infantry—all burst into a great cheer that swelled and rolled against the green hills until your heart beat loudly with the thrill of it. The sea, thronged with transports and cruisers, was suddenly ringing with the noise of steam whistles and cruisers, from the deep sealion roar of the great steamers to the wild screams of the launches."

At last it happened, wrote Crane. "A boat has been overturned. Men of the Tenth Cavalry, tied in blanket rolls and weighty cartridge belts, are in the water. It is horrible to think of them clasped in the arms of their heavy accoutrements. Wild excitement reigns on the pierhead; lines are flung; men try to reach down to the water; overboard from launches and cutters go blue-jackets, gallant blue-jackets, while over all the hubbub tears the sound of that same rasping voice, screaming senselessly to do this or that." Crane doesn't say so, but Captain Bucky O'Neill plunged fully clothed into the sea to rescue two Negroes who had slipped while climbing onto the pier. They were crushed before he could reach them. Horses were disembarked from the transports by throwing them overboard to swim for shore. Roosevelt says that some of the horses swam out to sea but that when a bugler blew the proper call they wheeled around and headed for the shore.

At the right of Daiquirí there was a blockhouse atop a sugar-loaf mountain rising sheer a thousand feet, a burnt-out ruin that had survived the bombardment of the village. At the side of the blockhouse there was a flagstaff, which Ed Marshall of the New York *Journal* felt should be flying the Stars and Stripes. He obtained a flag from his paper's dispatch boat and with artist William Bengough started up the mountain, but the heat and steepness were too much for them, and then some Rough Riders arrived at the summit with a silk flag donated by the women of Phoenix, Arizona. But no Rough Rider could shinny up the flagpole, and so a sailor from one of the transports climbed it and unfurled the flag to the breeze.

Crane describes the scene without identifying the persons involved: "Far on a high plateau overlooking this hamlet was silhouetted a band of men and a flagstaff. One man was hauling upon some halyards, slowly raising to the eager eyes of thousands of men the Stars and Stripes, symbol that our foot is firmly and formidably planted." In the blockhouse the Spaniards had left some bottles of wine, and Color Sergeant Wright and Trumpeter Platt of the Rough Riders were just about to drink from a bottle when Surgeon LaMotte snatched it to smash it against a rock. The wine was poisoned.

Crane thought the burnt-out blockhouse bore a certain resemblance to his own life, "his debts, other misfortunes, loves, prospects of happiness." He also reflected that to the troops landing at Daiquirí it was a great moment, but then, what did that "great moment" mean for the common man?

Nothing more than "an itch on his shin, a pain in his hand, hunger, thirst, a lack of sleep; the influence of his memory of past firesides, glasses of beer, girls, theaters, ideals, religions, parents, faces, hurts, joys."

The Rough Riders encamped haphazardly in dog tents in the beautiful valley of grass between two ranges of hills bordering the Daiquirí river, but the grass was higher than their tents and in that grass were lizards, suspicious-looking snakes, land crabs, and tarantulas. Photographer Burr McIntosh of *Leslie's Weekly,* enticed two tarantulas to race, after the fashion of land-turtle races he'd seen at Tampa, and they bit him. Sergeant Hamilton Fish failed to find any whiskey in camp, and so McIntosh drank sweet Spanish wine and, though the tarantulas didn't kill him, he felt bad enough on the morning of June 23 to wish that they had.

The tropical heat agonized not only General Shafter's huge bulk but also the troops in their heavy wool uniforms. "That evening [June 22] was a glory. A breeze came from the sea, fanning spirits of flame out of the ashes and charred remains of the sheds, while overhead lay a splendid summer night sky, a-flash with great tranquil stars. In the streets of the village were two or three fires, frequently and suddenly reddening with their glare the figures of low-voiced men who moved here and there. The light of the transports blinked on the murmuring plain in front of the village; and far to the westward Little Nell [as Crane calls himself in "God Rest Ye"] could sometimes note a subtle indication of a playing searchlight, which alone marked the presence of the invisible battleships, half-mooned about the entrance of Santiago harbor, waiting—waiting—waiting." (Not until the morning of July 3 did the battleship *Iowa* hoist her signal "Enemy Coming Out." The Spanish flagship *María Teresa* was making her doomed attempt to steam past our blockading fleet.)

General Shafter had promised Ed Marshall some horses at Tampa, but at the last moment he would not allow them on the transports. There was also a scarcity of mules. Marshall, however, had at least his saddle, which he lent to Colonel Roosevelt, who rode it into battle. Marshall, arriving from Tampa on the *Olivette,* was one of the first correspondents to land because there was a *Journal* dispatch boat to take him ashore; he was at the pier when the Rough Riders disembarked. The Cubans turned over to him a big bungalow for *Journal* headquarters, a wooden shanty built on posts with a porch across the front. Crane described it as a crude tavern and jokingly nicknamed it "Walkley's mansion." It had been General Castillo's headquarters, and men galloped back and forth to that bungalow with reports from scouting Cubans. The newsmen wore riding breeches, but thanks to General Shafter they had to walk. While "Walkley," in Crane's "God Rest Ye, Merry Gentlemen," discoursed from his hammock, "Point," who is photographer Burr McIntosh of gigantic frame, slept on the floor after foraging for food. Marshall ate only one meal during his first three days in Cuba. "What little we got we begged from soldiers, although all of us bore credentials from the Secretary of War, directing all commanding officers to furnish forage and rations for us at the cost price."

Perhaps it was on the porch of Marshall's bungalow that Crane and another correspondent were sitting when "a vast man on horseback" pulled up sharply on spotting Crane's friend and said: " 'Whoa! Where's that mule I lent you?' My friend arose and saluted. 'I've got him all right, General, thank you,' said my friend. The vast man shook his finger. 'Don't you lose him now.' 'No, sir, I won't; thank you, sir.' The vast man rode away. 'Who the devil is that?' said I. My friend laughed. 'That's General Shafter,' said he."

While Burr McIntosh snored on the floor of the bungalow, Crane nursed a sore left heel and a bottle of whiskey. He was up most of the night with Ernest McCready, attending him like a nursemaid, because McCready had been struck down by the heat of the sun.

At 1:30 that afternoon (June 23) the Rough Riders received orders to march the five miles to Siboney (Santiago harbor was five miles beyond Siboney), which—like Daiquirí—had been abandoned by the Spaniards. Scovel departed "tearlessly" for Jamaica, soon after he had bestowed upon friends his tinned goods and blankets. He wasn't going to walk it to Siboney, like Crane, McCready, McIntosh and Marshall.

Marshall says: "I shall never forget the terrible march to Siboney." On a hard coral road they followed the regulars and the volunteers (later famous as the Rough Riders). McCready, probably "Shackles" in "God Rest Ye, Merry Gentlemen," and McIntosh ("Point") disliked each other, and often quarreled foolishly over something or nothing. All the correspondents loathed McIntosh, and yet when men asked them the reason they grew quite inarticulate, says Crane. An old man of the world at twenty-six, he generously excuses McIntosh "since he was hideously youthful and innocent and unaware." McIntosh hugged to himself a bottle of lime-juice while his colleagues thirsted for a sip, and he imposed upon his three colleagues the burden of carrying his excess photographic equipment. They cursed him privately for being "a little ass," but said nothing. Crane wished to remark: " 'Point, you are not a thoroughbred in a half of the way. You are an inconsiderate, thoughtless little swine.' But in truth, he said: 'Point, when you started out you looked like a Christmas tree. If we keep robbing you of your bundles there soon won't be anything left for the children.' Point asked him dubiously: 'What do you mean?' Little Nell merely laughed with deceptive good nature."

There were some mounted infantry (not to be confused with the horse-less Rough Riders) and Crane and two colleagues posted after them on the path through dense thickets. In time we "met and passed the hospital corps, a vacant unloaded hospital corps, going ahead on mules. Then there was another long lonely march through the dry woods, which seemed almost upon the point of crackling into a blaze under the rays of the furious Cuban sun. We met nothing but blankets, shelter tents, coats and other impedimenta, which the panting Rough Riders had flung behind them on their swift march. In time we came in touch with a few stragglers, men down with the heat, prone and breathing heavily, and then we struck the rear of the column," says Crane in his dispatch.

At last they reached Siboney that night to watch a second disembarkment taking place. "It was one of the most weird and remarkable scenes of the war, probably of any war," Davis wrote. "An army was being landed on an enemy's coast at the dead of night, but with somewhat more of cheers and shrieks and laughter than rise from the bathers in the surf at Coney Island on a hot Sunday." Some men were dancing naked around the campfires on the beach, while others took a bath in the ocean. Crane and McCready, McIntosh and Marshall were picked up by a dispatch boat somewhere this side of that wretched little hamlet and disembarked from it on the beach just in time to see the last of our troops of mounted infantry wending over the top of a huge hill.

"Launches shouted, jack-tars prodded with their boathooks, and load of men followed load of men," says Crane in "God Rest Ye." It was the same scene as at Daiquirí. Parade-like on the shore "stood a trumpeter playing familiar calls to the troop horses who swam toward him eagerly through the salt water." On the morning of the 24th Crane and McCready shared a breakfast of stewed tomatoes, hard bread, and coffee with two officers, and Crane neglected to wash his own dirty dishes. In "War Memories" a year later he recalls having felt guilty about it. "I felt tremendously ashamed because my cup and my plate were there, you know, and—Fate provides some men greased opportunities for making dizzy jackasses of themselves, and I fell victim to my fury on this occasion. I was a blockhead. I walked away blushing." The officers had to wash Crane's dishes. One was Captain Bucky O'Neill, an iron-nerved fighter from Arizona, a sheriff whose name—Mayor of Prescott—was a byword of terror to every wrongdoer. He appears in "God Rest Ye" unnamed and in "The Second Generation" as General Reilly.

The old and grizzled Captain, says Crane in "God Rest Ye," was overjoyed to be on active service, and yet he suggested a note of pathos. "The war was come too late. Age was grappling him, and honours were only for his widow and his children—merely a better life-insurance policy. He had spent his life policing Indians with much labour, cold, and heat, but with no glory for him or his fellows. All he now could do was to die at the head of his men. If he had youthfully dreamed of a general's stars, they were now impossible to him, and he knew it. He was too old to leap so far; his sole honour was a new invitation to face death. And yet, with his ambitions lying half-strangled, he was going to take his men into any sort of holocaust, because his traditions were of gentlemen and soldiers, and

because—he loved it for itself—the thing itself—the whirl, the unknown."
Just before the charge of the Rough Riders at San Juan Hill a sergeant
warned Bucky O'Neill: "Captain, a bullet is sure to hit you." O'Neill took
his cigarette out of his mouth and, blowing a cloud of smoke, laughed.
"Sergeant, the Spanish bullet isn't made that will kill me." But then a
Spanish bullet got him in the mouth.[6]

The other officer at that breakfast around a fire of little sticks was
O'Neill's subaltern, a very young West Point lieutenant. He, too, was overjoyed to be on active service, and he was sure to emerge from it "either
horizontally or at the head of a company, and what more could a boy
ask?" Old man Crane compares himself with this very Young Personage.
He was a modest lad with "an expression of blissful contentment ever
upon his face. When a Mauser bullet caught O'Neill, the unlucky Rough
Rider, the West Point youth "arrived on the crest panting, sweating; but
unscratched and not sure whether he commanded one company or a
whole battalion."

Because of the insufferable heat Crane was indifferent about the rumor
of a battle that was shaping up on June 24. Marshall says: "I was amazed
at his apparent indolence." Nevertheless, he joined Marshall and McIntosh
to witness the ambuscade of the Rough Riders. Colonel Wood, former
Army surgeon in campaigns against the Apaches, was leading his men on a
hill trail toward Las Guásimas, while General S. B. M. Young took a parallel
road through the valley from Siboney. The Spaniards were at the junction
of the road and the hill trail, and that is where Young's First and Tenth
Cavalry discovered them—on a ridge to the left of Young's front, a ridge
separated from the hill trail by a deep ravine.

The Spaniards were using the same guerrilla tactics they had learned
from the Cuban insurgents. The Marines had learned it at Guantánamo.
"The Indian-fighting regulars know it anyhow, but this regiment of volunteers knew nothing but their own superb courage. They wound along this
narrow winding path, babbling joyously, arguing, recounting, laughing;
making more noise than a train going through a tunnel." Their laughter
rang through the woods, says Crane in "God Rest Ye." And then there
was the Spanish guerrilla wood dove, calling to his mate, and the firing
broke out in front, bullets speeding along the path and across it from both
sides. The thickets presented nothing but dense masses of light green
foliage, "out of which these swift steel things were born supernaturally.
It was a volunteer regiment [the First Cavalry under Young and Roosevelt]
going into its first action against an enemy of unknown force, in a country
where the vegetation was thicker than fur on a cat."

McCready and Crane ("Shackles" and "Little Nell") felt the thrill of
the orders. " 'Come ahead, men! Keep right ahead, men! Come on!' The
volunteer cavalry regiment, with all the willingness in the world, went
ahead into the angle of V-shaped Spanish formation. It seemed that every

leaf had turned into a soda-bottle and was popping its cork," says Crane. Richard Harding Davis with the Rough Riders says: "We were caught in a clear case of ambush."

The Spaniards permitted two scouts and Sergeant Hamilton Fish to pass down the trail unmolested, but then they fired into the lines as our men ran forward in single file. The two scouts were wounded, and Hamilton Fish was killed instantly. The men of Captain Allyn Capron's Troop L meanwhile lost their way, swung to the right, and fired into their own men. An order to cease fire was given, says Davis, and Colonel Roosevelt led the troops back to the left again, where the firing was fiercest. "It was here where Captain Capron was shot through the side over the heart and died in several hours. He was one of the most popular captains and one of the best officers in the regiment."

The smokeless powder used by the enemy helped them conceal their whereabouts.[7] "It was the hottest, nastiest fight I ever imagined. We never saw the enemy except glimpses. Our men fell all over the place, shouting to the others not to mind them, but to go on. I got excited and took a carbine and charged the sugar house, which was what is called the key to the position."[8] However, Davis later denied that the Rough Riders had been ambushed: "unless it is an ambush to find the enemy exactly where you expect to find him."

Crane in "Stephen Crane Calls It a Blunder" says that Roosevelt's men "marched noisily through the narrow road in the woods, talking volubly, when suddenly they struck the Spanish lines. Fierce fire was poured into their ranks, and there began a great fight in the thickets. Nothing of the enemy was visible to our men, who displayed much gallantry. In fact, their bearing was superb, and could not be finer. They suffered a heavy loss, however, due to the remarkably wrong idea of how the Spaniards bushwhack. It was simply a gallant blunder."

George Bronson Rhea, Crane's colleague on the *World,* reported that the Cubans had warned Colonel Wood, but he had refused to heed the warning. The Rough Riders, prepared to fight as cavalry, fought dismounted, and their inability to maneuver in the thickets cost them sixteen officers and men killed, with fifty-two wounded. Their baptism of fire taught the entire Army to use caution in fighting bushwhackers. Unlike Crane, who witnessed the ambuscade, Rhea and almost all the other correspondents except Davis and Marshall got their accounts of the fight at Las Guásimas second-hand from the wounded in the hospital at Siboney and from an officer who stampeded to the rear before the fight had really begun, an officer whom Roosevelt does not mention.

American newspapers condemned Colonel Wood and Colonel Roosevelt for having recklessly sacrificed their men in rushing foolhardily into an ambuscade, and one Congressman declared that Roosevelt ought to be court-martialed. But the fact is that the trail to Guásimas had been reconnoitered the previous afternoon by General Joseph Wheeler on being informed of the enemy's position by a Cuban officer, and then at Siboney he outlined his plan of attack to Colonel Wood and General Young. Crane and other correspondents knew nothing of this plan, but Davis did because he was present when it was discussed, and the odd thing is that they discussed their strategy in front of a war correspondent.

Teddy Roosevelt led his men with a rifle he had picked up from among the wounded and charged the iron building in which the Spaniards had fortified themselves. He borrowed the rifle because he had only a sword and afterwards discarded the sword because it kept getting between his legs.

Roosevelt says that when the fighting began the Cuban scout heading his column ran off into the tangled jungle, but two correspondents did not run away: Ed Marshall and Dick Davis "showed as much gallantry as any soldier in the field." But so did Crane, whom Roosevelt deliberately ignores in his *Rough Riders* story.

A soldier told Crane: " 'There's a correspondent up there all shot to hell.' He guided me to where Edward Marshall lay, shot through the body. The following conversation ensued: 'Hello, Crane!' 'Hello, Marshall! In hard luck, old man?' 'Yes, I'm done for.' 'Nonsense. You're all right, old boy. What can I do for you?' 'Well, you might file my despatches. I don't mean file 'em ahead of your own, old man—but just file 'em if you find it handy.' I immediately decided that he was doomed. No man could be so sublime in detail concerning the trade of journalism and not die. There was the solemnity of a funeral song in these absurd and fine sentences about despatches. Six soldiers gathered him up on a tent and moved him slowly off." A Rough Rider—a stern and menacing person— shouted at Crane: " 'Who are you? And what are you doing here? Quick!' 'I am a correspondent and we are merely carrying back another correspondent who we think is mortally wounded. Do you care?' The Rough Rider, somewhat abashed, announced that he did not care." So Crane tells it in "Stephen Crane at the Front for the *World*."[9] Davis saw Crane smoking a pipe and "badly rattled as he thought we were surrounded. He sat there a while and then went back to Siboney." Crane waited until Marshall regained consciousness and then took down the dispatch which Marshall dictated to him.

He admits: "I was frightened almost to convulsions," but—contrary to Davis' report—he did not sit out the skirmish or retreat to Siboney. While Marshall rested in the field hospital on the brow of the hill where the fighting had begun, Crane trudged some five or six miles to Siboney. He took with him the dispatch Marshall had written and cabled it to the *Journal,* a rival paper. He had to walk because he could get no horse or mule, and the temperature was around 100 degrees. At Siboney he found Acton Davies, of the New York *Sun,* aboard one of the *Journal*'s dispatch boats with two other correspondents, and the four colleagues trudged back to the field hospital. They brought Marshall a stretcher to carry him to the hospital ship *Olivette,* the ship that had brought him to Cuba.

The hospital at Siboney "was a spectacle of heroism. The doctors, gentle and calm, moved among the men without the common-senseless bullying of the ordinary ward. It was a sort of fraternal game. They were all in it, and of it, helping each other. In the meantime three troops of the Ninth Cavalry were swinging through the woods, and a mile behind them the Seventy-First New York was moving forward eagerly to the rescue. But the day was done. The Rough Riders had bitten it off and chewed it up— chewed it up splendidly."

Crane in "At the Front" modestly says: "I know nothing about war, of course, and pretend nothing; but I have been enabled from time to time to see brush fighting, and I want to say here plainly that the behavior of these Rough Riders [the First Cavalry] while marching through the woods shook me with terror as I have never been shaken." Thomas Beer says that Crane was "mute on Theodore Roosevelt's conduct as a commander in battle," but Crane praised Roosevelt: "Say, this fellow worked for his troopers like a cider press. He tried to feed them. He helped build latrines. He cursed the quartermasters and the—'dogs'—on the transports to get quinine and grub for them. Let him be a politician if he likes. He was a gentleman down there." It was Roosevelt who was mute about Crane, never mentioning him in his *Rough Riders* (1899). He had come to dislike Crane because of his tarnished reputation following the Dora Clark affair and his exposé of corruption in Commissioner Roosevelt's police force. His model was Richard Harding Davis.[10]

The Chicago *Evening Post*'s humorist "Dooley"—Finley Peter Dunne— reviewed Roosevelt's *Rough Riders* by depicting a blustering Teddy in command of the whole army with a blustering Davis as his bodyguard. Teddy sent the whole army home so that he could capture San Juan singlehandedly. He wanted to be "Alone in Cuba." With the same rifle he had used out in the West he sent a single bullet through the entire Spanish line, and that bullet not only ended the Cuban War but also killed off the Archbishop of Santiago eight miles away. The Archbishop was Teddy's rival candidate for the governorship of New York, and that explains why Teddy wanted to be alone in Cuba. In *Theodore Roosevelt, The Child,* Roosevelt's second wife is quoted as saying, when asked whether Teddy would accompany her on a certain journey: "For heaven's sake, don't put it into Theodore's head to go too; I should have another child to think of."

The Terrible Teddy and Dandy Davis were the perennial American boys. Slovenly Crane in his dirty, stinking clothes couldn't possibly fit Roosevelt's fixed ideal of the gentleman. And he had no patience with Crane's introspective kind of reporting. His own simple boyish ideas evoked in him simple teddy-bear emotions. He is criticizing Crane as a reporter when he says: "I did not see any sign among the fighting men,

whether wounded or unwounded, of the very complicated emotions assigned to their kind by some of the realistic modern novelists who have
written about battles."

In the advance on Las Guásimas Crane was with General Young with
the regulars on the right, while Roosevelt and Wood led the Rough Riders
on the left; and so Crane lost out by having attached himself to the less
newsworthy Young. The Rough Riders had been organized by Leonard
Wood and Teddy Roosevelt, when he was Assistant Secretary of the Navy,
and were recruited as the 1st Volunteer Cavalry at San Antonio, Texas.
It was an implausible collection of cowboys and frontiersmen, bluebloods
and socialites. It collected the Marshal of Dodge City and ace athletes of
the Boston Somerset and New York Knickerbocker clubs; the Mayor of
Prescott (Bucky O'Neill, killed at Kettle Hill) and Yale's most famous
quarterback, Princeton's tennis champion, and the world's greatest poloist.
Plainsmen Smoky Joe and Rattlesnake Pete served beside William Tiffany
of the New York City's *Social Register.* As there was a large contingent of
Harvard men, the band played the national anthem and then "Fair
Harvard." As Lieutenant Colonel, Roosevelt was second in command to
Colonel Wood, but the regiment became known as "Roosevelt's Rough
Riders." (Colonel Wood was promoted to Brigadier General on July 9.)

The newspapers exalted the society soldier such as Hamilton Fish and
reproduced oil paintings of Roosevelt's so-called Rough Riders, important
persons "limned as they were in the very act of being at the front," says
Crane in "Regulars Get No Glory." They are "proud young men riding
upon horses, the horses being still in Tampa and the proud young men
being at Santiago, but still proud young men riding upon horses." That is
Crane at his most caustic: the godly society soldier in the saddle of nonexistent horses, while the ungodly Nolan, the regular soldier under Young's
command (as distinct from the volunteers under Roosevelt), tears his
breeches on barbed wire. The same bullet that struck down Hamilton Fish
also struck Nolan, which name Crane derived from a man in Company C
at Guantánamo. Nolan is No Man,[11] the common soldier in military
harness—in "The Price of the Harness," which depicts the Army moving
up into the attack on Kettle Hill on July 1 under Sumner's Brigade. That
story, said Davis, of "the regular bleeding to death on the San Juan hills
is, so far as I have read, the most valuable contribution to literature that
the war has produced. It is only necessary to imagine how other writers
would have handled it to appreciate that it could not have been done
better."

In the two hours of fighting at Guásimas against a concealed enemy
"enough deeds of heroism were done to fill a volume," said young Henry
James Whigham of the Chicago *Tribune,* who had been wounded at
Guantánamo. The hero of "West Pointer and Volunteer," which Crane
renamed "Virtue in War" for his *Wounds in the Rain* volume, is Lige

Wigram. *Lige* is Old French for *liege,* a vassal bound by feudal law to give
service and allegiance to his liege-lord, who in this instance is the Major
Gates of Crane's story. Although Crane does not identify the location,
Gates' battalion is marching along the trail to Las Guásimas when he is
shot and bleeds to death. West Pointer Gates has reprimanded private
Lige Wigram for entering his tent without permission, and now Lige
Wigram lies on the ground beside the fallen officer and tries to ingratiate
himself. " 'I've been a-follerin' ye all day an' I want to say yer a good man.'
The Major turned a coldly scornful eye upon the private." Nothing has
changed. "The man bleeding to death was the same man to whom he had
once paid a friendly visit with unfriendly results. He thought now that he
perceived a certain hopeless gulf, a gulf which is real or unreal, according
to circumstances. Sometimes all men are equal; occasionally they are not."

When the private refuses to leave the dying officer, Gates "gazed at his
man with that same icy, contemptuous gaze. 'I'm—I'm a dead man anyhow. You go to the rear, do you hear?' 'No.' The dying major drew his
revolver, cocked it and aimed it unsteadily at Lige's head. 'Will you
obey orders?' 'No.' 'One?' 'No.' 'Two?' 'No.' Gates weakly dropped his
revolver. 'Go to the devil, then. You're no soldier, but—' " Lige pays his
allegiance to his officer by burying his body with a bottle containing his
name and regiment, "so's when they come fer to dig him up sometime an'
take him home, there sure wouldn't be no mistake." So ends Lige's token
devotion to the man he hated and by whom he was scorned for presuming
himself his friendly equal. Crane's germinal situation for this story derived
from an incident told him by Ed Marshall. Colonel Roosevelt, when asked
by a surgeon, "Who are you?" replied wrathfully: "I'm your superior
officer, sir; stand at attention, salute, and take your hat off." The Terrible
Teddy, who as war-monger was one of the worst offenders, was an arrogant martinet demanding liege-obedience from his inferiors.[12]

The code of the young Lieutenant Manolo Prat, in "The Clan of No
Name," is fidelity in love and war. His ambition is that he should be called
"a brave man by established brave men." Careless of life, he risks a death-
bullet while severing with his machete a barbed-wire fence; "and then he
ran on because he was all alone there in the fields of death and because it
was his duty. . . . He did not care to do it, but he thought that was what
men of his kind would do in such a case. There was a standard and he
must follow it, obey it, because it was a monarch, the prince of Conduct."
The Lieutenant has found five men in a saucerlike hollow, and from one
of the dead men he has taken a rifle and fired at the Spaniards. An enemy
Negro, whose face is "lit with an illimitable blood-greed," peers over the
saucer's edge, and the Lieutenant closes his eyes so as to avoid seeing the
flash of the machete swung down upon him.

In the final scene of this tale of war and love, Margharita is in the garden
of her house in Tampa and there she accepts the marriage proposal of the

rival suitor to Lieutenant Manolo Prat. She burns the photograph of Manolo on which he has inscribed his code of fidelity. In the opening scene Margharita's suitor, Mr. Smith, is introduced to her by her mother, who is "fat and commercially excited." These garden scenes encircle the war story of Manolo's heroic death. His last gesture is to reach for a photograph of his beloved. One wonders how he can look at a photograph when he has closed his eyes in fear of seeing the machete splitting his skull in that saucerlike hollow. There is pathos in Manolo's fidelity to that silly little flirt while he simultaneously believes in "the absolute treachery of his adored one."

Crane begins "The Clan of No Name" with this riddle:

> *Unwind my riddle.*
> *Cruel as hawks the hours fly*
> *Wounded men seldom come home to die;*
> *The hard waves see an arm flung high;*
> *Scorn hits strong because of a lie;*
> *Yet there exists a mystic tie.*
> *Unwind my riddle.*

To unwind his riddle: fidelity is the law of love. He who loves belongs—by "a mystic tie"—to the anonymous clan of no name. There need be no other identity. On the cartouche of Second Lieutenant Manolo there were two stars, one gold and the other silver. "One of his stars was bright, like his hopes; the other was pale, like death." Crane wrote George Wyndham: "Hope is the most vacuous emotion of mankind."

The day after the hot skirmish at Las Guásimas, he walked the trail again to recapture what had happened, but "he was unable to describe the fighting except in the most perfunctory way. 'To tell you the truth, there was too much going on,' he said: 'the details escaped me.'" There was an interlude of seven days when the correspondents had nothing to report, and Crane on June 30 took photographer Jimmie Hare on a tour of the Guásimas battlefield. He was then living in a hut not far from the beach at Siboney with Sylvester Scovel and Nichols, his *World* assistant, and there *Collier's* photographer Hare and George Rhea of the *World*—just in from the *Three Friends*—found them on June 29. Most of the war correspondents had gone on to Sevilla (just west of Guásimas), where General Shafter had his headquarters.[13] As Shafter was confined to a hammock by an attack of malarial fever, General Sumner commanded the advance of the cavalry division westward toward Santiago.

# XXIII

# ⊂ The Cuban War
# (Continued)

THE NIGHT before the impending battle Scovel assigned Crane to cover Brigadier General H. W. Lawton's advance to the hill village of El Caney, which he was supposed to capture in a couple of hours but didn't. Crane didn't go there. He and Jimmie Hare, who had just returned to Siboney from Jamaica, rose early to go to El Pozo, Scovel having gone ahead that morning of July 1 to establish a camp there. Crane hadn't slept much and was sluggish at dawn when Hare tried to wake him. Hare lost his temper, but soon Crane was trotting at his side and apologizing for his lethargy. "Nobody could stay angry with Stephen Crane for long," says Hare. Near El Pozo they took different paths, and at that moment, at eight o'clock, the American field guns opened their first volley on the fortifications of San Juan. " 'I should think they would tire of receiving these shells,' said the Swedish military attaché, Captain Gette. 'Have they, then, no artillery?' The answer came as he spoke. There was a swift, rushing shrieking sound in the air, and a shell burst thirty feet behind the battery and as many yards to the left, scattering a hail of shrapnel around. There was instant confusion," says Kennett Harris of the Chicago *Record.* Private Helm, standing at the breech of the gun, fell forward between the wheels, dead; a minute later a shell struck the earthwork in front of another gun, and private Underwood of A Battery was instantly killed.

"It was a fine morning and everybody—the doomed and the immunes— how could we tell one from the other?—everybody was in the highest spirits," wrote Crane. "We were enveloped in forest, but we could hear, from ahead, everybody peppering away at everybody. It was like the roll of many drums. This was Lawton over at El Caney [1 ⅓ miles north of El Pozo]. I reflected with complacency that Lawton's division did not concern me in a professional way. That was the affair of another man. My business was with Kent's division and Wheeler's division." Had he adhered to Scovel's assignment and covered Lawton's advance at El Caney he would have missed the battle of San Juan. Hare says that Scovel "usually found it very difficult to get Crane's copy," but it was just as difficult to commit Crane to a given plan and expect him to carry it out; he was by temperament a free-wheeler.

From the top of the hill he could see the Spanish trenches on the crest of a ridge, and in back of this position white buildings flying great Red Cross flags. "The jungle beneath us rattled with firing, and the Spanish trenches crackled out regular volleys, but all this time there was nothing to indicate a tangible enemy. In truth, there was a man in a Panama hat strolling to and fro behind one of the Spanish trenches, gesticulating at times with a walking stick. A man in a Panama hat, walking with a stick! That was the strangest sight of my life—that symbol, that quaint figure of Mars. The battle, the thunderous row, was his possession. He was the master. He mystified us all with his infernal Panama hat and his wretched walking stick. From near his feet came volleys and from near his side came roaring shells, but he stood there alone, visible, the one tangible thing. He was a Colossus, and he was half as high as a pin, this being. Always somebody would be saying: 'Who *can* that fellow be?' Later, the American guns shelled the trenches and a blockhouse near them, and Mars had vanished. It could not have been death. One cannot kill Mars."

Another "symbol" was the observation balloon of the U.S. Signal Corps swinging over the tops of jungle trees. "Whereat the balloon and the man in the Panama hat with a walking-stick—whereat these two waged tremendous battle." The cry was, "Follow the balloon, boys!" But when it got wind-blown over the Spanish lines, where the Spaniards fired at it vigorously, it was hauled down. It descended on the ford where the Rough Riders were crossing, and there it partly collapsed and remained. But it caused severe loss of life as it indicated the exact position of the infantry and the First and Tenth (Negro) Cavalry. Roosevelt got his men across the ford before that damned balloon floated down, but he would agree with Burr McIntosh that it was one of the most criminally negligent acts of the entire war.

From the crest of El Pozo, Crane, with the aid of glasses, could see the balloon mishap and to the right the battery of Captain Allyn Capron booming shells into the blockhouse at El Caney, a bombardment which had begun at 6:30. With Crane were Whigham, photographer McIntosh, and illustrator Fred Remington. Photographer Hare was also there and he took photographs of Captain George Grimes' battery cannonading the blockhouses surmounting San Juan and Kettle hills, which were about midway between El Pozo hill and Santiago. Nobody had expected that any action would occur at San Juan until General Lawton at El Caney accomplished what he had begun there. Captain Capron and his battery at El Caney were avenging the death of his son, who had fallen in the skirmish at Sevilla some days before.

Says Whigham of the Chicago *Record*: "It was impossible to locate the

Spanish guns, however, because their powder was smokeless and ours was not—our gunfire was painfully apparent. But their gunners tended to overshoot the mark and kept dropping shells into the sugar factory behind the hill at El Pozo, where the cavalry stood ready to advance and the hospital-corps had established their quarters." Whigham, who thought this July 1 fight "must rank as one of the glorious military deeds of the world's history," says that the British naval attaché declared he had never witnessed so gallant an attack, and that other attachés were amazed. Towards noon the firing ceased as if for siesta, and then Crane, Whigham and McIntosh went up the road from El Pozo to San Juan hills, while artist Fred Remington started off alone.

The infantry had advanced under General S. S. Sumner to Kettle Hill along the valley road from El Pozo before the Rough Riders crossed Aguadores ford at the foot of the hills of San Juan. Along that Valley of Death nothing could be seen on either side, although Crane and Whigham had somehow managed to escape the Spanish sharpshooters in the trees. Unlike Crane, young Whigham was witnessing his first warfare. He reports: "Bullets whistled through the trees, and one unfortunate soldier was hit in the thigh within a few yards of Stephen Crane and myself. The bullet was probably one of the large brass mounted kind used by the guerrillas, and it made a horrible wound. The pain must have been intense, for the poor fellow screamed with agony. The little incident corroborated exactly a similar instance in *The Red Badge of Courage* and, by a coincidence, Crane was there to see it. It may seem brutal to take a psychological view of the matter in the middle of so much suffering and agony, but for the inexperienced spectator the only way to prevent a condition of nauseating horror under such circumstances is to forget the claims and ties of humanity and regard each man as a mere pawn in the great kriegspiel."

At the first crossing of the Aguadores the enemy fire grew hotter. Crane reports that the whole front had burst out "with a roar like a brushfire. The balloon was dying, dying a gigantic and public death before the eyes of two armies. It quivered, sank, faded into the trees amid the flurry of a battle that was suddenly and tremendously like a storm. The American battery thundered behind the men with a shock that seemed likely to tear the backs of their heads off. The Spanish shrapnel fled on a line to their left, swirling and swishing in supernatural velocity. The noise of the rifle bullets broke in their faces like the noise of so many lamp-chimneys or sped overhead in swift cruel spitting. And at the front the battle-sound, as if it were simply music, was beginning to swell and swell until the volleys rolled like a surf."

Near Aguadores ford Crane and Whigham came upon Scovel writing his *World* dispatch during the noon lull in the firing. He was sitting under a tree writing rapidly while a man on a horse stood nearby to carry his dispatch to the *World's* base at Siboney. The three newsmen, along with

Burr McIntosh, had had breakfast of coffee, hardtack and canned tongue
at the camp Scovel had set up at the rear of the guns on El Pozo. Crane
noticed that Whigham stared over his shoulder and that "he waved away
the tinned tongue with some bitterness. It was a horse, a dead horse. Then
a mule, which had been shot through the nose, wandered up and looked at
Whigham. We ran away," says Crane in "War Memories."

At noon, having trudged along the trail from El Pozo, they found
Scovel at the ford at the foot of the hill, and he shouted: "Don't go up
there! Sharpshooters!" The trees on both sides of the road were full of
snipers. Photographer J. C. Hemment of the *Journal,* who had come to
Cuba on Hearst's private yacht, invited Crane, Whigham and McIntosh to
join him for lunch. Hemment with his Japanese servant holding an open
umbrella in one hand and a lunch basket in the other, said: "Won't you
join me in a bite?" He offered them fried chicken and even some napkins,
while a servant made coffee.

When the military balloon became lodged in the treetops and the
enemy had just begun to make a target of it, the Tenth Negro Cavalry
arrived along the jungle road at the crossing of the San Juan River and
rested there on orders to wait. Colonel Roosevelt complained to Captain
Hamilton of the Tenth Cavalry that his men were blocking his way, but
as Hamilton would take orders only from his own colonel he refused to
budge. "Then let my men through, sir," said Roosevelt as he rode through
the lines followed by the grinning Rough Riders. What Roosevelt said
is variously reported by Ed Marshall: "If you're not going up, get out of
my way, for I am." Crane in "Virtue in War" has Gates saying: "God
damn it, man, if you can't get your people to deploy, for God's sake give
me a chance! I'm stuck in the woods!" Just before the Rough Riders
charged and Bucky O'Neill was killed, Roosevelt shouted, "We'll have
to take that hill," and his men shouted it back along the line, "We'll
have to take that hill." And then they took it, Kettle Hill. The blue
bandana handkerchief with white spots that hung around Roosevelt's neck
became the "battle flag" of San Juan.

Some men in the 71st New York ran up to Roosevelt and, saluting,
said: "We want to go with you; our officers won't lead us." According to
First Lieutenant John J. Pershing, the 71st New York had become
"demoralized and well-nigh stampeded."

An unsigned dispatch in the *World* for July 16 reported the shaky conduct of the 71st Regiment, and the next day Hearst's *Journal* seized upon
it as a slander upon the heroism of New Yorkers: "Slurs on the Bravery
of the Boys of the 71st." When Hearst returned from Cuba he wrote a
defense of the heroism of the 71st, although he had not been at San Juan;
nor had Ed Marshall, who corroborated Hearst's piece of yellow journalism: "Editor of the *Journal's* Personal Experience of the Splendid
Heroism of the Seventy-First." Pulitzer's *World* tried to save face by

starting a fund for a battlefield memorial to be erected at San Juan as a tribute to the 71st and the New York men of the Rough Riders; whereupon Roosevelt declared that no Rough Rider could sleep in the same grave with the cowardly dead of the 71st. The *World* quit its memorial project and returned the money. The unsigned article was erroneously attributed to Stephen Crane, but it was Sylvester Scovel who wrote the piece.[1] It told the truth, but it wasn't diplomatic. Nor was Roosevelt diplomatic, although he was being boomed *in absentia* for the Republican nomination for governor of New York, and he was rebuked in the press for his slur on the 71st Regiment by the Secretary of War, Russell Alger.[2]

Back at the Bloody Bend of the Aguadores River the wounded were receiving first aid from the Red Cross men, who were shot at by Spanish guerrillas. Among the wounded was Reuben McNab, Crane's schoolmate at Claverack College, now a Corporal in the 71st New York Volunteers, with a hole through his lung. "Also, several holes through his clothing. 'Well, they got me,' he said in greeting. Usually they said that. There were no long speeches. 'Well, they got me.' That was sufficient. The duty of the upright, unhurt man is then difficult. . . . I had looked upon five hundred wounded men with stolidity, or with a conscious indifference which filled me with amazement. But the apparition of Reuben McNab, the schoolmate, lying there in the mud, with a hole through his lung, awed me into stutterings, set me trembling with a sense of terrible intimacy with this war which theretofore I could have believed was a dream—almost. . . . 'If you're goin' by the hospital, step in and see me,' said Reuben McNab. That was all." (Quoted from "War Memories.")

Jimmy Hare took a photograph of their reunion. Hare had met Crane on the terrible road when Crane was mounted on a pinto pony. But only the pony showed any trace of nervousness, although Crane in a gleaming white raincoat made a shining traget for some Spanish marksman. "Crane was cool and unconcerned as if he had been at a garden party," says Hare. " 'Hello,' he said casually and raised his chin toward the crest of San Juan Hill. 'I'm going on up. Want to come?' 'Up there?' demurred Jimmy. 'I've just come down from up there. It's not very attractive.' 'Oh, well come along anyhow. Maybe I'll get a story.' 'More likely an epitaph,' said Jimmy crossly, looking at the conspicuous pair. 'All right, I'll come if you want, but do get down off that pony! If you must take *him* with us, walk behind him.' 'Nonsense. If they aim at me, so much the better, no Spaniard ever hits the thing he aims at.' 'Well—d'you mind if *I* walk behind him?' 'Not at all. Only sorry he isn't larger.' "

On encountering the wounded Reuben McNab, Crane insisted on giving him the pony; but McNab could not be transported that way, and so Crane left the pony for Hare to use it. Horses, and even mules, were scarce. Horses were reserved for orderlies and for the immediate staff of General Shafter. Roosevelt had a pony, but he left it behind when the fighting began at Kettle Hill, where bullets rang against the iron sugar-boiling kettle that gave the hill its name. The horses that swam ashore at Daiquirí and Siboney (or were drowned there) were mostly military horses, wagon teams, pack mules. Two generals went into the battle of San Juan hills on foot, one of them finally getting there on a cargo mule.

In "Stephen Crane's Vivid Story of the Battle of San Juan" he says it was "a soldier's battle. It was like Inkerman, where the English fought half-leaderless all day in a fog. Only the Cuban forest was worse than any fog." (He compares the terrible road from El Pozo to San Juan with the sunken road at Waterloo, and the San Juan hills remind him of the sloping orchards of Orange County, New York.)

"The crash of the Spanish fire became uproarious," says Crane (in "War Memories"), "and the air simply whistled. I heard a quavering voice near my shoulder, and, turning, I beheld Jimmie—Jimmie—with a face bloodless, white as paper. He looked at me with eyes opened extremely wide. 'Say,' he said, 'this is pretty hot, ain't it?' I was delighted. I knew exactly what he meant . . . 'Yes, Jimmie,' I replied earnestly, 'you can take it from me that this is a patent, double-extra-what-for.' And immediately he nodded. If this was a big action, then he was willing to pay in his fright as a rational price for the privilege of being present. But if this was only a penny affray, he considered the price exorbitant, and he would go away. He accepted my assurance with simple faith, and deported himself with kindly dignity as one moving amid great things. His face was still as pale as paper, but that counted for nothing. The main point was his perfect willingness to be frightened for reasons." The pinto pony had run away with him and flung him into a ford. "He appeared to me afterward and made bitter speech concerning this horse which I had assured him was a gentle and pious animal."

"The air was absolutely crowded with Spanish bullets," Fred Remington reported. "The shrapnel came screaming over. A ball struck in front of me and filled my hair and face with sand. . . . It jolted my glass and my nerves, and I beat a masterly retreat, crawling rapidly backwards." But reckless Crane paraded up and down in his white raincoat within full sight of the Spanish riflemen. Richard Harding Davis, who encountered him with photographer Hare at Kettle Hill, remembered him as "most annoyingly cool, with the assurance of a fatalist." He walked leisurely and, though the bullets threatened, he never once ducked his head. "He wore a long rain-coat and, as he stood peering over the edge of the hill with his hands in his pockets and smoking his pipe, he was as unconcerned as though he were gazing at a cinematograph. The fire from the enemy was so heavy that only one troop along the entire line of the hills was returning it, and all the rest of our men were lying down. General Wood, who was then Colonel of the Rough Riders, and I were lying on our elbows at Crane's feet, and Wood ordered him also to lie down. Crane pretended not to hear and moved further away, still peering over the hill with the same interested expression. Wood told him for the second time that if he did not lie down he would be killed, but Crane paid no attention. So, in order to make him take shelter, I told him he was trying to impress us with his courage and that if he thought he was making me feel badly by walking about he might as well sit down.

"Hare said 'What's the idea, Steve? Did you get a wire from Pulitzer this morning reading: 'Why the hell don't *you* get wounded so we can get some notices, too?' There was a roar of laughter from the soldiers within hearing, and Crane, blushing, got down meekly and stayed there." But it was Davis's rebuke that brought Crane down to earth, not Hare's joke, for Crane respected Davis. Years later Davis retold the story in his *Notes of a War Correspondent* (1911): "I knew that, to Crane, anything that savored of a pose was hateful; so, as I did not want to see him killed, I called, 'You're not impressing anyone by doing that, Crane.' As I hoped he would, he instantly dropped to his knees. When he crawled over to where we lay, I explained, 'I knew that would fetch you,' and he grinned and said, 'Oh, was that it?' "[3] Crane got up once more, and then Davis seized him by the shoulders and forced him to the ground, and as Davis did so "a bullet knocked off his hat and another chipped the leather case of his field glasses."

Langdon Smith of the *Journal* reported in *Cosmopolitan Magazine* (September, 1898) how Crane on another occasion nonchalantly exposed himself to fire: "Crane was standing under a tree calmly rolling a cigarette; some leaves dropped from the trees, cut away by the bullets; two or three men dropped within a few feet. Crane is as thin as a lathe. If he had been two or three inches wider or thicker through, he would undoubtedly have been shot. But he calmly finished rolling his cigarette and smoked it without moving away from the spot where the bullets had suddenly become so thick." He was, said John Northern Hillard, "a courageous gentleman at all times, and as generous and kind-hearted as he was brave. I think that he was the coolest and bravest man I have ever known. He was, in a way, a fatalist, and his favorite saying was that 'what is to be is not to be dodged, and let worry go hang.' But his was not altogether the courage of a fatalist. It was in the blood. His people were pioneers and fighters." Crane told Hillard more than once that his fondest desire was to die in battle, as was meet in one whose ancestors had sacrificed their lives for their country.

General Shafter, because he discredited naval bombardment, or at any rate did not want the Navy to share in the glory of his campaign against Santiago, did not invite Admiral Sampson to shell the San Juan hills nor inform him of the location of the Spanish works there.[4] And so the brigades under General S. S. Sumner attacked Kettle Hill at one o'clock, almost simultaneously with the Rough Riders, without aid of naval bombardment. Colonel Roosevelt, then on horseback, paraded conspicuously in front of his men. He galloped his pony—Little Texas—toward the hill and then jumped off it when a wire fence blocked his path. He did not lead the charge up San Juan Hill; he and his Rough Riders assisted the advance of the regulars up San Juan by firing on the Spaniards from Kettle Hill. Some of the Rough Riders took shelter behind the huge iron kettle there, while the infantry of General J. F. Kent, led by General H. S. Hawkins, climbed Kettle Hill. Major General Joseph Wheeler, although he was ill with fever, rode by erect on his bay horse and called out: "Keep at 'em! The Yankees are falling back." Then he corrected himself "I mean the Spaniards," he said. But a great laugh went up, and the good old general joined in it heartily.[5]

In Crane's story "The Second Generation," the San Juan battlefield is more than Casper Cadogan can take. " 'By Jove,' he said, as he flung himself wearily on the ground, 'I can't stand much more of this, you know. It's killing me.' A bristly beard sprouted through the grime on his face; his eyelids were crimson; an indescribably dirty shirt fell away from his roughened neck; and at the same time various lines of evil and greed were deepened on his face, until he practically stood forth as a revelation, a confession. 'I can't stand it. By Jove, I can't.' " A lieutenant, suffering with fever, asks for water, and Cadogan—so named because he's a cad—denies that he has any in his canteen. " 'You lie,' said Ripley. 'I can tell the sound of a full canteen as far as I can hear it.' "

From the start the brigade detests Casper Cadogan as a selfish, bragging show-off who preens himself as their superior because as commissary officer he has a private stock of potted hams and can afford to scorn the common Army ration. Senator Cadogan obtained that post for his spoiled son. Through Casper Cadogan, who is not the only Rough Rider with a private stock of hams and crackers, Crane expresses his bias against the Rough Riders—not all of them were heroes.

In "The Price of the Harness" some troops charge up Kettle Hill. The common soldier Nolan is in "harness," rigged for death. Taking aim at the portico of a fortified house on the hill, Nolan lays his head to his rifle "as if it were his mistress."[6] When Nolan is struck down and is numb all over, he tells soldier Grierson that the ground is damp. Grierson pretends to agree, although he knows it is covered with blood. " 'You were right, Jimmie.' 'Of course I was,' said Nolan contentedly closing his eyes. 'This hillside holds water like a swamp.' " Some days after the battle of San Juan a soldier in the hospital at Siboney asks Grierson: "And where's Ike Watkins?" Grierson replies: "Well, he ain't dead, but he got shot through the lungs. They say he ain't got much show." Throughout Crane's fiction it is mostly the case of those who ain't got much show. Jack Martin asks Bill Grierson: " 'Where's Jimmy Nolan?' 'He's dead,' said Grierson. A triangle of raw gold light shone on the side of the tent." At the mention of the death of the common soldier Nolan a supernatural sign appears. As in *The Red Badge* Crane describes the Army as a machine: "It reminds one always of a loom, a great, grand steel loom, clinking, clanking, plunking, plinking, to weave a woof of thin red threads, the cloth of death." On striking off that passage Crane named his Cuban War tale "The Woof of the Thin Red Threads," but later changed it to "The Price of the Harness."

Grierson and Martin discuss the dead Nolan while they are recuperating in the fever tents at Siboney. Crane was there himself on July 8, fever-stricken and listening to the two soldiers recounting the death of Nolan. Fever, says Crane, "is the physical counterpart of shame, and when a man has the one he accepts the other with an ease which would revolt his healthy self." As in "An Episode of War," Nolan's friend Martin is wounded in the arm, and its galvanic effect makes him feel strange, dazed and sad. He trudges along a road to a ford and is grabbed by a surgeon. " 'Here, what's the matter with you?' Martin was daunted. He wondered what he had done that the surgeon should be so angry with him. 'In the arm,' he muttered, half shamefacedly." The surgeon, exasperated to the point of madness, glares at Martin and orders him to walk onwards down a road flanked by Spanish sharpshooters.

In "War Memories" Crane says that "the shooting subsided to little nervous outbursts," but that the road to the rear "increased its terror in the darkness. The wounded men, stumbling along in the mud, a miasmic mist from the swampish ground filling their nostrils, heard often in the air the whiplash sound of a bullet that was meant for them by the lurking guerillas. . . . The large tropic stars illumined the sky. On the safe side of the ridge our men had built some little red fires, no larger than hats, at which they cooked what food they possessed. There was no sound save to the rear, where throughout the night our pickets would be faintly heard exchanging shots with the guerillas."

In "An Episode of War," one of Crane's masterpieces, a lieutenant is pouring onto his rubber blanket the company's supply of coffee beans. In measuring them out precisely, he was just "on the verge of a great triumph in mathematics" when he is struck by a bullet, his arm shattered. Intruding upon his preoccupation with the precious coffee beans comes the "catastrophe which happened when catastrophes were not expected." At the hospital, the surgeon assures him that he won't amputate the wounded arm, and then he amputates it—in the schoolhouse, which is where one learns. The hospital is in the schoolhouse, and its door seemed to the lieutenant as sinister "as the portals of death."

After the battle of San Juan on July 1, late that Friday afternoon Davis in the company of Crane and Hare doubled over in a seizure of pain. "We'll all get shot," he said. Jimmy Hare retorted: "Aw, those Spaniards can't hit a haystack." They trudged back with him to the correspondents' camp at El Pozo.[8] "While the victim of sciatica was freshening up in his tent, Jimmy seized the occasion to question Crane. 'Who's this pal of yours we just brought down the hill?' 'Beg pardon, Jimmy,' said Crane. 'I thought you knew him. That's Richard Harding Davis.' That gave Jimmy food for reflection. He had heard stories to Davis' discredit, but they had been told by newspaper correspondents who were satisfied to stay miles in the rear and get their battle yarns from returning soldiers; Davis, it seemed, covered his subject at the front, even when in agony from sciatica."

In "War Memories" Crane says simply that a group of correspondents limped back to El Pozo and found hot coffee at their camp. "I have a vague sense of being very selfish over my blanket and rubber coat," he remarks, but in fact Davis accepted his offer of his blanket as he had no place to sleep and nothing to eat that night. On the way to El Pozo he protested that he didn't need help and pointed out the risk Crane and Hare were taking because the trail was under fire for over a mile of the way. When he "lay down in the road and refused to budge unless they left me, Crane called the attention of Hare to the effect of the setting sun behind the palm trees."[9] He heard an outcry: "Oh, my God, come quick." The hateful zip of a Mauser bullet sped close by Crane, and a lad at his rear wriggled on the ground. He was of New York's 71st Volunteers and was killed on returning from Aguadores ford with water for his canteen.

Sylvester Scovel had arranged for some food for the *World* correspondents at El Pozo, and Crane invited Davis and Hare to share it. Burr McIntosh, who also joined the *World* group, reported that Crane bunked on a pile of saddles and provender; Scovel stretched out near the campfire. Davis and McIntosh slept at a ruined farmhouse. Crane in "War Memories" says nothing about his thoughtfulness in having loaned Davis his blanket nor about his having sacrificed his blanket a week earlier for Ed Marshall's comfort. Hare says that he peeked over Crane's shoulder while he wrote about his reunion with Reuben McNab, but he did not write that story until August–September of 1899—in "War Memories." By then he had mellowed enough to remember the finer side of warfare. He is generous in praise of former colleagues and endearing in his memory of McNab as "a long lank boy, freckled, sandy-haired—an extraordinary boy in no way, and yet I wager a boy clearly marked in every recollection." He used the name of Reuben McNab, his Claverack College classmate, for the name of the barber in his Whilomville story "Angel Child."

That Friday night of July 1 was a most terrible night in the field hospital, and again Saturday night in the fever tents at Siboney. The bright moonlight shone upon a gruesome scene with the sick and wounded lying everywhere. "I have seen men who were shot in the throat, stretched out under the sun at the Division Hospital, who had been forty-eight hours without water, food, sleep, shelter, or medical attendance," says Frank

Norris. He made a roof for himself to sleep under out of boards that were glazed by dried blood. Stricken with fever somewhere between Daiquirí and Santiago, he remembered the whole war as "nothing but a hideous blur of mud and blood. There is precious little glory in war, if the Santiago campaign is a sample, and when you try to recall the campaign, it's only the horrors and the hardships and nothing of the finer side."

In spite of the July 1 victories the American position was none too tenable (the Spanish situation was also precarious); the casualties, lack of reserves and supplies, and the weather worried Shafter. He so notified the War Department, who in turn advised that a retreat would have a bad effect on the country. Shafter agreed and framed his famous reply: "I shall hold my present position." To carry out this plan was touch-and-go. It rained off and on during July 2 making the sector almost unmanageable, and the strain on the men was telling. Actual fighting was limited to artillery exchanges. In the evening Shafter held a conference at El Pozo to consider withdrawal. There was no agreement, but Shafter decided against retreat. Meanwhile Cervera was being urged to break out of the harbor by Captain General Ramón Blanco; he did not consider Cervera's objections pertinent. He told the Admiral to take "advantage of first opportunity, and go out with the ships of your squadron, following route you deem best."

The next morning Crane went up to San Juan Hill to watch General Lawton's division trotting under fire as they pushed on from El Caney to the west of San Juan within a mile of the city of Santiago. "There wasn't a high heroic face among them; they were all men intent on business. That was all," says Crane in "War Memories." He reports that among the two hundred prisoners taken at El Caney two squads were regular Spanish infantry in blue and white pajamas. "The others were native-born Cubans, *reconcentrados,*[10] traitors, guerrillas, of the kind that bushwacked us so unmercifully." Some were old men; some were sad-eyed boys. Crane— bored with it all—got back to Siboney and steamed off for Jamaica. And so he missed the destruction of Admiral Cervera's fleet in Santiago harbor. So, too, did Admiral Sampson. What happened was that on the morning of July 3, when the Spanish fleet escaped the blockaded Santiago harbor only to be destroyed, Sampson was on shore to meet Shafter; the meeting did not occur. Meanwhile Commander W. S. Schley directed the fleet's attack.

The Spanish ships steamed out of the harbor and fired vigorously at our blockading fleet, whose returning gunfire forced the flagship *María Teresa* and the *Oquendo* to run ashore and burn fiercely. The *Vizcaya* hauled down her colors, and finally the *Colón,* which had escaped, was beached when the *Oregon* fired five shells at her. Admiral Cervera was captured, and more than five hundred Spaniards were killed or wounded; their fleet was destroyed, while none of the American ships was seriously

jured, and only one man was killed and ten were wounded. Until
ervera attempted to escape Santiago harbor the blockading fleet could
ot get at his ships because the harbor was mined and forts guarded the
pproach. The Army was therefore ordered to attack these forts from the
ear, capture them, and sever their wires to the mines in the harbor. As
avis wittily put it, this was "probably the only instance when a fleet has
lled upon an army to capture another fleet."

That evening Crane steamed back from Jamaica to Siboney with Scovel
d heard the great news of Cervera's defeat from one of the yacht
nboats hailing him by megaphone over the water: " 'Hello! Hear the
ws?' 'No; what was it?' 'The Spanish fleet came out this morning.'
h, of course, it did.' 'Honest, I mean.' 'Yes, I know; well where are
ey now?' 'Sunk.' Was there ever such a preposterous statement? I was
miliated that my friend, the Lieutenant on the yacht gunboat, should
ve measured me as one likely to swallow this bad joke. But it was all
ue; every word."

He glanced back at the squadron in its usual semicircle with every
ip's nose pointing at the mouth of the harbor, precisely as he'd seen it
e day before. It was as though nothing had happened during his
urney to Jamaica. "The squadron hadn't changed a button. There it sat
ithout even a smile on the face of the tiger. And it had eaten four
moured cruisers and two torpedo-boat-destroyers while my back was
rned for a moment."

At Siboney the shore was ringing with the great news mixed with
mpathy for the Spanish Admiral as "poor old boy." The Spanish fleet
reaking clear of the harbor entrance became one by one a band of
ame; they sank or were driven ashore. Neither on sea nor on land could
e Spaniards hit anything except by chance, by a fluke. If the Spaniard
d been an able marksman, like the Rough Riders' Arizona sharpshooters
oodwin and Profft, our two unsupported divisions never could have
tained San Juan Hill. "They should have been blown to smithereens,"
ys Crane. "The Spaniards had no immediate lack of ammunition, for they
red enough to kill the population of four big cities. I admit neither
elásquez nor Cervantes into this discussion. . . . Velásquez? Yes.
ervantes? Yes. But the Spanish troops seemed only to make a very
pid fire. Thus we lost many men. We lost them because of the simple
ry of the fire; never because the fire was well-directed, intelligent."
rane says he doesn't understand why Velásquez and Cervantes should
gure in any discussion about Cuba.

The next day he rode over to El Caney, with a youth of the Second
avalry he names "Leighton." At El Caney they encountered refugees
om Santiago on Monday morning. They were numbed, tearless and
onderously casual. There was no sign of fatalistic theory." Dressed for
e exodus, the girls "wore corsets which captivated their forms with a

steel-ribbed vehemence only proper for wear on a sun-blistered road to distant town." The girls had fled Santiago because the Governor ha issued a decree permitting the exodus of noncombatants so as to avoi unnecessary slaughter. The American forces were supposed to bombar Santiago at noon of July 5. Actually, there was only a mock bombardmen on the 10th, arranged diplomatically so that the Spanish General Jos Toral could surrender Santiago with dignity while under fire. Captai Allyn Capron's battery began it with instructions not to hit anything.

Pushing through the throng in the plaza at El Caney on the 4th, Cran and "Leighton" entered a church which had been turned into a hospit: for the Spanish wounded. What Crane here describes is extraordinary though he calls it simply "a strange scene." The interior of the churc was too cavelike in its gloom for the eyes of the operating surgeons, s they had had the altar table, which they were using for operations, carrie to the doorway, where there was a bright light. Framed in the black arch way was the altar table with the figure of a man upon it. "He was nake save for a breech-clout and so close, so clear was the ecclesiastic sugges tion, that one's mind leaped to a phantasy that this thin, pale figure ha just been torn down from a cross. The flash of the impression was lik light, and for this instant it illumined all the dark recesses of one's remotes idea of sacrilege, ghastly and wanton. I bring this to you merely as a effect, an effect of mental light and shade, if you like; something done i thought similar to that which the French impressionists do in colou something meaningless and at the same time overwhelming, crushing monstrous."

The Church of San Luis de Caney, where Cortez, according to legen had prayed before venturing on his conquest of Mexico, had recently bee used as a fortification. It was stripped of sacred vessels, and its walls wer perforated with loopholes for rifles. From the altar space a figure of Ou Lady of Sorrows looked compassionately down upon a dying Spaniard. Hi comrade, says Kennett Harris of the Chicago *Record,* "called to him word of consolation and prayed fervently with his eyes fixed on the Mate Dolorosa on the wall." Crane in his *World* dispatch of July 5 depicts Spanish commander, sorely wounded, lying in the center of the churcl where American surgeons treated fifty-two wounded Spaniards. Th commander had believed that his position had been impregnable. "Ho any mortal could cross the zone of fire and survive was a matter beyon his ken. By the saints, it was a miracle! Three thousand Mausers, he kne to his knowledge, were trained down the slope he guarded. Yet the Ameri cans plunged through the rain of death and [had] driven all before them.

Crane described the scene also in "War Memories": Over the pron figure on the altar an American surgeon, Dr. Bangs, and his assistant worked in white aprons, and in the surgeon's hand something small an silvery flashed. "An assistant held the merciful sponge close to the man'

ostrils, but he was writhing and moaning in some horrible dream of this
rtificial sleep. As the surgeon's instrument played, I fancied that the man
reamed that he was being gored by a bull. In his pleading, delirious bab-
le occurred constantly the name of the Virgin, the Holy Mother. 'Good
iorning,' said the surgeon. He changed his knife to his left hand and gave
ie a wet palm."

Frank Norris, whose "Comida" sketch appeared on the same page of the
*Vorld* as Crane's "Spanish Deserters," was there at the hospital-church
vhen Crane was there, but neither rival admits the presence of the other
a their *World* sketches. Norris tied his horse to the communion rail as to
saddle-rack, while in the flaring light of commissary candles Mary the
Iother of God looked down upon that disordered chapel. It was an in-
ongruous scene, says Norris: 'The shattered chapel, the bayonet scabbards,
ie Mauser cartridges clinking underfoot, the prim stiff calicoes and ging-
ams from Waltham [Massachusetts], and the cow-puncher's pony shying
om an altar cloth woven by fingers that were dust two hundred years
go." Amid this incongruous scene Dr. Bangs exclaimed in his thunderous
umpet voice: " 'Well, fellows, here's something I do every night that you
an't do at all!' and with the words he took out his left eye and polished
on a leg of his trousers. I was faint in an instant, the thing was so unex-
ected, so positively ghastly. Not even the sight of the division hospital, a
veek before, had so upset me." (That was the hospital at Siboney.)

Many other incidents upset Frank Norris at El Caney, including the
ight of a seventy-year-old woman carrying on her back a woman of
inety-two. In an abandoned house he discovered the body of a little girl
who had been raped and then knifed to death just before the beginning
f the battle.[11] I want to get these things out of my mind and the fever
ut of my blood. . . ." The fever got "a twist" on Norris somewhere be-
ween Daiquirí and San Juan and laid him out once he got to Santiago.
Crane never got the fever (malaria) out of his blood. It is no wonder that
ever and dysentery spread; the bodies of Spaniards were only partly buried
r were thrown into the rivers, along with the carcasses of horses.

Crane scarcely mentions the sufferings of the refugees at El Caney, since
e was in the town only a short while. Some 20,000 emigrants from Santi-
go invaded that town of 200 houses, provisions were soon exhausted,
nd the people lived mostly on mangoes and mamoncillos. Among the
efugees were the kindred of Cuban insurgents who greeted them with joy.
Crane in his dispatch about Spanish deserters, whom he saw at El Caney
n July 4–5, says that the kindness of the American soldiers amazed the
efugees, but "meanwhile Spanish sharpshooters picked off our ambulance-
ien and surgeons. They bowled them over at every chance. Yet three of
iese miscreants [who] fought among the trees, wearing clothes stripped
rom our dead, have been set to work about headquarters."

On July 6 he went to San Juan Hill to witness the ceremony of the

exchange of Spanish prisoners for the men of the sunken *Merrimac*. Lie‑
tenant Richmond Hobson had sunk that large collier on June 3 so as 1
cork up the harbor at Santiago and thus prevent the escape of Cervera
fleet. That was Admiral Sampson's idea, but it failed. The *Merrimac*‑
fitted with torpedoes that were electrically fired—sank in the narrowe
part of the channel and her men floated around in the harbor's wate
until a Spanish launch steamed out to their rescue, Admiral Cervera hin
self aiding Hobson and his men in that ironic rescue. Now the *Merrimac*
heroes, liberated by the enemy, were being brought into the America
lines while two bands played the "Star-Spangled Banner" and our soldie
lolled on the grass in the hot sunshine of July 6. At sight of hero Hobsc
they arose *"en masse* and came to 'Attention.' Then the men of the regul;
army did another thing. They slowly lifted every weather-beaten hat a
dropped it until it touched the knee. Then there was a magnificent silenc
broken only by the measured hoof-beats of the little company's horses ;
they rode through the gap. It was solemn, funereal, this splendid sile:
welcome of a brave man by men who stood on a hill which they had earn(
out of blood and death—simply, honestly, with no sense of excellenc
earned out of blood and death. Then suddenly the whole scene went 1
rubbish." Jokes between Navy and Army men deflated the heroics.

The exchange of prisoners of war occurred in the shade of thickly leave
trees. There in his chair General Shafter met hero Hobson, Shafter's "bel'
sticking ridiculously out before him as if he had adopted some form ›
artificial inflation. He looked like a joss," Crane recalls in "War Memories

Crane survived the procession of the *Merrimac*'s crew at San Juan H
by swallowing half of a brandy flask, says Beer, "and as soon as his bra
drunk in the show, he let himself flop in the grass, asleep at once. Scov
and Rhea tried to feed him, but everything save soft fruit was an abomin;
tion. He could not even ride the Jamaican polo pony and men who ha
heard of his marvelous horsemanship saw the gaunt adventurer tumb
from the saddle." After the exchange of prisoners of war at San Juan Hi
Crane went with Davis to Siboney, but en route there he stopped at Ge
eral Shafter's headquarters at Sevilla and wrote his *World* dispatch "Ca
tured Mausers" (datelined: "Gen. Shafter's Headquarters, July 7").

Crane says he "caught a fever,"[12] but he evidently recovered enough 1
expend himself on this dispatch. He complains the location of America
troops using the Springfield (vintage 1873) was known to the enemy t
the smoke of every rifle shot, whereas the position of the Spaniards cou:
not be detected because their Mausers were smokeless. He scorches tl
War Department: "In war anything is justified save killing your own me
through laziness or gross stupidity." Not only the Spanish batteries b
also their infantry used smokeless powder. "We cannot without cruel i:
justice send men using black powder into action against men who use
fair grade of smokeless."[13]

When Crane got to Siboney from General Shafter's headquarters on
July 7, *The Three Friends* was not there. Scovel had taken the boat to
Jamaica to file Crane's dispatch about Spanish deserters. But Davis' dispatch boat was at Siboney. When Davis started to write his story of the
exchange of the *Merrimac* heroes, Crane laughed and declared his intention of preventing him from writing it because he himself could not send
his own story. (He wrote about the *Merrimac* prisoners only in "War
Memories," not in any dispatch for the *World*.) Crane, says Davis, "did
all he could to break me up, but I worked on. Finally he began to tell a
story of the Greek war. Now, there was no one would ever tell a story
like Stephen Crane, and time after time I would find myself stopping to
listen to the narrative. Crane apparently was telling the story to others in
the room, but in reality he was talking to me, and never was I so distracted
in my work. I really think that if any one could write while Stephen Crane
was telling a story, he could write anywhere."[14]

Negotiations for cease-fire occurred during the week of July 3, and on
the 17th a squad of Spanish cavalry surrendered General Toral's sword
to General Shafter at his tent in Sevilla. The Spaniards then returned to
Santiago, and General Shafter and his staff followed them to the Governor's
Palace in the Plaza de Reina in the oldest city in the New World, the city
whence Cortez sailed to conquer Mexico. As the clock in the cathedral
tower struck twelve, up went the Stars and Stripes to the top of the flagpole
(above the legend "Viva Alfonso XIII"), and the band played "Rally
Round the flag, boys" and Sousa's "Stars and Stripes Forever," while the
soldiers tossed their hats into the air and gave rousing cheers.

Before the flag was raised, however, reckless Sylvester Scovel had
climbed to the roof of the palace; he grasped the halyards of the flag and
was about to hoist it when soldiers pulled him down. Scovel rushed out to
Shafter to argue against this interference, this insult to the Special Commissioner of the New York *World*. Shafter told him to shut up or be
locked up, and Scovel was locked up because he swung at the General's
double chin and marked it with a red scratch visible for some days. As
Scovel had defied a military edict he faced the possibility of being shot.
"Of course he ought to be shot," cursed Shafter. "He ought to have been
shot down in his tracks. But the people at home think this war is a pink-
tea party. . . . It is none of your damned business what I do with him. You
have carried out your mission by appearing in behalf of the fool." Shafter
thought Scovel crazy and sentenced him to deportation. Ralph Paine tells
that story, and Richard Harding Davis sums up the General: "His self-
complacency was so great that in spite of blunder after blunder after
blunder, folly after folly, and mistake upon mistake, he still believed himself infallible, still bullied his inferior officers, and still cursed from his
cot."

# XXIV

# ⌘ Havana

CRANE says that his sickness began with "a langorous indiffer
ence to everything in the world." His veins burned and boiled, and on the
morning of July 8 George Bronson Rhea of the *World* staff got him aboard
the transport *City of Washington* and filed at Siboney the next day hi
"Regulars Get No Glory."[1] It is a tender and bitterly sympathetic accoun
of the death of the typical Army private, the same Michael Nolan we have
encountered in Crane's short story "The Price of the Harness," and who
reappears in "The Private's Story" and in "Memoirs of a Private."

Crane narrates his homecoming from Cuba in "The Private's Story,"
not published in the New York *Journal* until September 26. He says that
one day he happened to think of an ice cream soda while in a camp some
where in the woods between Santiago and Siboney. That would be at Gen
eral Shafter's camp at Sevilla on July 7. "I hadn't drunk anything but bee
and whiskey for fifty moons, but I got to dreaming of ice cream soda and
I came near dying of longing for it. I couldn't get it out of my mind, try a
I would to concentrate my thoughts upon the land crabs and mud with
which I was surrounded. All I could do was to swear to myself that if
reached the United States again I would immediately make the neares
soda water fountain look like Spanish fours. I decided upon the flavor. I
a loud, firm voice I would say: 'Orange, please.' "

Aboard the *City of Washington* an Army doctor ordered Crane to iso
late himself. "So I wandered away and ended up on the deck aft, with
my head against the flagstaff and my limp body stretched on a little rug
I was not at all sorry for myself. I didn't care a tent-peg. And yet, as
look back upon it now, the situation was fairly exciting—a voyage of fou
or five days before me—no food—no friends—above all else, no friend
—isolated on deck, and rather ill." At the start of the grim voyage north
ward the Captain of the transport had asked: " 'Have you got your ow
food? I hope, for Christ's sake, you don't expect us to feed you, do you?
Whereupon I went to the rail and weakly yelled at Rhea, but he was al
ready afar." As for the Captain: "The insults of this old pie-stuffed scoun
drel did not affect me then; they affect me now. I would like to tell him

at, although I like collies, fox-terriers, and even screw-curled poodles,
do not like him. . . . I—in fact I hate him—it is all wrong—I lose what-
ver ethics I possessed—but—I hate him, and I demand that you imagine
milch cow endowed with a knowledge of navigation and in command
f a ship—and perfectly capable of commanding a ship—oh, well, never
ind."

There were numerous complaints by the wounded and sick men aboard
e transport because the principal meal consisted of coffee, bacon and
ardtack, and there were times when even this ration was not available,
id the New York *Tribune*.[2] Flying the yellow flag—grim ensign of the
e Cuban fever—the *City of Washington* reached Hampton Roads in
irginia, opposite Old Point Comfort, at ten o'clock in the morning of
ly 13, and the wounded soldiers and sailors were taken to the field
ospital that Wednesday afternoon. A vast crowd on the piers cheered the
ounded heroes as they walked or were carried. The first man lifted from
e lighthouse tender *Holly* was a Negro trooper of the 9th Cavalry, both
whose legs had been shot away.

Crane on the verandah of Chamberlain's Hotel at Old Point Comfort
atched the procession of his wounded shipmates en route to the hospital
Fort Monroe. He had been among the first to disembark from the *City
f Washington* because he had by now recovered, or almost so, and he
eaded for the nearest soda fountain to order an orange soda in keeping
ith his vow. When the fever first struck him a week before he had craved
ot only orange soda but also pickles. He had talked about pickles in his
reams. In "War Memories" he contrasts his feverish craving for pickles
ith the man "who went mad that way over tinned peaches and who
andered over the face of the earth saying plaintively, 'Have you any
eaches?'" That was Burr McIntosh, nicknamed "Peaches."

The verandahs of the two big hotels at Old Point Comfort were thronged
ith women and officers in new uniforms, and a company of volunteers
ug a path through the crowd for the wounded, who were carried on
retchers or were loaded upon a flatcar towed by a trolley car. "When
at crowd began to pass the hotel the banks of flowers made a noise which
uld make one tremble." Those "flowers" were the women weeping. The
ng of bandaged, dirty, ragged, emaciated, half-starved cripples "hung
eir heads like so many jailbirds. Most of them seemed to be suffering
om something which was like stage fright during the ordeal of this
ance but supremely eloquent reception. No sense of excellence—that was
. Evidently they were willing to leave the clacking to all those natural
orn major-generals who after the war talked enough to make a great fall
the price of that commodity all over the world."

Mrs. Bolton Chaffee was on the verandah of the Chamberlain Hotel, and
e did not recognize Crane at first because he was unshaven, hatless, and
soiled khaki. She had dined at Ravensbrook three months before. Floyd

Bemis, a gossiping Southerner, joined them while Crane sat on the arm ⟨
Mrs. Chaffee's chair. They had met in March, 1893, and Bemis had cast
gated Crane as "an eccentric who spent all his time in dives of the Bowe⟩
and was the outcast son of an Episcopal Bishop," which of course ⟩
wasn't. Bemis had written a satire on religious life in Georgia, but he ha
failed to publish it. He liked Crane's free-thinking verses in *The Blac*
*Riders* and was thrilled by his definance of orthodxy. He mistook Mr
Bolton Chaffee to be the wife of General A. R. Chaffee, the hero of ⟩
Caney,[3] and later jested with Crane that it was rumored he was having a
adulterous affair with the General's wife, although Mrs. Bolton Chaffee wa
old enough to be Stephen's grandmother.

Later he wrote Mrs. Chaffee, whose husband had sent him some cigar:
"Mr. Bemis informs me that you and I are sinners and that we have flow
to San Francisco. They have promoted you to the rank of Mrs. Brigadi⟨
General Chaffee. Perhaps it is not known to you—and it has not long bee
known to me—that my name in New York is synonymous with mud. Giv
my regards to your husband and tell him the cigars made many correspon⟨
ents happier. My friends will pile a mountain of lies on me but they wi
smoke my cigars as freely as I smoke theirs. That is cynicism." Bem
called on Crane at Brede Manor early the next year to renew their sligl
acquaintance, and Crane thanked him for having tipped him off on th
rumor about his "affair" with Mrs. Chaffee.

As he had been wearing the same clothes for three months, fordin
streams and sweating in them from heat and from fever, Crane bougl
himself a complete new outfit at Fortress Monroe for twenty-four dollar
Shortly after July 16, when the *World* published the unsigned article a⟨
cusing the 71st New York Volunteers of panic, he was in New Yor
and called at Pulitzer's *World* offices. Don Carlos Seitz, the busine:
manager, no doubt accused him of writing that damaging article (as lat
as 1933 Seitz was saying the same thing), and Crane very likely shrugge
his shoulders at the accusation so as to shield his friend Scovel from blam⟨
The other count against him was that he had filed for a rival newspap⟨
Edward Marshall's dispatch at Siboney when Marshall was wounded ⟨
Las Guásimas on June 24.

According to Seitz, the *World* had paid Crane $3,000 and now Seit
and the *World's* financial manager, Norris, refused to pay him th
twenty-four dollars expended on a new outfit. Seitz, who had known Cran
at the Lantern Club in 1895 and who evidently disliked him, persisted i
damning him by repeating his untruths in his 1933 *Bookman* sketch ⟨
Crane as a war correspondent, even though the fact that Crane did n⟨
write the article which "imperiled the paper" had been made known i
1899 by Davis and by Marshall.

It is ironic that on the transport *City of Washington* en route from Cub
(July 8) Crane was berthed with the 71st New York Volunteers. Th

men in the ranks did not deserve the "shrill shouts of scandal"; as Marshall explained, it was their officers who had flunked. The men were the victims of some "incompetent and unpleasant officers." Nor did Crane deserve the gross injustice done him by Seitz and by subsequent historians repeating Seitz's misaccount, which included the malicious untruth that Crane repaid the *World*'s advance of $3,000 "with only one dispatch of any merit." As Harold Frederic's wife later remarked, "Historians lie so."

Seitz encountered the financial manager of the *World* gleefully rubbing his hands and remarking that he had "just kissed your little friend Stephen Crane goodbye." Said that gentleman, according to Seitz, Crane "came here asking for another advance. 'Don't you think you have had enough of Mr. Pulitzer's money without earning it?' I asked. 'Oh, very well,' he said, 'if that is the way you look at it.' So we're rid of him."[4] Fired by the *World,* Crane went to Hearst's offices and signed on as a *Journal* correspondent. The same *World* that sacked Crane later rendered an obituary of ambivalent praise in the title: "Madcap Genius Stephen Crane." What Seitz knew and concealed was what the *World* then acknowledged, that Crane's dispatches "were masterpieces of description. If he had a fault as a war correspondent it was that his enthusiasm took him too deeply into the thick of the fighting." That fault he shared with Sylvester Scovel, head of the *World*'s staff.

As war correspondent he thought of himself as a soldier. Some three months after the sentimental scene of women weeping at the sight of the wounded at Old Point Comfort, he declared: "And let me tell you, it brought something to my eyes which I was ashamed to have seen, and my sabre arm went stiff and strong as steel and I swore that, despite legislation and the appointment of incompetent quartermasters, I would live and die a good soldier, a true, straight, unkicking American regular soldier."

Because he was having trouble with his lungs, he went to see a specialist in the Adirondacks, Dr. Edward Livingstone Trudeau, who later assured Cora "it was not serious. . . ."[5] But Crane was coughing blood when Richard Harding Davis saw him in December, 1898, in New York.

Toward the end of July he got to Pensacola Naval Base (on the western end of Florida) and as *Journal* correspondent boarded a tug to shove off for the final phase of the war: the Puerto Rican campaign. The handsome youth who was photographed in an Athens studio in 1897 now seemed a decade older. Charles Michelson of the *Journal* says that he was more debilitated physically than he had been at San Juan a month before. "Crane revealed the wreck of an athlete's frame—once square shoulders crowded forward by the concavity of a collapsed chest; great hollows where the once smooth pitching muscles had now wasted; legs like pipestems—he looked like a frayed white ribbon, seen through the veil of green as the seas washed over him." Everything now reminded him of death.

He told Michelson the story of the shipwrecked *Commodore* while the

Pensacola tug wallowed in the cross-currents of the Gulf Stream, and
recited portions of his "Open Boat" story. He pointed to the seasick shipmates aboard the Pensacola tug: the convulsive jerk of their shoulders as
they bent miserably over the rail reminded him that soldiers died with
"just such a spasm." He was not unsympathetic or callous about their
plight. "It was simply that motion-picture mind of his registering impressions. It was an instinct stronger than pity, or love, or fear. I don't know
that he was a braver man than those who went through the same experience
in war reporting, but I do know that while these were wondering if the
next volley would spatter their way he was commenting on the rigidity of
men in columns of four, and the imperturbability of birds scolding each
other while the bullets cut the bushes on which they perched. He endowed
his heroes with the same mental attitude."

The cruiser *Minneapolis* swept up to the *Journal* tugboat to ascertain
her identity in the blockade zone off Puerto Rico, and then she sheered
off and ignored the tugboat, "like a fat dowager duchess," commented
Crane, "who has been asked by a scrubwoman where she had bought her
hat." Off San Juan, Puerto Rico, on July 30 or 31 "a Spanish destroyer
was strutting to and fro under the guns of the land batteries trying to
decoy the American warship within range of the heavy shore forts," Michelson reported. The American warship was the improvised cruiser *Prairie,*
and the tugboat was asked to go in near enough to lure the Spanish destroyer out. In the tugboat's pilot house Crane baited the Captain to run
in close, and when asked by others why he was going so near the Spanish
destroyer, the Captain answered fervently: " 'You don't think I'm going to
let this damned frayed tholepin think he's got more guts than me, do
you?' Until the joke staled, Stephen was Lord Tholepin." (A *tholepin* or
*thole* is a metal pin set in the gunwale of a boat and serving as fulcrum
for the oar.) It didn't take much to amuse half a dozen men jailed together
in a tugboat for a week, and the fiction was created of Crane "as a liverish
British squire, with an East Indian background, and the ancestral mansion [Brede Manor] was christened Mango Chutney. Innumerable varia-
tions of the theme were suggested, and Lord Tholepin of Mango Chutney
had more fun out of it than anybody else." Then another ship signaled
the *Journal*'s tugboat to lay to, but she was satisfied and megaphoned that
she knew who they were and why they were there, and so she went about
her business.

During his week's cruise off Ponce, Crane had rotten luck at poker. So
bad was his usually bad gambling luck that a tugboat mate suggested "he
must be the very devil with the women. That started Stephen on a whimsical lament of his unsuccess with the sort of women they were talking
about. 'If the five of us started out and gathered in four girls, I'd be the
odd man ten times out of ten.' " It was not hard to believe on the deck of
a tugboat, for Crane, says Michelson, "was one of the most unprepossessing

figures that ever served as a nucleus for apocryphal romances; shambling, with hair too long, usually lacking a shave, dressed like any of the deck-hands, hollow-cheeked, sallow, destitute of small talk, critical if not fasti-dious, marked with ill-health—the very antithesis of the conquering male."

What a contrast between Crane and model war correspondent Richard Harding Davis—immaculate in a tailored uniform, his deep chest striated with service ribbons, as Michelson describes him. Perhaps Crane resented or scoffed at the contrast. Wherever correspondents gathered Davis "glit-ered not only by his accoutrements but by his accomplishments. He would borrow a banjo and to its accompaniment sing 'Mandalay' and other ballads, and between times carry his full share of the burden of conversa-ion, always ready, always interesting; while Stephen, in his old campaign clothes, sat tongue-tied. They would try to talk to him about his books, but Crane was willing to talk shop only with shop people. It was neither sullen-ness nor diffidence, nor self-depreciation; he had a normal appreciation of his achievements and endowments, and was reasonably militant and loquacious in verbal battles over the true and false in literature, but it was not his kind of company."[6]

The Puerto Rican expedition turned out to be an almost bloodless anti-climax. The American forces under General Nelson Miles departed Guan-tánamo Bay on July 21, and the invasion began at Guánica on the southern coast west of Ponce, Puerto Rico. The original plan—to occupy Fajardo on the northeast corner of the island—was abandoned because the enemy knew about it. A shell from the USS *Gloucester* surprised the garrison at Guánica, and bluejackets landed from Lieutenant Commander Richard Wainwright's saucy yacht, infantry and artillery soon following them. In the skirmish half a dozen Spaniards were killed, and then the troops pushed on to Yauco (towards Ponce), while the native Puerto Ricans assured them that they were most welcome; they called upon everyone to accept the Americans as brothers and to revere the memory of George Washington.

When the ships steamed into Guayanilla harbor they were met by boat-loads of welcoming natives shouting "Viva los Americanos." On the 28th the flag was raised in Ponce at 6 A.M., and here again the people went delirious with joy. Americans themselves could not have shown a greater reverence for the flag than did the Puerto Ricans, says Henry Chamberlin of the Chicago *Record,* and the "Star-Spangled Banner" was to them the music of liberty from Spanish oppression and misrule. Then on Sunday, July 31, the 3rd Wisconsin Volunteer Infantry gave a concert in the plaza while the people cheered themselves hoarse amid the strains of patriotic music.

Crane had assumed that General Miles would keep his original plan of beginning the invasion at Fajardo and so he missed out on the opening campaign and these celebrations at Guayanilla and Ponce. He got to

Ponce (on the belly of the island) shortly after that festive Sunday. The next day Arroyo—the third harbor on the southern coast—was taken, and then General Miles put into operation his strategic plan for a three-pronged attack—launched from the three ports—against San Juan and the triangular island; the Spaniards, to avoid being cut off in the roadless interior, would have to retreat to the northern port. The plan succeeded even better than anticipated because the Spaniards showed a remarkable lack of eagerness to defend much of anything. The entire campaign turned out to be a farce, and Crane in his last attempt to see warfare was denied any sort of combat.

He landed at Ponce with Charles Michelson, and very early on the morning of August 3 they rode with a group of correspondents vainly seeking breakfast along the road to Juana Díaz; all the inns were preempted by the officers. The night before in Ponce, which had surrendered four times to as many different American officers, Davis proposed to Crane that they go out together and take Juana Díaz by surprise, demanding its surrender. That night they tossed a coin to see who would wake the other, and Davis won the toss. But he lost the town because Crane did not wake him. Michelson, Crane's *Journal* manager, saw no reason for letting Davis' rival paper share the honors of capturing that doomed garrison, and so he sent Crane on ahead of all the other war correspondents very early that Wednesday morning.

Smoking a cigarette, Crane approached the town's square. "His khaki suit, slouched hat and leggings were all that was needed to drive the first man he saw, or rather, the man who first saw him, back upon the town in disorderly retreat," Davis reports. "The man aroused the village and ten minutes later the Alcalde . . . surrendered to him the keys of the cartel. Crane told me that no general in the moment of victory had ever acted in a more generous manner. He shot no one against a wall, looted no churches, levied no 'forced loans.' Instead, he lined up the male members of the community in the plaza and organized a joint celebration of conquerors and conquered. He separated the men into two classes, roughly divided between 'good fellows' and 'suspects.' Anyone of whose appearance Crane did not approve, anyone whose necktie even did not suit his fancy, was listed as 'suspect.' The 'good fellows' he graciously permitted to act as his hosts and bodyguard [they constituted the First Families of his Aristocracy!]. The others he ordered to their homes. From the barred windows they looked out with envy upon the feast of brotherly love that overflowed from the plaza into the by-streets and lashed itself into a frenzied carnival of rejoicing."

The next morning Crane, taking coffee in front of the town's sole café and surrounded by some of his "bodyguards," saw approaching an American scout dodging from one side to the other along the white highway of the Ponce road, his rifle at the ready. He was followed by a "point"

of five men creeping close to the bushes and concealing their advances
in the sheltering palms. Then came cautiously behind them the advance
guard, "and then boldly the Colonel himself on horseback and 800 men
of his regiment. For six hours he had been creeping forward stealthily in
order to take Juana Díaz by surprise."

The commanding officer could not see "how necessary and proper it
was that any town should surrender to the author of *The Red Badge of
Courage*," Davis wrote in his May, 1899, *Harper's Magaznie* sketch. But
in a subsequent account Davis says the Colonel's sense of humor did not
desert him. The officer's pleasure at spotting Crane was no less great than
his astonishment. "He knew that it did not fall to the lot of every Colonel
to have his victories immortalized by the genius who wrote *The Red Badge
of Courage*. 'I am glad to see you,' he cried eagerly. 'Have you been marching with my men?' Crane shook his head. 'I am sorry,' said the Colonel.
'I should like you to have seen us take this town.' 'THIS town!' cried
Crane in polite embarrassment. 'I'm really very sorry, Colonel, but I took
this town myself before breakfast yesterday morning.'" He had done
this by announcing that the American Governor of Puerto Rico was on his
way, and he ordered breakfast for His Excellency and staff—and for himself. Some correspondents had come into town, and Crane appointed the
most imposing member to play the role of His Excellency. He was Jack
Mumford, who fit the role because he happened to be dressed in immaculate whites. The preposterous strategy worked because innkeepers had a
toga-kissing respect for official rank and insignia. His Excellency—Jack
Mumford—gave instructions that he was not to be disturbed during his
breakfast, Michelson says.

Through a shuttered window Crane espied a Brigadier General waiting
on his horse while Mumford was eating his breakfast. Crane whispered to
the other reporters, constituting His Excellency's staff, that the important
General was pulling on his moustache impatiently. He went outside, and
the Brigadier General asked him who the Governor was. "Governor? Oh,
I guess the people here heard us call Jack Mumford governor, he looks
so much like one," Crane glibly lied. "There's nobody here but a bunch of
newspaper reporters." Crane never mentions this amusing incident of his
capture of a Puerto Rican town, but Richard Harding Davis twice told the
story at his own expense: "How Stephen Crane took Juana Días."[7]

Davis' public appraisals of his rival, as distinguished from his envious
notes about Crane in letters to his mother, were very generous, and he did
not wait until Crane was dead to sing his praises. Davis "captured" another
town a week after Crane took Juana Díaz, but conceded that Crane's
"victory" would be ranked in history as higher than his own.

In the countryside beyond Juana Díaz Crane came upon thirty men in
civilian garb assembled on the steps of a country store or leaning against
trees. "As we appeared they turned their heads, and as we rode slowly

up every eye swung to our pace. They preserved an absolute, stony silence. Now, here were men between the lines," says Crane in "The Porto Rican 'Straddle.'" The Spaniards who were on one side, while the Americans were on the other in this Puerto Rican straddle, knew nothing about the American advance beyond Ponce. "We drew up and looked at them. They looked at us. Not a word was said." Other Puerto Ricans had greeted the Americans with a salute or with hat in hand, but these natives were "as tongue-tied and sullen as a lot of burglars met in the daytime. Not one of them could endure a straight glance, and if we turned suddenly we were likely to catch two of them whispering."

But they changed face when four American scouts and a sergeant galloped by, followed by forty troopers scouting for the enemy. They knew then which way the wind blew and they began to ingratiate themselves and by the time the General "clattered forward with his staff they were happy, excessively polite, overwhelming every one with attentions and shyly confessing their everlasting devotion to the United States. The proprietor of the store dug up a new English and Spanish lexicon and proudly semaphored his desire to learn the new language of Porto Rico. There was not a scowl anywhere; all were suffused with joy. We told them they were a lot of honest men. And, after all, who knows?"

Crane returned to Ponce during the seven days American troops occupied that coastal city. While other correspondents settled themselves comfortably in decent hotels and cafés, he went off alone to a back-street cantina, says Michelson, "with the wastrels of Ponce—drunkards, drabs, and tin-horn gamblers. They did not know a word of his language nor he a word of theirs. Moreover, this was a conquered city and he was one of the invaders. That made no difference. He was accepted into the easy brotherhood of the thriftless without question. 'Todos son ladrones [all are bandits],' said our guide, the Porto Rican policeman whose beat had been taken over by an American soldier, waving us toward the group in the midst of which sat Stephen drinking bottled beer and local colour." Perhaps they were thieves, but they didn't exercise their professional skill on him, "though his loose-fingered way with his money was a constant invitation." The Army and Navy officers were intensely curious about him; they made much of Davis, the star of their parties, but Crane shunned their dinners. They wanted to hear a literary lion roar, but he preferred listening to the adventures of the wastrels of Ponce and acting the role of a "social bankrupt."

On August 5 he filed his sketch describing a strange funeral procession, entitled "A Soldier's Burial" (*Journal:* August 15, 1898). Two American women are burying their dead man. The hearse waits before their home, and a crowd of natives emit "a high-pitched babble of gossip concerning this funeral." A company of American regular infantry presents arms; six blue-shirted privates carry the coffin. "The little band of Americans seems like beings of another world, with their gently mournful, impassive faces, during this display of monkeyish interest." Then the cortege moves off, followed by the curious natives, and in the suburbs "women hurried out to the porches of the little wooden houses, and naked babies, swollen with fruit, strutted out to see, sucking their thumbs. A man walking directly behind the hearse was hailed interrogatively from a distance. He answered loudly, waving his arm toward the graveyard. A girl called greetings to some friends in the crowd. Suddenly, close to the road, a woman broke out in a raucous tirade at some of her children. The crowd still babbled. All these sounds beat like waves upon the hearse; noisy, idle, senseless waves beating upon the hearse, the invulnerable ship of the indifferent man."

The Americans are calm, stoical, superior; deaf to this mockery of the burial ritual. At the open grave they stand bareheaded, and the natives—noting this—take off their hats as the chaplain says: "I am the resurrection and the life." A high wall surmounted by broken bottles sunk into the mortar circles the graveyard, and there some enterprising curiosity-seekers cling while shrilling "like parrots." The chaplain, beset, badgered, drowned out, goes on imperturbably. Then the American infantry fires a salute, and at the sound "many jumped like frightened rabbits and then a moment later the whole mob burst into wild laughter.

"A bugler stepped forward. Into a medley of sounds such as would come from a combined baseball game and clambake, he sent the call of 'taps,' that extraordinary wail of mourning and song of rest and peace, the soldier's goodbye, his night, the fall of eternal darkness, the end. The sad, sad, slow voice of the bugle called out over the grave, a soul appealing to the sky, a call of earthly anguish and heavenly tranquility, a solemn heartbreaking song. But if this farewell of the soldier to the sky, the flowers, the bees and all life was heard by the natives their manner did not betray it."

The Protocol of Peace—signed in Washington on August 12—concluded the three-week Puerto Rican campaign. Crane got to Key West on the *World* tugboat by the 16th, when he cabled Cora in England. The blockade of Havana had been lifted on the 13th, and a few days later Crane slipped illegally into that "interesting city" by posing as a tobacco buyer. "I came into Havana without permission from anybody. I was at a hotel while the Government was firmly imprisoning nine correspondents on a steamer in a harbor. But no one molested me." In an untitled holograph manuscript, written on the back of the stationery of the Grand Hotel Pasaje, where he stayed until about September 1, he wrote that Havana since about August 23 had witnessed "an unregenerate and abandoned collection of newspaper correspondents, cattle men, gamblers, speculators and drummers who have lived practically as they pleased, without care or restraint, going—most of them—wherever interest or whim led, with no regard for yellow fever or any other terror of the tropics."

On August 23 he filed his *Journal* sketch, "Havana's Hate Dying." "When I first landed here it was difficult to withstand the scowls that one met everywhere, particularly from Spanish officers, who at that time were all exaggerating their gaits and generally improving and rearranging their 'fronts.' That has now changed for the better, and one can now inhabit the hotels, cafés and streets without meeting any particularly offensive looks." The changed atmosphere was brought about by what the Spanish newspapers were now saying about "the temperance and justice of the Americans as well as their courage and prowess." Cuban opinions of the Americans had entirely changed, "and names like Sampson, Schley, Shafter and McKinley are spoken with a change of voice. Nobody—popularly speaking—has ever heard of Dewey, mainly because the existence of the Philippines is not a particularly well established fact. The Spaniards may hate us, or, at least many of them hate us, but they will never again despise us."

Even the police showed good manners. "What might be called a correspondent's corral was established out in the harbor, and nine birds fluttered therein. On a certain night one escaped and was trying his wings in Havana when the police swooped down on him. It is said that the air of distinguished consideration which surrounded the incident was beyond words. Spectators informed me the next morning that at a late hour they had left the correspondent and four police officials drinking cognac with almost supernatural courtesy in the Café Ingleterra."

Crane returned to his Grand Hotel Pasaje on the east side of the Parque de Isabel la Católica, half a block south of the Parque Central with its Hotel and Café Ingleterra. The Grand Hotel Pasaje, one of the finest in the city, had an arcade or passageway (*pasaje*); hence its name. Four stories high with an elevator and electricity, its roof afforded the best panorama of the city and the surrounding countryside—flat and rolling, with scattered hills a few hundred feet high.[8]

Havana was a sad, filthy and deadened city. Food was scarce, prices were inflated, scavengers flourished. Havana harbor was "a soundless vacancy" save for four gunboats and "the emaciated cruiser *Alfonso XII*, with no engines and no guns." Sanitation was primitive and endangered health. There were thousands of open privies; when they did not serve, the streets did. The open privies were in the immediate vicinity of Havana's kitchens—black holes emitting odors, "while flies swarmed on the meat and vegetables which were to be served."[9] Crane in his Havana dispatches ignored these unpleasant realities. It suited him that the city was a dead and lonely place, for he himself was war-weary and physically exhausted. His Havana sketches betray a world-weariness, an uncommon lassitude and an occasional bitterness.

That he had not told Cora in his mid-August cable from Key West that he intended to return to Cuba is apparent from her letter to Henry Sanford Bennett of September 3: "Stephen was sent from Cuba to Hampton Roads on an army transport as a typhoid suspect. Then he felt obliged to go to Porto Rico and is now said to be in Havana. If you have a line from him let me know instantly. His family can not give me an address. I am so anxious."

Enamored of Havana, Crane was writing story after story for agent Paul Reynolds and sketch after sketch for the New York *Journal*. He "began to think of spending the winter in the lazy old city." To Reynolds he sent "brief penciled scrawls on cheap ruled-pad paper; sometimes his vehement notes were written in a shaky hand on old telegraph blanks. Always they glowed with enthusiasm over his work and appealed for instant payment."[10] He was living on his Reynolds account and the money paid him for his *Journal* dispatches and sketches.

Cora nobly endured his outrageous neglect of her without criticism except to note in her journal: "When a man does exactly what he likes and with a perfectly natural air his friends allow him latitude so long as his domestic circle remains outwardly untroubled." So she kept up the mask. The important thing was to shield Stephen's reputation. What would damage it would be gossip that he was not returning to England or that he was trapped in Cuba because he was too broke to pay for his passage back.

On getting the news that Stephen had disappeared, in the "Cuban Gossip" of a Florida newspaper for September 10, Cora on the 24th wrote John Hay, Ambassador to the Court of St. James: "Knowing you to be a personal friend of my husband, Stephen Crane—I appeal to you to use your influence to find him. News has reached me that he is missing from Havana. He went there for the N. Y. *Journal* as you doubtless know. And was watched, I understand, by the Spanish police. He was stopping quietly at Hotel Pasaje—and disappeared about September 8th. I am almost distracted with grief and anxiety. I am sure you will personally ask the President to instruct the American Commission to demand Mr. Crane from the Havana police." The Honorable John Hay, however, was vacationing in New Hampshire before assuming his new duties on October 1 as our Secretary of State. Not having heard from Stephen since August 16, Cora cabled the Secretary of War, Russell A. Alger, and wrote him that same day, September 25.[11]

She also wrote the British Consul in Havana and cabled Judge William Howe Crane at Port Jervis. She wrote Paul Reynolds on September 25: "I am in *great* distress of mind as I can get no news through the *Journal* office here. Mr. Crane's affairs here need his attention. I am in great need of money. And I fear that we will lose our home here [Ravensbrook] if I cannot get money to pay some pressing debts. The *Journal* is behaving very shabbily. I have been served with two summonses; so you can see how bad matters really are. If you can collect any money due to Mr. Crane please cable it to me without delay. This being so helpless in a foreign country together with my fears for Mr. Crane are almost driving me mad. Will you use your influence with Mr. Hearst? He has no right to allow a man like Stephen Crane to be missing for over three weeks without using means to find him. And if he allows Stephen Crane's wife to be turned out of her home, while Stephen is risking his life in his service, I have told Mr. Creelman I would let every correspondent in London know about it. Both Harold Frederic and Robert Barr would let the world know over their own signature. I beg you to let me hear any news by cable." But Crane wasn't risking his life in Hearst's service; the peace had been signed a month before. As the British Consul was in charge of the *Journal*'s affairs in Havana, Stephen could readily have cabled her had he cared to and probably without paying for the cablegram.

Judge Crane thought that some of Cora's cables and letters were "not judicious. She cabled a very talkative newspaper man she had known in Jacksonville, and he put a yarn around that Steve had abandoned her. There was a great deal of nasty talk about it." On September 22 Cora received the story her Jacksonville newspaper friend sent her, a clipping from the Florida *Times-Union and Citizen* for September 10: "Cuban Gossip / Stephen Crane Missing." The novelist and member of the *Journal* staff, "who entered Havana as a tobacco buyer about ten days ago and was stopping quietly at the Hotel Pasaje, is missing, and fears for his safety are entertained by his friends. The police had been shadowing him for several days before he disappeared."[12]

Cora's newspaper friend was Bertram Marburgh, now in Havana for *Leslie's Popular Weekly,* and he got the news that Crane was missing from two correspondents—Matthews and Nicols of the *American*—at the American Bar in Havana. Marburgh had noticed "a mysterious slight figure in a white suit that used to slink along the street around eleven o'clock every night near the house where he was stopping." He did not learn that this was Stephen Crane until the white figure came into the American Bar one evening and introduced himself: "I'm Stephen Crane." Marburgh apologized then for having issued the report that he was missing. "Well," said Crane, "certain dignified and venerable ambassadors, not to mention a few Cranes, had been sorely upset by the news."

On September 9 Cora wrote Paul Reynolds, on whom she relied for getting word to Stephen: "Will you let me know if Mr. Crane gets my letters and where he is at the time this reaches you. The report that he was 'missing from Havana' caused me great distress. Will you tell him when you write that 'Illustrated Bits' have written asking to see him twice. I referred them to Heinemann—who has the matter in hand. They plagiarized 'The Bride Comes to Yellow Sky.' I transferred the copyright to

Heinemann who is suing. My letters seem to go astray; so I will be glad if you can tell Mr. Crane this."

Robert Barr explained Cora's plight to the New York *Journal*'s chief of staff in London, James Creelman, and on September 27 he wrote the North German Lloyd line asking for deferred payment for passage to New York City by Mrs. Stephen Crane. He said that her husband had been captured by the Spaniards in Havana, although Barr knew that Crane was hiding out there in some rooming house. "He is certain to be released as soon as the Americans get in there. Mrs. Crane is naturally very anxious about him and wishes to get to Havana. As soon as Mr. Crane reaches New York he will pay the amount due you, should you see your way to let Mrs. Crane cross on one of your boats."

Another idea was to raise money from Stephen's publisher Heinemann, but if that failed, then Barr and other friends must raise the passage money to New York on the hope that Hearst "would forward you on to Havana." Creelman said he would contribute two pounds. But nothing came of these plans. Creelman with his black goatee was a fierce fellow known as "Mr. Creelman" even to his closest associates, a formal and forbidding personage. He felt certain that some of Cora's letters had reached Crane and told Barr: "If in these circumstances you think it worth while to go after such a man, then there is nothing to do but consider the ways and means." Creelman, who had captured the Spanish garrison's flag for Mr. Hearst and was wounded in the assault on the blockhouse at El Caney on July 1, the same day that Crane contemptuously disregarded Spanish bullets at San Juan Hill, obviously considered him an irresponsible heel.

Robert Barr concurred, and Joseph Conrad privately felt the same way. Barr wrote Cora that if what Hearst "cables is true, then I should hate to put down in black and white what I think of S. Crane. If he has not disappeared, and if he has been drawing money for himself while leaving you without cash, then that article about his disappearance in the Florida paper is a put up job, and he does not intend to return." The Hearst press declared that Stephen Crane was hiding out in a Havana rooming house.

He had moved out of the Grand Hotel Pasaje about the first of September to take a room in the lodging house of Mary Horan, a tough old saddlebag who bullied her tenants with kindness and forced Crane to take nightly walks to relieve his built-in tensions. He was hiding out there for at least a month before he felt obliged to write Cora, and then ironically his October letters never reached her. Why not? It happened that he used to give a servant in Mary Horan's lodging house his letters to mail for him, but as the letters he wrote brother William were never received, it seems likely that the servant pocketed the postage money or soaked the stamps off to trade them in. That theory might spare Crane from the charge of utter neglect of Cora from mid-August until almost mid-November, but it does not explain his defaulting on sending her money. Since his letters and manuscripts to Reynolds arrived safely, one conjectures that Crane did not intrust them to the servant but mailed them himself. However, one wonders why Reynolds never disclosed the Havana address to William and Cora.

It would seem that Crane had pledged Reynolds to secrecy; as late as November 10, William was asking Reynolds for his brother's address. What flushed Stephen out from his hiding place was finally the cablegram to Secretary of War Alger which Cora sent on September 25. It got lost and was not transmitted from the Adjutant General's Office to General J. F. Wade in Havana until October 9. General Wade then inquired of some newspapermen and reported back to Washington on October 27: "After these inquiries Mr. Crane called and expressed regret at having caused so much trouble. I do not know his business or why he has not communicated with his family."

Meanwhile, William and Edmund were very much upset and "pulled all the wires we could think of to locate him." The story of Crane's disappearance was flashed throughout the United States and England, and Cora went almost crazy, says Wilbur's daughter, Helen R. Crane. Helen detested Stephen's brothers, especially William, and she says spitefully that they "suddenly realized that he was an extraordinary nice kid, and they started routing editors out of bed and consuls, too. The American Ambassador cabled to Washington, and Washington cabled everybody." British Consul Lucien Jerome in Havana wrote Cora not to worry about Stephen's disappearance, his health, and rumors about the Havana police. He did not know where Crane was living, but he frightened Cora by saying that Stephen was no longer with the New York *Journal*. He was in fact writing for the *Journal* until November 17, the day he sailed on the *Vigiliancia* from Havana for Manhattan.

Jerome's letter of October 18 disturbed Cora into writing Reynolds that same day that the letter gave "the impression that something is wrong, that Mr. Crane is in some sort of trouble." She feared that "Mr. Crane is having money trouble" and she begged Reynolds to write Stephen that his important work was to be done in England. "I am very much worried and will be glad if you will use every effort to induce Mr. Crane to leave Cuba & return to his work." Reynolds certainly reported her message, but Stephen simply ignored Cora's pleas. Lucien Jerome advertised in a local (Havana) paper that he held letters and cables for Stephen Crane, and it seems likely that Stephen retrieved them and responded to Cora and William in letters that were never mailed.

Joseph Conrad had grave misgivings about Crane's intentions of returning to Cora and he was irked that he had not yet paid off his indebtedness to William Blackwood of *Blackwood's Edinburgh Magazine*—£60— since last April. There was the possibility of raising another loan from Blackwood, but the old man must be approached diplomatically through his London consultant, David S. Meldrum—an admirer of Crane and most friendly. Conrad wrote Cora on October 28: "What kind of trouble is Stephen in? You make me very uneasy. Are you *sure* you can bring him back? I do not doubt your influence mind! . . . In Stephen's coming back to England is *salvation;* there is no doubt about that. Will he come? *Can* he come? I am utterly in the dark as to the state of affairs."

Cora had gone with Mrs. Ruedy last August to Conrad's Ivy Walls, but her visit with the Conrads was "marred by her very real anxiety as to his whereabouts, and a fierce jealousy as to his possible fancy for someone he might meet. In vain I assured her of my complete conviction," says Jessie Conrad, "that Stephen was deeply attached to her and that his first thought as soon as he was able to get a letter through would be of her." But no letter came for almost two months (William was mistaken in saying it was but twenty days she had no word from Stephen). Intuitively Cora was right in her jealousy; there was another woman on Stephen's mind—Mrs. Lily Brandon Munroe.

Writing Cora on November 1, Conrad said that he had suggested to Blackwood "a loan of £50 on three securities. *One* (for which they would care most) *Stephen's work, second* your property [some furniture at Ravensbrook], *third* my own understanding to furnish them copy to the amount advanced should unforeseen circumstances prevent you and Stephen from paying him back as soon as he may expect." He warned Cora: "Before you give bill of sale on furniture make sure the furniture dealer or dealers (from whom you bought) are paid in full as in the contrary case you would make yourself liable to prosecution. . . . I am sure you are doing and planning for the best. That is the way to rescue poor Stephen. I only wish I had something to pawn or sell; you would not have to wait long for means. As it is I've only my work and that I've offered to B'wood for what it is worth."

On November 3 he wrote Cora again: "Would Stephen come back by himself if written to? Would he tell us how much is wanted to enable him to leave Havana? Would he recognize the engagements we would enter into here for means to bring him back? His future is here—I firmly believe—but will he see it? Whatever happens the matter must be kept quiet, and his reputation shielded. I know of personal knowledge that B'wood is a little angry. A short letter from Stephen saying that he could not send anything would have made all the difference. It is too late now. What do you think of writing him a strong letter urging his return and saying that we keep £50 ready for that purpose if he gives his word."

Blackwood had written Conrad (August 30): "Have you heard anything from Stephen Crane or his wife—how he has come out of the American & Spanish War? He was to have sent me some articles whenever he got the opportunity, but I have heard nothing yet from him."

Crane had written Reynolds: "Now this is IT. If you don't touch big money for it I wonder! Cable me when you make sale and how much. English copy goes to Blackwood." That was "The Price of the Harness," about which he again wrote Reynolds in early October: "Did you get my story: 'The Price of the Harness'? I am worried for fear it is lost. Cable. I am now sending you a *peach*. I love it devotedly. Sell to anybody if the price is grand enough. Otherwise remember that Blackwood's have a call on me. Send all letters here. I *love* this story."

He wrote Reynolds again on November 3 that if Blackwood can't take "The Price of the Harness" for December, "ask them to give it to Pinker. Somebody must have it. With Pinker it is worth £36. We can't lose it." Blackwood took it for the December number of his *Edinburgh Magazine,* and Reynolds placed it in the *Cosmopolitan,* whose editor was probably a man named Walker. "Damn Walker," Crane wrote Reynolds. "The name of the story is 'The Price of the Harness' because it *is* the price of the harness, the price the men paid for wearing the military harness, Uncle Sam's military harness; and they paid blood, hunger and fever. Let him if he likes conjure some inflammatory secondary title. He is a fool." There were disagreements about the *World*'s reimbursement and wrangles over his account with the *Journal* and probably with Reynolds' account also. He also owed sums to his London agent, James B. Pinker.

Meldrum wrote Blackwood at the end of November that he thought Crane's "Price of the Harness" very remarkable; "but his later thing, which I enclose, does not seem to me to be up to the mark and I do not advise its publication. The price to be allowed for the story in the present Number is a difficult question. His price is very high . . . and, then, he is greatly in your obligation. I think the question must remain open until he gets back, if he ever does." So Blackwood loaned Crane no more money, and although Crane twice tried to wipe out his debt, he never repaid Blackwood in full because Meldrum did not think his manuscripts good enough.

If Meldrum had doubts about Crane's returning to England, so did Cora. Her desperation is indicated by her extravagant plan of October to go to Havana and fetch him home; had he then refused, she would have quit Ravensbrook while owing all their Ravensbrook debts. Her salvation depended upon his returning; otherwise their financial mess would doom her in bankruptcy. She was living on credit as usual and her grocer served her with a summons. Robert Barr promised to make himself personally responsible for that debt. "The trouble is that the butcher may do likewise [he did] & his bill is more serious. I will stay in town on Friday night & come right through to Oxted on Saturday, bringing this summons with me, when I will see the grocer. Of course the grocer is perfectly within his right in doing this. It has been noised about the place that you are going to leave & he knows he wont have your custom much longer anyhow; so doubtless having been bilked before, he fears he is going to be cheated again. [Cora had obtained Brede Manor for Stephen's new home, and it was known to her grocer and butcher that she'd leave Ravensbrook once he returned. This grocer's summons, so Barr thought, was provoked by "spite and servants' talk."] The only person at fault is Stephen Crane, & as he is not within cursing distance there is no use in swearing. I am sure, however, that the cash will be in from the *Journal* before many days, & then everything will run smoothly again."

Barr got advice from a lawyer about the summons that all Cora had to do was to give notice "that you are a married woman, that it is your husband's debt, and that he is in America and will pay when he returns." Barr found the grocer's bill so small he was amazed at his action. Meldrum advised Blackwood on November 30 that Mrs. Crane's offer of her furniture as a bill of sale and her promise that Crane would someday repay his debt with some short story were not sufficient security. "The promise of a story is none; for, apart from the fact that Crane, I know, is tied to Heinemann for his next novel, and is bound to you to offer [the] first free one, Mrs. Crane's promise on behalf of her husband is, legally, absolutely worthless."

Meldrum had considerable belief in Crane as a writer; but even so he didn't see how his boss in Edinburgh would recover money already lent if Crane didn't get back to England to work. "I fancy he is far more foolish than you know," he wrote. "I can find no justification for the man, though I can [find] many excuses for one with such a strange and all-on-edge temperament as his." Meldrum chiefly "wished to oblige Conrad whom I admire as a writer and like as a man, and wished to keep attached to the House. So I promised Conrad to do what I could among friends of my own by becoming security myself. His friend Nairn unfortunately was in America, but John Maqueen (a London publisher) might very well agree to advance the money to Mrs. Crane. I could not, and do not advise you to lend the Cranes money further, but I have thought it best to have your refusal for my own guidance before I put Maqueen . . . in communication with Mrs. Crane."

So Blackwood washed his hands of Crane, and Meldrum told Conrad and Cora that he could do no more. Conrad's plan thus fell through. It was a token of his devoted friendship to Crane and should be remembered in the face of later criticism claiming that Conrad spoke of him condescendingly.[13]

Cora these several months had to keep up a brave front, saying things about Stephen which Conrad agreed was the "golden truth." However, the truth was that Stephen resented returning to her and their Ravensbrook debts; he postponed doing so as long as it was possible. He did not cable her until the first week of October, as we know only from Meldrum's letter to Blackwood on October 10.[14] Conrad had sent Meldrum a note a day or two before about the lost Stephen Crane having now turned up; but Cora didn't say when he was coming back. He hadn't yet committed himself. "I cannot help vanishing and disappearing and dissolving," Crane had written Ripley Hitchcock in 1896. "It is my foremost trait."

# XXV

# ⊂ "*Intrigue*"

IN "Stephen Crane Sees Free Cuba," filed on August 26, Crane reports that the Spaniards feared possible retaliation from the Cubans and probably would welcome the arrival of American troops in unconquered Havana. "Four Havana thieves talking yesterday said, 'We must steal as much as possible before the Americans come, for then we will get into great difficulty if we steal.'" Feeling was growing stronger for the annexation of Cuba by the United States. The change in the spirit of this city was something wonderful, he reports on the 28th. At first there were scowls at the Americans, then toleration, then courtesy. There were only about thirty Americans in the city, and most of them were not supposed to be there.

Again on September 4, in "Stephen Crane's Views of Havana," he reports that some unarmed American soldiers strolling the streets of Havana drew much attention because they were very tall, "giants to the people of Havana." Newsboys excitedly peddled a translation of the Constitution of the United States "as if it were a war extra. So much so that two or three Americans were misled into buying it, expecting to read of the fall of New York." Captain General Ramon Blanco, whose reign in Cuba was regarded as prudent and conciliatory, refused to return the $800,000 which had been donated for the purchase of a warship by Spanish merchants of Havana. "The Spanish patriots want that money back, and they want it badly. They say with a deal of dry humor that they have discovered that a Spanish warship is not a good investment. . . . The Havana merchants now see themselves in the position of people who got over-patriotic at the wrong time. Their only solace now is to burst into tears." There was much agitation also over the bones of Christopher Columbus, it being rumored that the United States was going to seize the alleged bones of the venerated discoverer. (The remains of Columbus were in Santo Domingo, having been transported there in 1542, some thirty-six years after the Admiral's death.)

The Spaniard here "is making a laudable effort to take every possible dollar out of Cuba before leaving it," Crane says in his dispatch of September 20. "We do not stop the Spaniards from robbing the Cubans because we are a very generous people and we so want to be kind to our fallen enemy"—a shrewd insight on the naïveté of America in international affairs. Our generosity "is all very charming as a sentiment; but it is doubtful if Bismark's stern, quick terms to a conquered France were not more truly merciful than this buttermilk policy of ours. . . . In our next war our first bit of strategy should be to have the army and the navy combine in an assault on Washington. If we could once take and sack Washington the rest of the conflict would be simple."

Negotiations, after the Protocol of Peace on August 12, lasted until December 10, when the Treaty of Paris was signed. (The terms included Spain's withdrawal from Cuba and her cession of Puerto Rico, Guam and the Philippines to the United States.) Because of the indecision of our spineless administrators the intervening months, said Crane, were likely to be more disastrous for Cuba than were the months of the war. "The lack of a spine is not mentioned by any available authority as the supreme virtue of mankind." The war was at least "a tangible condition, plain as your nose." But now the Cuban "finds a grim and inexplicable fate fall from a sky which he thought was the sky of promise."

In "The Grocer Blockade" Crane tells the story of the greedy Havana grocers who at the beginning of the war declared that they had nothing to sell. They hid their stocks and said they had not so much as a pound of rice. They declared that the war had ruined them. Crane's barbs expose their hypocrisy. "Ah! those devils of Americans, thus to torment the honest grocers. In time, however, wealthy citizens might be seen wending their way with much gold to secret conferences with a grocer. Oh, no. Impossible! At no price! A pound of bread is worth more than a pound of gold. It is impossible. Well, if I sell some to you I would have to take it probably from the mouths of my own children, who are in danger of starving. A little, a very little; yes, perhaps. Thereupon ensued the spectacle of a respectable citizen digging into his own bowels for gold to buy a little of the flour which the grocer had cleverly made to appear like pounded pumice stone."

In August when the rumor spread that the blockade was to be raised, the market had slumped. These grocers, "as men with honest faces," says Crane, would either have to lower prices and thus give themselves away as cheats or they would have to lose money. "What did they do? Did they lose money, like men who would care for an appearance of consistency, or did they give themselves away rather than lose a centavo? In one day they lowered the price of rice 60 per cent. They lowered other staples proportionately. There had been no influx to the market. There had been simply a rumor that the blockade was about to be raised." (It was raised in mid-August.) "It was shameless. Our chill-blooded Northern race would have hung each grocer to his own signboard. These people, so fiery, so dangerous in temper, so volcanic, alive with p-p-passion, they did nothing."

In "Stephen Crane in Havana," filed on October 3, he characterizes the Cubans as "children of pellucid chance, and if Havana was a tub and they were a lot of rubber balls prancing and bouncing within they could not be more joyously irresponsible and incompetent." "Nature is usually seeking to alleviate, to mend," he writes, but chance or "circumstance is always perverse, aggravating." These chance events are neither predestined nor inevitable nor unalterable. He believed that man can shape his destiny if he has the will to do it.

Several days later he boarded the *Alfonso XIII* just before she sailed for Spain with sick soldiers, Spanish families, and some priests, and then descended her gangplank to a small boat, while people in other small boats waved handkerchiefs and shouted "Adios!" A woman sobbed because she was being parted from her husband, a Spanish officer who stood immovable on the ship and made no sign. "Sometimes men express great emotion by merely standing still for a long time. It seemed as if he was never again going to move a muscle." Crane's boatman "spat disdainfully into the water. 'Serves her right. Why didn't she take up with a man of her own people instead of with a Spaniard?' But that is of small consequence. The woman's heart was broken. That is the point. . . . But, after all—and after all—and again after all, it is human agony and human agony is not pleasant."[1]

While Cora waited for him to return, Crane philosophized: "Men seek the women they love, and find them, and women wait for the men they love, and the men come, and all the circumlocution and bulwarks and clever football interference and trouble and delay and protracted agony and duennas count for nothing, count for nothing against the tides of human life, which are in Cuba or Omaha controlled by the same moon." And Cora was writing in her journal: "There is no spirit of Evil, we are betrayed by our own passions and the chief of these passions is love. . . . I passed one of those days that outweigh an eternity, a day full of useless feeling; a day of self-forgetfulness and waking dreams, when what one has longed for in visions in the night actually stands before one. . . . But I may come to feel as if all this had been a dream, as if it had happened to some other girl I once knew, not to myself."

In another sketch[2] Crane describes a typical Sunday morning in Havana. "When in other cities of the world the church bells peal out from their high towers, slowly and solemnly, with a dignity taken from the sky, from the grave, the hereafter, the Throne of Judgment—voices high in air calling, calling, calling, with the deliberation of fate, the sweetness of hope, the austerity of a profound mystic thing—they make the devout listen to each stroke, and they make the infidels feel all the height and width of a blue sky, a Sunday morning golden with sun drops." Then he deflates this grandiloquent mood with the comic contrast of Havana's uninspired bell noises. At blear dawn when a man in an adjacent belfrey "begins to hammer the everlasting, murdering Hades out of the bell with a club—your aroused mind seems to turn almost instinctively to blasphemy. Religion commonly does not go off like an alarm clock, and, as symbolized by the bells, it does not usually sound like a brickbat riot in a tin store. However, this is the Havana method. I fancy they use no such term here as 'bell ringer'; they probably use 'bell fighter.' But, such passion! Such fury!" And on fast days the clamor is so endless and inane that it "simply shakes out of one all faith in human intelligence."

"I enclose a 'personal anecdote' thing for McClure," Crane wrote Paul Reynolds on October 20. "Hit him hard. Hit him beastly hard. I have got to have at least fifteen hundred dollars this month, sooner the better. For Christ's sake get me some money quick here by cable." One wonders why he needed that much money unless he was changing his mind about staying in Havana all winter and planned now to return to New York as soon as he earned enough for his passage. There was an S. Crane on the passenger list of the liner *Paris* for November 10, 1898,[3] but if that was Stephen Crane he canceled his reservation and stayed on until mid-November. The three months he spent in Havana, mainly in Mary Horan's lodging house, was one of the happiest periods of his life. He describes that place in "This Majestic Lie," which is no doubt the "personal anecdote thing" he sent Reynolds, who failed to sell it to *McClures's Magazine*.

In "This Majestic Lie" the American spy, Charles H. Thrall, who had hidden in Mary Horan's lodging house in May, figures as Johnnie. Crane tread the spiral staircase in Mary Horan's house that Thrall had descended from the gallery after the Spanish police had searched the upper chambers and had failed to find him. Perhaps he inhabited Thrall's former room, one of the three sleeping rooms off the gallery. He sat in Thrall's old chair in the courtyard "between the winding stairway and the door near the orange tree" and breathed the heavy odor of old straw, the odor of Havana itself. He had quit the Grand Hotel Pasaje to move into this lodging house because Thrall had lived there and also because he had to economize. After the blockade was lifted on August 13, there was food in quantity, but food in quality was very dear or nonexistent. The superb feast he and "Johnnie" enjoyed was in fact all in Johnnie's imagination—it was his Majestic Lie.

Crane rechristened his landlady, Mary Horan, as "Mary Clancy," who peered at him through her spectacles and was old enough to be his grandmother. She had been born in Ireland, "bred in New York, fifteen years married to a Spanish captain, and now a widow, keeping Cuban lodgers who had no money with which to pay her." A huge woman, she bullied the men and then nursed them when they were ill as she would her own children. She did not approve of Stephen's hours of work, says his niece

Helen R. Crane. She "used to go in and hover over him with a great tray of food. 'I don't want to eat, please go away.' 'Go away, me eye, you're goin' to eat this if I have to feed it to you spoon by spoon.' "

At Mary Horan's house he wrote all but a few of his *Journal* sketches of Cuba, worked at his novel *Active Service,* wrote a number of poems and completed Cuban War tales. In October he began a novel which he intended to be longer than anything he had yet done (says James Huneker), a novel about a boy prostitute: "Flowers in Asphalt." He also had with him the manuscript of a short story written in February, 1895, "Vashti in the Dark." In this story a Methodist preacher finds his wife has been raped by a Negro in a forest and kills himself. Acton Davies, who typed that tale for him, thought it marvellous, but Crane is said to have burnt it. He was thinking about Port Jervis in another story said to have been written in Cuba and typed by Acton Davies, who had been a drama critic on the New York *Sun* and was now a correspondent. "The Cat's March," which Huneker liked, was about an artist's model who marries an artist (Pennoyer of *The Third Violet*) and settles in a small town where the respectable women give her a bad time of it. Apparently Crane was brooding on Cora's plight were she to settle in some small American town like Port Jervis.

Poor destitute Cora with debt-ridden Ravensbrook seized (or about to be seized) by creditors at Oxted and at London, while Crane in Havana was writing a batch of poems about his love-conflict between her and Lily Brandon Munroe! He called these poems *Intrigue,* which defines his enigmatic situation. In a manuscript poem,[4] the husband regards his marriage ring as a ring of gold, while his wife and her lover regard it as of iron:

> *One came from the skies*
> *—They said—*
> *And with a band he bound them*
> *A man and a woman.*
> *Now to the man*
> *The band was gold*
> *And to another, iron.*
> *And to the woman, iron.*

The lover ought to have rescued his lady from her husband, and he regards himself as coward for not doing so:

> *But this second man,*
> *He took his opinion and went away.*
> *But, by heavens,*
> *He was none too wise*
> *For shackles fit apes.*

> *He is not brave*
> *Who leaves the iron on doves.*

Crane remembers their passion:

> *I have seen thy face aflame*
> *For love of me,*
> *Thy fair arms go mad,*
> *Thy lips tremble and mutter and rave,*
> *And—surely—*
> *This should leave a man content?*

But Lily had declared an end to their affair when last he saw her in April, and he remained distraught because he could not forget her.

> *Thou lovest not me now,*
> *But thou didst love me,*
> *And in loving me once*
> *Thou gavest me an eternal privilege,*
> *For I can think of thee.*

In Poem VI the lover says:

> *I have heard your quick breaths*
> *And seen your arms writhe toward me;*
> *At those times*
> *—God help us—*

Once they knew each other intimately:

> *I said: "Sweetheart."*
> *Thou saidst: "Sweetheart,"*
> *And we preserved an admirable mimicry*
> *Without heeding the drip of blood*
> *From my heart.*

His heart bleeds for her who once was happy with him and is now unhappy. He declares "I am no fool / To poll stupidly into iron," but he knows now that he was a fool not to shear off her marriage band.

> *I was impelled to be a grand knight,*
> *And swagger and snap my fingers,*
> *And explain my mind finely.*
> *Oh, lost sweetheart,*
> *I would that I had not been a grand knight.*[5]

"Oh, lost sweetheart."

> *I heard thee laugh,*
> *And in this merriment*
> *I defined the measure of my pain;*
> *I knew that I was alone,*

> *Alone with love,*
> *Poor shivering love,*
> *And he, little sprite,*
> *Came to watch with me,*
> *And at midnight*
> *We were like two creatures by a dead camp-fire.*
>
> (*Intrigue* VII)

He remembers an earlier time, when her evenings had "not yet been touched with flame"—

> *I wonder if sometimes in the dusk,*
> *When the brave lights that gild thy evenings*
> *Have not yet been touched with flame,*
> *I wonder if sometimes in the dusk*
> *Thou rememberest a time,*
> *A time when thou loved me*
> *And our love was to thee thy all?*

Something has come between them:

> *Is the memory rubbish now?*
> *An old gown*
> *Worn in an age of other fashions?*
> *Woe is me, oh, lost one,*
> *For that hope is now to me*
> *A supernal dream,*
> *White, white, white with many suns.*
>
> (*Intrigue* VIII)

When Crane visited Lily in Washington in April she was an unhappy woman, not yet divorced.

> *Love, forgive me if I wish you grief,*
> *For in your grief*
> *You huddle to my breast,*
> *And for it*
> *Would I pay the price of your grief.*

Crane, a veteran of two wars and a realistic reporter, could still write romantic verses with the same heart-tugging pathos as his sentimental melodrama "Drama in Cuba," an unfinished two-act play written at the same time.[6]

> *God give me medals,*
> *God give me loud honors,*
> *That I may strut before you, sweetheart,*
> *And be worthy of—*
> *The love I bear you.*

His strutting before her like a grand knight impresses her not at all; his

medals and honors mean nothing to her. She is frightened by their "af-
frighted love," and he doubts her loyalty to him.

> Beware of my friends,
> Be not in speech too civil,
> For in all courtesy
> My weak heart sees spectres,
> Mists of desire
> Arising from the lips of my chosen;
> Be not civil.
>
> (*Intrigue* II)

Her courteous speech incites "mists of desire":

> Love—reckless imp of the night—is a bungler,
> And I cursed him,
> Cursed him to and fro, back and forth,
> Into all the silly mazes of his mind,
> But in the end
> He laughed and pointed to my breast,
> Where a heart still beat for thee, beloved.
>
> (*Intrigue* IX)

*Intrigue IV* recalls a time when his beloved was "chattering girlishly to
other girls, / Bell-voiced, happy, / Careless with the stout heart of unscarred womanhood, / And life to thee was all light melody." "Unscarred
womanhood" rather cruelly sets into contrast Lily and Cora. Between
these two women he is torn and miserable. He is "ashamed of my open
sorrow."

> I thought of the great storms of love as I knew it.[7]
> Torn, miserable, and ashamed of my open sorrow,
> I thought of the thunder that lived in my head,
> And I wished to be an ogre,
> And hale and haul my beloved to a castle,
> And there use the happy cruel one cruelly,
> And make her mourn with my mourning.

The twice-married Cora who could not get a divorce is the subject of
*Intrigue V*:

> Tell me why, behind thee
> I see always the shadow of another lover?
> Is it real,
> Or is this the thrice damned memory of a better happiness?
> Plague on him if he be dead,
> Plague on him if he be alive—
> A swinish numskull
> To intrude his shade
> Always between me and my peace!

The longest and the least satisfactory of the ten *Intrigue* poems is No. I, where each stanza begins "Thou art my love" and ends "Woe is me." His loved one is "a tinsel thing," and in the second stanza "a weary violet," while in the third stanza she is the ashes of other men's loves; she is Cora, former hostess of the Hotel de Dream.

In mockery he reverses his loved one as a temple of love with his heart on its altar (stanza 7), but the priestess of that temple is a murderess with a bloody dagger (stanza 9), who plots to stab his heart upon the altar— unless he murders her first: "And if peace came with thy murder / Then would I murder— / Woe is me." *Intrigue* I ends:

> *Thou art my love,*
> *And thou art my death,*
> *Ay, thou art death,*
> *Black and yet black,*
> *But I love thee,*
> *I love thee—*
> *Woe, welcome woe, to me.*

"And I doubt thee," says Crane of Cora. But it was she who had cause for doubting him. Yet her faith in him is a record of unsoiled devotion. "Are faithfulness, and love, and sweet grateful memories no good? Is it no good that we should keep our silent promises on which others build because they believe in our love and truth?" Cora wrote in her little red manuscript book, while Stephen hid out in Havana and wrote poems about rescuing Lily from her "moated castle" (when he couldn't afford the upkeep of Castle Ravensbrook, nor even the cost of ship passage to get there).

"And I doubt thee / For I am come to where I know your lies as truth / And your truth as lies— / Woe is me." Stephen had no grounds for imputing treachery to Cora, who might well have doubted his fidelity during his nine-month separation from her.

"The 'Intrigue' lot goes to Heinnemann," he wrote Reynolds on October 20 when sending him the batch of love poems from Havana, but Heinemann did not publish *War Is Kind* and probably thought the *Intrigue* poems not in good taste. Only Frederick Stokes in America published them, in *War Is Kind* (1899). Mainly interesting as biography, these poems have been ignored or slighted by Crane's biographers and critics. They are memorable not as poetry but as poetic documents of personal feeling. Crane was at odds with the conventional verse of his age, and that displacement (to quote Amy Lowell) "is at once his plume and his forfeit." He used to amuse himself with the American poems in Stedman's anthology (1900) by cutting them down to the minimum of idea or emotion which they actually contained.

Crane's close friend Harold Frederic had a stroke in August, which a

pecialist diagnosed as embolism of the brain and endocarditis, but he
was skeptical of doctors and stuck it out with cigars and whiskey. A
Christian Scientist practitioner, Mrs. Mills, "nursed" the dying man during
his final week. Not of the faith himself, he assented to her "healing" to
please Kate, who was a Christian Scientist.

Robert Barr visited Frederic a few days before his death. He realized that a serious change had set in. The sick man contended that nothing
could cure him, but Barr implored the aid of Cora, who had tried before
and this time succeeded. "The Christian Scientist was driven out, the
doctors brought in, and also two nurses from Guy's Hospital. But it was
too late, for thirty hours afterward Harold passed quietly away. Those
who know the desperate pain of seeing the dead face of a great leader
and friend will forgive these lame words in which I tell of this cruel
thing. I loved him with his large, tender heart and rough big voice, his
great brain, his vast plans for his own dear country and the Ireland of
his dreams."[8] Said the New York *Times,* whom Harold Frederic served
in London for fourteen years, "he was the most thoroughgoing American
who ever lived in the British Isles."

Cora, although herself deeply troubled by Stephen's silence and by her
financial plight, had taken the Frederic children—Helen, Heléïse and
Barry—into Ravensbrook when their father had his heart attack in August;
after his death she also took in Kate Lyon upon her release on bail from
the court charge of manslaughter. Frederic had willed to Kate and her
children his American copyrights and royalties, and to his legal wife,
Grace, his English copyrights and royalties. But this latter possible source
of revenue "is so heavily mortgaged that it must be some considerable
time before any income, however small, can be looked for from this
direction," said a printed circular distributed by Grace Frederic's friends
and signed by clergymen. Cora wrote them and obtained donations for
Harold's unlawful children, as well.

Conrad wrote Cora on October 28: "We recognize your good heart
in your acts. God forbid that we should throw the first—or even the last
stone. What the world calls scandal does not affect me in the least. My
sincere approval and high recognition of the course you've taken is not
based on Christian grounds. I do not pretend to that name—not from
irreverence but from my exalted idea of that faith's morality. I can't
pretend to such morality but I hold that those that do pretend and boast
of it should carry it out at the cost of personal sacrifice, and in every
respect. My admiration of your courageous conduct exists side by side
with an utter disapproval of those whom you (in your own extremity)
befriend. They invoke the name of a Faith and they've dragged its substance pretty well through the mud. It may be only folly—of course—unutterable folly. But it looks worse. The only Christian in sight in this whole
affair is you, my dear Mrs. Crane—exercising that rarest of the Creed's

virtues: that of Charity." In charity he'd contribute to the Kate Lyon fund except that "the exact truth is I've only £8 in the bank and am in debt to publishers so heavily that I can't go to them for more. Or else I would do it, believe me."

Henry James, who had signed the appeal of the committee for Grace's legitimate children, contributed five pounds then and, months later, fifty pounds to Cora's fund, which Cora and Jack Stokes had instigated for Kate Lyon's children. (Stokes had a high position in the London Post Office and had known the Cranes at Ravensbrook.) Bernard Shaw contributed five pounds and wrote Cora with inappropriate wit: "My impulse is to repudiate all extra orphans with loud execrations. . . . I should simply take them out into the garden and bury them." Henry James said: "Deeper than I can say is my commiseration for those beautiful little children." Garnett much later sent Crane "a week's keep" for the Frederics' children fund: "I'm sorry it's no more." Hall Caine, author of *The Christian* and *Home, Sweet Home,* whom Crane later damned as "Christ on the Mount," wrote Cora: "As I never approved of Mr. Frederic's course in life I do not feel called upon to contribute to the support of his illegitimate children now that he is dead." To the photograph of Hall Caine hanging in Crane's study at Brede Manor, Stephen gave a sneery curl of his thin lips, and Cora said: "God, how I loathe him!" The photograph, which Caine sent Crane, was of "the Master in his Quaker hat and his enveloping cape, the wind of the Channel blowing his Buffalo Bill hair."[9] George Gissing had a common-law wife and thus shared the same social situation as Frederic, H. G. Wells, and Stephen Crane. His sympathy was for Kate Lyon. He wrote Cora: "I feel that everyone who has read with understanding and pleasure any of Frederic's recent work owes to her a vast debt of gratitude, that but for his true companion, his real wife, this work would never have been done. I cannot express the loathing with which I regard any man or woman who speaks slightingly of her. Surely it must be some solace to her to remember that she did play that part in Frederic's life—that she saved him and enabled him to do admirable things. Impossible that she should want for friends, so long as our world does not go quite brash and brainless."[10] Cynic Crane had years ago observed in one of his *Black Riders* poems: "Charity, thou art a lie."

James Creelman of the New York *Journal* in London, who had offered to contribute a couple of pounds to a fund for paying Crane's ship passage back to England, was out of the city when Cora's letter of appeal to contribute to the fund for Kate and her children reached his wife, Alice Creelman. She opened the letter and replied that she had "a great scorn for Kate Lyon and the evil influence she has exerted over a morally weak man." Cora responded (December 30, 1898): "Dear Madam: I thank you for your reply to my letter asking for private subscription for the support of the three youngest children of the late Harold Frederic. In

ustice to their mother, let me say that she refused, absolutely, to join in
a public appeal for help, thinking, as I do, such an appeal in shocking
aste. Nor did she have any knowledge until yesterday when I wrote in-
orming her, of this fund for the children. The people whom you have
heard 'discuss this unfortunate scandal' are, naturally, not the people one
would look to for help in this matter. The nasty taste that such discussion
would leave in their mouths would strike through to the organ which
hey use solely to pump blood—blood soured by lack of true charity—
o the brain. One wonders if they think themselves Christians? And how
hey dare to set themselves up as models of virtuous morality, when they
have the example of Christ's loving kindness to sinners before them. How
can we judge another, we that are so full of sin and weakness? And how
can any creature knowing itself mortal lose an opportunity to be chari-
able in the true sense? Judging not!

"To me, the supreme egotism of women, who never having been
empted, and so knowing nothing of the temptation of another's soul, set
hemselves upon their pedestals of self-conceit and conscious virtue,
udging their unfortunate sisters guilty alike, is the hardest thing in life.
f we women who are beloved and sheltered would help those less fortunate
of our sex to help themselves (and this is not done by using a club or
urning ourselves into shrews under the cover of outraged innocence) the
world would be a sweeter, purer place to live in and we ourselves would
be more worthy of happiness. . . . For those who have no charity I ask
God's mercy; they are so poor a lot! You say you are surprised that I
hould ask anyone to help Miss Lyon with the burden of her children.
My surprise is that people can visit the sins of the parents upon those
nnocent babies. If self-respect can come to mankind in proving their
oathing of sin (and how can we judge the laws of God—by laws of state,
or those of our theological brothers?) by not helping these children to
read and shelter, let them so get what comfort they can . . . with the
knowledge of their own loved ones warm and fed. I have sheltered these
children for five months in my own home and with my own name—and if
all the world line themselves up to fight these babies, I will shelter them
& God will help me ["until such time as their mother can take them,"
cancelled]. . . . I would say it is my wish to board the children with some
very good Catholics in the country."[11]

Mrs. Julia Field-King, on contributing six pounds to the committee
nitiated by Jack Stokes on behalf of Kate Lyon, wrote Cora that Kate
was not a true Christian Scientist. "God's edict is—we must reap what
we sow—then the way out of undesirable reaping is to cease sowing, and
hat is what Christian Science tells us how to do." Had Kate been a true
Christian Scientist she'd not have engaged in "undesirable reaping"—
she'd not have sown at all. One concludes that the Catholics regard illegiti-
nate children more charitably than the Christian Scientists and that Cora

for that very reason intended to board Kate's children with some Catholics.

Frank Harris, a friend of Harold Frederic and editor of the London *Saturday Review,* wrote a fine obituary, but he defaulted on his pledge to pay the legal expenses of the trial of Kate Lyon and Mrs. Mill for manslaughter. Somebody named Lawrence then footed the whole bill and was furious. As Mabel Barr wrote Cora, "How small rich men can be."

The London *Academy* in October reported that Crane was in Havana recovering from yellow fever (Cora said it was yellow fever, but it was malaria), and that on his return he would settle at Brede Place. This was advance publicity on Cora's part; she was addicted to jumping the calendar. Crane had not yet committed himself, and he remained undecided about returning to England as late as the end of November.

"More and more are wealthy Americans settling in this country," said the *Academy*. Crane, far from wealthy, was sitting in the Café Ingleterra one morning "when some of the waiters suddenly crowded toward the door and stared in the plaza. Being interested in what so attracted them, I looked also, and saw a young man in a white duck uniform of the American navy crossing the plaza. It was Lieutenant Marsh of Admiral Sampson's staff. This to the greater part of Havana was the arrival of the American commission. It was an event, of course, but never a spectacle. Havana opinion of the conquerors faded 50 per cent in a single day." The Cubans had expected "a magnificent ceremony of gold lace and cocked hats." The evacuation commission entered Havana on September 10, and then in Paris the American and Spanish commissioners negotiated terms of the peace, while the Cuban insurgents wondered what was to become of them. In " 'You Must!'—'We Can't!' " Crane explains their plight. " 'Are we Americans now? What are we anyhow? When are the Spaniards to be put out? When? When? When?' In polite deadlock, the American commission says 'You must,' while the Spanish commission replies 'We can't. We must wait until we hear from Madrid.' "[12]

Some day, says Crane, we will get over considering these Spaniards as clever. He thought the Spaniards "shockingly stupid. They are of the Mediterranean, that accursed sea in which in modern times bathes only the feet of liars. . . . Catch any Spaniard in a lie—it ωay be a Havana cabman or it may be the redoubtable Weyler—and he fights you off with the unthinkable desperation of a cat in a corner." This is unfair to General Weyler; he had nothing to do with the Cuban situation after he was removed from office in late 1897, when General Blanco replaced him.

The Spaniard's mind "has no knowledge of the tremendous and terrible art of the half truth." As for the Americans, "We're First in War but Not in Peace" said Crane's dispatch to the *Journal* of November 4. He reports instances of drunken American sentries and of promiscuous shootings at night in Santiago on the testimony of Santiago's *La Lucha,* a newspaper which was against us as much as it dared. Havana citizens, said that paper, wondered if they would be subjected to the same irresponsible misbehavior when the American troops occupied the city. These articles "are meant to establish a fear of American rapacity in the minds of the people of Cuba; their intention is thoroughly vindictive." Nevertheless, ill-feeling against Americans would never have occurred," Crane says, "if a certain number of our soldiers could completely understand that whenever they wear the uniform of a United States soldier they carry upon their shoulders the weight of the honor and dignity of their country, and that their responsibility has increased a million fold." He tells of drunken sentries and joyous privates who order drinks in a Santiago café and then "hilariously refuse to pay for them." These yarns stir much apprehension, but so it goes—"man spills some claret down his cuff and the report goes abroad that he has been drowned in a wine vat."

In "Our Sad Need of Diplomats," cabled on November 9, Crane says that Americans "know as much about diplomacy as we do about hatching fighting cocks by holding eggs over a gas jet, but unconsciously and without any virtue of our own, we have in certain places men who perfectly understand the business which, by mandate of Government, they are required to manipulate. These are invariably subordinate officers. The great men, the high-steppers, they come for a time, lean heavily upon the shoulders of the wheel horses and then retire to oblivion or Congress. The wheel horse puts some liniment upon his shoulder and stands then ready to pull the next high-stepper out of a mudhole." Subordinate officers in American diplomatic offices end in some obscure abyss. The great man—the Ambassador or the Minister—goes home "with his very boots full of laurels, but the wheel horse in all probability gets flung into some adjacent abyss without anyone taking trouble to listen whether or not he hits a projecting ledge."

Crane's bias is for the unknown wheel horse, such as James H. Springer, consular agent in the province of Santa Clara, who departed the island just previous to the war, with Fitzhugh Lee of Civil War cavalry fame. Springer at the end of the war is forgotten, sacked. "The young men who were under Springer's consular tutelage before the war are here, officially. Everybody is here but Springer. Springer has no influence. Heaven help Springer. I often think of the fate of White,[13] the first secretary of our Embassy in London. He has pulled Ambassadors through knot holes and up through cracks in the floor until he is prematurely gray, and at last he will be flung out somewhere to die—all same Springer."

"In Havana as It Is To-Day / Stephen Crane Writes of Our New Acquisition" was Crane's last dispatch to the *Journal* (November 12). He tells about his visit with two other correspondents to an insurgent camp outside Havana to see Lieutenant Colonel Jones on General Mario García Menocal's staff. The livery people who transported them charged fabulous sums, so he couldn't afford to get there alone. Jones—an American—had served three years in the Cuban army as an artilleryman, and as artillery-men in that army were as scarce as the guns themselves he was promoted steadily by General Maximo Gómez "until he has now reached a position second to no artillery officer in the Cuban service. We had some money for Jones; we had some tobacco for Jones. We expected a welcome. Did we get it? We did. We got one of those open-armed, splendid welcomes which are written for the coming of dukes. . . . We could see him breathe in the outright Americanism as if it were some perfume wafted from the folds of the flag and we were not too noble representatives, either."[14]

Crane found the horseflesh in Cuba in bad condition, "but no worse than the Spanish mounts. They were all old, unmatched little beasts, with an infinite variety of accoutrement ranging from ragged and war-worn saddles with the padding leaking out to dazzling tan equipments from the best Havana saddlers, the latter being gifts of joyful friends since the pause in the conflict. In fact, the donations of Havana were everywhere plain. The officer of the day, for instance, wore a gorgeous crimson sash embroidered in white. "The beloved, the sweetheart, has again entered the life of the lonely insurgent." Crane sets in contrast the pitiful sight of the *reconcentrados* hanging around the camp: "Miserable women and babes, ragged, dirty, diseased, more than half famished. They are in desperate straits. Such, indeed, is the condition that a gift of a little bread sometimes brings the virtue of women to the feet of the philanthropist."

Later, in London, a friend asked him about the future of Cuba: " 'That is a large question to ask a small man,' he replied. 'The island has passed through practically thirteen years of continuous war. A very small war can destroy a very enormous commerce. Outside the American garrison the island now contains about one-fifth of the normal population. But its industries of tobacco, sugar, and ore are vast in possibility, and must exert an influence upon the shifting masses who are always searching for work. The New Government will develop Cuba in a way of which the oldest Cubans could not dream. No one wants to speak of the Americans as an immaculate race; but I feel sure that my own people stand well in honesty with the rest of the world—else they would not accuse themselves so vio-lently and continually. . . . I think it can fairly be said that nations move without regard for either pledges or men; but the word that "Cuba shall be free" has so freely been given through every city and village of the United States that I am confident it will be kept. I am sure that it has become almost a national creed that we shall do as we declared in the beginning. And now the sore part,' resumed Mr. Crane. 'The Cubans have not behaved well in the most prominent cases. And this makes the common American soldier very angry. And the common soldier is the common American man. The Cubans say, "We took San Juan Hill." Any of us who were there know that there were no Cubans present within any other range than spent-shell range. The common American soldier, having died to some extent in Cuba, does not like these statements. Moreover, when he was in a hurry, the Cuban back of the firing line stole his blanket-roll and his coat, and maybe his hat.' "

Cora wrote to Reynolds (November 9, 1898): "I understand that Mr. Crane is wanted to do some work here, and that the *Saturday Review* has cabled to him and offered him money to return to England (£50). I *know* that a friend has written him and that the letter should reach him not later than the 11th of this month, offering to cable him enough money to get home if he needs it. It is the opinion of all the men who know, that Stephen's future is in England. No matter what he writes, there is always favorable notices in every English paper. He has a great vogue here and now he must return if he is ever going to do more great work. A man must have pure wholesome air if he wishes to succeed in art. I beg you will advise Mr. Crane to return to England. He has a great future and a wonderful home awaiting him. I will write to the people who have written about stories and tell them you have stories of Mr. Crane's. . . . P.S. I will be glad of any news of Mr. Crane." Cora had had no news of Stephen since his noncommittal cablegram of October 10. The London *Saturday Review*'s offer of fifty pounds was an advance against some future article, but he was too trapped by other commitments to accept it.

On the same day Cora was writing Reynolds, Stephen was cabling William, who reported to Reynolds on the 10th that Stephen "telegraphs me from Havana to loan him some money and asks me to notify you. Can you tell me what the urgency is or whatever you may have to do with it? I shall be greatly obliged. I have written him at Havana, but my letters were returned uncalled for. Do you know his city address there?" That Stephen asked William to notify Reynolds and to send the money to him indicates that he had overdrawn his Reynolds account and couldn't get out of Cuba without borrowing from his brother. He did not reveal to William his Havana address, and he did not write Cora that he intended to return to Manhattan.

What shook him into deciding to quit Havana was an urgent letter from Conrad, also the embarrassment of General Wade's reprimanding him for having caused so much trouble by not communicating with his family, and his own recognition that he had exhausted his "bank account" of personal experience about Cuba. If he had nothing more of consequence for *Journal* sketches, he could not possibly spend the winter in Havana—which is what he might have done had he not been broke. And then a miraculous thing happened. Jack Stokes, who had cabled on November 11 an urgent appeal, repeated his message on the 14th, with an added note this time: "Money shortly through General Wade." He was sending an advance from Heinemann of £50, which was enough to get Crane to

Manhattan. Stokes sent the money to General Wade, not to Crane himself, and on November 17 Stephen cabled Stokes through Thomas Cook & Son that he had sailed that day for Manhattan. He arrived in New York on the 21st, on the steamship *Vigiliancia.*

He dined in the city on several occasions with music critic James Gibbons Huneker at the Everett House or in some German restaurant "where talk might be unbridled and the frothing outpour of Huneker's conversation need not shock ladies." On November 23 they had cocktails at Delmonico's bar. After they left, Richard Harding Davis, who had ordered dinner for himself in a quiet corner, overheard a noisy argument going on at the bar about Stephen Crane. Davis went over to the bar, where he confronted a group arguing whether it was true that Crane had tried to kill himself in Cuba.

Why should a famous young writer try to kill himself? Said Thomas McCumber: Crane was dying of nameless and disgusting diseases, and that was why he tried to get himself killed by a Spanish bullet. McCumber, a photographer, had joined the bar talk uninvited, and some newspaper reporter disputed him. There were men coming in for dinner who stopped to listen, and Davis tried to silence the gigantic photographer who wanted to use his fists on the reporter. McCumber repeated his indictment of Crane, towering in defiance before Davis in evening dress, and an alarmed waiter pulled at his coat. The anonymous reporter, a smaller man, was suppressed by force until Davis "towed the big gossip out of the place and came back with his customary dignity and a cut lip to ask such men as he knew to forget the affair."

Crane, we may remember, had no liking for McCumber, and he and Huneker had probably quit Delmonico's bar when they spotted him there. McCumber, who died of paresis in 1904, had eight years earlier spread the malicious gossip that Crane took morphine. Ripley Hitchcock had diplomatically asked Crane his views on the taking of drugs, and he plainly did not approve of such habits. His liberalism (to quote Beer) "had certain inset features. The ordinary prejudices of formal codes simply washed down from his mind, but drug-taking was a habit of fools, and he had seen the dreary end of it on the East Side. A man of sense would not take drugs, and two years later he repeated the opinion to James Huneker"—at Delmonico's bar, before McCumber took over.

From the Everett House's dining room Crane and Huneker looked out on Union Square and talked about literature. Crane asked him if he had read anything of Joseph Conrad, a Polish sea captain who was writing the most wonderful things in English. That was the first time Huneker had heard of Conrad, but some years later he went to England mainly to meet his favorite contemporary novelist and talked with him for three hours at Conrad's farmhouse in Kent (in October, 1912). He found him "just a simple-mannered gentleman, whose welcome was sincere, whose glance was veiled, at times far away, whose ways were French, Polish, anything but 'literary,' 'bluff' or English."

Huneker, who was thirty-eight in November, 1898, and eleven years older than Crane, shared an interest in paintings and at one bar or another they competed in explosions of adjectives as though while talking in words they were painting in oils. The charm of Crane's talk, said Huneker, "defies description. It was all adjectives and adverbs. He spoke of his friend Conrad as the devout speak of the B. V. M. [the Blessed Virgin Mary]. Harold Frederic's case was dragging through the papers still and the bourgeois in Park Row used to bore Crane about it a good deal. He was a great individualist and he resented the twaddle about suicide intensely as he knew that Frederic could not have recovered anyhow. I saw him last about Christmas time."[15] Except for paintings and music, Crane and Huneker had little in common as the older man was almost ignorant of Crane's writings and did not know much about literature, although he later wrote two volumes of short stories. In the *Musical Courier,* where he conducted his potpourri column (1887 to 1902) he makes no mention of Crane's works and in his obituary notice there in 1900 he simply says that Crane "was a good fellow and a promising writer."

He very likely kidded Stephen about the parody of his Cuban War dispatches he had published in the *Musical Courier* on August 3,[16] and told him that he was referred to as an illiterate writer in Vance Thompson's unsigned *Courier* column. "An illiterate writer describes illiterate people in their own and his own locutions—the result is realistic literature of an excellent sort [as in *Maggie*] . . . . Mr. Crane and his fearful partners in fiction are the forerunners of the great writers to come." Although Crane was not erudite, he knew much more about literature—and painting and music—than Vance Thompson gave him credit for.

Huneker rightly surmises that "there must have been people who hated the boy monumentally. Three or four times when he had been spending the whole evening with Ryder [the American painter] and myself I would be told in the morning how drunk and disorderly he had been the night before by men who had not seen him. For a mild and melancholy kid he certainly had fallen completely into the garbage can of gossip." Crane's picturesque person and reputation provoked the gossip-mongers into turning "a little Flaubert into a big Verlaine."

Not yet decided whether he cared to return to England, Stephen wrote Mrs. William Sonntag on November 28: "I am very anxious to have Mrs. Crane come to this country. Mrs. Crane is very anxious to have me come back to England. We are carrying on a duel at long range, with ink. How do you persuade anybody to do anything by cables and letters?" They had been dueling for about two weeks, probably since the 14th, when the money for ship passage reached him in Havana. He entertained a notion of settling in Texas; meanwhile he was hunting for a house in New York

City. And then the same day he sent Mrs. William Sonntag his note about trying to induce Cora in England to return to America, he went to the theater with her and was almost arrested by a policeman. It was this unhappy entanglement with the police that decided him to return to Cora and England.

Mrs. Sonntag, her seventeen-year-old son Henry, his cousin the Reverend Patrick Hart, and Crane were leaving a theater, when someone in the lobby called: "Oh, there's Stephen Crane!" He attracted a good deal of attention, and two or three men spoke to him, Acton Davies perhaps one. Suddenly a policeman "shoved through the people, asked if his name was Stephen Crane and then said, 'Come 'round to the station, you drunken bum!'" Mrs. Sonntag, white-haired at forty-three and a cripple using crutches, spoke up in her lisp, and the policeman yelled at her: "That will be enough from you, you goddam French whore!" Crane's friends tried to intervene, while he stood silently by. Then the priest stepped forward, and at sight of the priest's costume the policeman mumbled something apologetic and fled. The newspapers did not report the incident, but young Henry Sonntag was asked about it at school.

Someone at the Jefferson Market Police Court had sent out word that Crane was back in the city and "to get" him booked on one pretense or another—probably Charles Becker, who had arrested Dora Clark in Crane's presence two years ago. Becker's grudge simmered, and decades after Crane's death senior detectives hated his memory, as indeed did some newspapermen who had worked with Crane. Their bias was felt by A. J. Liebling at the time that he became a reporter. Crane's having intervened publicly in favor of some street girls who were being shaken down by plainclothesmen "marked him indelibly, in the copy mind, as one subversive of public order."

And thus it was that Crane decided to quit New York and "to stay in England for some time. It seems that in New York, outside the immediate circle of men who know me well, I am some kind of Simon Legree who goes around knocking women into the gutter and then walking on them. If I was a grocery boy or a hired man or a bank clerk no one would give a cuss what I did. But I am a writer; so all bets are doubled." The committee on admissions to one of the most eminent literary clubs had notified William Dean Howells that the proposal of Crane's name for membership would not be acted upon favorably. Howells gave a luncheon for him at Delmonico's with the grandees of criticism assembled (to quote Beer), but it was a failure because Crane, exhausted by the Cuban War, sat silently turning the stem of a wineglass, and then at Howells' that afternoon he fell asleep on a couch. He thought of himself now as an old man, and elderly Howells was amused by his references to "my youth" and "when I was young."

He ate nothing at that luncheon because he was ill. Louis Senger later wrote Hamlin Garland: "I saw him only once after the Cuban War. He was sick and joked mirthlessly that they had not got him yet. You know that he was essentially a soldier. He would have elected to die in battle rather than wait for the slower death of which I believe he had a prophetic knowledge."

Ill and listless, he slept endlessly and put off necessary visits to see his agent Reynolds and his publisher Frederic Stokes. He was making excursions to the city from Edmund's house on the pond in the Hartwood forests via the single-track railroad to Port Jervis. He had no place in Manhattan to bum a bed as most of his friends were gone: Corwin Linson was in Palestine, John Willard Raught was no longer in Linson's studio, Hamlin Garland was in the West.

Sometime in early December[17] he went to Washington, D.C., presumably in hope of seeing Lily Brandon again, although her affair with him had terminated when last they saw each other in April. While there he again mingled with Congressmen and watched Congress from its gallery. To quote Beer, "he was presented to some Senator who told him gravely about the failures of the war and the discomforts undergone by a nephew in the Rough Riders. 'I understand now, that Congressmen and Senators all rolled in august pain by night and sat weeping by day over our lot,' said Crane. 'This warhorse told me so. He told me that he visited the War Department hourly on July First. I asked him what good that did and he said it showed his interest in the campaign. Nobody would believe in him. I can't believe in him but it is true that I saw him.' "

The story told him by that Senator became "The Second Generation," Crane's story of the Senator's son who by political influence obtains the post of commissary officer in Reilly's brigade, lands at Siboney, and at San Juan is exposed as a coward for not sharing his canteen with wounded men needing water. His father later tells him: "I guess you are no damned good."

Whether or not he got to see Lily, her destiny was not his, and on December 20 he cabled Cora that he was returning. Since his arrival from Havana he had lingered an entire month, not in any hurry apparently to rejoin Cora.

She had finally won the "duel at long range, with ink," and Conrad on December 4 responded to her good news, or rather her anticipations of Stephen's not yet declared intentions: "Do you think Stephen will be in England before Christmas?" *Blackwood's Edinburgh Magazine* had just published "The Price of the Harness," and Conrad wrote Cora that it was magnificent. "It is the very best thing he has done since the *Red Badge*— and it has even something that the *Red Badge* has not—or not so much of. He is maturing. He is expanding. There is more breadth and somehow more substance in this war-picture. . . . It is Stephen all himself—and a little more. It is the very truth of art. There is an added ampleness in his method which makes me augur a magnificent future for his coming work. Let him only come—and work!" Conrad's genuine admiration for that story, although it is by no means the best thing Crane had written since *The Red Badge,* comforted Cora. He repeated the same praise to Blackwood on the 13th. "The man will develop. I find this story broader, gentler, less tricky and just as individual as the best of his work. It is the best bit of work he has done since the Red Badge." And again to Meldrum he said the same thing on the 21st: "I think the *Harness* is first rate. . . . Several men wrote to me about it in almost the same terms."

Conrad wrote Cora a Christmas note on December 23: "I wish you could have given us some news from Stephen. Well, please God you will have your mind and your heart at rest soon. I need not tell you it is the fervent wish of those who live here and however ineffectually, but none the less sincerely take part in your anxieties and hopes. May the Xmas be a season of joy indeed and the new year a year of peace to you. Amen . . . Let us share in all that befalls you as you have done me the honor to allow me heretofore. I am dear Mrs. Crane your faithful friend and servant / Jph Conrad." But Crane sent Cora no New Year's greeting. Pawling of Heinemann wrote her on January 2: "I thought he would be home by now, as the money from Heinemann was sent some weeks ago." And Conrad that same day wrote Meldrum: "Mrs. Crane still without news. I don't know what to think."

Huneker's "I saw him last about Christmas time," suggests that Crane quit the city for the holiday week at Edmund's house. At the end of December Edmund took train with Stephen to New York to catch the *Manitou,* which sailed for England on December 31. Crane had neglected to tell Cora, and she had been so embarrassed by his disregard for her that she lied to Garnett when writing him in early January: "From the Cooks tourist people, I learn that Stephen starts from Havana this week." She knew, of course, that he was lingering in New York, but his hiding out in New York was too much of a personal wound for her not to conceal the truth from Garnett. She had written Moreton Frewen on Christmas Day: "The horror of the last few months is almost at an end. Mr. Crane is in New York settling up some business affairs, but sails next Saturday [December 31]." Then, on January 10, she wrote Garnett that she would meet Stephen at Gravesend "if I have time." Gravesend is that sea reach of the Thames at London, and the ominous connotations of that name are played upon in Conrad's "Heart of Darkness," the opening scene of which Conrad wrote just prior to Crane's arrival on January 11 (1899). One end of Crane's journey was Hartwood; the other, physically and financially, was Gravesend.

# XXVI

## ⊂ *Brede Manor*

"I AM, at every moment, expecting a wire saying that the ship which carries my dear one is sighted," Cora wrote in her letter to Garnett. "The 'Manitou,' she is due today or tomorrow morning and I shall, if I have time, go to Gravesend to meet Stephen. I am so hoping bad weather has not detained the ship." The *Manitou* by luck missed a gale across the English Channel by a week and made port just a day before another violent storm ripped across England, washing out railroad tracks and halting Channel traffic. The ship reached Gravesend on the 11th.

Stephen returned with Cora to Ravensbrook, and on the 13th he sent Joseph Conrad two telegrams, repaying him 50 guineas in one and mentioning in the other Garnett's *Academy* appraisal. It was the first thing he read after settling down at Ravensbrook.

Garnett's "Mr. Stephen Crane: An Appreciation" was the best critical study published during Crane's lifetime. He had sent Cora a copy, remarking that there were things in it she would like and things she wouldn't. He felt that Crane had reached his creative limits, but of course Cora shared Conrad's conviction of a magnificent literary future for Stephen. "Mr. Crane's technique is far superior to Mr. Kipling's," wrote Garnett, "but he does not experiment ambitiously in various styles and develop in new directions as Mr. Kipling has done. I do not think that Mr. Crane will or can develop further." Two decades later he concluded that "the dice of fate were loaded by all his circumstances against his development as a craftsman. . . . He had written his best things without advice or encouragement, urged by the demon within him, and his genius burned clear, with its passionate individuality, defying all the inhibitions and conventions of New England."[1]

Conrad, on the 13th, wrote from Pent Farm: "My dear Stephen—I am more glad than I can say to hear that you are here at last. You haven't lost time in looking up the old *Academy*. I only heard of it today. Thanks very much for your second wire. All this would be damnable bosh but for the 50 gs. which just save me from battering my head against the walls. I long to hear your news. . . . I feel a new man since this morning's wire.

*443*

It was good of you to think of me at once. I intended to wire myself today inquiring. Well, that's all over now. I mean where to locate you when I think of you—which is often—very. I've been nearly dead and several times quite mad since you left. This is no joke, it is the sober truth. I haven't been able to write and felt like cutting my throat. Not a ghost of a notion in my head, not a sentence under the pen. Well. Never mind. It's a little better now. What have you got in *your head?* You must be full of stuff. I suppose the 'Dead Man' ["The Upturned Face"] story will have to wait till you unload your new experience. I know whatever it is it will be *good.* It will be great! You think I might have given a whole sheet of paper for your welcome, but may I be shot if I can find another piece. I am coming to see you directly I finish a rotten thing I am writing for B'wood [*Blackwood's Magazine*]. It *is* rotten—and I can't help it. All I write is rotten now. I am pretty well decayed myself. I ought to be taken out and flung into a dusthole—along with the dead cats—by heavens! Well. Enough. I don't want to bore you into a faint in your first week in merry England." Conrad characteristically belittles his own work, while praising Crane's; what he calls his rotten thing—"Heart of Darkness"—is of course incomparably superior to Crane's "The Price of the Harness," which Conrad in this same letter rated above *The Red Badge:* "There is a mellowness in the vigour of that story that simply delighted me."

No sooner had Crane landed in England than creditors leaped at him with summonses. He owed one year's rent at Ravensbrook and long-standing debts to the Oxted butcher, grocer and dairy. He was threatened with bankruptcy and a three-cornered correspondence soon began between the Cranes, London literary agent James B. Pinker, and solicitor Alfred T. Plant. More than four decades after Stephen's death a solicitor's firm in Surrey, Nightingale & Nightingale, still maintained a file on his debts: overdrawn bank accounts, dishonored drafts, and tradesmen's pleas for remittances.[2]

He had more reason than Conrad to think of himself as "pretty well decayed"; he was ill again from malaria. David Meldrum wrote William Blackwood on February 2 that Crane had arrived in England a fortnight before and had written him the next day, "and I had expected him to call about the beginning of this month, but from what Conrad tells me [I] fear that he is still too ill to do so. I enclose the personal letter I had from him, so that you may understand his wishes, and I should be glad to know from you how you stand with him—that is to say, how much of the £50 advanced him was wiped out by the story [which had] appeared in Maga [*Blackwood's Edinburgh Magazine*]. I never doubted we could get material from him to make up the account, and now that he is home it is certain. The present story ["Clan of No Name"], though good, does not strike me as so good as the "Price of the Harness," of which, I know, I had possibly too high an opinion however. In any case, it would be well to know how much is still due to you by Crane, so that Pinker (his agent now) may give me the selection of his best to wipe off the score."

Crane had written Pinker on February 1: "Of course, you will understand . . . our affairs at this time are in a woeful condition." Three days later he wrote to Pinker again, explaining his difficulty in paying off the debt to Blackwood: "The idea of writing stories for the purpose of getting them buried forever in Scotland makes me very unhappy. Please tell Meldrum that I am unwell so that he won't be indignant because I haven't come to see him. . . . 'God Rest Ye, Merry Gentlemen' is coming on finely. If you conclude that 'The Angel Child' is not a good opening gun, bury it in the heather i.e. send it to Blackwood. The next story will be a better one." He couldn't afford to send Blackwood one of his better stories, and he wasn't sure that "The Angel Child" was good enough for his first shot at the English market. Actually, it is one of his best *Whilomville Stories*. He had sent it to Reynolds along with "Lynch Hunting," and they appeared in *Harper's Magazine* in August and September, 1899.

He went back to London to interview Dominick, the London representative of Frederick A. Stokes & Company, and returned to Ravensbrook exhausted. He owed Whiteley's Department Store £98 9s, part of which was for the unpaid balance on the purchase of a piano in 1897. Morrisons & Nightingale (as the firm was then known) were solicitors for the store, and Crane assured them that he would pay his debt. "Dominick says that he will have no hesitation in giving the Solicitors to understand that Stokes and Co. will come to my assistance to some extent at least," he wrote Pinker. Dominick "wishes me to write a letter (which is to remain in your hands) setting forth an acknowledgement of a little temporary mortgage upon the royalties of my four Appleton books vis: *The Red Badge of Courage, The Little Regiment, Maggie,* and *The Third Violet,* the royalties being at fifteen per cent and free of all claims."

On February 9, he wrote Pinker: "Morrison and Nightingale have been seen and they expressed themselves willing to stand off the rent *if* you will give them a guarantee that the rent will be payed, time not specified. They said: 'If Mr. Crane's money for *ms.* comes through Mr. Pinker's hands of course Mr. Pinker will be willing to guarantee the amount of the rent.' " Maybe so, but Crane had already mortgaged his royalties on the four Appleton books according to Dominick's plan; hence, Morrisons & Nightingale were cut off from that income. "Of course I don't want to let you in for any strange game but this seems to me to be my *only* way clear. Really your position would be simply that of a buffer-state. I hesitate to ask you to do it but there is absolutely no other way. If you think you can stand it do so and God be with you. This will enable me to move almost at once to Brede and get a fair chance at myself. Morrison[s] and Nightingale are an old fashioned English firm of solicitors and they require of me that you write to them first. This is an added indignity but I hope you will see your way clear to do it and to make your letter to them very strong. Answer me, if you can, by the first post."

Although still at Ravensbrook, Stephen used newly printed stationery headed *Brede Place, Brede, Northiam, Sussex, England;* but not when writing Pinker, only when corresponding with those he wished to impress. Extravagant Cora couldn't afford the fancy, embossed stationery, but then neither could she afford Brede Manor, or the three hundred choice roses she had planted at the entrance grounds so as to impress Stephen on his first sight of the ancient manor. Obsessed with a desire for respectability, she wrote Charles Woodruff Woolley, an elderly genealogist at Buffalo, in the hope that he might trace the ancestral Stephen Crane of pre-Revolutionary stock back to some remote Surrey baronetcy. Woolley replied that he was not interested in royal blood, coats of arms, crests and quarterings; nor did he believe that "our Stephen Crane was a descendant of Sir George Carteret." (No connection exists.)

Cora had intended to show off Brede Manor to Stephen the week he arrived in England, but they did not get there until the next week when he suddenly decided on Tuesday afternoon (January 17) to see it. Well-informed about the history of the baronial manor house, Cora conducted Stephen from room to room and he fell as much in love with the place as she. The realist and cynic shared what Ford Hueffer called Cora's "amiable romanticism." Stephen felt that he could utilize the fabulous house for future fiction, which he did in "The Squire's Madness" and in *The O'Ruddy.* He also saw—through Cora's eyes—the prospect of Brede Manor providing them social status, which was especially important to her.

They had taken the train to Hastings, and then, wrote Cora, "we drove out and of course it was very dark—Stephen was mad over the place. We tramped, later, after a supper of ham & eggs beside the kitchen fire—to a cottage in the village and put up for the night there." (Brede village is about 1 1/2 miles from Brede Place, or Brede Manor.) After visiting Brede Place the next day, they returned to Ravensbrook, and on the 19th Cora wrote Edward Garnett: "We are going to move Heaven and Earth to get there. Stephen said that a solemn feeling of work came to him there; so I am delighted. Come see us soon." She was, in effect, thanking him for having proposed Brede Place. Architect Cowlishan (brother-in-law of Constance Garnett), who advised on repairs to the manor before the Cranes moved in (and again in 1900), spoke of it as "lyric" in its architecture.

One of the greatest treasures of Sussex, Brede Manor stands halfway up a steep incline, and eerie is the windswept, damp valley below it. When William the Conqueror landed at Hastings in 1066, he could rely on Brede as a Norman foothold through his alliance with Emma, the Lady of Fecamp. "Without Brede, William might not have landed, might perhaps never have ventured. But he could count on these few square miles, a convenient bridgehead."[3] It was an outpost of Normandy for 363 years and was referred to by King Canute in a charter dated 1017. Brede village is approached by one of the loveliest lanes in Sussex with high hedges on either side and overshadowed by ancient oaks. Some parts of the roads to Brede Place give the impression that they have hardly changed since the days when the Oxenbridges, arrayed in armor, rode them. At the bottom of a steep hill one crosses Groaning Bridge, and a long narrow road through the park brings one suddenly in view of the Manor.

"It's a pretty fine affair," Stephen wrote Sanford Bennett before moving from Ravensbrook. "Cora believes that Sir Walter Scott designed it for her. One wing of the manor was begun in 1378 and somebody kidded it with heavy artillery in Cromwell's time. We shall move in as soon as we can. I enclose 10 pounds. Do I owe you more than that?" (Crane was paying off loans that had aided him in getting to Cuba.)

The front door of Brede Manor, as Crane describes it in his Irish romance *The O'Ruddy,* was of iron-studded oak set into a stone arch of Gothic design; it looked like "the Gothic entrance of a church." The steps leading to the so-called porch were steep and irregular, worn by age, and the stone supports had carved heads and emblems worked upon them. A second stairway brought Stephen and Cora to the inner entrance, a massive oak door made for defense, which opened into the spacious antechamber. At the summit of that second stairway, inscribed on stonework at the left-hand jamb of the doorway, was the name "John Oxenbregg," probably the brother of the famous Sir Goddard Oxenbridge, and near it in very ancient characters "Mychell Hyll 1489."[4] From the antechamber a great room extended the whole length of the house. The walls were paneled in oak, and the stone over-mantel carved with a Tudor rose and fleur de lys. On the east side the windows gave a view of the sloping gardens, and on the west the trackway down to the stream below.

At an early date a chapel had been added to the manor house at its most southerly end, and its cinquefoil windows suggested the medieval and ecclesiastical. With the addition built by Sir Goddard in Queen Elizabeth's time the ground plan of the house took the form of an E in honor of the Queen, as was customary in buildings of her reign. The little room over the porch in the E, Stephen made his study, writing incessantly like a spider giving its entrails to nourish a wilderness of parasites, as Ford Hueffer says.

Before quitting Ravensbrook, Crane on February 7 sent Mrs. Moreton Frewen an inscribed copy of *The Open Boat and Other Stories:* "You, with the rest of the world, have herein a further proof of my basic incapacity. However there are some stories of Americans and some stories of America in the book which may remind you of somebody better but, in any case, allow me to present my esteem." By "somebody better" he probably had in mind Ambrose Bierce and Bret Harte, whom Mrs. Frewen might have met, since they had both lived for a time in London. Crane's Western story "The Five White Mice" is reminiscent of Bret Harte, and the melodramatic Bierce is echoed in the macabre situation of the war tale "Death and the Child." But neither Bret Harte nor Ambrose Bierce could have written "The Bride Comes to Yellow Sky" or "The Open Boat," two of Crane's masterpieces of fiction. As she had been brought up in New York, Mrs. Frewen may well have liked the "Midnight Sketches," which were included in Heinemann's edition of *The Open Boat,* but not in the American edition.

In his inscription, Crane assumed a humble guise. Not so humble was his letter to the Reverend Charles J. Little, written the previous day on Cora's new Brede Manor stationery. Now President of the Garrett Bible Institute, Dr. Little had been professor of history and logic at Syracuse University when Stephen was there in the spring of 1891. Crane wanted his former professor to know that he had arrived as a literary figure and had attained social respectability. He confesses that at Syracuse "I had not the ability to impress myself upon you through my mental endowments, but I remember your telling me once that I impressed myself upon you through a resemblance to 'John' whom you knew when you were at Dickinson College." He remembers that the Reverend Dr. Little had called him to his desk after an examination on the French Revolution and told him to beware—"that I was going very wrong indeed. It has stuck in my mind for years that some of the information you had received of me was quite false. Candidly, I was worse than I should have been, but I always had a singular faculty of having it said that I was engaged in crimes which are not of my accomplishment. Indeed, this singular faculty has followed me out of college into real life. I am not one of the foolish ones who would say to you that your talk to me directed or changed my life, but I *would* say to you that I remember with so much gratitude the words you spoke; they have been to me so much of a strength in life that my first fear is that amid your interest in the hundreds of students who year by year pass under your eye, you have totally forgotten your one-time interest in me." As to his literary career: "It is a little thing to talk about, but I have written several little books which have editions in New York, London, Paris, Leipzig, Vienna and in the English colonies."[5] Crane hopes that Dr. Little "will remember the lad who resembled 'John'."

Dr. Little, replying on the 23rd, says that Stephen had reminded him of "John" because he, too, was "a young Apollo, lithe, vigorous, handsome," a clever lad, but too eager "to tread the floors of hell." He had feared that Crane's "potencies of various kinds" might end "in blight as 'John' did. The ruin of 'John' that you recall to me is still a poignant recollection; I should be glad to be quit of all responsibility for it. We teachers,

I fear, handle life rather carelessly, and 'John's' blood has not yet ceased crying from the ground. Well! I am glad you have kept to the highway. There are so many cross-cuts to hell that I wonder always when a full-blooded adventurous lad gets safely established on the main road."

In anticipation of the Cranes' departure, Mrs. Edward Pease, their neighbor at Limpsfield, sent Cora the gift of a warming pan, and Cora reciprocated by sending her two manuscripts belonging to Stephen's projected *Whilomville Stories:* "The Angel Child" and "The Lover and the Telltale." Young Michael Pease (age eleven) was infatuated with Helen (age seven), daughter of Grace Frederic, and Cora mistakenly assumed that their romance inspired Crane's stories. She wrote Mrs. Pease: "I was going to send you by tonight's post the enclosed Ms. of a little story that comes before Michael's 'story.' I thought you would like them both. You can see that Michael for the moment is 'Jimmie' and he writes to 'The Angel Child.' Tell him, I shall ask him to bring the pigeons down to Brede. This is to be our P. O. address—but you must run in as you're going by— and give us a chance of seeing you once again before we go." Michael Pease, decades later, disputed the identification: "I'm afraid the story of the Tell Tale, the fight, and the School Mistress was Stephen Crane's romance—or rather, I should say the hero was not me."[6] Jimmie Trescott was Stephen Crane in his Port Jervis boyhood, and little Cora was Cora Crane.

Stephen and Cora moved from Ravensbrook on Sunday, February 12, proceeding by train to Hastings, and then nine miles by carriage. The railway station nearest to Brede Place, as Crane describes it in "The Squire's Madness," was a mere wayside halt well-concealed by "hop-fields and sheep-pastures." In the welcoming party was Ford Madox Hueffer. Frederic's children—Barry and Heloïse—had been sent ahead with their governess, Mrs. Burke, and they were playing near the house when the Cranes and Hueffer arrived there by carriage from Hastings.

Cora wrote Mrs. Pease the day after their arrival: "This is just a line to say we are here. We came yesterday with the dogs and are camping out until our things arrive. It is very jolly and we are happy. The children were so very glad to see us. They look better already." She regretted being cut off from the Peases, "but we shan't lose you altogether; you will write to us and you will come often to visit us." But they visited the Cranes only once.

One part of the ancient beams in the manor was formed exactly like a gallows, as the poet Coventry Patmore had pointed out to some friends in 1897. It had a great iron hook in it, and Patmore said: "That's where the old lord used to hang his vassals." Two or three years later Patmore, who lived at nearby Hastings, revisited Brede Manor when the Cranes were there, and the butler, having forgotten Patmore's previous visit, "showed the beam to the party, repeating my own words as authentic history, and

I am told that the place is never shown now without the relation of this tradition."

When Curtis Brown came down from London to visit the Cranes (he was now a London literary agent) Stephen gave a turn of the screw to Patmore's story. He pointed to a crane projecting high up from the wall of the great two-storied kitchen and claimed that a certain unpleasant tenant used to hang from that crane such cooks as had not prepared food to his liking. There had been two or three unfortunate women ghosts in that left wing part of the house, but Brown did not meet them.

When an English friend arrived at the Rye railway station at nightfall of a dull November day, Crane met him and drove his high-mettled horses through the dripping Sussex lane at breakneck speed and in utter darkness. As they came through a large park the house loomed up before them, an enormous stone structure with only faint glimmering lights in a few of the windows. A kind of ancient and decayed servingman opened the door, holding a flickering candle. Within, the huge stone-vaulted rooms were mostly quite bare and dark. In a few of them the occupants seemed to have camped, putting in a little simple furniture and making cheer with an open fire and a few candles. The visitor that night was to sleep in the "priest's chamber," a great room with a tiny oratory and a writing closet opening from it. He said nothing about believing in ghosts, but he declared that such an unearthly patter and rattle and moaning went on in his bedchamber that night that he never slept a moment, but lay shivering in nervous agitation. The visitor was not a man given to nervous fears, but he remembered the occasion as the most curious experience of his life. A well-known cricketer, he was probably the writer Edwin Pugh, whom we shall meet again.[7]

Another visitor, the novelist A. E. W. Mason, slept in a room enclosed by two doors which he was not warned to leave unopened. He opened them in the dark and "found that if I had taken one step forward I should have stepped down about thirty feet into the chapel, this being the private pew or box of the owners of the house. We had, I remember, rushes on the floor instead of carpets, and there were other disadvantages which meant nothing to us, for we were all of us young." Bats flew about the ceiling until Mason put out the candle, and then they settled down to share the room with him. Other disadvantages included the lack of toilets, and so visiting gentlemen relieved themselves outside in the shrubbery. There was no plumbing, no gas or electricity, no way of heating the house except by fireplaces; wood and water had to be fetched by servants. In *The O'Ruddy*, one of O'Ruddy's men on entering the house falls through a trapdoor whose rusty bolts had broken, and he is let down into a dungeon that has no other entrance.

"Indeed this was a queer house entirely," Crane writes in that novel, "with many odd nooks and corners about it besides the disadvantage of

Sir Goddard Oxenbridge tramping through the rooms in two sections." He adds that many a good cask of brandy had gone down that trapdoor, and in fact Brede Place because of its lonely location was used by smugglers in the eighteenth century as their hideout for kegs of spirits and parcels of lace and silk. Legend has it that these smugglers gained access through an underground passage, the entrance being located in the valley below. Crane in jest locates its opening near the parish church in Brede village. In 1826 a bricklayer, working in the cellars of Brede Place, discovered a secret hiding place which had evidently been used for smuggled goods. He found there an ancient gold cross, which is still in the possession of the Frewen family.

In the parish church there is the altar tomb of Sir Goddard with a full-length figure of him as a knight in plate armor. His head rests on a helmet, and his feet on a lion; his hands are folded in prayer.[8] In *The O'Ruddy* Crane recreates the legends about him. A caretaker tells O'Ruddy: "Bullets wouldn't harm him, nor steel cut him, so they sawed him in two with a wooden saw down by the bridge in front. He was a witch of the very worst kind, your honour. You hear him groaning at the bridge every night, and sometimes he walks through the house himself in two halves, and then everybody leaves the place. And that is our most serious danger, your honour. When Sir Goddard takes to groaning through these rooms at night, you'll not get a man to stay with you, sir; but as he comes up from the pit by the will of the Devil we expect his Reverence to ward him off." And so O'Ruddy's men are no longer frightened by a ghost because "no imp of Satan could appear in the same county as Father Donovan." His Reverence holds Mass in the little chapel in Brede Place, and this had "a very quieting effect on the men, especially as Oxenbridge had not walked during the night."

Brede Manor with its imposing and picturesque front, was, as Crane came to realize, a house symbolic of the empty shell of his own self. Windswept from the valley, the house was damp and cold, certainly not a healthy place for a consumptive whose doctor later concluded that he should never have lived in that house. As Mason said, if Crane "had been a little less 'Early English' just to suit Brede Place, it is possible that he might have lived longer." Karl Harriman, a young American who spent several months with the Cranes, caught severe colds because of the damp chill and the drafts, with the wind whistling through the casements day and night. Stephen's study was "the draughtiest of all"; Harriman declared in the London *Critic* (July, 1900) that Brede Manor killed him. Ford Hueffer—inclined to give the screw of truth another turn—complained not of its dampness but rather that the sunlight filtered into dark green places and was ghastly! The mullioned, leaded windows of that massive gray-stone mansion offered "a proud and sinister front to sunlight coming through the lowering clouds."

Crane wrote Pinker from Brede Manor in late February: "My stories are developing in three series. I. The Whilomville stories (always to Harpers). II. The war tales. III. Tales of western American life similar to 'Twelve o'Clock.' It might be well to remember this. For instance if you could provisionally establish the war tales with one magazine and the western tales with another as the Whilomville yarns are fixed with Harper's, it would be very nice." He sent Pinker a short story, reminding him to send solicitor Alfred Plant £10 for another installment payment, and hoped "you will send me a further cheque of £25 by next post." Again, "Please send me a cheque for £40 so that I will get it on Sunday morning. If you have to dispose of the U. S. rights of any of the stories you had better consult me. I know my U. S. market. . . . P.S. I should think this would go to the Strand. How am I going? Strong?"

*Strand Magazine* published a Cuban War sketch in September: "The Revenge of the *Adolphus*," one of the least interesting pieces in *Wounds in the Rain,* Crane's Cuban War tales and sketches[9] recreate in semi-fictional form the same adventures he had reported in war dispatches to the *World* and *Journal,* but with the difference that he now disguises the identities of persons, places and ships and thereby attains a humorous and spoofing tone, which of course was not suitable for the war dispatches. (Two boats in "The Revenge of the *Adolphus*," for example, are named *Chicken* and *Holy Moses*.)

Behind a camouflage of fake names, however, he wanted to be accurate about the events he described, and so he sent a copy of "The Revenge" to a Naval Attaché now with the American Embassy in London—Commander J. C. Colwell—to check nautical terms, ship's gear, etc. He had in all probability met Colwell aboard one ship or another in June, 1898, and the Commander and his wife visited Brede Manor. Colwell wrote that he thought "Revenge of the *Adolphus*" hit off "the locale of the sort of thing admirably," quite true to life; but as the so-called *Chancellorsville* belonged to the class of the actual cruiser *Marblehead,* the fictional ship ought to have on board a couple of buglers and a drummer. Colwell, warming to his subject, advised Crane to inject into his manuscript "Beat to quarters!" and to follow that with the "quick notes of a bugle and the sharp roll-rat-rat-tat-roll of a drum stirred the decks of the *Chancellorsville*." That would do it; but Crane threw overboard the drummer and the buglers.

From then on he was writing against the clock, without time to let themes ripen in his mind, and he could not afford to tear up a first draft or start on a better line. To obtain advances from Pinker he was writing things that came easily to him such as "The Revenge" and "God Rest Ye" and Whilomville stories one after another. A week after moving into Brede Manor he mailed Pinker "a whacking good Whilomville Story—

4,000 words—and I am agitatedly wiring you at the same time. You are possibly able to forgive me by this time for the way I put upon you. I must have altogether within the next ten days £150—no less, as the Irish say. But, by the same token, I am going to earn it—mainly, in Whilomville stories, for they are sure and quick money. £40 of my £150 have I done yesterday and today, but for all your gods, help me or I perish."

Crane signed his letters "Yours faithfully." However, he was not faithful to Pinker, who during the first twenty days of February advanced him more than £200 to save him from bankruptcy. He was two-timing Pinker by dealing simultaneously with a Mr. Collis of another literary agency, The Author's Syndicate. He wrote Collis on the 18th: "Thank you very much for your kind note of the 15th—. Was the 'Blue Hotel' sold at all in England? If it was not I suppose you still have that typed copy? and I would be very glad if you would send it to me. Since it has already been published in America I suppose there is very little use of keeping it going here. However you might let me know to what papers and magazines you have sent it." To Collis also he is "Faithfully Yours."

On March 2 he wrote Collis again: "I am quite sure that the best thing to do with the 'Blue Hotel' is to take it to the *Westminster Gazette* and sell it for about fifteen pounds. I have always been a bit of a fad with them and whenever I have to sacrifice myself upon the altar of copyright, I have found them good priests. The Editor has changed since my day, but I think you will find them willing. This is the only thing which I can think of. I am very much obliged to you for the attention you have given the story. If you ever get down into this dark corner of the world, I am always free and at home on Thursdays." Collis sent him a check (for £6 / 12 / 3), but "The Blue Hotel" was not published in an English periodical. Crane in his double-dealings with Collis was risking his future with Pinker, and he must have recognized how foolhardy that risk was because his dealings with Collis ended here.[10]

Pinker had placed, or was about to place, the Cuban War tale "God Rest Ye, Merry Gentlemen," but when Paul Reynolds cabled him he withdrew it from circulation until this mixup was clarified. As Pinker wrote Cora (March 9) he wished they could make some arrangement to prevent Reynolds' and his operations overlapping. "Editors are not pleased if I go and talk a great deal about a story and ask them to pay special attention to it, and then withdraw it." In 1900 Reynolds made the same complaint to Cora about *The O'Ruddy:* "I wish I could also know where it has been offered by Mr. Pinker so that I might not offer it twice to the same people."[11] Reynolds placed "God Rest Ye" in the *Saturday Evening Post* in May, and Pinker placed it the same month in the *Cornhill Magazine*. Reynolds cabled Crane on March 5 that he had sold it for $300, but

Crane wasn't sure whether that included international serial rights or solely American rights, so Cora asked Pinker to withhold the story temporarily.

The next day she wrote Pinker indignantly that Crane's "stuff" was not being accepted in England as readily as it deserved to be: "I cannot understand what can be the reason for the English publishers refusing such stuff as those children stories and 'God Rest Ye.' They seem to fancy themselves as judges of literature but to me they appear to be a good set of idiots to refuse really clever and artistic stuff and to print the rot they do. Mr. Reynolds has pleased us very much by his prompt placing of these stories. We hope that you will be equally successful in placing the serial rights of 'Active Service' and in also, perhaps, by pointing out to London publishers that Harpers have not only thought 'Lynx Hunting' and 'The Angel Child' good enough, but have asked for all the 'Whilomville' stories that Mr. Crane may write, that they have a lot to learn and that the firm of Pinker are the people to teach them.[12] It is a good opportunity for you to let them know that there are others, as we say in America. We hope now to soon put at rest any doubts Messrs. Morrisons and Nightingale may have. Half of the novel should reach you by Thursday." She invited Pinker for a few days' visit at Brede Manor, and perhaps he got there; but if so, he stayed away thereafter; it must have been embarrassing for him to underwrite the upkeep of that costly house and be entertained there at his own expense.

Pinker replied to Cora on March 9: "In condemning English editors for their want of appreciation, one must remember that Mr. Crane's reputation is not established on this side as it is in the States, so that his name does not carry so much weight with the readers of sixpenny magazines, which are, after all, what one has most to depend on."

Crane had written Pinker the same day Cora wrote him that he expected £600 for American serial rights on *Active Service*. That was a lot of money. He undoubtedly didn't get nearly that much, but as a poker player he knew how to bluff his hand.[13] Ignoring Pinker's explanation that his name did not yet carry as much prestige in England as in America, he echoed (on March 17) Cora's complaint that the English editors lacked appreciation of his writings—as though that were Pinker's fault.

With springtime Brede Manor was gayer, says Beer: "*Active Service* was finished and in print. Half a dozen tales had been sold and he could cheerfully lend a hundred pounds without taking a note."

But things were not so cheerful at the Manor. Stephen wrote his brother, Judge William Crane, to borrow more money: "If you think I am not hustling to get out of this hole you are mistaken. But sometimes I think I can't quite do it. Let me know as soon as you see this letter exactly what are the prospects of your lending me five hundred dollars by the first of April. We are living very quietly, devoting all our attention to my work.

My wife is very helpful to me and feels the same interest in the stories that I feel myself. This makes it easier and if the month of March don't wipe me off the earth I hope by this time next year to be fairly rich so much confidence have I in the different life I am now leading and then I will be able to help Teddy [Edmund], which is one of my pet principles."

*Active Service,* which Beer thought had been mostly written in Havana. was not yet even half-written and did not see print until November. In his March 17 letter to Pinker, Crane said it was now at 48,000 words, "but the English market seems so stagnant that I have delayed sending you a copy of the first half of the book in order that I might get a copy off to Reynolds. I am confident that it will be the most successful book that I have ever published." Psychologically, it was necessary for him to think so. He hits Pinker as usual for more money, preferring £30 in cash *now* as better than £50 next month. "You grumble at the English market," wrote Pinker, "but it has not yet had a fair chance. It won't be sluggish when you give it what it wants and a reasonable time."

Cora sent him twenty-two chapters of *Active Service* on April 25 and again lectured poor Pinker: "Please do your very best to sell serially and give editors to understand that two weeks is the limit to keep Mr. Crane's copy. Please make this your fast rule for all of Mr. Crane's work. Editors have always subscribed to this for me, when I have been disposing of Mr. Crane's stuff." Crane wrote Reynolds (sometime after May, 1899): "As for 'Active Service.' Stokes and Company have, without my knowledge or permission, been attempting to sell it serially. I have told them that I wanted you to conduct that matter and in order to prevent confusion I send you word at the earliest possible moment." He could be a shrewd operator on occasion.

"We love Brede with a wildness which I think is a little pathetic," Stephen had written Mrs. Moreton Frewen in early March. "We have been in the old house nearly a month and every day it seems more beautiful to us." Later he wrote Moreton Frewen (April 10): "We will be greatly delighted to have the supply of fresh mushrooms and will have spawn placed as you direct. All does indeed go well and we are comfortable in our isolation. . . . If you succeed me here next year, we will depart with a sense of delightful sojourn. During these late heavy storms the whole house sang like a harp and all the spooks have been wailing to us. It is rather valkeric. The servants are more impressed than we would like them to be and we have not yet found maids who will sleep in the house." A month later he was expecting the Frewens to visit them, and he wrote Moreton on May 15: "If you can stay the night we will be very glad and can put you up comfortably. The ghost has been walking lately but we cannot catch him. Perhaps when the real Frewen sleeps under his roof he may condescend to display himself to all of us."[14]

Crane's usual routine before breakfast was to ride one of the two white carriage horses in the Brede stable: Glenroy and Gloucester, whom he renamed "Hengist" and "Horsa."[15] Before breakfast meant towards noon because he always wrote late into the night. One morning he encountered Maurice Hewlett, who was shocked to find him in muddy boots. Author of *Richard Yea and Nay,* a title which seems to fit his own character, Hewlett was a very proper Englishman, and "Baron Brede" (as Sanford Bennett called Stephen) liked to shock proper English gentlemen.

Willis Clarke interviewed Crane at Brede Manor for the biography of Crane he never wrote (he was baffled by too many conflicting statements), and Henry James gave him a list of persons for information about Crane's life. The list included Maurice Hewlett, who "heartily disliked Crane." Hewlett, however, attached no importance to tales of his dissipation. "He was envied," he said, "and the fantastic mode of his life grated on our English propriety."

Crane's English years brought him many friends, and their names read like a catalog of contemporary literature, but he was surrounded also by men who flattered him while envying him and who spread calumny against him. A popular English author wrote his publisher that Crane lived "in debauchery and died of its consequences." Conrad concluded that he "had the misfortune to be, as the French say, *mal entouré.* He was beset by people who understood not the quality of his genius and were antagonistic to the deeper fineness of his nature. . . . I don't think he had any illusions about them himself: yet there was a strain of good-nature and perhaps of weakness in his character which prevented him from shaking himself free from their worthless and patronizing attentions, which in those days caused me much secret irritation whenever I stayed with him in either of his English homes."

Calumny had it that Crane "could not write his tales without getting drunk," but although he always drank while he wrote, he drank whiskey from a tall glass filled with water. At Ravensbrook Conrad saw him again and again at work with a small jug of ale beginning at ten o'clock in his study and ending two hours later with the same ale in his glass—"how flat by that time I don't like to think! The most amusing part was to see Crane, as if moved by some obscure sense of duty, drain the last drop of that untempting remnant before we left the room to stroll to and fro in front of the house while waiting for lunch."

Edwin Pugh, who had played handball with Stephen in the damp garden at Ravensbrook just before he moved to Brede Manor, was hailed rather unceremoniously to come and stay with the Cranes as long as he liked. "Eternity's an entr'acte," Crane wrote Pugh.[16] He recalls that Stephen met him at the railway station, "bent that pale Mephistophelian face of his close to mine and said: 'This looks like Edwin Pugh.' That seemed the queerest approach to friendship I had ever known: It embarrassed me considerably. Hardly a word passed between us on the long drive to his home, but from time to time he hummed, and the refrain of his humming was: 'I'll be there, I'll be there! / When the Hully Gee is calling I'll be there— / Sure as you're born!' "

What was Crane like? "To say that he was rather tall," says Pugh, "inclined to stoop a little, very fair, with a slight moustache and resplendent hair of pale brown, seems trivial. To say that he was beautiful and brave and careless, that he was in short all those things the typical fool doesn't like, might be misleading. . . . He talked with a lazy American accent, and he flopped and lounged about a good deal. His hands were miracles of strength and cleverness. He could play hand-ball like a machine-gun. He would fire the ball at me from every conceivable angle, in that old damp garden of his, with a sort of wild-cat fury."

Writing Cora after Crane's death, Pugh expressed his grief: "I was more attracted to him than to any man I have known, & I believe he liked me too & was more frank with me than with most. I thought to be his friend for many years. He was of my age & temper, & I like to believe that any little light of talent had something in common with the pure white blaze of his genius. I can hear his voice as I write & see his face—his kind, grave smile & the eager, fearless earnestness of his wonderful eyes— eyes that saw clearly by the light of the soul they mirrored."

Ford Hueffer thought Crane's eyes with their long fringes of lashes "were almost incredibly beautiful—and as if vengeful. They were large, like a horse's. They frowned usually with the gaze of one looking very intently. But they shone astonishingly at times. His New York argot disappeared when he got excited, and then he talked a rather classical English." Small, frail, energetic, his voice at one moment could be harsh, "like a raven's uttering phrases like, 'I'm a fly-guy that's wise to the all night push,' if he wanted to be taken for a Bowery tough; or 'He was a mangy, sheep-stealing coyote,' if he desired to be thought of cowboy ancestry. At other times, he would talk rather low in very selected English. That was all boyishness. There surely was never a soul more gallant than Stephen Crane [says Ford]. Physically brave and of untiring industry, fearless and morally courageous, observant beyond belief," he was "infinitely hopeful, generous, charitable to excess."

When the Conrads visited Brede Place, Stephen rode out to meet them at the park gate. He looked his best on horseback, and that was their happiest memory of him. His face was "wreathed in smiles all the way to the front door. He looked about him at that bit of the world, down the green slopes and up the brown fields, with an appreciative serenity and the confident bearing of a man who is feeling very sure of the present and of the future. All because he was looking at life from the saddle, with a good morning's work behind him. Nothing more is needed to give a man a blessed moment of illusion.

"The more I think of that morning, the more I believe it was just that:

that it had really been given me to see Crane perfectly happy for a couple of hours; and that it was under this spell that, directly we arrived, he led me impatiently to the room in which he worked at Brede. After we got there he said to me: 'Joseph, I will give you something.' I had no idea what it would be, till I saw him sit down to write an inscription in a very slim volume. He presented it to me with averted head. It was *The Black Riders.* He had never spoken to me of his verse before. It was while holding the book in my hand that I learned that they were written years before in America. I expressed my appreciation of them that afternoon in the usual half a dozen, or dozen, words, which we allowed ourselves when completely pleased with each other's work. When the pleasure was not so complete, the words would be many. And that was a great waste of breath and time.''

Kate Frederic, living on the charity of the credit-ridden Cranes and the fund Cora elicited after Harold Frederic's death from his many friends, was there at Brede Manor with her five-year-old son Barry and both the Frederic daughters, Helen and Helöise, the former born of Grace in 1892 and the latter the child of Kate in 1893. These orphans ran barefoot in the park, but at dinner they were clothed in "coarse bronze plush frocks, terribly ornate, their socks mended with weird cobbled darns in some colour that swore violently with that of those pitiful little garments," Jessie Conrad recalls in her "Recollections of Stephen Crane" (*Bookman:* April, 1926). Stephen would sit in one of the windows of the big drawing room while twanging a guitar and singing in a low voice some haunting Neapolitan air, "his wonderful eyes fixed on space. He never varied his tune, but I always noticed an expression of serenity and quiet satisfaction on his face at these times."

The Conrads, with Jessie's sister Dora, arrived on June 3—Saturday noon—and stayed a fortnight or more at Brede Manor. Jessie Conrad describes Cora as a somewhat monumental figure affecting "a statuesque style of dress." The chances of dinner at eight were unpredictable because the cook had to be bribed to stay with a bottle of brandy. She'd announce she was departing, and then Cora at wit's end would appeal to Stephen, and he in turn would ring a bell summoning butler Heather, who in turn would hand over the brandy bottle to the thirsty cook. She would then prepare the dinner, complete in every detail. As the house was almost constantly occupied by visitors and permanent guests, including semi-bohemian associates from London, Conrad seldom visited Brede Manor. He told Hamlin Garland: "I didn't enjoy his crowd, but I liked him and valued his work." Crane's greatest extravagance was his hospitality. "You are too good-natured, Stephen," Conrad told him, and after a period of silence, he replied, "I am glad those Indians are gone." One of those Indians was probably Edwin Pugh. He disliked Conrad and impugns him for an affectation of humility in Crane's presence, an irritating note of patronage as though Crane were "something of a simpleton." But Conrad had genuine reason to be humble before this American genius, for Crane was then his superior as literary artist; Crane was "my senior," he said, "as I ventured to remind him now and then with affected humility, which always provoked his smiles."

The reversal of that situation began after the publication of "Heart of Darkness" and *Lord Jim,* and became more pronounced after Crane's death, as Conrad progressed from one masterpiece to another. Pugh's notion that Conrad "during his whole career never rose to Crane's level" is nonsense, and so is his contention that any impartial comparison between Crane and Conrad must give the verdict of greater strength of character to Crane. Conrad's moral fiber was unassailable. He was just as insolvent as Crane, but he did not let his artistry deteriorate. What motivated Crane during the last fourteen months of his hectic life was constantly the need for "sure and quick money," a phrase which tells us how he regarded his Whilomville stories at the same time he was assuring Harper that his best efforts went into them. For quick money he hastily concluded *Active Service,* a novel which failed him in his hopes for a popular success. Writing Pinker about *Great Battles of the World,* another potboiler, he used the same phrase: "such sure quick money."

# XXVII

## ᙍ *Henry James and Others*

JUDGE William Howe Crane decided to send his eighteen-year-old daughter, Helen, to visit Uncle Stephen in England. He would pay for her board at Brede Manor and for sightseeing on the Continent, and brother Wilbur would go as her chaperon. "Helen's trip will, or ought to be, educational in its effects, and we expect it to cost us something," William wrote Cora. Helen was the difficult daughter who "might easily become reckless," and he was sending her on this expedition "as a venture worth the expenditure." He also wanted to get her "free from her mother's influence."

Helen, William's eldest daughter, was the great favorite of Stephen, says her sister Edna. When it was finally decided she should go, after much indecision, what great preparations were made! A dressmaker stayed for weeks while making her many wonderful dresses "which later she was to learn from Cora were all wrong. At the steamer, father gave her as a surprise, a Columbia chainless bicycle, for which he paid the fabulous sum of $100. In England she got into much difficulty with it by riding on the right side of the road instead of the left."

William saw her off on the Hamburg-American steamer *Pennsylvania* on June 10, and two days later he wrote Stephen from Goshen, New York: "I would like to have her make a good long visit and, if everything goes right, to stay long enough with you and in England for something like educational effect. . . . I want you and Cora to exercise oversight in respect to her choice of associates. She has never associated with undesirable people here, except from a social standpoint, and she is at an age now where she cannot afford to be too democratic."

On reaching Plymouth on June 19 Helen telegraphed Stephen that she and Uncle Wilbur would look for him in London at the Paddington Station, but Stephen met them instead at the station in Rye. On the train they had encountered a young man who was also on his way to meet the famous author. His name was Karl Harriman and he was a twenty-three-year-old University of Michigan graduate who wrote a column and Sunday stories for the Detroit *Free Press* at $25 a week. Harriman, who later published two sketches on Crane, spotted him at the Rye station "by the photographs I'd seen of him.

"Approaching him, too, was a man older than he, accompanied by a young girl. Stephen shook hands with the man and kissed the girl. Then he held out his hand to me. You see, I'd never met him. I'd been asked down at the suggestion of Barr [Robert Barr of the London office of the Detroit *Free Press*.] But that didn't make any difference. He made me one of the family immediately . . . our scant luggage—mine was scant, anyway—was stowed away in the brake; Stephen took up the reins and we were off. I don't know the road, though I was there again last year after a lapse of thirty-two. I had eyes only for the back of Stephen Crane's head then—the head that had created *Maggie, George's Mother,* and *The Red Badge of Courage.* He seemed a lot older than I, though his seniority was only a matter of four or five years. He was so quiet—I guess that was the reason. He wore riding-breeches and puttees, like a stable-boy, a flannel shirt, belt, and no coat—the sort of costume that so shocked Henry James. When Stephen learned that, he always affected the rig when he called on James as we frequently did that summer, or whenever James with official warning, so to speak, descended for tea on the lawn at Brede Place.

"As we drove on, Stephen would indicate with the whip this or that patch or covert, or bridge, or stream, and Helen would 'oh' and 'ah.' Brother Wilbur didn't speak once, as I recall. Not so much as a single 'ah.' He kept looking at the back of his younger brother's head, too. He was probably saying to himself, 'Who would have believed it?' I wonder if any doubt of the authenticity of Stephen's authorship did lurk in his mind. But there didn't in Helen's. I know that. She adored her thin-faced uncle and mixed with adoration, so patent in her eyes, was an enormous admiration and pride.

"We drove down a lane, as dusky as a cathedral's nave under the arch the trees made. At its end stood the ancient house, with its benign bishop without a nose, holding up his two fingers in blessing from his niche in the angle of the wall. And never a house needed a presiding bishop more, nose or no nose, for the place was notoriously haunted from the labyrinthine cellars that no one has ever completely explored, through every room, to the furthest angle of the immense hedge enclosing the garden." Heather (the butler) took the horses' bits when the brake stopped, and then there came into the sunlight of that early June day, through the Gothic arch of the ancient portal, "a woman whose appearance took my breath away. What it did to Helen I was not to know, but Wilbur, as I recall, gasped. What a woman was Cora Crane!"

She was dumpy, and her dumpiness was enhanced by her plaid skirt and mandarin blue smock (or middy blouse). She wore sandals and perhaps no stockings. But it was her face—her eyes—that most impressed sentimental young Harriman. "Her hair was the honeyist I have ever seen, and finer than any floss as real blond hair is likely to be. And Cora Crane's was real—no greenish grey at the roots. Honey all the way down and into her scalp, and through it, and on. Her eyes were just such eyes as her hair demanded. I have seen blue eyes in my time, looked deep into them once of a day, but never such eyes as Cora Crane's. . . . They were luminous, rather as the sky at its palest is still luminous when the sun is shining, and rarely was the sun not shining in Cora Crane's eyes.

" 'We'll not dress tonight,' she said as we crossed to where the tea table stood beneath the canopy of a gorgeous beech. 'Wilbur didn't bring his evening things.' How I happened to, God only knows," Harriman remarks.

In July, 1899, sixteen-year-old George Hyslop took a bicycle trip through southern England with his sister and Tom Wood, whose mother had known the Cranes at Newark, New Jersey, and given them a letter of introduction to Stephen. On biking over from Rye, they met the Cranes, who insisted that they stay at Brede Place a couple of days. Hyslop remembers Cora very pleasantly, and his sister took a liking to her at once. An odd-looking woman, Hyslop said, "Mrs. Crane did and said nothing that would upset anybody. If she had a 'past,' it did not do her much harm. But she was rather eccentric. She put in an appearance, the morning after we got there, in a weird kind of wrapper, her hair all down her back. (By the way, she had beautiful hair.) She blew into the bedroom where Tom and I were planted and asked if either of us was any good at grooming horses. The groom had a sore thumb. She and Stephen had to go to London to see his literary agent, and somebody had to be a stable boy."

Helen and the other young people at Brede Manor took Cora for granted, and noticed nothing unusual about her manner and talk. But every now and then she would say things which indicated that she knew too much about life. Henry Sanford Bennett and his young French wife lodged at nearby Rye for some days of July and for two weeks in August (1899); they never stayed at Brede Manor but frequently visited there. Bennett remembered an unfortunate discussion of Arthur Pinero's *The Second Mrs. Tanqueray,* in which Tanqueray marries his mistress Paula. Mrs. Crane, as Bennett politely called Cora, thought the tragic ending of the play "false and overdone. She was right, of course. But I remember wishing she would hold her tongue." He liked her a great deal, but "I have to admit that when she got sentimental she could be tedious. She sometimes told 'sob stories' which the American youngsters seemed to like. I recollect one about a man coming from San Francisco, every year, in order to lay a single rose on a dead woman's grave. Crane would get very wooden and depressed during these recitals." In front of seven or eight guests during a poker game Cora would let down her hair. "I suppose she was *farouche.*" Bennett felt that Crane "was miserable about her.

t may be that he married her from chivalry, but he had grown very fond
f her indeed. There was something very fine about her. It has hurt me
o describe her little vulgarities and eccentricities."

"Baron Crane" would dress for dinner in formal attire like a proper
English gentleman. If he could not boast of titles and heraldry, he could
brag about the captured Spanish flag he had brought back from Cuba to
hang in the entrance chamber of the Manor. Nothing pleased him better
than his role as Lord of Brede Manor, says Ford Hueffer. "He strewed
his floors with rushes; a vast pack of dogs clustered around his hearth . . .
and every passing tramp was welcome to a cut of beef and a draught of
ale. Yet, curiously enough, when the fit took him, he would assume the
dress and speech of an American plainsman and pace the sunk lanes of his
demesne, a picturesque figure with his shock of hair, piercing eyes and
rather weak mouth, his rough attire of shirt and breeches, with revolver
swinging at his hip."[1]

Sometimes "The Duke" (as Cora called him) affected an extravagant
Yankee accent when telling a story: "Say, when I planted these hoofs of
mine on Greek soil I felt like the hull of Greek literature, like one gone
over to the goldarned majority. I'd a great idea of Greece. . . . So I said
to the chocolate-box general of the Greek army: 'Can I go into the fighting line?' And he says to me like a Denver Method[ist]: 'Not in those
trousers, sonny.' So I got back at him with: 'How near may I get to the
fighting line, then?' And he says in his eloquent way, 'Not less than two
miles.' " Crane's wit was "like liquid silver, his humor profound; so profound that usually he practised it merely to amuse himself."

Ford avoided Brede Manor as much as possible, but Stephen would ride
over to his place and talk "with discouragement of the revival of medieval
places of sanctuary." He had two enormous carriage horses and astride
either one of them he gave the impression "of a fragile eagle astride a
gaunt elephant."

The Cranes and Karl Harriman drove over to Rye to visit Henry James
at Lamb House. They talked about the Rye annual mud-boat regatta,
which James refereed in knickerbockers, ghillie-shoes and a homburg,
while Stephen was dressed in breeches and puttees, much to Cora's amusement. Stephen gave James the copy of Knut Hamsun's *Hunger* which Harriman had bought in London. They talked about the "Swede," as Stephen
called Hamsun, and of Mrs. Humphrey Ward, whose writing he disliked
without ever having read a line she wrote. Cora expressed hope that
James would contribute to the fund for the Frederic children, although he
had already given five pounds last January. James cocked his head to one
side and said: "My dear Mrs. Crane, I am so sorry; I shall write you."

He later sent a check for fifty pounds, adding, "I only wish I could do
more." Cora wept when she read James' note, and Stephen smiled: "Did
you expect anything less?" She expressed her gratitude, and James re-

plied: "Dear Mrs. Crane: All thanks for your note. I am glad any sort of sum has been raised for the poor little mortals." James had the idea that all his friends must be illegally mated, says Ford, and "he had a personal horror of letting his more august friends come into contact through him with any one who might be evenly remotely suspected of marital irregularities."

He had a great affection for Stephen but little for Cora, and he used to groan to Ford over the necessity of visiting the Cranes. Cora no doubt invited him to Brede Manor right after they moved in (on Sunday, February 12), and on February 17 James wrote that he would try to get over before going to Italy "for several weeks on Monday next." He biked over from Rye and left his calling card: "Very sorry to miss you—had a dark foreboding it was you I passed 1/4 an hour ago in a populous wagonette Will try you soon again. H. J." What appalled him was their aping to absurdity the state of a feudal lord on Stephen's inadequate income of so many pounds per thousand words. Brede Manor is probably as perfect an example of a medieval home as is to be found in England, and, to quote Ford, it was is if James shuddered "at seeing a mock made of a settled and august mode of European life and a wonderful old house; and it made it all the more bitter that the mockery should be meant as a sincere flattery of imitation by a conspicuous compatriot."

Stephen's manor house and way of life were too much for brother Wilbur; he quit the place for a visit to London, and the Cranes with Helen joined him there in the first days of July. Stephen spent the evening of July 3 at the Savage Club and there encountered Mark Twain, whom he had first met in 1895 at the Lantern Club in New York. That noon Cora was at the Hotel Cecil for luncheon with the Society of American Women in London and met Lady Randolph Churchill, who was Mrs. Moreton Frewen's sister, and Mrs. Frances Hodgson Burnett, author of *Little Lord Fauntleroy* (1887). She also met Mrs. Lafayette Hoyt de Friese and other notables of the Society for Feminine Social and Intellectual Culture, of which Mrs. de Friese was an officer. She had sponsored Cora for membership. "We want the right kind of people," she said.

Wilbur sailed for America, while the Crane party, with Helen, Karl Harriman, Edith Jones, and others, left London on July 4 to stay at a little riverside inn, the Angel, to watch the Henley Regatta, and then they went on to Brede. Mabel and Mark Barr (an American chemist, not to be confused with the writer, Robert Barr) had probably joined the party by then, as had A. E. W. Mason and George Lynch, a war correspondent colleague of Stephen whom he called "the wild Irishman."

Henry James invited them to come over to Lamb House, where tea was poured by Mrs. Humphrey Ward. The tea talk was about the Boers, their rebellion against the British, and about the annual yacht race, *Columbia* versus *Shamrock*. In an unpublished manuscript Crane wrote

▪at if you can get on speaking terms with an Englishman, he says: " 'If the ▪up once gets over here you'll never get it back.' It was cried out in the ▪ffee-rooms of hotels, in clubs, in busses, everywhere people could meet. ▪he last stroke arrived yesterday when a lady looked at me over her tea-▪up and said 'If the Cup once gets over here you'll never get it back.' I ▪ssented at once; I knew enough to assent at once. She didn't know a ▪acht from a motor-car but she had been given the password, the national ▪assword, by her husband who had said to her: 'If the Cup once gets over ▪ere they'll never get it back.' So she said to me: 'If the Cup once gets over ▪ere you'll never get it back.' "[2]

Crane was critical of English smugness, their "colossal serenity." At ▪ames's tea-party he also remarked about the Boer situation: "People tell ▪e a couple of Guard regiments could whip them in a week. When a ▪ankee says such things he is bragging, but I guess an Englishman is just ▪gging the truth from some dark cave." The Englishman's boast about ▪cking those South African yokels collapsed in December with the ▪pectacular triumph of the Boers at the besieged town of Ladysmith in ▪atal, which the British Commander-in-Chief, Redvers Buller, failed to ▪elieve. Crane was to write about it in "Some Curious Lessons from the ▪ransvaal."

"It would be idle to say that British pride has not sunk down into the ▪ps of the national toes," he stated. "The bewildering thing to the British ▪ind has been the mauling received at the hands of bewhiskered farmers ▪y many regiments which were such favorites, whose records so blazed ▪ith glory that they were popularly accounted invincible. For instance, ▪he Black Watch' (Royal Highlanders), a regiment composed of the old ▪orty-second Foot and the old Seventy-third Foot, has traditions which ▪re superior to that of any regiment in the world, perhaps. Very well—▪n unimposing body of men who don't wash very often batter this regiment ▪ut of shape. . . . At this writing the brigade of Foot Guards is cut off ▪ith Lord Methuen, having already suffered severely." Lord Methuen's ▪eventy-fifth battalion, which had achieved a name second to none in ▪ampaigns against frontier tribes of northwest India, and the Ninety-▪econd under Sir George White had "been so hammered and pounded by ▪he 'unpricked bubbles' that they would do well in a representation of the ▪amous picture *Roll Call After Quatre Bras.*"

Henry James told Mark Barr "we love Stephen Crane for what he is; ▪e admire him for what he is going to be." He presented Stephen with a ▪opy of his book *In the Cage,* with an elaborate and affectionate inscrip-▪ion in French. Crane later sent the book to a friend, with instructions to ▪please be very careful of it, as you see that the inscription makes it a ▪ersonal affair. Hope that you find it interesting. I got horribly tired half ▪vay through and just reeled along through the rest. You will like some of ▪t a lot. But I do not think that this girl in the cage is exactly an underclass clerk in love with a 'man about town.' Women think more directly than he lets this girl think. But notice the writing in the fourth and fifth chapters when he has really got started."

After the Henley party finally left Brede Place, Crane stuck to his study for three days; Cora brought him food on a tray. With so many excursions, parties and visitors it's a wonder he managed to write anything at all.

H. G. Wells and Jane (as he called Catherine) were living at Sandgate not far from Folkestone, where the sailboat *La Reine,* belonging to Conrad and Crane, was moored. Within a half-circle around Wells' Spade House with its grass terrace overlooking the English channel lived—at distances from five to thirty-odd miles—Crane, Hueffer, Conrad, James, and W. H. Hudson. "It was not to be wondered at if we lived rather in each other's pockets and interested ourselves in each other's affairs," says Ford.

Conrad and Crane had bought the boat together from Conrad's friend Captain G. F. W. Hope, and their plan was to keep it half the time at Folkstone and half the time at Rye (five miles from Brede Place). Conrad in Stanford-Near-Hythe was close enough to Brede for the Cranes to take carriage there. But the arrangement turned out unsatisfactory because once the Cranes docked the boat at Rye she stayed there most of the summer and also because Stephen defaulted on payment of his half-share. "I'm so sorry Stephen worried about the payment," Conrad wrote Cora on August 27. "Thanks ever so much for the cheque—I've sent Hope yesterday £15 in Stephen's name." But Conrad the next year had to pay the rest of Stephen's debt. It left him speechless when Cora proposed (in mid-May 1900) that Crane's half-share in *La Reine* should be taken over by their local wood merchant "in payment for their wood-account."

The wood merchant went unpaid and Conrad had to pay off Captain Hope. Twenty-five years later a man named Hayter Preston and a friend were directed to Brede Place by an elderly lady, and when Preston said: " 'Mr. Crane lived here, I think?' her eyes grew hard. " 'He did—the rotter!' We were both shocked and not at all anxious to pursue the subject; but the lady went on: 'Yes, he is a rotter. He owes me twenty pounds for firewood! . . . . 'Well,' I apologetically said, 'I'm afraid you won't get paid now. Mr. Crane died twenty-four years ago.' Her eyes took on a reminiscent expression. 'Yes, I suppose he must be dead, or he would have paid me.' She softened somewhat and described Crane as 'a thin gentleman who rode a lot,' and, we also gathered, drank a little; no, she didn't know that he was a writer, but she 'thought that he looked delicate.' He was a kind man, and 'he certainly had a great many friends.' "[3]

As companion for Helen Crane, Edith Richie Jones (then nineteen, the sister of Mark Barr's wife, Mabel) was the guest of the Cranes all summer and remained at Brede Manor until January. In her 1954 memoirs of the Cranes Mrs. Jones claims that she never saw any uninvited guests ınd "never heard money mentioned while I was there." The destitute Cranes bravely camouflaged their pinched plight. "Mr. Crane" and "Mummy Crane" called Edith "Snubby" because of her short nose. That s all very charming, but Mrs. Jones's defense of Cora's innocence in the matters of money and of open-house hospitality collapses under scrutiny. 'The guests who came were invited by Cora at Stephen's suggestion." But Cora by inviting them did not protect Crane's privacy and later regretted it grievously.

True, Stephen and Cora loved to have guests, but they were frequently mposed upon by uninvited strangers—"lice" was Crane's name for them, 'lice" and "mummies." "If you don't tell some of these lice that Cora and I aren't running a hotel, I'll have to advertise in the *Times,*" he wrote Pinker. He also wrote Elbert Hubbard: "I must have Egyptian blood in me. Mummies rise from the tomb and come to pay calls for days." In July a journalist, who probably got an introduction to Crane from agent Pinker, complained about a servant who hadn't brought something to his guest room, and Stephen drawled: "Perhaps she has patrician instincts." The journalist stayed on day after day until Cora somehow managed to dismiss him through James Pinker.

An Englishman who saw Crane quite frequently at Lamb House, where Stephen visited Henry James after his return from Italy, said of the situation at Brede Manor: "I have nothing to say of the jolly young Americans who ran down there, but preserve me from some of the 'Fleet Street boys.' I greatly disliked the attitude certain journalists took towards Mrs. Crane. They seemed to regard her as a kind of superior servant who ought to be delighted to be up at all hours to do some eggs in a chafing-dish and find a bottle of wine for them. She said to me of one of these pests, 'I always expect him to tip me.' The lady was not a fool."

Unfortunately, Cora "rasped the more insular English. She made the mistake of so many Americans. She would discuss diseases at table. And I seem to recollect her telling a very gruesome murder story at lunch at Lamb House. But I liked Mrs. Crane. I knew there were unpleasant stories in regard to her early life circulated among Americans in London. But what of it?"

Cora had hoped that the perfect quiet and remoteness of Brede Place would free Stephen from the lots of "dear good people" who had consumed his time at Ravensbrook, but Brede Manor soon became another hotel. It was all right for James, Conrad, Garnett, Wells, or Ford Hueffer to come and go as they pleased; and the Cranes were glad to entertain the Bennetts, Frieses, Robert Barr, Mark Barr and Mabel, A.E.W. Mason, Crane's school chum C. T. Janeway, Mrs. Richie (Kate Frederic's sister, the mother of Mabel and Edith), or even a stranger like Karl Harriman, who with Edith Richie (Jones), Helen Crane and the Frederic children stayed all summer—not to mention transient guests like Edwin Pugh, or friends like

John Stokes and George Lynch. Some of them had "the kindness to let Cora know when they were coming, but would to God that some of the other Indians would write and ask." Crane remarked to Sanford Bennett: "How does it come to pass that anybody in England thinks he can come and stay with me before I've asked him and patronize my wife's housekeeping?"

Janeway, who heard from English friends about Henry James' intense sufferings when he had to endure Cora, recalls that James came over from Rye one day, probably in early August, with a carriage load of people "all stuffed shirts, and announced that he had brought them to lunch. Mrs. Crane was mad as a hornet, but did not show it. She vanished into the kitchen and concocted a lot of extra lunch in a chafing-dish." Cora impressed Janeway "very favorably. She seemed to be shrewd and plucky and very good humored. I do not know where some of those amazing stories about her conduct at Brede Place came from," he said.

Cora's strange fancy for inviting people in such shoals that even the huge manor house could not accommodate them each with a bedroom gave rise to much unfavorable gossip, says Jessie Conrad. "I fancy Cora's idea was that this lavish hospitality would bring to Stephen much popularity; and all the while he wrote feverishly, anxious—too anxious—to get the best out of himself." All day long a wagonette, drawn by horses Hengist and Horsa, plied between Rye station and Brede Manor for the convenience of friends, lice and Indians.

The Cranes collected "all things in the world that nobody wanted, children, dogs, men, old maids—like beachcombers washed up on green sands," to quote Ford. "And behind the facade; a rabbit-warren of passages with beer barrels set up at odd corners, and barons of beef for real tramps at the kitchen door, and troops of dogs and maids and butlers and sham tramps of the New York newspaper world, and women who couldn't sell their manuscripts. And poor, frail Stevie, with all the organs of his body martyred to the waters of Cuba. . . ." It was Ravensbrook all over again, with guests besieging Brede Manor's lavish hospitality.

"Troops of dogs and maids and butlers!" For servants the Cranes had butler Richard Heather—white-bearded Mack, who Conrad thought looked much like Tolstoy; Frewen insisted that he remain in charge of the staff, which included a very drunken cook, who was later replaced by housekeeper and cook Vernal (half-English and half-Swiss). They lived on the premises, while coachman Pat and his wife lived over the stables, and some slatternly girls and women from the village came in the morning and faded away at sunset, apprehensive that the house was haunted. Mack disapproved of Stephen's carefree American habits. He hoped that he had seen the last of the Cranes when he drove them to Folkestone in a big wagonette to visit H. G. Wells in September, but when they came back he left Brede Manor in a huff.

Stephen wrote the Frewens: "We are getting along happily at dear old

Brede; the ghost is behaving himself although the doors open in some uncanny way. As to Mack leaving us, the old man found it a bit too much out of the world for him. He missed the usual talk at the taverns, we think. We were very fond of him and he seemed fond of us, but when he wished to go we did not try to keep him. You see it is impossible to keep all beer and drink under lock and key, and the old man was tempted two or three times to take too much. With lamps and open fires it gave me an anxiety for the safety of your old house. You have been very kind to me about the rent. I've had a hard year of it, etc."

Mack complained of inconveniences and longed "for five or six footmen which of course we do not need."[4] "My man Heather," Stephen had written a friend in April, "can hire me a pair of maids while I ride to Rye and back. If I went to Russia I should come home and find Parliament in buttons and Marie Corelli in the kitchen." (The servants, whenever Crane rode off, took books downstairs from his study to read them in the kitchen. They liked Corelli's *Thelma*.[5]) Vernal had been the cook for Edith Richie's mother in Kentucky for ten years, and knew how to satisfy Crane's craving for the American dishes of his boyhood.

The dining room had a long refectory table and a carpet of rushes from the meadows by the brook; the chapel was used as a storehouse for apples; the bedrooms Cora furnished with old four-poster beds which had served as chicken coops in neighboring farmyards. She cleverly rubbed them down and fitted the mattresses. The big oak-paneled hall where everyone lived most of the time was filled with comfortable couches and chairs and pretty lamps with plants and books.

The dogs included a fox terrier bitch, named Flannel; Sponge (a cross between a retriever and an old English sheep dog), who was the wisest and best of dogs; and two Russian poodles, amiable but stupid. The dogs would scratch at Stephen's study door, and then he would get up from his desk without the least impatience to open the door for one of those spoiled animals, says Jessie Conrad. When he had almost returned to his desk, he would have to repeat the performance, except when butler Heather attended to their demands. Many times, Jessie said, she watched the farce of Heather escorting them to the head of the stone steps and solemnly kicking each dog down the steep flight. That old ruffian's face was set in the most benevolent expression. "Those dogs were the source of much tribulation in the village and were also very destructive to the sheep and lambs in the surrounding park. It happened unfortunately that Stephen either could or would not consent to pay for the damage, and the shepherd more than once threatened dire consequences. All this Stephen disregarded in a somewhat lofty manner. Then one day when we were returning from a long drive (we had been gone two days) we all gasped and held our noses as soon as the horses turned into the drive. A sheep's carcass hung from each of the four or five biggest trees bordering the drive in the park. Stephen's face turned deathly pale with anger while he muttered curses under his breath. The horses shied violently at the ghastly objects swinging on a level with their heads. Next morning when I went out the carcasses had all disappeared, and I never heard that Stephen did more than roundly curse the shepherd."

Young Edith Richie Jones mixed Stephen's drinks for him the way he wanted, "with about two teaspoonsfuls of whiskey in a tall glass of soda water. He might have three of these during the day. He always had a cigarette in his fingers, but most of the time it was out." His study over the porch was an austere place with a not-too-comfortable chair and a long table. When he was writing, they all stayed away from him. But sometimes he would say that he could think better if he had company and then he would bring his manuscript down to the hall and write while Edith and Cora sewed.

When Henry James visited, Cora would say: "Now, let's have a concert!" And then Edith would pick up the five puppies and sing while the puppies howled in anguish. Sometimes Cora would awaken Edith and tell her to slip into her dressing gown to come down into the huge old kitchen where the servants gathered in the daytime. "Stephen wants some music." The music was made by blowing upon tissue-paper stretched over combs, Stephen "conducting with the toasting fork as his baton" while we sang "horribly and happily through the combs. Such foolishness amused those brilliant minds!" Stephen and Henry James would become limp with laughter, says Edith Richie Jones; but if so it was a rare occasion, for Crane almost never laughed.[6]

The butler primed himself with brandy one summer night and knocked over a lamp in Stephen's study, setting fire to the table. Crane wrote Moreton Frewen about the accident only because Mr. Frewen might hear of it "in some exaggerated form." The fire had been put out "with no particular trouble. I did not scold Mack at all because his heart was quite broken."

He did not report to his landlord a much more serious fire that caused considerable damage when the fired logs in the Elizabethan fireplace set ablaze the rushes which carpeted the first floor.

After that fire, Crane had a dream that he was acting on the stage of some theater the part of a prisoner handcuffed and with ankles bound together. In his dream there suddenly came the cry of "Fire!" All the other actors and all the audience ran for the theater's exits, forgetting that he was tied up and helpless. Before writing about his dream he wondered "how long it might take him to inch along a corridor to an outside door. He got Cora and Edith to tie his hands and ankles together and then he spent the morning trying to hop or roll or work along like an inchworm over the given distance, all in deadly seriousness. The story he wrote afterwards was entitled "Manacled."[7]

William had sent Helen to England out of fear that his daughter might become reckless if she remained in Port Jervis, but at Brede Place she fulfilled his doubts about her character by committing a theft, an incident which Cora tactfully managed. It was a painful experience for her but, said William, writing Cora on August 14, it "would not be wise to give Helen to understand that she had squared the whole thing by a confession and an apology. She is now on probation, and the most she could ask from the most generous and forgiving nature is that confidence shall be freely and generously given to her as fast as she earns it."

His wife, Cornelia, had mismanaged their daughter, William said. Helen's mother was a good woman, etc., "but she is one of the impulsive, unreflecting creatures that, to a nature like Helen's, will frequently do more harm than good. She talks first and thinks afterwards. For a year or two, I have noted with deep anxiety that her mother was unwittingly, of course, cultivating in Helen a sullen and revengeful disposition. When Helen did wrong, her mother usually made the first contribution to the situation, and the effect would be such that what little I might say or do would do very little good. . . . I shall be grateful to you as long as I live for the loving interest you take in her welfare." Cora did indeed take a loving interest in Helen, but William a year later forgot all about his vow of gratitude to her.

In a subsequent letter William asked Stephen to send his autograph; a clerk in his office at Port Jervis had asked for it. An English book collector, Thomas Hutchinson, asked him to inscribe his books, and Stephen refused: "I wish to thank you for your sympathetic letter but I am sorry to say that at present I find it impossible to do as you ask. Later, if you will send me the books, I will be glad to write in them whatever is in my head at the moment although I am sure that it will be of no interest."[8] To Hutchinson's query about living authors, he answered that he was not "carnivorous about living writers. I have not read any of the books that you ask me to criticize except that of Mr. Howells, and it has disappointed me. My tastes? I do not know of any living author whose works I have wholly read. I like what I know of Anatole France, Henry James, George Moore, and several others. I deeply admire some short stories by Mr. Bierce, Mr. Kipling, and Mr. White [William Hale White, whose pseudonym was Mark Rutherford]. Mr. Hardy, since you especially inquire about his work, impresses me as a gigantic writer who 'overtreats' his subjects." The shelves at Brede Place were piled with books to the ceiling, and it is interesting to note the authors represented. Crane shortly after moving there from Ravensbrook made a list of his library: "List of Books / Brede Place."[9] In his study at Brede he read in one week Turgenev's *Smoke;* a volume on Greek vases; du Maurier's *Peter Ibbetson,* which he did not like; and Henry James' inscribed copy of *In the Cage,* which he forgot to include in his booklist.

William wrote Cora to tell Stephen that he had recently spent half a day with their Uncle Luther and that he would have been extremely bored with the old man "if I had not been interested in a little speculation of my own, as to how much Stephen owed to the Peck side of his make-up for his literary abilities. Uncle Luther read to me (and translated) extracts from the Greek poets and took down book after book from his shelves and read me little marked passages for the sole and only purpose of enjoying with me the literary beauties of his favorite authors. At times, the tears came into his eyes. He said, among other things, that 'The Open Boat' was worthy of being a book by itself. My point is that Uncle Luther lives among his books and has a very keen literary appreciation." Crane did not share his uncle's devotion to classical literature, but his Brede library included Luther's books.

His discovery of Anatole France's *Procurator of Judaea* excited him enough to tell Henry James and Edmund Gosse about it, as though they had never heard of that French writer. He disliked Twain's long novels for the same reason that he disliked Hardy's and he scoffed at Twain's acting like a society clown. Hardy's retirement, on the other hand, was "all right," and Kipling's absence from society was "the man's own business." He preferred W. E. Henley's less popular verses to his famous "Invictus"[10] because there was too much "I" in that—a fault of which Crane himself was not exactly guiltless.

He was arrogant in August, 1899, when he exploded: "I am, I think, sufficiently grateful to men who really did things for me and in particular to Mr. Garland, who, as you know, gave me sound advice about 'The Red Badge.' But just what is it to the credit of A and B that they bought things from me? I mean, what is my obligation to them? They saw a profit to their papers in buying my stuff and we break even. If it comes to that sultry point, why shouldn't they be grateful to me?" It seemed to Crane that "I am the only person who had nothing to do with bringing myself before the public." He forgets his deep debt to his literary agents Pinker and Reynolds. Without Pinker's trust in his talent and his constant advances of money against an always famished account, he could not have survived in his inflated role as Duke of Brede Manor.

Of Walter Besant, with whom Henry James had engaged in a literary duel about the modern novel, Crane said: "I will bet all my marbles and my best top hat that Walter Besant is forgotten in twenty years." He knew well enough that his own *Active Service* would be forgotten, admitting as much when in February, 1900, he wrote someone: "I hope that the new book will be good enough to get me to Colorado. It will not be good for much more than that."

The closing event of the summer was a bazaar to aid the parish and the district nursing association held in the rectory gardens of the ancient Norman church in Brede village. The South Eastern *Advertiser* reported that there was "a total absence of class lines that would have gladdened

he heart of a socialist." We see Stephen in a straw hat and white flannels
n a photograph taken by George Lynch, who was selling snapshots at
,ixpence each, and Henry James holding a doughnut from the kitchen at
3rede Place—he liked cook Vernall's doughnuts. James wrote Cora after-
vards to thank her for some snapshots—strange images, he called them.
'No, surely it can't be any doughnut of yours that is making me make
;uch a gruesome grimace. I look as if I had swallowed a wasp, or a
)enny toy. And I tried to look so beautiful. . . . But don't show it to
inyone as H. J. trying." Cora managed a rummage booth, Edith Richie
n gypsy costume sold love potions and forecast anyone's future in her
ortune-teller's hut, and Stephen carried potted plants to the carriages of
vomen who had purchased them at the bazaar.

Vicar Frewer of the Brede church had called on him before the bazaar
o ask for the gift of a hundred signed copies of one of his books and
vas shocked to find the famous author rolling dice on the floor of Brede
iall.

# ⊂ *"Whilomville Stories"*—
# *"The Blue Hotel"*

MR. CRANE needs a vacation, Cora wrote Pinker towards the end of August after the completion of *Wounds in the Rain*. He "must have a change or I fear he will break down & we can't have that." Stephen was planning to take his niece Helen to the Rosemont–Dezaley School in Lausanne, and William was sending money to cover her expenses, but his letter had not arrived. Would Pinker please send £20 for travel money?

There was another problem. The wine dealer "threatened to serve papers tomorrow if his bill for £35 is not paid at once (today)"—August 31. This meant another letter to Pinker. The Whilomville story he would receive before they left for Paris, wrote Cora, meant money from Harper's, and this would pay off the wine merchant, but "Please move—I was going to say Heaven & Earth, but publishers is better—to get every pennie you can." Meanwhile she had overdrawn the £35 on her bank account at Oxted, and on September 4 she repeated her request to Pinker. Stephen begged him to send the money at once! She promised that by Friday, the 7th, when they expected to leave for Paris, Pinker would receive Crane's second battle sketch for *Lippincott's Magazine*. (It appeared in the April, 1900, issue—"The Storming of Badajos.")

On their way at last, Stephen and Helen, with Cora and Edith Richie, stopped overnight with H. G. Wells and Catherine at Folkestone, where they had gone in the big wagonette driven by coachman Pat. After dinner there was music, with Catherine accompanying Edith on the piano. Cora asked Catherine how she had cooked the corn grown from the seed they had given her (which William had sent her to start a kitchen garden). "Cook it!" exclaimed Wells. "We didn't cook it. We cut it when it was six inches high and ate it for salad. Wasn't that right?"

While Stephen went on to Lausanne with Helen, Cora and Edith stayed in Paris at the Hotel Louis le Grand. When he returned to Paris, although he was ill with one of his recurrent attacks of malaria, he shut himself off from Cora and Edith at the hotel to write another Whilomville story and thus earn enough to pay for some of their expenses at the Louis le Grand. In other words, he had written one story to get to Lausanne and Paris and was writing another to get back home. Cora may have been having a vacation but plainly Stephen wasn't.

On returning to Brede he sent Pinker the second Whilomville story—3230 words worth $160 from Harper. Later in September he wrote Pinker that he was finishing a third story, and complained that Harper had short-changed him by three or four pounds. He returned the signed contract for *The O'Ruddy* with Frederick Stokes, the American publisher with whom he was under pressure now to complete *Wounds in the Rain,* his volume of Cuban War tales. On the 30th he expressed worry over the titles of two stories: "I would almost bet the two titles cover one story," he wrote Pinker. "We may be making a hideous blunder. Please find out." There were in fact two stories: "Virtue in War" and "The Second Generation"; he had forgotten one of them, "as I often did."

The war in the Transvaal was then getting into full swing and many of Crane's newspaper friends were already in South Africa. "I am getting serious about the Transvaal," he had written Pinker in mid-September. See if you can work it up." Cora was panic-stricken at the thought of Stephen's leaving her again to report on the Boer War. "I am so glad you wrote him *not* to go to the Transvaal," she told Pinker. "His health is not fit for it. He had a return of Cuban fever while we were in Paris and he is in no physical condition to stand a campaign no matter how short it may be. Then he has settled down to his work so well and ought not to leave home before Jan. or Feb. at least." "Please don't let Mr. Crane know I've said a word against the Transvaal," she added in a postscript.

Joseph Conrad had asked the Cranes to visit at Pent Farm in the second half of September, and now in mid-September he wrote again: "Could you come? You would make me happy. And will you pardon me for not writing to you. Dear Stephen, I am like a damned paralyzed mud turtle. I can't move. I can't write. I can't do anything. But I can be wretched, and, by God! I am! Jess sends her love to the whole house. Give my affectionate regards and compliments. Let me know the day before when you are coming. You are a dear old chap."

But Crane was having trouble with Stokes over *Wounds in the Rain.* He had cabled the American publisher that the book was finished and would he send the £100 to be paid on receipt of the manuscript. Stokes cabled back: "Yes on receipt of complete MS." He was undoubtedly amazed at Crane's response: "I withdraw the book." "We stand by the London Convention of 1884," Stokes declared.

Robert Barr[1] advised Crane not to break with Stokes, who was a thoroughly honest man. "You are right when you stick to the pen," said Barr, but you "are apt to be all wrong when you meddle with business. You are too much like Edgar Allan Poe. Our friend Kipling never writes

a business letter, and yet he gets into lawsuits, which is foolish of him.
. . . Write, write, write, anything but business letters." Barr had had
dinner with Admiral Dewey down at Monte Carlo. "He is one of the
loveliest men that any fellow is privileged to meet. He admires two literary
men, Stephen Crane and Rudyard Kipling. So *he's* all right, in every sense
of the word."

In this same letter of October 2 from Hillhead, Barr wrote that he saw
himself as a boy in the Whilomville stories and that "no one has ever
touched the inwards of the actual boy until those stories were written."
As only a few of the Whilomville stories had by then been published he
may have read in manuscript those still unpublished. His insight most aptly
applies to "His New Mittens," published in *McClure's Magazine* for
November, 1898 and excluded from *Whilomville Stories* because it was
included in *The Monster and Other Stories*—December, 1899).

In "His New Mittens" little Horace sadly watches other boys gleefully
snowballing while he must go straight home from school because his
mother has admonished him not to get his new red mittens wet. "A-fray-ed
of his mit-tens! A-fray-ed of his mit-tens," they sing, and though Horace
voices his denial he is alone in the screams of the mob, "fronting all the
traditions of boyhood held before him by inexorable representatives." A
mere baby strikes him with a snowball, and the beset and haggard Horace
in desperate withdrawal "suffered more than is the common lot of man.
Being a boy himself, he did not understand boys at all." He joins the
group and feels that he has "undergone an important change." But then
he hears his mother's shrill voice calling him home. Crane describes her
sad-lined and homely face as perhaps his own mother appeared to him
"in her widow's weeds" after his father's death.

Horace is made to sit alone in the kitchen, and in reprisal refuses to
eat his supper. He loathes life, the world, his mother; defeated, he "painted
in his mind scenes of deadly retribution." His plan is to run away down
Niagara Avenue to California, but a snowstorm forces him into Stickney's
butcher shop on Niagara Avenue. Mr. Stickney returns the boy to his
worried mother, "lying limp, pale as death, her eyes gleaming with pain.
There was an electric pause before she swung a waxen hand toward
Horace. 'My child,' she murmured, tremulously. Whereupon the sinister
person addressed, with a prolonged wail of grief and joy, ran to her with
speed. 'Mam-ma! Mam-ma! Oh, mam-ma!' She was not able to speak
in a known tongue as she folded him in her weak arms."

Crane's Whilomville stories are sentimental, but what perhaps saves
"His New Mittens" is the final scene with Aunt Martha turning defiantly
upon butcher Stickney with a gesture half-military and half-feminine:
"Won't you have a glass of our root-beer, Mr. Stickney. We made it ourselves." From little Horace's viewpoint he is doomed by his environment,
his Aunt Martha and "the merciless ferocity of his mother." It is she

who has thrust him into this wild storm, and she is perfectly indifferent
to his fate, perfectly indifferent." However, from the viewpoint of the
boy's mother and Aunt Martha, people brewed their own drink and their
own fate.

Whilomville is any boy's town (*whilom:* once upon a time). The stories
have their setting in the various New Jersey towns of Crane's boyhood:
Bloomington, Paterson, Jersey City, and Asbury Park, but mainly Port
Jervis. The town "drawled and drowsed through long months, during
which nothing was worse than the white dust which arose behind every
vehicle at blinding noon, and nothing was finer than the cool sheen of
the hose sprays over the cropped lawns under the many maples in the
twilight." The main street has arc-lamps whose shimmering blue is conquered by the orange glare of the outnumbering gaslights in the shop
windows. There is a crowd at the post office awaiting the evening mail
and at the corners the young men gather to review with critical insight
the passing scene. There is a shrill electric streetcar whose motor sings
"like a cageful of grasshoppers," and there is a little theater imitating in
miniature by its varnish and red plush the New York prototype.
Jimmie and Dr. Trescott (William Crane thought the portrait flattered
him) appear in both the Whilomville stories and in "The Monster"; but
there the center of interest is the Negro Henry Johnson rather than the
boy Jimmie, and so it is not a boy's story although it belongs to the
Whilomville saga. Peripheral to the saga is "An Illusion in Red and White"
(apparently a murder story but actually a satire on journalists), where
the stonily perverse Jones children behave not unlike the Whilomville
kids: "Young Freddy's mind began to work like ketchup." "An Indiana
Campaign," a Civil War episode, has the same mellow humor as some
of the Whilomville stories and might just as well be located in Whilomville
as in the village called Wigglesville.
In "Lynx-hunting" (*Harper's Magazine:* September, 1899) Crane remembers the incident of the cow he once "shot" with the toy gun William
gave him while their father was preaching at Middletown. Jimmie and the
daring Willie Dalzel and another boy hunt for a lynx to shoot in the hills
beyond Whilomville, but what they "kill" is not a lynx—it's only a cow.
They confess their crime to the farmer there, whose name is Henry
Fleming. " 'What you boys been doin' to my cow?' The tone has deep
threat in it. They all answered by saying that none of them had shot the
cow." Old Henry Fleming flourished a whip. "Their denials were tearful
and clamorous, and they crawled knee by knee. The vision of it was like
three martyrs being dragged toward the stake. Old Fleming stood there,
grim, tight-lipped. After a time he said, 'Which boy done it?' There was
some confusion, and then Jimmie spake. 'I done it mister.' Fleming looked
at him. Then he asked, 'Well what did you shoot 'er fer?' Jimmie thought,

hesitated, decided, faltered, and then formulated this: 'I thought she was a lynx.' " Old farmer Fleming and his Swedish farmhand lie down in the grass and laugh themselves helpless.

The very best of the Whilomville stories is "The Knife," another Negro story. The late gallant Henry Johnson, who was burned faceless by the fire from which he rescued Jimmie Trescott, is here remembered by Peter Washington as his ideal. Peter also remembers Henry Johnson's conquests in Watermelon Alley and in the hill shanties of Oakland Park (he knew how best to steal watermelons), conquests which "had proved him the equal if not the superior of any Pullman car porter in the country. Perhaps Peter had too much Virginia laziness and humor in him to be a wholly adequate successor to the fastidious Henry Johnson, but, at any rate, he admired his memory so attentively as to be openly termed a dude by envious people." (The envious people were Peter's competitive watermelon snatchers like Alek Williams, the deacon of their church.)

"The Knife" is located in the township of Whilomville in a countryside suburb of Port Jervis, between that Delaware River port and the mountains of Hartwood, and there in a hut clinging to the side of a mountain lives Alek Williams amid a scattered colony, descendants of Negroes who had drifted there during the Civil War. Peter Washington, after visiting Deacon Williams, stops on the way home at the fenced garden of white man Bryant's house, and meanwhile Alek approaches the same watermelon garden near the lakeside where the only sound is the chanting of frogs in the reeds. Peter in darkness climbs the fence and is just about to cut a melon at its stem when he discovers the agonized face of his friend Alek, at whom he hisses: "I got che. Steal Mist' Bryant's mellums, hey?" He takes Alek by the scruff and marches his prisoner up the road. "Come erlong, deacon. I raikon I gwine put you w'ah you kin pray, deacon. Come erlong, deacon." The old man, to whom religion is a personal dignity and who on Sundays is 'so obtrusively good that you could see his sanctity through a door," pleads that he hasn't come to steal any melons but "jes fer ter *feel* 'em." Alek's cur Susie attacks Peter, and he is frightened into releasing the old man.

Si Bryant, owner of the melon garden, confronts Alek the next morning with the knife Peter Washington dropped by the uncut melon. "I found a knife and thought it might be yours." When Alek denies owning it, Bryant tries another trick: "Is he a close friend of yourn?" At this the old man stammers: "Well, seems like he *was* er frien', an' then again, it seems like he. . . ." "It seems like he *wasn't?*" says Bryant. The deacon's only recourse is to lie. "The old man drew himself to a stately pose and held forth his arm. 'I gwine tell who. Mist' Bryant, *dish yer knife b'longs ter* Sam Jackson!' Bryant was startled into indignation. 'Who in hell is Sam Jackson?' he growled." White against Black, the Negro's salvation—as Deacon

Williams realized—lies in the fidelity of Negroes to each other, and so he saves Peter Washington by telling a "white lie."

As a chronicler of common, everyday talk heard on the streets Crane has no superior among small writers or great, said the Springfield *Republican* (August 26, 1900). "This fidelity has not deserted him in the transcription of boy life, and the Negro servant who looks after Jimmie Trescott's welfare is no less admirably portrayed." Jimmie in "The Carriage-Lamps" has secretly acquired a revolver and asks Peter Washington the cost of a box of cartridges, whereupon Peter exclaims: "Ca'tridgers! *Ca'tridgers!* Lan' sake! wut the kid want with ca'tridgers? Knew it! Knew it! Come home er'holdin' on to his hind pocket like he got money in it. An' now he want ca'tridgers." Peter tells Dr. Trescott about the revolver, and in reprisal Jimmie throws pebbles at him and breaks by chance some old carriage lamps stored in the carriage house. In punishment he is confined to the house, and while a prisoner there his friend Willie Dalzel attempts to rescue him from the "fortress"—in emulation of Tom Sawyer and Huck in the "lame ending" of *Huckleberry Finn,* as Crane rightly called it. As those carriage lamps could just as well have been on another shelf, the boy concludes the world is a bitter place where fate conspires to make him the victim of mere chance.

In "The Fight" and its sequel, "The City Urchin," Crane remembers well his own boyhood when he frequently changed schools and had to confront a new environment. "This whole business of changing schools was a complete torture. Alone he [Johnnie Hedge] had to go among a new people, a new tribe, and he apprehended his serious time. There were only two fates for him. One meant victory. One meant a kind of serfdom in which he would subscribe to every word of some superior boy and support his every word." Johnnie Hedge acquits himself like a hero, and Jimmie Trescott goes down in defeat. (Crane in recasting himself both as Johnnie, the hero, and as Jimmie, the coward, must have felt like Huck Finn: all good up one side and all bad down the other.) After Peter Washington stops the fight, the boys fight again, only to be stopped this time by Mrs. Hedge: "a dreadful woman with gray hair, with a sharp red nose, with bare arms, with spectacles of such magnifying quality that her eyes shone through them like two fierce white moons." Thenceforth the war for supremacy is over. Crane remarks: "The long-drawn animosities of men have no place in the life of a boy. The boy's mind is flexible; he readjusts his position with an ease which is derived from the fact— simply—that he is not yet a man."

The Negro Peter Washington in the *Whilomville Stories* reappears in two unpublished manuscripts partly written by Crane: "Brer Washington's Consolation" and "The Ideal and the Real." They are Southern Negro tales, not located in Whilomville township, and their Negro dialect makes them not easy reading for any Northerner. That the typescripts are corrected in Cora's hand is no proof that Cora wrote the originals, which were presumably written in collaboration. In "The Ideal and the Real" Crane recasts one of Cora's Southern reminiscences and ribs her by rendering the former hostess of a nightclub as a teacher of moral philosophy in a female school in Tennessee. The narrator of this tale aligns himself with the old Negro cook Dinah and intercedes on behalf of her complaint against Miss Cynthia of Boston, who locks the pantry cupboards so that Aunt Dinah cannot get access to them. Aunt Dinah distrusts Miss Cynthia because this Bostonian newspaper writer makes notes of everything Dinah and her husband talk about. Miss Cynthia is using them "ter solve sum' problem." She queries Dinah whether she doesn't now as a freed slave feel any soulful feeling, "enny stronger longin' fur immortality, an' desire to go upward an' onward; enny secret flutterin' ob de soul aroun' de innmos' chambers ob de heart," and the old Negro cook disclaims any soulful feelings. She suffers flutterings not in her heart but in her belly— from the cold cabbage she eats. "The Ideal and the Real" concludes: "I think I have already solved the Negro problem in the South," said Miss Cynthia. "How so?" asks the narrator. Well, says Cynthia, "once you owned the Negroes—now they own you."

Crane's East Side sketches of children in "An Ominous Baby" (1893) and "A Dark Brown Dog," written in early January, 1900, expose the hardships of childhood; the Whilomville stories expose children's cruelty to each other. They are savages, barbarians, gladiators, bullies and braggarts and gossips; but they are not social outcasts like the youngsters in the East Side sketches. Johnnie Hedge in "The Fight" is the outsider, a newcomer to Whilomville, and he redeems himself from the charge of cowardice on the "battlefields" of Port Jervis. The Hedge family has taken over the house which in "The Monster" belongs to E. J. Harrigan; it is next door to the Trescott house. Johnnie Hedge beats up Jimmie, and the bully Willie Dalzel runs away. They have been encouraged to fight it out by the savage cries of the bystanders, boys too timid to challenge anything. Crane comments on the situation: "It was a time when certain natures were impressed that only man is vile."

In "The City Urchin and the Chaste Villagers," Negro Peter Washington attempts to settle a dispute between the white boys, separating the Hedge boy from braggart Dalzel. "You two kids act like you gwine mad dogs. Stopper dat!" and then Peter turns his wrath upon Jimmie Trescott for encouraging them. The Hedge boy retreats with dignity, but his younger brother—at a safe distance from the Negro—plays his fingers at his nose and calls out: "Nig-ger-r-r! Nig-ger-r-r!"

In "Shame," Jimmie Trescott is baited by that brat Minnie Phelps, who "simply tore down the sky with her shrieks of derision. 'Got his *lunch* in it! In a *pail!*' She ran screaming to her mother. 'Oh, mamma! Oh, mamma! Jimmie Trescott's got his picnic in a pail!'" The boys don't care if Jimmie brings his lunch in a coal bin, "but such is the instinct of childish society that they all immediately moved away from him. In a moment he had been made a social leper."

Jimmie Trescott is not naturally vicious; his mother rationalizes his naughtiness as springing from "pure animal spirits," and from the bad influence of that naughty Dalzel boy, that "little predestined jailbird." But Jimmie is no more an angel child than little Cora, and he is as much of a bully as Willie Dalzel. "I kin lick you," says the Dalzel boy, and Jimmie also challenges the foreigner from Jersey City: "Kin you lick me?" Johnnie Hedge in reply pales before these gladiators, and so the other boys hoot him scornfully and escort Jimmie down the street amid acclamations, and then at school they all haw-haw at Hedge's name. "The new boy felt that his name was the most disgraceful thing which had ever been attached to a human being." "Oh, here's the new feller!" shout schoolboys at noon recess to taunt the newcomer. "The village school was like a nation. It was tight. Its amiability or friendship must be won in certain ways." One way to win it in this boys' world is to thrash the insider, and that's what the outsider Hedge does to Trescott and bully Dalzel.

The "joys of cruelty" among adults have their parallel among the children of Whilomville. In "The Lover and the Telltale," the "barbarians" who taunt Jimmie Trescott for having written a note to his sweetheart Cora become a yelping demoniac mob composed not only of his enemies but of his friends. His friends no more understand the poetry of his position "than they would understand an ancient tribal sign language. His face was set in a truer expression of horror than any of the romances describe upon the features of a man flung into a moat, a man shot in the breast with an arrow, a man cleft in the neck with a battle axe." It is Rose Goldege who spreads the gossip: "Oh! Oh! Oh! Jimmie Trescott's writing to his girl! Oh! Oh!" Jimmie thinks to attempt, "by an impossible means of strangulation, to keep her important news from the public." The informer Goldege causes a riot in which other children throng to the scene of Jimmie's destruction like blood-fanged wolves.

In "Making an Orator," Jimmie Trescott is "a child in torment," terrfied at the ordeal of reciting Tennyson's *Charge of the Light Brigade*. His classmates rustle with delight in the teacher's cruelty in snapping at him; she shares in their joys of cruelty. As for his classmates, "they were no better than a Roman populace in Nero's time." From thenceforth his incapacity for public speaking would remain with him until he died, as it did with Crane, who shared with Jimmie the feeling that death amid flames was preferable to reciting Tennyson's poem.

In "The Stove" Mrs. Trescott gives a tea party for her cousin Willis and his wife on their visit from New York, while Willis' daughter Cora, the angel child of a bewildered father, and Jimmie attempt to set up her toy stove in the stable, only to be confronted by Peter Washington. " 'An' have er fiah in it? No, seh! G'w'on 'way f'm heh!—g'w'on! Don' 'low no sech foolishin' round yer. No, seh.' 'Well, we ain't goin' to hurt your old stable, are we?' asked Jimmie, ironically. 'Dat you ain't, Jim! Not so long's I keep my two eyes right plumb squaah p'inted at ol' Jim. No, seh!' Peter began to chuckle in derision."

Crane spoils this scene by lecturing his adult readers: "Nothing affects children so much as rhetoric. It may not involve any definite presentation of common sense, but if it is picturesque they surrender decently to its influence. Peter was by all means a rhetorician, and it was not long before the two children had dismally succumbed to him. They went away." They relocate the toy stove in the cellar of the house and pretend that the turnips they burn in the stove are puddings. The stench brings their parents downstairs to discover the cause, and that ends the turnip party.

The tea party upstairs has been a great success, unprecedented in Whilomville. Willis' beautiful wife has suggested that good tea be served, as an innovation, but Mrs. Trescott is sure the ladies of Whilomville would not like it. The important thing is the style of the teacup. The party is pictured as a pagan ritual where latent enemies greet each other in a fanfare of empty affections while measuring to the inch what the others are wearing. "Those who wore old dresses would wish then that they had not come; and those who saw that, in the company, they were well clad, would be pleased or exalted, or filled with the joys of cruelty. Then they had tea, which was a habit and a delight with none of them, their usual beverage being coffee with milk." The habit of tea parties is "the result of a conspiracy of certain unenlightened people to make life still more uncomfortable"; the charms of Willis' beautiful wife make all the other women feel bad. And out in the stable little Cora, Jimmie's old flame, "made a serf of him in a few sentences." The stench from the burnt turnips in the toy stove is Crane's commentary on the social stench of the tea party upstairs.

"The Stove" is the most subtly designed of all his Whilomville stories. Sometimes charming but more often boring, most of them are lightweight stuff; only half a dozen seem to us today to rise above the commonplace. Their chief appeal is to readers who have experienced similar incidents in childhood and find pleasure in self-identification. It would be comforting, said the *Nation* (February 28, 1901), to think that Crane "meant to satirize one group of American children for the eternal good of all American children, but, on reflection, there is nothing to support such a kindly opinion."

*Whilomville Stories,* said the *Critic* (October, 1900), "shine superior to much of the late Stephen Crane's work. They are by no means masterpieces, these acutely human little sketches, for simplicity is ever lacking. They show observation and sympathy, but are in many places baroque, overweighted. Throughout his career Mr. Crane was a consistent victim of the shoddy in word or phrase. That which stood most in his way was an absence of fine, discriminating, aesthetic perception. Hence his splendors are largely tinsel, his triumphs often tawdry. Though brilliant and colorful, Mr. Crane's pages do not burn with anything approaching Pater's 'gem-like flame'; they are, after all, mere flashes in the pan."

Extremely slight they are, said the London *Academy* (December, 1900) "In some the framework is almost too frail to bear the canvas on which he paints; but everywhere in the treatment of these children, no less than in the minute touches by which his ultra-sensitised mind reflected the humours, the gaieties, the bizarreries of the struggle against an armed landscape that is modern war, you find the marks of the wonderful beyondness that was his convincing effect. The absurdities of the playground, the jealousies of rival heroes, the boastfulness of the coward, the complacencies of the lickspittle—it is pleasant to see these things exposed."

*Whilomville Stories* are as clever a study of the psychology of boyhood as has appeared since Kenneth Graham's *Golden Age,* said *Book News.* Howells' *A Boy's Town,* William Allen White's *Boyville Stories,* Charles Dudley Warner's *Being a Boy,* and the small-town boy depicted in *Huckleberry Finn* and in T. B. Aldrich's *The Story of a Bad Boy,* each had presented the American boy from a different point of view; Crane's was yet another.[2] In some ways his treatment of boys is unequaled, the Springfield *Republican* said, and his *Whilomville Stories* "represent the fiction art of their author as worthily as almost anything he has written. For one thing, the limitations of his art are less glaring when he writes of children than when he treats of those who have broader and more varied interests, while the external, bare, even hard style with which Mr. Crane was accustomed to write of adults becomes perceptibly softer and more sympathetic when he chronicles the acts of the little people. There is more moralizing over fighting, for instance, in the account of the new boy's fights with the neighborhood champions than in all the pages of *The Red Badge of Courage.*"

However, the true Crane style is the ironic style of *The Red Badge* and of *Maggie,* rather than the soft sentimental variety of *Whilomville Stories.* There is some truth to Edward Garnett's remark that when Crane "breathes an everyday, common atmosphere his aesthetic power always weakens."

One morning in early October Crane came down to breakfast and said: " 'Edith has never been to Ireland. Let's go to Ireland.' Bless him! He was writing *The O'Ruddy* and wanted some local color and I was a good excuse. So we packed our bags and off we went to London," says Edith Richie Jones.

While in Ireland Crane received £30 from Pinker, and then back at Brede Place by October 21 Cora sent Pinker a letter from their solicitor which explained why they were in urgent need of £50. At least that much, she explained, was due Crane from John Lane for "War Memories" (published in December in Lady Churchill's *Anglo-Saxon Review*), and something would be forthcoming from a few Whilomville stories not yet written. She sent Pinker the first two chapters of *The O'Ruddy* and promised that "Mr. Crane will just deluge you with stuff for the next two months." She figured that Pinker already held in favor of Crane's account three Wyoming tales (so-called because they are located in Wyoming Valley, Pennsylvania) and a Western tale called "Moonlight on the Snow." She judged them to be worth £115, but that sum did not materialize in Crane's lifetime; they were published posthumously, except for "Moonlight," which appeared in April, 1900, in *Leslie's Popular Monthly*.

Crane was by now heavily in debt to Pinker, who wrote him on the 24th: "I confess that you are becoming most alarming. You telegraphed on Friday for £20; Mrs. Crane, on Monday, makes it £50; today comes your letter making it £150, and I very much fear that your agent must be a millionaire if he is to satisfy your necessities a week hence, at this rate. Seriously, you pinch me rather tightly. Mrs. Crane says I have 'probably advanced money to Mr. Crane that I have not myself yet collected.' As a matter of fact, this sum, at present, is £230. I mention this to impress you less with an obligation to me than to yourself. There is a risk of spoiling the market if we have to dump too many short stories on it at once."

Crane had sent him the eleventh Whilomville story, and Pinker thought one more would suffice to complete that series unless *Harper's* thought of extending it. He had also received the beginning of the Irish romance *O'Ruddy* for Methuen Ltd. and for Stokes in America. He asked Stephen why he didn't do the battle sketches for Lippincott *(Great Battles of the World)*. As a sure thing towards solving his money crisis Crane had thought up a collection of battle sketches, beginning with the "Brief Campaign Against New Orleans." Crane chose the various battles "for their picturesque and theatrical qualities, not alone for their decisiveness. What he could best assimilate from history was its grandeur and passion and the fire of action," said Harrison S. Morris in his preface to *Great Battles* (1901). The American artist John Sloan did the illustrations. Kate Frederic not only researched the book but wrote most of it, perhaps all of it, but when it appeared posthumously there was no acknowledgment to her.

Pinker in his letter of October 24 promised to do his best "to try to manage *something* during the next ten days or a fortnight." Cora replied two days later that Stephen's Whilomville stories brought cash on delivery of the manuscript at *Harper's* New York office (at the rate of £10.10 per thousand words for the serial rights, as Pinker pointed out to Scribner's, who declined the three Crane manuscripts he submitted on the 26th). "I am *begging that you will send today* the amount due for one you received yesterday ('The Fight') £40 to Oxted Bank to my credit. Please *send it directly to my account.* The enclosed note from C. Hayles will explain the need. If this cheque [bill] for £32. 14. 6 is not paid these people will issue writ—at once—and give us no end of trouble." Another Whilomville story would be sent Pinker tomorrow, and he should advance its payment immediately to her account at Oxted, where the Cranes still owed everyone for the upkeep of their Ravensbrook establishment during 1897–1898.

"Now Mr. Pinker, how could you say to Mr. Crane not to dump too many short stories upon the market for fear of spoiling it? This is a fatal thing to say to a writing man. Particularly to Stephen Crane. And how can you think so with an utterly unspoiled and vast American market." He could sell a thousand short stories of Mr. Crane there if he had them. "If there is any doubt of your being able to get the amount that Mr. Crane must have, £150, will you write me and I will come up and see what I can do borrowing some on some of his stuff. Mr. Crane is now engaged in fighting his last creditors and they can be fought only with money."

Crane thanked Pinker for a check for £50 on November 4, hoped that he'd send another for that sum as soon as possible, and explained why his collections of stories were so slow in reaching completion. "I can do nothing save to continue to turn out the best work in my power and turn it out as fast as possible. Your remark upon the possibility of overloading the market struck me as being extremely wrong. I have been aware for some years that I have been allowing over half of my real market to languish without any of Stephen Crane's stories. I mean 'The Century' [and] 'Scribner's,' 'Youth's Companion' and a lot of newspaper syndicates in America which have made me personal requests to help fill their pages."

Perhaps as a kind of vacation from his evil monetary ghosts while his mind harked back to Port Jervis days in his Whilomville stories, Crane wrote "The Mesmeric Mountain: A Tale of Sullivan County." A remarkable fable, it aptly applies to his plight during his last English year. As in other Sullivan County sketches, here is the little man who gazes dim-eyed in the distance and ponders: "That road out yonder. I've been wonderin' what it leads to," and then sets off down the forest track in spite of being told by his friend that it leads only to Jim Boyd's house and the Lumberland Pike. Determined to ascend Jones' Mountain, whose summit was "a blaze of red wrath," he feels that the mountain is attacking him. "The mountain was approaching." And so he counterattacks and desperately gains the summit to gaze at the Western horizon, where the sun has sunk "in red silence." All that he finds at the top is that the world is unchanged beneath him: " 'Ho!' he said. 'There's Boyd's house and the Lumberland Pike.' The mountain under his feet was motionless."

The futility of climbing a mountain only to discover what one already knew existed in the valley below epitomizes Crane's climb to fame in early 1896. The image also serves as a sustaining metaphor of his life since then. It was uphill again and again, and always the happy gardens below belonged to "impossible distances."

He sent Pinker on November 4 "a double extra special good thing" which he then called "The Burial," and which was retitled as "The Upturned Face." He was wonderfully keen on its 1500 words; it is, indeed, one of his best. Pinker placed it in *Ainslee's Magazine* for March, 1900. "It is so good—for me—that I would almost sacrifice it to the best magazine in England rather than see it appear in the best paying magazine. I suppose many men stir you with tumultuous sentiments concerning work which they have just completed but—anyhow you take a copy of this story home with you and read it and let me know your opinion. This is something which you do not always do. I can go all over the place and write fiction about almost anything and if you give me a racing tip from time to time it is extremely handy."

Cora wrote Pinker a few days later with Chapter XIV of *The O'Ruddy,* now at 36,800 words, which she typed in four copies, and suggested that he offer to the *New Magazine* in New York City both "The Burial" (as she calls it) and another Spitzbergen tale (linked with "The Upturned Face" and other Spitzbergen tales), "And If He Wills We Must Die." Its variant title is "The End of the Battle," and it was published—like so many things Crane wrote in his last months at Brede Place—posthumously. He was killing himself to write them now, he did not live long enough to see them in print, and he died too soon to collect the profits.

In December, 1899, Harper published the American edition of *The Monster and Other Stories,* containing "The Blue Hotel," which Crane had written at Ravensbrook in February, 1898, and sold to *Collier's Weekly* for $300. "The Blue Hotel" in its germinal idea follows Stevenson's formula for a story, that terrain and atmosphere suggest the correlative action and persons for that particular locality, and are so used as to express or symbolize it. The atmosphere of the old blue hotel, the psychic quality of its screaming blue, impels and foreshadows the action that expresses it—the fistfight in the blue snowdrift on the sheltered side of the hotel. Crane begins his story: "The Palace Hotel at Fort Romper was painted a light blue, a shade that is on the legs of a kind of heron, causing the bird to declare its position against any background." The blue hotel, standing alone on the prairie, was "always screaming and howling," and the snow-covered land also was "blue with the sheen of an unearthly satin."[3] As the blue-legged heron declares his position against his background, so does the Swede with his fixed idea that some of these Western places are dangerous enough for him to be killed there. He, too, like the heron, is at odds with the environment, and he is identified with that bird by Johnnie's calling the Swede "the wildest loon I ever see."

He is blustering and arrogant, but frightened. He supposes that a good many men have been killed in this hotel and that he is going to be killed before he leaves it. And killed he is, but not here in the hotel where he expects his murder but in a saloon, and there by an utter stranger. The trouble with this Swede from the East is that he has been reading dime novels about the badlands, says the Easterner, " 'and he thinks he's right out in the middle of it—the shootin' and stabbin' and all.' 'But,' said the cowboy, deeply scandalized, 'this ain't Wyoming, ner none of them places. This is Nebrasker.' 'Yes,' added Johnnie, 'an' why don't he wait till he gits *out West?*' The travelled Easterner laughed. 'It isn't different there even—not in these days. But he thinks he's right in the middle of hell.' "

And so the Swede—convinced that he is formidably menaced and about to be killed—assumes a tragic attitude and makes "the gesture of a martyr." But he is mistaken about the place being hell; on the contrary, the hotel resembles a church complete with icons and a priest—Patrick Scully looks "curiously like an old priest," and like the priest he declares: "A guest under my roof has sacred privileges." He conducts his new guests on their arrival in this prairie town through the portals of the hotel into a small room, which "seemed to be merely a proper temple for an enormous stove"—it hums "with godlike violence." The three guests—the Swede, the cowboy, and the silent Easterner—wash themselves in three basins of cold water, and by these "small ceremonies" they are made to feel that their host is very benevolent and of philanthropic impulse. The icons are photographs of Scully's son Michael and of his dead daughter, and he proudly shows them off to the blasphemous Swede, whose glance burns with hatred as the eager little Irishman insists that his guest share the bottle of whiskey secreted in his upstairs chamber, but this libation offered in friendship is misconstrued—the Swede thinks his host is trying to poison him.

The three travelers are mock figures of the Three Wise Men who came out of the East. The wisest of them is the Swede, who knows it all. He has divined the whole plan of the father and son; they are out to get him. And sure enough he is tricked by the son. "You are cheatin'!" he screams at Johnnie as they play a game of High-Five around the mock altar of the stove. The five men are sitting around one side of the stove in a crescent. Now they rise in consternation, and their boots trample the scattered cards whose painted kings and queens gaze "with their silly eyes at the war that was waging above them." The "peace-compellers" are the priest-like Pat and the silent Easterner, who importunes in a voice that goes unheeded: "Oh, wait a moment. What's the good of a fight over a game of cards?"—a game not played for money, but for the joy of it. The son, who has defaulted on his father's trust, challenges the outsider and goes down in defeat.

The Swede quits the hotel and walks in a blizzard to the town's saloon, whose indomitable red-lighted lamp makes the blue snow the color of blood. He dies of a knife wound inflicted upon him by a gentleman gambler whom he seizes by the throat to force him to share a drink of whiskey. "What! You won't drink with me, you little dude? I'll make you then! I'll make you!" The saloon scene echoes the hotel scene in several ways: The gambler refuses to drink with the outsider, just as "the wise man" from the East—suspicious of his host—had declined Scully's offer of the whiskey bottle. He had jerked his hand away from it "and cast a look of horror upon Scully. 'Drink,' said the old man affectionately."

Johnnie cheats at cards, and so does the saloon gambler, although otherwise "this thieving card-player was so generous, so just, so moral, that, in a contest, he could have put to flight the consciences of nine tenths of the citizens of Romper." Prior to the quarrel between the Swede and Johnnie, there are two quarrels between an old farmer and Johnnie, who was probably cheating in these card games also, and then at the end there is the Swede's quarrel with the gentleman gambler. Quarrels pattern the story and bind the scene of the hotel as temple with the scene of the red-lighted saloon as hell, where the corpse of the Swede "had its eyes fixed upon a dreadful legend that dwelt atop of the cash machine: 'This registers the amount of your purchase.' "

To the dramatic ending of the story Crane attached a second ending, a moralizing appendix whose subsequent scene is months later near the Dakota line where cowboy Bill and the silent Easterner (presumably the author) recount over their campfire what happened back at Romper. The Easterner now admits that he knew Johnnie was cheating, but "I refused to stand up and be a man. I let the Swede fight it out alone. . . . We are all in it! This poor gambler isn't even a noun. He is a kind of an adverb. Every sin is the result of a collaboration. We, five of us, have collaborated in the murder of this Swede." So, then, the Swede's tragic end was brought about not by the Swede himself but by his environment—comprised of the blue hotel and its proprietor, his son Johnnie, cowboy Bill, the Easterner, and the saloon gambler. At the end of the story Bill protests against the Easterner's "fog of mysterious theory: 'Well, I didn't do anythin', did I?' " From the Easterner's point of view, which is Crane's point of view, the cowboy shares with him in the blame, but is not the cowboy exempt in that he didn't know Johnnie was cheating? That is the fog in the Easterner's mysterious theory.

This second ending of the story, with its trumped-up theory that the Swede's death was brought about through his environment, stands at odds with the ironic first ending of the story declared by the cash register's legend. The two endings contradict each other in their philosophical import. What traps the Swede is his fixed idea of his environment, but according to the second conclusion it is the environment itself that traps him. The two endings thus confound each other and negate the artistic unity of "The Blue Hotel." *Maggie* had fulfilled Crane's declared intention "to show that environment is a tremendous thing in the world and frequently shapes lives regardless." But in "The Blue Hotel," he belittles the importance of environment, in the scene where the Swede accuses Johnnie of cheating, by remarking that such scenes often prove that "there can be little of dramatic import in environment. Any room can present a tragic front; any room can be comic."

The second ending was originally much longer than in its published form. Robert Collier of *Collier's Weekly* wrote Paul Reynolds (April 26, 1898) his acceptance of "The Blue Hotel" shortened to 7,500 or 8,000 words, and then on September 20 he wrote again: "I had intended publishing it before Christmas, or the week immediately after, but I cannot lay my hands on it at present. Do you remember the date on which you left the shortened version here? It was in manuscript, not typewriting, was it not?" Then Collier found the manuscript and published it in two parts (November 26 and December 3). "The Blue Hotel," Crane had written Reynolds in early February, 1898, should be conjoined with "The Monster," and together they'd make 32,000 words, enough for a dollar book. ("His New Mittens" was added later.)

Crane spent two months trying to find an effective title for his Cuban War tales. Of all war correspondents who published their Cuban War reminiscences only he achieved a unity in his collection, by repetition of the themes which pattern the whole: "wounds" and "rain." He was excited by the title, demanding that Methuen stick to it and writing Pinker that he would not change it "unless I am compelled to do so." He completed the book by the end of August, 1899, and dedicated it to Moreton Frewen, proprietor of Brede Manor: "This small Token of Things Well Remembered by his Friend Stephen Crane."

*Wounds in the Rain,* said the *Critic* (January, 1901), is the work of a born story-teller, and his experiences here are as vividly recorded as in his imaginative *Red Badge.* It is one thing to imagine how one would have felt and acted in a certain battle, as Mr. Crane did in *The Red Badge,* and quite another to tell what one actually felt and did under fire as he recounts it here in his Cuban War tales. "Any experienced story-teller could have written them, whereas no one but Crane could have written *The Red Badge.*" In reading Mr. Crane's extraordinary work, said the London *Academy* (October 16, 1900), no one can escape from the reflection that this last war book ridiculously resembles his first, *The Red Badge,* where almost every impression was preconceived. "For verisimilitude the author might have stayed for the one as for the other in his own armchair and never have gone at all to the wars. This might lead to either of two conditions: that the reporter was obsessed by the author's battles in the brain, or that the author had successfully divined truth which the reporter's observation could but verify."

Crane boasted to Pinker that *Wounds in the Rain* was the only decent book that had yet been written on the Cuban War. He was right in that he alone of all the war correspondents had recast his experiences in the form of fiction, but in the matter of actual war dispatches Richard Harding Davis' *The Cuban and Porto Rican Campaigns* (1899) is the best of the more than two dozen contemporary journalistic books on the Cuban War. Most of the pieces in *Wounds in the Rain* are low-pressure writings without design or significance as short stories and are in fact mere tales or sketches. "God Rest Ye, Merry Gentlemen," said Willa Cather, is done in the out-worn manner considered smart in the days when Davis was a romantic figure. The chesty manner which came in with Kipling, and the pompous humor, seemed quite the thing. The London *Athenaeum* singled out as the best of the stories "The Price of the Harness," and so it is. But it just misses fire; it is not worth its length. The best thing in *Wounds in the Rain* is "War Memories," a semifictionalized account of Crane's Cuban War experiences reprinted from the *Anglo-Saxon Review* (December, 1899).

"War Memories" reads with livelier interest today than almost all the eye-witness accounts by contemporary reporters of the Cuban War. Crane, said the *Nation* (November 29, 1900), writes in the manner of a clever journalist aiming to give literary effectiveness to descriptions of episodes "in which the note of life is distressing or violent or brutal." Crane debunked sentimentalism and stood apart from his times, exemplifying Henry James's credo that "art should be as hard as nails, as hard as the heart of the artist," and that even lyrical poetry should consist of "stony-hearted triumphs of objective form." In Henry James's now famous declaration of June 1896, "But I have the imagination of disaster—and see life indeed as ferocious and sinister," one is reminded of the lines from Crane's *Black Riders:* "In all drink/ He detected the bitter."[4]

# XXIX

## ⊂ə *The Beginning of the End*

EXPLOITING the legend of Brede Manor as a haunted house, Crane devised "The Ghost," a play to be written by ten collaborators.

"We of Brede Place are giving a free play to the villagers at Christmas time in the school-house, and I have written some awful rubbish which our friends will on that night speak out to the parish," he wrote H. B. Marriott-Watson, author of *The Heart of Miranda,* on November 15, 1899. "But to make the thing historic I have hit upon a plan of making the programmes choice by printing thereon a terrible list of authors of the comedy and to that end I have asked Henry James, Robert Barr, Joseph Conrad, A. E. Mason, H. G. Wells, Edwin Pugh, George Gissing, Rider Haggard and yourself to write a mere word—any word 'it,' 'they,' 'you'— any word and thus identify themselves with this crime."[1]

It was sketched out by A. E. W. Mason, said the London *Daily Chronicle,* "and then sent round to be filled in by a number of eminent hands. One wonders what the Sussex peasantry think of the work of Mr. Henry James, who is now settled among them at Rye. It should be added that no London manager need apply for *The Ghost.* It is laid."[2]

A combination of farce and comedy, opera and burlesque, "The Ghost" has been called a literary curiosity unrivaled, but it is unrivaled only in its authorship. Joseph Conrad contributed one line to the play: "This is a jolly cold world," and George Gissing another: "He died of an indignity caught in running after his hat down Piccadilly." Edwin Pugh submitted: "A bird in the hand may be worth two in the bush, but the birds in the bush don't think so."

Mason acted the role of the ghost; an experienced actor, he was very realistic. He also performed the duties of stage manager in a very satisfactory manner, said the *South Eastern Advertiser.* He was the only one of the ten collaborating authors to participate in the play, "probably the most amazing play ever produced." The cast of characters stepped right out of novels: Doctor Moreau from H. G. Wells' *Island of Doctor Moreau:* Peter Quint (son of Doctor Moreau) from Henry James's *The Turn of the Screw.* The character Suburbia derived from Edwin Pugh's first success,

*Street in Suburbia.* Miranda is an echo from Mason's *Miranda of the Balcony* and Marriott-Watson's *Heart of Miranda.* Rufus Coleman came to the stage out of Crane's *Active Service,* where we first met that war correspondent for the *Eclipse* (Hearst's *Journal*).[3]

The play was performed on December 28 in the old schoolhouse in Brede village, before an audience of Sussex yokels leavened by Crane's distinguished guests. The house party began the day before and concluded with a ball in the Great Hall on the night of the 29th. The house was festooned with ropes of holly and ivy, and forty plum puddings, sauced and burning, were prepared for the banquet by servants "hired for the week." Because of a tremendous snowstorm that night none of the local countryside friends (including the merchants who supplied the food and wine and wood for the party) attended this festival, but it was a good thing they didn't get there, as the nonsense of the house guests would have staggered them. They were playing a game of racing on broomsticks amidst the rushes on the floors, a game invented by H. G. Wells. He and Catherine had arrived for this marvelous Christmas–New Year's party in a Sandgate cab rather in advance of guests from London, and so they were given one of the four available bedrooms, which they furnished with their own bedding and blankets.

Cora had invited thirty or forty guests with only four bedrooms habitable! She rented from the local hospital some truckle-beds or cots for the unfurnished and icy bedroom, large as a hall and nicknamed the Girls' Dormitory, while the men—separated from their wives—retreated to an array of shakedowns in the cold attic. The sanitary facilities dated from the seventeenth century, says H. G. Wells, and such as there was indoors was accessible only through the Girls' Dorm. "Consequently the wintry countryside next morning was dotted with wandering, melancholy, preoccupied men-guests. Anyhow there were good open fires in the great fireplaces, and I remember that party as an extraordinary lark—but shot, at the close, with red intimations of a coming tragedy."

They danced until two or three in the morning in the big oak-panelled room downstairs lit by candles stuck in iron sconces improvised by Cora and the Brede blacksmith, and then near noon they breakfasted on beer, eggs and bacon, and sweet potatoes from America. Wells and his old schoolfellow Sidney Bowkett swapped yarns while playing poker, which they didn't take seriously, and Crane in a peeve quit instructing them in the game. "In any decent saloon in America," he said, "you'd be shot for talking like that at poker." Wells describes him as a "slow-speaking, perceptive, fragile, tuberculous being, too adventurous to be temperate with anything and impracticable to an extreme degree. He liked to sit and talk, sagely and deeply. . . . He was profoundly weary and ill, if I had been wise enough to see it, but I thought him sulky and reserved." He had no critical chatter, and when they compared impressions of their contem-

poraries Crane would simply say: "That's great." Or he'd grunt "Gaw!"
Was so and so any good? So and so was "no good." He never talked over
his projects with Wells.[4]

The Conrads were there, and Jessie talked with Cora in the Great Hall
while that golden-haired amazon made preparations to retire. Jessie kissed
Cora goodnight, and then she stole a look into her "bedroom." Cora had
chosen for her bedroom what had been used that night as the ballroom
(the large first-floor drawing room running east to west), "and her big
four post bedstead standing on the raised dais (where the musicians were
meant to sit) looked like a tiny doll's bed. All the necessary bedroom furniture was grouped close together in a small island, and the light from the
two tall candles threw the rest of the vast apartment into ghostly shadow.
At the extreme end of the big room appeared a small opening like a tube
railway; far in the distance I saw Stephen and my husband seated in
close conclave . . . I remember thinking that when Stephen escorted his
friend through as they parted for the night Cora would be sleeping too
far away to be visible, even with the light of the candles burning close
beside her. Hardly a comfortable room to have chosen for sleeping, especially in winter."

No sooner had the musicians packed up their instruments and departed,
after the ball on the 29th, than Crane collapsed with a lung hemorrhage;
it was the beginning of the end. He fainted against the shoulder of a
guest while strumming his guitar, and then he spouted blood. He tried
to conceal it from Cora, who in great alarm appealed to Wells, although
Stephen "didn't want anyone to bother." Wells sensed the crisis; he himself had had tuberculosis as a young man. He grabbed a bicycle and rode
that wintry night seven miles into a drizzling dawn to call up a doctor in
Rye.

In the irony of his Western tale, "Twelve O'Clock," appearing in *Pall
Mall Magazine* that December, one recognizes Crane's obsession with
death in the murder of three cowboys who shoot each other in the Placer
Hotel, their meaningless end mocked by the wooden bird that springs from
the cuckoo clock and cries "cuckoo" twelve times. His Western tale might
be read as a parody of the extravagant and idiotic life at Brede Manor,
except that it needed no cuckoo clock to tell Crane how senseless it was,
a comic opera that was destined to end quite otherwise.

In September a fistula had kept him from riding and from sailing the
boat he shared with Conrad, and the Cuban fever troubled him enough
to ask George Wyndham what he knew about the Black Forest. "I mean
as a health resort? The truth is that Cuba Libre just about liberated me
from this base blue world. The clockwork is juggling badly. I have had
a lot of idiotic company all summer."

Crane made a good deal of money, says Jessie Conrad; but it all went toward keeping up that expensive house, which was always filled "with what Joseph calls 'free lunchers'—and all the while the poor man was dying!" Their open hospitality and gay extravagance was Cora's program for giving her ailing Stephen always a good time, and she carried it out with excessive vigor, says H. G. Wells.

Crane wasn't the master of his home, and although Cora was not alone to blame for that pretentious Christmas–New Year bacchanalia, "his life was altogether out of control; he was being carried along. What he was still clinging to, but with a dwindling zest, was artistry." He kept up the front that as artist he could not condescend to write potboilers and refused Pinker's request for a Christmas story for Tillotson's. Stephen will not write a "seasonable story," Cora wrote Pinker. He said that he "has never written Xmas stories of the kind which seems to be specified and declared that he will not begin now." (He conveniently ignored that in his desperate 1894 days he had written "Christmas Dinner Won in Battle"—for the *Plumbers Trade Journal!*)

The money situation was so bad that in December Cora wrote Pinker: "Mr. Crane says that he has not time to stop & do a story of 7500 words for which he will have to wait some weeks for return. So he will put this story aside now as he did with the 'Irish Romance' and return to short stuff which will bring in money at once. After the holidays, perhaps, he can settle and do them both." Had he survived, the situation would have been the same: living day to day from hand to mouth, always in debt to butcher, baker, candlestick maker, and always writing the "short stuff" that would pay off at once. Although he was pleased at being asked by Lady Randolph Churchill to write for her *Anglo-Saxon Review,* a new venture in style and cultural ideals, he was yet more pleased with the £50 she paid him, even though he told Pinker that that was "not a commercial transaction." He was writing "to order," delivering "copy" to meet his commitments and debts. "I got to do them," he told Wells, "I got to do them."[5]

Crane recovered rapidly from his ominous attack and on New Year's Day he wrote Moreton Frewen of Chesham Place, London, while abed in his immense long and narrow study at Brede: "I am desolated by your request because I fear it is the result of a misunderstanding. It is true that we gave a play in the village school house but the whole thing was a mere idle string of rubbish made to entertain the villagers and with music frankly stolen from very venerable comic operas such as 'The Mikado' and 'Pinafore.' The whole business was really beneath contempt to serious people and it would be inconsiderate, even unkind, of me to send it to you. The names of the authors was more of a joke than anything. Still, we made it genuine by causing all these men to write a mere word or phrase— such as 'It's cold' or, in fact anything at all—and in this way we arranged this rather historic little program. Allow me to wish you a very fine shining

1900."[6] On New Year's Eve he lifted his glass in a toast to friend Mark Barr: "Let's drink to the twentieth century—in spite of your objection, Mark." Barr had assured him that the new century did not begin on the 1st of January.

Ford Hueffer visited on January 2, and Crane probed him about certain ill-willed gossipings and grudges against him he had heard of. Were they true? Ford probably evaded that query, but he had no reason to invent the situation. Crane had a hideout house up the bank from that lugubrious manor house, and there he greeted his unexpected caller on what was to be their last visit together. "Hueffer, thank God, it's you. I always say you bring me luck." The luck Ford brought him was that of his not being the tax collector from whom Crane was hiding. "He had the theory that if in England you did not pay your taxes on New Year's Day you went to prison." Ford assured him it was not so and that he had two or three more months before the tax collector would visit him.

Mrs. Edith Richie Jones, who insists that the house "radiated with happiness," scoffs at Ford's exaggerations in his reminiscences of the Cranes, but in spite of Edward Garnett's calling him the archliar there is always some truth behind his smoke screen; Ford's exaggerations frequently prove to be just the way things were.

On the same Tuesday (January 2, 1900) Cora wrote Pinker: "Mr. Crane is ill again—in bed but is still keeping at his work. The pressing of his creditors is so distressing. Now I simply loathe bothering you again, but I can't help it." She begs again for another £20 to be put to her credit at the London bank of Brown & Shipley, as she is obliged to draw against it for things which can't be put off. The Irish romance *O'Ruddy* ought to bring a good round sum from Stokes and Co., especially if the serial rights on it could be gotten in, and she felt sure that there was some money still due from Stokes on *Active Service* that "would put Mr. Crane straight. But as it is we have to keep begging you to put cheques in bank all the time. I don't know what Mr. Crane would do without your kind help through these long days of trying to get straight, but I'm sure you feel that in the long run he will prove his appreciation of your simply saving him from going smash." He should wire her what Stokes says because every moment saved means so much less worry for Mr. Crane. By Thursday he had almost written one *Battle* sketch and another chapter of *The O'Ruddy* but Pinker's promised wire did not come, and so she explained that Miss Helen Crane needs money for her ticket to Lausanne today (January 4) as she leaves this weekend for Paris. "She can't leave until money reaches her. Then, as I explained, if the money is not deposited with Brown & Shipley, & cheques are returned again, they may ask me to close my account."

William Crane had written Cora on December 22, 1899, a letter of apology for his prolonged silence. Although he was in arrears now on money to Stephen for getting Helen back to Lausanne from Brede, he never mentions it. When Stephen had taken Helen to the Lausanne school the previous September, he not only left her without any pocket money, but borrowed from Mme. Eytel-Hubbe—through his niece Helen—the sum of thirty Swiss francs and never paid it back. William repaid it when Mme. Eytel-Hubbe, proprietress of the Rosemont-Dezaley School, wrote him about the loan, but he could not forgo mentioning it now in his Christmas letter, although he himself had defaulted in sending Helen travel and pocket money, letting Stephen advance such sums. He claims that he is financially embarrassed by the closing of the doors of the Port Jervis bank, forced out of business temporarily by having been robbed of a sum large enough to make Port Jervis almost bankrupt if outstanding claims are pressed against it. The robber was Lew Goldsmith, whom Stephen once knew.

William hopes that Stephen's health has improved since a month or so ago, doubts that he can afford visiting him in 1900, and decides that he cannot afford to send Edmund's daughter Agnes to Lausanne. He defends the Port Jervis public schools as very good against Cora's remarks that they could not teach Helen this or that. The fault is with her, or rather was with her because she was so indolent in her studies, careless in her choice of associates, and so persistent in her ways; hence it was a godsend that the Cranes invited her to Europe. "She needed a tremendous moral and intellectual awakening, and I think she is getting it. I am not defending Port Jervis. I am telling you facts, in order that you may fully understand Helen's case. I appreciate your goodness to her."

William adds that he does not know how *Active Service* is selling. The public library has it, and he sees it occasionally on private tables; it is very much liked. People in Port Jervis would like to know what Stephen's views are about the Transvaal matter in the Boer War. "We are almost all pro-Boer here. I have looked in vain for your name [Cora's] among the American women who are fitting out the hospital ship." That was Lady Randolph Churchill's hospital ship *Maine,* christened in honor of the American battleship sunk in Havana Harbor in 1898. The idea of equipping a hospital ship to be sent to the Transvaal with funds jointly subscribed in England and America was launched by Lady Churchill as a symbol cementing the ties between the two countries.

Crane wrote Pinker on January 5 that he had to have more money, could not get on without it. "If you cannot send £50 by the next mail, I will have to find a man who can. I know this is abrupt and unfair, but self-preservation forces my game with you precisely as it did with Reynolds." He was threatening his sole benefactor and patron with breach of contract, and once more Pinker drew the line. Cora on the 7th replied to his telegram that Mr. Crane intended no threat and would keep all engagements as per agreement. She mailed him a little story: "The Tale of a

Dark Brown Dog," written the past week, and Stephen on the 9th wrote Pinker in softened tone: "you are a BENEFIT." However, solicitor Plant was kicking for £10, and Her Majesty would be calling tomorrow for income tax, and Cora's bank account was overdrawn. That same day Pinker was writing Cora that he had deposited £30 in her bank. "I am sure it is not necessary for me to tell you that you and Mr. Crane may always count on all the help I can give, but as you know, the demands on my help have been greater in extent and persistency than was ever contemplated, and I was therefore much surprised to receive Mr. Crane's letter of the 5th."

Cora protested that Stephen had no idea of putting any of his work in other hands than Pinker's and could not understand why Pinker should have received such an impression. Stephen was very faithful to any agreement, she wrote, and appreciated Pinker's having advanced money upon stories before he received payment for them himself. By Friday several more chapters of *The O'Ruddy* would be finished. Pinker should ask Methuen if they will advance £100 on it; for Crane's next book they are to pay £200 (the novel on the American Revolution, which he abandoned). "Mr. Curtis Brown, who is an old friend of Mr. Crane's, and of whom doubtless you know, is anxious to buy a book from him and says that he will give a bigger price than anyone." Curtis Brown, it will be remembered, had served under Edward Marshall on the New York Sunday *Press* in 1894 when Crane was selling sketches to the *Press* at five dollars per column. He had come down from London, where he was beginning his literary agency, to visit Stephen at Brede Manor and see if he had anything for him to handle.[7]

By January 20 Crane was well enough to get to London with Cora and retrieve from Pinker two *Great Battles* sketches because they weren't good enough—he had mailed them the day before. He mentioned to Pinker his idea of going to Texas for his health. Pinker asked about the New Year's party. "I've heard it was a Babylonian orgy," said Stephen, echoing the opinion of the Brede natives.

Several days later, Robert Barr wrote to an American friend: "England has been kind to Stevie in many ways, but some of his cherished friends have said things too carelessly about his most generous but not too formal hospitality, and I have heard some gossip that must wound him deeply. His skin is very thin, and he is subject to a kind of jealousy that knows how to hurt him worst. His present plan is to take some land in Texas and live in the open air,[8] but, between ourselves, it is all over with the boy. He may last two years, but I can not bring myself to hope for more than that."

Crane in a mood of disgust intended to sail by February 1, but solicitor Alfred Plant could hardly have failed to point out that if he left the country then he would lay himself open to the charge of running out on his creditors. Barr had urged him to go to South Africa, and Moreton Frewen advised the south of France. Cora wrote Mrs. Frewen, now at Innishannon in Cork County, Ireland, that they had been disappointed the Frewens did not visit them in early January: "You will not forget us at the end of January," she hoped. The Frewens, however, never visited the Cranes.

"How splendid it is that you are going to plant trees and shrubs at Brede Place," Cora wrote. "We often say: 'Oh, if we could only replace every tree that has been cut in the Park,' and we have said: 'we must plant an avenue of oaks to mark our time.' Then we are forced to say, 'we can't do it now,' and publishers are behaving so badly at the moment that we now say: 'Well, we must plant *one* oak to mark our time.' Nervous people can't endure Brede Place to stay at. It simply gets on some people's nerves, but I don't believe we have any, for we love it most when 'the children cry' and the house rings as if it were filled with telegraph wires. I hope when you are here it's a wild night so that you may really enjoy it. Don't let me frighten you, we will make you comfortable and warm, but it's very jolly to sit by the fire and have things moan & hum, particularly if you have someone to tell good ghost stories. Does that sound childish?"

Late in January, the Cranes went to a luncheon in their honor given by Thomas Parkin of Hastings, nine miles from Brede. A bibliophile, ornithologist, amateur artist, and country magistrate, Parkin had inquired if there might be any chance of "The Ghost" being published; if so, he would like a copy of it as he considered it "a real curiosity" because of the names of its authors. Cora sent him the letters of some of the authors and the printed program of the play, along with a copy of *George's Mother*.[9] Miss M. Bothim-Edwards, who met Stephen at this luncheon, recognized at once that his years, if not months, were numbered. "Painful was the contrast between the young author of the 'Red Badge of Courage' and the other guests, all of whom were in good health and spirits. Poor Stephen Crane had that white, worn-out, restless look betokening complete nervous exhaustion. He took no tea and did not join in general conversation, but moved about uneasily as if in search of something he could not find." Among other guests at Parkin's literary luncheon was that somber genius William Hale White, known as "Mark Rutherford." He and Crane spent two hours in each other's company without exchanging so much as a syllable.

John Floyd Bemis, the Southerner who had absurdly hinted to Crane that his friendship with Mrs. Chaffee at Old Point Comfort (in 1898, at the end of the Cuban War) was a subject of New York gossip, called on Stephen and was cordially received. Crane told Bemis the intended plot of the Irish romance, beyond the eighteen chapters he'd so far written. O'Ruddy at the end was to be entangled with a middle-aged courtesan and dragged into court again, an episode not appearing in Robert Barr's conclusion of that novel. But at Dover in May, just before crossing the Channel for Calais, he told Robert Barr what had yet to be written about the hero, and Barr worked it out that way: O'Ruddy rescuing the girl and barricading Brede Place against her father.

What had realist Crane to do with writing a romance? some of his friends complained. He remarked to one of them: "I get a little tired of saying, 'Is this true?' But that frame of mind isn't, in the long game of writing a deliberate romance, just the weapon, or shovel, needed." At the same time he was also reporting again for the New York *Journal*—about the terrible execution done in South Africa by the British guns, and how much the British soldier had yet to learn about the modern rifle. In another dispatch he maintained that the Englishman Watson, who was out of sympathy with his country in the Boer War and who had been challenged in the London *Daily News,* was not unpatriotic. And in "The Talk of London" he reported on the political situation in Europe and Ireland.

He writes satirically of the proposal to establish an American Academy to foster American literature and honor her leading authors. Why imitate that silly custom of the English Academy when it is an institution which accomplishes nothing! Let any forty men choose to elect themselves to positions of literary eminence and photograph these dignitaries in a group. "A tidy little sum might be raised from the sale of this photograph, for it is certain that we can show more fine old literatures* with manes of snow white hair than any country on the face of the globe." Another plan would be an academy composed of *any* ten college presidents. "There would be no difficulty about persuading them to accept the distinction, because no college president in normal health ever abandons to another individual anything which by the due exercise of personal charm may be induced to remain under his benign care. But the very simplicity of this solution may defeat it. These pious men probably should be left to the business of raiding Chicago's wealth."

A better plan would be an academy composed of but one author. Give him a set of by-laws and let him convene himself to discuss literary matters. And who is Crane's candidate for the American Academy's singular member? It is a man of virile manhood who appears in public in his shirtsleeves; "a strong man, mark ye; no apish child of fiction; a veritable eagle of freedom, and, withal, kindly, tender to the little lame lamb—aye, bold, yet gentle, defiant of all convention, and yet simple in his manner even to kings. Such a man is Edwin Markham."

Former sheepherder and farmer, poet Markham attained international renown in 1899 with the publication of "The Man with the Hoe," a didactic poem inspired by Millet's painting of the same title. With its protest against the wrongs done the laborer and the exploitation of the poor, Crane was in sympathy, but not with its sonorous rhetoric. In proposing this picturesque, bearded Walt-Whitman personality he is spoofing the

---

* litterateurs

whole notion of an American Academy—to be represented by this "one leonine old man in his shirt sleeves" (Markham was then forty-seven). Who is worthy of membership in the academy other than this coatless poet? Crane asks in "Stephen Crane Says: Edwin Markham Is His First Choice for the American Academy" (*Journal:* March 31).

William Dean Howells and Mark Twain were the leading candidates for first membership in the proposed American Academy, but are they worthy to take a place by the side of the illustrious coatlessness of the farmer-poet Markham, who preaches the virtues of a man with a hoe? No. Howells wears collars and never has his photograph taken when in shirt-sleeves or while enwrapped in a carelessly negligent bath towel. "In the name of God, let us have virility; let us look for the wild, free son of nature. Mark Twain? At first it seems that he would have a chance. He growls out his words from the very pit of his stomach and is often uncivil to strangers. But no; he, too, wears collars and a coat." Howells the "progressive realist" whom Crane worshipped in 1891, and Mark Twain, now struck him as stuffed shirts. In November (1899) Stephen had visited with William Dean Howells in London, and Cora made a sketch of him: "Mr. Howells enjoying a joke." (In *Cora Crane,* p. 210.)

And so he kept writing, hour after hour and day after day, in the upstairs section of the E of Brede Place over the arched entry. To see him finish a page filled you with concern, says Ford Hueffer, because it meant he'd begin another page, and so until his death. The house was "a nightmare of misplaced hospitality, of lugubrious dissipation."

One afternoon, after a night of poker, he led a party of unshaven friends to a tavern in Rye, where someone intruded to say that Lamb House was not open to strangers and only by appointment could they see Henry James. "O, sire," said Crane, "I know that the duel is not practised in this country, but I am prepared to waive that for your benefit." James had sent him some manuscripts for his opinion and he was returning one of them. He and his unshaven friends were invited to dine with James and some ladies at Lamb House.

At times Stephen would assume his Bowery role for the sole purpose of teasing the Master, and he'd rein up before his door on one of his two immense coach horses and, going inside, tell the titled guests that he was a fly-guy that was wise to all the all-night pushes of the world. The effect on Henry James was devastating, but the titled guests liked it and thought it characteristic of Americans.

James suffered infinitely for that dying boy, says Hueffer. He referred to Crane as "my young compatriot of genius" who was "of the most charming sensitiveness . . . so truly gifted . . . so very lovable." James "was forever considering devices for Crane's comfort. He telegraphed Wanamaker's for a whole collection of New England delicacies from pumpkin pie to apple butter and sausage meat and clams and soft shell crabs and minced meat and . . . everything thinkable, so that the poor lad should know once more and finally those fierce joys. Then new perplexities devastated him. Perhaps the taste of those far off eats might cause Stevie to be homesick and hasten his end."

Crane had begged Pinker to send him one hundred pounds by Monday, February 12, and asked that he phrase his telegrams about money ambiguously because the postmaster who delivered them was also his unpaid grocer. His checks to grocer and butcher bounced back as worthless, and so late the next month he again petitioned Pinker to send him £16 and to solicitor Alfred Plant £22 before Wednesday (March 28), "or a bailiff will be here." Also, deposit £20 to his wife's bank account. "This does not include the £15 which I asked from you today. . . . Would you take my note for £100?" Crane's notes of debt to Pinker already totaled several thousand dollars. He questioned the prudence of abandoning "my lucrative short story game for this long thing [*The O'Ruddy*] which doesn't pay (much) until the end." He sensed that he would never see the end of it. He wrote ten or twelve thousand words at a stretch and then, resting a day or two, went at it again; by March 24 he had written about one-fourth of the entire thing. "Some folks call it ripping—but I don't know; tell me what you think of it when you get your copy," he wrote Karl Harriman.

Crane's last appeal to Pinker for money was on Saturday, March 31, when Cora had gone off to Paris to meet Helen, who was arriving from Lausanne to buy some clothes. The next day, while patting one of his dogs during lunch, his mouth filled with blood, and the following day he had another hemorrhage.

On Tuesday, April 3, Cora's housekeeper, without Stephen's knowledge —he had forbidden the servants to upset her—secretly cabled Cora in Paris that Crane had suffered two hemorrhages. Cora immediately cabled Moreton Frewen, William Crane, and Hoyt de Friese; on Wednesday, Mrs. de Friese obtained at the American Embassy a note of introduction to an eminent "lung specialist," Dr. J. T. Maclagen, and arranged for a nurse to go down to Brede Place on the same train with the physician. Cora and Helen caught the night boat from Calais. The so-called lung specialist was nothing more than a fashionable physician, a Scotsman of singularly attractive manner who had numbered among his many well-known patients Thomas Carlyle and the Duchess of Albany. Crane scoffed at "commercial physicians," but to Cora with her social pretensions the society status of Dr. Maclagen added to his importance, although he knew no more about tuberculosis than what the less fashionable Dr. Skinner of Rye had diagnosed of Crane's lung trouble in December. They both pronounced that Crane's right lung was entirely unaffected.

"Mr. Crane is ill," Cora wrote Pinker on April 6; she also wrote Lippincott to beg them to deposit with Pinker or in her bank a check of £50 to cover the sum she had to give Dr. Maclagen. "I don't think they will hesitate as it was a matter of saving Stephen's life," she said. The London specialist was encouraging and the report was favorable, she wrote Pinker the next day, at the same time revealing her panic in assuring him: "If Mr. Crane should die I have notes of end of novel [*The O'Ruddy*] so it could be finished & no one will lose—if that should occur." Crane had already known in November that he was "just a dry twig on the edge of the bonfire," but when someone remarked on his health he wrote: "Please have the kindness to keep your mouth shut about my health in front of Mrs. Crane hereafter. She can do nothing for me and I am too old to be nursed. It's all up with me but I will not have her scared. For some funny woman's reason, she likes me. Mind this."

When Sanford Bennett learned that Crane had collapsed he came over from Paris and found a desperate woman pacing the floor and lashing her skirt with one of Stephen's riding crops. She broke into a frantic denunciation of herself for allowing so much entertainment at Brede. It was a ghastly quarter of an hour for Bennett. "She finally sank into a chair, sobbing. . . . She had no real hope of his recovery. But she showed her courage, and cheered him up."

"There has been no hemorrhage now since Monday last. The doctors say if he pulls through until next Thursday [April 19]—ten days—that he will be out of danger. Then the future plans will have to be made. I fear that we shall have to give up Brede Place & go to a more bracing place, on the sea," Cora wrote H. G. Wells on April 15, thanking him for his kind letter. "Stephen sees his letters today for the first time. He is much better & very cheerful." She had written Pinker on the 11th that "my husband seems a little better today. He had a quiet day and night with no hemorrhage, and takes his nourishment well. His illness will be a long one and I shall be under great expense. . . . Ready money is an absolute necessity in illness. I have two nurses who cost £2.4.6 each per week beside their expenses. Then there are the medicines and living expenses— so do your best to get serial money in. My niece is typing the battle article which you shall have this week. I hope my husband will be able to dictate the remainder of the last one from notes so that I can get the £100 from Lippincott." Helen was typing "The Battle of Solferino."

Pinker was much put out that Cora had approached Lippincott directly. He also questioned the wisdom of engaging a physician who charged the outrageous fee of fifty pounds. Cora, of course, defended her decision to have Doctor Maclagen down from London. "Now Mr. Pinker, it was a matter of life & death to have the Specialist down. I could not leave any stone unturned. You might not have gone to office on Saturday or Friday. I had to write to Lippincott at the same time & I wrote you. One cannot stand upon ceremony at such a moment, and indeed I was almost distracted. Pray forgive any seeming lack of courtesy to yourself."

Dr. Skinner, the local physician, now concluded that the trouble "seems only superficial, not deeply rooted" and that it would divert Mr. Crane's mind to continue his writing once he was better for work in two or three weeks; so Cora wrote Pinker on April 17. With hopes thus bolstered, she assured him that Stephen could write one more battle sketch needed to complete the *Great Battles* and satisfy Lippincott's contract.[10] "I am so glad to hear Mr. Crane is better," Pinker wrote her on the 20th.

With good care Stephen seemed to be pulling through the crisis, and friends tried to cheer him with affectionate messages. Moreton Frewen rejoiced: "Please God this desperate load of anxiety will be resolved. . . . That such danger and distress should have overtaken him and you under our old rooftree is a matter of sadness indeed to us both." Mrs. Frewen then in Ireland, had telegraphed her husband to let her know if there was anything she could do, and Robert McClure offered to come to Brede Place if he could be of any help to Cora.

When Kate Frederic first heard of Stephen's illness (very likely in January), she wrote Cora in sympathy and reported on her progress with *Great Battles of the World:* "My dearest girl: What is the matter with Stephen? I could not tell from your letter. I need not say how sorry I am, you blessed and dearest and best two, that any trouble should come to you. But whatever it is, the dear boy will be sure to throw it off at once, I am sure. . . . keep a brave heart, dear girl. God is sure to be good to you. You have been so good to others. What wouldn't I give to be able to help you now." Kate Frederic was then writing "The Battle of Solferino," and she asked Cora whether Stephen "is not well enough to go over what I write?" She would send it "in a shape that won't positively disgrace Stephen." Kate felt indebted to the Cranes for providing a home for her children; she expected no acknowledgment for writing *Great Battles*. Robert Barr, however, saw to it that *The O'Ruddy*'s authorship included his name.[11]

After Crane's first hemorrhage on December 29 the newspapers on both sides of the Atlantic reported on the condition of his health. Walter A. M. Goode, of the Associated Press in London, a correspondent friend, was instructed to get reports telegraphed from Brede Place daily "until my old friend is out of danger." He wrote Cora how glad he was to learn of Stephen's improvement. Crane was now front-page news, and in Port Jervis William read the reports on his "progress." William wrote on April 7 to express his alarm and anxiety over Stephen's illness. However, he could not help with money because his bank account was depleted. "We are very anxious over your sickness," he wrote Stephen on the 13th. "There is in our morning paper every day a London dispatch, giving the latest news from you. We find this unsatisfactory, and are awaiting anxiously for letters." Cora had not yet written him. She had not asked him for money, but he anticipated that she would and begged off in advance. He advised Stephen to come to America.

On April 21 Crane made his will, witnessed by Dr. Skinner. He left to Cora all his personal effects and—until she should marry—all the income from his estate (comprised of royalties due him on his published works).[12] But Cora in fact obtained no cash from Stephen's estate. William Crane maneuvered it to his benefit, not hers.

The same day that Stephen made his last will William wrote Cora that he was delighted to learn that Stephen was improving. Her letters and Helen's, he said, were "always a little belated, when they relate to a question of life and death; but as long as they are not contradicted by the newspaper dispatches, we take a great deal of comfort out of them. I wish you or Helen would write almost every day, as we are very anxious. We also have many inquiries from his friends in Port Jervis and elsewhere." He would try to send Stephen a book "written by Dr. Buckley, one of father's old friends, on 'A Consumptive's Struggle for Life.' He had hemorrhages when he was a young man and began the use of Dr. Howe's breathing tube, which Stephen knew about. He recommends it very highly, and also makes some valuable suggestions about climate. Stephen can tell you that I have blown on Dr. Howe's tube over twenty years, and I am sure that it has done me great good." (Dr. Howe's breathing tube, although it inflated Judge Crane, could not possibly have done Stephen any good.) All the relatives were in good health, William reported, except Uncle Luther, at whose burial in early April he had served as pallbearer. "The people of Port Jervis take a certain pride in Stephen and they are very much concerned about his health." But their sympathy was to the dying Stephen as hollow as Dr. Howe's breathing tube, and especially by the time William's letter reached him.

# XXX

# ⟡ The End

DURING his last five months Crane saw himself in print monthly in one periodical or another, but meanwhile he no doubt felt despondent; he knew he had cheated on his talent, writing so much second-rate stuff to make quick money.

That his feelings for Cora were not unmixed would seem to be indicated in his story, "The Squire's Madness," in which the poet Linton of "vacant Oldreshthan Hall" writes:

> *The garlands of her hair are snakes;*
> *Black and bitter are her hating eyes.*
> *A cry the windy death-hall makes—*
> *O, love, deliver us.*
> *The flung cup rolls to her sandal's tip;*
> *His arm—*

Squire Linton cannot complete his verse about "the poisoned lover" who is "dying at the feet of the woman." His wife insists that he is ill, and in his poem he describes her as mad. She looks at him with "the expression of a mother watching her dying babe." Why, Squire Linton asks himself, "does she look at me with such hopeless despair in her eyes? These kindly eyes that had hitherto been so responsive to each glance of his own. Why did she think that he was ill, she knew well his every mood. Was he mad? Did this thing of the poisoned cup that rolled to her sandal's tip—and her eyes, her hating eyes—mean that his— No, it could not be." Linton's conviction that he is not mad prepares for the story's ending. "Night and day his wife watched Linton. He would awaken in the night to find her face close to his own, her eyes burning with feverish anxiety." A London brain specialist finally tells him: *"It is your wife who is mad! Mad as a Hatter!"*[1]

Crane was ill when he wrote this tale, but Cora in her reckless extravagances was something of a mad hatter. She might very well have uttered the same words as Grace Linton, who bites "her underlip nervously" and moans: "Oh, Jack, you are ill, you are ill."

Cora wrote Mrs. Moreton Frewen on April 25 that the last two days had been such anxious ones that she had not been able to reply to her letter. "We moved my husband on Monday night [April 23] downstairs in the oak room. He seems to get weaker every day and my anxiety is very great. There has been no return of hemorrhage but he suffers so horribly from the abscess, which is too deep-seated to open from the outside while he is in such a weak state. We are in hopes to get him out in the sunshine on warm days." To Pinker she confides: "We are bringing Mr. Crane to a room on the ground floor today, so he can be taken out in the sunshine every day. . . . He has had an abscess which has given great pain and which is still not finished with. Otherwise he is getting on wonderfully well." But Crane was not getting on wonderfully well; he was dying.

Cora refused to believe it. She tells Pinker, "the doctors say that a sea voyage is the thing for Mr. Crane. Is there any way in which you can raise money for him?" Could Pinker get some English newspaper to pay her expenses and Stephen's to St. Helena for a month there, for which Stephen would send them "some interesting letters & interview Group." Crane had the impossible idea of going to the Boer prison camp at St. Helena to interview soldiers interned there and report for the New York *Journal* and the London *Daily Chronicle* and *Morning Post*. Cora must have realized that his writing days were over, but she persisted in hoping otherwise and encouraged his illusory voyage to St. Helena. She wrote William for permission to take his daughter there, and he replied on the 30th that he'd be glad to have Helen go there if the cost were about the same as her schooling.

In view of Stephen's condition, there is an element of grim humor in William's bookkeeping reminder: "Stephen paid me $500 on account of $1250 which he was to pay me for a one-eighth interest in Hartwood. He has no deed and even hasn't a contract—which, however, makes no difference. Now, if he does not wish to complete the transaction, the situation is about like this: I credit him with $500; I charge him with various items, including the 100 which I sent him in March, 1899, and he is still in my debt $155.27 this date. Of course, I do not expect him to pay this, until he gets ready. I am merely setting forth the business situation of the Hartwood transaction. If he is able to think of business matters, kindly show him this letter and I think he'll concur. We are overjoyed to hear of Stephen's improvement."

Cora thought now of renting Brede Place. "Do you think this is a good plan?" She asked Pinker to write his answer on a separate paper lest Stephen see it and worry. Also to please send every check immediately as every post delay might make Mr. Crane's temperature fly up. "We want to get him to Bournemouth if possible among the pines for a time."

Crane was spared the irony of spending his last days at Bournemouth, where the shade of Robert Louis Stevenson still lingered in a yellow-brick house on the edge of Alum Chyne. Stevenson retreated to the favorable climate of the South Seas because of his tuberculosis and lived there fourteen years. He exerted himself in heavy outdoor labor and rode horseback; in the end he did not die of tuberculosis. It is conceivable that Crane, but for his stubborn refusal to accept the rigorous discipline of a sanitarium, might have prolonged his own life as did Stevenson, and it would not have cost him much more to get to the South Seas than it did to remain at Brede Place with two nurses and several doctors. But on April 30 he suffered another relapse and Dr. Skinner abandoned hope, although he had pronounced Crane out of danger five days earlier.

H. G. Wells had written Stephen on the 22nd that he had just heard through Pinker "you are still getting better and I rejoice mightily thereat. I was hugely surprised to hear of your haemorrhaging for you're not at all the hectic sort of person who does that with a serious view in end. As an expert in haemorrhages I would be prepared to bet you any reasonable sum—I'll bet an even halo only I am afraid of putting you on that high mettle of yours—that haemorrhages aren't the way you will take out of this terrestial Tumult. From any point of view it's a bloody way of dying, and just about when you get thirsty and it bubbles difficult and they inject you with morphia. I know few, more infernally disagreeable. And confound it! What business have you in the Valley? It isn't midday yet and Your Day's Work, handsomely started I admit, is still only practically started. The sooner you come out of that Valley again and stop being absolutely irrelevant to your work, the better!"

Cora replied on the 25th: "Dear Mr. Wells: Stephen is not up to letter writing; so I am answering your very cheerful letter to him. The lung trouble seems to be over! The doctor today, after an examination, said that the right lung was entirely un-affected. The trouble is that this dreadful abscess which seems to open from time to time in the bowels—or rectum—makes him suffer the most awful agony. And it takes away his strength in an alarming fashion. The abscess seems to have upset the bowels too. So he is very weak. Then the fever (Cuban fever) comes for an hour or two each day. The chills seem to have stopped the past week. And he hopes within three or four weeks to go on a sea voyage. Write to him when you can. Sick people have fancies that their friends neglect them and wonder at small number of letters, etc. Of course, I have up to date read all letters first and there are many which I think best he should not see—you understand." One surmises that she is tactfully implying she did not show Stephen that "bloody-way-of-dying" letter.

"I thought you were going to utilize the Lippincott money to take Mr. Crane to Bournemouth," Pinker wrote Cora in late April. (The Lippincott money had been advanced against the not yet completed *Great Battles of the World.)* But she was presently interested in the restoration work going on at Brede Manor. Stephen—himself beyond restoration—had not yet been brought downstairs into the sunlight when the workmen exposed for the first time in centuries an old wall extending from the brick buttresses of the house and curving down the hillside. They found some old tiles, very old ones, and bits of charcoal at a depth of four feet; "so there may have been a fire there. In the wall we found half of a battle axe head. It is of hard limestone and a curious outer surface, like a shell. I shall save it for you of course," Cora wrote Mrs. Frewen. She made a drawing of the wall that faced the chapel, tower, and porch of the front of the old house, the wall curving away from it and forming a courtyard. She traced on her map where possibly there had been certain buildings inside the fortified courtyard. "Your old oak table is a very good one but dreadfully worm eaten. We are treating it with vinegar. That horribly new varnish should come off and the table done with wax and vinegar."[2] Cora's mind seems a piece of floating tinsel unattached to the grim realities confronting her: Stephen was dying while she busied herself about restoring the old house.

His friends began urging his removal to a sanitarium on the Continent. The choice now was between the cure at Davos in the Swiss Alps or the celebrated "Nordracht treatment" in the German Black Forest area. The Duchess of Manchester (the Cuban-born Consuelo Yznaga, known as the American duchess) wrote Cora sometime in April: "I think Mr. Crane would be very comfortable at Davos. It is the Nordracht cure without the brutality. You could not get anyone in at Nordracht, under six-eight months. I am not even sure Dr. Doughty has a vacancy as his limit is sixty in the Sanitarium—but if you decide I will write and bring the case before him." An intimate friend of the Frewens, the Duchess had lost two daughters by tuberculosis.

Stephen Crane was lying at the point of death, said an English newspaper. "His recent work has called forth unstinted praise from England's greatest critics, and though perhaps he is the most American of all the Americans in England, no one in English literary circles is spoken of more lovingly and admiringly than the author whose career threatens to end before he reaches his thirtieth year."

"The doctors say that Mr. Crane's life can be saved and that perhaps a cure can be made by his going to the Black Forest for the 'Nordracht' treatment," Cora wrote Pinker on May 1. Now I give you an outline of what has to be done. He is carried on an air bed on a stretcher to Rye. There an invalid carriage will take him, the nurses, one doctor, and myself to Dover. Here we rest for one or perhaps two weeks at the Lord Warden Hotel to have sea air & rest, then a deck cabin to Calais, & there an invalid carriage awaits us. It costs sixteen first class fares and there is no change to the Black Forest. . . . With the expense at the Hotel Dover it will mean £100—to get there and I must have this within the week. Now you know the situation.[3] Try to get someone to take Brede if you can even if they pay running expenses only for two months until I can pull matters together again. This is a matter of life and death; so please do your best. The lung has healed over, and he has a chance to get well & live for years if we can get him out of England."

Five days later Cora wrote Pinker again that the move to the Black Forest must be made within the week. "Mr. Crane is no worse & the right lung holds out, only this change must be made without delay. We will go to some small Inn in the Black Forest & rent Brede Place as it stands. I shall have to take nurse, & Doctor will go with us. It's a very expensive journey but it's a matter of life or death and it must be done."

Moreton Frewen underwrote this extravagant and futile expedition to Badenweiler by raising £100, of which he contributed something of his own. He approached the American banker J. P. Morgan on Crane's behalf and Morgan replied that he would be "very glad" to see Moreton "about Mr. Crane at any time"—either at his office or at his Hyde Park home. Walter Goode of the Associated Press cabled Andrew Carnegie and obtained £50 for his dying compatriot. Frewen twice called on his solicitor, Alfred Plant, at Plant's office in Gray's Inn, to ascertain how much Crane lagged in accounts payable. Frewen, although not himself a wealthy man, presumably settled all Crane debts known to him through Plant's list.

Hoyt de Friese, "broken hearted," wrote Cora a note: "Seldom in my life have I found such affection for anyone. . . . and now to lose him in his very youth! I can't realize or believe it." The de Frieses, just back from Paris, wanted to come to Brede Place to see Stephen and comfort Cora, and later in May came Mark Barr, also on a visit from Paris, to peep into the sickroom but wanting "to rush in and grip Stevie's hand till he swore!"

Conrad wrote John Galsworthy on May 5 that he was going to visit Stephen the next day, but, ill himself, he was unable to get to Brede. He wrote Cora on the 10th that her plight distressed him beyond all measure. "You may imagine that had it been in my power to render you any sort of service I would not have waited for any sort of appeal. I've kept quiet because I feel myself powerless. I am a man without connections, without influence and without means. The daily subsistence is a matter of anxious thought for me. What can I do? I am already in debt to my two publishers, in arrears with my work, and know no one who could be of the slightest use. It is not even in my power to jeopardize my own future to serve you. If it had been, such is my affection for Stephen and my admiration of his genius that I would do so without hesitation, to save him. But my future, such as it is, is already pawned. You can't imagine how much I suffer in writing thus to you. I have been almost distracted since I had your letter." Then on the 13th he wrote: "What awful news you are giving us! And yet people given up by the doctors have been known to live for years." He didn't offer to come to Brede Place, "knowing myself powerless to help you, not wishing to bring my sympathy and my helpless sorrow only to hinder you who are fighting the battle. Believe our hearts are with you. May heaven give you strength and the supreme consolation of faith. I can't give you an idea how unhappy I am since I have received your letter."

The same day that Conrad asked Cora, "Won't Stephen's relatives come forward?" William wrote her that he had received her telegram and a letter from Dr. Skinner of Rye. "We are grieving over the situation; but I really cannot send money in any amount to make it worth while, at present. It has been years since I have been so hardly pressed as I am now." He says that their older brother George is donating various books written by the Reverend J. T. Crane to the Drew Theological Seminary, and wants Stephen's consent because his interest in the Crane library—by his mother's will—"is larger than the interest of any one of the rest of us." These books, William assures Cora, possess "only nominal value."

Crane dictated a note to Sanford Bennett the day before quitting Brede Place: "My condition is probably known to you. . . . I have Conrad on my mind very much just now. Garnett does not think it likely that his writing will ever be popular outside the ring of men who write. He is poor and a gentleman and proud. His wife is not strong and they have a kid. If Garnett should ask you to help pull wires for a place on the Civil List for Conrad, please do me the last favor. . . . I am sure you will."

That was Crane's last letter. His last message was a telegram to Moreton Frewen, probably an expression of gratitude. His last dedication of a book was to Cora: "May—1900 / Brede Place / Sussex, England / To / My Wife / Stephen Crane." However, when *The O'Ruddy* was published three years later this dedication was not included.

"We got Stephen safely here today," Cora wrote H. G. Wells on May 15 from the fashionable Lord Warden Hotel in Dover. The hotel was near the Admiralty Pier from which steamers departed for Calais and Ostend thrice daily, and the rooms offered a fine view of the sea. The Empress Eugenie had stayed there with the Prince Imperial. "Hope she liked the carpet!" Stephen said. Cora planned to stay there one week "and then if I can arrange it and all goes well, I take him on to the Black Forest. Dr. Mitchel Bruce said one lung is all right so far and that there is the chance of recovery—I should say, the chance of *life!* The doctor and two nurses have to go with us. The wound needs constant care. I've done all a mortal can do and I hope! I wish I could have seen you and the dear wife before going—My best love to you both." She had brought along not only Doctor Bruce and two nurses, but also Helen Crane, the butler of Brede Manor, and the dog Sponge. Cora filled in Stephen's passport on May 18 at Dover, before the Channel crossing to Calais, stating that he intended "to return to the United States within six months with the purpose of residing and performing the duties of citizenship therein."

"Went to see Crane yesterday at Dover," Conrad wrote John Galsworthy from Pent Farm on May 17 (Thursday). "Been with him 20 minutes. Supported move from Brede pretty well. I was awfully shocked of course and had to put on jolly manners. He may yet escape. The Frewens (owners of Brede) pay all his transit to the Black Forest,—rather more than £100. A doctor friend goes with him. It is a long good-bye to England and Stephen seems to feel it very much. And it may be for ever! He is not too hopeful about himself. One lung quite intact at any rate." H. G. Wells had been there the day before, and intended to come over from Folkestone again, but Cora wrote him on May 20: "Nurses think best for Stephen not to see any one before starting. Best for him to be quite alone tomorrow; so I must ask you not to come & I am sorry. I will write you of our journey. Love from us all to your wife. Faithfully yours, Cora Crane. If ever a good book or magazine turns up send it to us in the wood [the Black Forest]."

Before Conrad saw Stephen at Dover, Jessie Conrad had a dream in which she beheld Stephen lying on a stretcher being placed in an ambulance with two nurses in attendance and Cora. "The ambulance was driven to the coast as quickly as possible. The dream was curious because we had not spoken of the Cranes or seen anyone connected with them for some months. When the post arrived an hour later a letter told us the exact substance of my dream and begged us to go that morning to the 'Lord Warden' in Dover, where the poor fellow lay awaiting a calm sea to cross and try to reach the Black Forest in search of health. For poor Cora it was a pitiful business; she had not the means to pay for meals in the 'Lord Warden.' The nurses were fed outside, but I know that the wife often went without." Jessie Conrad caught a glimpse of Stephen in his hotel bed while Joseph talked with him, Stephen answering only by signs and a few panting words scarcely above a whisper. His eyes were fixed on the ships that showed through the open window, while Conrad brooded upon the stretcher that was to carry his friend on his last journey.

"It is the end, Jess," Conrad said to his wife. "He knows it is all useless. He goes only to please Cora, and he would rather have died at home!" Stephen before the open window had turned his pillowed head to stare at the sails of a cutter yacht gliding across the sea, "like a dim shadow against the grey sky," and that was the last glimpse Conrad had of him. His wasted face was enough to tell Conrad that it was the most forlorn of all hopes. The last words Stephen breathed to him were: "I am tired. Give my love to your wife and child."

Robert Barr got to Dover on the 19th and gave in to Stephen's plea that he finish writing *The O'Ruddy* in spite of his feeling that only Kipling was adequate to the task. Cora wrote Pinker the next day that "Mr. Crane wants Robert Barr to finish it & perhaps Mr. Kipling may edit (don't mention this yet). You should get a big serial price." Moreton Frewen, whom Crane characterized as seeming "like a search-light on a hungry boat at sea," later (June 3) approached Kipling, whom he had once done a considerable favor, but Kipling refused to touch another author's novel. Barr's excuse for hesitating was that Crane had genius and style: "The contrast in the work would be too horrible, and I should be hopelessly handicapped with the knowledge of my own deficiencies. With pretty near any other man except Kipling and a few others, I would have the cheek to try, but with Stephen the discrepancy would be too marked." Barr later wrote Karl Harriman that the unfinished manuscript (65,000 words) struck him as different from anything Crane had ever written: Stephen "thought I was the only person who could finish it, and he was too ill for me to refuse. I don't know what to do about the matter, for I never could work up another man's ideas." But he did it splendidly once he finally settled down to do the job, writing so skillfully that it is impossible to detect the page where Crane had left off in Chapter XXV.

"Can't you understand," said Crane to Cora as she hovered over Barr while he was reading the manuscript, "there are times when men like to be left alone together?" Before Barr's futile efforts at cheerfulness Crane, who looked already dead, quipped: "You damned humbug, you know I'll take no more rambles in this world." Years ago he had written these lines in *Black Riders* (1895): "Mystic shadow, bending near me / Who art thou? / Whence came ye? / And—tell me—is it far? / Or is the truth bitter as eaten fire? / Tell me! / Fear not that I should quaver. / For I dare—I dare. / Then, tell me!" "When you come to the hedge that we must all go over," he told Barr, "you feel sleepy—and—you don't care."

"Even your vivid imagination," Barr wrote Karl Harriman, "could hardly conjecture anything more ghastly than the dying man, lying by an open window overlooking the English channel, relating in a sepulchral whisper the comic situations of his humorous hero [O'Ruddy] so that I might take up the thread of his story."

Wells remembered Stephen "lying still and comfortably wrapped about before an open window and the calm and spacious sea. If you would figure him as I saw him, you must think of him as a face of a type very typically American, long and spare, with very straight hair and straight features and long, quiet hands and hollow eyes, moving slowly, smiling and speaking slowly, with that deliberate New Jersey manner he had, and lapsing from speech again into a quiet contemplation of his ancient enemy. For it was the sea that had taken his strength, the same sea that now shone, level waters beyond level waters, with here and there a minute, shining ship, warm and tranquil beneath the tranquil evening sky. Yet I felt scarcely a suspicion then that this was a last meeting. One might have seen it all, perhaps. He was thin and gaunt and wasted, too weak for more than a remembered jest and a greeting and good wishes. It did not seem to me in any way credible that he would reach his refuge in the Black Forest only to die at the journey's end."

Wells wrote Cora on May 24 to apologize for "my absence from that last sight of Stephen today but indeed if I could have brought myself to see him I would not have failed you. These things however affect me so darkly, I should have found so little comfort and so much distress in this encounter and I have the memory of him in still comfort before that open window of the sea so vividly in my mind, that I do not care to disturb or weaken it by meeting something that was no longer him. The last few days I have been very much with him, with the ample portion of him that will not die, for, at the request of Messrs. Harper I have been making an impression of his work and of his significance in literature as they appear to English eyes. There I have tried to say without exaggeration and without cant the essential greatness of his work." And that is what Wells accomplished in his splendid tribute to his friend: "Stephen Crane from an English Standpoint" (*North American Review:* August, 1900). "The good things in his life had slipped by him," Wells remembered in 1934.

Henry James was on the point of going to Dover to see Crane on the 21st when he was prevented by the arrival of a mass of page proofs needing instant attention.

Regardless of cost, Cora had charted a salon-carriage to wait at Boulogne to convey Stephen and her extravagant entourage to Basel, (Bâle), Switzerland. She wrote Pinker about this on May 23, the day before the Channel voyage. "Address there at Hotel Trois Rois until later address comes. I thank you for your letter. Mr. Robert Barr will call to see you and will explain our wishes about Romance [*The O'Ruddy*]. Please *register* all contracts you have to Bâle for Mr. Crane to see. He asks you to please do this at once."

The Channel voyage had to be postponed several days until the 24th, when the rough sea became calm enough for Stephen to endure the crossing to Calais. He rested on a stretcher, and his dog Sponge lay at his side.

At Basel's Hotel Trois Rois, which was about as expensive as the fashionable old Lord Warden at Dover, Cora "economized" by taking rooms on the top floor. She was charged 68 marks a day because the party did not take all meals in the hotel, "and everywhere it's 'pay extra' because of my husband's illness." From Switzerland the group got by train to Badenweiler. It was a funeral entourage on the grand scale fit for the hero of a tragi-comic opera. They moved into Villa Eberhardt or Haus Luisenstrasse 44, which Dr. Albert Fraenkel rented for his sanitarium patients from Herr Albert Eberhardt. Badenweiler, in the Baden district of Lörrach (in the southeast corner of Germany), had been discovered as a health spa by medical authorities in the sixteenth century. Situated on the slope of a mountain, it affords a superb view of the Alps. But Stephen, carried into his second-floor bedroom in the Villa Eberhardt, saw nothing of the Alps, the thermal baths, and the fashionable promenade through the tree-lined park. All was meaningless to him. He knew that he had come here to die—to go out on the same stretcher that brought him in. Only Cora persisted in hoping for his restoration.

She had exhausted the hundred pounds Frewen had sent her. The frantic tone of her letter to Pinker on the 29th reflects her acute emotional disturbance. What is being done about the serial rights of *Wounds in the Rain?* she asks. She returns the page proofs amidst her agony of watching Stephen die. Why doesn't Pinker sell the Wyoming Valley tales through Paul Reynolds?[4] "I simply must have money for Mr. Crane." Has Pinker seen Robert Barr? "Now this is a matter that must be attended to. I can sell the American serial rights myself [*The O'Ruddy*]."

A letter from Frewen arrived on June 2 with twenty-five pounds, and Stephen told Cora: "Say to Moreton Frewen that it will ever be my joy to follow his wishes in every way. Tell him that if Robert Barr finishes the *O'Ruddy* and if Kipling goes over the book, adding to it as he thinks fit, I shall be glad. Robert Louis Stevenson left in his will that Quiller-Couch was to finish his book [*St. Ives*] and the world calls it *his* book (R. L. S.'s) and I shall be happy if my book goes through Kipling's hands." Stephen "also has 2 or 3 acts of a war play finished," and Cora would try to get "some good man" to finish it,[5] she wrote Frewen on June 3, thanking him for the £25. "The journey from Brede Place to this villa cost £150. It seems awful"—that the journey cost so much and that Stephen—as Cora now realized—was not going to survive. "We have a small villa on the edge of the forest. 90 marks a week. A German cook who cleans, etc., for 2½ marks a day. It's difficult to get any woman simply. One big item is washing. Sometimes Mr. Crane's bed is changed 3 times a day. It is too dreadful to have to think or write that if God takes my husband from me I shall not know what to do. What shall I do! I can't write more about it."

A. E. W. Mason, at James Barrie's suggestion, had written in late May while Stephen was en route to Badenweiler that the Royal General Literary Fund lent money to any author crippled in his working powers by age or illness. Later there were efforts by Cora to secure aid from the Fund with Henry James writing the Committee in support of her application in October, 1900. But nothing came of that prospect.

Cora had invented an army canteen with a filter, and lawyer Hoyt de Friese drew up an agreement between Cora and Frederick L. Bowen, a young engineer who contributed improvements to her canteen design, for their joint manufacture and merchandising of the product in England and abroad. It is likely that she then approached Moreton Frewen (he knew a great many influential people) for financial backing of this enterprise. In her letter of June 3 from Villa Eberhardt she wrote him that her canteen filter invention "seems the best way to get money. It's really a good thing—I send you a clipping from 'The Hospital' which might interest you. Stephen is not quite clear in his mind tonight.

"I've only sad news to write you. There seems little hope of cure. The fever seems the thing that cannot be conquered. It is not due alone to the lung but is remains of the yellow fever and the Cuban fever. Dr. Frankel [Fraenkel] cannot see why the lung trouble was not discovered when Mr. Crane was examined in Dec. He will not take responsibility of Mr. Crane's case alone; so I've consented to a consultation tomorrow with Professor Bruiler of Freiburg, to whom Dr. Mitchel Bruce wrote & through whose advice we came here. I wired you but have received no reply. There is nothing for me to do but to consent to consultation. Dr. Frankel said that Professor Bruiler would only ask about 125 marks. . . . He [Stephen] worries so about his debts and about our not being able to live well. So I told him yesterday that I had £300—cash & since then he has been satisfied. I think it is really worry about my future. So I do everything possible to ease his poor tired mind."

Henry James sent fifty pounds, begging Cora to consider it simply as a convenience and to "dedicate it to whatever service it may best render my stricken friend. It meagerly represents my tender benediction to him."

From his bedroom Stephen could see nothing but a corner of the sky. His tormented mind took him back to the dinghy where once he had rowed against waves that were "most wrongfully and barbarously abrupt and tall." "A singular disadvantage of the sea," he had written, "lies in the fact that after successfully surmounting one wave you discover that there is another behind it just as important and just as nervously anxious to do something effective in the way of swamping boats." Now in his feverish dreams he must have recalled the burden of that doom-eager youth in the dinghy: "If I am going to be drowned—if I am going to be drowned— if I am going to be drowned, why, in the name of the seven mad gods who rule the sea, was I allowed to come thus far and contemplate sand and trees?"

"My husband's brain is never at rest," Cora wrote Frewen. "He lives over everything in dreams and talks aloud constantly. It is too awful to hear him try to change places in the 'Open Boat.' "

# XXXI

# ⊂ *The Journey Home*

"GOD took Stephen at 11.5. Make some arrangements for me to get the dog home," Cora cabled Alfred Plant.[1] Getting the dog home, the *O'Ruddy* completed, and the canteen-filter invention financed seem to have competed in Cora's distraught mind with the death of her beloved Stephen. That it did not occur 11.5 on June 4, as she said in her telegram, suggests that she was not at his bedside when he died. The hour and the day—three o'clock in the morning of June 5—are given in his death certificate, which strangely claimed that Stephen Crane was of the Lutheran religion. At his death-bed was his dog Sponge.

Cora cabled Frewen at Brede Manor, and he went to Lamb House to tell Henry James the sad news. "What a brutal needless extinction—what an unmitigated, unredeemed catastrophe!" James wrote Cora. "I think of him with such a sense of possibilities & powers! Not that one would have drawn out long these last cruel weeks—! But you have need of all your courage. I doubt not it will be all at your service. Shall you come back—for any time at all—to Brede Place? You will of course hate to—but it occurs to me you may have things to do there, or possessions to collect. What a strange, pathetic, memorable chapter his short—so troubled, yet also so peaceful—passage there!"

On the morning of June 5 Cora cabled the German Embassy in London and thereby set in motion the diplomatic machinery for removal of the body to Calais.[2] The American Consul at Freiburg—E. T. Liefield—went to Badenweiler to supervise the transportation, and accompanied the entourage homeward to Basel from Mulheim (four and one half miles west of Badenweiler), thence to Brussels via Mannheim and Cologne and thence to the coast of France for the Channel crossing to Dover. The funeral cortege was in Freiburg by June 8, where a pathologist embalmed the body. Meanwhile, at the Embassy in London, J. R. Carter was writing the Secretary of the President of the Board of Agriculture to obtain special permission for admitting Stephen's dog Sponge back into England. No dog could be imported into Great Britain unless specially authorized by

*516*

the Board of Agriculture and then, if granted admission, it must be "detained and isolated at the expense of the owner" for six calendar months![3] Carter begged Mr. Arbuthnot, Secretary of the Board, to waive this provision on the grounds that the dog had always lived in England, except for his short stay in Germany with his master Stephen Crane, "a young and brilliant Author." The extraordinary Mr. Arbuthnot conceded the exception, and Sponge was granted reentry to England. Cora, faithful to Stephen's loyalty to his dogs, took Powder Puff as well as Sponge with her later when she and Helen Crane accompanied Stephen's body on the *Bremen* for burial in New Jersey.

"Tomorrow, Saturday (June 9) I go again to Dover to meet his body," Robert Barr wrote Karl Harriman. "He will rest for a while in England, a country that was always good to him, then to America, and his journey will be ended." Cora was determined that Stephen should be buried in his native soil and William sent money for transporting the body back to America. "Port Jervis is in mourning," he wrote. "So many people here knew him, that the village claimed him as one of her sons and always felt pride in his achievements. I suppose Stephen's wish was to be buried in our family plot at Elizabeth, New Jersey." (However, he was not buried there). And so William, having begged off in sending money during Stephen's illness, finally provided the money to bring his brother home, but that sum he would account for later in balancing the books of Stephen Crane's estate.[4]

Stephen's body lay in a London mortuary, after arrival at Dover, and Cora, from her St. James Park hotel, the Queen Anne's Mansions, sent announcement cards (handwritten by Helen): "Mrs. Stephen Crane has arranged that friends of her late husband may see him to say goodbye, at the Mortuary, 82 Baker St., on Thursday between the hours of 3 and 5 o'clock [June 14]." The Conrads and others looked through the glass lid of the coffin for a last sight of Stephen and left their cards at the small undertaker's shop opposite the house where Sherlock Holmes was supposed to have lived. The body was lying outside the shop in a stable yard approached through an archway and surrounded on three sides by covered bays. There were horses in two or three of the bays, and carts were piled up in the middle of the large, square stable yard.

In one of the bays, Curtis Brown recalls, "there was a coffin on trestles, with the face of my old friend exposed through the glass. He looked as if he had suffered greatly. There was no one else about. I stayed for a time, thinking over our talks together; and then went slowly away, with a heavy heart." "I always thought it was a terrible pity the poor corpse should have to lie in a London mortuary waiting for a passage to America so long (one week)," said Jessie Conrad.

Robert Barr was coming to see Cora at her hotel, and she wanted to know whether there might be an answer from Kipling by that time as to his finishing *The O'Ruddy*. The American serial rights on it had been sold, and so that ought to mean £500 (of which £100 would go to pay Pinker for advance money) for Plant to give creditors. That would save the unpaid-for furniture at Brede Place from being reclaimed. "It is so good of you to let it remain at Brede Place until my return to England," she wrote Frewen. "I hope to be back in six weeks or two months, only staying long enough to see about Mr. Crane's play and getting some material of his life, then back to work and earn my own living." Nothing came of Crane's play or Cora's biography; her attempt to earn her living by writing in London collapsed in April, 1901, when she gave up and returned to America. But just now she had hopes also that her canteen filter would make her fortune, and she asked Frewen to show the filter to the war office.

"I hope you will feel that you can do as I asked and divide my share with me. I shall have plenty to live my life—only my dear one's dog to care for beside myself—and if the filter, first thought of at your dear old place, were to add a stone to it, it would be such a joy to me, and my joys will not be many." And (as we shall see) they were few indeed. As for the horses, if Frewen kept them out for rent they'd be cared for and fed. "For all that you and your dear wife have done for us only God can reward you. I never, never could tell you of all the love and gratitude my dear one had in his gentle heart for Moreton Frewen."

Among the many letters of sympathy was one from Walter Goode, who had known Crane through Robert McClure. "Dear Mrs. Crane: I can't tell you how sorry I was to hear of poor Stephen's death," he wrote on June 7. "The world loses a man, who, as Richard Harding Davis said, was one of the few, *very* few, who possessed the spark of genius. And I lose a good friend, a man whose sincerity and bravery—a rare bravery it was, too,—I admired more than I say. And your loss—I am so sorry for you." Henry James wrote Cora that same day but did not visit the mortuary, and H. G. Wells stayed away because such things affected him "so darkly." His letter of sympathy—sent to America—didn't reach Cora until she was back in London (in late July).

Several obituaries compared Crane with Poe, Stevenson, or with journalist George Steevens. Young Steevens and Crane each had that rare gift of seeing things for himself and knowing in a flash just what was essential to bring a picture vividly to the reader, said the London *Academy* (June 9). Crane "was the type of the nervous, nimble-minded American, slight in figure, shy and kind in manner, speaking little, with a great power of work, a fine memory, and an imagination of astonishing psychological insight. . . . His gifts of presenting the critical or dramatic moments in the lives of men and women was supreme."

On the other hand, the New York *Tribune,* where Crane had begun his journalistic career, belittled his literary achievement and said he had not attained a well-balanced view of life. "If he saw life clearly upon occasion he never saw it steadily; he never saw it whole. A sense of proportion was missing from his equipment." The *Tribune* commentator was most probably the young poet Wallace Stevens, who was a *Tribune* newsman at that time and attended Crane's funeral.

The New York *World,* under the lurid headline of "Madcap Genius Stephen Crane" (June 10), declared it "a mistake to say that he began life as a reporter. His nature could not brook the drudgery and discipline of reporter's work. He preferred to hover on the ragged edge of starvation, earning a precarious pittance by writing sketches and stories of city life for newspapers. . . . An engaging genius was Stephen Crane, intensely human in all his impulses, lovable in his very frailties. Men lament his untimely taking off because he was such a fine, brave, madcap, generous comrade; women because he had the winning gift of eye and speech whose secret cannot be told in words. . . .

"Although it was not until after years that he developed consumption, he was always more or less delicate. His build was as frail as his stature was small. But so aflame was he with energy, so incessantly did his nervous force goad him into vigorous action that one lost sight of his physical deficiencies. . . . His face expressed both his intellectual strength and his physical weakness. It was an interesting face: lean, sharp-featured, sallow, eager, a mirror of every emotion. The eyes were restless, searching, eloquent and deeply blue. In speech he used the vernacular with vigor; he was without affectation."

Edward Marshall, who had hired Crane for the Sunday *Press* in 1894, said in the *Herald* (June 10) that America in losing Crane had lost "one of her most promising young writers. But his friends lost more. They lost a chap whom they all knew to be a real man as well as a talented acquaintance."[5]

Cora sailed with Helen Crane—and the dogs, Sponge and Powder Puff —on the German Lloyd *Bremen* from Southampton on June 17, with Stephen Crane's body in the hold of the ship. Cora had been held up at Ostend "by the English quarantine against dogs, probably the strictest law since Medes and Persians. Poor Mrs. Crane had either to sacrifice the dog or desert it. She chose to go to Dieppe and out to the Southampton boat by lighter. It was one of the most pitiful stories I ever heard," said Rupert Hughes, editor of *Godey's Magazine.*[6]

In New York City, while resting in a hotel before the funeral service, Cora looked at herself in a mirror. In the presence of William's wife Cornelia and Stephen's sister, Mrs. P. Murray Hamilton, she remarked that if Stephen could only see her now in her widow's weeds "how he would laugh"; she was wearing a mourning dress of black nun's veiling with a full skirt. Cornelia and Mary Helen knew nothing about the shocking life of "Mrs. Stephen Crane," but her remark unnerved them.

The Reverend Dr. James M. Buckley, editor of the *Christian Advocate* and a lifelong friend of the Crane family, delivered the eulogy at the funeral service in the Metropolitan Temple (Seventh Avenue near 14th Street). Dr. Buckley "spoke of the life of Mr. Crane and of the inheritance of many of the traits of character of his father. He said that Stephen Crane's career might well be said to have been like that of a meteor which gleams brilliantly in the sky for a time and then sinks to rest," according to the New York *Tribune* (June 29). William and Edmund had taken the body in charge as soon as it arrived on the *Bremen*. Among the pallbearers were Ripley Hitchcock, Stephen's editor at Appleton, and Willis Hawkins, to whom Crane had mailed the manuscripts of *The Red Badge of Courage* (on January 27, 1896).

Wallace Stevens went to the funeral that Thursday morning of June 28 and noted in his journal that the Metropolitan Temple was a small church and was about a third full. "Most of the people were of the lower classes and had dropped in apparently to pass away the time. There was a sprinkling of men and women who looked literary, but they were a wretched, rag, tag, and bob-tail. . . . The whole thing was frightful. The prayers were perfunctory, the choir worse than perfunctory with the exception of its hymn 'Nearer My God to Thee' which is the only appropriate hymn for funerals I ever heard. The address was absurd. The man kept me tittering from the time he began till the time he ended. He spoke of Gladstone and Goethe. Then—on the premature death—he dragged in Shelley; and speaking of the dead man's later work he referred to Hawthorne. Finally came the Judgment day—all this with most delicate, sweet, and burial gestures—when the earth and the sea shall give up their dead. A few of the figures to appear that day flashed through my head—and poor Crane looked ridiculous among them. But he lived a brave, aspiring, hard-working life. Certainly he deserved something better than this absolutely commonplace, bare, silly service I have just come from. As the hearse rattled up the street over the cobbles in the stifling heat of the sun, with not a single person paying the least attention to it and with only four or five carriages behind it at a distance, I realized much that I had doubtingly suspected before—there are few hero-worshippers."

The *Tribune* reporter was mistaken in claiming that Crane's body was taken to the Evergreen Cemetery in Elizabeth, New Jersey. Not one of that town's three cemeteries holds his remains. In the First Presbyterian churchyard in Elizabeth there are three earlier Stephen Cranes, but author Stephen Crane's grave is in the Evergreen Cemetery in Hillside, New Jersey. It is marked by a large gray granite stone inscribed: Stephen Crane —Poet—Author—1871–1900.[7]

After Stephen's funeral Cora visited with Judge William Howe Crane's family on East Main Street in Port Jervis and met Edmund and his family in the nearby village of Rio where they were camping out because the babies—Harold and Stephen—were ill with whooping-cough. She had written Edmund from Europe before she ever saw his three daughters to advise him to have them taught dancing to improve their carriage and bearing. "We all thought she was lovely," said Edith—in 1900 she was fourteen. Aunt Cora, as they called her, went hiking with Stephen's nieces in Sullivan County and took her turn in telling stories when the young girls entertained each other in that game. When Agnes told of ghosts who lived on the tombstones of a cemetery, Cora quipped: "A good solid diet!"

Stephen used to lie on the couch at Edmund's house in Hartwood and read the press clippings he had pasted into a scrapbook, Edith recalled. "He would read them over and over and chuckle and even laugh aloud," she wrote Thomas Beer in 1922. "He always enjoyed them immensely. I can remember his delight when some big critic said he would 'like to officiate at the Hanging of the Crane.'" The scrapbooks were given by my father to Aunt Cora when she visited us. We all regretted that he did so afterward, but my father thought at that time that she should have them."

# XXXII

# ⊂⊃ Cora—The Aftermath

CORA, in her black mourning gown, sailed back to England on July 19, 1900, with a friend identified only as Mrs. Brotherton. She took lodgings at 47 Gower Street in South Kensington, where David Belasco left a note on the 28th that he was disappointed in having missed her that day by a few minutes. "I will undertake the dramatization of your brilliant young husband's new story *The O'Ruddy,* as well as his former book, *The Red Badge of Courage.*" It was wonderful news. It buoyed her spirits for the next eight troubled months.

In "The Genius of Stephen Crane" in the *Metropolitan Magazine* Belasco told of his attempted interview with "Mr. Crane's widow for the purpose of obtaining permission to dramatize *The Red Badge of Courage.* It was Mrs. Crane who put the unfinished manuscript of *The O'Ruddy* into my hands. The unfinished manuscript was her husband's dying legacy, and the last incomplete chapter were the final words written by his pen. As one for many years interested in plays, I could personally give no greater proof of my admiration for Stephen Crane than my enthusiasm for, and my determination to produce, the last creation of his great mind."

Crane, said Belasco, "by his directness and wealth of imagination, possesses eminently the qualities of a dramatic writer. He reveals the great human drama, its struggles and tragic climaxes, in a flash of the pen. His creations seem to rise in the flesh, vibrating with life and pulsating with passion. This is dramatic instinct par excellence." He invited Cora to meet him in Paris at his expense on August 16, but she went to see his London dramatic agent, Elizabeth Marbury, instead; Belasco had instructed Miss Marbury to offer a contract on most favorable terms for the unfinished novel *O'Ruddy.* But the new novel, Paul Reynolds explained, "could not be dramatized until it had been brought out as a book." Belasco, irritated that *The O'Ruddy* was still not completed, wrote Cora: "One thing is very certain—I can make no arrangements until the book is published." By the time Robert Barr finally completed it in 1903 the flamboyant Broadway czar had lost interest.

Cora did sign a contract with Belasco for the dramatization of *The Red*

*Badge* but in doing so she was overriding Crane's contract terms with Appleton, which included dramatic rights on *The Red Badge,* and the fact that these rights, as Reynolds wrote her on July 21, "are in my hands to place." Reynolds did not complain; he simply said that he understood "you wished me to sell the dramatic rights of *The Red Badge of Courage,* and I was trying to sell it." Belasco may have learned of this situation; in any event, he dropped his projected dramatization.

Cora reveals herself also as rather ruthless in asking Pinker to obtain a typescript of *The O'Ruddy* "even if we have to take it away from someone else." She also asked him for money for her landlady. Through Poultney Bigelow,[1] who had visited Brede Place the previous spring, she began negotiating with his London agent, G. H. Perris, and obtained an advance on some of Crane's stories which she completed.

She was in a bitter mood as she watched the vans truck off her furniture and some paintings by contemporary artists which she and Stephen had collected at Brede Place. (She placed them with a London art dealer, but he had no luck in selling even the Beardsley.) "Poor darling Cora, I would like to see you. I think you are sure of our sympathy," Jessie Conrad wrote, and Joseph sent a check and promised to send her another as soon as possible. She appealed to Wells, presumably for a loan, but nothing came of it. The wife of playwright Arthur Pinero deeply sympathized with Cora's great sorrow, but "I never for one moment imagined you desired charity!"

She wrote Hamlin Garland on August 8 that she hoped to settle in "a tiny house in London. But ways and means are a puzzle just now." Her hope was to write a little book of Stephen's life, although it would have "little commercial value, no value at all except, perhaps, to those who knew his work." She asked Garland for anything of interest he might contribute, and also wrote Linson, Bacheller, Howells, Louis Senger, and other friends of Stephen, including Professor Smalley of Syracuse University, who belonged to Crane's fraternity Delta Upsilon and was proud of Stephen's connection with the university.

She wrote Garland on September 17 that she had been trying to write some short stories, "but they are woefully bad, though I have sold two. I am of the opinion that it is criminal for people to write who know nothing about it—but one must live, and I must work to live." She thanked him for his *Saturday Evening Post* appraisal of July 28 ("Stephen Crane: A Soldier of Fortune") and hoped he would review Crane's forthcoming books because that would mean much to making his work live: "So very few people understood Stephen or even knew him." She felt sure that Hamlin Garland would see how much better work there was in *Wounds in the Rain* than in *The Red Badge of Courage.* As for *The O'Ruddy,* although not completed, she felt it to be "really splendid work. I feel sure that my husband's best work was done the last year of his life.

*He* thought so." It was as necessary for Cora to believe this as it had been for Crane himself.

Garland thought otherwise and said as much years later in "Stephen Crane as I knew him" (*Yale Review:* April, 1914): "He was not born for long life and he was not born for development. His work did not change except for the worse. It remained fragmentary and severe." Garland had come to be more and more affected by moral disapproval of Crane's character after the police "exposé" of his underworld life with Chinatown opium pots and Tenderloin fleshpots, and he concluded that "there was something essentially unwholesome about his philosophy." Again, in his diary for 1922, he wrote Crane off as essentially unwholesome in character. The rift between them was not aided by Crane's neglecting to write him; when he visited England he snubbed Stephen and called on Joseph Conrad instead. Garland had written Crane (November 29, 1897) that he was very glad "to hear from you and from Mr. Conrad. I wish you had written another page to tell me how you were getting on and what you intended to do." Stephen never wrote him again, although he always felt kindly to his benefactor and grateful. Just before he went to Cuba in 1898 he told Louis Senger to write Garland in case anything happened to him there. He had no particular message but simply wanted Hamlin to know through Senger "that the appreciation shown for his early work by yourself and Mr. Howells was the first of that particular success which he so much craved."

"Stephen said that he supposed you had reason to believe that he had neglected you and so [you] did not care to reply," Cora wrote Garland after Crane's death. She mentioned the breach in their former friendship to Louis Senger, who then wrote Garland on October 9 that Stephen had often spoken of him "and always with a sense of blame for himself lest you should think him ungrateful. He was never that." In her letter of September 17 she had expressed thanks to Garland's wife "for her kind sympathy. No one can realize how great my loss is or how difficult it is to fight for an existence which I don't want. But my faith bids me believe that we shall be together again. Our life was too beautiful, too full of work and sunshine not to be continued, under new conditions perhaps, but still I am sure that I shall be with him again."

Cora was so pinched for money that on August 29 she had sent her companion, Mrs. Brotherton, to agent Perris with the manuscripts of three tales of Crane's which she had completed.[2] She begged Perris to advance her five pounds because "I have just had a terrible run-in with the woman who keeps this place and must leave today. I am short just £3.10 in paying her. These things and kinds of people are new to me, and I am unfit to go out or I would come personally to see you." The run-in with her Gower Street landlady in South Kensington occurred three days after she had begged Pinker to say nice things for her application to rent a mall house in Millborne Grove at £70 per year (at the same time she vas double-dealing with Perris as agent for Stephen's works). Pinker had io interest in her writings and cared not how she sold them, but he had a vested interest in Stephen Crane's work and hoped, he told Alfred *lant, to recover Crane's debts to him.

William Heinemann disliked Cora and thought her extravagant and vain, and Pinker had more reason than Heinemann to dislike her. She iad the notion that all the obligations of the estate could be "paid off quickly so that the executors' work will be finished," she wrote Pinker on August 26. "Please think how very distressing all this is to me and how long to be settled and to get to work doing what I know my dear one vould have me do." It doesn't seem to have occurred to her that Pinker lso was distressed about retrieving the money he had advanced. Her usiness relations with him came to an end in an interview on the 27th, nd thereafter she didn't care to see him again nor did he care to see her. I explained my position to you yesterday," she wrote him. "And so I nust ask you to return to me all the Ms. and the verses to see what I can lo about them personally. I have instructed the boy to bring them with iim."

The verses were the *Intrigue* poems and "The Battle Hymn"—found in Stephen's saddlebags which he had left behind in Cuba with Charles Michelson of the New York *Journal*. "The saddle bags and contents will e sent to you immediately," Michelson had written her on July 8. "Among he things you will find an autograph battle hymn, probably written while 'our husband was in Cuba. I sent a copy of this to the *Pall Mall Magazine Gazette*]—which I see now I should not have done. Will you kindly keep ne advised of your address in order that I may forward to you the check he magazine will doubtless send if they publish the hymn."

Cora wrote Corwin Linson on September 28: "I am . . . working very iard trying to write woefully bad stories—pot-boilers!"[3] Stephen had onged to see his old friend during his last months, but his query to McClure's for Linson's address did not reach him until April 1, the day f his hemorrhages while Cora was in Paris, and then he wired Cora to o and see Linson at his Paris address; but she didn't go. "Stephen does iot seem lost to me; only gone upon a journey which I will take one day, o that we may be together again to work & live under the new condi- ions." In her notebook she wrote "I feel like one having started out upon . journey which led for a while through pastures green and waters still. 'hen suddenly to have lost the turning—henceforth the desert and the larkness of loneliness forever."

This same journey theme reappears in her October 17 letter to Elbert Hubbard (written on black-bordered stationery with the monogram "CC"). 'he regrets that Hubbard had not visited Crane at Brede Place. "Stephen alked so often to me of you, and your photo was always in his study, so it seems as if I knew you too. I want to know you and to keep in touch, if they will let me, with all my dear one's friends. If you ever come to London please come and see me. I should like to tell you of Stephen's last year; he seemed to grow so, and to have the power of wonderful speech. You will remember how slowly he used to talk? And he did so much that was good for helpless people the past two years. We had the little children of Harold Frederic, you know. I have two now, but must give them up as life is a struggle for me at present."

Linson wrote on October 12 that he and his wife hoped Cora would visit them in Paris, and she optimistically responded that she might get to Paris and see them en route to revisiting Badenweiler. But it was not to be; they never met. It would be "such a delight to hear you tell of the early days when you lived—on potato salad, was it not?" she wrote. "Stephen always made me shudder at the idea of potato salad for breakfast! How I wish you could have seen him as the Squire at Brede Place. I used to call him 'The Duke.' The old house would have delighted you. Stephen was so very happy there. I could not drag him into town or indeed off the Place. We had a little park of 100 acres, and Stephen would take his morning ride within the fence, over the turf. It is such a joy to me now to remember that his last years here were so filled with comfort; with comfort bought by work. His life was so filled with good. We had the two children of Harold Frederic, you know, and there was always some poor-in-luck or health chap staying with us. Sometime I hope to tell you about Stephen's charity—and no one, not even himself felt it to be charity. His character the last year was wonderful! He could see all things clearly. His mind was too wonderful to stay here, and that is why God took him."

She wrote Linson's cousin Louis Senger on October 27 that she had so far been unable to settle down to writing her biography of Stephen, on which project Senger had offered to aid her. "Of course I want to put in the work the best that is in me and you can appreciate how difficult that is, when my mind is worried by the lack of £. s. d. However, that is only a temporary matter. I am writing some woefully bad short stories and also a series of papers on the British regiments that served in the war of the American Revolution. By Xmas I hope to have this work ended. All sorts of information comes to me of Stephen's struggle before the 'Red Badge' success. Will you write me about this work we want to do?"

A month later Cora had not rented out her Milborne Grove rooms, and she wrote agent Perris whether he knew of any man or wife wanting comfortable rooms, with bath and good attendance by a maid (Mrs. Brotherton doubling in that task?) "who can valet and look after a gentleman's clothes. Pardon me asking you but I must leave no stone unturned to support myself." As she was too ill to go to see Perris that day she sent her friend W. F. Richie (whose daughter Edith had lived at Brede Place) to deliver for sale only in England four short Crane pieces.[4] "Will you buy

ese things outright or let me have an advance of £10?" she wrote Perris:
f so please let me have cheque by the bearer, Mr. Richie. This will be
great accommodation." She would bring him other stories shortly for
m to sell on the usual commission. Money from the Wyoming stories
erris had sold belonged to Alfred T. Plant as English executor of Crane's
tate. "I suppose you know that my late husband got high prices for his
ork, at least £10—a thousand words." She had collected by then—
id-November—59,260 words toward a new book and sent Perris that
uch. "Some of these pieces are of Mr. Crane's latest," written after his
*ounds in the Rain* stories, which were now in their fourth edition on
oth sides of the Atlantic. She told Perris: "I want £100 *advance* royalty.
50 now and £50 when remainder of ms. is delivered which can be
side 2 months, and 15 per cent royalty, for English publication & colo-
ies." In America, Frederick Stokes would not gamble more than £50
n this new book, which Paul Reynolds recognized as not up to Crane's
andard: "a rather heterogenous mass of matter." Because Cora balked
the £50 offer, *Last Words* never appeared in America, and for the
nglish edition Perris obtained only £50. I "think that one obstructing
fluence must be the prices which have been asked and obtained [by
rane] in the past and which have created a sort of tradition of expensive-
ess, which cannot be maintained now that his personality is not behind
em," he explained. *Last Words,* with eight pieces published here for the
st time (in 1902), was at first entitled *Reluctant Voyagers* until Cora
otested to Perris against that title. A good many pieces were not Crane's
st words; they were early writings.

Paul Reynolds had cabled Cora to ask whether the sketch "A Deser-
on," which he had just sold for the November, 1900, *Harper's Magazine,*
ad yet been sold in England, and Cora sent the cablegram to Perris
ecause she was broke and could not afford to cable. On October 23
e asked Perris to advance her five pounds and to try to get some money
 her by the first of the month; then she'd be "very, very glad."[5] On
ovember 10 she sent Mrs. Brotherton to Perris to obtain a check for
x guineas. "I hate to ask but I am at my wit's end over being dunned by
 man who wants £7." On the 23rd she urged him to sell the serial
ghts of the incomplete *O'Ruddy.* "Mr. Pinker has had it to sell but has
one nothing with it." Crane creditors were besieging solicitor Plant, and
e needed to pay them "a dividend with as little delay as possible," he
rote Pinker in October, and on December 19 asked him to turn over to
m "all contracts and papers in your possession." "As you are aware,"
inker replied, "I advanced money to Mr. Crane on the security of the
ontracts and Mss. which I hold, and I scarcely think I can give up all
ontrols and papers until my account is settled." He was stuck with ne-
otiations about Crane's works until 1914.

Cora sent Perris a copy of *The O'Ruddy*'s 65,000 words in hope of get-

ting £300 for the sale of its English serial rights and asked him to plac
*Great Battles of the World* in England. Perris sold *Great Battles* to Chap
man & Hall. "And now I must ask if you can manage me an advance, a
much as you can make it. This is not particularly business-like I know, bu
under the circumstances I hope you will try to think it business-like. I
would be impossible for me to sign a contract giving you the exclusiv
rights in my late husband's (published) works. We will leave the contrac
until I come to see you. . . . I shall go over what manuscripts you have . .
and send the stories for you to sell for me, but of course you will nc
charge me 15%. 10% is the usual rate everywhere." By November 2
Perris had two book-rights to sell, one long serial, and a lot of shor
pieces. She sent him then a story of her own: "José and the Saint." Poult
ney Bigelow and Lewis Hind of the London *Academy* thought them good
she said. "The *Strand* refused it but said it was good and powerful bu
they did not dare print it. (Rubbish, the public can't want all love an
milksop!) The *Traveler,* the *Graphic,* & *Pall Mall* have said 'nice things' bu
have refused it. Do your best & let me know who refuses it."

On December 3 she wrote Perris again: "In thinking over what Mr
Radford said to me I can't quite see *what* he means by saying 'it can't g
on, this hand to mouth business.' Perhaps he does not understand that al
my late husband's estate is mine, but that until the small estate is settle
I cannot draw any money—hence my present difficulties." But in fact sh
had no title to Stephen's estate because she was not his legal wife, a poin
by which William Howe Crane maneuvered to shut her out from mone
accruing from Stephen's royalties. In August he had promised cooperatio
but could not send her any money, and in November he reminded her tha
he had returned (in April, 1899) the $500 Stephen had paid on his invest
ment in the Hartwood acres, and so he was still owed that sum. But h
assured his "dear sister, your interests will be more than safe in my hands."
More than safe, since she got nothing from her "affectionate brother."

Paul Reynolds would release money to Cora "as soon as he consents,'
but Judge Crane did not consent. Reynolds wrote her on May 14 tha
he had asked Judge Crane whether he, as executor of Stephen Crane'
will, had any objections to paying Cora Crane moneys received from sal
of Stephen's current publications. William replied that while he was no
prepared to say he objected, at the same time he did not consent. "Yo
will see that if I paid this money to anyone but the person who has lega
authority to receive it [Judge Crane himself], I may render myself person
ally liable for the amount of such money," Reynolds wrote.

Cora meanwhile had pleaded with him to send her the money he ha
obtained from Henry T. Coates of Philadelphia for the American rights o
*Last Words,* for otherwise she would land in New York City "withou
money and must send money back here to save my things." Judge Cran

rote her that she had better consent that the money with Reynolds be
aid to him, and to Reynolds he wrote that he might take "this letter as
ly agreement to indemnify you against any further payments to her."
his cut Cora off from the $250 Reynolds had from Coates (and from
ther sums), and then Judge Crane decreed that all writings by Stephen—
ublished or in manuscript—belonged to the estate, not to Cora Crane,
though he consented that she be paid by Plant the $100 she asked for
er services in preparing for the printer the pieces she collected for *Last
'ords*. Cora had thought that by the codicil to Stephen's last will, which
lant had drawn up, the income from royalties and copyrights belonged
» her, but in this legal issue Judge Crane had the last words![6] When
tephen's will came up for probate hearing in December, 1904, the court
itation named Cora not as Stephen's wife but only as "one of the next of
in;" hence she had no legal status. Judge Crane had known his brother had
ever married Cora, but he did not let her know that he knew it, and
ius he misled her as she had deceived him. She finally recognized that he
ad duped her, and declared her defeat to Alfred Pinker on July 9, 1905:
Judge Crane has not acted as a gentleman should."

In December, 1900, Cora gave a reception at her little house in Mil-
orne Grove, and that little house "was a crush" (she wrote Edmund
'rane's daughter Agnes) with such distinguished guests as the Frewens
f Brede Place, Walter Crane (that "great artist") and his wife and
aughters, Mrs. Cornwallis-West (the former Lady Randolph Churchill),
ie society beauty Lady Hamilton (friend of the Prince of Wales), and
heaps of other distinguished men and women. They all know it's a ques-
on if I get my next meal or not," she let young Agnes know so as to
npress the Crane family with her social status among the English elite
·hile simultaneously letting them know how destitute she was.

Although she had no idea where her next meal would come from, she
eld Sunday evenings for artists, musicians and literary friends such as
.ewis Hind of the London *Academy* and magazine writer Edwin Pugh.
·he invited the artist Clement T. Flower to do a portrait of Stephen
'rane, hoping that Judge Crane would pay for it. William, however, was
atisfied with some snapshots. He wrote for some autographs of Stephen,
·ho in his letters to his brother never signed his full name; some college
·ad asked him for an autograph. "If it's not asking too much, I'd like to
·ave you send me two autographs of Harold Frederic. . . . How many
*Maggies* would you like to have?" He owned twenty-seven copies and
·ad not sold them "for the reason that I could get no offer for the same,
·lthough I have offered to sell them to several booksellers."

"Last year at this time we were so gay and happy at Brede Place,"
'ora wrote Agnes Crane with regrets that she could not send "a good

Xmas box to you all."[7] She couldn't afford it, and she was ill with a ba
leg resting high in the air on a pile of pillows—"my gouty leg!" You ca
fancy, she said, "how miserable a time this is for me." Mabel Bar
Edith Richie and Florence Bray had visited her in December; and th
Frasers, who had lunched at Brede Place one Saturday in March, entei
tained her for Christmas dinner (John Foster Fraser, M. P., admire
everything Crane had written). Other friends such as George Lynch an
Poultney Bigelow had kept in touch with the lonely woman ghost-ridde
by memories of Stephen and of her former husband, Captain Donald Wi
liam Stewart. His family's home in South Kensington (73 Harrington Ga
dens), a fashionable part of the London West End, was not far fro
Cora's Milborne Grove house in the Boultons.

Henry James responded to her Christmas greeting on December 3(
"I echo heartily your words of woe over the rather ghostly business. I ca
well imagine how little of anything but heaviness it must have had for yo
—in the dark & dreary town [London] or with little but ghosts at you
fireside. Here [at Rye], however, it has not been brilliant: deluges of we
a howling gale & a very quiet state of mumps for me (as I've been, int
the bargain, unwell) being the order of the day. The midwinter here is a
best gruesome, & I am longing for an absence." Catherine Wells wrote t
wish Cora "very sincerely that the New Year may give you some day
of brightness and hopefullness and happiness among your friends."

Cora wrote Flower, the artist, about his proposed painting on Januar
22: "I have been waiting to see if my late husband's brother, Judge Cran
would order the picture. He does not write to me about it and to b
quite frank with you, I cannot pay for it until the estate is quite settle
and that seems months off. In the United States the executor has 1
months. It is causing me simply endless worry and it is so unnecessary, bu
the fact remains. Now, if under these circumstances you are willing t
undertake the portrait I shall be glad to have the 'head.' " Flower decide
to paint a larger picture ("as it would be so much nicer to have the hand
in") and wrote her on April 28—the day Cora was sailing for America—
for an appointment to show her the painting at his studio.

In February, Frederic Remington, whom Crane had known in Cuba
and whose drawings of cowboys and Indians had inspired him to see th
West in 1895, returned the manuscript of a Spitzbergen tale which Cor
had sent him in hope that he could complete it. "It is utterly impossible,'
he wrote her on February 26, "that I should undertake what you suggest—
for the reason that I could not imitate Crane's style and that I have a
very pronounced one of my own. Again I am laborious in my writing—
having little facility. I am not the man to do the work although from m
regard for Mr. Crane I would do anything in reason for his widow. I hav
a great fear that you cannot find a man who can carry Crane's master-han

through so mysterious a scheme as the Fire-Tribe story but that's how-ever."[9]

On April 25, Cora notified Perris that she was "obliged to go suddenly to the States. Please give any money for Ms. in your possession to Mr. Plant (the English executor of Stephen's estate)."[10]

Moreton Frewen wrote from Ireland that he thought she had made a wise decision. If she got a quiet year in the country in Kentucky ("not in Louisville or any of their horrid towns"), it would do her much good. She needed a rest "after the awful strain of the past year. He sent her twenty pounds and asked that she write him later how the world was treating her. One of his senatorial friends in Washington might find something for her with a reasonable salary attached. "Don't please give me any charge on the rent of your house; if times turn out well later on you can return me this tiny loan." He would try to get her a pass on the rail-road to Kentucky, for the more dollars you arrive with in America "the better." She sublet her furnished house (leased for two years) through solicitor Plant; offered the Conrads another of Stephen's dogs, Tolstoi;[11] made a gift to the Society of American Women in London of the captured Spanish flag Crane had brought back from Cuba; and threw a last party, which as usual she could not afford. Henry James begged off that he was "fast down" at Lamb House. "I am afraid your recent stay in Eng-land has not had much convenience for you and I can't help congratulat-ing you on your decision to bring it to a close. That America may be easier for you is the hope of yours very truly." A cold note, colder than his chilly note of the previous December, it implies that he was not anxious to see her again.

Cora took ship from America on April 28. She was skipping the country on her creditors.

In September, 1904, William, then in permanent residence in New York City, wrote Cora at her Aunt Mary Holder's apartment in that city to ask that she sign "a consent and waiver" for his accounting of Stephen's estate. Instead of signing it she petitioned the Surrogate of Orange County, New York (where Stephen's last will was filed), to have royalties paid not to Judge Crane but to her. However, she erred in filling out the legal forms and in sending them to Crane's publisher Appleton instead of to the Surrogate. When she finally wrote the Surrogate on New Year's Eve of 1904 she gave as her permanent address her Aunt Holder's and said that she was now on a visit to Georgia so as to conceal the fact that she was—and had been since 1902—in Jacksonville managing her house of joy, the Court.

On returning to America in May, 1901, she had spent several weeks with her aunt in New York City, where she suffered a breakdown. She had vacationed six or seven months at Owensboro, Kentucky, gone to New Orleans for a while and then returned to Owensboro. Finally she went to Jacksonville, Florida, and built the Court in 1902.

On June 1, 1905, she married Hammond McNeil while they were on a spree in New York, and in her marriage license she claimed it was her second marriage (she had been twice married before she met Stephen Crane), and that she was thirty-six (she was forty-one). Hammond—age twenty-five—said his occupation was railroad conductor. He was soon set up in business, probably by Cora, as proprietor of the Annex Saloon in the Everett Hotel. He ran a saloon, and she ran a house of joy. She set aside a room for him at the Court and apparently gave him money from time to time.[12]

Two years later he became jealous of her supposedly flattering attentions toward a railroad boy of nineteen named Harry Parker. Parker had flashed a wad of money and boasted that it was from his girl, and McNeil suspected that the girl was his wife Cora. He accused her of intimacy with Parker, exacted a promise from him to stay away from his wife, and then went out and bought a gun. Cora was playing her new gramophone, and McNeil taunted her that she was playing for the other fellow. There was an exchange of blows and violent words. "After what you said, you are as dead as in your coffin," McNeil said. The next morning (May 31, 1907) he left a note: "My feelings for you are as dead as if in the grave. I never had any friend except my mother."

Cora took lightly his threat to kill her. She went on a picnic with Hattie Mason, housekeeper at the Court, and Mabel Wright, the housekeeper at Palmetto Lodge, whose boyfriend just then was Harry Parker. They were driving in a carriage when they came upon Parker walking to the railroad station, and he, having missed his train, joined their picnic party in Floyd's saloon in East Mayport. And now McNeil suddenly made his appearance. "Ah, I have caught you at last!" he exclaimed. 'I'm going to kill you both!" He threatened to kill both Cora and Harry Parker. Mabel Wright jumped out of the front seat of the carriage, and McNeil warned: "Stand back, Mabel, or I'll kill you too." He fired four times, the second shot wiping the smirk from rival Parker's face, while Cora hid behind Mabel and cried: "He is going to kill me!" On the dead Parker's necktie was Cora's diamond ring, her wedding ring.

As McNeil was now threatened by death in the electric chair for the murder of Harry Parker, his father persuaded Cora to flee the country with the star witness Hattie Mason, whose testimony had been most damaging at the preliminary trial on August 13, when Cora refused to testify against her husband. The coroner's jury had returned a verdict of "willful murder," and the newspapers represented McNeil and Parker as the dupes of McNeil's "alleged" wife, "keeper of a disorderly house" and "woman of the underworld."

Cora fled America for Dover on the S. S. *Finland* on October 19. In London she spotted in St. Paul's crypt the brass inscription to her former husband. "I did not know he was dead. Poor old Don!" (Sir Donald Stewart had died at Nairobi; he had been Governor of the British East Africa Protectorate, now Kenya.) She was staying at the Charing Cross Hotel, where she had stayed with Stewart at the time of their marriage, and then she moved into her London lodgings at 47 Gower Street. She went to Paris by crowded train ("Was ass enough to go in carriage 'For ladies only ' "), saw Versailles by magnificent auto with Hattie of the Court, and then back in London Hoyt de Friese took her to the theater and supper at the Carlton. She revisited the countryside near Brede Place—Bodiam Castle, the Queen Elizabeth oak tree, and went on to Rye's Mermaid Inn for tea, then took the train back to London. At Rye she walked past Lamb House without going in, Henry James having curtly told her that he was then in London and that "a call at Lamb House will not find yours truly." She visited the Conrads for lunch with Hattie (presented as Mrs. Barrett, as Mathilde years ago had been presented to them as Mrs. Ruedy), and she visited next the Frewens at Brede Place after tea with Mr. and Mrs. H. G. Wells the day before. Then off to Ireland where word reached her that her dog Sponge died—"the dearest and best treasure I had, my old faithful dog!! This will always be the reproach of my life & it is surely a punishment." He died, she was convinced, of a broken heart because of her absence, and she cabled Nell at the Court to bury him in the courtyard. By mid-December, 1907, she and Hattie were homeward bound on the American liner *New York*.

Hammond McNeil, against whom Cora refused to testify when he was tried for murder, testified against her in a bill of complaint for divorce proceedings that she had an "ungovernable temper" and had beaten him on the head with a shoe and physically assaulted him many times. These charges were sworn to by Mabel Wright, Cora's friend at the picnic where McNeil had shot down Harry Parker two years earlier, and by Cora's housekeeper (Edith Gray) and chambermaid (Bessie McPherson) at the Court. Her former friends testified that she had said: "Yes, I did it, I would do it again, and I only wish I had beaten him to death. I have lost all respect for him—and I will never live with him again!"[13]

Prior to her marriage to McNeil, Cora had gone by the name of Cora Taylor in Jacksonville and "Miss Cora" at the Court, but some of her friends knew her as Mrs. Stephen Crane. Among them was Ernest Christie Budd, a real-estate operator and horse-racing gambler who made small bets for her. He wanted to marry her in spite of the scandal, but his wife refused him a divorce and had him arrested for nonsupport when he quit her house and moved into the Court.

In January, 1910, Cora suffered a stroke. She resigned the management of the Court to her housekeeper, then Edith Gray, and made out a will

leaving her property and personal things to Ernest Budd. On Septemb
4 she collapsed and died after helping to push a stranded automobile o
of the sand before Palmetto Lodge in the hot sun.

Cora's grave in the Evergreen Cemetery at Jacksonville, Florida,
marked by a white marble block inscribed: *CORA E. CRANE—1868
1910.*[14]

# *Appendix*
# *Notes*
# *Checklist*

# ☙ *Appendix*

## 1. "DAN EMMONDS"*

Of several unsolved mysteries about Crane the most puzzling problem has to do with "Dan Emmonds," which was published for the first time in my article discussing it ("New Short Fiction by Stephen Crane") in *Studies in Short Fiction*, Vol. I, No. 1 (Fall 1963).

The confusion arises partly from the fact that when *George's Mother* was coming off the press the *Bookman* for May 1896 announced that the London publisher Edward Arnold will have "a new novel by Mr. Stephen Crane ready for publication in June with the probable title *Dan Emmonds*." The *Bookman* got its news from the *Illustrated London News* for April 18, which said that Crane's next novel would be called *Dan Emmonds*. In June the *Bookman*, having said that it would be ready for publication in June, corrected itself by saying that *Dan Emmonds* "will not be ready until the autumn. Mr. Edward Arnold will publish immediately, however, a new story by Mr. Crane entitled *George's Mother*." Berryman in *Stephen Crane* confounds *Dan Emmonds* by guessing that it is "evidently the old short novel *George's Mother*," but he very likely never saw the typescript of ten pages. The difference between that short satirical sketch entitled "Dan Emmonds" and the novel *George's Mother* is absolute.

Is the difference also absolute between the short sketch "Dan Emmonds" and the projected novel called *Dan Emmonds*? Crane wrote Hitchcock of Appleton on March 26, 1896, that he gave his schoolmate Harry Thompson of Edward Arnold "a satirical sketch," an "old thing, strong in satire but rather easy writing—called Dan Emmonds . . ." Reconsidering my viewpoint of 1963 and 1964 (in *Studies in Short Fiction*), it is possibly true that Crane had begun a novel called *Dan Emmonds*, but the hard fact is that what he gave Harry Thompson was *George's Mother*, which Arnold published in May 1896. If he gave him also the beginning of a novel called *Dan Emmonds*, the question arises why Crane did not retrieve it in 1899 to offer it to agent Curtis Brown who visited him at Brede Place to see if Crane had anything for him to place. All he had were contracted-for books which exhausted him in the attempt to complete them and some uncollected sketches, including no doubt the short sketch "Dan Emmonds," which Cora was still trying to

* (Chapter I, fn. 16)

537

peddle in 1900 through agent Pinker. His label on the typescript reads: "PRICE: 10. 10/—for serial rights." Cora queried Pinker on November 5, 1900: "What has become of the story Dan Emmonds? If you have it please send it to me to copy." As she preserved the typescript of the sketch, she probably would have preserved the manuscript of the novel *Dan Emmonds,* had it existed.

Announcements in various journals in 1896 about Mr. Crane's forthcoming novel called *Dan Emmonds* is no proof of its existence. Crane began and dropped many book projects, some of which never got beyond their title. The *Book News* for October 1896 claimed that Mr. Crane sails for England "this month for a brief stay, returning probably a short time before the holiday. This will interrupt his work on his new novel *Dan Emmons* [sic], and will probably postpone its publication until spring." In September the book Crane intended to write was about New York City police, a project which was announced in the papers but which he never carried out. The *Book News* for October added that a few chapters of *Dan Emmonds* have been written and that "they give promise of something quite unlike any of Mr. Crane's former work. Dan is an Irish boy, and the story as far as written deals with life in New York City."

In the short sketch again Dan is an Irish boy, but what Crane called "a satirical sketch" does not deal with New York City. In 1897 he wrote Edmund on September 9 from Ireland to send on "any odd bits of writing you find at H. [artwood] . . . Some of them will come in handy. Have you noticed a ms devoted to the adventures of a certain Irishman? Try to get it." (A new Crane letter in the *Stephen Crane Newsletter:* Spring 1967.) This seems to refer to a small manuscript rather than to one of several chapters, for were it bulky it would be readily noticed. Assuming that it was the short sketch, Crane recast it to include the near-shipwreck adventures of Cora on the Black Sea aboard a ship which Cora in her journal called a "terrible old tub" carrying a cargo of 5000 live chickens and having "little hen coops for cabins." What saves Dan when he finds himself alone on the sea is a floating hen-coop, the ship having gone down and left nothing but the hen-coop and the dead body of "a pig named Bartholomew, who had been a great favorite with the ship's cook." The Irish humor here and the echoing of Cora's dreadful Black Sea voyage would date the sketch for 1897 or later, whereas I had thought it "an early Crane voyage fantasy in imitation of Defoe." However, the first scene on land might have been written earlier, and a hint of this is in the naming of the ship "Susan L. Terwilliger." The Terwilliger Funeral Parlor was in Port Jervis, New York.

The fact that Cora's near ship-wreck is described in Dan Emmonds' shipwreck scene has seemed to Lillian Gilkes additional evidence for her theory that Crane was with Cora all the way to Constantinople and Athens, as given in *Cora Crane* (1960). We have argued the issue in *Studies in Short Fiction,* I, No. 4 (Fall 1964), an issue having importance because if Crane was with Cora on the overland route to Varna on the Black Sea he then faked his dispatch about the Powers' Fleet off Crete with its dateline: "On Board French Steamer *Guadiana.* . . . Leaving Marseilles." Miss Gilkes contends that Crane "could not possibly have come from Marseilles, going direct to Crete, and also have been in Athens on the 17th." But the Guadiana left Marseilles on April 3 and was off Crete on the 8th, spending "Half a Day in Suda Bay," as given in the variant title of Crane's dispatch in the New York *Sun*. The *Sun's* dateline of April 22 is the only item faked, since Crane was then in Epirus, but the *Sun* editor or Crane himself could have faked it. Any number of Crane dispatches in the Cuban War as well as in the Greco-Turkish War have tampered datelines. Finally, Miss Gilkes points out that Stephen wrote brother William: "I have been in . . . *Turkey* and Greece." That seemingly proves that Crane got to Turkey *before* he got to Greece, got there with Cora via the Orient Express and then suffered with her that near-shipwreck on the Back Sea. "This was their second honeymoon, the real one, and all the more delicious after doubts and separations!" I contend that Crane was not with Cora enroute to Greece and that he was in Turkey *after* reaching Athens from the *Guadiana;* on April 17 he left Athens for Epirus, which was then Turkish soil. And that settles that.

## 2. *MAGGIE* IN REVIEW*

Appearing six years before Norris' *McTeague, Maggie: A Girl of the Streets* was the first social exposé in fiction to render truthfully "how the other half lives"—the title of Jacob Riis's sociological study of New York City tenement-life. *Godey's Magazine* of October 1895 reviewed the 1893 edition of *Maggie* along with Edward Waterman Townsend's *Jimmie Fadden* ("a household familiar . . . whose vivid language has infected the nation"), the book by which the Bowery was then best known. *Maggie*, it granted, was probably the strongest piece of slum writing we have; in keenness of wit, minuteness of observation, and bitterness of cynicism, *Maggie* compares with Arthur Morrison's *Tales of Mean Streets* (London, 1895). Crane renders the "foredoomed fall of a well-meaning girl reared in an environment of drunkenness and grime," and his plainness of speech may "give a shock to spasmic prudishness, but there is nothing to harm a healthy mind, and they [*i.e.,* the novels here under review] all should have the effect of creating a better understanding and a wiser, more active sympathy for the unfortunates who must fill the cellar of the tenement we call life. To do this," the reviewer (Rupert Hughes) concluded, "is far better even than to be artistic."

*Maggie* "is a powerful sermon on the need of missionary work among the heathen in the tenements of our big cities, and it cannot fail to open the eyes of many who have only taken a sentimental interest in a class that seems to be no nearer to them than the natives of the Congo" (San Francisco *Chronicle:* August 9, 1896). *Maggie*, said the London *Academy* (January 16, 1897), "is one of the most downright earnestly-written books ever published. The gruesome tragedy of environment, with all its sordidness of detail, is hammered in with brief, pitiless sentences. Mr. Crane's command of language is remarkable: he does not spare his readers one jot or tittle of the horror of New York slum life." Crane's heroine is doomed from the start—by her environment. "From the

* (Chapter V, fn. 14) Abridged from my *Houses That James Built* (1961), where reviews were first quoted.

first, Maggie was forced to bear heavy burdens which should have been carried by the older and stronger members of her family. Then, too, heredity and environment, the two bugbears of to-day, are strong factors to contend with and when, as in this case, their chief elements are drunkenness and even worse vices, the end is not hard to foresee" (Denver *Republican:* July 26, 1896).

"I recall no tale that approaches 'Maggie' in the illustration of drunkenness, promiscuous pugilism, joyless and repellent dialogue, and noise. Of course," says this reviewer, "I like it. Mr. Howells has educated me in realism, and I hope I know a good thing in that line when I see it" (New York *Town Topics:* June 25, 1896). In the 1896 Heinemann edition with revised title *Maggie: A Child of the Streets,* Howells in his Foreword remarked against "the many foolish people who cannot discriminate between the material and the treatment in art, and think that beauty is inseparable from daintiness and prettiness." (An unidentified London journal commented on the Heinemann edition: "Mr. Heinemann has given to Mr. Stephen Crane's 'Maggie' something of the appearance of an old-fashioned Sunday school prize-book.") It is a terrible satire, said the London *Mail & Express* (November 6, 1896), "but the writer has stopped short of cynicism—not far enough, however, to make 'Maggie' palatable to the lovers of only pleasant things." Howells, in the New York *Press* of April 15, 1894 (remarking on the 1893 *Maggie*), had admitted: "There is so much realism of a certain kind in it that unfits it for the general reading, but once in a while it will do to tell the truth as completely as Maggie does." In announcing the forthcoming Appleton edition *The Critic* (February 22, 1896) summed up briefly the history of *Maggie* since its first appearance in paper-bound mustard-yellow covers with a pen-name for the author and with no name at all for the publisher: " 'Maggie' was not an immoral story, as many persons imagined from its title; it was coarse in the way that 'Chimmie Fadden' is coarse; but there was more objection to bad language from the mouth of a girl-tough than from a boy." Bowery slang, "of which other writers have given us a taste, reaches its perfect flower in Mr. Crane's chronicle," the Indianapolis *News* conceded (August 14, 1896). Crane "has gone to the lowest depths of degradation for material, and he does not spare the reader in telling of his observations." The *News* concluded: "This is by no means a cheerful tale. There is something inexorable in the movement of the incidents of the girl's life. It is all very pitiful, and it is told with power. There is no halfway in Mr. Crane's realism." The *News* added, however: "The great question is not of veracity, but is as to the right of an author to use an undeniable power in presenting a tale of unrelieved misery, despair and sin. It is to be hoped that Mr. Crane will turn his talents to the writing of some less wretched tale." The same squeamish note appeared the next day in the Nashville *Banner.* Like the Indianapolis *News,* the *Banner* recognized *Maggie's* realism; "it is a magnificent piece of realism, which loses its artistic value because its shadows are too deep and its lights too faint and evasive, missing, indeed, the highest aim of literature, which is to give some small degree of pleasure, at least, to the world, and to prove itself not a clog, but an inspiration in the uplifting of humanity's heart."

The obsession with the idea that art aims to inspire, please, and enlighten by tender and uplifting sentiments was the aesthetic malady that afflicted the 1890's. *Maggie,* said the *Banner,* is not an immoral book; it's rather "a strong sermon urging the need of greater charity of sentiment, as well as of gold for the poverty-hardened people of the slums." Nevertheless the reviewer was of the opinion that "it is too hopeless, too full of misery, degradation and dirt. The reader flounders in a mire of pessimism, never once receiving from the author the offer of a helping hand or a word of encouragement, and the memory of the book is a nightmare, and the thought of it inexpressibly hopeless and depressing." The *Banner* reviewer wanted it both ways: realism minus the degradation and dirt, and realism touched up with noble sentiments.

*Maggie,* said the New York *Advertiser,* "is as realistic as anything that Emile Zola has ever written. Though some of its chapters are enough to give one the 'creeps,' none can deny that the characters which he draws with such a master hand are absolutely true to life." Echoing Howells, the New York *Advertiser* (June 1, 1896) praised Crane's artistry: *Maggie* "is free of maudlin sentiment." The *Advertiser* scored an important insight: "No missionary ever ventures near 'Rum Alley.' Its denizens are left to their own resources, and they simmer in them." As the San Francisco *Chronicle* observed: "There is no attempt, as in Ned Townsend's latest story, to idealize the characters. The coarseness, the sordidness of life in these overcrowded buildings of New York is something which affects one like the reek of the Mulberry Bend gutters on a hot August night. The genius of the writer is revealed in the simplicity of his means of producing powerful effects." One of the best English reviews is unfortunately unidentified; it is worth quoting in full here:

> It is surely a fine tribute to the art in a book that the reviewer should be compelled to praise it against his will. And this tribute must certainly be given to Mr. Stephen Crane's latest story. 'Maggie' is a study of life in the slums of New York, and of the hopeless struggle of a girl against the horrible conditions of her environment; and so bitter is the struggle, so black the environment, so inevitable is the end, that the reader feels a chill at his heart, and dislikes the book even while he admires it.

*Maggie,* in sum, is thwarted by her environment, but what gives the book its artistry is Crane's realism:

> Mr. Crane's realism is merciless and unsparing; in these chapters are set before us in cold blood hideous phases of misery, brutality, drunkenness, vice; while oaths and blasphemies form the habitual speech of the men and women who live and move in this atmosphere of vileness. Yet every scene is alive and has the unmistakable stamp of truth upon it. The reader does not feel that he is reading about these horrors; he feels as if the outer walls of some tenement houses in the slums had been taken away and he could see—and see with comprehension—the doings of the teeming inmates. Over the whole grimly powerful tragedy is the redeeming grace of the author's implied compassion; but he never mars the effect of the story by speaking this compassion or by pointing a moral. He has drawn a vivid picture of life at its lowest and worst; he has shown us the characters as they would be, with no

false glamour of an impossible romance about them; and the moral may confidently be left to look after itself, since it stares from every page. Maggie herself is a wonderfully well-drawn character, and the book, repellent though it is, is in its way a triumph.

As for the American reception of *Maggie,* as the *Academy* explained in reference to the failure of the 1893 edition: *"Maggie* is not a pleasant book, and in those days the public was not ripe for the reception of instantaneous literary photographs of slum life. . . . But we have changed all that," stated the *Academy.* As a matter of fact, however, *Maggie* received a considerable number of very favorable American reviews. The San Francisco *Argonaut* of August 31, 1896, after reviewing *Maggie* on July 13, introduced excerpts from the novel with the explanation that "its popularity has grown to such an extent that we have decided to put before our readers a few of the more striking scenes. . . ." The New York *Times* (May 31, 1896) praised Crane as artist in rendering his pictures "with such vivid and terrible accuracy as to make one believe they are photographic. Mr. Crane cannot have seen all that he describes, and yet the reader feels that he must have seen it all. This, perhaps, is the highest praise one can give the book."

Other reviewers went *"Maggie-*mad," but not in the way Crane hoped for. "This unpleasant story," said the Pittsburgh *Bulletin* (August 8, 1896), "will make Stephen Crane's admirers wish they had stopped at his 'Red Badge of Courage.' Its heavy vulgarity leads nowhere and effects nothing." A certain English critic was similarly offended, and the Boston *Globe* (November 5, 1896) quoted him: "The fame of Stephen Crane has spread abroad in the wild way in which it has here, and a London critic writes in this wise of the young and glowing colorist: 'Mr. Crane always shouts in his writings; in fact he positively blares, with never a pause. To read his latest book, "Maggie," is to put one's ears into the bell of a cornet blown by giant lungs. It leaves one limp, exhausted, mistreated. The book is like a lump of red, raw beef. It is food for tigers, not for women and men. Mr. Crane may be as clever as Mr. Howells makes him out to be, but he is abusing his talents. Even supposing he does split our ear drums with his loud bass what shall it profit him or us?' "

These *Maggie* reviews document the literary and moral barometer of the 1890's, the impact of Crane's sociological iconoclasm upon the Gilded Age, and the contemporary reputation of a very young American writer destined to survive all his anonymous reviewers. He survived also his reputation in Port Jervis. So shocked were the ladies of Port Jervis after the 1896 publication of *Maggie* that several of them consulted his brother "as to the propriety of receiving Stephen Crane in their homes. . . ." (Thomas Beer in the Appendix to his *Stephen Crane,* 1923). They probably took their stance from the *Home Journal* of July 8, 1896: "One of our most noted contemporary literary critics, preëminent for his good taste, fairness, and discrimination, has sharply castigated this book. But whatever may be the general trend of the notices it has received, it is inconceivable that any reader, even with moral tone not above the average, could go over these pages without a shock to his sensibilities, and the pressure of the old question, 'Cui bono?' No good at all, must be the answer that springs to the lips of every right-thinking man or woman that turns over the leaves of Mr. Crane's 'Maggie.'" Reeking with profanity, blasphemy, the low, brutal dialect of the slums, etc., how could such a book "find acceptance among the better and purer classes of the reading world?" It didn't. But it found acceptance among those who recognized the importance of its "aggressive and pitiless realism" and felt that this picture of tenement-house life "in its sordidness and pathos amounts to a positive revelation" (Boston *Beacon:* June 27, 1896). As the Boston *Times* (July 12, 1896) pointed out: "The pitiful tragedy of the plot is being enacted over and over again all about us. It tells of a girl whose dormant soul was never kindled, who was ruined by the overwhelming forces of heredity and environment." After concluding that "Despite the sadness of her death one does not wish that she might have lived longer," the *Times* added: "There is not a gleam of sunshine in the whole book, but in Mr. Crane's hands this simple, ordinary story is so horribly real that it makes an indelible appeal to the fortunate portion of mankind, to right the wrongs which are making such hideous mischief all about us."

In "New York Low Life in Fiction," appearing in the New York *World* of July 26, 1896 (reissued in the 1896 Heinemann edition of *Maggie* as "An Appreciation"), Howells said: "I think that what strikes me most in the story of 'Maggie' is that quality of fatal necessity which dominated Greek tragedy." Chelifer (Rupert Hughes, a fraternity brother of Crane) echoed Howells in *Godey's Magazine* of September, 1896: "It has the inevitableness of a Greek tragedy, and the reader that grants to the fate of Euripides's fanciful 'Medea' an import and significance he refuses to see in the predestined ugliness of the end of this well-meaning 'Maggie,' has an outlook in life that is too literary to be true. Indeed he has misread his classics, if the woes of their creatures leave him uneducated into sympathy with the miseries of the miserables of his own town."

Many readers will find it impossible to become interested in *Maggie: A Girl of the Streets,* remarked the Richmond *Times* (July 26, 1896), "because, as they will tell you, 'it deals with such low people.' These will belong to the class who consign Mr. Dickens to the back shelves, or tolerate him coldly, as a person who devoted great talents to a low use. Mr. Crane can afford to dispense with their admiration. As a matter of fact, in the ghastly story of this girl of the streets, he has revealed the tragedy in the degradation of the lowest ten thousand with the pen of a master." *Maggie,* said Hamlin Garland in his June 1893 *Arena* review of the 1893 edition, "deals with poverty and vice and crime also, but it does so, not out of curiosity, not out of salaciousness, but because of a distinct art impulse, the desire to utter in truthful phrase a certain rebellious cry. It is the voice of the slums."

Frank Norris, on the contrary, thought Crane concerned himself too much with style at the expense of truth-to-life; and in one sense he was right, namely the fact that Crane is more stylist than realist. Reviewing *Maggie* in the San Francisco *Wave,* Norris complained that Crane's characters seemed deficient in psychological realism. "It is as if Mr. Crane had merely used the 'machinery' and 'business' of slum life to develop certain traits or to portray certain emotions and passions that *might happen anywhere.*" Norris wanted *Maggie* to be otherwise than it is. Psychological realism is not to be found here, but rather in *The Red Badge.* In both novels the realism is an invented, imagined realism;

not studied from life but created—created in such a way as to render an illusion of reality. The reader, Norris said, "is apt to feel that the author is writing, as it were, from the outside. There is a certain lack of sympathy apparent. Mr. Crane does not seem to *know* his people. You are tempted to wonder if he has ever studied them as closely as he might have done. He does not seem to me to have gotten *into* their life and to have written from what he saw around him" (*Wave:* July 4, 1896). The Boston *Ideas* that same day expressed just the opposite viewpoint: "The writer must have absorbed the meaning of the life here described deeply into his consciousness; it must have lingered there, to enable him to so accurately depict characters and scenes of which the average intelligent reading public catches but incidental outward glimpses without sympathetically understanding their causes and interludes." This reviewer noted the inevitableness of Maggie's end ("Circumstances are too strong for her") and, as though replying to Frank Norris, he pointed out that *Maggie* necessarily is quite different from *The Red Badge of Courage*.

The publisher's blurb for the Appleton 1896 edition of *Maggie* (priced at 74 cents, whereas the unsaleable 1893 edition was priced at 50 cents) proclaimed it "a real and strenuous tale"—and strenuous it was; but as the *Literary Digest* said, it is more "impressionistic" than "real," and "true to the impressionistic practice, alike in paint and in letters, the essential figure is the least delineated. Maggie is far less important to the canvas than her brother Jimmie, or her sottish mother, or the coarse and tawdry Bowery bartender who is the villain of the piece, and her destroyer" (August 8, 1896). But Maggie is of course just as important as the other characters who comprise her enforced destiny; to distinguish the latter as dominant because delineated with more detail is to blur the relationship of the one to the other. They represent her environment: "None of the dirt of Rum Alley seemed to be in her veins." Of course, people in fiction are composed of words, not of flesh and blood, and to identify them with reality is absurd. Though the characters in *Maggie* are not individuals but types, individualized characters are no more true to life than "mere types"; their anonymity reflects Crane's intention.

"Every sentence bristles with the steely sinews of the Nemesis that lays its heavy burden upon the dwarfish development of these poor, puny lives. Every phrase is a noteworthy one, a revelation of a people waiting for a savior." The reviewer for the Boston *Courier* was very perceptive. So too was the reviewer of the Springfield, Ohio, *Womankind* (August 1896). *Maggie* "is not the story of 'A Girl of the Streets'—rather a record of her evolution, how she unwittingly and unwillingly became the thing she despised." He points out: "In a line or two—without saying anything about them, himself, at all, Mr. Crane shows the utter futility of the ordinary 'mission' methods for reaching such people as Maggie and her brothers; again in a line he reveals the contemptible Pharisaical spirit of certain of the clergy; and in the brutal laugh and jest that greet the successive appearances of the old drunken mother in the police court, he hints at the wickedness and folly of our present methods of dealing with such pitiable creatures." The Boston *Saturday Evening Gazette* (June 20, 1896) saw *Maggie*, similarly, as having perhaps some sociological effect: "In the hands of an artist like Mr. Crane the simple story becomes an awful arraignment of our humanity. Such books are needed to impress upon the fortunate portion of mankind the truth that their fair cities bear ulcerous spots which threaten hideous mischief." *The Daily Tatler* in its first review of the book (November 11, 1896) remarked on the *Literary World's* comment that "there is nothing pleasing or pretty about Mr. Crane's work; but it has its place undoubtedly"—what the *Literary World* means, said the *Tatler*, is that "the complacent among christians need the lesson conveyed by Maggie's wicked life and consequently untimely death." The highest office of the writer, so Chelifer thought in *Godey's Magazine* (October, 1895) is the education of human sympathy. "Literature is the greatest of all democratizing forces." One gets more into sympathy with *Maggie* than with *George's Mother*, the New York *Press* opined (July 12, 1896): "It is assured from the beginning that in the ordinary course of events she will go to the bad. Mr. Crane makes one feel the morally downward pull of her surroundings with a power all the greater because he skillfully avoids all hint of sermonizing and almost all comment of any sort."

Edward Garnett complained in 1921, "If America has forgotten or neglects Crane's achievements, above all in 'Maggie' and 'The Open Boat,' she does not yet deserve to produce artists of rank."

## 3. "A PROLOGUE"*

Sometime after the Philistine banquet Crane dashed off "A Prologue," which Hubbard published in his *Roycroft Quarterly* and simultaneously in *A Souvenir and a Medley:*

> *A gloomy stage. Slender curtains at a window, centre. Before the window, a table, and upon the table, a large book, opened. A moonbeam, no wider than a sword-blade, pierces the curtains and falls upon the book.*
> *A moment of silence.*
> *From without, then—an adjacent room in intention—come sounds of celebration, of riotous drinking and laughter. Finally, a swift quarrel. The din and crash of fight. A little stillness. Then a woman's scream:*
> "Ah, my son, my son."
> *A moment of silence.*

CURTAIN

In its dramatic form "A Prologue" echoes a passage in the Reverend Thomas de Witt Talmage's *Night Side of New York Life* (1878):

> *Act the first* of the tragedy: A young man starting off from home; parents and sisters weeping to have him go. . . . Ring the bell and let the curtain fall. *Act the second:* The marriage altar. Full organ. Bright lights. . . . *Act the third:* a woman waiting for staggering steps. Old garments stuck into the broken window pane. Marks of hardship on the face. . . . Ring the bell and let the curtain drop. *Act the fourth:* Three graves in a dark place. . . . Oh, what a blasted heath with three graves! Plenty of weeds,

* (Chapter XI, fn. 6)

but no flowers. Ring the bell and let the curtain drop. *Act the fifth:* A destroyed soul's eternity. No light. No music. No hope. . . .

## 4. *THE LITTLE REGIMENT* IN REVIEW*

We cannot call Crane a story-teller, said the Boston *Literary Review* (March 15, 1897); he is rather a sketcher with decided impressionistic tendencies. "Neither do his sketches hold for us what they tell; instead, it is by the manner in which they tell it. However, Mr. Crane's war episodes are like clippings out of the great book of war itself, realistic in the best sense, and in *The Little Regiment* he fully sustains the surprising power he first displayed in *The Red Badge of Courage.*" The London *Academy* (February 20, 1897) said the same thing but noted that the bold and dangerous task of writing two books on exactly the same subject, from exactly the same standpoint and background, has proved a stumbling-block to many more experienced writers, and so it is high praise to say that this companion volume to *The Red Badge* "is not one whit behind it in power or picturesqueness. . . . As a word painting *The Little Regiment* is truly wonderful. In every sentence we can hear, even more clearly than in *The Red Badge of Courage,* the panther-like screaming, the witches' crooning of the shells, the cracking of the skirmishers, the spattering and zipping of the bullets, while through all these pulsates the fierce elation of the men amid the horrors. Great dashes of crimson and blobs of blue break occasionally through the dim and mystic clouds of grey mist, and the whole demoniacal howling of the battle quivers in our brain for hours. . . . Mr. Crane's peculiar genius is admirably adapted to the exigencies of the short story."

They are rough sketches of war and carnage done in glaring pigments, said the Chicago *Record* (January 16, 1897). "Mr. Crane is above all an impressionist, who obtains now and then a happy combination of colors, but more by chance than by intention. There is a superficiality about the tales of *The Little Regiment* which is unfortunate." It is noticeable and significant, said the New York *Press* (November 19, 1896) that opinion about this author has been more positive, one way or the other, than about any other writer of the day. Although Whitman's influence is rather negligible, the *Press* thought that Crane resembles Whitman remarkably in style, in independence of tradition, and in general philosophy of life. Also his adjectives "are as striking as Walt Whitman's. Many of them are strokes of genius, and in this latest work fewer of them than formerly create a suspicion of affectation."

Crane's *Red Badge,* said the Brooklyn *Daily Eagle* (December 20, 1896), was a revelation because no one had ever before attempted anything of the kind; but having done it once, is it possible for him to keep on doing it. After the title story "The Little Regiment," which makes the same portrayal of primary emotions as *The Red Badge,* the most striking tale is "A Mystery of Heroism." Here Crane brings out the fact "that the most daring deeds are oftentimes performed under stress of passion, and with no realizing sense of

* (Chapter XI, fn. 7)

the risks that are run. A soldier ventures upon a dangerous enterprise simply because he is thirsty and because in some queer way his pride has been touched. It shows a clearer insight into the mainsprings of human action than is found elsewhere in any of these sketches."

The *Book Buyer* for January, 1897, declared that most readers prefer depictions of war evoking the human traits of loyalty, faith, deliberate self-sacrifice, and cool-headed heroism; whereas *The Little Regiment* stories present man as an animal. (The reviewer ignored the heroism of Collins in "A Mystery of Heroism" and of Henry Fleming in "The Veteran.") "The power of Mr. Crane's art is undeniable but his stories are seriously handicapped by morbid psychology and by mannerisms. Interesting as is the color-notation, for instance, it is frequently obtruded upon the reader at the very moment when his attention should be engrossed with the personages or the action of the story. A sympathetic spectator of the struggle would not notice—nor wish to notice— many of the nuances of atmospheric effect to which Mr. Crane invites his scrutiny, and it is sometimes difficult to resist the conclusion that the author himself did not at bottom care so much for the essentials as for the picturesque incidents of the tale. He takes great risks, likewise, as every impressionist must, in his phraseology."

The New York *Daily Tatler* (November 9, 1896) scored Crane for his bizarre color schemes, his profanity and bad English, and his magnificent collection of adjectives; also for his decided talent for exaggeration, "which is perhaps the keynote of his popularity. But 'nothing is reprehensible if you're clever at it,' and clever at his exaggerations Mr. Crane certainly is. It goes without saying that these war stories cannot compare with *The Red Badge of Courage* in merit." (The London *Athenaeum*'s appraisal that they equal *The Red Badge* and excel *Maggie* flatters the truth.) There are three Stephen Cranes, said the *Daily Tatler:* the one who is advertised by his loving friends; the one who is reviled by his adverse critics; and the man he really is. Said the London reviewer for *Lady's Pictorial* (October 2, 1897): "I am amongst the very few who are enthusiastic admirers of Mr. Crane. I acknowledge his cleverness and his gift of graphic description, but his themes are so uniformly gruesome that I have never been able to enjoy thoroughly one of his books." This reviewer—probably a woman—preferred these tales to *The Red Badge* because they have less bloodshed and more real heroism in them. The *Lady's Pictorial* thought that Crane's men exhibit the best side of human nature. Jeannette Gilder in the New York *World* (October 25, 1896) thought *The Little Regiment* as much superior to Crane's slum stories—*Maggie* and *George's Mother*—as it is possible to imagine. In the title story the two brothers belonging to the same regiment are bitter enemies, and there is something of sameness in these Civil War tales, but also "there is a vividness and virility about them that is refreshing, and I would advise Mr. Crane to give up looking about him for experiences and turn his attention to imaginative stories, for it is in these that his best work is to be found." Crane might have profited by that advice, but he did not heed it.

The London *Spectator* thought *The Little Regiment* showed a distinct advance on *The Red Badge* because it depicted not only the horrors of war but also the humors and romance and ironies in campaigning. (The English reviewers had catapulted *The Red Badge* into fame, but now they overpraised its sequel.) Said the London *Bookman:* "Mr. Crane is already a master who has earned the right to be recognized as comparable to Tolstoy in seeing warfare the same way."

The London *Academy* pointed out that the women who figure in "Three Miraculous Soldiers" and in "A Gray Sleeve" seem only half realized, and that "An Indiana Campaign" "is a pleasant piece of comedy, which comes as a relief amid the all-pervading gloom; but Mr. Crane lacks the necessary lightness of touch."

Not adulatory was the San Francisco *Examiner* (January 10,1897), claiming that a reader of Crane "will find that that erratic writer has much in common with Hamlin Garland. Both men show much affection in style and both make dead sets against literary rules; both are young, too [Garland was thirty-six and Crane twenty-five], and they have good knowledge of the language. But as an offensive stylist Mr. Crane leads Mr. Garland. He is more violent, and at the same time his work is more permeable by the light by which we discern superficiality. For, in his case, the superficial is very poorly concealed. He is not easy reading. You are constantly annoyed by the blare of his word-trumpets, which, like the steam whistles of factories, soon become an intolerable nuisance when they toot intermittently throughout the day. . . . There is no denying the value of Stephen Crane's work, and that he has his place in letters is not to be gainsaid. It is really astonishing to us civilians that a young man who had never seen a battle could write *The Red Badge of Courage and The Little Regiment,* and we must still accept them against the solemn averments of not a few old soldiers that Mr. Crane's batles are sham fights with nothing of reality in them. But Mr. Crane must flit more easily or he will never soar. For the present he insists upon a literary style that flies up and flaps its callow wings in your face, sometimes emitting in that unpleasant proximity an adolescent crow." This San Francisco reviewer was one of those Ambrose Bierce bird-watchers on the Pacific Coast who disliked and pot-shotted any bird not named Bierce. They included bird-watchers Pollard, Gertrude Atherton, and Frank Norris.

President McKinley, himself a soldier, spoke favorably about the Civil War stories in *The Little Regiment,* and when Crane heard about the President's compliment he drawled: "He would know if the stuff was real or not, even if he can't write good English."

## 5. THE COMMODORE DISASTER—
## THE TREACHERY QUESTION*

Many Cubans in Jacksonville believed that a traitor to the Cuban insurrection sabotaged the steamer (said the New York *Herald*). A Spanish spy in Jacksonville had watched the loading of her cargo of ammunition and exclaimed: "Load up with your guns, but you will never get them to Cuba in that old tub." Some Spaniard had removed the valves from the pumps; a traitor in Spanish

* Chapter XIV, fn. 12)

pay was the cause of the disaster, said steward (or cook) Montgomery. "This was absolute proof of treachery, and we realized that some one had planned diabolically to send us all to the bottom of the sea." It's a sentence that Joseph Conrad or Crane might have written, but not likely the *Commodore*'s cook Montgomery. The reporter for the New York *Journal* wrote it, and other reports of pure conjecture were repeated from one newspaper to another by journalists eager to file a story. The newspapers exploited Montgomery because he alone gave them "good copy."

The *Herald* quoted him again on January 5 that he had had premonitions of "treachery and disaster." Said Montgomery: "We had struck on the ground twice in the St. John's, and it did not look right. My fears became more decided when Franco Blanco came to me with tears, saying: Charlie, the ship doesn't mind her wheel. Somebody must have tampered with her steering gear. I had good reason to feel uneasy, because, before leaving, a Spaniard, whom I met in New York, sent word from shore that he wanted to see me. I replied that I could not see him. He came to the ship and begged me not to go, but I told him I was going. He sent this word to me five minutes before the ship left. 'My God, Charlie! Don't go on that ship. You risk your life.' "

But Henry Fritos, who supervised the loading of the arms cargo, affirmed that the *Commodore*'s passengers had been hand-picked by the Cuban Junta and that "every one was above suspicion." Also Dr. Castille of the Cuban Junta affirmed the seaworthiness of the *Commodore* as above suspicion. She had been thoroughly overhauled before leaving Jacksonville (in the *Herald* for January 3). Fritos was quoted in the *Herald* of January 4. Simultaneously the *Herald* was issuing Montgomery's treachery theory.

# 6. THE COMMODORE DISASTER—
# HOW MANY MEN IN THE DINGHY?*

With seven men in the ship's boat and sixteen in the remaining two lifeboats, what's left are four men for the dinghy—not five, as Berryman conjectures. Steward Montgomery in the *Journal* says "the four of us," and Crane does not acknowledge a fifth man either in his *Press* interview or his short story. Berryman, ignoring three dozen newspaper accounts (although a number of newspapers did incorrectly list the total as twenty-eight) *and* the log of the *Boutwell*, puts five men in the dinghy because the New York *Press* for January 4 (datelined Jacksonville, January 3) reported that five men reached shore at Daytona Beach at noon on the 3rd: Captain Murphy, Stephen Crane, the Cook, and *two* sailors, one of whom (oiler Higgins) died of injuries.

As the mistaken *Press* is Berryman's main source, so the mistaken Florida *Times-Union* is the main source for William Randel's more recent investigation of how many passengers had the *Commodore* and how many were in the dinghy. Although Randel cites the *Times-Union* (in *American Literature:* November, 1962), which says the total was twenty-eight passengers, the *Times-*

* (Chapter XIV, fn. 15).

*Union* also contradicts itself by printing the names of the passengers—a total of twenty-seven!

Both Berryman and Randel ignore "Captain Murphy's Story" as given not only in the *Press* and the *Times-Union* but also in the New York *Journal, Herald, Times* and *World*, wherein Murphy lists the crew as twenty-seven (and therefore four in the dinghy). But the proof is primarily in the log of the *Boutwell*:

> Date: January 1, 1897.
> Location: St. Johns River, Florida.
> Steamer *Commodore*. Home port, New York, N.Y.
> Number persons on board, 27.†

## 7. THE COMMODORE DISASTER—
## THE CONDITION OF THE SEA*

Whether or not Crane's short story is equated with the "Fact" of his experiences is irrelevant, but not irrelevant is the question of possible discrepancies between Crane's *Press* account and the fact. The alleged discrepancies include the charge that no rough seas prevailed during the dinghy's voyage. No especially high winds existed on January 2 and 3, according to the records of the weather stations maintained in 1897 at New Smyrna and Jacksonville. When the *Commodore* sank at about 7 A.M. on the 2nd, there was a gentle breeze at Jacksonville, and during that day the wind increased to a maximum of nineteen miles per hour, which is a "moderate to fresh" wind. When the dinghy came ashore at Daytona on the morning of January 3, there was a light breeze at Jacksonville, a light breeze being at the speed of six to eight statute miles per hour. A fresh breeze (at the speed of nineteen to twenty-four miles per hour) can produce whitecaps, but it cannot raise the "monstrous waves" and the "wilderness of breakers" that Crane claimed in his *Press* dispatch. "Not combers, then, but rollers were coming in from the Atlantic during the early morning hours of January 2 (1897)—large waves with rounded crests, far apart from one another, and comparatively harmless, even to men in a ten-foot dinghy"—says a recent investigator, Cyrus Day. He contends that the physical hardships endured by the men in the dinghy "have been grossly exaggerated." In high seas, he contends, the maneuver of fending off the dinghy from the ship with an oar would have been impossible. Crane "would have been struggling desperately (and probably vainly) to keep the dinghy from being swamped or stove." But, to answer Day, because the ship provided a sheltered position from wind and sea, Crane *could* fend it off from the ship by an oar—*even in heavy seas*. Common seagoing procedure dictates the launching of a small craft on the leeside of the ship to afford the craft

---

† In *Report of the Chief of Division of Revenue Cutter Service*, 1897 (Washington, D.C., 1897), page 52. This report adds: "Munitions. From Jacksonville, Fla., for Cuba." The table on page 49 provides additional proof: "Steamer *Commodore*/Tonnage 178/Cargo Arms, etc. . . . ./Persons on board 27/Persons saved or assisted 27."

* (Chapter XIV, fn. 17)

more protection and maneuverability as the ship's leeside is not facing the wind. Even in a gentle sea a timorous dinghy heavily laden confronts the hazardous, and especially so once the dinghy stands off from the ship's protection.

Steward Montgomery mentioned "blinding winds" and "thick spray," and the telltale thing here is "thick spray" because that is impossible without winds high to moderately high. Secondly, the condition of wind velocity a dozen miles from shore cannot be ascertained by examining wind-velocity charts recorded at the weather stations of New Smyrna (fifteen miles south of Daytona) and at Jacksonville (eighty-five miles north of Daytona). Thirdly, what has to be reckoned with in the seas off Daytona is the unpredictable Gulf Stream, which causes ground swells on the sea's surface *even when there is no wind.* In the area north of Cape Canaveral where the Gulf Stream diverges from the Florida coast occur random countercurrents, a backwash of the Gulf Stream. The combination of these conditions makes it plainly possible that seas of considerable turbulence could prevail in the waters where the *Commodore* sank and the dinghy journeyed to shore. For a heavily ladened small boat these seas would in all likelihood be dangerous. At this point in my investigations I obtained the logs of the steamers *Newark* and *Roland.* Just before midnight of January 1 the steamer *Newark* stood about forty miles east-northeast of Daytona Beach, heading for the St. Johns River, and while on this course she was "rolling from 21 degrees to port to 19 degrees to starboard. With this biased roll—taking into account her northwesterly course and the fresh and persistent northeast to east-northeast winds—it is plainly evident that a strong sea was running forty miles off Daytona Beach on the nights of January 1 and 2" (I quote here oceanographer George Rumney). As for the position of the floundering *Commodore,* anywhere from twelve to twenty miles offshore, the moderately heavy seas under a fresh wind not far from where she went down were plainly of "a dangerous magnitude for a very small, overloaded, open-boat." Again, the log or journal of the steamer *Roland,* a German vessel off the east coast of Florida on January 1 (1897) and heading for the Delaware Breakwater, reads: "Moderate gale," *"rough sea."* Then for January 2: "Moderate gale and strong breeze . . . *chopping sea."* Then for January 3: *"Strong breakers* from 9 to 11 P.M. Moderate gale . . . *Sea rough high* from east."† So, then, Crane in his *Press* dispatch did not exaggerate the condition of the sea.

† In National Archives, Record Group No. 27. The *Newark's* log is in No. 24. In order to obtain such logs one must first know the names of the ships. Several newspapers reporting the *Commodore* disaster mentioned that the *Roland* and the *Newark* were in the vicinity of the shipwrecked *Commodore.* The location of the *Newark* is also noted in the journal of the *Boutwell,* entitled "Transcript from the Journal of the U.S. Revenue Steamer 'Boutwell,' Captain W. F. Kilgore Commanding, for the week ending Saturday, January 2, 1897." In Record Group No. 26. Crane mentioned the *Boutwell* in his *Press* dispatch.

I have been aided in my readings of ship logs, ocean-and-wind conditions, and weather-station records by Professor George Rumney at the University of Connecticut, an oceanographer intimately acquainted with the Daytona Beach and Florida area.

## 8. PARODIES OF STEPHEN CRANE AS
## WAR CORRESPONDENT*

Snide commentaries on Crane as journalist appeared in newspapers across the country: "Stephen Crane and Grover Cleveland are running a mad race in the use of the personal pronoun 'I,' with 'Steve' a neck ahead." Said the Buffalo *Express* for May 17, 1897: "Now we know what the war in the East is about. It is about Stephen Crane. . . . The war has not interested him and there was another correspondent detailed to write on the entrancing subject of Stephen Crane. The other man has done his work well." (The other man was John Bass.) "Two men were sent to Thessaly to name a blind puppy and to cable back the news at enormous expense for the benefit of admirers of the Yen-yen Journalism." Stephen Crane had better stick to fiction, said another newspaper. "Regular war-correspondents can do the real article much better." Said the Denver *Post* on May 17: Crane "cables that during a recent fight he was under the weather. It is a safe two to one bet that Steve would get under the first thing that came handy when the guns began to pop." Newspaper slams are meant to tickle and not to hurt, Corwin Linson remarks, but this one from the Lewiston (Maine) *Journal* reprinted in the New York *Tribune* (May 18, 1897) is a wisecrack having a nasty undercurrent of insinuation:

> *I have seen a battle.*
> *I find it is very like what*
> *I wrote up before.*
> *I congratulate myself that*
> *I ever saw a battle.*
> *I am pleased with the sound of war.*
> *I think it is beautiful.*
> *I thought it would be.*
> *I am sure of my nose for battle.*
> *I did not see any war correspondents while*
> *I was watching the battle except*
> *I.*

The parody by Charles Battle Loomis in the *Critic* on May 1, 1897, has Crane reporting the war from Italy, where as war correspondent he is in no danger from stray bullets. "From what the critics say, I know all about war without ever having been near one. What have I to expect by being on the scene except an incapacitating wound? It is far more fair to those who sent me out as war correspondent that I stay here in Italy. So I will give my imagination free play and sling in lots of color, and there's not one man in a million can tell where I'm wrong if I am."

In Loomis' parody Crane is informed at Brindisi, Italy, that a desperate battle had been fought at Mati. That much scorches Crane for not having been at Mati (but neither was Richard Harding Davis). "The fight must have

* (Chapter XVI, fn. 8)

been between the Greeks and the Turks, and so it was full of my favorite color, red—Turkey red. The Turkish and Greek troops lay encamped before Mati. A huge and laborious fog wallowed and pirouetted by turns, shutting out the operations of the armies from the knowledge of my contemporaries, Richard Harding Kipling and Rudyard Davis. Now and again, a Greek youth filled with patriotic fire of an exceedingly effective shade of scarlet would swear volubly in Greek, but as I am not a linguist I am unable to spell his conversation either phonetically or after my own system. The effect of the Greek fire, which is of course in constant use in the army, was to color the fog beautifully and make Richard Harding think he was at a pyrotechnic display at Coney Island. Shortly after four o'clock the Turks were ordered to win the battle and they pressed forward with religious frenzy, waving their bundles of shoestrings, just as they do on Broadway. A giant Turk stubbed his toe and fell to sobbing piteously, but unmoved at the sight the rest swept on uttering huge yellow oaths that it would tax even my ingenuity to spell. One Turk who had been in business in New York and had returned to fight for his country ran along crying irrelevantly, 'This is a heluva note. Wanta shoestring? This is a heluva note. Wanta shoestring? Five cent.' ") Crane in *The Red Badge* has it "a heluva row.")

Loomis good-naturedly mocks *The Red Badge of Courage:* "A squirrel sat upon a cannon and cracked cannon balls with saucy gibberings, unspellable. Red and brown and green ants hurried this way and that as if scenting the coming danger. The Greek youth remembered his mother. She would be making doughnuts full of grease about this time, and he cried silently. A short Greek by his side looked blue for a minute, and then at a remark from the youth he changed color. The fog, as if rejoiced at balking the efforts of Davis and Kipling, wallowed at intervals of five minutes. Then there was a Turkish crash, cream color with a selvage of red, and the ants and the youth and the squirrel were gone, and the Turks had won the battle of Mati."

The Cleveland *Leader*'s parody was entitled "Just Before the Battle."

'Halt!' exclaimed the Turkish commander. 'Adjutant, call the roll.'
'Rudyard Kipling!'
'Here.'
'Stephen Crane!'
'Here.'
'Richard Harding Davis!'
'Here.'
'All right! Let the word to advance be given.'

And here is Frank Norris' parody in the San Francisco *Wave* (December 24, 1897): "The Green Stone of Unrest/by S——N CR——E."

A Mere Boy stood on a pile of blue stones. His attitude was regardant. The day was seal brown. There was a vermilion valley containing a church. The church's steeple aspired strenuously in a direct tangent to the earth's center. A pale wind mentioned tremendous facts under its breath with certain effort at concealment to seven not-dwarfed poplars on an un-distant mauve hilltop. . . . The blue Mere Boy transported himself diagonally athwart the larger landscape, printed in four colors, like a poster. On the uplands were chequered squares made by fields, tilled and otherwise. Cloud-shadows moved from square to square. It was as if the Sky and Earth were playing a tremendous game of chess.

By and by the Mere Boy observed an Army of a Million Men. Certain cannon, like voluble but non-committal toads with hunched backs, fulminated vast hiccoughs at unimpassioned intervals. Their own invulnerableness was offensive.

Norris images an officer waving a sword "like a picture in a school history," which uncannily anticipates what Crane was yet to write in "An Episode of War" about a lieutenant who is wounded and withdraws from the real world into an imaginary one. He was puzzled what to do with his unsheathed sword. The Mere Boy of Norris' satire echoes *Maggie* in: " 'Go teh blazes b'Jimminey,' remarked the Mere Boy. 'What yeh's shooting fur? They might be people in the field.' He was terrific in his denunciation of such negligence. He debated the question of his ir-removability. 'If I'm goin' teh be shot,' he observed; 'if I'm goin' teh be shot, b'Jimminey—' " Which also mocks "The Open Boat" with its refrain: "If I am going to be drowned—if I am going to be drowned."

Next Norris comes at *The Red Badge of Courage* with this imitation of its image of the "red sun pasted in the sky like a wafer." Norris; "The yellow sun was dropping on the green plain of the earth, like a twenty-dollar gold piece falling on the baize cloth of a gaming table." In *The Red Badge,* Henry Fleming has been bruised on the head, and Norris' parody has the Mere Boy "struck with seventy-seven rifle bullets. Seventy had struck him in the chest, seven in the head. He bore close resemblance to the top of a pepper castor. He was dead. He was obsolete. As the blue serge officer bent over him he became aware of a something in the Thing's hand. It was a green pebble. 'Gee,' exclaimed the blue serge officer. 'A green pebble, gee.' The large Wind evolved a threnody with reference to the seven un-distant poplars."

Norris did not like Crane when later he met him aboard the tug the *Three Friends* during the Cuban War, and from the start he wrote of Crane's works "with a coolness not untouched with envy."

James Huneker's parody is quoted in footnote 16, Chapter XXV.


## 9. "LIST OF BOOKS/BREDE PLACE"*

Crane's library at Brede Manor contained the poetical works of Shelley, Browning, Meredith, Swinburne, Heine, Lowell, Longfellow, Rossetti, Dryden, Shakespeare, Grey's *Elegy,* and copies of Ossian. Also Stevenson's *St. Ives,* Hall Caine's *The Scapegoat and the Christian,* and Richard Le Gallienne's *The Quest of the Golden Girl.* An odd collection!

Also, books written by his mother's father, the Reverend George Peck:

* (Chapter XXVII, fn. 9)

*Seven Wonders of the New World; Our Country, Its Trial and Its Triumph;* and *Early Methodism from 1788 to 1828.* And by his mother's uncle, Bishop Jesse T. Peck: *Christian Perfection; Central Idea of Christianity; Rule of Faith; History of the Great Republic;* and *County Families of the United Kingdom* (1868). And by Stephen's Uncle Luther: *Luther Peck and His Five Sons.*

His library included Yeats' *The Secret Rose,* three titles by Edwin Pugh, and bound volumes of the *Bookman* (1896–1897) and of *Town Topics.* On the Spanish-American War he owned only Stephen Bonsal's *The Fight for Santiago* (1899) and Burr McIntosh's *The Little I Saw of Cuba* (1898). Also, *Mr. Dooley in Peace and War* (1898), satirical sketches by Dunn—including one on Teddy Roosevelt, ex-Rough Rider and now Governor of New York. At the time he tallied his book shelves at Brede he had three copies of *Maggie* in the German translation, four copies of *Pictures of War,* four copies of *The Third Violet,* three of *The Black Riders,* and one copy of *George's Mother.* But no copy of *The Open Boat* or *The Red Badge of Courage. War Is Kind* (April, 1899) had not yet been published.

Crane had Henry James' *The Princess Casamassima; The Real Thing; Stories Revived; The Spoils of Poynton;* and *The Bostonians;* but the copy of *In the Cage* which James inscribed for Crane is not listed—it was out on loan. He had Conrad's *Almayer's Folly* (1895), *An Outcast of the Islands* (1896), *The Nigger of the "Narcissus"* (1897), and *Tales of Unrest* (1898).

He owned I. Zangwill's *Children of the Ghetto;* Elizabeth Robbins' *The Open Question* (and other titles); Robert S. Hichens' *An Imaginative Man;* George Gissing's *In the Year of Jubilee* (1897); Turgenev's *A Lear of the Steppes.* And much Kipling: *Captains Courageous; Soldiers Three; The Day's Work; An Almanac; Many Inventions; Recessional; Seven Seas; Departmental Ditties, Barrack-Room Ballads and Other Verse.* Also Frank Harris' *Elder Conklin* and Harold Frederic's *Illumination* and *March Hares;* Robert Barr's *Countess Tekla* and *A Woman Intervenes;* George Eliot's *The Mill on the Floss;* Mark Twain's *A Connecticut Yankee in King Arthur's Court;* and *Quo Vadis.* Also Anthony Hope's *Chronicles of Count Antonio;* Marie Corelli's *Thelma;* and Amiel's *Journal* in translation by Mrs. Humphrey Ward; Garland's *Jason Edwards* and other books of his; Henley's *Lyra Heroica;* Dredge's *Modern French Artillery;* Count De Segur's *Napoleon's Expedition to Russia* (2 vols); Ella Wheeler Wilcox's *Poems of Passion;* Westcott's *David Harum;* and Darwin's *Cross and Self-fertilisation of Plants.* (This list is in CUCC.)†

Not included in his list of books was *Wyoming: Its History, Stirring Incidents and Romantic Adventures* (1858), by George Peck, D. D., with a picture by Mary Helen Peck (Stephen's mother) among the illustrations. At Brede Place Crane wrote in September-October 1899 his "Wyoming Valley Tales," drawn from Peck's *Wyoming.* Wilbur Crane brought the book with him on his visit to Brede in July. " 'Ol' Bennet' and the Indians," which Crane probably recast there from an early draft (1892?), contains a passage almost copied from *Wyoming.* The old Bennet of that tale was Stephen's great great grandfather.

† Columbia University Crane Collection.

## 10. "THE GHOST"*

The performance of "The Ghost" caused stir in local newspapers and in the *Manchester Guardian* (January 13, 1900):

> A remarkable piece of literary patchwork has lately been allowed to waste its sweetness on the Sussex air. This is the play which has been written for an amateur performance by a string of our most popular novelists. . . . One is deeply sorry that it is not to be published. . . . When the London theatres are so devoid of good plays as is the present case, it seems unkind to deprive managers of such an opportunity. The expense of scenery could hardly be an objection, for both acts passed in the same locality—an "empty room in Brede Place."

The Sussex *Express* (January 5, 1900) reported that Stephen Crane paid all the expenses incurred in the production, and the *South Eastern Advertiser* (Sussex, England) described the play as a combination of farce, comedy, opera, and burlesque. The *Advertiser* summarized the plot as follows:

> The ghost first introduces himself to the audience, the inference being that he appears on special occasions at midnight for the special delectation of the antiquary or tourist, the latter of whom is held in abomination by the said ghost. A couple of tourists then appear, followed by "three little maids from Rye," Holly, Buttercup, and Mistletoe, and these ladies [Mrs. Mark Barr, Miss Bowen, and Miss Edith Richie] were rapturously encored for their rendering of the selection, "Three Little Maids from Rye," which bore a suspicious resemblance to an air from a popular opera [The Mikado, by Gilbert and Sullivan]. Miss [Florence] Bray, in the capacity of caretaker, gave one the impression that the greater part of her life had been spent in showing visitors over the place. Miranda [Miss Sylvia Bowen] delighted the audience with a castanet dance, which she was compelled to repeat. A poem was then recited by Surburbia [Miss Ethel Bowen] which convulsed the audience, and so moved one of the party he wiped away tears with his ample whiskers. A very amusing chorus, "We'll be there," was rendered, Miss Richie singing the chorus capitally.
>
> In the next act Rufus Coleman [Cyril Frewer, son of the rector of Brede Village] appears in the haunted room at 11:30, and whilst waiting for the apparition Mistletoe enters and unbosoms her sorrow to Rufus in an original up-to-date song, "The Sussex Volunteers," which depicts the call to arms of "The Absent-Minded Beggar," and the forlorn condition of the girl he left behind him. . . . As the hour of midnight approaches Doctor Moreau [Mr. F. L. Bowen] gives a correct imitation of cockcrowing, followed by "Simon the Cellarer," and a pleasing selection by Miss Bowen. At midnight the company are paralysed by the sudden appearance of the ghost from apparently nowhere, and he commences his weird history, but reminds himself that he can relate it better with soft

* (Chapter XXIX, fn. 3)

musical accompaniment, and this is accorded him. He states that in the
year 1531 he was sitting in that very same room, consuming six little
Brede boys, and washed down his meal with an appropriate quantity of
beer. This overcame him, and whilst in a stupor four courageous Brede
men enter, and saw him asunder. . . . The caretaker constantly corrects
the ghost during the time he is making his statement, and she emphatically
denies that it was beer he was drinking. She said he knew it should
be "sack," and that he will get the "sack" from his post if he commits
such glaring historical errors again. At this juncture the ghost makes a
speedy exit, and reappears partially divested of his ghostly raiment, when
he causes laughter by going round with his hat, his fee to each batch
of tourists being "two bob." A grand chorus and dance, taken part in by
the ghost and tourists, concluded the piece. (The time of the play is
1950.)

### Manuscript Page of "The Ghost"

*The ghost:* "I am the ghost. I don't admit this because I am proud. I admit
it because it is necessary that my indentity [sic] should be established.
My identity has been desputed for many centuries—how many, I forget
—anyhow, it was some time ago. It is difficult to be a ghost here. I would
like to have an easier place. Tourists come here and they never give
me a penny although I had my last pipe of 'baccy two hundred years
ago and I drank my last pint of bitter [beer] in '53. . . . Ha, a noise—
Perhaps some terrible tourist—Will I fly? No; despite my constitutional
timidity, I will stand my ground.
(Enter tourist with white whiskers and his wife.)
*Tourist with white whiskers:* "Now, you see, my dear, there is no such
things as ghosts. Really there is not. It is all a superstition. There is no
such thing as a ghost.
*The Ghost:* (approaching unnoticed.) "Aw—pardon?"
*Tourist with w.w.* (jumping) Beg pardon?
*Ghost* Oh, nothing. Only I thought I heard you denying the existence of
ghosts.
*T. with w. w.* (excitedly) Well, you did. I can prove to you mathematic-
ally that it is impossible——"
*Ghost* (holding up his hand) Don't. I couldn't bear to hear that.

Crane's holograph of the above was reproduced in *Stephen Crane: Letters*
(1960) from the original in Cora's Notebook in the Barrett Crane Collection.
A typescript of seven pages is in the Berg Collection, and there are five pages
(three in holograph) in CUCC. A facsimile of the first page of the printed
program giving the title and names of the authors appeared in the London
*Academy* (January 6, 1900).
"The Ghost" is discussed by C. Lewis Hind in *Authors and I* (1921), by
H. G. Wells in *Experiment in Autobiography* (1934), by Edith Richie Jones
in *Atlantic Monthly* (July, 1954), and by Lillian Gilkes in *Cora Crane* (1960).
Beer and Berryman mention the play, but the first detailed account of it
was given by John D. Gordan in "The Ghost at Brede Place," *Bulletin of the
New York Public Library* (December, 1952).

## 11. THE O'RUDDY*

The day Cora began her voyage to bring Stephen's body back to America she received a sympathetic note from Moreton Frewen saying that he and Alfred Plant would watch over her affairs until she returned to England, and then he'd talk over her plans "and future and see what is best to do." He was sorry that Rudyard Kipling had refused to complete Crane's Irish romance *The O'Ruddy.* He had expected a different answer because he had once done the then young Kipling a favor.

"My own opinion is," Kipling wrote Frewen, "and I hold it very strongly that a man's work is personal to him, and should remain as he made it or left it. I should have been glad to have done him [Crane] a kindness, but this is not a thing that a man feeling as I do can undertake." He and Crane had never met, but when Kipling was stricken with pneumonia in New York during the winter of 1897 Crane had cabled him hopes for his recovery. Admiral Dewey admired two literary men, Crane and Kipling (so Robert Barr reported to Stephen after having dined with Admiral Dewey at Monte Carlo). Crane had read Kipling's *The Light That Failed* (1891) before completing *Maggie* and *The Red Badge,* and Kipling's novel about an artist influenced Crane's own novel about an artist, *The Third Violet.* Crane was influenced by Kipling, notably at the beginning of his career but also even at the end, and he owned a good many of Kipling's books.

Robert Barr had promised Stephen at Dover that he would complete *The O'Ruddy,* but Cora indiscreetly sent him Frewen's letter with Kipling's refusal, and so Barr changed his mind. He wrote Cora: "I think Kipling is quite right in saying that no man should touch another man's work. I have read the story over from the beginning to end once more, and have also gone over two or three times the sketch you gave me of the completion, but the latter is so vague and incomplete in itself that it gives little guidance for another to go upon." Barr proposed that Cora herself complete the novel, but she rightly knew that she wasn't much of a writer. If she'd do it, Barr would proofread it and try to get Kipling to go over it as well. Cora explained to agent G. H. Perris that by finishing "The Squire's Madness" she meant "that I 'conceived' the finish. . . . I trust it is not *too* bad! I worked so much with Mr. Crane and knew his work so well that it is not difficult to picture the ending of his stories—but of course to attempt to finish them as *he* would have done is impossible!" And she couldn't conceive what to do with *The O'Ruddy* because writing a novel was beyond her talents. Nor could Robert Barr conceive what to do with it when in September, 1900, he tried to write a chapter and made hash of the attempt. However, when he finally committed himself to complete it, what he wrote surpassed what Crane had written —not even Crane or Kipling could have done better.

When Barr first decided not to touch *The O'Ruddy,* Cora turned to Marriott-Watson, but he knew that Barr had been Crane's first choice and he declined to play second fiddle to Robert Barr. Marriott-Watson, an admirer of Crane's work since reviewing *The Red Badge* in the London *Pall Mall Gazette,* had

* (Chapter XXVIII, fn. 11)

misgivings about undertaking "so solemn and responsible a task" of adjusting to another mind, especially when Crane had gotten so thoroughly into the swing and style of the novel that it would be "a forlorn hope for any other to follow him." Next, Cora turned to novelist A. E. W. Mason, and he replied on August 24 asking for anonymity in the authorship if he undertook the job. Had Cora asked him at the start he could then have done it, but now he was leaving England. Also, he thought that Robert Barr was going to complete *The O'Ruddy*—his ghost confronted every prospective author. Cora bungled the affair once more by telling the publisher that Mason was to complete the manuscript, and he was named as co-author in the *Critic* for March, 1901. Jeannette L. Gilder, who had reviewed in the New York *World* almost all of Crane's early works, announced Mrs. Crane's plans for completing and publishing Stephen's last works, including a novel on the American Revolution ("in which she will introduce historical personages from whom Stephen Crane was directly descended"), as well as the Irish romance to be completed by Mason, and a travel sketch relating how Mrs. Crane "went through the Cuban war with Crane at Santiago." (She meant the Greco-Turkish War.) The *Critic* published photographs of Crane in Ireland and at Brede Place which Karl Harriman furnished along with notes about Stephen.

This advance publicity infuriated Mason: "It is no use bustling me." Crane's notes as to how the adventures of O'Ruddy should end were mere hints and not of much use, and so there remained a good deal of the plot to be invented, Mason wrote Cora, and "one wants to get it in accordance with what is done." Crane had asked Mason in the spring of 1900 to read the manuscript and "he told me its history," and later Mason read it. Crane had begun this Irish romance while at the same time he was "scoffing at some of us who were writing that sort of romantic tale, but, as he went on with it, he got bitten by the theme and the treatment and the period, and was enjoying himself writing it. I read it very carefully. I think there must have been, even at that time, a suggestion or hint that if he did not come back [from Badenweiler], I should finish it, but of that I can't be sure. Certainly I read it carefully and inclined to realize that this was not his pigeon at all. However, I think I told him that he must get well and finish it himself. After he died, Cora wrote to me and asked me to undertake it. I didn't, for although I guessed that Stephen's affairs were not very flourishing, I did not think that *The O'Ruddy* would add either to his estate or his reputation. It was a little time afterwards that Barr finished the book and justified my reluctance."* Robert Barr completed the novel by mid-July, 1903.

Barr had reversed his standpoint by the end of 1902, but once he took possession of the manuscript he refused to turn it back unless he was paid £ 220. However, solicitor Alfred T. Plant threatened action and thereby succeeded in forcing Robert Barr "to carry out his Agreement." †

* Letter of A. E. W. Mason to Vincent Starrett (October 4, 1945), which Mr. Starrett kindly supplied me a decade ago.

† Alfred Plant wrote Cora: "I think he is behaving abominably in the matter as he knows perfectly well we have no money and the arrangement I made with him was that he should have the serial rights for publication in 'The Idler' as payment for his work upon the book." (Barr co-founded the *Idler* with Jerome K. Jerome

When the novel was published in November, 1903, Cora sent Mrs. Moreton Frewen a copy of the American edition and wrote her: "There has been so much said in English papers about the tale ending at Brede Place that I write to tell you that Mr. Robert Barr finished the story (the last chapters) from notes which I gave him as I knew, having discussed the story (and typed it) with Mr. Crane, that he wished to have it end at Brede Place." But Barr in fact wrote three-fourths of the novel, not just the last chapters. He told Willis Clarke that he simply did what he could to put himself into Stevie's place in carrying on where Crane left off, that only a fourth of the book is really Crane's, and that he was obliged to drop out "one episode toward the end as I really did not know in what spirit the poor boy wanted it written. . . . He would be sure to scold me for some of my work, but I am not a chameleon, like Quiller-Couch, and it was impossible for me to do as Q [Quiller-Couch] did with Stevenson's *St. Ives.*" Crane intended *The O'Ruddy* as a satiric romance—satiric of Robert Louis Stevenson's swashbuckling adventure novels. Barr caught the spirit of Crane's beginnings and brilliantly concluded the manuscript by improvisations so engaging that neither Crane nor Stevenson could have bettered them.

*The O'Ruddy*, said the *Book News* (December, 1903) is a brilliantly witty Irish tale. "The Irish effervescence of spirit permeates it through and through; the Irish impulsiveness and dash gives it its color. The O'Ruddy was a young Irish blade, daring and clever. His adventures, his duels and his romance make a story that never stops once it has started till the very end. And then we wish that there was more of it. We lost a pleasing novelist in Stephen Crane. There is a quickness of spirit, a rapidity of action, a liveliness and a rollicking humor in his last book that makes it go. And the character study presents an all-alive man, a bit of a swashbuckler and a true Irish egoist, but a man for a' that. We could stand much more of the amusing O'Ruddy. Mr. Barr has finished the story with fitness. He has entered into the spirit of his deceased friend and has tried to carry out the latter's ideas and to make his own style conform to that which goes before. It all makes a thoroughly good novel."

## 12. OTHER OBITUARIES*

"Mr. Crane's mental attitude was that of one for whom there were to be no surprises. His confidence in himself was thorough. His belief in the excellence of his work was complete, but not often expressed; and toward the last he frequently made light of the early style in which he placed too much dependence upon adjectives of color, and in some stories of child life (commenced on board a despatch-boat in the Santiago blockade) he was trying for that finish and nicer use of language which his critics had said he lacked. Notwithstanding a kind of shyness of manner, he was always self-possessed.

---

in London in 1887.) Except for this incident, of which the full details remain unknown, Barr sustains the image of a splendid person: generous and outgoing, a true friend. However, he struck Karl Harriman as "a funny fellow, though why he does some things that he does I have never been able to tell."

* (Chapter XXXI, fn. 5)

In the matter of social conduct, few conventions were permitted to interfere with what he felt inclined to do; and as war-correspondent, on the top of the encircled hill at Guantanamo and in the field before Santiago, he showed absolute fearlessness of danger." (New York *Evening Post.*)

In "Stephen Crane: A Wonderful Boy" the *Literary Digest* (June 23) said: "In seeking to gather from what Stephen Crane has done indications of what he might have done, had he lived, it is necessary to take into account his youth and his handicaps. He was only a boy when he began to write. He undertook *The Red Badge of Courage* before he was twenty-one. He was little more than a boy when death stopped his writing forever. He started upon his literary career with no equipment but such literary powers as nature had given him. He had not even the technical equipment that common scholarship gives to a writer. *The Red Badge of Courage* shows that, at the age of twenty-one, he could never be sure whether or not he was writing commonly correct English. It also shows that he then lacked literary good taste and discrimination. He had to learn as he went along. During all his literary career he seems never to have been free from the necessity of doing a great deal of hack-work. . . . His working days were few and far from free of distractions. And yet he wrote 'The Open Boat' and 'The Monster.' "

The London *Spectator* declared Crane "a writer of singular force and originality, whose studies in the psychology of peril had the clairvoyance nothing short of magical." The London *Criterion* in July reappraised his achievement, lamenting that Crane got to write his Whilomville stories so late. These stories about children have better qualities than his other works in that they have "not only true, warm color, but also sympathy and sincerity. It is a pity that Mr. Crane got to these stories so late. If he had reached them earlier his first reputation, the reputation which will last among many readers, would have been based upon something firmer than a grotesque, *The Black Riders;* an apparent imitation of another book [Zola's *La Débâcle*], *The Red Badge of Courage;* and the uglinesses, *Maggie* and *George's Mother.*"

During his last years, said the July *Bookman*, "his work showed no marked diminution of his literary powers, but to those who had intelligently followed his career it was obvious that some years must elapse before he would be ready to give the work of his maturity."

Elbert Hubbard in the September *Philistine* compared Crane with Chopin: "Both were small in stature, slight, fair-haired, and of that sensitive, acute, receptive temperament—capable of highest joy and keyed for exquisite pain." In the nature of each was a trace of iron that often manifested itself in their work. Crane was an artist in conveying feelings by just the right word, or by "a word misplaced, like a lady's dress in disarray, or a hat askew. This daring quality marks everything he wrote. The recognition that language is fluid, and at best only an expedient, flavors all his work. He makes no fetish of a grammar—if the grammar gets in the way so much the worse for the grammar. All is packed with color, charged with feeling, yet the work is usually quiet in quality and modest in manner."

# ◖ Notes

1. Almira Blanche, Jessie Peck, Elizabeth Blanche and Jesse Peck. (Mrs. Crane's maiden name was Mary Helen Peck; Jesse was the first name of her uncle, Bishop Jesse Truesdell Peck.) Still another child had died before Stephen was born—Elizabeth Townley (1861–1866).

The Cranes' first born, Mary Helen (1849–1933), was named after her mother; the second, George Peck (1850–1903), after Mrs. Crane's father, the Reverend George Peck. The third child, Jonathan Townley (1852–1909), was given his father's name. Then followed William Howe (1854–1926), Agnes Elizabeth (1856–1884), Edmund Brian (1857–1922), Wilbur Fiske (1859–1918), Luther Peck (1863–1886), and finally Stephen (1871–1900). Thus, of the thirteen Crane children who preceded Stephen, only eight were living at the time of his birth.

The above information is drawn from the "Newark Chart" in the Newark, N. J. Public Library, which differs radically from *Genealogy of the Crane Family,* by Ellery Bicknell Crane (Vol. II, 1900, pp. 518–519), in respect to the names of the four children who immediately preceded Stephen.

2. Another Crane (Ralph) accompanied Sir Francis Drake to America on his voyage of 1577, and Sir Robert Crane was a member of the first company coming to Massachusetts Bay in 1630.

Crane's accounts of his ancestors are in his 1896 letters to John Northern Hilliard and to Editor of Newark *Sunday Call,* in *Stephen Crane: Letters,* edited by R. W. Stallman and Lillian Gilkes, with an Introduction by R. W. Stallman (New York and London, 1960).

3. Peaslee's theme is the theme of Daniel G. Hoffman's *The Poetry of Stephen Crane* (1957), and one strand of it was pointed out by Professor Charles Kelsey Gaines in his "Rise to Fame of Stephen Crane," Philadelphia *Press* for March 15, 1896, some four months prior to Peaslee's *Monthly Illustrator* sketch: "The College Days of Stephen Crane." No mention is made of the Gaines and Peaslee articles in Hoffman's otherwise scholarly (and critically perceptive) study.

4. Crane mistakenly claimed: "My great-great-great-grandfather was one of the seven men who came and solemnly founded Newark. He was Jasper Crane.

. . . His son, Stephen Crane, M. C. moved to Elizabeth, where my grandfather and my father were born." However, that Stephen Crane—born by 1640 and married in 1663–was not Jasper's son, although he was probably closely related to him. Jasper was one of the first settlers of New Haven in 1639 and of Newark in 1666 (but more than seven men were involved). In *History of Elizabeth*.

5. After graduation from the College of New Jersey (Princeton University) in 1843, J. T. Crane was licensed to become a local preacher the next year, and then, after two years as an itinerant Methodist preacher, he served as pastor of several churches (1846–1848). For the next ten years he served as Principal of the Pennington Seminary and returned to preaching again in numerous churches during the next decade (1858–1868). Then followed eight laborious years as presiding elder of the Newark and then the Elizabeth district before he became pastor at Paterson, N. J., and finally at Port Jervis, New York, in April, 1878.

The degree of Doctor of Divinity was conferred on him in 1856 by Dickinson College in Carlisle, Pa.

6. Amy Lowell in her Introduction to *The Work of Stephen Crane,* edited by Wilson Follett, Vol. VI (1926). She rightly declared the Bible as the source for the form of Crane's poems: "Its cadences, its images, its parable structure" must have been "ground into his consciousness."

7. Just as little Jimmie Trescott does in *Whilomville Stories* (1900).

8. In Mrs. George Crane's "Stephen Crane's Boyhood," New York *World,* June 10, 1900.

9. The official church records at Drew Methodist Church state that Dr. Crane died at "11 A.M. after about one hour's sickness of paralysis of the heart." The board minutes for their meeting of April 1, 1878, state that preparations were being made to receive Dr. Crane as their new pastor. This data was provided me by the Reverend Eric Kullberg, B. D., pastor of the Drew Methodist Church in Port Jervis. (Reverend Kullberg to R. W. S., November 5, 1962.) He also kindly provided me with a photograph of the church, which remains—except for the missing steeple—the same as in the Reverend Dr. Crane's days there. The most noteworthy thing in that church is its large stained-glass window of the Madonna and Child.

10. Edna Crane Sidbury (William Howe Crane's daughter) said that Mary Helen Peck was a graduate of the College of the City of New York. In "My Uncle, Stephen Crane, As I Knew Him," *Literary Digest International Book Review* (March 1926). This is not true; for while Mrs. Crane was educated, she was not educated in any college or university. She was long dead before the College of the City of New York admitted its first women. This note corrects *Stephen Crane: Letters* (1960), for which note I am indebted to Mr. Louis Zara.

The same mistaken notion was repeated by Helen Crane (Wilbur's daughter) in "My Uncle, Stephen Crane," *American Mercury* (January 1934).

11. A man named Collier, who helped lynch the Negro, took the body to the

Carley and Terwilliger Funeral Home, where he worked. He told Judge William Howe Crane that he could use the $25 he would get as undertaker. Another enterprising resident displayed Robert Lewis' shoes and the rope for $5 a week in Worth's Museum until the novelty wore off. Negro Lewis had committed no crime, however. He had been tricked by Peter J. Foley into meeting Lena McMahon at Cuddeback Brook near its junction with the Neversink River; and then white man Foley spread the story that the Negro had raped her and severely bruised her about the head, limbs and body; whereas it was Foley himself who had beaten her up. Foley had been extorting money from the girl, who filched it for two months from the grocery store of her foster-father. Mr. McMahon, on learning the truth about Foley's blackmail of his adopted daughter, swore out a warrant on June 3 (Friday), and Peter Foley was arrested just as he was making preparations to leave town. Another mob assembled, this time to get the man who had defamed the innocent Negro, but Port Jervis' police out-tricked the mob and brought him by train to the jail in Goshen. When he was released from jail Peter Foley ran away with Lena!

12. This article declares that the sale of novels has been prohibited by the Ocean Grove Association and that the bathing suit in question "is again agitating the people of Asbury Park, and chief of police Bailey has been instructed to intercept all bathers who attempt to enter the water when not properly attired." Stephen no doubt wrote this *Tribune* article (1888).

13. Post Wheeler—as George P. Wheeler was later known—in his *Dome of Many Coloured Glass* (1955).

14. She spoke probably for the last time in July, 1899, at the New Jersey W. C. T. U. meeting at Ocean Grove, reading a paper there on "Press Work."

15. Henri Stefan Opper de Blowitz was the internationally known and immensely influential correspondent in Paris of the *The Times* during the last quarter of the nineteenth century. His life and times are related by Frank Giles in *A Prince of Journalists* (1962).

16. On "Dan Emmonds" see Appendix I.

Lillian Gilkes says it is late writing, but Crane in 1896 called it an "old thing." A portion following the ship's near wreckage, however, was no doubt injected into the earlier version after Cora Crane experienced near shipwreck in 1897.

Berryman in his *Stephen Crane* persists in calling it "evidently the old short novel *George's Mother*." The confusion arises partially from the fact that when *George's Mother* was coming off the press, the *Bookman* (May, 1896) announced that the London publisher Edward Arnold will have "a new novel by Mr. Stephen Crane ready for publication in June with the probable title *Dan Emmonds*." To explain the confusion: Crane had on hand in 1896 an old piece called "Dan Emmonds," which he probably intended to expand; but not having the time to do it when he was besieged by Harry Thompson of Edward Arnold, he gave him instead *George's Mother*, then lying in a publisher's safe until the author called for it. He told Ripley Hitchcock on March 26 that he had given his "old school-mate" Thompson a sketch—"an old thing, strong in satire but rather easy writing——called Dan Emmonds. . . ." One concludes that Crane deceived Hitchcock; for the difference between "Dan Emmonds" and *George's Mother* is absolute.

## II

1. For researching these matters I am indebted to Paul Gabriner, my former graduate student at the University of Connecticut. At this writing (October 1967) the mystery about Stephen Crane's middle name remains unsolved. The inscribed AUTOGRAPHS is in the Barrett Crane Collection at the University of Virginia Library, and is quoted here for the first time.

One conjectures that the "H" in the New York City Directory was a misprint and that Stephen's middle name was Truesdell, after Bishop Jesse Truesdell Peck, uncle of Stephen's mother. For searching the baptismal records of the First Methodist Church in Newark, I am indebted to the Reverend Vergil Mabry.

Stephen attended the Pennington Seminary from September 1885 to December 1887.

2. One afternoon some boys in military uniforms of blue and gold and some girls in fluffy ruffles strolled along the Great North Road, but at the fork leading to a by-way the girls refused to go along and the boys in a huff retaliated by declaring themselves an association of misogynists and named themselves S. S. T. Girlum. *(Sic Semper Tyrannis Girlum.)* The Claverack magazine *Vidette* joked Stephen for his Biblical name and his girl friend Harriet with her red hair: "Stephen was the first martyr. He seems also to be the last. Anyway, these red sunsets must be very Harrying. Why, oh why, did the S. S. T. Girlum have to be, just now when the Indian summer is coming on?" Harvey Wickham in "Stephen Crane at College," *American Mercury:* March 1926.

3. Crane experienced such a panic in a burning theatre in a dream during the summer of 1899, and from this dream came his tale "Manacled." A good many of his *Black Riders* poems also derived from dreams.

4. In *Stephen Crane: Letters* (1960), which is also my source for other quoted matter pertaining to Crane's college days. Other sources include: *Delta Upsilon Quarterly* (February 1891); Mansfield J. French, "Stephen Crane: Ball Player," Syracuse University *Alumni News* (January 1934). Claude Jones, "Stephen Crane at Syracuse," *American Literature* (March 1935). Jerry G. Mangione, "Stephen Crane's Unpublished Letters," Syracuse University *Chap Book* (May 1930). Thomas Martin, "Stephen Crane: Athlete and Author," Syracuse University *Argot* (March 1935). Frank W. Noxon, "The Real Stephen Crane," Chicago *Step Ladder* (January 1928). C. L. Peaslee, "The College Days of Stephen Crane," *Monthly Illustrator* (August 1896). L. U. Pratt, "The Formal Education of Stephen Crane," *American Literature* (January 1939). Thomas L. Raymond, *Stephen Crane* (1923). Ellwood M. Smith, "Stephen Crane, Ex '94," *Syracusan* (December 1, 1917). Harvey Wickham, "Stephen Crane at College," *American Mercury* (March 1926).

The above articles are listed in *Stephen Crane: A Bibliography,* by Ames W.

Williams and Vincent Starrett (1948). Additional articles on Crane's college days include:

*Delta Upsilon Quarterly,* IX (1890). Ralph Chamberlin, "Lafayette's Most Notorious Flunk Out," Lafayette College *Marquis* (February 1961). Frank W. Noxon to Mansfield J. French, an unpublished letter (June 29, 1934) in Syracuse University Crane Collection. Also an unpublished letter (March 20, 1930) from A. Lincoln Travis to Mansfield J. French. Thomas F. O'Donnell, "John B. Van Petten: Stephen Crane's History Teacher," *American Literature* (May 1955). Col. Ernest G. Smith in *Lafayette Alumnus* (February 1932). Lester G. Wells, "Steph Crane—Syracusan Extraordinary," Syracuse University *Alumni News* (October 1946).

5. Three unfinished manuscripts describing Edmund's black mastiff Jack exist, one of which I published in holograph copy as the cover to the *Fine Arts Magazine* of the University of Connecticut in 1961. With Jack, Crane explored the forests on the hills between Port Jervis and Mongaup Valley during visits to William's house on East Main street in Port Jervis.

6. From the Syracuse Library *Courier,* III (September, 1963): "Stephen Crane's Bugs," by Ames Williams (unsigned). The sketch was first reprinted in the *Courier* for March, 1963, along with Johnson's rejoinder of June 2, 1891.

The Syracuse *Standard* for June 1, 1891, published only the first half of the sketch, with a commentary. The Syracuse *Daily Journal* on June 2 reprinted the entire *Tribune* hoax and with it verbatim Johnson's editorial. "The Bugs of Onondaga" is reprinted in *The New York City Sketches of Stephen Crane and Related Pieces,* edited by R. W. Stallman and E. R. Hagemann (1966).

## III

1. In a letter of October 29, 1897: "Try to get it at Asbury Park," Stephen wrote William. Townley—now remarried—was probably living in the house his mother had spent her last years in at Asbury Park. In 1899 Townley and his wife Fannie moved into Wilbur's household at Binghamton, N.Y., because Townley's health had collapsed. His death certificate at Binghamton, where he died in 1908 at fifty-four in the New York State Hospital, has the legend: "Newspaper Correspondent." However, he ended his career not as journalist but as Superintendent of Streets," supervising street-cleaning in Port Jervis.

2. In "The Launching of Stephen Crane," *Literary Digest International Book Review* (April, 1926), Johnson says: "One day in the summer of 1891 he brought me a big bundle of manuscript and asked me to read it and tell him what to do with it. I found it to be not a Sullivan County sketch, but a tale of the slums of New York; the first draft of *Maggie: A Girl of the Streets.*" That same summer Crane, on first approaching Johnson, brought him two Sullivan County sketches. Even if Johnson is mistaken about the date of Crane's visiting him with *Maggie,* Frank Noxon says that he saw sheets of *Maggie* in the Delta Upsilon house at Syracuse in the spring of 1891, and implied consent to that statement was given him by F. K. Congdon, another fraternity brother. Clarence Peaslee, in his published memoir for August, 1896, says that *Maggie*

was "detailed to some of his acquaintances" at the Delta Upsilon Chapter house. The importance of this evidence is that Crane was simultaneously writing *Maggie* and some Sullivan County sketches, as well as articles for various Syracuse dailies and for the Detroit *Free Press,* in 1891.

3. Crane reported it in "Howells Discussed at Avon-By-The-Sea," in New York *Tribune* for August 18, 1891; unsigned. In 1894 Crane reported "Howells Fears Realists Must Wait," in the New York *Times* for October 28. Howells praised Crane in "New York Low Life in Fiction," in the New York *World* for July 26, 1896. These articles were collected in *The New York City Sketches of Stephen Crane and Related Pieces,* edited by R. W. Stallman and E. R. Hagemann (1966).

4. Stephen signed the register again in March, 1892, and so did H. F. Carroll of Easton, Pa., who was perhaps a Lafayette College classmate. "Hob" Senger remembers that there was a poker party on that occasion. Stephen and William signed the Hartwood Club register on May 17, along with their relatives of Lyons Farms, N.J., Mr. and Mrs. Fred W. C. Crane and R. T. Crane. Stephen now gave his home address as Port Jervis, since he was staying at William's house while writing his Sullivan County sketches. He signed it again on February 21, 1896, and inscribed to Mr. George E. Dimock a copy of *The Red Badge of Courage:* "Stephen Crane, Hartwood, February 1896." He signed the register for the last time on August 23, 1896. Cora Taylor signed the Hartwood Club Register on July 7, 1900 as "Mrs. Stephen Crane, Brede Place, Sussex, England." This account is quoted here for the first time from Judge E. J. Dimock's unpublished address of February 1953 before the Minisink Valley Historical Society: "Stephen Crane and the Minisink Valley."

5. Of the six newly discovered Sullivan County sketches, five are hunting sketches from the *Tribune* for 1892: "Hunting Wild Hogs" (February 28), "The Last Panther" (April 3), "Sullivan County Bears" (April 19), "The Way in Sullivan County" (May 8), and "Bear and Panther" (July 17). They are companion-pieces to such Sullivan County pieces as "Killing His Bear," in the *Tribune* for July 31, 1892.

In addition to these five, discovered with the aid of my graduate student Kelly Flynn, I have also traced in the *Tribune* (February 21, 1892) a sixth, entitled "The Last of the Mohicans." Although unsigned, it bears the unmistakable signature of Crane's metaphoric style and device of contrast. (It was traced from an unidentified newspaper clipping belonging to Judge E. J. Dimock, who kindly sent me a copy in 1966. Its dateline of Hartwood, N. Y., provided me the clue for researching the *Tribune* for 1891 and 1892. For grant in aid of research on this project I am indebted to the University of Connecticut Research Foundation.

6. Reproduced for the first time in "Stephen Crane and Cooper's Uncas," by R. W. Stallman, *American Literature:* November, 1967. A new edition of *Stephen Crane: Sullivan County Tales and Sketches,* edited with an Introduction by R. W. Stallman, is forthcoming in 1968 from Iowa State University Press.

7. James Colvert in *Modern Fiction Studies* (Autumn 1959): "Structure and Theme in Stephen Crane's Fiction."

8. First published from the typescript (originally owned by Edith Crane) in "Stephen Crane: Some New Stories," *Bulletin of the New York Public Library:* January 1957.

The relation of "The Mesmeric Mountain" to *The Red Badge of Courage* is aptly summarized by James Colvert: "It is at once a summary of the plot of the novel and an expansion of the metaphor by which Henry interprets his victory. There are the familiar elements—the terror and the rage of the hero, the hallucinatory imagery, the antagonism of Nature, the delusive victory, the heroics, the narrator's ironic commentary. By the time Crane started writing *The Red Badge* in 1893 he had repudiated the Sullivan County stories as immature and unworthy; but he was never to repudiate the basic elements of these tales, for they are expressive of his deepest sense of the meaning of life." In *Stephen Crane: A Collection of Critical Essays,* edited by Maurice Bassan (1967).

9. In *Stephen Crane: Letters.*

10. An undated quotation in Melvin Schoberlin's Introduction to *The Sullivan County Sketches* of Stephen Crane (1948). The subsequent letter to Copeland and Day is in *Stephen Crane: Letters.*

11. Mrs. Crane had been seriously ill for several months in 1886, when she was fifty-nine. The Asbury Park *Shore News* for March 11 that year reported that Mrs. Crane "is now suffering from a temporary aberration of the mind and is in a critical condition." The Asbury Park *Journal* for March 13 said that "though her mind is yet feeble it is hoped with returning strength her mental troubles will disappear." As stated in a recent article on Stephen Crane at Pennington Seminary, by Professor Jean Cazemajou of the Université de Toulouse, France (in *Études Anglaises,* XX, No. 2, 1967).

12. Today there is a sign—"The Stephen Crane Pond"—at the millpond from which Edmund cut ice to ship to Port Jervis, which is by no means the fifty miles from Hartwood that John Berryman supposed. In his *Stephen Crane,* Berryman says that Hartwood consisted of "a store, a blacksmith shop, and a tavern." However, the hamlet of Hartwood in fact never had any store, blacksmith shop or tavern, according to the Dimocks, who still live there.

13. Edmund's daughter Edith, born in 1886 and two years younger than Agnes, kept and treasured Stephen's flute, some of his books and other mementos, and typescripts of then unpublished sketches. Her letters to Thomas Beer (once in the Alfred A. Knopf files, now in mine) are indispensable for background material.

Edmund's daughter Agnes was named after Stephen's sister, who died in May, 1884. William Howe Crane had five daughters, one of them named Agnes. His daughter Helen visited the Cranes at Brede Manor in 1899, accompanied by her Uncle Wilbur, who also had a daughter named Helen.

## IV

1. Riis's exposé brought about reform of the child labor laws, improvement of playgrounds and water supply. His *Out of Mulberry Street* (1898) brought about the elimination of the notorious slum, Mulberry Bend, in New York City.

2. In "Joys of Seaside Life / Amusements, Stationary and Peripatetic," *Tribune:* July 17, 1892.

3. In "Meetings Begun at Ocean Grove," *Tribune:* July 2, 1892.

4. In "The Seaside Assembly's Work at Avon," *Tribune:* August 29, 1892.

5. In *Tribune:* August 15, 1892. The *Tribune* also reported that "Hamlin Garland of Boston, who is going to deliver a course of lectures here on American and English literature, will arrive at the Sylvan Lodge next week."

6. In *Tribune:* September 11, 1892.

7. "On the Boardwalk," *Tribune:* August 14, 1892.

8. Oliver shared with Wheeler an office in the Monmouth building for their Wheeler-Oliver Correspondence Bureau in Asbury Park. Oliver had served his journalistic apprenticeship on the *Daily Spray,* a pink sheet edited by Billy Devereaux. Arthur Oliver published his "Jersey Memories—Stephen Crane," in *New Jersey Historical Society Proceedings,* Vol. 16. Indispensable is Victor Elconin's "Stephen Crane at Asbury Park," *American Literature* (November 1938). And W. F. Johnson, "The Launching of Stephen Crane," *Literary Digest International Book Review* (April 1926). Johnson scorches Beer for claiming that Crane was fired by the *Tribune,* but nothing by Crane appeared in the *Tribune* for 1893–94. (I have had the 1893 *Tribune* researched.) On Crane at Asbury Park I have used also Post Wheeler's posthumously published *Dome of Many Coloured Glass* (1955).

9. William Crane told an inquirer in after years that Townley was thereafter a broken man. After his Asbury Park summers, Stephen saw little of Townley and Wilbur; he never had much contact with his oldest brother, George.

10. It is identifiable by the same stylistic characteristics: ingredients of color adjectives or of Hawthornesque chiaroscuro; contrast, and the "musical device" of a reiterated leitmotif or a phrase repeated in variant versions.

11. From notes recorded by Ames W. Williams after his interview with Lily Brandon years later when she was Mrs. Smillie. For the transcript of these notes I am indebted to Williams.

This important document records Lily's admission that Stephen was very much in love with her "and she with him, but he seemed to have no concrete plans for the future and was melancholy and anxious in that respect. He was a troubled spirit seeking happiness which always seemed beyond reach. She believed him to have a degree of feminine intuition. . . . Crane begged Lily to elope with him and she considered the proposal seriously before declining. Her family was wealthy and not too eager for a marriage between the two, and strangely enough his family was also opposed. Crane appeared to have little use for his family except [for] his mother of whom he was very fond."

"Once when Crane dined with Lily and her father in New York he directed a few words in French to Mr. Brandon, who rebuked him thus: 'My daughter does not speak French, Mr. Crane.' Lily was a beautiful blond in her youth. Crane once took her to an artist friend of his in New York, David Ericson, for a portrait. She sat for several sketches, but the painting was never completed." Lily first met Crane in the summer of 1892 at Asbury Park, where they enjoyed watching the surf; he told her "that whenever she saw the ocean she would think of him. She has." She was with him at the parade of American Mechanics and recalls his being discharged by the *Tribune* for his undiplomatic sketch of it. She notes that he was indifferent to dress and would "use his cuffs for making notes" and that because he was so prudish about the then daring bathing-suits she "has never been swimming in her life." He was then writing *Maggie,* "and he gave her the manuscript, which her husband later destroyed through jealousy. She had many letters and pictures, most of which were also destroyed. Lily is very fond of violets. . . . Could S. C. have had her in mind in *The Third Violet?*" After 1892 they met several times later, once in January 1895 before Crane left for Mexico and again in 1897. "He told her about Cora's kindness to him."

12. John Berryman in his *Stephen Crane* decided that the beautiful Lily felt no "special interest in her unkempt, dry, taciturn junior." But the evidence proves quite the contrary.

13. A beginning draft was written on the back of "The Holler Tree," a Sullivan County tale, and also on verso of that manuscript Crane wrote two pages of *George's Mother.* The manuscript is in the Barrett Crane Collection at the University of Virginia Library.

14. Retold here from Linson's *My Stephen Crane,* edited by Edwin Cady (1958), and from Linson's "Little Stories of 'Steve' Crane," in the *Saturday Evening Post* (April 11, 1903).

15. The *Journal* sketch (August 16) became "Stephen Crane at Asbury Park" in the Kansas City *Star* (August 22, 1896).

## V

1. "Most of *Maggie* was written at our house in two or three nights," says Helen R. Crane in "My Uncle, Stephen Crane," *American Mercury:* January, 1934. She, too, was duped by Crane's boast, but what her note indicates is that he wrote his December, 1891, second draft at Wilbur's house in Port Jervis, where Wilbur had moved in hope that its mountain air would enable him to throw off his asthma.

2. Crane shared the belief of most Americans that the Bowery "is the most interesting thoroughfare in America" (as Julian Ralph puts it). In English colonial days it was the beginning of the Boston Road, but its later-day name is all-inclusive of adjoining streets such as Doyer Street, a queer and crooked relic of the English days with wooden houses; a street, Ralph continued, that "turns and dodges in several directions like a thief eluding a policeman. It is not a nice street, and it looks as if it were doubling upon its own unsavory reputation. The Bowery is something less than a mile in length. It reaches from

Chatham Square to the little wedge in front of the Cooper Union at Eighth Street which splits it in twain, sending one half uptown to be the great Third Avenue and one half close beside it to be the Fourth Avenue." In 1891 on the fourteen-block long street there were sixty-five bars on its east side and seventeen on its west side, an average of six per block. For eight cents one could get a meal of large portions of meat with bread and potatoes included and a bed at the East Side House for fifteen cents or at the America Hotel "Lodgings for Men Only / Nice Rooms, 25 cents."

3. Crane submitted a copy of its title page and one dollar to the Library of Congress to register it for copyright on January 18, 1893: "Enclosed find a printed copy of the title page of a book written by me." But what Crane in fact submitted was but a typewritten sheet (not a printed copy) bearing the legend: "A Girl of the Streets, / A Story of New York." She was not yet *Maggie*.

Beer was incorrect in assigning Crane's note to McHarg for February 1892. William did not christen the heroine until late in February 1893, as pointed out by Ames W. Williams and Vincent Starrett in *Stephen Crane: A Bibliography* (1948), p. 14.

4. Under that tigerish proprietor Bennett, with his fickleness and brutality, men were unjustly fired or demoted. Even the most deserving staff members were reduced in rank or in pay through young Bennett's erratic and contemptible conduct. Serving his evil system of ill-usage was as desperate as serving in the French Foreign Legion, says Don Carlos Seitz, advertising manager of the *Herald* in 1895. He later became business manager of Pulitzer's *World* and fired Crane mid-way through the Cuban War. Seitz in 1895 was treasurer of the Lantern Club, of which Crane was a charter member.

5. One of these was Ripley Hitchcock, then literary adviser at D. Appleton & Co. and a friend of journalist Willis Johnson. He hesitated to recommend acceptance of Crane's Bowery novel in 1893. After he became Appleton's editor, he dared to publish *Maggie* in 1896, but only because of the success of *The Red Badge* (1895). He issued a hardcover edition in tan buckram in June, 1896, with swear words and a passage or two expunged, and later remarked to Johnson, "That boy has real stuff in him."

6. They "did me the dirt," Crane said. They also had him sign a statement that he was twenty-one.

7. Wilbur's daughter Helen when a girl played with stack of unsold *Maggies* in her attic. Her mother, Mattie, had no respect for them and burned them during a house-cleaning spell. In the 1930's that fifty-cent first edition brought at auction for an inscribed copy $1200 to $3700; it was described then as "the rarest in modern literature." William Howe Crane had some copies stacked in a barn for the mice to nibble because the family believed *Maggie* was "not nice"—until they discovered in 1935 that it brought a nice price. When his daughter Florence (Mrs. Coughlin) attempted to sell the 1893 *Maggie*, the Anderson Galleries forced her to declare how many copies she owned. "As far back as I could remember there had always been a small pile of paper-bound 'Maggies' in our storage-room, but when I spoke of this to my mother

she said she didn't believe there were any left as my two oldest sisters had burned them, believing they were 'not nice.' " Florence owned eleven copies, and the enforced exposure of her holdings tumbled the price considerably. One of her copies was uncut and "almost as fresh as on the day it left the printer's hands." (In *American Art Association Catalogue:* April, 1935.)

8. Unable to find another copy, Crane gave Charles J. Pike his own signed copy. The inscribed one he gave to Elbert Hubbard sold in 1930 for $1200. In inscribing it, arrogant Crane played the role of humble Crane in counterpoint to Hubbard, who was himself by turns arrogant and humble: "My dear Hubbard: This tawdry thing will make you understand the full import of the words: 'It is more blessed to give than to receive.' I am very sensible of the truth of the sentence when I give book of mine." But Crane, after all, was giving away a fifty-cent paperbook that no bookseller could sell, and he was at the same time jesting at Hubbard's editorial policy of no reimbursement to *Philistine* contributors.

9. "Yeh seem t' be in a pretty bad way, boy?" said a cheery voiced man, who took the bewildered youth firmly by the arm. When in the distance he sees a campfire he chuckles with glee and self-satisfaction. " 'Well, there's where your reg'ment is. An' now, good-by, ol' boy, good luck t' yeh.' A warm and strong hand clasped the youth's languid fingers for an instant, and then he heard a cheerful and audacious whistling as the man strode away. As he who had so befriended him was thus passing out of his life, it suddenly occurred to the youth that he had not once seen his face." When Crane tramped it to Lake View with the farmer he saw the lamps of his brother's house, and that light in the distance might indeed have been the source of the campfire of Henry Fleming's regiment.

10. Crane went out a good deal with R. G. Vosburgh, whose studio he shared in 1893. A young illustrator from Chicago, he illustrated some of Crane's New York City sketches and in 1901 published his memoir—"The Darkest Hour in the Life of Stephen Crane." He says that the fortunes of Crane reached their lowest ebb in "the months following the sinking of the money inherited from his father's estate in the unsuccessful publication of *Maggie: A Girl of the Streets.*"

11. The remark dates this incident prior to midsummer of 1893. Brother Edmund moved from Lake View, N. J., to Hartwood, N. Y., not far from brother William in Port Jervis, probably in early April, 1893.

The account cited is drawn from the Philadelphia *Press* for April 22, 1894, by E. J. ("Holland") Edwards. Edwards, a descendant of the Puritan writer Jonathan Edwards, was graduated from Yale Law School in 1873 and was then forty-six years old (Crane was twenty-two). "Holland" is identified by Marston LaFrance in *American Literature:* May, 1965.

12. Crane made token payment of his debt to Howells by sending him a note of "veneration and gratitude" inscribed in a prepublication copy of *The Red Badge* on August 17, 1895. Then on New Year's Day, 1896, he wrote Howells: "Every little time I hear from some friend a kind thing you have said of me, an interest which you have shown in my work. I have been so long conscious

STEPHEN CRANE

of this that I am grown uncomfortable in not being able to express to you my gratitude and so seize the New Year's Day as an opportunity to thank you and tell you how often I think of your kind benevolent life."

13. Crossed or confused identity fashions nearly all of Crane's best work, as it does the novels of Conrad, Ford Maddox Ford, Joyce, Scott Fitzgerald, Hemingway, Faulkner, Graham Greene, and, of course, Henry James.

14. For contemporary reviews, see "Crane's *Maggie* in Review," Appendix 2.

15. He also sent one to his Pendennis boardinghouse friend Lucius L. Button, who—like Wallis McHarg—was then studying medicine in Germany.

My data on Dr. Parkhurst draws from Lloyd Morris' *Incredible New York* (1951). On the relation of *Maggie* to Zola's *L'Assommoir* and to the background of reform preachers such as Thomas DeWitt Talmage, I have used Marcus Cunliffe's "Stephen Crane and the Background of *Maggie*," *American Quarterly*: Spring 1955. That Crane got the stuff and craft of *Maggie* from Flaubert's *Madame Bovary* was first pointed out in my *New Republic* essay for September 1955: "Stephen Crane's Primrose Path." Recast in "Crane's *Maggie*: A Reassessment," *Modern Fiction Studies*, V (Autumn 1959).

16. It moved into the American Fine Arts Society Building at 215 West 57th Street. Its component societies were the National Academy of Design and the Architectural League of New York. The 57th Street building still houses the Art Students League today.

17. Gordon, Ericson, and Vosburgh shared the same studio (it seems), which explains why each apparently contradicts the other in claiming that Crane wrote *The Red Badge* in his studio. David Ericson's pen-portrait of Crane appeared in the *Bookman's* review of *Maggie* and *The Black Riders*.

18. A portion of this sketch from the Crane Pocket Notebook first saw print in my "Stephen Crane: Some New Stories" (1956). It was published in its entirety for the first time in *The New York City Sketches of Stephen Crane* (1966). Here also appeared for the first time "A Mournful Old Building."

19. Crane had a proclivity for reading human temperament into animals' actions. At Hartwood, for example, Crane's brother Ed has a Belton setter named Judge, whose soul became so filled with hatred of the world when the girls ran him out of the kitchen that he would pounce on the first dog he met outside. "This is all right if it happens to be one of the hounds. They are only pups. He whales them and they roar. But sometimes the first dog he meets is the collie and then the collie, after recovering from his surprise, simply wipes up the place with him. But this causes no change in Judge's ways. Little dog, or big dog, hound or collie, put him out of the kitchen and he pounces on the first one. This is the way I felt up at the pond. But there was nobody there," Crane wrote Willis Brooks Hawkins from Hartwood (November, 1895) during a bitter mood.

20. The six-page manuscript was not published until 1966 in *The New York City Sketches of Stephen Crane*.

21. Crane jokingly wrote Henry Sanford Bennett in 1899: "Met him in a

whorehouse when we were kids." Berryman (page 139) mistakenly reverses the name to Bassett Holmes.

22. According to Beer in *Hanna, Crane, and the Mauve Decade* (1941), p. 286. All page references to Beer's *Stephen Crane* (1923) are cited from this 1941 reprint edition.

## VI

1. Linson was making drawings for a never published volume celebrating the 1893 Chicago World's Fair. Stephen had often posed for him. Linson's partner in his West 22nd Street studio, Reeves, was a watercolorist of ability who held a twice-a-week class. "Gee! All C. K.'s friends are at the Faur, usin' up the space. Who's that girl on Reevesy's arm? Ain't he a dude!" Crane once remarked. The friends who took turns posing for Linson were artist John Willard Raught, illustrator Fred S. Coburn, and painter Jesse L. France.

2. "Confound their cheek; they even parody my verse," said Crane. (Linson in his "Little Stories of 'Steve' Crane,") *Saturday Evening Post,* April 11, 1903.

3. Linson errs in claiming that Crane "had a marked indifference to reputations." That was true only of his studio friends who had not yet made their mark. He was fully cognizant of the importance to him of persons of literary reputation, such as Garland and Howells, and important persons meant much to him during his English years.

4. Hamlin Garland recalls this occasion in his 1900 *Saturday Evening Post* sketch: "Stephen Crane: A Soldier of Fortune." In 1914 he wrote another version for the *Yale Review* ("Stephen Crane as I Knew Him"), and later other variant accounts in the *Bookman* and in his *Roadside Meetings* (1930). Nothing could be more confusing than to unriddle what happened when; for in his *Post* sketch and *Roadside Meetings* he had Crane bringing him first his poetry and then the manuscript of *The Red Badge,* but in his *Yale Review* version he reversed this sequence of events. In the *Bookman* (1930) he forgot to mention Crane's visit with his sheaves of poetry!

In "The Garland-Crane Relationship" (*Huntington Library Quarterly:* November 1960), Donald Pizer corrects Garland's "tangled accounts" of his relationship with Crane. Drawing on the Hamlin Garland papers, Pizer in this invaluable contribution to the Crane chronology corrects thus my account in *Stephen Crane: An Omnibus* (1952).

5. This letter of March 23 is misdated for 1893 in *Letters.* Crane slipped in saying of his poems, "I wrote the things in February of 1893," for he wrote them in January or February of 1894. He turned on the "poetic spout" again in May and in September, 1894. He wrote some poems out of his disillusioned love affair with Helen Trent, his first poems in late 1891. By February of 1893 Crane had not yet experienced Howells' reading of Emily Dickinson's verses. Later that year, however, he showed John Barry "thirty poems in manuscript, written, as he explained, in three days." Barry in *Bookman,* 13 (1901).

6. Garland in his 1914 account—"Stephen Crane As I Knew Him"—complained that *The Red Badge* "in its printed form did not in my judgment have

the quality that was in the manuscript which came to me in the boy's pocket. The prodigious opening sentence which so impressed me on that memorable day (the image of the two armies facing each other like monstrous beasts) disappeared entirely from his copy, and the printed book lacked many other of the most notable pages of the original manuscript." Garland could not have seen any manuscript subsequent to the one Crane brought him in April, 1894, because he left for Chicago on the 25th and did not return to the East until December, 1895, when he read the book in print. Crane probably expunged the image when he prepared the first and second or final hand-written manuscripts for Appleton's editor Ripley Hitchcock and his typist. The penciled marginal questions and grammatical corrections in the final manuscript are not in Crane's hand. Some few insertions which he later retraced in ink indicate that this manuscript was being read while he was recasting the whole thing.

John Berryman in his *Stephen Crane* (1950) said: "None of the innumerable persons who claim to have once had in their possession a manuscript of *Maggie* or of *Red Badge* has ever produced one. Two pages of the first draft of the war novel are said to be among Cora Crane's papers." By querying Rosenbach of Philadelphia I found that the manuscripts of *The Red Badge* existed, and in December, 1951, Mr. C. W. Barrett gave me a photocopy of them (in the book-form binding by which Willis B. Hawkins had preserved them). They were published for the first time—both the Short Version Manuscript and the Long Version Manuscript—in my *Stephen Crane: An Omnibus* (Knopf, 1952; Heinemann, 1954). Five additional pages belonging to MS. LV were reproduced for the first time in my Signet edition of *The Red Badge of Courage* (New American Library, 1960).

7. Dick, a great friend of Crane, borrowed the $15 from his *Godey's Magazine* boss and gave it to Crane, but the boss had already refused Crane this very loan and on noticing the canceled check with Crane's endorsement felt tricked. Dick did not get any more commissions from *Godey's* and Crane never repaid the loan, according to Rupert Hughes in a letter to Thomas Beer.

8. Bacheller had been a newspaperman since his early twenties and had founded his newspaper syndicate in 1884. Now forty-four years old, he was the author of two novels: *The Master of Silence* (1890) and *The Still House of O'Darrow* (1894). Nothing that Crane ever wrote, not even his *Red Badge,* attained the popular success of Bacheller's *Eben Holden* (1900), which sold more than a million copies.

9. Stangé's account, quoted here, mistakenly places his visit on "a fearful day in March," whereas it occurred the same February day that Linson and his brother found Crane in bed towards noon the day following his Bowery experiences during a blizzard of rain and snow. This corrects the confused account by Linson in *My Stephen Crane* (1958), edited by Edwin Cady (1958). Not noticed by Cady is Linson's variant account in the *Saturday Evening Post* (1903).

10. "The youth went to the studio of an artist friend, who, from his store, rigged him out in an aged suit and a brown derby hat that had been made long years before. And then the youth went forth to try to eat as the tramp

may eat, and sleep as the wanderers sleep." This passage is part of the opening portion of the *Press's* text, which was reprinted for the first time in my *Stephen Crane: An Omnibus* (1952), together with the ending, a passage in the original text. Crane expunged these two passages from the text of his *Open Boat and Other Stories* (London, 1898).

11. Crane stayed at 111 West 33rd until he quit the city in mid-May 1894 for Hartwood and Port Jervis, and then in the autumn he was again back in the Art Students' League building (in the studios of Fred Gordon or R. G. Vosburgh or David Ericson). When he wasn't sleeping in a hammock or a borrowed cot there, he was bumming a couch at Linson's studio at Broadway and West 30th, or else he shared Charlie Pike's third-floor flat at 281 Sixth Avenue (1894 into 1896). In November, 1894, he was back at Fred Gordon's studio in the old Needham building, but just before leaving for Port Jervis for the Christmas holidays he had a room at 33 East 22nd Street, and there he again lived in early March, 1896, before his journey to Washington, D. C. On returning, he moved into a large studio at the top of a house in the center of the city, at 165 West 23rd, where he had lived in October, 1895.

12. In 1892 James L. Ford, managing editor of *Truth*, wrote a series attacking the quality magazines, mainly the *Century*. "Ford thought that American literature needed more stories of tenement realism and 'low life.' He charged that the editors of the *Century*, Richard Watson Gilder and Robert Underwood Johnson, had erected a barbed-wire fence at Fourteenth Street in New York City and kept out of their magazine all stories that dealt with the lower East Side. Such restrictions, thought Ford, along with the use of the pruning hook in editorial policy, were creating a literature that was sentimental and false to life." W. R. Linneman in *American Literature*, XXXIV (1962).

13. First published in *The New York City Sketches of Stephen Crane* (1966).

14. This passage occurs only in the handwritten Pocket Notebook of 1892–1894. Crane in his *Press* recast of this sketch (1894) rephrased it: "I think that if a squadron of Napoleon's dragoons charged into this place they would be trampled under foot before they could get bisquit. They were great soldiers, no doubt, but they would at once perceive that there were many things about sweep and dash and fire of war of which they were totally ignorant."

15. Henry McBride in "Stephen Crane's Artist Friends," an important memoir of Crane, in *Art News*, XLIX (October 1950). That McBride once intended to write a biography of Crane, a legend initiated by John Berryman in *Stephen Crane*, does not seem to have basis in fact.

16. In Hawkins' column "All in a Lifetime," appearing in some unidentified paper. First reprinted in *The Stephen Crane Newsletter* for Spring, 1967. Hawkins met Crane through Irving Bacheller sometime in the winter of 1893–1894 and soon became a close friend and staunch admirer of Crane's "extraordinary mental and moral courage."

17. However, the philosophy expressed is Crane's in that it is opposed to fatalism: "The laws of the universe sometimes appear to be toying with compensations, holding back results until death closes the eyes to success, blud-

geoning a man of benefactions, rewarding them who do evil. It is well that we do all in our power to defeat these things." As for the contrariness of nature, "Let us then struggle to defeat this ironical law of fate." Crane had already written in *Maggie* his implied critique of those who submit to their environment as though doomed.

A poem prefaces his prose sketch: "A soldier, young in years, young in ambitions / Alive as no grey-beard is alive / Laid his heart and his hopes before duty / And went staunchly into the tempest of war." (That much of the poem is worth quoting.)

None of the Memorial Day tributes which have been claimed (by Thomas Gullason) to be Crane's is his except this unsigned one, of which the manuscript is in CUCC. What Crane published in the New York *Press* always bore his signature.

# VII

1. Linson published this passage for the first time from Crane's manuscript in *My Stephen Crane* (1958). It was reprinted with "In the Depths of A Coal Mine," which *McClure's Magazine* published for August 1894, in *The New York City Sketches of Stephen Crane* (1966). The sketch first appeared on July 22 of 1894 in the St. Louis *Republic* as "Down in a Coal Mine." This title is not listed in the Williams-Starrett Crane Bibliography (1948), and neither title is mentioned in *My Stephen Crane* as edited by Edwin Cady.

2. Anna Wells in a letter to R. W. S. To Miss Wells, then the librarian of the Poughkeepsie Public Library, I am indebted for a photocopy of that rarity known as "The Pike County Puzzle," the newspaper Crane and Senger edited at Twin Lakes in the summer of 1894. (It has just recently been issued in facsimile by *The Stephen Crane Newsletter.*)

3. He began in May 1894 where he had left off writing in 1893 the starting two pages of *George's Mother* on the clean back of "The Holler Tree" manuscript, on verso of which he also had begun "The Reluctant Voyagers," also in 1893.

4. Not collected during Crane's lifetime, they were first issued as a unit—several dozen of them—in *The New York City Sketches of Stephen Crane* (1966).

5. "When Man Falls" was reprinted in a shortened version as "A Street Scene in New York" in *Last Words* (1902). In his scrapbook of newspaper clippings Crane wrote the title "When Men Stumble" on a clipping of the *Press* sketch actually entitled "When Man Falls."

6. No such tenement fire could have occurred because none was reported in any of the New York City papers of late November, 1894, according to John S. Mayfield in his *American Book Collector* articles (December, 1956, and January, 1957): "Stephen Crane's Curious Conflagration." Bibliographer Ames W. Williams, apparently believing the sketch genuine, had privately published it in pamphlet form under the title "Fire."

7. Of these seven poems five never saw print, and all that remains of these

five are their opening lines: "A god it is said / Marked a sparrow's fall"; "A god came to a man / And spoke in this wise"; "The traveller paused in kindness"; "Should you stuff me with flowers"; "One came from the skies" (from an unpublished Copeland and Day letter—new to *Letters*).

Two of these seven poems were printed in 1899 in *War Is Kind:* "To the maiden" and "There was a man with a tongue of wood."

8. Sillier still was Will Bradley's design for *War Is Kind* (1899), printed on dark gray paper like blotting paper with outrageous drawings. The worst of these ghastly pictures was appended to Crane's poem "Fast Rode the Knight," first published in Hubbard's *Roycroft Quarterly* (May, 1896). Bradley depicts the knight's horse, presumably dead and certainly upside down, brandishing wild, stiff legs against a castle "which wavers up from a striped ground in sections shaped like daffodil leaves" (to quote Amy Lowell).

9. When Linson visited his cousin Louis Senger at Port Jervis that summer and happened upon a volume of poetry by "Ossian," he shrewdly observed: "Why that's poetry just like Steve's." Linson's making this link brought Crane to jest that Linson talked as if he expected Ossian "to write about Port Jervis Sunday-school picnics."

10. Talcott Williams, L. L. D., reviewed Crane's *The Open Boat and Other Tales of Adventure* (1898) in *Book News* for May, 1898. By then he had become more critical while still admitting that Crane remained "the most original and interesting prose figure in American letters." He said that whereas Crane "once waited in some city and wrote things as they came," he is today the most active-footed of men and is too busy to do more than Kodak his impressions. The result is "he never thinks." The profundity of "The Open Boat" obviously escaped Talcott Williams, but not other reviewers.

11. Some editor had expunged not only the final three chapters but also such phrases as "hell's fire" and "Good Lord." About midway through the typescript he quit his revisions, and from then on the soldiers freely utter their oaths, drop their g's, and speak in Crane's soldier dialect of "t'morrah" and "behint."

## VIII

1. Crane wrote Ripley Hitchcock on February 12, 1895, from Lincoln, Nebraska: "I would be glad to have Appleton and Co. publish the story on those terms." Not until he returned from the journey into the West and Mexico did he sign the Appleton printed contract, specifying 10% of the retail price of all copies sold. He signed it in New York on June 17, 1895. (The original contract with Daniel Appleton is in the Lilly Library at Indiana University.)

2. "The famous 'Red Badge of Courage' bristles more with false grammar than with bayonets," said Chelifer (Rupert Hughes) in *Godey's Magazine* for September, 1896. He listed examples by the dozen. "Mr. Crane, in his remarkable aptitude for bold and striking effect, is not only led into a frequent neglect of the time-hallowed rights of certain words, but is so tireless in the pursuit of color and vividness that he falls occasionally into almost ludicrous

mishap, like the mention of Henry's mother's cheeks as 'scarred' by tears, or the reference to a 'dauntless statue,' as if a statue could be either dauntless or dauntful; on page 106 we have 'terror-stricken wagons'; on p. 195 smoke is 'lazy,' which one can understand; but it is more, it is 'ignorant.' Page 211 gives us human auricles as 'perched ears,' and compels one to wonder if their noses had gone home to roost."

3. Willa Cather, "When I Knew Stephen Crane," *Library*: June 23, 1900. Willa Cather also wrote the Introduction to *The Work of Stephen Crane,* edited by Wilson Follett, Vol. 9 (1926).

4. In "Mardi Gras Festival," which was postponed for publication until the next year in the Philadelphia *Press* (February 16, 1896).

5. In addition to corrections Crane deleted many passages (a total of about 2,000 words). The first American publication of these deleted passages appeared in my *Stephen Crane: An Omnibus* (Knopf, 1952; Heinemann, 1954).

6. Not published until November 16, 1900, in the London *Westminster Gazette,* headlined "By the Late Stephen Crane."

7. Quoted here for the first time from the untitled holograph manuscript in CUCC, to which I've given the title: "Apaché Crossing."

8. The five Western tales appearing in English magazines are "One Dash—Horses!" in the *New Review* (February, 1896); "A Texas Legend" in *English Illustrated Magazine* (June, 1896); "The Bride Comes to Yellow Sky" in *Chapman's Magazine* (February, 1898); "Twelve O'Clock" in *Pall Mall Gazette* (December, 1899); the fifth appears as a portion of "London Impressions," written at Ravensbrook for the London *Saturday Review* (July and August, 1897).

Crane's Wyoming Valley tales are located not in the West but in Pennsylvania, and they were published posthumously.

9. In Philadelphia *Press:* July 21, 1895. It was subheaded: "The Brilliant Author of 'The Black Riders' Describes a Trip as Picturesque as Any to Be Taken in America." Another *Press* edition this same day is headed: "Stephen Crane in Mexico. / From San Antonio to the Ancient City of the Aztecs. / Through Cactus and Mesquite," datelined "City of Mexico, July 4." But it is the same sketch as the *Press's* "Ancient Capital of Montezuma," which is datelined "City of Mexico, July 12."

A press copy in CUCC is headed "For July 21," but this sketch did not appear in the *Press, World* or *Herald* on that date. *Stephen Crane: An Exhibition* (1956) is in error in listing as a new title "Stephen Crane in Mexico." datelined: "City of Mexico, July 12. Both dates were faked by the Bacheller, Johnson & Bacheller Syndicate. Crane was back in the East by May 16 (1895).

The press copy in Columbia University Crane Collection is the one cited above: "Stephen Crane in Mexico." Press proof "For July 21." It is a variant title, but not a new sketch, as it appears to be in its listing in *Stephen Crane: An Exhibition of His Writings,* arranged and described by Joan H. Baum (1956), page 57. It lists, page 55, three news articles from "City of Mexico," signed. These unpublished sketches, new to the Crane canon, are here assigned the title "City of Mexico." See Note 11.

Crane wrote a prose fable about the old man Popocatepetl in "The Voice of the Mountain," in *Pocket Magazine* for November 1896.

10. In Louisville *Courier-Journal* and as "Mexican Sights and Street Scenes" in Philadelphia *Press,* also for May 19, 1895, but with a variant text.

11. These three signed untitled holograph manuscripts in CUCC are here given the title "City of Mexico." Crane in his dateline left blank the space for the date, which the Bacheller, Johnson & Bacheller Syndicate would supply. He is bitingly critical of American capitalists, and perhaps for this reason Bacheller rejected these sketches. These three sketches were first published in *Bulletin of the New York Library* (November, 1967): "Stephen Crane: Some New Sketches," by R. W. Stallman.

12. In Philadelphia *Press* (August 11, 1895), sub-headlined: "A Country Where One Drink Will Fill the Vision with Sea Serpents."

13. Here I am quoting from one of the three holograph manuscripts comprising "City of Mexico."

14. The holograph manuscript (in the Huntington Library) differs only slightly from the printed *World* text.

## IX

1. Hawkins became one of four executors of Crane's 1896 will, and, as an expression of gratitude, Crane sent the original manuscripts of *The Red Badge:* "Thought maybe you'd like it." The two friends appeared side by side in *The Lanthorn Book* (1898), a collection of tales and verses "Read at the Sign O' the Lanthorn."

2. Crane gave his address as the Hartwood Club rather than Edmund's house and then gave his New York address as c/o The Lantern Club at 126 Williams Street instead of Linson's studio, where he would actually stay. He was always fond of patent-leather addresses.

3. Mr. Brentano had been cool to *Maggie* in 1893. "To this hour," said Howells in 1913, "I cannot understand the attitude of the dealers. I saw several of them personally and tried to interest Mr. Brentano. If Crane had cared to try that trick he might have disposed of *Maggie* through certain stores which had the reputation of selling obscene paperbacks. I suppose that the profanity of his masterpiece would have appealed to High School boys. But he did not descend to the method and, on my suggestion, mailed copies to Dr. Parkhurst and another minister who were then interested in the condition of the slums. Neither acknowledged the gift, and Crane told me afterwards that a Roman Catholic notable wrote that *Maggie* was an insult to the Irish. I shall never understand what was found offensive in the little tragedy."

4. Crane boasted to Harvey Wickham that he had written *The Black Riders* in three days at Twin Lakes, Pa., in the summer of 1894. But some of the

poems were written as early as 1891. In his last meeting with Wickham, Crane told him that his poems had been the outcome of a fit of desperation. "No one would print a line of mine, and I just had to do something odd to attract attention."

5. Thomas Beer claimed that *The Black Riders* was dismissed as a freakish thing ("the reading nation was told at once that Stephen Crane was mad"), and John Berryman reiterated Beer's unjustified statement in saying that the ferocity of attacks on *The Black Riders* has been "if anything, understated."

Elbert Hubbard kept a scrapbook of reviews of *The Black Riders,* and he cited from these reviews such epithets as "idiocy, drivel, bombast, rot, nonsense, puerility, untruth, garbage, hamfat, funny, absurd, childish, drunken, rant, bassoon-poetry, windy, turgid, stupid, pompous, gas-house ballads; etc." The scrapbook no longer exists, but there is no proof among known reviews for Hubbard's claim in the *Lotus* that no American writer was so thoroughly hooted and abused as Stephen Crane in the latter half of 1895.

6. The Philistine Society's banquet for Crane was also celebrated in two pamphlets, companions to *A Souvenir,* entitled *The Members of the Society* and *The Time Has Come.* The latter leaflet issued a new Crane poem: "I Have Heard the Sunset Song of the Birches." Harry Taber printed them at a little plant of his own in East Aurora called the Roycroft Printing Shop (the name harks back to early English printers, the Roycroft brothers, and means the "king's craftsmen"). All of the poems in *A Souvenir and a Medley* had appeared in *The Philistine* except "Fast Rode the Knight."

The Philistine Society's banquet for Crane is depicted in my *Stephen Crane: An Omnibus* (1952) and in *Stephen Crane: Letters* (1960).

For the source of Crane's "A Prologue" see Appendix 3.

7. According to Dr. Frederic Lawrence, Crane wrote him (in early 1893 ?) from Fredericksburg "giving a graphic account of the recollections of Confederate veterans who had seen the Union troops cut down 'in winnows' as they attempted to cross the river." In *Stephen Crane: Letters,* p. 332: "I remember also his first trip to Fredericksburg and other Virginia towns, his delight in the reminiscences of the old soldiers whom he met there and his determination to write a real story of the Civil War. . . ."

## X

1. What Crane first wrote was "a little warm badge of courage." He changed this to "a little red badge of courage," then deleted the word "little." Afterward he crossed through the early title, "Private Fleming / His Various battles," and wrote above it: "The Red Badge of Courage. / An Episode of the American War."

2. As given in MS. SV. The previous quotation is in MS. LV. Both passages belong to Chapter X, immediately following the death of Jim Conklin at the end of Chapter IX. Critics who assert that the youth directs his fist-shaking at the battlefield have ignored these passages in the manuscripts, first published in my *Stephen Crane: An Omnibus* (1952). Five new manuscript pages (Manuscript LV, Long Version) were brought together for the first time

in my 1960 Signet edition of *The Red Badge of Courage.* Copyright 1952, by Alfred A. Knopf, Inc., copyright 1960 by R. W. Stallman.

3. Edmund Wilson's objection (in the *New Yorker,* May 2, 1952) that "Crane's parents were not Catholics but Methodists" is ill-founded. The two churches utilize the same ritual, and Methodists as well as Catholics have used—or do still use—wine and the wafer. But Crane need not have been Catholic *or* Methodist to have the knowledge and liberty to use the symbolism common to both. (I am indebted to Methodist Bishop Herbert Welch, replying to my query on these matters.)

4. First identified in 1951 by Scott C. Osborn in *American Literature.* Discussed in "The Scholar's Net: Literary Sources," by R. W. Stallman, in *College English:* October 1955. And in "The Origins of Stephen Crane's Literary Creed," by James Colvert, in University of Texas *Studies in English* for 1955.

5. The New York *Tribune* scoffed at "The Genius of 1896" and explained that London is always hungering for a literary hero, once a year at least. For a while it had been Oscar Wilde, but he lasted longer than London wanted him to, and so the genius reputations have been restricted to brief periods. "Mrs. Caffyn sailed along for a time on a bubble so iridescent that when her husband wrote anything it was advertised as 'by the husband of the author of *The Yellow Aster.*' When Mr. Crane turned up with his *Red Badge of Courage* (it is curious, this passion of the English for colors), there was a void that ached for him. He filled it, this 'genius of 1896.' It will be interesting to see who takes his place."

6. The English edition is dated 1896, but it was published during the month of November, 1895.

7. The Cleveland *Plain-Dealer* erred in saying: "It is perfectly apparent that the experiences described were those of the author."

## XI

1. In fashionable homes the "Turkish corner" was the upstairs sitting room reserved for the daughter and her beau. This cozy corner was a tentlike affair of red draperies festooned on spears with a divan inside, a brass lantern, and a Moorish tabouret. "By its titillating suggestion of Oriental lasciviousness, the Turkish corner was destined to the rites of courtship." From Lloyd Morris' *Incredible New York* (1951).

2. Crane told this story to Willis Clarke at Brede Place when Clarke visited there in November, 1899, to gather material for a biography of Crane he intended to write. Clarke's brother had reported a rumor circulating in 1896 at the Cairo restaurant, one of the rowdiest night resorts in New York City, that Crane was the father of a child by a girl who was loose on the town.

3. On January 2 he wrote Elbert Hubbard in flattering praise of Hubbard's insipid novel *No Enemy* (1894): "Your manipulation of the life in Indiana and Illinois is out of sight. There are swift character sketches all through it that strike me as being immense. . . . Your flowers on the water—good god, that is magnificent. A thing that I felt in the roots of my hair. Hell and

blazes, but I do envy you that paragraph. The book strengthened me and up-lifted me / It is a peach." In *The Stephen Crane Newsletter,* No. 2 (Winter 1966).

4. The March issue of the same London journal published another story, "A Tale of Mere Chance," a piece of outright imitation of Edgar Allan Poe, which was reprinted, along with "A Detail," in *Best Things From American Litera-ture* (1899). They are second-rate Crane.

5. This new Crane letter, written on verso of the photographs taken by Mr. King on January 24–25, 1896, is in the Lilly Library of Indiana University. This photograph of Crane in cravat and stiff collar was reproduced in the London *Mail & Express* for January 21, 1897, and elsewhere.

6. "The terrific assault of the Union army on the impregnable had something in it of the fury of despair. It had been goaded and hooted by the sit-stills until it was near insane and just as a maddened man may dash his fists against an iron wall, so did the Union army hurl itself against the hills back of Fredericksburg. . . . I want to understand Fredericksburg," Crane wrote Phil-lips (on January 9), "completely as far as the books will teach it and then after that, the other things."

7. *Pictures of War* (1898), *War Is Kind* (1899), *Active Service* (1899), *Wounds in the Rain* (1900), and *Great Battles of the World* (1901). *The Lit-tle Regiment* was published in the first week of December, 1896. For reviews, see Appendix 4.

8. Of the four books one was the English edition of *The Black Riders,* one the revised *Maggie,* and the other two were new works: *George's Mother* and *The Litle Regiment.*

9. This new Crane letter, tipped into Richard LeGallienne's copy of *The Black Riders,* is in the Alderman Library at the University of Virginia. The subsequent data is from a letter of Elbert Hubbard II to R. W. S.

10. Written on lined pages of a pocket notebook, the holograph manuscript of three pages in CUCC lacks a title. It is quoted here for the first time.

11. Crane's letter to Bacheller (the only one known to be extant) is quoted here for the first time from the original in the St. Lawrence University Library. (I am indebted to Librarian Andrew K. Peters for bringing it to my attention.)

### XII

1. Hitchcock, editorial adviser for Appleton and Harper, was thirty-nine in 1896 (Crane was then twenty-four). Art critic for the *Tribune* (1882–1890), he published in 1896 *Etching in America* and was now editing in seven vol-umes *The Story of the West* (1895–1902). He also wrote *David Harum,* a play which was an immensely popular stage success. He did not risk much in publishing *The Red Badge,* but he took a risk on *Maggie* and on *The Third Violet.* Hitchcock had as much literary insight as any editor of his day.

2. Just before going to Washington Crane lived at 33 East 22nd and sent a note from that address to a certain Mr. Shipman: "Hope you can find it in

your heart to pardon. I indeed feel too ill this morning to leave the house."
Shipman was probably a poker-playing crony. (This note, quoted here for the
first time, is in the Barrett Crane Collection.)

3. Huneker, who was influenced by Saltus' style, portrayed him in *Painted
Veils* (1920). All that was petty and foolish in Saltus' life was unintentionally
exposed by his third wife in her biography, *Edgar Saltus the Man* (1925), and
that put "the kiss of death on his literary fame."

4. Thomas Beer to Edith Crane (January 2, 1923), in the former Knopf files.

5. Written in January, 1899, just after Crane returned from Havana, "A Self-
Made Man" appeared in the *Cornhill Magazine* for March, 1899.

6. Maurice Bassan in his account of the early draft of *George's Mother*
(*American Literature:* January 1965) makes no mention of the first draft of
"The Reluctant Voyagers" appearing on verso of page three of "The Holler
Tree" holograph manuscript (in Barrett Crane Collection). But this is impor-
tant because we can establish its date of composition by Corwin Knapp Lin-
son's *My Stephen Crane* (1958) and his *Saturday Evening Post* article for
April 11, 1903, an important memoir not noticed by the editor of *My Stephen
Crane,* Edwin Cady. In all probability, then, Crane wrote *George's Mother*
after *Maggie* went to press in early 1893, began it then or by June. Harry
Thurston Peck declared in the *Bookman* (July 1896) that on the basis of
internal evidence "its first draft must belong to the time when [Crane] wrote
and published *Maggie.*" He guessed that it might be "even earlier, and probably one of Mr. Crane's first attempts at serious composition." However, his
first serious compositions were *Maggie* and then *The Red Badge.*

7. Crane's letters to H. P. Williams, here quoted for the first time, were kindly
supplied me by Mr. Charles E. Feinberg of Detroit. One of the three, not
quoted above, occurred prior to July 6, 1896: "If you will come tomorrow
about 3 o'clock I will talk as well as I am able."

8. Probably at 141 East 25th Street. A curious volume by William Astor
Chanler, *Through Jungle and Desert, Travels Through Eastern Africa,* published by Macmillan in 1896, has the fly-leaf signature: "Hamlin Garland, 141
East 25th Street, New York" in his hand. Under this is "Stephen Crane, Hartwood, Sullivan County, New York" in Crane's hand. And under this is "Frank
Snathis—Players—vol. presented by Chanler." My surmise is that Snathis
gave Crane his gift-copy and Crane in turn gave it to Garland. The volume
shows no signs of ever having been read by anybody, says David Randall,
Librarian of Indiana University Libraries (in letter to James B. Stronks, to
whom I am indebted for this item).

9. The New York *Press* in a two-column spread by its Sunday editor, Edward
Marshall, reported: "Realists at the Lanthorn Club," a banquet honoring
Cahan, Garland and Crane. In *Press,* Sept. 27, 1896.

10. Crane misdated it for August 15. Howells replied on the 15th.

11. Crane's name appeared not only in the headline of this Sunday *World*
sketch (October 25, 1896), but also in facsimile signature, and *The Third*

*Violet,* his first love story, was announced as forthcoming in the evening edition of the *World* next November 4, to begin then in serialized form with illustrations by Powers.

# XIII

1. In Ellen Moers' "Teddy Roosevelt, Literary Feller," *Columbia University Forum: Summer,* 1963.

2. "I am sure that if you read the police news in next Sunday and Monday mornings' papers and go to Jefferson Market Police Court on Monday morning, you will get the material for a good Tenderloin story to start with. I suppose that if you are going there on Monday you would be glad to have a reporter (who knows the ropes) meet you there." Huxton wrote Crane on Sunday, September 13, that he had written that morning the city editor of the *Journal* and had it from him that a reporter "will ask for you at Shanley's tomorrow, Monday morning at a quarter before nine." (The Huxton to Crane letters, here quoted for the first time, are in CUCC.)

3. In a typed manuscript with autograph corrections (six folio leaves) Crane wrote a first draft for his September 20 *Journal* account of the Dora Clark affair. Here Crane, uneasy in mind, says to himself: "Now, this arrest is wrong. This girl may be nothing but a prostitute. I know nothing whatever as to that. I have no information on that subject, but as to the facts of her soliciting two men between the time she left the Broadway Garden and the moment of her arrest I know that to be untrue. I have a small reputation; not as light as a feather perhaps, or not so heavy as a penny, but one which I have earned by hard work—the thing—a little structure which has taken me years to build up. Now, this common prostitute is being done a wrong. But shall I risk all this? Shall I risk all this for a girl who is alleged to be a common walker of the streets? I have friends who are conventionally particular. Citizens of New York, men of character and reputation, perhaps witness these things from time to time, but do they then interfere? No, they go home and attend seriously and solemnly to their own affairs. Shall I become a ridiculous figure for the benefit of a prostitute? Or, shall I go home? 'Well,' continued the reluctant laggard witness, 'this girl be she a prostitute or whatever, was under your protection and while in your escort she has suffered an injustice, and a wrong to a prostitute is as great a wrong as to a queen.'" (MS in Barrett Crane Collection, here quoted for the first time.)

4. Attorney for Becker and Conway, lawyer Louis Grant, is not to be confused with Commissioner Grant (Frederick D.), son of President U. S. Grant.

5. Reproduced for the first time in *The New York City Sketches of Stephen Crane* (1966). Also reproduced here for the first time are the manuscripts: "A Blackguard as a Police Officer: (in CUCC); "Notes About Prostitutes" (in Barrett CC): and "Adventures of a Novelist," reprinted from the New York *Journal* (September 20, 1896), another addition to the Crane canon.

6. Herbert Asbury, *The Gangs of New York* (1927). Neither Asbury nor Jonathan Root in his *Life and Bad Times of Charlie Becker* (1962) mentions Becker's encounter with Stephen Crane in 1896.

7. *The Gangs of New York.*

8. B. A. Botkin's *New York City Folklore* (1956).

9. "The 'Tenderloin' as It Really Is" (October 25), the first of a series of "Striking Sketches of New York Life by the Famous Novelist" was commented on by the *Literary Digest* for November 7, from which I traced the original *Journal* sketch.

## XIV

1. An addition to the Crane canon, quoted here for the first time. (I am indebted to Professor William Gibson for bringing it to my notice.) Other contributors to this birthday party *Journal* included Howells, Edgar Saltus and Julian Ralph. There were pen-drawings of them and of Crane.

2. Cora wrote this in it and added: "This book belongs to / Mrs. Stephen Crane / 6, Milbourne Grove / The Boltons / South Kensington." She lived there in 1898 when Crane was in Cuba and again after Crane's death and her return to England.

On the front end-paper to *The Seven Seas* she had written when Crane gave her the book: "Cora / Jacksonville / 1896." In later years she pasted over that inscription, so as to conceal her connection with Jacksonville, two pieces of paper containing Kipling's signature and his printed address: *"The Elms, / Rottingdean, / Nr Brighton."* These pieces of paper she evidently cut from one of Kipling's replies to Cora's attempts to persuade him to complete *The O'Ruddy* in 1900, at the time of Crane's death.

The account, with some changes added, derives from "Cora's Mouse," by Matthew Bruccoli in *Papers of the Bibliographical Society of America,* LIX (1965).

During Crane's English years Mark Barr, an American chemist, called on Hamlin Garland, then in London, and spoke of Stephen Crane's marriage to Cora. "He quoted Crane as saying, 'I brought Cora back.' He married her over here [in England] in the presence of Wells and one or two others. . . . The fact of Wells [H. G. Wells, whose common-law wife Catherine he finally married] being a witness at the wedding would not add anything to its legal aspect, for so far as I know he does not believe in the home or marriage." If any such wedding ceremony between Stephen and Cora actually occurred, it was a mock-marriage having no legal status because Cora's husband refused her a divorce.

Garland in his journal for August 22, 1922 adds that Joseph Conrad wrote about Crane "saying that he was surrounded by a lot of third class people"— at Villa Ravensbrook in 1897–1898 and at Brede Manor in 1899–1900. Garland goes on to say that Crane "was never given to really fine associations. . . . With all his endowments he was not an admirable character. He gave out the effect of being an alley cat so far as habit went. And during the days when I first knew him in New York City he was living like an outcast. Although not a drinking man, he smoked incessantly and sometimes was thought to have used a drug of some kind." As for Cora, Mark Barr considered her a woman of education and "an ample 'Negro mammy' sort of person." (Mark

Barr's wife Mabel was the sister of Kate Lyon, common-law wife of Harold Frederic, whose illegitimate children were boarded and mothered by Cora at Brede Manor after Harold's death in October 1898 until October 1900.)

For copy of Hamlin Garland's 1922 journal I am indebted to Professor Donald Pizer of Tulane University.

3. If Crane's date of November 4 in Jacksonville were accurate, it would mean that he left Cambridge on October 31 for Jacksonville and then returned to Cambridge for the November 7 football game between Harvard and Princeton, and then went down to Jacksonville again. The letter to Catherine Harris of November 12 was written *not* in Jacksonville, as erroneously given in *Letters* (page 132). The most reasonable conjecture is that he went to Jacksonville for the first time on the 13th, as reported in the Syracuse University *Herald*.

4. The Hotel de Dream, technically speaking, was not a whore-house but rather a night-club, according to Miss Gilkes in *Cora Crane* (1960); and "technically" Cora was not a madam. However, to newspaper reporters visiting Jacksonville her house was a house of joy and she was the madam. Although her girls did not live in her so-called night club, also known as a boarding-house, couples did "drift upstairs."

5. Miss Gilkes speculates on this slight evidence that "it is evident that Stephen Crane had some sort of dealings with her at the very time he was falling in love with Cora."

6. E. W. McCready of New Brunswick, Canada, to B. J. R. Stolper of New York City: January 22, 1934. He says that he and Paine were dining "in one section of the house and did not that night encounter Crane, but only heard distantly the Murphy party. But we returned some nights later—Christmas eve —sojourned—and sat in at the 'family' board next day for Christmas dinner— Paine carving the noble bird." However, Paine was at Key West on December 24 and was still stuck down there in early January, and so McCready has confused the chronology here; for the dinner he describes occurred on Thanksgiving Day 1896, whereas his overhearing the Murphy party occurred after the *Commodore* disaster. A portion of this letter was first published in *Stephen Crane: Letters*, pages 339–340.

7. By my reading, Crane was appeasing a broken-hearted and mentally-ill woman. This squares with Joseph Katz's recent discussion of the Crane–Amy Leslie Affair (in *Mad River Review:* Winter 1964–1965), which provides new data to the above account. Gilkes sees it as the story of a depraved woman betrayed by Crane, to whom she looked for rescue.

8. Hawkins wired Crane the requested fifty dollars at Jacksonville on December 28, 1896. Crane's telegram in *Letters* (1960) is misdated for December 28, 1898.

9. Her cargo contained cartridges, powder, forty bundles of rifles, three hundred machetes, drugs and clothing; total value: $4,465. As there were two steamers named the *Commodore*, the identity of the shipwrecked *Commodore* is to be established by data about her given in the log of the *Boutwell*. There her home port is given as New York. "Built in 1882 in Philadelphia, gross

tonnage 178.25, net tonnage 99.25, length 122.5 feet, home port New York," in *Twenty-Eighth Annual List of Merchant Vessels of the United States* (1896), page 228. The record of her expeditions to Cuba, 1895–1897, is found in *International Law and Diplomacy of the Spanish-American War*, by E. J. Benton (1908).

10. These include "The Wreck of the New Era," "The Raft Story" (also entitled "Six Years Afloat"), "The Captain," "The Ghostly Sphinx of Metedeconk," and "The Reluctant Voyagers."

11. The *Commodore* was beached again at Mayport, changing pilots, and then she dragged herself off the sandbar and headed for the open sea. Captain Kilgore of the cutter *Boutwell* hailed: "Are you fellows going to sea today?" Captain Murphy called back, "Yes, sir." Captain Kilgore doffed his cap as the *Commodore's* whistle saluted him: "Well, gentlemen, I hope you have a pleasant cruise."

The *Boutwell* knew the *Commodore's* record as a filibustering vessel; yet instead of making arrests and seizing the vessel, the revenue cutter abetted breach of U. S. neutrality laws by towing these Cuban insurrectionists and ammunition.

The *George S. Boutwell* "was built in 1873 and owing to bad design is not now, and never was, a seaworthy vessel. It is a twin-screw boat, very slow, and unfit for the work of a revenue cutter. . . ." In *Annual Report of the Secretary of the Treasury . . . for the Year 1897*, pp. lviii-lix.

12. The story on treachery which Captain Murphy on another occasion called "a damned lie" is reported in Appendix 5. My study of the *Commodore* disaster appears in shortened form in "Journalist Crane in That Dinghy," *Bulletin of the New York Public Library*, 72 (April, 1968).

13. Crane in "Flanagan and His Short Filibustering Adventure" (London *Illustrated News:* August 28, 1897) describes it again. "As for the stokers, death might have been with silence in this room. . . . In the unholy red light and grey mist of this stifling Inferno they were strange figures with the silence and their immobility." Crane here calls the *Commodore* the "Foundling," which has "a quality of unholy medieval despair." This fictional account differs from Crane's *World* account of January 5.

14. The *Herald* wrongly reported on January 4 that this second boat "was washed ashore at Port Orange, bottom upward." This was one of dozens of false reports that came from the *Commodore* wreck. In 1899 in "War Is Kind" Crane wrote: "A newspaper is a collection of half-injustices." It is a court where every one is "unfairly tried / By a squalor of honest men." It is "a game / Where error scores the player victory / While another's skill wins death. / A newspaper is a symbol; / It is feckless life's chronicle, / A collection of loud tales / Concentrating eternal stupidities, / That in remote ages lived unhaltered, / Roaming through a fenceless world."

15. For the argument on how many men in the dinghy (and therefore the number of passengers aboard the *Commodore*), see Appendix 6.

16. The attorney for the notorious filbustering tug the *Three Friends,* J. M.

Barrs, sent the Secretary of the Treasury, Mr. Carlisle, a telegram on January 3 at 2 P.M. "Telegram from Ormond says steamer foundered. Eight men on rafts at sea. Please answer Collector's request and permit *Three Friends* to save lives. If not now too late." (The number eight and the fact of the rafts can have been only a guess.) But the Collector of Customs at Jacksonville was unwilling to let the *Three Friends* go to the rescue without authorization by the Secretary of the Treasury, the tug being under the Treasury's custody. Because of administrative redtape and the timidity of Mr. Bisbee, Collector at Jacksonville, the *Three Friends* was not permitted to go on its life saving mission until it was much too late.

The tug *Three Friends* with McCready and Paine and a group of Cuban insurgents in Florida sneaked out of Fernandina (a few miles north of Jacksonville) on the night of December 13, deposited them and a cargo of ammunition at No Name Key, eluded the Revenue cutters *Raleigh* and *Norfolk* sent out to intercept the *Three Friends*, which was seized when she put into port at Key West on Christmas Eve. The Collector of Customs at Key West escorted the tug *Three Friends* back to Jacksonville, and there an officer of the *Boutwell* took command of her. She got into Jacksonville on December 31 and "received an enthusiastic welcome. The crew hastened ashore and disappeared. None would talk further than to admit they had met and returned the fire of a Spanish coaster and cruiser," said the New York *World* (January 1, 1897). Her officers and crew were arrested on a charge of piracy in early January, 1897, and passengers McCready and Paine holed up in a twenty-five-cent lodging house until the affair blew over. The *Three Friends* made seven more hazardous filibustering adventures and passed through them all unscathed. (From T. Frederick Davis' *History of Jacksonville, Florida,* 1925.)

The *Three Friends* was so named because she was owned by A. W. Fritot, George Foster, and N. B. Broward (then Sheriff of Duval County and later Governor of Florida), and she was the so-called flagship of the "Cuban Fleet." That "fleet" included also the *Dauntless,* the *Commodore* and the *Bermuda.* Shortly after the *Three Friends* was stopped trying to get arms to Cuba, the Jacksonville Junta wired Washington (on January 29) to clear the *Dauntless* with arms for Cuba, and Washington granted her clearance. The possible answer to that puzzle is the fact that the *Dauntless* was owned by the son of Cyrus Bisbee, Collector of Customs at Jacksonville. But before the request was sent, the *Dauntless* had already sailed for No Name Key to pick up the Cuban insurgents and arms deposited there by the *Three Friends.* Soon after war was declared in 1898 the *Three Friends* was chartered as a dispatch boat by the New York *World,* and the *Dauntless* by the Associated Press.

17. Cyrus Day's contention—in "Stephen Crane and the Ten-Foot Dinghy," *Studies in English,* III (Winter, 1957)—that Crane falsified the stormy condition of the sea, impugns Crane as a journalist. More evidence that Day is in error is given in Appendix 7.

18. Cyrus Day says it took the Captain sixteen to eighteen hours to muster up "the courage to take the dinghy through the surf." Day's biased account ignores the facts.

19. "Stephen had to throw away his gold and a part of his garments to get in

and was near losing his life at that," says Irving Bacheller in *Coming Up the Road* (1928). "He was to send us articles from the island as often as possible and if war came he was to write of that. . . . Soon the thrilling tale of 'The Open Boat' came to us. We sold it to *Scribner's Magazine* for three hundred fifty dollars." Bacheller is mistaken in claiming that Crane got off to Cuba in a tugboat chartered by Sylvester Scovel of the New York *World* and that they "had to fight their way back in an open boat." Scovel was with Crane in Greece (1897) and again in Cuba (1898), but he was not with him on the *Commodore's* expedition to Cuba.

20. Some of my data here has been drawn from the Odell Hathaway interview with Fred Niver and other Daytona Beach residents who had witnessed the dinghy and who offered aid to the survivors. Hathaway submitted his article about this interview to the Daytona Beach *News-Journal,* which scooped him by using his articles for its own rewrite: "The Day that Stephen Crane Was Shipwrecked" (*News-Journal,* April 22, 1962). In *Cora Crane* Gilkes is mistaken in saying that "a special train was at last got off to Daytona —eighty-five miles away—to bring back the other survivors of the shipwreck, Crane among them."

# XV

1. *A Farewell to Arms* expresses the same philosophy except that here nothing redeems the unconcern of the universe; Frederic Henry thinks only of himself. He pours water on a burning log full of ants and steams them. Some escape, but most of them fall into the fire. He pours water on the burning log not to put out the fire but selfishly to empty his cup and ready it for some whiskey. In contrast, the men in the dinghy think only of each other's welfare.

2. A recent literal-minded critic (P. Rahv) sees nothing in "The Open Boat" as ironic. To answer *that,* one might quote the Cook's murmur: "What kind of pie do you like best?"

3. Said the Newcastle *Daily Chronicle:* "Mr. Stephen Crane has got a literary art as complete and high in its way as that of Walter Pater—a literary art that has the candour of spirit, the intimate sense of personality, and the economy of style." The *Athenaeum* declared its signs of "extraordinary ability, amounting to genius, distinguish all the prose of Mr. Crane." The English edition added nine Midnight Sketches to the American edition of *The Open Boat,* and so it was a collection comprised of odds and ends: "excellent odds, laudable ends," said the London *Academy* (May 14, 1898). Mr. Crane, when he is objective, is a cinematograph; when he is subjective, he is "the analytical chemist of the subconscious and the occasional betrayer of the night side of heroism." The Edinburgh *Scotsman* remarked: "There is more than cleverness and originality; there is a power that can only be called genius in almost every page of the remarkable volume entitled *The Open Boat.* It contains pieces which will raise the reputation even of the author of *The Red Badge of Courage.*" The *Outlook* for May 7, 1898, said that Crane in "The Open Boat" has given us the realism of shipwreck, as the late Charles Dickens, in the "Wreck of the *Golden Mary,*" gave us the romance.

4. This corrects the version of this letter in Beer, *Stephen Crane: Letters* and in Thomas Raymond's *Stephen Crane* (1923), where it first appeared. In *The Stephen Crane Newsletter,* I, No. 2 (Winter, 1966).

5. Robert H. Davis in Introduction to *The Work of Stephen Crane,* Vol. II (1925). The street walker seemed to Davis like an opalescent moth preening herself and then fluttering into the indigo night; but to Crane she must have seemed another Cora, for her eyes were blue and her hair sunny.

6. As I said in my Introduction to *Stephen Crane: Letters* (1960). The evidence is in the letters. Berryman in 1962 scoffed at this judgment, but further evidence is in Linson's *My Stephen Crane* (1958). What inconveniences Edwin Cady's theory of Crane as gentleman is in the above data, as well as the fact that Crane was not scrupulous about repaying his debts. He deliberately deserted Cora by hiding out in Havana after the Cuban War and left her destitute, on the brink of bankruptcy, while he gambled away hundreds of dollars in card games aboard one tug or another.

7. Thomas Beer was mistaken in his notion that Crane never read Bierce.

8. Undated clipping in CUCC, here noted for the first time. Bitter Bierce said of Percival Pollard, editor of *Echo,* that he "has dragged to upper day two worse writers than Stephen Crane and names them out loud. I had thought there could be only two worse writers than Stephen Crane; namely, two Stephen Cranes." (In New York *Press:* July 25, 1896). The two "worse writers" were H. W. Philips and Rupert Hughes; they were not named in the *Press* article.

9. In *Dark Rider,* a novel based on the life of *Stephen Crane* (1961), Louis Zara conjectures that Cora was on the same train with Crane, Jacksonville to New York City, and that Crane converted that occasion into the train ride of Potter and his bride in "The Bride Comes to Yellow Sky," an ingenious theory.

10. Crane had difficulty spelling the millionaire's name. First he wrote Salifa, then Shalife, and finally "Sharefe millionaire." Below he multiplied 35.50 by 16—money matters. This holograph scrapnote is in CUCC.

11. Beer's misdating the Savoy Club luncheon for March 26 would seem to be guesswork, since Crane did not reach London until March 29. *Letters* also is thereby in error.

12. Crane's sketch appeared on May 3 in the London *Westminster Gazette,* but without any dateline: "Impression of the 'Concert' " (the Concert of the Powers). Again it appeared in the Louisville *Courier-Journal* on May 9 with the dateline misspelling the steamer as "Guardiana." And here the title was "Stephen Crane's Pen Picture of the Powers' Fleet off Crete." This syndicated dispatch also appeared in the Detroit *Free Press* on May 27.

13. When the Orient Express made its inaugural trip in 1883 it left the Gare de l'Est in Paris with its sleeping cars and restaurant on a Thursday and arrived in Constantinople 82 hours later at 6:30 in the morning. The present-day route runs from Munich through Venice into Yugoslavia. Henri de Blowitz, a journalist who wrote of his experiences in Turkey, took the inaugural 1883 Orient Express from Paris to Constantinople, as Frank Giles reports it in *A Prince of Journalists* (1962).

14. Downey Fairfax in *Richard Harding Davis: His Day* (1933) says that Davis sailed from Patras "in company with Stephen Crane of the New York *Journal*." But Crane was in Athens by April 17 and got there from Crete aboard the *Guadiana*, while Davis did not start for Greece until Turkey declared war on April 17—he was still in Florence.

## XVI

1. In "Stephen Crane's Pen Picture of the Powers' Fleet Off Crete," in Louisville *Courier-Journal* for May 9, 1897, reprinted for the first time in *The War Dispatches of Stephen Crane*, edited by R. W. Stallman and E. R. Hagemann (1964).

The importance of this dispatch is in its dateline. "On Board French Steamer *Guadiana*. April 26.—Leaving Marseilles. . . ." What this proves is that Crane got to Greece by ship from Marseilles—not, as Lillian Gilkes claims in *Cora Crane* (1960), by the overland route with Cora on the Orient Express. Additional evidence is contained within Crane's dispatch by the fact that an Englishman aboard the steamer—misspelled "Guardiana"—was cocksure that the Cretans could never be conquered, whereas unknown to him and to Crane the island had already been subdued. The *Guadiana* arrived from London March 30 and sailed April 3 from Marseilles for Greece, Turkey, and the Black Sea via Piraeus, Smyrna, the Dardenelles, Constantinople, and finally Batum. As Crane's dispatch tells us, the *Guadiana* was off Crete in the Bay of Suda on the fourth day (April 8).

No dateline was given in the London *Westminster Gazette's* issue of this dispatch on May 3 with the title: "An Impression of the Concert." The Ames Williams and Vincent Starrett *Stephen Crane: A Bibliography* (1948) lists only that title. The same dispatch appeared in the New York *Sun* for May 9 with the title: "Half a Day in Suda Bay." Here the dateline reads: "On Board French Steamer *Guadiana*, April 22."

2. In Turkey there was anarchy also. Mountaineers of Taurus put the city of Marash in terror over the strife between them and the Turks, and the local governor at Ak-Hissar ordered the killing of fifty Armenian men, while in Constantinople two hundred Armenians—most of them innocent even of the possession of arms—were shot down. "At no time in the history of Turkey has the situation been so serious as it is now. Armenians and Moslems seem to be about equally desperate and both to have lost all hope of succor from the Powers of Europe on the one hand or their own government on the other," said *Harper's Weekly* in November, 1895. Cursed by Christians and Arabs, as well as by Turks, the Sultan was shut up in his palace—afraid of his life. Massacres occurred in October. In Trebizond on the 30th a priest was shot down while seeking an audience with the Governor, and then came four hours of carnage, "in which not less than 400 men were killed," and then looting began, the Turks destroying what they could not carry off from the shops— *Harper's Weekly* (December 28, 1895): "The Armenian Massacres."

3. The Englishman Steevens was—like Crane—a man of letters who became a war correspondent from love of adventure and the desire to experience the vivid realities of life. Both had the rare gift of knowing in a flash just what was

essential for pen portraits of battle to affect the reader. Both were born in 1871 and died before they were twenty-nine. Steevens' *With the Conquering Turk* (1897) remains today one of the few first-rate books on the Greco-Turkish War.

4. Arthur Gaye, "The Greeks and Their Lesson," *Macmillan's Magazine:* September, 1897.

5. Bennett Burleigh in "The Greek War as I Saw It," *Fortnightly Review:* July 15, 1897.

6. The fight at Domoko (or Domokos, as variously given) was an exception. It was the greatest battle seen in Europe since the days of Plevna. Crane wrote of the battle of Plevna in his *Great Battles of the World,* published posthumously in 1901.

7. The *Journal* headlined Cora's April 29 Athens dispatch: "Imogene Carter Braves Perils of the Field of War / Only Woman on the Scene." But Cora as "Imogene Carter" was not the only woman on that battlefield. Hearst's *Journal* had another woman reporting the war and claimed her in a May 5 dispatch as "Only Woman Correspondent at Front." The other woman correspondent was Harriet Boyd, who was in Athens as a Smith College student of Greek when the war broke out. Crane later found out about that situation and cast Harriet Boyd as the daughter of a Professor of Greek trapped in Epirus by the advancing Turkish Army and saved by reporter Coleman in *Active Service.*

8. See Appendix 8.

9. Bass tells the story flatly with no irony in "Gallant Greeks Would Continue War" (*Journal:* April 30, 1897). He explains that the safety of the King was the result of the shrewd removal guards. Bass wrote his article on the spot, whereas Crane took more time writing his—for the London *Westminster Gazette* series entitled "With Greek and Turk," where it did not appear until June 18, a month after the war had ended.

10. Bass deserted Cora's project to interview Prince Constantine in Pharsala. She had obtained a letter of introduction from the American Minister in Athens, Eben Alexander.

11. This—to quote Bennett Burleigh—was the absolute abandonment of all Thessaly to the enemy. "The Crown Prince retreated without trying his fortune in a general engagement, though his position at Pharsala was all but impregnable. The Turks did not win the place, however, without a fight; for an advanced force of Evzoni and the Philhellenic Legion held a low ridge seven miles north of Pharsala for several hours." General Smolenski, on receiving the Crown Prince's order to withdraw, was furious at the news of a second flight without battle or defeat. "The Prince's men are the same as mine. They can win battles against the Turks if some one will lead them."

12. The Turks had made three attacks on Velestino on three different days and had been repulsed each time, and then on May 4—a week later—they came

back again and the fighting continued for two days more. This was called the Second Battle of Velestino. (From Davis' *A Year from a Reporter's Note-Book,* 1898.)

13. The text here is a variant on "Crane at Velestino," reprinted in *The War Dispatches of Stephen Crane* (1964). The New York *Journal* issued two editions on May 11, one with "Crane at Velestino" and the other with "Stephen Crane at Velestino." Crane's dispatch was sent to Athens by courier from Volo, probably on May 7.

14. Constantine Smolenski was a general only by courtesy of Crane's dispatch. He was one of ten senior colonels in the Greek Army and "the ablest Greek artillery officer." He had served as Minister of War prior to the outbreak of hostilities. Said the *Illustrated London News:* Colonel Smolenski "has a strong face, black piercing eyes, and an abrupt manner. In his dress he is very particular, always wearing white gloves, and he emphasizes any orders he gives with his small riding-cane." He came from an old Slav family.

15. A wounded evzone told Crane that he blamed the royal family for these retreats. "They are cowards. They are not Greeks. They are foreigners."

16. Datelined "Athens, May 22 (On board the *St. Marina,* which left Chalkis, May 18)." Crane in his text says: "This is Wednesday, I think." But it was Tuesday. Crane's spelling of Stylis is Stylida.

17. G. W. Steevens stuck to the principal rule that a journalist ought to believe only what his eyes saw and ought to consider the opposite point of view. In *With the Conquering Turk* he says: "People talk of the sufferings of the Armenians and the grievances of the Greeks"—this at the start of the war—"but what about the Turk? The Greek and Armenian take Government contracts and grow rich; the Turk takes his rifle and his bandolier, and grows poor." The Turks, in contrast to the Greeks, were disciplined. Pillage and violence were forbidden, and so the Turkish soldiers—simply, unquestionably, and even childishly obedient to their officers—obeyed.

18. Wells was mistaken in his notion that all Crane got out of his expeditions to Greece and Cuba was "The Open Boat"; he never read the war dispatches. Of Wells, who prided himself as journalist rather than as artist, Crane remarked: "I should say that Mr. Wells will write better and better when he sticks to character altogether and does not so much concern himself with narrative. I may be wrong but it seems to me that he has a genius for writing of underclass people more honestly than Charles Dickens."

19. Although Cora later admitted that she was without talent as a writer, she was half competing with Crane as reporter. In reference to the London newsletters he and Cora composed after the Greco–Turkish War, in October, 1897, he wrote his agent Paul Reynolds that he might go to Curtis Brown, then Sunday editor of the New York *Press* and later a literary agent in London, "and say how-how from me. Tell him this in the strictest confidence that a lady named Imogene Carter whose work he has been using from time to time is also named Stephen Crane and that I did 'em about twenty minutes on each

Sunday, just dictating to a friend." He added: "Of course they are rotten bad," but he hoped that "the nature of the articles I mean to write" will be much better. From here on Crane was in quest of the quick buck.

20. Nora Black, the *Daylight*'s woman reporter, had been a dancer and actress in the London production of *Fly by Night*. Amy Leslie—like Nora Black—was a newspaperwoman who had been a dancer and actress. Cora Taylor had quit her Jacksonville nightclub and its fly-by-night prospects to become a *Journal* reporter and "compete" with Crane. Nora Black has with her some servants and also an old lady on a very little pony. Cora's companion in Greece, although probably not an old lady, was Mrs. Charlotte Ruedy of the Hotel de Dream in Jacksonville, and Cora's servants were the Ptolemy brothers, whom the Cranes took back to England at the war's end. *Active Service* is, in sum, autobiographical in almost all of its details of persons, places and things. It is no coincidence that Nora Black is called the "tigress," which makes her lover Coleman a mouse in her tigress paws to taunt, and a mouse he is for falling for that insipid Marjory. Cora in her journal mentions Crane as "mouse." As Cora was lioness to Crane's mouse, so in the novel Nora is tigress to Coleman. Coleman is a composite of Crane himself and of Richard Harding Davis, whose sister—coincidentally—was named Nora.

Gilkes in *Cora Crane* (1960) complains that "the autobiographical elements of this novel have been widely misrepresented as well as overstressed." However, I find it just the opposite in that the autobiographical elements have never been extensively explored and identified. The novel has been read only by Crane biographers and then carelessly. Gilkes, for instance, says that Marjory's mother objects to Coleman's courtship, but it is Marjory's father who objects. Crane is remembering here how his courtship of Lily Brandon Munroe was strongly objected to by her father, a colonel. Beer misreads the novel in saying that Coleman wins his sweetheart by the mere merit of being the chance rescuer of her parents—"and through no virtue whatever." But Coleman's rescue of the Wainwrights is surely a heroic adventure, even though Coleman modestly discounts the heroism, and in abstaining from the hussy Nora he also is virtuous.

21. The legend of Crane as Channing persisted for more than a decade. It prompted Davis to write Mrs. Charles Sidmore (June 11, 1913) that although Crane had acquired an "ugly halo" of gossip, we should have had better sense than "to believe what we came to believe." "May I repeat that I had no intention of attacking Stephen Crane's memory in the story? The facts are as I have stated them." Thomas Beer thought that the illustrations for the *Derelict* "happened to resemble Crane somewhat and Mr. Davis suffered a deal of comment for which he was not responsible." But the illustrations do not resemble Crane. One must conclude with Berryman that Davis' Channing is a caricature of Crane. Author Channing, a correspondent in the Spanish-American War, is an indolent, illdressed "genius," who "ought to brace up." Like Crane, Channing is author of *Tales of the Tenderloin*, and is praised by English reviewers.

In his comedy *The Galloper* (in *Farces*, 1906) Davis possibly modeled after Cora Taylor the actress who is "an attractive, dashing-looking woman of the adventuress type" (to quote Scott C. Osborn).

## XVII

1. Crane's letters to Cora have yet to come to light. Nor has any Crane letter in Beer's *Stephen Crane* appeared on the market since 1923.

2. When Chester was a pup, Edmund Crane taught him to lie down at the command "Charge!" One of the Crane brothers, says their niece Edith, "began to quote: 'Charge, Chester, charge! On, Stanley, on!' Thereupon the dog was named Chester, and when he appears in *The Third Violet* he is called Stanley. He was a dog with a soul, and I am sure has been in heaven these many years."

3. Ophelia gives to Queen Gertrude *rue* for sorrow and *daisy* for light-hearted love: "There's a daisy. I would give you some violets, but they withered all when my father died."

4. Lily Brandon Munroe was very fond of violets and speculated in after years that Crane could have had her in mind in *The Third Violet*. "However, it was only in old age that she talked about Crane, and when teased about him she would indignantly deny any romance. Although she was so far ahead of her generation getting a divorce in the 'nineties, she still had many of the strait-laced ideas of that period and could be easily shocked." (Letter of Mrs. Frederick B. Smillie, here quoted for the first time from the Barrett Crane Collection.)

5. When applying for an Army post in World War I, Ford chose the signal squad and was examined at Cardiff in 1915 for signaling. The receiving sergeant took down his message—a line of Sappho's poetry in Latin—and wiped it off his tablet on the notion that anything in a foreign language must of necessity be obscene.

6. This version is quoted from Douglas Goldring's *The Last Pre-Raphaelite* (1948); it differs from the version Ford gives in *Mightier Than the Sword* (1938).

7. Ford characteristically hedges by adding that even if Crane had remained on Limpsfield Chart's hilltop, "perhaps his writing would have grown thinner." (In *Portraits from Life*, 1937, the same as the English edition entitled *Mightier Than the Sword*.)

The description of Ravensbrook in Ruth Franchere's *Stephen Crane* (1961) is inaccurate. Over the brook—no more than four feet in width—was a culvert, not a bridge; and the garden was not "a wild tangle of grass and weeds and vines." Gardeners in 1897 could be had cheaply, and so untidy gardens were most unusual. A huge rooks' nest, says Franchere, "hung from a great copper beech tree near the entrance." But rooks nest in colonies and in elm trees; not *hanging* from a copper beech tree—rooks build their nests *on* branches. And Adoni Ptolemy was not a "Greek boy"—he was a young man of about twenty-five. (Some of this data draws from Nicholas A. Pease's letter to R. W. S., March 6, 1962.)

8. Ford says this of Ravensbrook, but he obviously means Brede Place. Any future occupant there would need to be "a stockbroker" because its upkeep is

very costly. The present-day owner and occupant of Brede Manor is in fact a stockbroker—Roger Frewen.

9. Two letters to Cora from her brother-in-law, Sir Norman Robert Stewart, contain inferential evidence that Cora had not been successful in obtaining a divorce from Captain Stewart. (These letters of March 9 and November 17, 1901, are in CUCC.) Captain Stewart in *Who's Who* did not cite himself as having been married!

10. The so-called wedding was reported by Mark Barr in 1922 to Hamlin Garland in London, Garland recording it in his diary for "August 2–3, 1922." (Mark Barr and his wife were Crane's guests at Brede Manor in 1899.) For Garland's note I am indebted to Donald Pizer and the Huntington Library.

11. When the Cranes moved into Brede Manor in early 1899, the Mark Barrs took Adoni Ptolemy as servant for a while. Adoni next went into the business of importing tins of honey from Greece, and then finally he returned to his homeland.

12. "Fresh Bits of Gossip" belongs with the sketches Cora submitted to Curtis Brown signed "Imogene Carter." Crane proposed to Paul Reynolds to continue this Sunday series of sketches and instructed him to ask Curtis Brown "if he wants them, signed and much better in style, and how much he will give. Then if he says all right you might turn up a little syndicate for every Sunday." That is, locate a syndicate to issue them in other newspapers. "You can figure out that I should get about £10 per week out of it. Then—you do the business— I do the writing—I take 65 per cent and you take 35. The typewriting expenses in New York we share alike. You do a lot of correspondence, that's all—and keep your eyes peeled for new combinations."

## XVIII

1. Quoted here for the first time from a clipping in Crane's Scrapbook in CUCC. "Flanagan" falls grievously below the level of "The Open Boat," to which it is a companion-piece. It is a variant version of "The Open Boat" with Captain Murphy here as "Flanagan."

2. The men with gun cases were out to stalk deer in Scotland, where deer-stalking nowadays opens on August 12.

Euston Station was built in 1838 by P. C. Hardwick. It was threatened by demolition a few years ago in spite of efforts by the Society for National Monuments to preserve it. (For some of my data here I am indebted to Mr. Michael des Tombes.)

3. A sequence of five sketches appearing in the London *Westminster Gazette*, beginning on October 19, 1897. "Queenstown" is a recent discovery and is here quoted for the first time. (This note corrects *Letters,* page 148.)

4. Michael F. Morahan, a retired constable, in his "Rejoinder to Mr. Stephen Crane," pointed out that a Royal Irish constable "moves and is welcomed in a social class a step or two higher than that from which he came into the service. In the Irish villages the Constable mixes freely with the dispensary doctor, the school-master, the farmers, and the shopkeepers; and if he be a well-informed

and well-conducted man, even his reverence the priest is glad to exchange views with him on matters of social or political interest. Want of society, indeed! So far from such being the case too much company is generally the young Constable's stumbling-block. . . ."

As for girls not being allowed to speak to the Constables, "Nonsense! For whom are the girls looking out at the church on Sunday, or at the fair on Monday, but the Constable? And as he is everywhere regarded as a connoisseur in female charms, proud and very proud is the girl that wins him. . . ." (In *Westminster Gazette:* Dec. 3, 1897.)

Crane got scorched also in the New York *Sun* (Nov. 6, 1897): "Mr. Stephen Crane, we see by the *Westminster Gazette,* has discovered the Irish policeman; at least the Irish Policeman in a light that never was on land or sea. Mr. Crane's Irish Constable is a poetical, pensive, almost intangible personage who holds no discourse with plain-clothes Pat, and is unloved of Irish girls. . . . What a difference it might make in the relations of the two countries if we could have Mr. Crane with Mr. Gerald Balfour as an Irish Under-Secretary!"

5. The text in *Work* has a variant opening sentence: "The brook curved down over the rocks, innocent and white, until it faced a little strand of smooth gravel and flat stones."

6. Elbert Hubbard published these two Irish sketches in his *Philistine* in July and in August, 1899. Cora and the English publishers of *Last Words* (Digby, Long & Company) did not use the *Philistine* texts. Hubbard could not resist tampering with the spellings of words so as to make Crane's descriptions more colorful; hence Hubbard's text has it "smokt and talkt" and the old man is "melankoly." He goes "A-Wooing." Etc.

7. Silas Weir Mitchell was a famous American physician known throughout the medical world for his writings on neurology and clinical medicine, an assistant surgeon with the Union Army during the Civil War, and a novelist mainly of the Civil War.

8. Quoted here for the first time from the holograph letter (written on stationery embossed *Ravensbrook / Oxted / Surrey*) belonging to the Public Library of Mason City, Iowa. Copy kindly supplied me in 1963 by Ray Smith, Library Director.

9. He told Pinker that the *Youth's Companion* "once offered me £22 per 1000" (eleven cents per word), but that was in late 1895 when *The Red Badge* brought him his first flush of fame; he never sold anything to the *Youth's Companion.* He told Reynolds that the New York *Herald* "pays me $100 per article of between 3000 and 4000 words" (about 2½ cents per word). Mr. Crane, said Pinker, "is receiving 1 10. 10 / —per thousand words for the serial rights" of his Whilomville stories (5¼ cents per word); but *Black and White* in 1899 paid only 1⅕ cents for British serial rights to "The Clan of No Name," after *Blackwood's Magazine* had refused it. *Scribner's* refused to pay more than $300 for "The Open Boat"; and *Collier's Weekly* finally bought for $300 "The Blue Hotel," which had been declined at Paul Reynolds' asking price of $500 for the quality magazines: *Harper's Monthly, Harper's Weekly, Scribner's,* the *Atlantic,* and *Blackwood's Magazine.* Crane didn't expect to get more than

2¼ cents for "The Monster" because of its length, but he hoped *McClure's Magazine*—although McClure's paymaster was "artful"—would pay him four cents per word for "The Bride Comes to Yellow Sky." These four stories, although among Crane's very best, brought him a total of about $1225 at an average of only 2 ⁷⁄₁₀ cents per word or less. The hard facts thus contradict the legendary reputation of Crane's high rate of payment during his English years.

The standard rate for quality magazines in America was about ¾ cent per word in 1890; to unknown writers they paid about ½ cent and as high as fifteen cents to a few famous ones, said Howells in 1895, and that was "far higher prices than any others in the world." Crane's two or three cents per word was a respectable rate, but he seldom got the higher prices he asked. Howells received more than the ten cents per word he was offered (and rejected) for serial rights to all his fiction in 1890; Hamlin Garland got five cents per word for the serialization of his book-length life of Ulysses S. Grant in 1897; Rudyard Kipling, twenty-three cents per word and sometimes more. But Crane earned at most only five cents and in his best later fiction only half of that.

Some of my data in this account draws from James B. Stronks' article in *Papers of the Bibliographical Society* (Third Quarter, 1963): "Stephen Crane's English Years: The Legend Corrected." Stronks does not mention Ford's *Evening Post* article and Beer's rejoinder there on November 19, 1924. Ford, forgetting Beer's rejoinder and what he himself had said in his *Post* article (July 12, 1924), reinstated the terms of twenty pounds per thousand words in his *Return to Yesterday* (1932).

10. Beer says that Crane lagged in writing his novel *Active Service* that fall and "took up other tales and finished *The Monster* one day in early December, having spent a week of interrupted evenings on the long story, which shows every strength and every weakness of his armory." But he'd finished it in early September, at least the first draft.

The weakness of *Active Service* is instructive, as the London *Times Literary Supplement* remarked (November 25, 1960). "It fails because it tries to go beyond war, beyond the first palpable shock of battle and danger. The correspondent is covering a war, but he is also 'on active service of the heart'; it was a form of service beyond the scope of Crane's imaginative insight. His one novel wholly about a love-affair, *The Third Violet*, is his one almost total failure. . . ."

## XIX

1. Conrad in his Introduction to Beer, 1923. In *Under Western Eyes* (1911) Sophia declares to Razumov: "You have not the face of a lucky man."

2. Quoted from Conrad's "Stephen Crane: A Note Without Dates," in London *Mercury* for December, 1919, and in Conrad's *Notes on Life and Letters* (J. M. Dent & Sons, Ltd., 1921). Reprinted as the Introduction to Thomas Beer's *Stephen Crane* (1923). Jessie Conrad's "Recollections of Stephen Crane" appeared in the London *Bookman* for April, 1926. There she dates the occasion

of Conrad's first meeting with Stephen Crane as "a little more than seven weeks before our eldest boy, Borys, was born." Borys was born on January 14, 1898. However, they had met several times in October–November.

3. According to Ford, Crane with extreme vigor and intonation, his eyes flashing, said: "By God! when Stevenson wrote 'With interjected finger he *delayed* the action of the timepiece,' Stevenson put back the clock of English fiction one hundred and fifty years!" Not Crane, however, but Harold Frederic said it. Then Crane repeated it to Ford, who years later ruminated: "No, it was when Rossetti at eighteen wrote *The Blessed Damozel* that the art of writing in English received the numbing blow of a sandbag." (Ford's error was corrected by Thomas Beer in the New York *Evening Post* for July 19, 1924. This note corrects my *Crane Omnibus,* page xxxvii.)

4. A year later when Crane was on the rebound from Cuba, he and Huneker dined at the Everett House, looking out onto Union Square in New York City, and he asked Huneker whether he had read anything by Joseph Conrad, the Polish sea captain who "was writing the most wonderful things in English." That was the first time Huneker had heard Conrad's name, and later when he visited Conrad at Kent, he noticed on his desk a photograph of the late Stephen Crane.

5. Crane here refers to the Tirah campaign against the Afridis in the Northwest Province of India, begun October 18, 1897. The British forces under General Sir William Lockhart stormed the Dargai heights on October 20 and lost 199 killed and wounded. Crane wrote up the campaign, or some portion of it, and sent Paul Reynolds a thousand words for him to place in some paper. (*Letters,* page 147.) On January 14 1898: "It might go to the *Press* and be syndicated, or else to the *Journal*." (*Letters,* page 168.)

6. The closest Crane ever got to Africa was in writing about it in "The King's Favor," published in Syracuse University *Herald* in May, 1891, and in "The Great Boer Trek," posthumously in *Cosmopolitan* in June, 1900.

7. Crane wrote William (October 29, 1897): "Sometimes I think you and old Ted worry about me and you may well worry! I have managed my success like a fool and a child but then it is difficult to succeed gracefully at 23. However I am learning every day. I am slowly becoming a man. My idea is to come finally to live at Port Jervis or Hartwood. I am a wanderer now and I must see enough but—afterwards—I think of P. J. & Hartwood."

8. Conrad's style, said W. L. Courtney, "though a good deal better than Mr. Crane's [in *The Red Badge of Courage*], has the same jerky and spasmodic quality; while a spirit of faithful and minute description—even to the verge of wearisome—is common to both." The example of Crane is obvious and potent upon Conrad, who "has determined to do for the sea and the sailor what his predecessor had done for war and warriors."

9. There is no record of a translation. In 1956 Alain Bosquet translated three Crane poems with the note that this poet, "concis et rageur, est de ceux qui ont fait le plus pour dénouncer l'absurdité d'un monde matérialiste; il n'est pas

sans rappeler Corbière et LaForgue." (In *Anthologie de la Poésie Americaine des Origines à Nos Jours*.) With Francis Veilé Griffin, Davray translated *The Red Badge of Courage* under the title *La Conquête du Courage*, in 1911. Other recent translations into the French are *L'Insigne rouge du Courage*, translated by Dominique Awry (1960); *Le Canot* (*The Open Boat*); and two translations of *Maggie: fille des rues*.

10. From the holograph manuscript in the Berg Collection, New York Public Library. Cf. *A Personal Record* (1912), but also "A Note Without Dates" (1919) in *Notes on Life and Letters* (1921). In the latter book Conrad contradicted what he said in the former.

11. Ford in "Techniques," *Southern Review* (July, 1935).

12. *Ibn* signifies an Algerian titled hero.

13. From the photocopy of the original supplied me by Charles Feinberg. It is obvious from the typescript of Crane's letter (dated March 2, 1899) that he was then learning the keys of his newly acquired typewriter—that "machine," as he called it. "Since we have had this machine I have lost some of my habits of being an ill correspondent."

14. "No other story in our literature," says Leslie Fiedler, "defines so clearly the opposition between the demands of male loyalty and the claims of polite female society; and in none is the Negro more brutally portrayed at the limits of mindlessness and nauseating horror." In *Love and Death in the American Novel* (1960).

15. "I call this an outrage on art and humanity; and the splendid descriptive ability of the author, his vividness and veracity, only render it more flagrant. Something is fundamentally out of gear in a mind that can reconcile itself to such a performance. . . . Of constructive ability he shows not a vestige. His outfit for literary purposes consists of a microscopic eye and a keen sense of the queer, the bizarre, the morbid. His minute analysis produces nothing. He is anything but an artist." Julian Hawthorne—Nathaniel Hawthorne's son—reviewed *The Monster and Other Stories* (1899) in *Book News* for February, 1900. His review first appeared in the Philadelphia *North American*.

16. Ralph Ellison in his Introduction to his Crane collection (Dell editions: 1960). Ellison does not mention the racist story "Vashti in the Dark." *Harper's* rejected this story, and Crane burned it "in one of his rare fits of pique" after Acton Davies had typed the revised manuscript for him when he was in Cuba (1898).

## XX

1. Ford never dates the events he writes about and is ambiguous even when attempting to be precise, as when he says that he "entered the world two years and forty-five days after" Stephen Crane. Ford was born December 17, 1873, and Crane on November 1, 1871.

2. Berryman says that Conrad and Crane wrote "The Blood of the Martyr," but the play of their intended collaboration was "The Predecessor."

3. Here a hole is torn in Conrad's letter. He called Cora Mrs. Crane, and Jessie in her reminiscences speaks of "Stephen Crane's wife Cora." If Joseph guessed the truth, Jessie didn't.

Conrad's inscription is not signed, but it is in his handwriting. On the back of the flyleaf torn from an unidentified book, probably *The Nigger of the "Narcissus"* Cora later wrote an account of "Joseph Conrad. Both these names are Christian names. . . .He is a Pole of noble family. His father died in Siberia and he was there when an infant with his mother. Their estates were confiscated. He was educated in France and speaks and acts like a Frenchman. Went to sea when seventeen and has had the most wonderful adventures, particularly in the South Sea Islands. He is a master in Merchant Service. In 1898 he lived at Ivy Wall's Farm, Stanford-Hope, Essex. His son Borys was born there on January 15, 1898. 1899 he moved to Pent Farm near Hythe, Kent." (Actually, the Conrads moved to Pent Farm in October, 1898. Borys was born on January 14, 1898).

4. *The Red Badge of Courage*, which Frederic reviewed in the New York *Times* for January 26, 1896.

5. In his Introduction to Beer's *Stephen Crane,* Conrad misdates this letter for 1899.

6. The sinking of the *Maine* in Havana harbor on February 15 was the talk now in London clubs. The battleship had arrived at Havana on January 25 on presumably a friendly visit, and the Spanish officials seemed cordial enough; but now the ship had sunk and American newspapers were whipping up war fever.

7. This letter—in Beer undated—Crane wrote on Sunday, March 20, 1898. The quoted passage is obviously from the same letter.

8. Berryman is in error in claiming that Crane wrote "The Blood of the Martyr" while on board the ship taking him to Manhattan (en route to Cuba): "The Play perhaps occupied him on shipboard, for he gave it to Curtis Brown in New York for the *Press,* where it appeared on April 3rd, and it must have been very shortly indeed after their evening together that Crane was racing madly over London, white-faced with excitement, with Conrad, trying to raise sixty pounds to get immediately to war." However, Crane and Conrad were in London some days after April 11 trying to raise money to get Crane to Manhattan, and since the *Press* had already published "The Blood of the Martyr" on April 3, Crane must have written it long before he quit England. He could not possibly have handed it over to Curtis Brown, but very likely Brown showed him the *Press* clipping of it when Crane reached Manhattan (April 21–22).

9. One surmises that Crane had tuberculosis even before the *Commodore* shipwreck and that his exhausting experience in the dinghy "caused the infection to spread to his intestines." He told his family in early 1897 that his "equatorial zone" caused him considerable unrest. It is possible that he then paid a first visit to Dr. Edward Livingstone Trudeau, a specialist, at Saranac. (See note 5, Chapter XXIV.)

# XXI

1. It was a rather dull sketch: "The Little Stilettos of the Modern Navy which Stab in the Dark," published in the *Journal*, April 24.

2. He gave his occupation as journalist, his address the *World* bureau, and his permanent address as Hartwood, N. Y. Crane's passport—dated "23 *day of* April *18* 98"—reads:

*Age: 26 years.*      *Mouth:* with moustache
*Stature: 5 feet 8 inches, Eng.*      *Chin:* round
*Forehead:* high      *Hair:* brown
*Eyes:* grey blue      *Complexion:* medium
*Nose:* straight      *Face:* oval

Other passports have his *eyes* grey, *nose* aquiline, *mouth* moustache *tawny*, *hair* light, *complexion* clean, *stature* 5 feet 8½ inches (January 15, 1897). On his last passport of May 19, 1900, when he was near death, his complexion was dark, his eyes light blue, and his mouth had no moustache. His age was mistakenly given as 29.

3. Hare, born in London, was forty-two in 1898, when Crane was twenty-six. He became one of the great war photographers of his day. During World War I he was a pioneer in aerial photography.

4. Whereas Crane was independent of the chief of correspondents and the censor at Key West, "smaller men," as Frank Norris puts it, had to submit their dispatches first to the chief and then to the censor, whose job it was to cut the big news, such as the movement of the fleet. But on this occasion one reporter tricked the censor by wiring his paper: "*Newspaper* fleet have gone to Porto Rico." A few hours later, when the censor—swamped by other dispatches—had forgotten this one, the reporter wired: "Omit first word of my last dispatch," thus revealing Cervera Sampson's whereabouts.

5. Crane to Robert Barr on May 23 from Key West. Jack Oakhurst, a character right out of Bret Harte, becomes the gambler Tom Larpent in "Moonlight on the Snow," a companion Western story to "The Blue Hotel."

Crane in this same letter to Barr adds: "Now I owe Harold [Frederic] an apology for laughing when he said they would tear me in pieces the minute my back was turned. Hi, Harold! I apologize! Did you know me for a morphine eater? A man who had known me for ten years tells me that all my books are written while I am drenched with morphine. The joke is on me."

6. The *World* in early June poked fun at Dandy Dick Davis: he "has had his portrait published as a war correspondent attired in a Norfolk jacket with twenty-four pockets, golf trousers, cavalry boots, hat and gauntlets, a field glass, a notebook, a revolver, a cartridge belt, and a practicable flask. In fact, no war correspondent on the stage has ever surpassed the equipment of Mr. Davis when facing the camera, and we naturally accept the judgment of a war correspondent whose costume is so correct."

7. E. W. McCready to B. J. R. Stolper (January 12, 1934), quoted here for the first time. Stolper kindly sent me the McCready letters a decade ago. A por-

tion of them was first quoted in *Stephen Crane: Letters* (1960). The three McCready letters are dated January 12, 22 and 31, 1934.

8. Gregory Mason in *Remember the Maine* (1939). Remington had been sent to Cuba in 1897 to draw sketches of rumored Spaniard cruelties. He became bored with it all and telegraphed William Randolph Hearst, impresario of the Cuban drama: "Everything is quiet. There is no trouble here. There will be no war. I wish to return." Hearst, so legend has it, cabled Remington: "Please remain. You furnish the pictures and I'll furnish the war." Hearst was as good as his word.

9. Only the Chicago *Record's* veteran reporter Henry Chamberlin witnessed aboard the *Hercules* the destruction of Cervera's fleet at Santiago de Cuba.

10. Whigham, then thirty-four years old, was a colorful and unique man. A native of Scotland, a graduate of Queen's College, Oxford (1893), he became drama critic of the Chicago *Tribune* and had been a prisoner of the Spaniards in Cuba (in 1897?).

11. Written after Crane returned to England and published in Lady Randolph Churchill's *Anglo-Saxon Review* in December, 1899.

12. The Army has no official burial service, and chaplains may use any variation. The original for Timothy Lean was a Marine, and, according to *Naval Customs and Traditions*, the Episcopal Prayer Book burial service is the one most commonly used for burials at sea: "Unto Almighty God we commend the soul of our *brother* departed, and we commit *his* body to the deep; in sure and certain hope of the Resurrection unto eternal life, through our Lord Jesus Christ; at whose coming in glorious majesty to judge the world, the sea which gives up her dead, and the corruptible bodies of those who sleep in him shall be changed, and made alike unto his glorious body; according to the mighty working whereby he is to subdue all things unto himself."

13. Timothy Lean of "The Upturned Face" reappears in other sketches about the Kicking Twelfth Regiment in the imaginary Spitzbergen Army's skirmishes against the Rostina Army: "Kim Up, The Kickers!" and in "The Shrapnel of Their Friends." Also in an unpublished Spitzbergen sketch, "The Fire Tribe." This last one concludes the action of the sequence. Here the war is over, Spitzbergen is victorious over Rostina, and Captain Lean is sent to pacify a native tribe from whom the Rostinians had exacted a tribute. Kipling's influence shows up here, although Crane had claimed to have abandoned Kipling half a dozen years earlier. The names "Rostina" and "Spitzbergen" derive from Norwegian islands in the Arctic Ocean east of Greenland and 400 miles northwest of Norway.

14. Lieutenant Colonel Cochrane in May, 1899, sent Crane the kind regards of Colonel Huntington (commander of the *Panther*), Captain G. F. Elliott, and another officer named Harrington. "We all have a welcome for you." (Letter in CUCC.) Captain Elliott, the commanding officer of the Marine detachment at Guantánamo, officially commended Crane to the Secretary of the the Navy. Colonel Huntington told the story of this engagement against the Spaniards on June 11 in *Commandant: Annual Reports to the Navy Department* (1898): Huntington to Commandant: June 17, 1898.

15. From the McCready to Stolper letters, here quoted for the first time, in CUCC and in my files by gift of Mr. Stolper.

16. John Dunn to Cora: October 10, 1900. Letter in CUCC.

17. This dispatch—"In the First Land Fight 4 of Our Men Are Killed"— appeared in the *World* for June 13. A recent discovery, it is quoted here for the first time. McCready probably considered it a co-authored dispatch in that he wrote it and Crane dictated it; hence it appeared unsigned. The *World*'s byline reads: "Special Cable Dispatch to the *World*," whereas the usual *World* byline for Crane reads: "Special from a Staff Correspondent." All other known Crane dispatches in the New York *World* bear his name.

18. Paine retells the story of the steam-boiler incident in his *Roads of Adventure* (1922). Paine dedicated his book "To / Ernest W. McCready / My Old Comrade Afloat and Ashore / and to the Memory of / Stephen Crane."

19. Crane says that their firing interrupted "in some degree the services over the graves of Gibbs and some others," but by Crane's own statement elsewhere the death of Surgeon Gibbs occurred on the third night (June 9) after the Marines landed at Guantánamo on June 7. Accuracy is frequently missing in "War Memories" because Crane wrote that account in 1899.

## XXII

1. Addressed from Washington, D. C. (December 30, 1899) to "My dear Crane"—letter in CUCC. McCawley was Captain in the Marine Corps during the Cuban campaign.

Crane reported on the Cuzco expedition in "The Red Badge of Courage Was His Wig-wag Flag," in "Marines Signalling under Fire," and in "War Memories." Also in some of his Cuban War tales, such as "The Sergeant's Private Madhouse."

2. "First American Newspaper to Open Headquarters on Cuban Soil Is the *World*." Datelined: Mole St. Nicholas, Haiti, June 19.

3. In this passage of two sentences I have paraphrased one of Crane's *World* dispatches, but elsewhere the text is from "War Memories" (1899). Exceptions are noted.

Scovel's list of ships (in the *World* for June 19) did not include the *Pluton* and the *Furor* and differs from Crane's list by adding "the old *Reina Mercedes*." Behind them in "the green-fringed harbor" lay also some torpedo boat destroyers and some smaller craft.

4. The above reports by Munson and on Kilbourne derive from Kennan's *Outlook* articles. Daiquirí was frequently misspelled in the newspapers as Baiquirí or Baquirí.

5. So C. K. Linson reports it in *My Stephen Crane* (1958). Linson does not give his brother's name, and he misspells the name of the ship *Vigiliancia*. On that same ship Crane sailed from Havana on November 17 for Manhattan.

6. T. R. Roosevelt in *The Rough Riders* (1899). What follows is from Crane's "God Rest Ye."

7. Davis in the *Herald:* June 26, 1898: "How Hamilton Fish and Allyn Capron Died, Fighting Bravely." Allyn Capron was the son of Captain Allyn Capron, hero at El Caney.

8. Davis in *Adventures and Letters of Richard Harding Davis* (1918). Davis, himself a socialite, claimed that socialite Hamilton Fish was the first soldier of the war to be killed in battle, but this ignores the fact that six Marines had been killed in the opening days of the first engagement with the enemy at Guantánamo, an important engagement which Davis missed out on. The press exploited the wartime exploits of socialites and Rough Riders and tended to ignore as not equally newsworthy the heroism of the common soldier. Crane redressed this injustice by eulogizing the common soldier in several Cuban War dispatches and tales.

9. Filed at Siboney on June 24 but not published until July 7. Crane retells the story about Marshall in "God Rest Ye" and in "War Memories." Marshall tells the same story in "Stories of Stephen Crane," *Literary Life* (December, 1900) and in his *Story of the Rough Riders* (1899).

10. When Roosevelt was President his secretary, Cortelyou, handed him a copy of Crane's *Wounds in the Rain* (1900) in the presence of James Hare. " 'You knew this fellow Crane rather well, didn't you, Jimmy?' 'Yes, sir, very well indeed.' Again the Roosevelt teeth clicked decisively. 'I remember him distinctly myself. When I was Police Commissioner of New York I once got him out of serious trouble. "Oh, yes,' said Jimmy slowly. 'I recall the occasion. It was while he was collecting data for his book, *Maggie: A Girl of the Streets.*'

" 'Nonsense!' retorted Roosevelt vigorously, careless that Jimmy had come to his feet with a face anything but pale as paper. 'He wasn't gathering any data! He was a man of bad character and he was simply consorting with loose women.' Bristling at every whisker, a hundred pounds of human dynamite exploded. 'That is absolutely not so!' flared a man who defended his friends. 'Nothing could be farther from the truth!' Roosevelt stared, and Cortelyou gasped. Admittedly, it was no way to talk to the President of the United States, even if the incumbent himself happened to be a two-fisted wielder of words. Jimmy knew instantly he had been guilty of a lapse in good taste; he forced down his choler and spoke more calmly. 'I'm sorry,' he said, a trifle too shortly to be convincing. 'You see, I happen to know the story behind that incident. My friend, Crane, was merely taking the part of an unfortunate young woman who was being hounded by the police; that was the whole reason for his getting into a scrape with the law.'

"Roosevelt was still staring, but a fiery gleam that had lighted his eyes now died away. He nodded understandingly. 'All right, Jimmy,' he said. 'Have it your own way.' " (In Cecil Carnes' *Jimmy Hare,* 1940, pages 128–129.)

11. The socialite's military salary was of course more than Nolan's. A private's pay in the Army was $13 per month; a sergeant's pay ranged from $18 to

$23; for sergeant major, $36 to $41. Officer pay ranged from $1,400 a year for second lieutenants to $7,500 for major generals.

12. Crane wrote a sketch of a military martinet, an unpublished manuscript; he was one himself, a martinet on the drill-field at Claverack College.

13. Among the correspondents were Richard Harding Davis, photographer Burr McIntosh, Casper Whitney of *Harper's Weekly* and his friend John Fox, Jr., future author of two best sellers: *The Litle Shepherd of Kingdom Come* (1903) and *The Trail of the Lonesome Pine* (1908). Crane no doubt had heard of him, for he was a writer of sketches and short stories: *A Cumberland Vendetta* (1895) and *Hell fer Sartain* (1897). John Fox of *Harper's Weekly* said that Las Guásimas (variously spelled La Guásima, Las Guásina, and Las Guásinas) was named thus after the guásima trees which grew there—trees with low, widespreading boughs bearing a nut used to feed hogs.

## XXIII

1. Don Carlos Seitz, business manager of Pulitzer's *World*, damaged Crane's reputation as journalist in 1924 (in his *Joseph Pulitzer*) and again in his 1933 *Bookman* article on Crane, where he deliberately repeated the same misinformation. Journalist Crane has been impugned for four decades because historians such as Walter Millis and W. A. Swanberg lifted from Seitz, without checking the facts. Even a Crane scholar, Thomas Gullason, fell into the same trap. In *The Martial Spirit* (1931) Millis said that Pulitzer had very bad luck in hiring Crane because the only dispatch he sent Pulitzer's *World* "incautiously told the truth about the conduct of the Seventy-first New York at San Juan. It 'imperiled the paper.'" Swanberg in *Citizen Hearst* (1961) copied Millis' errors, including the one about Crane sending only one dispatch to the *World*, whereas Crane sent more than a dozen and a half dispatches to the *World*.

Margaret Leech in *In the Days of McKinley* (1959) says that New Yorkers "were especially touchy about their gallant Seventy-first, whose prowess the newspapers had glorified without regard to the facts. The *World*, in an inadvertent moment, had printed a truthful account of the panic in this regiment under fire, as described by a young correspondent named Stephen Crane, who was known as the author of a cynical novel about the Civil War." Also in error is Gregory Mason in *Remember the Maine* (1939). Ed Marshall had set the record straight in 1899 in his *Story of the Rough Riders*.

See also Ames W. Williams' "Stephen Crane: War Correspondent," in *New Colophon*, April, 1948.

2. When Roosevelt was Governor of New York he dismissed Major Clinton Smith from the service of the National Guard for his failure in taking command of the 71st Regiment at the battle of San Juan Hill to lead it into the fight when Colonel Downes, its commander, had failed to do so. Captain Malcolm Rafferty of Company F in the 71st declared, at a banquet held in his honor three weeks after Governor Roosevelt sacked Major Smith, that he refused to support entreaties to save Smith and that were he Colonel of the 71st Regiment "I would try to have two-thirds of its officers dismissed."

3. First published in *Harper's New Monthly Magazine* for May, 1899. Following that quoted passage is a note from Fairfax Downey's *Richard Harding Davis: His Day* (1933).

4. Margaret Leech, *In the Days of McKinley.*

5. Kennett F. Harris, in *The Chicago Record's War Stories* (1898).

6. Added in the text of *Wounds in the Rain* (1900): "He laid his face to his rifle as if it were his mistress." Not in text of *Cosmopolitan:* December, 1898.

7. Because of the scarcity of coffee beans the lieutenant doles them out with great care. On the trail beyond Siboney on June 23 the exhausted troops had discarded their packages of coffee, says Kennett Harris in *The Chicago Record's War Stories*. Cautioned that they would need their coffee, one of the men filled his pockets with coffee beans just before the command "March" was given.

8. Cecil Carnes in *Jimmy Hare* errs in saying that the camp was at Sevilla and that they camped in Davis' tent, enjoying a hardy meal from his well-stocked larder. Carnes failed to collate Hare's story with the accounts by Crane and Davis.

9. Davis in his *Notes of a War Correspondent.*

10. So-called because of an order issued by Captain General Valeriano Weyler on October 2, 1896, the results of which brought untold horror and suffering upon the Cubans. Briefly, the order required "all the inhabitants [noncombatants] of the country or outside the line of fortifications of the towns" within a period of eight days to "reconcentrate themselves in the town occupied by the troops. Any individual who after the expiration of this period is found in the uninhabited parts will be considered a rebel and tried as such." In Elbert J. Benton's *International Law and Diplomacy of The Spanish-American War* (1908), page 27.

11. Howard Chandler Christy's drawing of this scene appears under the caption "An Awful Tragedy of the Spanish War" in Frank Freidel's *The Splendid Little War* (1958). He quotes war correspondent James Archibald's eye-witness account. In an old house Archibald came upon the tragic scene of a beautiful young girl, dressed in a loose gown, with a knife sticking from an ugly wound in her breast, "while her blood had formed a black pool on the tiled floor. A few feet away a Spanish officer sat with his head on the table, drunk. Through the barred window one could see the little old church [at El Caney], and at the opposite side the open door led into a beautiful court-yard. No amount of shaking could arouse the man, and he slept on, heedless of the evidence of a horrible crime. I had him carried away and never saw him again. I pulled the knife from the body and drew a sheet over it, and wondered if there was no limit to the horror of war."

12. Beer is mistaken in saying that Crane did not have a fever and was simply exhausted and improperly fed and suffered from intestinal consumption. He had malaria. As George Kennen wrote in *Outlook* (August, 1898): It comes suddenly with a chill and a violent headache, the temperature rising to 105;

if the attack is not severe, it subsides in a few days—yielding to treatments of sulphate of magnesia at the outset and then quinine with calomel or sulphur. "The patient is not allowed to take any nourishment while the fever lasts, and if he keeps quiet, avoids sudden changes of temperature and does not fret, he generally recovers in a week or ten days. He suffers from languor and prostration, however, for a fortnight or more, and if he overeats, moves about in the sunshine or exposes himself to the night air, he is liable to have another chill with a relapse, in which the fever is higher and more obstinate, perhaps, than at first."

13. However, not all the Spanish batteries employed smokeless powder. Crane never got to Santiago and probably did not know that the arsenal there consisted mainly of antiquated brass cannon for which there were no shells proper for its bore (vintage "Marquis de Austrian, 1733"), and so the Spaniards at Santiago fired misfit shells which curved too high and came so slowly that the eye could trace them en route. And yet those relic cannons held in check Admiral Sampson's fleet. His flagship *New York* expended in ammunition 2 million dollars with no results other than damaging the lighthouse and dismounting one gun, says Howbert Billman of the Chicago *Record*.

14. In "Adventure Filled Life of Richard Harding Davis," New York *Post:* April 15, 1916—published shortly after Davis' death.

## XXIV

1. Berryman is in error in claiming that Crane's last dispatch from Siboney was on August 9 and that Crane sailed from Daiquirí. In Berryman's *Stephen Crane* the Cuban War occurs in twenty pages; Beer has it in eight pages. Beer, who never read Crane's war dispatches, claims that Crane could not report.

2. *Tribune* for July 14, 1898, does not mention Crane, but says there were nine newspapermen aboard the transport, a major and five members of the Rough Riders, and a large contingent of wounded 71st New York Infantry; all in all, twenty officers and two hundred noncommissioned officers and privates.

3. General Chaffee bore the brunt of the fighting at El Caney and for that action he was appointed Major General on July 8. He had early won military immortality on the Western plains in a skirmish with the Sioux when he shouted to his Indian-fighting troops: "Forward! If any man gets killed I'll make him a corporal!"

4. As already indicated (see Chapter XXIII, footnote 1), Seitz was responsible for initiating the false charges damaging Crane's reputation as journalist. Beer's prejudice in this respect can be attributed to Seitz. What saved Berryman was Ames Williams' *Colophon* article (April 1948): "Stephen Crane: War Correspondent."

5. Crane visited Dr. Trudeau at Saranac sometime between his arrival on July 13 at Old Point Comfort on the transport bringing back the wounded from Cuba, and his trip to Puerto Rico in August to cover the campaign there. Cora learned of his visit to that sanitarium and wrote Dr. Trudeau to find out the

truth. Dr. Trudeau replied (September 16, 1898): "Your husband had a slight evidence of activity in the trouble in his lungs when he came back here this summer, but it was not serious and he has improved steadily, I understand, since he came."

6. An Introduction to *The Work of Stephen Crane,* Vol. XII (1927). Charles Michelson writes on Crane also in his *Ghost Talks* (1944).

7. First published in the collection *In Many Wars,* edited by George Lynch and Frederick Palmer (Tokyo, 1904), a book difficult to come by. Davis' sketch is here collated with his earlier version in *Harper's New Monthly Magazine:* "Our War Correspondents in Cuba and Puerto Rico"—May 1899. I have quoted sometimes the *Harper* version, but mainly the later book recast. Here Davis says erroneously that "Charlie Michaelsom" was manager of Crane's paper, the "New York *World.*" But it was the *Journal,* not the *World,* and the business manager spelled his name Michelson. Here he says "Crane crept forward," whereas in *Harper's Magazine* he says Crane "rode into Juana Díaz." In the book version Davis spells it Días.

8. From *Norton's Complete Hand-Book of Havana and Cuba* (1900), page 138. The Hotel Pasaje was built in 1871.

9. From *Annual Reports of the War Department, 1899.*

10. In *Paul Revere Reynolds* by Frederick Lewis Allen (1944).

11. Cora's letter to John Hay, first reproduced in the *Stephen Crane News-letter* (No. 3, Spring 1967), is in the John Hay papers at Brown University Library.

Cora's cable to the Secretary of War: "Mrs. Stephen Crane desires information concerning the whereabouts of her husband, Stephen Crane, who entered Havana September 1st as a tobacco buyer. Missing since Sept. 6th or 8th."

Cora's letter to the Secretary of War:
"Dear Sir: If there is any way in which you can communicate the fact of Stephen Crane's disappearance to the U. S. authorities at Havana will you do so! He entered Havana about September 1st as a tobacco buyer. Stopped quietly at Hotel Pasaje and was watched by the police and was missing about Sep. 6th to 8th. If you receive any information about him I beg you will send it to me as I am very much alarmed as to his safety." In *Letters,* p. 187.

12. Crane, as we see by what follows the above account, had been living in Mary Horan's lodging house for some time prior to the dateline of this Havana dispatch to the Florida *Times-Union,* which is datelined Havana, September 7, via Key West and Miami (September 9). Crane entered Havana not ten days before but three weeks before as indicated by the substance of his first cabled *Journal* sketch of August 25: "Havana's Hate Dying."

13. Conrad in 1908 wrote Cora: "I can not sufficiently thank you for the memento of poor Stephen. I had for him a very deep affection; hardly a day passes without my thoughts turning to that genius so soon lost to the world. I am deeply grateful for this proof of your continued friendship for us both."

14. The letters of David S. Meldrum, William Blackwood, and Joseph Conrad quoted above are drawn from *Joseph Conrad: Letters to William Blackwood,* edited by William Blackburn (1958).

## XXV

1. "How They Leave Cuba," *Journal,* October 6, 1898.

2. "Stephen Crane On Havana," *Journal,* October 28, 1898.

3. Beer to Edith Crane (October 30, 1922), in Knopf files.

4. In CUCC.

5. This poem—*Intrigue* VI—was published in the *Syracusan* in 1917 by Crane's friend M. Ellwood Smith, under the heading "Stephen Crane, Ex '94." Smith had been a freshman with Crane at Syracuse University in the spring of 1891.

6. In *The War Dispatches of Stephen Crane* (1964).

7. In CUCC the typescript is numbered X. For *Intrigue* II the typescript is numbered VII.

8. Obituary in the New York *Times:* October 23, 1898. Unsigned (by Robert Barr).

9. Hall Caine was then in America lecturing to society ladies assembled in the Golden Room of the Astor Gallery at the Waldorf-Astoria, and the New York *Journal* drama critic (Alan Dale) ripped him to shreds in "Mr. Caine at the Waldorf." On the dark, drab and spirit-crushing morning of November 10, in an atmosphere of damp ladies, the melancholy voice of rain-soaked author Caine "sprouted and flourished. It was a soft, gentle voice, like unto that of a minister who is about to plead a great and merciful cause, and then ask for a collection. He alluded to the weather and asserted with tearful jocularity that it was thoroughly English and must have been turned on for his benefit." His lecture about his next novel—*Home, Sweet Home*—was introduced by an Edinburgh Scotsman (Major Pond), who pronounced Caine's lachrymose lecture equal to "the best acting to be seen on the stage." In the New York *Journal,* November 11, 1898: "Mr. Caine at the Waldorf."

10. In CUCC.

11. From the original in CUCC, a portion of which is not reproduced in *Letters.*

12. The American Peace Commissioners met the Spanish Peace Commissioners in Paris on September 29 and demanded on October 31 the complete cession of the Philippines. The Spaniards rejected this demand, while admitting they were powerless to oppose it. On November 28 they declared they were constrained by force to cede the Philippines and Sulu Archipelago in exchange for the indemnity of twenty million dollars, which the American Commissioners had offered the Spanish Government on November 21. As for Cuba, they had argued over the meaning of evacuation, whether in the sense of military or both civil and military evacuation, and over the property rights of

Spain in Cuba. The date for the evacuation was set for January 1, 1899, but the last of the Spanish troops did not quit Cuba until February. In E. J. Benton's *International Law and Diplomacy of the Spanish-American War* (1908), page 233.

13. Henry White, who had been Secretary of the Legation under Robert Todd Lincoln and Envoy Extraordinary and Minister Plenipotentiary to Great Britain, 1889–1893.

Fitzhugh Lee of Confederate cavalry fame in the Civil War served as United States Consul to Havana, 1896–1898. He took over command of the 7th Army Corps in May, 1898; later he was named Military Governor of Havana (1899).

14. Next, they visited with General Menocal, a young man of thirty-two and a graduate of Cornell University in civil engineering (1888). Menocal was Calixto García's chief of staff and had much to do with General García's success in the eastern end of Cuba. "He will be one of the men who will comprehend the American point of view. He will know how honestly we mean in this affair." (In 1913–1921 Menocal was President of Cuba, succeeding Gómez.)

15. Beer is mistaken that Crane reached decision suddenly after Christmas to return to England, and he silently corrects himself in his March 1934 *American Mercury* article: "Mrs. Stephen Crane."

16. "The American fleet came redly on like a bunch of waving bandana handkerchiefs. The air was full of prunes as a plum pudding. . . . The Spanish met the onslaught with a mauve determination. . . . The two fleets hurtled in a magenta hurtle. They feinted and thrust with a deep canary-yellow vigor. The battle looked like two overturned garbage-cans on a hot night. The shells whistled seal-brownly. The death screams of the Spaniards were full of purplish pink despair. One Spaniard with a cerise voice like the aftermath of an aurora borealis screamed paintily his desire to kill the Americanos. Then with a blackish white tremor, strong battleships sank greenly chromely black into the water. A gauntly greenish smell tore the air. The whole thing looked like a German pouring dark wine into a dingy funnel. Admiral Dewey had won." Four parodies of Crane, including Huneker's and one by Frank Norris, are reprinted in *The War Dispatches of Stephen Crane* (1964). On Huneker I have drawn on Arnold T. Schwab's letters to R. W. S. (1953, 1956) and on his *James Gibbons Huneker* (1963).

On Parodies of Crane, see Appendix 8.

17. Beer says: "In October he got to New York after a stay in Washington," but Crane did not reach Manhattan until November 21.

## XXVI

1. Americans reading the *Literary Digest* for January 21, 1899, learned of Edward Garnett's praise of their young countryman. Garnett's judgment on Crane in his *Friday Nights* (1922) was echoed soon after by Rebecca West, who wrote that Crane "at his best was superior to Rudyard Kipling at his best."

2. Ames Williams in Syracuse *Courier* (December, 1962).

3. In Clare Sheridan's *My Crowded Sanctuary* (London, 1945). No mention of Emma, the Lady of Fecamp, occurs in books about the Norman Conquest.

4. John became a clerk in holy orders and in 1509 Canon of Windsor. Another brother, Adam Oxenbridge, was one of the Barons for Rye who bore the canopy at the coronation of Richard III in 1483. Sir Goddard, Knight and Justice of the Peace, attended the Lord Legate Cardinal Wolsey at Canterbury on May 24, 1522, and also was in the Cardinal's retinue at the landing of the Emperor Charles V at Dover two days later. The Oxenbridges had possessed the estate of Brede Place since the reign of Richard II, retaining it for 225 years. In 1708 Sir Edward Frewen purchased a portion of its 700 acres, but as he lived in nearby Northiam and had no need of the Brede Place manor, he rented it to farmers and later to laborers, and so the house became infested with bats and rats and owls. Throughout the eighteenth and nineteenth centuries the place was reported to be haunted because strange noises were heard there; hence the legendary ghosts of Brede Manor. Although Sir Goddard was deeply religious, a just administer of the law and a champion in fighting for the rights of the oppressed, legend prevailed for several centuries that Sir Goddard Oxenbridge had been a giant or ogre who loved no dish so well as a succulent infant. "No doubt it was smugglers who kept alive the old legend of the giant—Sir Goddard Oxenbridge—and his cannibal feasts, culminating in his tragic ending by being sawn asunder by a wooden saw near Groaning Bridge." Edmund Austen, *Brede: the Story of a Sussex Parish* (1947). My data on Brede Place draws also from the articles in the *Sussex County Magazine* (mainly for October 1929 and July 1931), from my visit to the manorhouse in 1954 and subsequent correspondence with its present-day owner Mr. Roger Frewen, who gave me copies of the *Sussex County Magazine*, Clare Sheridan's *My Crowded Sanctuary*, and Hugh Frewen's *Imogene* (1944). Moreton Frewen's wife was one of the three beautiful Jerome daughters; her sister was Lady Randolph Churchill, mother of Winston.

5. In 1897 H. G. Wigand in Leipzig, Germany, published *Maggie: A Girl of the Streets*, translated into the German by Dora Landé.

6. Letters of Mr. Michael Pease to R. W. S. (June 3 and 15; August 25, 1962).

7. Reported in the *Saturday Evening Post* (July 28, 1900): "The Ghosts of Brede Place."

8. In Brede church is the crib of the great Jonathan Swift, albeit no mention of it is made in any of the histories of Brede. Perhaps the legend of Sir Goddard as an ogre relishing a succulent infant became embellished by Swift's *Modest Proposal* that Irish mothers breed infants succulent enough to sell on the English market.

   The Brede parish church—in its south arcade of the nave—dates back to 1180. In nearby Northiam are the ruins of Bodiam Castle, complete with a moat and swans in the moat. An inn there dates back to Queen Elizabeth's time, and legend has it that she once rested under the still-remaining huge oak which fronts the old inn.

9. A sketch, as distinguished from a story, is simply a report of an incident or an adventure. Most newspaper dispatches are sketches, and so are many of

Crane's so-called Cuban War tales. Sketches like "The Revenge of the *Adolphus*" lack the ingredient of thematic import by which such a short story as "The Price of the Harness" transcends mere reporting. "The Revenge" is a series of vignettes, a descriptive account of what happened.

10. The letters to Collis were given to me years ago by Vincent Starrett. The last one is handwritten; the others are typed. All three are on the familiar embossed notepaper.

11. This letter of December 14, 1900, continues: "You spoke of its having been offered to McClure, the *Journal* and Tillotson. Has it been offered elsewhere? I spoke of it to *Pearson's Magazine* and found it had been offered there; so apparently Pinker or his agent has offered it widely. I would like to know so as not to make a fool of myself offering it to people who have already seen it."

12. If *Active Service* "is published serially," said Pinker, "Methuen's novel will have to come out first." Methuen had advanced Crane £ 100 on the American Revolution novel which he abandoned. Through Phillips-McClure *Active Service* was serialized in America; Heinemann published the novel in November. For serial use of "The Monster" in *Harper's Magazine* (August, 1898) Harper's had paid Crane via Reynolds $450, which he frittered away somehow during the Cuban War, and on March 8 Harper's advanced Crane $250 at 15 percent royalty on *The Monster and Other Stories* ("The Blue Hotel" and "His New Mittens"), Reynolds signing the contract for "Stephen Crane, a citizen of the U. S. temporarily residing in England." On May 3, Harper's told Reynolds that they had purchased serial rights for four Whilomville stories (9600 words) for $481.75. They desired to make a book of them but needed a dozen more stories to total 40,000 words by November, 1899. If Crane agreed on their terms for a book of Whilomville stories they would advance him $250 against royalty of 15 percent retail. If Crane failed to supply the stories, Harper's would have the right to include in *The Monster and Other Stories* the four Whilomville stories already contracted for: "Making an Orator," "The Lover and the Telltale," "Lynx Hunting," and "The Angel Child." Reynolds, replying for Crane, accepted the terms and urged haste in the letter accompanying a check for $250. The above data draws from Contract Books in the Pierpont Morgan Library, quoted here for the first time. (For these items I am indebted to Louis Zara.)

13. Crane had boasted in the same vein to Pinker in late February that Harper & Bros. would pay Pinker's account $50 per thousand words or something over forty pounds for another Whilomville story he had sent him. He asked Pinker to send him £ 30 "by next post. I need it badly. If you can stick to your end, all will go finely and I would bombard you so hard with ms that you will think you are living in Paris during the seige."

14. These new Crane letters are reprinted here from Anita Leslie's *Mr. Frewen of England* (1966), by permission of Miss Leslie.

15. "Hengist" is old German for a male horse, and "Horsa" figures in the Anglo-Saxon Chronicle. These horsey names reappear in Scott Fitzgerald's *Tender Is the Night* in the characters of "Major Hengist and Mr. Horsa."

16. An ex-socialist and anarchist, Pugh was a magazine writer and author of *A Street in Suburbia, King Circumstance,* and *Man of Straw.* Crane had these books at Brede Manor.

## XXVII

1. Hueffer, now Ford Madox Ford, interviewed by Wilfred Partington, editor of the London *Bookman's Journal and Print Collector* for August, 1923: "The 'Lost Souls' of Stephen Crane and His Sussex Days."

Karl Harriman is quoted here from his "Last Days of Stephen Crane," *New Hope,* 2 (October, 1934). Other information is drawn from Harriman's "A Romantic Idealist—Mr. Stephen Crane," *Literary Review,* 4 (April, 1900), and from Thomas Beer's "Mrs. Stephen Crane," *American Mercury,* 31 (March, 1934).

Not noticed by Gilkes in *Cora Crane* (1960) is Harriman's account of Henry James' donation of "a crossed cheque for fifty pounds" to Cora's fund for Frederic's children, in addition to the five pounds he had already given.

2. Quoted here for the first time from the holograph manuscript in CUCC. In Cora's hand: "*Journal* Oct 31 '99." And in pencil: "*Journal* did not print it."

3. Ignorant that Brede Place dates from the fourteenth century, Preston calls it "a mock antique, fifty years old at most." His article—pretentiously titled "The Real Stephen Crane"—appeared in *First Edition and Book Collector* (September–October, 1924).

4. Quoted from *Mr. Frewen of England* by Anita Leslie (1966), by permission of the author and Alfred A. Knopf Inc. Miss Leslie says that Frewen loaned Brede Manor for a rent of £ 40 a year on condition that Crane continued restorations, but my sources have it that the rent was £ 120.

5. Heinemann in 1967 reissued Corelli's *Ziska, Vendetta!, The Soul of Lilith,* and *The Life Everlasting.*

6. Edith R. Jones in *Atlantic Monthly* for July 1954: "Stephen Crane at Brede." A splendid essay by a grand old lady, Mrs. I. Howland Jones, who with her sister—Mabel Barr (wife of Mark Barr, the American chemist)—had attended the Rosemont-Dézaley School in Lausanne. Helen, William's daughter, went there when she was eighteen; Edith in 1899 was nineteen.

7. At a theatre we watch a convict in prison-garb as he pants in rage against two warders who fasten his wrists and ankles with handcuffs. Brutality and betrayal fashion the plot of the drama on stage, and they dominate the audience as people scramble for the exits at the cry of "Fire! Fire! Fire!" Women "cried out tender names; men, white as death, scratched and bleeding, looked wildly from face to face. There were displays of horrible blind brutality by the strong. Weaker men watched and clawed like cats. From the theatre itself came the howl of a gale."

The actor convict has been handcuffed by the actor warders with real handcuffs. He beats his handcuffs against the wall as the flames begin to consume him and curses the actor warders: "They've chained me up!" If only they had used handcuffs of paper-mache! But everything else on stage had been real:

real horses had drunk real water out of real buckets and afterwards dragged a real wagon off stage. Crane's unexpressed theme in "MANACLED" is that no theatrical version of life—no matter how realistic it seems—can equal life, the real thing.

8. Typescript letter owned by Vincent Starrett, with interpolated hand-written corrections. Copy in the Thomas Beer papers. Not in *Letters*. Here reproduced for the first time.

9. See Appendix 9.

10. W. E. Henley edited Heinemann's *New Review*, beginning in January, 1896, and he was first to make known Crane, the new American author, by publishing there the next month Crane's "One Dash—Horses!" Henley encouraged Conrad by publishing his *Nigger of the "Narcissus,"* and he made known another unknown writer—H. G. Wells—by serializing Wells' fantastic *The Time Machine.*

## XXVIII

1. Twenty years older than Crane, this Scotsman, educated in Toronto, had taught in Canada and then joined the Detroit *Free Press*, establishing in London its weekly edition in 1881. He edited the magazine *The Idler* until 1895, and had written four novels. After Crane's death he completed The O'Ruddy (1903).

2. To Booth Tarkington, the sequence of boys' stories was *"Tom Sawyer, Helen's Babies, Whilomville Stories,* Owen Johnson's *Lawrenceville Stories, The Tennessee Shad*, etc. No doubt there were realistic 'realistic children' before Mark Twain—bits in Dickens and elsewhere—and, of course, Tom and Huck are realistic only in character. He gave 'em what boys don't get, when it came to 'plot.' All that the boy, Sam [Clemens], had wished to happen, he made happen. Through all the years—over fifty?—since I read *Helen's Babies,* I seem to remember that they really were children. But when it comes to the Whilomville series, there's no seeming about it. Crane's children *were* children. . . ."

3. "The light blue legs designate not the kind of heron but the age of a heron, a young one. The bird Crane had in mind was the Little Blue Heron with whitish blue legs until it is two or three years old, changing to dark purplish blue in adult years. Though Crane was a close observer of Nature, he was not an ornithologist." (From R. L. Hough's article in *Notes and Queries:* March, 1962.)

4. In *Henry James: Letters to A. C. Benson,* edited by E. F. Benson (1930).

## XXIX

1. Marriott-Watson jokingly replied on the 18th from Chiswick with a cryptographic contribution to the comedy: "Most are publishers fools d—d." Which —unscrambled—reads: most d—d publishers are fools. (He pasted each word of that message onto his letter as a puzzle.)

2. But the ghost was not yet laid, for Beerbohm Tree asked Mason if "The Ghost" couldn't follow "Midsummer Night's Dream" at Her Majesty's Theatre, 1900. Mason said no. (So Cora wrote on her copy of the printed program which she pasted into her scrapbook.) And an editor of *The Ladies' Field* asked to reproduce any photographs of the play, if any were taken. The ghost, however, eluded that fate. "A remarkable piece of literary patchwork has lately been allowed to waste its sweetness on the Sussex air," said the Manchester *Guardian* on January 13.

3. On "The Ghost" see Appendix 10.

4. So Wells said in writing Vincent Starrett (December 8, 1927): "My dear Sir / I am very sorry to say I can't help you to disinter any unknown work (?) by Stephen Crane. I wish I could. But he never talked over his projects with me that I can remember & I lost touch with his wife after his death." (This letter in Starrett's possession is here quoted for the first time.)

5. At the same time that they were planning the Christmas party for forty guests, Cora was so hard up that she asked Pinker to retrieve from Robert McClure the £ 5 he owed Crane. She is rather spiteful about their friend Robert McClure in this letter of December 7 to Pinker: "Mr. McClure is just playing the 'artful' to keep from paying up." But who other than Cora played it artful to keep from paying up the local merchants who subsidized the Crane Christmas party with unpaid-for wood, wine, meat and forty plum-puddings! She had received £ 20 from Pinker and in her letter of December 7 she asked for still another £ 20 as she was £ 39 overdrawn at her Oxted bank—as usual. On December 12 she begged Pinker to send *"at once* upon receipt of this letter" £ 18 to solicitor Alfred Plant. It is *absolutely necessary* that he has it without delay. Mr. Crane will be in town and come to see you toward the week's end. He will bring you the first article for Lippincott"—for the *Great Battles* series.

6. A new Crane letter, reproduced here for the first time from the Barrett Crane Collection.

7. Crane had no book project to offer Curtis Brown, only some unpublished sketches (collected in *Last Words,* 1902), and what books he was then trying to complete exhausted him.

On August 26, 1899 he had writen the Secretary of the New Jersey Historical Society for titles of books on the manners and customs in the Province of New Jersey, particularly Elizabethtown, because he was about to attempt a novel upon Revolutionary times. Lippincott's London agent, J. Garneson, was still trying to retrieve the books he had obtained for this project from the United States when in March 1901 he wrote Cora a second letter reminding her to return the missing volumes of *Proceedings of the New Jersey Historical Society.*

8. Crane had been in Texas in March, 1895, and had fallen in love with San Antonio and with Texas, where he might have survived for many years had he returned in time. He had been in good health there, and living was cheap.

9. Cora wrote Parkin on September 9, 1908, from Palmetto Lodge at Pablo

Beach, Florida: "Have you quite forgotten Mrs. Stephen Crane! If not, drop a line to this address & let me tell you the adventures of a book."

10. In the first American edition of *Great Battles* (Lippincott: December, 1900) "The Battle of Solferino" concludes the series of nine sketches, whereas in the first English edition (Chapman & Hall Limited: 1901) it is the penultimate sketch, followed by "The Battle of Bunker Hill."

11. Rightly so since Barr wrote most of *The O'Ruddy*. Robert Barr was a generous person. He loaned his house at Woldingham to the Frederics and later opened it to wounded Canadian volunteers of the Boer War in 1900, where they were nursed through their convalescence.

The completion of *The O'Ruddy* is reported in Appendix 11.

12. However, should Cora marry, one-half of Crane's estate was then to be divided between William and Edmund, the other half going to his namesake Stephen (Edmund's baby son, born in early 1900). William was made executor of the American branch of his estate, and Crane's London solicitor Alfred T. Plant the English executor, with power over the income from America, which was to be sent to Plant after payment of debts. A portion of Crane's last will is in the Pierpont Morgan Library. Judge William Howe Crane filed a copy of Stephen's last will of 1900 in the Goshen Courthouse (Orange County, New York); I located it there a decade ago.

## XXX

1. Cora completed the manuscript of "The Squire's Madness," whose ending Crane had plotted in his poem. Squire Linton has an income of £ 800 per year, and Crane earned about the same sum. Linton's complaint that "sometimes I can write like mad and other times I don't seem to have an intelligent idea in my head" was Crane's complaint.

2. Cora to Mrs. Frewen, in the BCC. Here quoted for the first time.

3. The situation included innumerable other debts. Alfred Plant, Moreton Frewen's solicitor, wrote to Cora on May 7: "I am in receipt of your letter of the 5th inst. and can only say it was at Mr. Frewen's express wish that I asked you for the list of debts, as he was most anxious that this trouble should be, if possible, removed. . . . I believe he has written direct to Dr. Skinner, and am certain that he is doing all in his power to help you."

The "invalid carriage" Cora chartered to take Stephen from Boulogne, near Calais on the French coast, to Basel is not mentioned in *Cora Crane* by Lillian Gilkes, although this extravagance tells us much about that woman. H. G. Wells errs in saying she hired a special train.

4. Crane showed Wallis McHarg a Wyoming Valley tale in January 1893, "in clippings from the New York *Tribune*" (says Beer); but no such *Tribune* tale has come to light. Possibly it was "Ol' Bennet' and the Indians," which in substance is taken from *Wyoming* (1858 by George Peck, D. D., Stephen's maternal grandfather. His "List of Books Brede Place" includes George Peck's *Our Country: Its Trials and Its Triumph, Seven Wonders of the New World,* and *Early Methodism.* Not included is *Wyoming,* a history of the Wyoming

Valley in Pennsylvania, recounting the wars of the early settlers with the Indians. Crane wrote Pinker on September 30, 1899: "Here is the first story of a series which will deal with the struggles of the settlers in the Wyoming Valley (Pennsylvania) in 1776–79 against the Tories and Indians. Perhaps you had better hold it until I finish two or three more and then deal with some wealthy persons for the purchase of the lot, eh?" By mid-October he had written two more: "The Battle of Forty Fort" and "The Surrender of Forty Fort." Cora wrote Pinker on October 21 that the three "Wyoming Stories" should bring £ 115, against which expectation she asked for £ 30 to get the Cranes to Ireland. But Pinker never sold them. Cora included the last two in *Last Words* (1902) and placed in *Cassell's Magazine* for December 1900 " 'Ol' Bennet' and the Indians." She wrote Pinker about the tales on May 20 from Dover: "Wyoming Tales should bring big prices. It will be a long time before there are more." In August 1900 she asked agent G. H. Perris whether *Cassell's* might take more Wyoming Tales if she wrote them—probably from notes Stephen left for continuing the series. (Also see Appendix 9, last paragraph.)

5. The Cuban War drama, "Drama in Cuba," remains unfinished. It was first published from the untitled typescript in CUCC in my "Stephen Crane as Dramatist," *Bulletin of the New York Public Library* (October 1963).

Stevenson's *St. Ives* was in Crane's library at Brede Place.

## XXXI

1. The "queer telegram for their man of business" is quoted from Jessie Conrad's *Joseph Conrad and His Circle* (1935). This item and other matters are not given in her "Recollections of Stephen Crane," London *Bookman:* April 1926. On June 6, Crane's death certificate was registered at Badenweiler by the owner of the house where he died (as was the custom in Germany for deaths and births, and still is), Herr Albert Eberhardt of the Villa Eberhardt signing himself as The Registrar. The Villa Eberhardt was one of the villas of Dr. Fraenkel's sanitarium, which was modeled after Dr. Trudeau's Adirondack Cottage Sanitarium. It remains today unchanged since Crane's time and is pointed out to tourists as a literary landmark, the death place of a famous American author.

My copy of Crane's death certificate was obtained from Mayor Dr. von Siebold after my visit with him at Badenweiler in 1958. I am indebted to him also for other documents, too numerous to mention here. John Eidson published the same certificate in *Notes and Queries,* 7 (April, 1960). A variant certificate in facsimile appeared in *The Stephen Crane Newsletter,* Vol. I, No. 4 (Spring, 1967), without citing Eidson's *N & Q* article of 1960. In both documents Crane's death is given as 3 a.m. of June 5, 1900.

Some of my data stems from E. R. Hagemann's "The Death of Stephen Crane," *Proceedings of the New Jersey Historical Society* (July, 1959); but it does not include the death-certificate of Stephen Crane.

2. The German Embassy in London notified the American Ambassador to Great Britain (J. H. Choate), who replied that the "German Embassy here has no jurisdiction in matter" and advised application to the American Consul

at Kehl (Alexander Wood) or if necessary Embassy Berlin (A. D. White), and that afternoon the Secretary of the American Embassy in Berlin (J. B. Jackson) directed the American Consul at Freiburg (E. T. Liefield) "to facilitate remains of Stephen Crane. . . ."

3. Heinemann's editor Sydney Pawling had cabled Cora that the Board of Agriculture "cannot make exceptions. Have tried hard. Might arrange if dog started for America in within a very few days."

4. Stephen Crane's debts at his death totaled almost £ 1000 ($5000), but his as yet unpublished works—so Pinker thought—might realize "a sum not less than that amount." Stephen otherwise left no assets except some royalties forthcoming. The copyright on his published and unpublished writings (manuscripts and letters) found no buyer until Alfred A. Knopf purchased those rights from William Crane in 1925 for $5000.

5. For other obituaries see Appendix 12.

6. Hughes to Thomas Beer (December 24, 1921). As "Chelifer" (Rupert Hughes) had reviewed *Maggie, The Black Riders, War Is Kind, Active Service,* and *The Monster.* A member of Delta Upsilon at Cornell, he never met Crane (so far as is known). Hughes got the above story from Hoyt de Friese. Rupert Hughes's letter to Beer, here quoted for the first time, is in the Beer papers which I examined many years ago by the kindness of Miss Alice Beer.

7. Berryman and Beer mislocated the grave at Elizabeth, New Jersey. Berryman, page 260, is again in error in his notion that "There is no separate marker." Three other Stephen Cranes are buried in the First Presbyterian Churchyard at Elizabeth: the Stephen Crane who died in 1780 (at the age of seventy), the Stephen Crane who died in 1796 (age fifty-eight), and the Stephen Crane who died in 1846 (age sixty-four). Lillian Gilkes, page 262, errs in saying that Stephen was interred "in the family plot at Elizabeth, in what is now Hillside, N. J." Hillside stands separate and has never been Elizabeth. Stephen was buried in Hillside's Evergreen Cemetery in 10t 168, Section C; whereas the Crane family plot was in Evergreen Cemetery in Elizabeth.

The *Tribune's* reporter—Wallace Stevens—falsely identified the cemetery. He probably did not bother to go there after the awful Metropolitan Temple service he describes in *Wallace Stevens: Letters* (1966), p. 42.

## XXXII

1. A popular American lecturer on politics, Bigelow publicly denounced Rough Rider Teddy Roosevelt as a flashy politician in the Cuban War. Crane would agree with that but not with Bigelow's accusation of Harold Frederic as liar and plagiarist. Bigelow's praise of Cora's writings ("you have an effective style") encouraged her, and in September she sent him for criticism her long story "José and the Saints."

2. One was The Squire's Madness," which Cora completed from Stephen's notes dictated in his dying days; Perris placed it in *Compton's Magazine.* Another was probably "The Surrender of Forty Fort," one of Crane's Wyo-

ming Valley tales (not published until *Last Words,* 1902). Would *Cassell's Magazine* take more of that series of Wyoming Valley tales if she wrote them? Cora asked Perris.

3. Most of Cora's writings never saw publication. She sold to *Smart Set* her prose poem of bitter disillusionment, "What Hell Might Be," written in late 1898 when Stephen in Havana had deserted her. In one of his *War Is Kind* poems, probably written in 1897, Crane had queried: "Where, then, is hell?" She completed some of Crane's writings, including "The Man from Duluth" and others already noted, and she sold her own sketches "The Red Chimneys" and "Cowardice" to newspaper syndicates in America.

Not sold were "The Lavender Trousers," an offtake from Crane's "Angel Child" story, and another Whilomville story: "Eldridge Carter's Dream." Two others, possibly written jointly by Cora and Stephen, are: "Brer Washington's Consolation" and "The Ideal and the Real." Not sold, also, were "The Poor Soul" and "An Old World Courtship" and two other nonfiction pieces: "Arundel Castle" and "The Seventeenth Regiment of Light Dragoons." The latter Cora recast from Stephen's notes for the Revolutionary War novel he had abandoned prior to his fatal illness at Brede Place. It is an historical account of an Irish cavalry troop fighting on the side of the British in the American Revolutionary War. "José and the Saints" (a lost manuscript) the *Graphic* considered good and powerful but dared not print as it seemed "too gruesome for the present editorial frame of mind on this side of the Atlantic."

The *Pall Mall Gazette* did not publish Crane's "The Battle Hymn," nor did Cora publish it, although she submitted it to a few magazines. It was reproduced from Cora's copy in CUCC for the first time in *The Poetry of Stephen Crane* (1957). This poem provides supporting evidence for my 1951 reading of religious symbolism in *The Red Badge of Courage,* with Jim Conklin as a surrogate for Jesus Christ, a reading which is buttressed and extended by Daniel G. Hoffman in the introduction to his edition of *The Red Badge of Courage and Other Stories* (1957), pp. xv–xxiv, as well as in his *Poetry of Stephen Crane,* pp. 160–161.

4. The four Crane manuscripts were "The Man from Duluth," which Perris placed in *Crampton's Magazine* for May, 1901, two sketches now not known to exist, "Hartwood Park" and "The Crowds from N. Y. Theatres," and a little play, which "can be sold both in England and U. S." The play was "Drama in Cuba."

5. On October 26 she thanked Perris for his advance of £ 5. She listed works of Stephen which had been printed in America or were held by Reynolds for American serial rights. "I have been reading over a copy of the little story of my own which I sent to you, 'The Lavender Trousers,' and it seems like dough that wants to be worked up, and so if you will return it to me I will try to improve on it."

6. Judge Crane also had the last words in deciding the inscription for Stephen's tombstone. Cora had asked W. D. Howells for his suggestion, and he wrote her (July 29, 1900): "I would so willingly help you about words for your husband's monument if I were good for anything in that way. But I am not, as I find once more after trying in this case."

7. Cora and Agnes Crane had a considerable correspondence, but only one of Cora's letters (written on black-bordered stationery) was kept. Edith sent a copy to Beer, but it is not among Beer's papers. Cora wrote Agnes: "Your Uncle Stephen wanted to give you a year or two at school," and perhaps some day "you can visit me and see things for yourself." Agnes had asked whether the poor and the rich are separated in England, and Cora answered: "No. Wealth makes less difference here than in any country in the world. But *Class* distinction *does* make a difference. For instance, a servant is always a servant. A servant marries a servant and their children and grand-children are servants. They have no chance to become anything else and they do not see the need or feel the need of any different life. In another class are the tradespeople who keep shops, but unless they are great manufacturers they are not received by the gentry. In America, a new country, all the conditions of life are different. It's a wretched life for any man, no matter how much wealth he may have, if he is not in business. . . ."

8. Remington wrote "With The Fifth Corps" (*Harper's:* November, 1898). "A thoroughly academic painter, he wrote in a stilted style that is dated," said the New York *Times* review of *Frederic Remington's Own Outdoors* (1964).

9. "The Fire-Tribe" story is the last of the Spitzbergen tales written at Brede Place. It belongs with the Spitzbergen series of which "The Upturned Face" is one of Crane's greatest short stories. "The Fire Tribe and the White-Face" is a fictional fizzle. Crane recast it in variant version as a drama.

10. On the day she sailed she wrote Perris that she was sorry not to be able to come to see him: "Now about the £ 17 advance on the MS., you said you could value my work in collecting, re-writing and revising the book of short stories [*Last Words*] at £ 50—to be paid me by the estate. Mr. Plant wants you to value the work, if you can value it at £ 50 and will let me know; we can arrange to have the £ 17 paid out of that money. And that will leave the MS. free to sell as Mr. Plant directs." In June, 1902, when Cora was in Jacksonville she heard from Plant that her Milborne Grove tenants were vacating her house and that the various Kensington creditors—he warned her—"are very angry and will certainly commence proceedings as soon as they hear you are in England."

11. The Conrads already had one of Stephen's dogs: Escamillo—as Conrad renamed him—had been the puppy Pizzanner, so named because the spread of his legs was like a grand piano's. Another of Stephen's Brede Place dogs— Puff—grew fat at William's house in Port Jervis, where Cora had left him after her voyage to America with Stephen's body.

12. What follows here—the story of Cora's last years—is recast from Lillian Gilkes' *Cora Crane* (1960). In the preceding sections of this chapter I have drawn on the original materials in CUCC, the Knopf file of Edith Crane letters to Thomas Beer, and other sources. I have kept to the name "Mathilde" for Mrs. Charlotte Ruedy because Cora spells it that way in her diary of loose sheets (pages 11A–22A), whereas Miss Gilkes spells it "Mathilda."

13. Six years after Parker's murder, McNeil in a quarrel with his new wife— a girl younger than he—threatened to shoot her, but his gun went off awry in

his direction during their scuffle. The drunkard McNeil died with a bullet at the base of his brain, the same place where his bullet had lodged in Parker.

14. Cora was actually born in July, 1865. Thomas Beer wrote Edith Crane on January 2, 1923, while his *Stephen Crane* was in the press: "It may interest you to know that Cora Crane died in March of 1921 at Pablo Beach, Florida. I have employed a lawyer in Jacksonville to trace her effects." Beer's misinformation came from the detective he and his publisher, Alfred A. Knopf, had hired to do Beer's research for him about Cora of Jacksonville. Cora in fact died on September 4, 1910, at the age of forty-five by cerebral hemorrhage.

CUCC = Columbia University Crane
        Collection
BCC = Barrett Crane Collection

# ⋐ Checklist

## I. WRITINGS BY STEPHEN CRANE

This list presents, in alphabetical order, the titles of Stephen Crane's books and his collected writings beginning with *The Little Regiment* (1896) and ending with *The New York City Sketches of Stephen Crane* (1966) and the forthcoming edition of *Stephen Crane: Sullivan County Tales and Sketches* (1968). It includes titles of articles presenting Crane manuscripts for the first time, such as "A Foreign Policy in Three Glimpses" in "Stephen Crane: Some New Stories," *Bulletin of the New York Public Library* (1957). Original periodical publications of stories, sketches, and war dispatches are cited under the titles of books in which they were collected. Not so cited are the periodical publications of Crane poems—too numerous to list.

Writings by Crane not collected in *The War Dispatches* and *The New York City Sketches* are grouped under the following topics (arranged in alphabetical order): The Boer War, Book Reviews, The Cuban War, English Notes and Sketches, On the New Jersey Coast, and Western and Mexican Sketches. Of Crane's published writings nothing of consequence is missing from this checklist. For new Crane poems I have drawn on the manuscripts in the Columbia University Crane Collection (coded hereafter CUCC). Since I have already published most of the manuscripts in CUCC and in the Barrett Crane Collection (coded hereafter Barrett CC), nothing of consequence among unpublished letters and manuscripts is missing from this checklist. For new letters by and about Crane not included in *Stephen Crane: Letters* (1960), I have drawn on Barrett CC, CUCC, and other sources such as Mr. Charles Feinberg of Detroit, *The Stephen Crane Newsletter*, St. Lawrence University Library. Most of these special instances are source-identified in footnotes to my text.

*ACTIVE SERVICE.* New York: Frederick A. Stokes Company, 1899. London: William Heinemann, 1899. Copyrighted by S. S. McClure on July 21, 1899, for serial publication. In Buffalo *Courier*, October 2, 1899.

In *The Collected Poems of Stephen Crane.* New York: Alfred A. Knopf, 1930. In *The Poems of Stephen Crane: A Critical Edition*, edited by Joseph Katz. New York: Cooper Square, 1966.

*THE BLACK RIDERS and Other Lines.* Boston: Copeland and Day, 1895. London: William Heinemann, 1896.

*BOWERY TALES: George's Mother. Maggie.* London: William Heinemann, 1900. With an Appreciation, by W.

*625*

D. Howells, reprinted from *Maggie: A Child of the Streets* (London, 1896).

GEORGE'S MOTHER: New York and London: Edward Arnold, 1896. In *Bowery Tales*. London: William Heinemann, 1900. Prior to publication this work was tentatively entitled *A Woman Without Weapons*.

GREAT BATTLES OF THE WORLD. Philadelphia: J. B. Lippincott Company, 1901. Illustrated by John Sloan. London: Chapman & Hall Limited, 1901.
CONTENTS: "The Battle of Bunker Hill," *Lippincott's Magazine* (June 1900); "The Siege of Plevna," *Lippincott's Magazine* (May 1900); "The Storming of Burkersdorf Heights," *Lippincott's Magazine* (November 1900); "A Swede's Campaign in Germany (I, Leipzig; II, Lutzen); "The Storming of Badajos," *Lippincott's Magazine* (November 1900); "The Brief Campaign Against New Orleans," *Lippincott's Magazine* (March 1900); "The Battle of Solferino," *Lippincott's Magazine* (October 1900).

LAST WORDS. London: Digby, Long & Co., 1902.
CONTENTS: "The Reluctant Voyagers" "The Kicking Twelfth," *Pall Mall Gazette* (February 1900); *Ainslee's Magazine* (August 1900); "The Upturned Face," *Ainslee's Magazine* March 1900); "The Shrapnel of Their Friends," *Ainslee's Magazine* (May 1900); "And If He Wills, We Must Die," *Illustrated London News* (July 28, 1900) and *Frank Leslie's Popular Monthly* (October 1900); "The Surrender of Forty Fort," "Ol' Bennet and the Indians," *Cassell's Magazine* (December 1900); "London Impressions," *Saturday Review* (July 31, August 7 and 14, 1897); "Great Grief's Holiday Dinner [Stories Told by an Artist]," *New York Press* (October 28, 1895); "The Silver Pageant"; "A Street Scene [When a Man Falls]," *New York Press* (December 2, 1894); "Minetta Lane," Philadelphia *Press* (December 20, 1896); "Roof Gardens [Evening on the Roof]," *Washington Post* (August 9, 1896); "In the Broadway Cars," "Assassins in Modern

Battles," New York *Journal* (April 24, 1898); "An Old Man Goes Wooing," *Philistine* (July 1899); "Ballydehob," "The Royal Irish Constabulary." "A Fishing Village," *Philistine* (August 1899); "Four Men in a Cave," New York *Tribune* (July 3, 1892); "The Mesmeric Mountain." "The Squire's Madness," *Crampton's Magazine* (October 1900); "A Desertion," *Harper's Magazine* (November 1900); "How the Donkey Lifted the Hills," *Pocket Magazine* (June 1897); "A Man by the Name of Mud;" "A Poker Game;" "The Snake," *Pocket Magazine* (August 1896); "A Self-Made Man," *Cornhill Magazine* (March 1899); "A Tale of Mere Chance," *English Illustrated Magazine* (March 1896) and *Pocket Magazine* (April 1896); "At Clancy's Wake;" "An Episode of War;" "The Voice of the Mountain," *Pocket Magazine* (November 1896); "Why Did the Young Clerk Swear?" *Truth* (March 1893); "The Victory of the Moon," *Pocket Magazine* (July 1897).

THE LITTLE REGIMENT and Other *Episodes of the American Civil War*. New York: D. Appleton and Company, 1896. London: William Heinemann, 1897.
CONTENTS: "The Little Regiment," *McClure's Magazine* (June 1896) and *Chapman's Magazine* (June 1896); "Three Miraculous Soldiers," St. Paul *Pionier Press* (March 15, 1896), *Inter Ocean* (March 15, 1896) and *English Illustrated Magazine* (May 1896); "A Mystery of Heroism," Philadelphia *Press* (August 1 and 2, 1895); "An Indiana Campaign," *Pocket Magazine* (September 1896); "A Gray Sleeve," Philadelphia *Press* (October 12, 14 and 15, 1895), *English Illustrated Magazine* (January 1896), *Pocket Magazine* (May 1896) and *Leslie's Weekly* (May 28, 1896); "The Veteran," *McClure's Magazine* (August 1896).

MAGGIE: A Girl of the Streets (A *Story of New York*), by Johnston Smith. [New York, printer unknown, 1893.] *Maggie: A Girl of the Streets*, by Stephen Crane. New York: D. Appleton and Company, 1896. *Maggie: A Child of the Streets*. London:

William Heinemann, 1896. Facsimile reproduction of the First Edition of 1893 with an Introduction by Joseph Katz. Gainesville, Florida, 1966. Also the 1893 edition in *Stephen Crane's Maggie: Text and Context,* edited by Maurice Bassan. Belmont, California, 1966.

*THE MONSTER and Other Stories.* New York and London: Harper & Brothers, 1899. Reprints "The Monster," *Harper's Magazine* (August 1898); "The Blue Hotel," *Collier's Weekly* (November 26, December 3, 1898); "His New Mittens," *McClure's Magazine* (November 1898) and *Cornhill Magazine* (November 1898).

*THE MONSTER and Other Stories.* London: Harper & Brothers, 1901. Adds to the 1899 edition of *The Monster and Other Stories:* "Twelve O'Clock," *Pall Mall Gazette* (December 1899); "Moonlight on the Snow," *Frank Leslie's Popular Monthly* (April 1900); "Manacled," *Argosy* (August 1900); "An Illusion in Red and White," New York *World* (May 20, 1900).

"New Short Fiction by Stephen Crane," edited by R. W. Stallman. In *Studies in Short Fiction,* Vol. I, No. 1 (Fall 1963), 1–7. Presents for the first time "Dan Emmonds" from the ten-page typescript in CUCC. In *Studies in Short Fiction,* Vol. I, No. 2 (Winter 1964); "Art in Kansas City," "In the Country of Rhymers and Writers." (With comments on "The Camel.")

*THE NEW YORK CITY SKETCHES of Stephen Crane and Related Pieces,* edited by R. W. Stallman and E. R. Hagemann. New York: New York University Press, 1966.
CONTENTS: Preface, pages ix–xiv [includes Crane's journalistic hoax: "Great Bugs in Onondaga," New York *Tribune* (June 1, 1891)].
1. New York City Sketches: "Travels in New York," New York *Tribune* (July 10, 1892); "The Landlady's Daughter," from the MS in CUCC; "The Art Students' League Building," from Crane's Pocket Notebook in Barrett CC; "A Mournful Old Building," from the MS in CUCC; "Why

Did the Young Clerk Swear?" *Truth* (March 18, 1893); "At Clancy's Wake," *Truth* (June 3, 1893); "Some Hints for Play-Makers," *Truth* (November 25, 1893); "Matinee Girls," in *Bulletin of the New York Public Library* (September 1960); "A Night at the Millionaire's Club," *Truth* (April 21, 1894); "An Experiment in Misery," New York *Press* (April 22, 1894); "An Experiment in Luxury," New York *Press* (April 29, 1894); "Billy Atkins Went to Omaha," New York *Press* (May 20, 1894); "The Gratitude of a Nation," from the MS in CUCC; "An Ominous Baby," *Arena* (May 1894); "An Ominous Baby—Tommie's Home Coming," from the MS; "Youse Wants 'Petey,' Youse Do," from an undated New York *Herald*; "Mr. Binks' Day Off," New York *Press* (July 8, 1894); "Coney Island's Failing Days," New York *Press* (October 1894); "Stories Told by an Artist [Great Grief's Holiday Dinner]," New York *Press* (October 20, 1894); "In a Park Row Restaurant," New York *Press* (October 28, 1895); "The Silver Pageant," *Last Words* (1902); "Howells Fears Realists Must Wait," New York *Times* (October 28, 1894); "The Men in the Storm," *Arena* (October 1894) and *Philistine* (January 1897); "When Every One Is Panic Stricken [Fire!]," a literary hoax in New York *Press* (November 25, 1894); "Heard on the Street Election Night," New York *Press* (November 1894); "When Man Falls," New York *Press* (December 2, 1894); "The Duel That Was Not Fought," New York *Press* (December 9, 1894); "Sixth Avenue," from the MS in CUCC; "Louise Gerard—Soprano," *The Musical News* (December 1894); "A Christmas Dinner," *The Plumbers' Trade Journal* (January 1, 1895); "A Lovely Jag," New York *Press* (January 6, 1895); "The Judgment of the Sage," *Bookman* (January 1896); "A Great Mistake," *Philistine* (March 2, 1896); "A Dark-Brown Dog," *Cosmopolitan* (March 1901); "A Tale of Mere Chance," *English Illustrated Magazine* (March 1896); "Sailing Day Scenes," from an undated clipping in CUCC; "Opium's Varied Dreams," New York *Sun* (May 17, 1896); "A Prologue," *Roycroft*

*Quarterly* (May 1896) and *Philistine* (July 1896); "New York's Bicycle Speedway [Transformed Boulevard]," New York *Sun* (July 26, 1896); "An Appreciation," by W. D. Howells, New York *World* (July 26, 1896); "Evening on the Roof [Roof Gardens]," Washington *Post* (August 9, 1896); "Yellow Undersized Dog," Denver *Republican* (August 16, 1896); "In the Tenderloin: A Duel," *Town Topics* (October 1, 1896); "The 'Tenderloin' as It Really Is," New York *Journal* (October 25, 1896) and *Literary Digest* (November 7, 1896, entitled "A Picture of the Tenderloin"); "In the 'Tenderloin,'" New York *Journal* (November 1, 1896); "A Tenderloin Story, Yen-Nock Bill and His Sweetheart," New York *Journal* (November 29, 1896); "Diamonds and Diamonds," *Bulletin of the New York Public Library* (October 1956); "A Detail," *Pocket Magazine* (November 1896); "Stephen Crane in Minetta Lane," Philadelphia *Press* (December 20, 1896); "In the Broadway Cars," *Last Words* (1902); "A Desertion," *Harper's Magazine* (November 1900); "The Auction," *The Open Boat* (London, 1898); "A Poker Game," *Last Words* (1902); "A Man by the Name of Mud," *Last Words* (1902); "A Self-Made Man," *Cornhill Magazine* (March 1899); "Manacled," *Argosy* (August 1900) and *The Monster* (London, 1901); "The Man From Duluth," *Metropolitan Magazine* (February 1901) and *Crampton's Magazine* (May 1901).

2. Stephen Crane, Dora Clark, and the Police: "Adventures of a Novelist," New York *Journal* (September 20, 1896); "A Blackguard as a Police Officer," from the MS in CUCC; "Notes About Prostitutes," from the MS in Barrett CC; "A Desertion," from the MS in Syracuse University CC; "An Eloquence of Grief," *The Open Boat* (London, 1898); "A Girl Arrested for Stealing," from the MS in Barrett CC; and other articles, not by Crane.

3. On the New Jersey Coast: "Howells Discussed at Avon-by-the-Sea," New York *Tribune* (August 18, 1891); "Joys of Seaside Life," New York *Tribune* (July 17, 1892); "On the New Jersey Coast": "Summer Dwellers at Asbury Park and Their Doings," New York *Tribune* (July 24, 1892); "On the New Jersey Coast": "Guests Continue to Arrive," New York *Tribune* (August 21, 1892); ["Selections from the Mail," New York *Tribune* (August 24, 1892)]; with the *Tribune's* editorial of apology; "The Pace of Youth," New York *Press* (January 19, 1895); "Stephen Crane at Asbury Park," Kansas City *Star* (August 22, 1896) and New York *Journal* (August 16, 1896, entitled "Asbury Park as Seen by Stephen Crane").

4. Excursions: "In the Depths of a Coal Mine," *McClure's Magazine* (August 1894) and St. Louis *Republic* (July 22, 1894, entitled "Down in a Coal Mine"); "The Devil's Acre," New York *World* (October 25, 1896).

*THE OPEN BOAT and Other Stories.* London: William Heinemann, 1898. CONTENTS: "The Open Boat," *Scribner's Magazine* (June 1897); "A Man and Some Others," *Century* (February 1897; "The Bride Comes to Yellow Sky," *McClure's Magazine* (February 1898) and *Chapman's Magazine* (February 1898); "The Wise Men," *The Lanthorn Book* (1898); "The Five White Mice," *Westminster Gazette* (November 12, 1897) and New York *World* (April 10, 1898); "Flanagan and His Short Filibustering Adventure," *Illustrated London News* (August 28, 1897) and *McClure's Magazine* (October 1897); "Horses—One Dash," Philadelphia *Press* (January 4 and 6, 1896), *New Review* (February 1896) and *Pocket Magazine* (June 1896); "Death and the Child," *Harper's Weekly* (March 19 and 26, 1898); "An Experiment in Misery," New York *Press* (April 22, 1894); "The Men in the Storm," *Arena* (October 1894) and *Philistine* (January 1897); "The Duel That Was Not Fought," New York *Press* (December 9, 1894); "An Ominous Baby," *Arena* (May 1894) and *Philistine* (October 1896); "A Great Mistake," *Philistine* (March 1896) and *Roycroft Quarterly* (May 1896); "An Eloquence of Grief;" "The Auction;" "The Pace of Youth," New York *Press* (January 18 and 19, 1895) and San Francisco *Examiner* (June 30,

1895); "A Detail," *Pocket Magazine* November 1896).

*THE OPEN BOAT and Other Tales of Adventure.* New York: Doubleday & McClure Co., 1898.

*THE O' RUDDY: A Romance;* by Stephen Crane and Robert Barr. New York: Frederick A. Stokes Company, 1903. London: Methúen & Co., 1904. Crane wrote only the opening portions.)

*PICTURES OF WAR.* London: William Heinemann, 1898. Reprints *The Red Badge of Courage;* "The Little Regiment," "Three Miraculous Soldiers," "A Mystery of Heroism," "An Indiana Campaign," "A Grey Sleeve," "The Veteran." With "An Appreciation," by George Wyndham (his review of *The Red Badge* reprinted from *The New Review,* January 1896).

*PIKE COUNTY PUZZLE.* Written and published (August 28, 1894) by Stephen Crane and Louis Senger, a mock newspaper composed by their fellow campers at Twin Lakes, Pennsylvania, in August 1894.

*THE RED BADGE OF COURAGE: An Episode of the American Civil War.* New York: D. Appleton and Company, 1895, 1896. With Introduction by Ripley Hitchcock, 1900. London: William Heinemann, 1896. In Philadelphia *Press,* December 3–8, 1894; New York *Press,* December 9, 1894; Nebraska *State Journal,* etc. In *Stephen Crane: An Omnibus,* edited with Introduction and Notes by Robert Wooster Stallman. New York: Alfred A. Knopf, 1952. London: William Heinemann, 1954. Text of the First American Edition (1895) with the final handwritten manuscript and the earlier handwritten draft here together in print for the first time. (MSS in Barrett CC.) In *The Red Badge of Courage and Selected Stories,* edited with an Introduction and Notes by R. W. Stallman. New York: New American Library, 1960. Copyright 1960 by R. W. Stallman. Text of the First American Edition (1895) with the holograph manuscripts and—here

for the first time—five handwritten manuscript pages.

"Stephen Crane's First Story," edited by Daniel G. Hoffman, *Bulletin of the New York Public Library,* Vol. 64 (May 1960), 273–278. Presents for the first time Crane's holograph manuscript of "Sketches from Life: Uncle Jake and the Bell-Handle."

*STEPHEN CRANE: Letters,* edited by R. W. Stallman and Lillian Gilkes. With an Introduction by R. W. Stallman. New York: New York University Press, 1960. London: Peter Owen, 1960. Incorporates the letters first collected in *Stephen Crane: An Omnibus,* edited by R. W. Stallman (1952, 1954), and in *Stephen Crane's Love Letters to Nellie Crouse,* edited by Edwin H. Cady and Lester G. Wells (1954).

"Stephen Crane's New Jersey Ghosts," edited by Daniel G. Hoffman, *Proceedings of the New Jersey Historical Society,* Vol. 71 (October 1953), 239–253. Reprints for the first time: "Ghosts on the Jersey Coast," New York *Press* (November 11, 1894); "The Ghostly Sphinx of Metedeconk," New York *Press* (January 13, 1895).

"Stephen Crane: Some New Stories," edited by R. W. Stallman. *Bulletin of the New York Public Library,* Vol. 60 (September 1956), 455–462. Presents for the first time Crane manuscripts: "Gustave and Marie," "The Art Students' League," "Matinee Girls," and "Heard on the Street Election Night." In *Bulletin,* Vol. 60 (October 1956), 477–486. Quotes from "Notes About Prostitutes," reproduces for the first time "Raft Story" and "Diamonds and Diamonds." In *Bulletin,* Vol. 61 (January 1957): comments on "The Ghost" and "Jack," quotes from "Greed Rampant," and reproduces for the first time "Across the Covered Pit" and "A Foreign Policy in Three Glimpses."

*STEPHEN CRANE: Sullivan County Tales and Sketches,* edited by R. W. Stallman. Ames, Iowa: Iowa State University Press, 1968. (In preparation.) Presents seven newly discovered

Sullivan County pieces: "The Last of the Mohicans," New York *Tribune* (February 21, 1892); "Hunting Wild Hogs," New York *Tribune* (February 28, 1892); "The Last Panther," New York *Tribune* (April 3, 1892): "Sullivan County Bears," New York *Tribune* (April 19, 1892); "The Way in Sullivan County," New York *Tribune* (May 8, 1892); "Bear and Panther," New York *Tribune* (July 17, 1892). Reprints: "The Snake," *Pocket Magazine* (August 1896); "Four Men in a Cave," New York *Tribune* (July 3, 1892); "Across the Covered Pit," *Bulletin New York Public Library* (January 1957); "The Octopus," New York *Tribune* (July 10, 1892); "A Ghoul's Accountant," New York *Tribune* (July 17, 1892); "The Black Dog," "A Night of Spectral Terror," New York *Tribune* (July 24, 1892); "A Tent in Agony," *Cosmopolitan* (December 1892); "An Explosion of Seven Babies," *Home Magazine* (January 1901); "The Cry of a Huckleberry Pudding," Syracuse *Chap Book* (May 1930); "The Holler Tree," *Golden Book* (February 1934); "The Mesmeric Mountain," *Last Words* (1902); "How the Donkey Lifted the Hills," *Pocket Magazine* (June 1897).

*THE THIRD VIOLET.* New York: D. Appleton and Company, 1897. London: William Heinemann, 1897. Prior to publication this novel was tentatively entitled "The Eternal Patience." In *Inter Ocean* (October 25, November 1, 8 and 15, 1896) and New York *World* (November 4–14, 1896).

*THE WAR DISPATCHES of Stephen Crane,* edited by R. W. Stallman and E. R. Hagemann. New York: New York University Press, 1964. London: Peter Owen, 1964.

CONTENTS:

1. Introduction, The Greco-Turkish War, pages 3–11. "Stephen Crane's Pen Picture of the Powers' Fleet Off Crete," Louisville *Courier-Journal* (May 9, 1897), *Westminster Gazette* (May 3, 1897, entitled "Impression of the 'Concert' ") and New York *Sun* (May 9, 1897, entitled "Half a Day in Suda Bay"); "The Spirit of the Greek People," from the MS in CUCC; "Stephen Crane Says Greeks Cannot Be Curbed," New York *Journal* (April 30, 1897); "Gallant Greeks Would Continue War," by John Bass, New York *Journal* (April 30, 1897); "Lew Wallace Tells How Greece May Win," New York *Journal* (April 30, 1897); "Salonica Expecting a Bombardment," by Julian Ralph, New York *Journal* (April 30, 1897); "Woman Correspondent at the Front," by Imogene Carter [Cora Taylor], New York *Journal* (April 30, 1897); "Imogene Carter's Pen Picture of the Fighting at Velestino," by Imogene Carter, New York *Journal* (May 10, 1897); "Crane at Velestino," New York *Journal* (May 11, 1897); "The Blue Badge of Cowardice," New York *Journal* (May, 12, 1897); "Yale Man Arrested," New York *Journal* (May 14, 1897); "War's Horrors and Turkey's Bold Plan—I" by Julian Ralph, II by Stephen Crane, New York *Journal* (May 23, 1897); "How Novelist Crane Acts on the Battlefield," by John Bass, New York *Journal* (May 23, 1897); "The Dogs of War," New York *Journal* (May 30, 1897); "Greeks Waiting at Thermopylae," New York *Journal* (May 24, 1897); "Four Parodies of Crane as War Correspondent;" "The Eastern Question," from the MS in CUCC; "A Fragment of Velestino," *Westminster Gazette* (June 3, 4 and 8, 1897); "Some Interviews," *Westminster Gazette* (June 14 and 15, 1897); "The Man in the White Hat," *Westminster Gazette* (June 18, 1897); "Death and the Child," *Harper's Weekly* (March 19 and 26, 1897).

2. Introduction, The Spanish-American War, pp. 107–111. "The Little Stilettos of the Modern Navy," New York *Journal* (April 24, 1898); "Sampson Inspects Harbor at Mariel," New York *World* (May 1, 1898); "With the Blockade on Cuban Coast," New York *World* (May 9, 1898); "Frank Norris' Pen Portrait of Stephen Crane," *McClure's Magazine* (May 1898); "Thrilling Adventures of World Scout in Cuba," by Charles H. Thrall, New York *World* (May 8, 1898); "Stephen Crane's Pen Picture of C. H. Thrall," New York *World* (May 8, 1898); "Hayti and San Domingo Favor the United States," New York *World* (May 24,

1898); "Narrow Escape of *The Three Friends*," New York *World* (May 29, 1898); "First American Newspaper to Open Headquarters on Cuban Soil Is the *World*," New York *World* (June 20, 1898); "Crane Tells the Story of the Disembarkment," New York *World* (July 7, 1898); "The Red Badge of Courage Was His Wig-Wag Flag," New York *World* (July 1, 1898); "Marines Signalling Under Fire at Guantánamo," *McClure's Magazine* (February 1899); "Stephen Crane at the Front for the *World*," New York *World* (July 7, 1898); "Roosevelt's Rough Riders' Loss Due to a Gallant Blunder," New York *World* (June 26, 1898); "Hunger Has Made Cubans Fatalists," New York *World* (July 12, 1898); "Artillery Duel Was Fiercely Fought on Both Sides," New York *World* (July 9, 1898); "Chased by a Big Spanish Man-O-War," New York *World* (July 3, 1898); "Night Attacks on the Marines," New York *World* (July 16, 1898); "Stephen Crane's Vivid Story of the Battle of San Juan," New York *World* (July 14, 1898) and *Harper's Weekly* (July 23, 1898, entitled "In Front of Santiago"); "Spanish Deserters Among the Refugees at El Caney," New York *World* (July 8, 1898); "Captured Mausers for Volunteers," New York *World* (July 20, 1898); "A Soldier's Burial That Made a Native Holiday," New York *Journal* (August 15, 1898); "The Porto Rican 'Straddle,'" New York *Journal* (August 18, 1898); "How Stephen Crane Took Juana Dias," by Richard Harding Davis, from *In Many Wars* (1904); "Havana's Hate Dying, Says Stephen Crane," New York *Journal* (September 3, 1898); "Stephen Crane Sees Free Cuba," New York *Journal* (August 28, 1898); "Stephen Crane Fears No Blanco," New York *Journal* (August 31, 1898); "Stephen Crane's Views of Havana," New York *Journal* (September 7, 1898); "Americans and Beggars in Cuba," from the MS in CUCC; "Stephen Crane Makes Observations in Cuba's Capital," New York *Journal* (October 2, 1898); "The Grocer Blockade," New York *Journal* (September 23, 1898); "Memoirs of a Private," New York *Journal* (September 25 1898); "The Private's Story," New York *Journal* (Septem-

ber 26, 1898); "Stephen Crane in Havana," New York *Journal* (October 9, 1898); "How They Leave Cuba," New York *Journal* (October 6, 1898); "How They Court in Cuba," New York *Journal* (October 25, 1898); "Stephen Crane on Havana," New York *Journal* (November 6, 1898); "'You Must!'—'We Can't!'" New York *Journal* (November 8, 1898); "Mr. Crane, of Havana," New York *Journal* (November 9, 1898); "Spaniards Two," New York *Journal* (November 11, 1898); "Our Sad Need of Diplomats," New York *Journal* (November 17, 1898); "In Havana as It Is To-Day," New York *Journal* (November 12, 1898); "Mr. Stephen Crane on the New America," *Outlook* (February 4, 1899); "The Price of the Harness," *Cosmopolitan* (December 1898) and *Blackwood's Edinburgh Magazine* (December 1898); "The Sergeant's Private Madhouse," *Saturday Evening Post* (September 30, 1899); from "War Memories," *Anglo-Saxon Review* (December 1899).

3. Introduction, South Africa and the Boer Wars, page 299. "Some Curious Lessons from the Transvaal," New York *Journal* (January 7, 1900); "The Great Boer Trek," *Cosmopolitan* (June 1900). Appendix, Crane as Dramatist, pp. 315–317. "Drama in Cuba," from the typescript in CUCC first published in *Bulletin of the New York Public Library* (October 1963).

*WAR IS KIND.* New York: Frederick A. Stokes Company, 1899. In *The Collected Poems of Stephen Crane.* New York: Alfred A. Knopf, 1930. In *The Poems of Stephen Crane: A Critical Edition,* edited by Joseph Katz, 1966.

*WHILOMVILLE STORIES.* New York and London: Harper & Brothers, 1900. Illustrated by Peter Newell. New York edition copyrighted by Stephen Crane; London edition copyrighted by William Howe Crane.
CONTENTS: "The Angel Child," "Lynx-Hunting," "The Lover and the Telltale," "'Showin' Off,'" "Making an Orator," "Shame," "The Carriage-Lamps," "The Knife," "The Stove," "The Trial, Execution, and Burial of Homer Phelps," "The Fight," "The

City Urchin and the Chaste Villagers," "A Little Pilgrimage." Appeared monthly in *Harper's Magazine* beginning in August 1899 with "The Angel Child" and ending with "A Little Pilgrimage" in August 1900. Not included is "His New Mittens."

*THE WORK OF STEPHEN CRANE,* edited by Wilson Follett. Twelve uniform volumes. New York: Alfred A. Knopf, 1925, 1926, 1927. Vol. I, Introduction by Joseph Hergesheimer. II, Introduction by Robert W. Davis. III, Introduction by Wilson Follett. IV, Introduction by Carl Van Doren. V, Introduction by William Lyon Phelps. VI, Introduction by Amy Lowell. VII–VIII, Introduction by Thomas Beer. IX, Introduction by Willa Cather. X, Introduction by H. L. Mencken. XI, Introduction by Sherwood Anderson. XII, Introduction by Charles Michelson. The Davis and Michelson introductions are important biographically.

Knopf's house usage was inflexibly Oxford; hence the English spellings, which were not Crane's, are therefore not textually valid.

*WOUNDS IN THE RAIN: A COLLECTION OF STORIES RELATING TO THE SPANISH-AMERICAN WAR OF 1898.* London: Methuen & Co., 1900. New York: Frederick A. Stokes Company. Entitled *Wounds in the Rain: War Stories.* Dedication to Moreton Frewen: This Small Token of Things Well Remembered by His Friend Stephen Crane.

CONTENTS: "The Price of the Harness" ["The Woof of Thin Red Threads"], *Cosmopolitan* (December 1898) and *Blackwood's Edinburgh Magazine* (December 1898); "The Lone Charge of William B. Perkins," *McClure's Magazine* (July 1899); "The Clan of No-Name," "God Rest Ye, Merry Gentlemen," *Saturday Evening Post* (May 6, 1899) and *Cornhill Magazine* (May 1899); "The Revenge of the Adolphus," *Strand Magazine* (September 1899); *Collier's Weekly* (October 28, 1899); "The Sergeant's Private Madhouse," *Saturday Evening Post* (September 30, 1899); "Virtue in War," *Frank Leslie's Popular Monthly* (November 1899, entitled "West Pointer

and Volunteer"); "Marines Signalling Under Fire at Guantánamo," *McClure's Magazine* (February 1899); "This Majestic Lie," New York *Herald* (June 24, July 1, 1900); "War Memories," *Anglo-Saxon Review* (December 1899); "The Second Generation," *Saturday Evening Post* (December 2, 1899); *Cornhill Magazine* (December 1899).

"The Wreck of the New Era." Reproduced from the typescript in Barrett CC for the first time in University of Connecticut *Fine Arts Magazine* (April 28, 1956).

## THE BOER WAR

"Stephen Crane Says Watson's Criticisms of England Are Not Unpatriotic," New York *Journal* (January 25, 1900); "Stephen Crane Says the British Soldiers Are Not Familiar With the 'Business End' of Modern Rifles," New York *Journal* (February 14, 1900); "The Talk of London," New York *Journal* (March 11, 1900).

## BOOK REVIEWS

"Harold Frederic," Chicago *Chap Book*, Vol. 8 (March 15, 1898), 358–359; "Ouida's Masterpiece," *Book Buyer*, Vol. 13 (January 1897), 968–969.

## THE CUBAN WAR

"The Terrible Captain of the Captured *Panama*," New York *World* (April 28, 1898); "Inaction Deteriorates the Key West Fleet," New York *World* (May 6, 1898); "Sayings of the Turret Jacks in Our Blockading Fleets," New York *World* (May 15, 1898); "In the First Landing 4 of Our Men Are Killed," New York *World* (June 13, 1898, unsigned, dictated by Crane to Ernest McCready); "Denies Mutilation of Bodies," Philadelphia *Press* (June 26, 1898); "Pando Hurrying to Santiago," New York *World* (July 1, 1898); "Stephen Crane in Havana: Why Cuba Is by No Means a Klondike," New York *Journal* (November 6, 1898).

## ENGLISH NOTES AND SKETCHES

"New Invasion of Britain," Omaha *Daily Bee* (May 9, 1897); "Concerning the English Academy." *Bookman* (March 1898); "The Scotch Express," *McClure's*

*Magazine* (January 1899) and *Cassell's Magazine* (January 1899); "Talk of London," New York *Journal* (March 11, 1900); "At the Pit Door," *Philistine* (September 1900).

## ON THE NEW JERSEY COAST

*Unsigned; authorship conjectural:* "Temperance Women at the Seaside," New York *Tribune* (July 10, 1889); "Interested in Bible Lessons," New York *Tribune* (July 18, 1889); "Crowds at Ocean Grove," New York *Tribune* (August 17, 1889).
*Unsigned; by Stephen Crane:* "Gay Bathing Suit and Novel Both Must Go," New York *Tribune* (August 5, 1888); "Meetings Begun at Ocean Grove," New York *Tribune* (July 2, 1892); "Crowding into Asbury Park," New York *Tribune* (July 3, 1892); "The Captain," New York *Tribune* (August 7, 1892); "On the Boardwalk," New York *Tribune* (August 14, 1892); "Along the Shark River," New York *Tribune* (August 15, 1892); "On the New Jersey Coast . . . Parades and Entertainments," New York *Tribune* (August 21, 1892); "Seaside Assembly's Work at Avon," New York *Tribune* (August 29, 1892); "Seaside Hotel Hop," New York *Tribune* (September 11, 1892).

## WESTERN AND MEXICAN SKETCHES

"Nebraskans' Bitter Fight for Life," Philadelphia *Press* (February 24, 1895); "Merry Throng at Hot Springs," Philadelphia *Press* (March 3, 1895); "Grand Opera in New Orleans," Philadelphia *Press* (March 24, 1895); "Mexican Sights and Street Scenes," Philadelphia *Press* (May 19, 1895) and Louisville *Courier-Journal* (May 19, 1895, entitled "In Old Mexico"); "Free Silver Down in Mexico," Philadelphia *Press* (June 30, 1895); "Ancient Capital of Montezuma," Philadelphia *Press* (July 21, 1895); "Jags of Pulque Down in Mexico," Philadelphia *Press* (August 11, 1895); "Apaché Crossing," from MS in CUCC; "Mardi Gras Festival," Philadelphia *Press* (February 16, 1896); "Freight Car Incident," Brooklyn *Daily Eagle* (April 12, 1896), Philadelphia *Press* (April 19, 1896, entitled "Caged With a Wild Man") and *English Illustrated Magazine* (June 1896, entitled "A Texas Legend"); "Hats, Shirts and Spurs in Mexico," Philadelphia *Press* (October 18, 1896); "Galveston, Texas, by the Late Stephen Crane," *Westminster Gazette* (November 6, 1900).

## II. WRITINGS ON STEPHEN CRANE

Of the extraordinary number of writings on Crane which appeared with accelerated pace after 1952, I am indebted mainly to the articles of biographical information for this book and only in certain instances to critical writings for my reading of Crane's works. Sources to which I feel especially obligated are cited in the text or in the footnotes.

The source of unidentified passages in the text is mainly Thomas Beer's *Stephen Crane* (1923) and/or my *Stephen Crane: Letters*, co-edited with Lillian Gilkes (1960). *Letters* corrects and fills in numerous gaps in Beer's chronology. Of writings on Crane not included in *Letters*, I've drawn from the Columbia University Crane Collection, which is Miss Gilkes' source for her *Cora Crane* (1960) and Daniel G. Hoffman's source for his *Poetry of Stephen Crane* (1957), namely the manuscript poems.

To footnote every quoted passage in a text which juxtaposes on the same page quotations from disparate sources would encumber this biography with an elephantine appendix of data irrelevant to the text. For the same reason it is impossible to provide a complete checklist of writings on Crane. Such a listing of more than eight hundred items requires a book in itself, and so the Crane scholar is asked to consult my forthcoming *Stephen Crane: A Bibliog-*

*raphy* (Iowa State University Press). This book incorporates the Ames W. Williams and Vincent Starrett *Stephen Crane: A Bibliography* (1948), bringing their twenty-six pages of writings on Crane up-to-date and adding critical annotations.

# III. RELATED BACKGROUND WRITINGS

Sources are grouped according to the following topics: Brede Manor, The Dora Clark Affair, The *Commodore* Disaster, The Greco-Turkish War, The Spanish-American War.

## BREDE MANOR

Austin, Edmund. *Brede: The Story of a Sussex Parish* (Rye 1947).
Frewen, Hugh. *Imogene: An Odyssey* (Sydney, Australia, n.d.).
Leslie, Anita. *Mr. Frewen of England* (London, 1966).
"The 'Lost Souls' of Stephen Crane and His Sussex Days," (London) *Bookman's Journal* (August 1923).
Sheridan, Clare. *My Crowded Sanctuary* (London, 1945).
*Sussex County Magazine*, V (May, July, August 1931). On Brede Manor by Viscountess Wolseley; on Brede Place by Shane Leslie and David McLean.

## THE DORA CLARK AFFAIR

See *The New York City Sketches of Stephen Crane* (1966). Additional articles include the following:
Anonymous. "Stephen Crane as Champion," New York *Times*, September 17, 1896. ———Editorial in Boston *Herald*, September 21, 1896. ———"Stephen Crane on the Stand," New York *News*, October 16, 1896. ———"Novelist Crane Backed," New York *Sun*, October 17, 1896. ———"Red Badge Man on a Police Rack," New York *Press*, October 17, 1896. ———"Dora Clark in Court," New York *Times*, November 2, 1896. ———"Stephen Crane; the Unfortunate Girl," Rochester *Times*, November 3, 1896. ———*Bookman*, July 1900.

## THE COMMODORE DISASTER

Anonymous. "The *World*'s Dispatch Boat," Florida *Times-Union*, January 1, 1897, 5. ———"*Commodore* Starts for Cuba," New York *World*, January 1, 1897, 7. ———"A War Cargo for Cuba," Philadelphia *Record*, January 2, 1897, 1. ———"*Commodore* Clears for Cuba," Florida *Times-Union*, January 1, 1897, 6. ———"The Wreck of *The Commodore*," Florida *Times-Union*, January 3, 1897, 1. ———"Filibustering *Commodore* Lost," New York *World*, January 3, 1897, 7. ———"The Tug *Commodore* Sunk," New York *Times*, January 3, 1897, 1. Many of the facts here are erroneous, including the notion that the *Commodore*'s Mate Gaines reached shore and that "the sea was smooth." ———"*The Commodore* Sunk Off Florida," New York *Herald*, January 3, 1897, 4. Lists Murray Nobles among crew; but in fact Murray Nobles did not join the *Commodore*'s crew. ———"*Commodore* Lost; Her Crew Saved," New York *Journal*, January 3, 1897, 1. Mistakenly reports Sylvester Scovel among the passengers. Nor was the crew saved. ———"*Commodore* Lost at Sea," New York *Sun*, January 3, 1897, 1. ———"*The Commodore* Sunk," Philadelphia *Record*, January 3, 1897, 1. ———"To Stop Filibusters," New York *Herald*, January 3, 1897, 4. ———"*Vesuvius* to Watch Filibusters," New York *World*, January 3, 1897. ———"Uncle Sam's Vessels Ordered to Watch Cuban Filibusters," New York *Journal*, January 4, 1897. "The Loss of *The Commodore*," New York *Sun*, January 4, 1897, 6. ———"Loss of *The Commodore*," New York *Times*, January 4, 1897, 1. ———"Steamer *Commodore* Sunk," Boston *Evening Transcript*, January 4, 1897, 1. ———"Crane Knocks Down a Coward," New York *World*, January 4, 1897. ———"*The Commodore* Was Scuttled," New York *Journal*, January 4, 1897, 1–2. ———"Twelve Men Lost Through

Treachery," Florida *Times–Union*, January 4, 1897, 1. ———"Seven Are Missing," New York *World*, January 4, 1897, 7. ———"Eight Men Still Missing," New York *Journal*, January 4, 1897, 2. ———"Sixteen of the *Commodore*'s Men Were Lost," New York *Herald*, January 4, 1897, 3. ———"15 Drowned, In the Sinking of *The Commodore*," Boston *Record*, January 4, 1897. ———"*Commodore* Men Adrift," New York *Sun*, January 4, 1897. ———"More of the Filibusters Safe," New York *Press*, January 4, 1897, 1–2. ———"Stephen Crane and His Work. How He Came to Be on the Unlucky *Commodore*," New York *Press*, Monday, January 4, 1897, 2. ———"Little Doubt of Treachery," New York *Herald*, January 4, 1897, 7. ———"Capt. Murphy's Story," New York *World*, January 5, 1897. ———"*Commodore* Said to Be Overladen. Many Think That Fact, and Not Treachery, Sunk Her," New York *Press*, Tuesday, January 5, 1897, 1. ———"Captain Murphy's Shipwrecked Crew," Florida *Times-Union*, Tuesday, January 5, 1897, 6. ———"Were Traitors on *The Commodore*? Some of the Survivors Say There Were and Others Stoutly Deny It. . . . Number of Lost Reduced to Eight Americans Who Were in the Crushed Lifeboat," New York *Herald*, January 5, 1897, 9. ———"Twelve Men Lost Through Treachery," Florida *Times-Union*, Tuesday, January 5, 1897, 1. ———"Cuban Castaways Seen on a Raft," New York *Journal*, January 5, 1897, 1–2. ———"Stephen Crane Safe," New York *World*, January 5, 1897, 1. ———"Men on the *Commodore* Likely to Be Accused of Law Breaking," New York *Herald*, January 5, 1897, 9. ———"The *Commodore*'s Lost Men," New York *Times*, January 6, 1897. "It seems to be settled that the seven men missing from the crew of the foundered steamer *Commodore* have been drowned." The steamer *Three Friends* and the cruiser *Newark* have made a fruitless search. ———"Rescuing Party Returns," Florida *Times-Union*, January 6, 1897, 5. ———"The Filibustering Cases," New York *Times*, January 7, 1897, 7. ———"The *Commodore* Investigation," Florida *Times-Union*, January 7, 1897, 4. ———"One of the Dead," Florida *Times-Union*, January 8, 1897. ———"S. S. *Commo-*

dore*, Filibuster. Her Loss Described by Mr. Stephen Crane," London *Mail*, January 21, 1897. A press clipping in the Crane Scrapbook in CUCC. The London *Mail* is quoting from the Chicago *Record*'s reprinting of "Stephen Crane's Own Story" in New York *Press* for January 7. The *Mail* article contains a photograph of Crane.

Hubbard, Elbert. "Of Stephen Crane," *Philistine*, IV (February 1897), 84.

### Logs of "Boutwell" and "Newark." Weather reports, etc.

*Atlantic Coast: Cape Henry to Key West* (U.S. Coast Pilot No. 4, 1959, Sixth Edition), pp. 109–110. "St. Johns River to Miami."

Bowditch, Nathaniel. *American Practical Navigation* (1958). On the effect of winds on the tides, page 771, and on ocean waves, page 774; on landing in a surf, pages 243 ff.

*Log of the United States Steamer Newark*, January 1, 2, 3, 4, and 5, 1897. (In National Archives, Group No. 24.) Arriving off St. Johns bar, January 1st. Records the wind and sea conditions. On 4th sighted wreckage of *Commodore*: "a piece of the side of a deck house painted reddish brown on inner side, which side was up. . . ."

*Record of Movements, Vessels of the U.S. Coast Guard 1790—December 31, 1933.* On the *George S. Boutwell: 1873–1907*, page 152. In United States Coast Guard Library, Washington, D.C.

*Report of the Chief of Division of Revenue Cutter Service* (Washington, Government Printing Office, 1897), pp. 49, 52. *Table*, page 49; Date: January 1, 1897. Place: St. Johns River, Florida. By: *Boutwell*. Vessel assisted: Steamer *Commodore*. Tonnage: 178. Cargo: Arms, etc. Estimated value of vessel: $20,000. Of cargo: $5,000. Total: $25,000. Persons on board: 27. Persons saved: 27.

*Report of Marine Meteorology.* (For January 1897.) In National Archives (Group No. 27). *The Roland,* off the east coast of Florida, reported for January 2, 1897: "Chopping sea."

Report on the Wreck of *The Commodore*. From the Keeper of Mosquito Inlet Light Station, Florida, January 4, 1897. (In National Archives, Group No. 26.) "One of the boats beached at 10:30 a.m., on the 2nd inst. with Mr. Rojo, chief of the expedition and eleven men. Another boat beached at 12:30 noon with four men, and a third boat beached 12 miles north of this light at 8 p.m. with master and three men, one of whom was killed in beaching."

Transcript from the Journal of the U.S. Revenue Steamer *Boutwell*. (In National Archives, Group No. 26). On Friday, January 1, 1897 "mate of steamer *Commodore* came aboard reporting that vessel had grounded and requested assistance. 7:00 underway, and stood down river to aid *Commodore* as there was no tug available. ... Took line from her, and steamed ahead. 7:40 vessel floated, took her in tow down stream while she was getting steam. 11:00 steamer touched on sand shoal in turning round." (*Commodore* grounded for a second time.) Saturday, January 2: "Moderate breeze from east, and partly cloudy."

*U.S. Department of Agriculture, Weather Bureau*. Record of Observations at Jacksonville for the month of January, 1897; at New Smyrna, month of January, 1897. (Additional data from National Weather Records Center, Asheville, North Carolina, letter to R. W. S. for 16 March 1962.)

Letter from the Keeper of Mosquito Inlet Light Station, Florida, January 4th, 1897. In National Archives and Record Service (Washington, D.C.): "Sir: I enclose report of the wreck of the Commodore. One of the boats beached at 10:30 a.m. on the 2nd inst. with Mr. Rojo, chief of the expedition and eleven men. Another boat beached at 12:30 noon with four men, and a third boat beached 12 miles north of this light at 8 p.m. with Master and three men, one of whom was killed in beaching...." Here,

again, is proof that there were only four men in the dinghy.

Interviews with persons who were at Daytona Beach in January 1897 when the dinghy came ashore, an article written by Odell Hathaway and published in recast form without acknowledgment by the Daytona Beach *News-Journal* (April 22, 1962): "The Day Stephen Crane was Shipwrecked."

"Journalist Crane in That Dinghy," by R. W. Stallman, *Bulletin of the New York Public Library*, 72 (April, 1968).

## THE GRECO-TURKISH WAR

*Annual Cyclopedia and Register of Important Events*, 1897 (London, 1900). On the Cretan situation, pp. 241–253.

*Annual Register, 1897* (London, 1898).

Anonymous. "The Armenian Massacres," *Harper's Weekly*, December 28, 1895, 1249–1250. ———"Anarchy in Turkey," *Harper's Weekly*, November 16, 1895, 1098. ———Florida *Times-Union*, February 19, 1897. A press release about Greek interference in Crete. ———"Greece and Its Rulers," *The Saturday Review*, September 1897. ———"The King of Greece and Ourselves," *The Saturday Review*, October 1897. ———"Greece and Its People," *The Saturday Review*, October 1897. ———"Anarchy in Turkey," *Harper's Weekly*, November 16, 1895, 1098.

Bass, John. "Gallant Greeks Would Continue War," New York *Journal*, April 30, 1897. ———"How Novelist Crane Acts on the Battlefield," New York *Journal*, May 23, 1897, 37.

Burleigh, Bennet. "The Greek War, As I Saw It," *Fortnightly Review*, July 15, 1897.

Callwell, C. E. "A Glimpse of the Late War," *Blackwood's Edinburgh Magazine*, CLEII (August 1897), 178–179. An interesting account of what seems to be the same voyage Crane took.

Davis, Charles Belmont, editor. *Adventures and Letters of Richard Harding*

*Davis* (New York, 1917). On Crane in Greece, pp. 200, 207.

Gaye, Arthur. "The Greeks and Their Lesson," *Macmillan's Magazine*, September, 1897.

Nevinson, Henry W. *The Thirty Days' War Between Greece and Turkey* (London, 1898). Reviewed by Huyshe Wentworth, "The Thirty Days' War of 1897," *Saturday Review*, May, 1898.

Norris, Frank. "The Green Stone of Unrest: by S– – – – –n Cr– –e," San Francisco *Wave*, 24 December 1897. (A parody.) In *Frank Norris of the "Wave,"* edited by Oscar Lewis San Francisco, 1931), pp. 82–85. Reprinted in *The War Dispatches of Stephen Crane* (1964), pp. 52–53.

Steevens, George. *With the Conquering Turk* (London, 1897). The best study of the Greco-Turkish War.

Tyler, Mason Whiting. "The European Powers and the Near East, 1875–1908," *Research Publications of the University of Minnesota*, No. 17 (1925).

## THE SPANISH-AMERICAN WAR

Abbot, Willis J. *Blue Jackets of 1898* (New York, 1917).

Alger, Russell A. *The Spanish-American War* (New York, 1901).

*Annual Reports of the Navy Department* (Washington, D.C., 1898).

*Annual Reports of the War Department* (Washington, D.C., 1898).

Anonymous. "The Story of Cuba," Brooklyn *Daily Eagle*, June 7, 1896, 19. The story of Murat Halstead's visit to Cuba. ———"Great Misery in Pinar del Rio," New York *Herald*, January 4, 1897, 3. ———"Cubans Warned Col. Wood in Vain of an Ambush," New York *World*, June 26, 1898. ———"Newspaper Men in the War," *Literary Digest*, October 15, 1898. ———"Attacks 71st Officers," New York *Tribune*, June 29, 1900. ———"Major Smith Dismissed," New York *Tribune*, June 7, 1900.

Archibald, James F. J. "The First Engagement of American Troops on Cuban Soil," *Scribner's*, August 1898.

Atkins, John Black. *The War in Cuba* (London, 1899).

Azoy, A. C. M. *Charge! The Story of the Battle of San Juan Hill* (New York, 1961). A splendid little book.

Hagedorn, Hermann. *The Rough Riders* (New York, 1927).

Halstead, Marat. "Our Cuban Neighbors and Their Struggle for Liberty," *Review of Reviews;* April 1896. *Full Official History of the War with Spain* (Chicago, 1899).

*Harper's Pictorial History of the War with Spain* (New York, 1899), 2 Vols.

Harris, Kennett F. "Cavalrymen at Guásimas," in *The Chicago Record's War Stories* (Chicago, 1898). An important article with relation to the scarcity of coffee beans at Siboney on June 23, which in turn suggests the situation Crane describes in the opening of "An Episode of War."

Hemment, John C. *Cannon and Camera* (New York, 1898).

Hilliard, John Northern. "Letters to a Friend," New York *Times Supplement*, 14 July 1900, p. 407. New Crane letter not in *Letters* (1960). Quotes Richard Harding Davis on Crane at Guantánamo.

Hobson, Richmond Pearson. *The Sinking of the "Merrimac"* (New York, 1899).

Hubbard, Elbert. *A Message to García* (East Aurora, New York, 1899).

Kennan, George. "George Kennan's Story of the War," *Outlook*. A series of articles of which the following are especially useful: XI "The Fever Outbreak in the Army," *Outlook*, 59 (August 20, 1898); XII "Fever Experiences," *Outlook*, 59 (August 27, 1898); and "The Santiago Campaign," *Outlook*, 59 (October 22, 1898).

*Campaigning in Cuba* (New York, 1899).

Langford, Gerald. *The Richard Harding Davis Years* (New York, 1961). A rather superficial account with only eleven pages to cover the Cuban War. Reviewed in New York *Times Book Review*: 5 March 1961. "Davis was never the objective reporter; each military operation, large or small, was a personal experience to him; had the letter 'I' been removed from his typewriter, he would have been in dire straits," says Quentin Reynolds.

Lee, Arthur. "The Regulars at El Caney," *Scribner's*, October 1898.

Leech, Margaret. *In the Days of McKinley* (New York, 1959). On Crane, pp. 304–305. In error on Crane and the 71st New York Volunteers, repeating Walter Millis' misidentification.

McClernand, E. J. *Recollections of the Santiago Campaign* (Washington, 1922).

McIntosh, Burr. "Perils of the Front," *Leslie's*; August 18, 1898. ——— *The Little I Saw of Cuba* (London and New York, 1899). One of the best books on the Cuban War; important on Crane.

Manchester, William. "The Spanish-American War," *Holiday*, 30 (September 1961).

Marshall, Edward. "How It Feels to Be Shot," *Cosmopolitan*, September 1898. ———"A Wounded Correspondent's Recollections of Guasimas." *Scribner's*, September 1898. ———*The Story of the Rough Riders* (New York, 1899). On Crane at Las Guásimas, 76, 85, 143.

Mason, Gregory. *Remember the Maine* (New York, 1939). A very lively account. On Crane, however, copying Millis' error, he repeats the false charge that Crane wrote the *World* article charging panic among the 71st New York Volunteers.

Mathews, Joseph J. *Reporting the Wars* (Minneapolis, 1957).

Meriwether, Walter Scott. "The Unremembered *Maine*," *Harper's Weekly*, July 11, 1908. ———"Remembering the *Maine*," *United States Naval Institute Proceedings* (Annapolis, May 1948).

Michelson, Charles. Introduction. *The Work of Stephen Crane* (New York, 1927), Vol. XII. Important on Crane in Cuba. ———*The Ghost Talks* (New York, 1944).

Baker, Ray Stannard. "How the News of the War is Reported," *McClure's* September 1898. ———*American Chronicle* (New York, 1945).

Bigelow, John Jr. *Reminiscences of the Santiago Campaign* (New York, 1899).

Bonsal, Stephen. *The Fight for Santiago* (New York, 1899).

Brisbane, Arthur. "The Modern Newspaper in War Time," *Cosmopolitan*, September 1898.

Brooks, Van Wyck. *Sketches in Criticism* (New York, 1932).

Brown, Charles H. *The Correspondents' War* (New York, 1967). An important book, but superficial in its account of the Santiago campaign.

Carnes, Cecil. *Jimmy Hare, News Photographer* (New York, 1940). An eyewitness report on Crane in Cuba; important.

Cather, Willa. Introduction. *The Work of Stephen Crane* (New York, 1926), Vol. IX.

Chadwick, French Ensor. *The Relations of the United States and Spain* (New York, 1911), Vols. II and III.

Chamberlain, Joseph E. "How the Spaniards Fought at Caney," *Scribner's*, September 1898. (Not to be confused with Henry Barrett Chamberlin of the Chicago *Record*.)

*Chicago Record's War Stories* (Chicago,

1898). Important eye-witness accounts by Howbert Billman, Kennett F. Harris, James Langland, and Henry Chamberlin ("The Destruction of Cervera's Fleet").

Churchill, Allen. *Park Row* (New York, 1958).

Creelman, James. "Crisis in Spain Almost at Hand," New York *Journal*, January 3, 1897, 1, 7. ———*On the Great Highway* (Boston, 1901). Creelman and Hearst at the battle of El Caney. A defense of Yellow Journalism.

Davis, Richard Harding. "How Hamilton Fish and Allyon Capron Died, Fighting Bravely," New York *Herald*, June 26, 1898. ———"The First Shot of the War" and "The First Bombardment," *Scribner's*, July 1898. ——— "The Rocking-Chair Period of the War" and "The Landing of the Army," *Scribner's*, August 1898. ———"The Rough Riders' Fight at Guasimas," *Scribner's*, September 1898. ——— "The Battle of San Juan," *Scribner's*, October 1898. ———"The Porto Rican Campaign," *Scribner's*, November 1898. ———*A Year From a Reporter's Note-Book* (New York, 1898). ———"Our War Correspondents in Cuba and Puerto Rico," *Harper's Monthly*, May, 1899. On Crane, page 942; retold in *Notes of a War Correspondent* (1910). ———The Cuban and Porto Rican Campaigns (New York, 1899). ———"How Stephen Crane Took Juana Dias," In *Many Wars by War Correspondents*, edited by George Lynch and Frederic Palmer (Tokyo, Japan, 1904), pp. 43–45. Important. ———*The Notes of a War Correspondent* (New York, 1910). On Crane at San Juan Hill, pp. 125, 127, 128. "Adventure Filled Life of Richard Harding Davis," New York *Evening Post*, April 15, 1916. Downey, Fairfax. *Richard Harding Davis and His Day* (New York, 1933). Davis, Charles Belmont, editor. *Adventures and Letters of Richard Harding Davis* (New York, 1917).

Dunne, Finley Peter ("Dooley"). *Mr. Dooley on Ivrything and Ivrybody,* edited by Robert Hutchinson (New York, 1963).

Freidel, Frank. *The Splendid Little War* (Boston, 1958). The best short summary of the war, although mainly a picture book. The photograph of correspondents at Tampa which claims "Stephen Crane in white suit" does not contain Crane (page 66).

Goode, W. A. M. *With Sampson Through the War* (New York, 1899).

Graham, George E. "The Destruction of Cervera's Fleet," *McClure's Magazine*, September 1898, 403–421.

Miley, J. D. *In Cuba With Shafter* (New York, 1899).

Millis, Walter. *The Martial Spirit* (Boston, 1931). Misidentifies Crane as author of the article in the *World* reporting panic among the 71st New York Volunteers (Sylvester Scovel wrote it). This error is repeated by Mason (1939), Leech (1959), and Swanberg (1961).

Mott, Frank Luther. *American Journalism: 1690–1960* (New York, 1962).

Muller y Tejeiro, José. "Battle and Capitulation of Santiago de Cuba," *Notes on the Spanish-American War* (1900).

*New York Times Illustrated Weekly Magazine* (New York, 1898).

Norris, Frank. "News Gathering at Key West," *McClure's Magazine*, May 1898. ———"Life at Key West," New York *Daily Tribune*, July 3, 1898, 4. ———"Comida! Comida!" *Atlantic Monthly*, March 1899. ———"With Lawton at El Caney," *Century*, June 1899.

*Our Islands and Their People,* edited by William S. Bryan. Introduced by Major-General Joseph Wheeler (New York, 1899), Vol. I.

Paine, Ralph D. *Roads of Adventure* (Boston and New York, 1922). Important; much here on Crane and Ernest McCready.

Pershing, John J. "The Campaign of

Santiago," *Under Fire With the Tenth Cavalry* (Chicago, 1902).

Post, Charles J. *The Little War of Private Post* (Boston, 1960).

Rea, George Bronson. *Facts and Fakes about Cuba* (New York, 1897). "The Night of the Explosion in Havana," *Harper's Weekly*, March 5, 1898.

Remington, Frederic. "With the Fifth Corps," *Harper's*, November 1898.

Roosevelt, Theodore. *The Rough Riders* (New York, 1899). Disdains to make any mention of Crane.

Rowan, Lieutenant Colonel Andrew. "My Ride Across Cuba," *McClure's Magazine*, 11 (August 1898), 372–379. Reprinted by Elbert Hubbard in his *Philistine* for March 1899. By 1913 over forty million copies had been published. A. S. Rowan wrote another version for a pamphlet published in 1923 in San Francisco: *How I Carried the Message to García*. Crane considered Rowan a sham hero; he scolded Hubbard in May 1899 for publicizing that military charlatan. In *Stephen Crane: Letters* (1960).

Sampson, William T. "Sampson Withdraws Charge of Mutilation," Philadelphia *Press*, June 26, 1898. ——— "The Atlantic Fleet in the Spanish War," *Century*, April 1899.

Sargent, Herbert H. *The Campaign of Santiago de Cuba* (London and Chicago, 1907).

Shafter, William R. "The Capture of Santiago de Cuba," *Century,* February 1899.

Seitz, Don Carlos. *Joseph Pulitzer* (New York, 1924). Important for his mistaken charges against Crane as *World* reporter, which damaged Crane's reputation as journalist ever since they were repeated by Walter Millis in *The Martial Spirit* (1931). One of his charges was that Crane wrote the *World* article claiming panic among the 71st New York Volunteers, whereas Seitz as business manager of the *World* could readily have ascer-

tained that the author was Sylvester Scovel. ———*The James Gordon Bennetts* (Indianapolis, 1928). ——— "Stephen Crane: War Correspondent," *Bookman*, February 1933. Seitz here repeats his unfounded charges of 1924 against Crane.

Sigsbee, Charles D. *The "Maine," An Account of her Destruction in Havana Harbor* (New York, 1899).

"Some Men Who Have Reported This War," *Cosmopolitan*, September 1898, 556–557. Compares James Creelman and Stephen Crane as war correspondents. Mr. Creelman "cares less for the form of the telling than for the fact to be told. Mr. Crane's interest in life is not so much to tell what happens as to make telling it interesting. Mr. Creelman went to the war for facts; Mr. Crane went for a chance to write good descriptions and to see with his eyes what had been seen by his imagination. Creelman got the facts and also got shot. Crane wrote very good articles, lived through a Red Badge of Courage experience in real life and got the fever." Quotes Langdon Smith of Hearst's *Journal*, who describes "Mr. Crane's conduct under fire as entirely worthy of the coolest hero that Mr. Crane's imagination ever devised."

Snyder, Louis L., and Richard B. Morris, editors. *A Treasury of Great Reporting* (New York, 1949). Reprints, pp. 236–238, "A *World* Correspondent Immortalizes an Incident on the Shores of Guantánamo Bay," which is the editors' invented title for "In the First Landing 4 of Our Men are Killed," New York *World*, June 13, 1898. That dispatch Crane dictated to Ernest McCready, who filed it for Crane on June 12 for the New York *World*. (McCready was of the *Herald*.)

*Spanish-American War ... by Eye-Witnesses* (Chicago, 1899). Important. Multiple points of view by various newsmen, some of them reporting also in *The Chicago Record's War Stories*, Chamberlin, Billman, Harris. Useful are Langdon Smith's "Landing of General Shafter's Men," Harris' "With

Grimes' Battery," and H. J. Whigham's "Fighting at Guantánamo." On Crane, page 98; but Whigham's account is in error. Also in gross error is Malcolm McDowell's fabrication that "one of the Seventy-first New York men, Scovill by name, brought a wounded comrade to the field hospital. He stooped over to aid the surgeon when a Spaniard in a tree 200 yards away put a bullet in Scovill's head, and he fell dead." *Contra* McDowell, Sylvester Scovel headed the *World* Staff and had no connection with the 71st New York Volunteers. Crane—not "Scovill" (Scovel) —brought Ed Marshall to the field hospital at Sibony. Scovel never "fell dead." He ended his career as newsman after punching General Shafter in the jaw.

Stallman, R. W. and E. R. Hagemann. Introduction. *The War Dispatches of Stephen Crane* (New York and London, 1964).

Starrett, Vincent. "Stephen Crane: An Estimate," *Sewanee Review*, 28 (June 1920), 405–413. On Crane with Burr McIntosh in Cuba; also in Starrett's essay in *The Colophon* (New York, 1931).

Steep, Thomas W. "First Fighting Days in Cuba," *Leslie's*, July 14, 1898. On the death of Assistant Surgeon Gibbs at Guantánamo.

Swanberg, W. A. *Citizen Hearst* (New York, 1961). On Crane; repeats the erroneous charges against Crane which Walter Millis instigated among historians since 1931.

Thrall, Charles H. "Thrilling Adventures of World Scout in Cuba: How Charles H. Thrall, Yale Graduate and Prominent Business Man, Three Times in One Week Entered and Left Havana," New York *World*, May 8, 1898, 19.

Walker, Franklin. *Frank Norris* (Garden City, New York, 1932). ———editor, *The Letters of Frank Norris* (Book Club of California, 1956).

"War History in Private Letters," *Outlook*, August 13, 20, 27, 1898; 919, 969–972, 1016–1021.

*West Point Atlas of American Wars* (New York, 1959), Vol. I.

Wheeler, Joseph. *The Santiago Campaign* (Boston, 1898).

White, Trumbull. *Our War With Spain for Cuba's Freedom* (Chicago, Philadelphia, 1898).

Williams, Ames W. "Stephen Crane: War Correspondent," *New Colophon*, April 1949. Important.

Zogbaum, R. F. "The Blockading Fleet," *Harper's Weekly*, May 14, 1898.

# ⊂⃛ *Index*

648 STEPHEN CRANE